THE GUN
AND ITS DEVELOPMENT

BY

W. W. GREENER

AUTHOR OF " MODERN BREECH-LOADERS," " CHOKE-BORE GUNS," " MODERN
SHOT-GUNS," " THE BREECH-LOADER, AND HOW TO USE IT,"
" SHARPSHOOTING FOR SPORT AND WAR,"
" THE BRITISH MINIATURE RIFLE "

NINTH EDITION

Rewritten, and with many Additional Illustrations

BONANZA BOOKS · NEW YORK

Library of Congress   67-27420

This edition published by Bonanza Books, a division of
Crown Publishers, Inc.
i j k l m n o p
MANUFACTURED IN THE UNITED STATES OF AMERICA

PREFACE TO THE NINTH EDITION.

THIS book, first published in 1881, was written with a view to supplying such information relative to fire-arms as is most frequently sought by a sportsman. Owing to numerous recent inventions it became necessary not only to rearrange the matter, but to rewrite the book when the sixth edition was needed.

The author thanks those critics who have pointed out literal faults in this book, and he has done his best to remove ambiguities and correct errors. He sees no reason to make any alteration of importance, and, in matters of opinion, adheres to what he has already written, so that this ninth edition is, with the exception of a few minor alterations and some additional pages upon Gun Trials, "Single Trigger" mechanisms, Miniature rifles and the "Rifle Club" movement, practically a reprint of the last one.

In the arrangement of this treatise the author has followed a method which appears to him the best suited to convey an accurate idea of different small arms and of their capabilities under varying conditions.

From the nature of the subjects treated it is impossible that the book could be wholly free from technicalities, but no endeavour has been spared to make the contents readable ; intricate mechanisms, instead of being described in detail, have been freely illustrated ; technical data are presented in tabular form, and theories relative to the action of explosives, the flight of bullets and shot pellets, have been concisely explained.

The thanks of the author are due to many sportsmen and others who by their investigations and experience have added to his knowledge of guns and gunnery ; possibly in some instances the sources upon which the author has drawn have not been acknowledged, but the omissions are unintentional.

The object of the author has been to supply trustworthy information relative to fire-arms and their history, but, owing to the quantity and diversity of the contents, it is improbable that all errors have been eliminated ; for such as remain the author asks the indulgence of readers and critics. Any mistake notified will be corrected in future editions and a continuous effort made to render THE GUN AND ITS DEVELOPMENT still more useful to those who have need to consult a shooter's cyclopædia.

W. W. GREENER.

BIRMINGHAM,
1910.

W W Greener

INTRODUCTION

An appreciation of the author extracted (by permission) from G. T. Teasdale-Buckle's book, "Experts on Guns and Shooting," published by Sampson Low, Marston & Co.

MR. W. W. GREENER, successful before the choke bore, became noted by his introduction of it. The history of the firm commences when the late William Greener (father of W. W. Greener) returned from London, where he had been working for John Manton, and established himself in 1829 at his native town of Newcastle.

Almost immediately he commenced experimenting, with the intention of publishing his first book, "The Gun," which appeared in 1835. This work dealt nearly exclusively with small arms, and it contains many ideas then new with deductions from his numerous experiments supporting them. At this time there was scarcely a work on the subject of gunnery, with the exception of Baker's book on the rifle, even then out of date. This was followed six years later by "The Science of Gunnery," dedicated to Prince Albert, which, besides embodying "The Gun," dealt with cannon, and contained criticisms of other workers in the same field.

In November, 1844, finding himself much retarded by the difficulties of obtaining materials from Birmingham, W. Greener moved his business to that town, and there began to make greater progress. An enlarged edition of his second book was published in 1846, and in 1845 the pamphlet "The Proof House, The Present Company the Bane of the Trade," was the chief means of promoting the Gun Proof Act of 1855.

We are informed that W. Greener was the first to discard vent holes in the breeches, relics of the old flint lock gun. He was also instrumental in improving the hardness and quality of barrels, by introducing more steel into their manufacture. He also improved the pattern of the Harpoon Gun, and his was the one adopted for the Scottish Fisheries; it is still to be found in use. But, undoubtedly, his greatest achievement in gunnery was the discovery of the expanding principle for muzzle-loading rifle bullets. The musket to which W. Greener adapted his bullet was eleven bore, and although the trial of his invention proved that the rifle could be loaded as easily as a smooth bore while still retaining its accuracy, no notice was taken of it by the Government, yet, in 1852, the Government awarded Minié (a Frenchman) £10,000 for a bullet on the same principle as Greener's invention of 1836. The method used was that of a plug driven by the powder gas into the base of the bullet. Mr. Greener considered himself aggrieved by this, and the Government ultimately admitted the justice of his claim and gave him £1,000 in the Army Estimates of 1857.

W. Greener did not confine himself to gunnery, and among his numerous inventions were Davy Lamps, a life-boat, self-righting by means of water ballast, and a mechanism by which four gates could be worked at once for level crossings. He also, in 1847, patented an electric light system.

As a sporting gunmaker, W. Greener had now (1845-58) arrived at a very high position, proved by the fact that he was appointed to make guns for the Prince Consort, and at the 1851 Exhibition he received a highest award "for guns and barrels perfectly forged and finished," and later, too, at the New York and Paris Exhibitions of 1853 and 1855 silver medals were awarded him. In the palmy days of the Southern States of America, before the War, very highly finished weapons were sent there, as much as £75 being paid for a gun of W. Greener's make. It was with the money obtained by the supply of South Africa with two-groove rifles that Mr. Greener erected his factory at "Rifle Hill," Aston, in 1859, and the more prosperous time of the firm may be dated therefrom. Just before this W. Greener had published his last work, "Gunnery in 1858," which was written in the warlike spirit, as he challenged the statements of other authors very freely. Though he lived until 1869, he never took kindly to the breech-loaders, and died in the faith in which he had lived. His son differed from him in this respect, and struck out a line of his own in breech-loaders, producing in 1864 his first patent, an under-lever pin-fire half-cocker with a top bolt entering the barrels underneath the top rib.

After the death of W. Greener the two businesses were amalgamated and carried on by W. W. Greener, whose next patent was the self-acting striker—a method only superseded by the rebounding lock. This was not of so much importance as the patent that followed it, the famous cross bolt, produced as a single top bolt in 1865. In 1873 this was combined with the bottom holding down bolts to form the "Treble Wedge Fast," one of the strongest breech actions ever invented, and one that has become much used of late, wherever an extended rib is thought to be necessary. Even London makers are now employing it to withstand the heavy charges in rifles of Express character.

W. W. Greener having written five books,* of which two have reached a sixth edition, has emulated his father in authorship. His first effort was the "Modern Breech-loaders," in 1871.

The introduction of choke boring may be regarded as W. W. Greener's greatest achievement: his previous inventions had shown his cleverness; this one made him famous throughout the world. Mechanism in a mechanical age like ours is not easy to grow famous upon. But choke boring, as brought out by Greener in 1874, altered the whole system of gun boring, and made close shooting the servant of the gun-maker, where before it had been his Will-o'-the-wisp.

We are aware that Mr. Pape, of Newcastle, considers himself the inventor of choke boring, and has been awarded a Cup as such by a committee. We do not agree with that award. That his patent proves him to have had some idea in May, 1866, that he thought might be worth protecting, is a fact. But although he described the method in a patent having to do with mechanisms of the actions of breech-loader fastenings, he made no claim in the patent for the invention of the method of boring he describes. We believe that (whether he knew or did not know what was possible from choke boring) he did not work the principle foreshadowed in his patent, or if he did, he did not work it in the modern successful method. We are of this opinion, because we happen to know that when asked in '73 or '74 to do his best by way of pattern, he sent out a weapon that could not put 100 No. 6 shot in the 30-inch circle at 40 yards. And having regard to the extreme care with which the cartridges sent to try the gun were loaded, we have every reason to believe that he was doing his best. Good shooting guns at that time were accidents to a great extent; with such an accident Mr. Pape had won at a public trial with a pattern of less than 130. That is our opinion of the matter, and moreover, no English maker could guarantee any such pattern as 130 until Mr. Greener showed the way in 1874. We speak from the results of our own trials with the guns of many of them, including Mr. Pape's. The information we are able to give on this subject was more particularly derived from trials made of a number of guns from a large number of makers, sent by them for the purpose, when we formed one of the shooting party in Leicestershire in 1873 or 1874. The whole of the shooting at this trial was

* Since the publication of Mr. Buckle's book, two more books have been written by the author and two of the earlier books have reached nine editions. They have been translated into the French, German, Italian, Spanish, Russian and Japanese languages, and over 80,000 volumes have been distributed in all parts of the world.

done by ourselves, and as some of the most fashionable London makers, and the most successful at that time at pigeon shooting, sent their guns, we became well aware of the state of barrel boring immediately prior to the introduction of the choke bore. Mr. Greener was one of the makers who sent guns to us on the particular occasion of which we speak. These were sent back to him, and as a result we probably saw the first choke bore he made. This was sent up to us in Scotland, in the autumn following the trials of which we speak, and the difference between its performance at the target and that of any of the guns previously tried was astonishing to all who saw it at that time.

Choke boring has been more or less adopted by all gun-makers since that date, and it is for this reason that we say that Mr. Greener's reputation is based on the introduction of the invention. Mr. Greener makes no claim to be the inventor of choke boring; what he claims is that he improved an American invention to such an extent, that in 1874 and 1875 no one who had got hold of the American method had any chance of making such patterns as he could get out of his guns.

This was clearly established at the 1875 gun trials, when Mr. Pape, who advertises himself as the inventor of the system, exhibited guns against Mr. Greener's winning weapons, but although he had then got choke bores of some kind, like all the other makers, which he had not the year before (if our Leicestershire trials were the test we believe them to have been), he could not, any more than they, get shooting from them that approached that of Mr. Greener's specimen guns of almost all the various bores.

CONTENTS.

CHAPTER I.

EARLY ARMS.

CHAPTER II.

THE INVENTION OF GUNPOWDER.

CHAPTER III.

EARLY ARTILLERY.

CHAPTER IV.

EARLY HAND FIRE-ARMS.

Contents.

CHAPTER XVII.

HOW TO USE THE GUN.

CHAPTER XVIII.

TRAP SHOOTING.

CHAPTER XIX.

DOUBLE GUNS WITH SINGLE TRIGGERS.

CHAPTER XX.

MISCELLANEOUS.

CHAPTER XXI.

MODERN PISTOLS.

CHAPTER XXII.

EXPLOSIVES.

CHAPTER XXIII.

INTERNAL BALLISTICS.

CHAPTER XXIV.

AMMUNITION AND ACCESSORIES.

CHAPTER XXV.

THE HISTORY OF RIFLING AND ITS DEVELOPMENT.

CONTENTS.

CHAPTER XXVI.

MODERN SPORTING RIFLES.

CHAPTER XXVII.

EXTERNAL BALLISTICS.

CHAPTER XXVIII.

SINGLE-SHOT MILITARY RIFLES.

CHAPTER XXIX.

EARLY REPEATING RIFLE MECHANISMS.

CHAPTER XXX.

MODERN MILITARY MAGAZINE RIFLES.

THE GUN AND ITS DEVELOPMENT.

CHAPTER I

EARLY ARMS.

WEAPONS which would kill at a distance were possessed by man in the prehistoric age ; but what those arms were the archæologist and ethnologist must decide. For the purpose of this treatise it is of small moment whether primitive man was better armed than the modern Ainu or the African pigmy. It is probable that the races of men coëval with the mastodon and the cave-bear were better armed than is generally supposed ; the much-despised Australian aborigine, notwithstanding his lack of intelligence, is the inventor of two weapons—the boomerang and the throwing-stick for hurling spears—which races much higher in the scale of humanity could not improve upon. So other weapons, as the sling and the bow, appear to have long preceded civilisation, and their use has been traced to times of remotest antiquity. The throwing of sticks and stones was doubtless the readiest method by which the aggressor could effect a result at a distance. Even monkeys will pelt their assailants with nuts ; and the throwing of stones in the primitive fashion was one method of fighting generally practised throughout all ages. It was indulged in by the French and English even so recently as the battle of Alexandria (1801).

It was as an instrument of the chase that the weapon which would kill at a distance was developed ; it may be that a flint used for some domestic purpose, and found handy because it was the particular flint most often used, led to the securing of that one flint to the wrist or waist by a thong ; thus could the chosen weapon be recovered, and quickly used time after time until the prey was taken or the foe vanquished. This weapon, flint-and-thong, is the first form of the sling-shot, an arm still favoured by the Scotch Highlanders ; from it too, probably, the sling was developed. Possibly accident caused to be noticed the increased power of the sling-hurled missile over that of the flint thrown by unaided arm. The use of the sling is, or has been, almost universal. Its invention by the Phœnicians or Acarnanians, or the Ætolians, is clearly as mythical as the legend relating to Apollo and the production of the bow. The Achaians and Balerians were extremely expert in the use of the sling, and even prior to the Christian era made use of lead missiles. The sling was used for many centuries as a weapon of war; it still exists as a savage weapon; but its last appearance for military purposes in Europe was at the siege of Sancerre in 1572.

The bow, although possibly a later invention than the sling, can be traced to the earliest times in the annals of every country. It was held in high repute as a weapon of war, but was pre-eminent as a hunting weapon; by striking down the most renowned as well as the most insignificant of warriors its use was deprecated by men of heroic character.

The ancient method of warfare among the most civilised of nations was inferior to that now practised by the most untutored of savages. The two armies—if a few fighting men and a rabble on each side may be so termed—were usually encamped within a half-mile or so of each other. In the space between the camps single combats took place. The heroes of either side would advance and challenge the other side; thus Goliath before the Jews: Goliath having found his David, and fallen, the Philistines ran away. So in the Trojan war Hector could only be fought by Achilles or some "hero" of equal rank.

The bows and the other engines of war were not available at a greater distance than about four hundred yards, and in the heroic age it may be assumed that it was contrary to the usage of war to fire arrows at champions when engaged in mortal combat. This rule was sometimes broken, as the readers of the "Iliad" will remember; the exploits of the archer Pandarus being there referred to in flattering terms.

The method of war changed when Alexander marched his phalanx successfully against every army in the civilised world. The fiercest champion was powerless against the compact body of men acting as one machine; the tricks of the savage— ambush, stealth, surprise, treachery—were more successful. Then the bow and the sling, the weapons of the hunter and the herdsman, were requisitioned for military purposes. It was sought by their use to destroy the solidity of the phalanx. Terror played an important part in all war manœuvres; the array of elephants before the Carthaginian phalanx, the strange engines of war, were designed to dismay the enemy; so the archers and slingers, but more particularly the archers, struck terror alike into the hearts of mounted warriors and foot soldiers. They were particularly successful in disorganising the cavalry; for the horses, wounded with the barbed darts and driven mad as the shafts changed position with each movement, became uncontrollable.

The weapon which would kill at a distance has always been the weapon of the hunter ; the Roman warrior, with his bossed shield and short sword, was unconquerable in hand-to-hand conflict ; and in the Roman wars with Gauls, Helvetians, and Britons the bow played no part ; the untrained barbarians met their foe in battle array, and were routed. The Greeks were not a hunting race, and they learned the use of the bow from the Scythians, who were hunters one and all ; so the ancient Norsemen, although they made frequent use of the bow, and thought highly of it as an instrument of the chase, rarely employed it in war. The Anglo-Saxons, in like manner, regarded the bow as of little use in war.

The first bow is supposed to have been made by thinning down the horns of the ox and joining them at their base. This gives almost the correct form of the

Saxon Bowmen.

classical bow. The bow of Pandarus is said to have been made of the horns of the wild goat ; the Grecian bows, originally of horn, were later made of wood ; the strings were of horse-hair or hides cut into narrow thongs. The arrows were of light wood or were reeds tipped with barbed points. The bows of the northern nations were longer and were of wood, and when unstrung were almost straight ; it is from them that the English long-bow was developed.

The illustration shows the shape of the Saxon bow ; it is from the Cotton MS., and represents two sportsmen of the eighth century. In the Saxon Chronicles there is little relating to archery. That Harold, William II., and Richard I. were killed by arrows is every-day history; but it was not until the middle of the fourteenth century that the English bow attained its reputation. It would appear that the bandits and outlaws of Britain—living, as they did, by the chase—knew well the power of the bow; when the King's forces were sent against them they used their bows to such advantage that it was deemed advisable to employ archers in the war in France. Creçy, Poictiers, and Agincourt were won by the long-bow; and almost by the bowmen alone. The bow likewise played the most prominent part at the battle of Homildon Hill, and at Shrewsbury. Long after the use of fire-arms for military purposes it was retained by the English as the chief weapon of war. As much as could be done by legislation was done to encourage its use. The learned Roger Ascham was commissioned to " write up " the sport of archery; later Sir John Smith advocated the use of the bow in preference to the hand-gun, but although it lingered beyond the Tudor period it was in only a half-hearted fashion, and the bands of archers raised to defend the King in 1643 appear to have done very little.

The feats of the bowmen have been greatly exaggerated, but there can be little doubt that a skilled archer was a formidable antagonist. The arrows, made with square heads, would pierce armour quite as well as a musket-ball. Possibly the account of Pandarus's prowess is not exaggerated; at any rate, there are well authenticated records of feats as surprising as that of the effect of his arrow upon Menelaus.

> " It struck
> Just where the golden clasps the belt restrained,
> And where the breastplate, doubled, checked its force.
> On the close-fitting belt the arrow struck;
> Right through the belt of curious workmanship
> It drove, and through the breastplate richly wrought,
> And through the coat of mail he wore beneath—
> His inmost guard, and best defence to check
> The hostile weapon's force : yet onward still
> The arrow drove."—*Il.* iv. 119.

Giraldus Cambrensis states that some archers belonging to the Ventna, a warlike Welsh tribe, shot clean through an oak door, behind which some soldiers had concealed themselves, the door being no less than four fingers in thickness. A party of 100 archers shot before King Edward VI., at doubtless considerably over 220 yards (the recognised minimum range), and pierced an oak plank one inch in thickness, several of the arrows passing right through the plank and sticking into the butts at the back. The renowned Douglas found that armour was no protection ; his first suit of mail, of splendid temper, was pierced in five places at one battle fought in 1402. The North American Indian has been known to drive an arrow right through a buffalo.

With reference to the range of the bow, the measured mile of Robin Hood and Little John, known by honoured tradition, is as fabulous as the wondrous shooting recounted by Firdusi, the Persian poet, of the heroic Arish, whose arrow sped over five hundred miles. The longest well-authenticated distance for shooting with flight-arrows is about 600 yards, and at 400 yards hazel-rods were frequently cleft by experts. Modern archers have in a few instances shot their arrows over 400 yards. The Turkish Ambassador shot an arrow, from a short Eastern bow of horn, 480 yards at one of the early meetings of the Toxophilite Society. By a statute of Henry VIII. it was forbidden that any man over twenty-four years of age should shoot at a mark nearer than 220 yards with a flight-arrow or 140 yards with a sheaf-arrow.

As to the method of shooting, the Persians drew the bowstring to the right ear by means of the thumb, on which not infrequently a ring was worn to strengthen the grip ; the ancient Greeks drew the bow-string to the right breast ; the English drew to the ear, gripping the arrow and pulling on the string with the fingers.

Under Edward IV. every Englishman was required to

Henry VIII., in Archer's Costume, shooting at the Field of the Cloth of Gold.

have a bow of his own height, made of yew, wych, hazel, or ash, according to his strength.   The arrows were required to be of the length of a man's arm or half the length of the bow.   Practice was enjoined under certain penalties.   In the reign of Henry VII. the use of other bows than the long-bow was forbidden ; in the next reign a fine of £10 was ordered to be paid by whomsoever might be found to possess a cross-bow ; and during the reigns of Elizabeth, James, and Charles I. the Legislature repeatedly interfered to protect archery.

Contemporary with the English bow was the Continental cross-bow or arbalist, a weapon developed from the most ancient engines of war known as catapultæ.

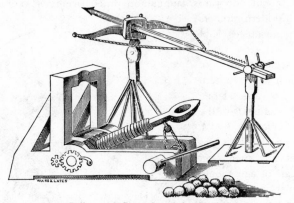

Balista and Catapulta of the Greeks.

Though its invention has been attributed to the Normans, others state that it was invented by the Cretans and introduced into Europe after the first Crusade.   In all probability it was a modification of well-known engines of war used in besieging and defending fortified towns.   These engines were often of huge proportions ; one used by the fifteenth legion against Vespasian at the battle of Cremona, according to Tacitus, discharged stones large enough to crush whole ranks at once.   The first mention of such machines is in 2 Chronicles (xxvi. 15), where it is stated that Uzziah "made in Jerusalem engines, invented by cunning men, to be upon the towers and upon the bulwarks, to shoot arrows and great stones."   Josephus states that the Jews shot the corpses of men and horses from these machines—a common practice of the Carthaginians, who thought thus to strike terror into their assailants. The catapultæ were sometimes made to shoot at once a whole sheaf of arrows or a number of javelins ; the *balistæ* were used to throw stones chiefly.

The cross-bow was looked upon as a most cruel and barbarous weapon, and Pope Innocent III. forbade its use among Christian nations, but sanctioned it in fighting against infidels. Richard I. introduced the cross-bow into the English army against the wish of the Pope ; and, he being killed a few years later by a shot

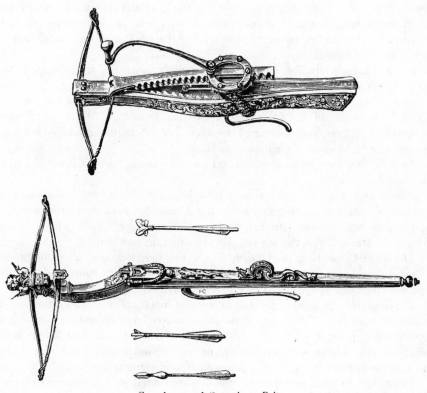

Cross-bows and Quarrels or Bolts.

from one whilst besieging the castle of Chaluz, his death was considered as a judgment from Heaven inflicted on him for his impious conduct.

The cross-bow continued to be much used by the British ; the cross-bowmen were second only to the long-bowmen in the expedition fitted out against the Scots by Edward II. In 1572 Queen Elizabeth engaged to find a number of cross-bowmen to aid Charles IX., and it is said that in 1627 some of the English in the attack upon the Île de Ré were armed with cross-bows.

The cross-bows were of several varieties ; in the illustration on page 7, the shorter, called the goat-foot, was the type more generally used for military purposes.

The bow is of steel, and the string is pulled by a hooked rod with a ratchet edge.   The ratchet is wound up by means of the lever and cogs until the string is pulled over a movable nut or button fixed to the stock.   By depressing the lever underneath the button is brought to the level of the stock, and, the string slipping over it, the bow is released.

In some cases a windlass with ropes and pulleys was used ; it was fixed to the stock of the cross-bow after each discharge, but at the time of shooting or marching it was removed, and hung from the soldier's girdle.   This type is shown in the illustration of bow-men of the fifteenth century from Froissart.   Others were cocked by means of a lever, and some had a pulley fastened in the stock, with a rope passing over it, to which a stirrup was attached.

To bend this bow, its head was rested on the ground, the foot inserted in the stirrup and depressed.

Others were light enough to be set by hand ; the one which belonged to Catherine de Medicis is still preserved in the Musée des Invalides, Paris, and is a light ornamental weapon, discharged by a lever trigger which, when pressed towards the stock, lowers the nut or hook clutching the bow-string.

The smaller cross-bow, used chiefly for sporting purposes, was called the prodd ; with some such weapon Margaret of Anjou shot deer in Northumberland, and this type was employed by Queen Elizabeth at Cowday.

The bows of the lighter cross-bows were of wood, of wood and horn, or of combined materials.   An early Spanish cross-bow was recently examined, to ascertain the material of which the bow was composed.   It was found to be mainly of yew, backed with whalebone, the two bound together with sinews, and the whole embedded in a glutinous composition and varnished.

In addition to bolts and quarrels, the cross-bow fired long arrows, occasionally "fire-arrows," and not infrequently was specially designed to propel pellets or stones.   The long-bow has also been adapted to the same purpose, for pellet-bows are still not uncommon in the East Indies.

A small cross-bow intended to be concealed about the person, and used as a secret weapon, is preserved in the Birmingham Museum ; and the collection of the United Service Institution, London, includes a specimen of a repeating cross-bow— this last a modern Cingalese production.

Cross-bowmen of the Fifteenth Century. (*After Froissart.*)

The arbalist or cross-bow was a clumsy weapon ; it fired a variety of missiles, mostly of the type termed *quarreaux*—that is, square bolts, later known as quarrels. These, by reason of their barbed heads and their great weight, caused dangerous wounds ; they pierced armour, and not infrequently they were poisoned.   An ordinary wound was not easily cured, owing to the clumsy surgery of those days ;

English Long-bowman.

some of the remedies proposed, and used, must have been worse even than the wounds. The point-blank range of the military cross-bow was about sixty yards, but, if elevated, some were available at more than double that distance.

The cross-bowman was sometimes mounted ; the long-bow was quite unsuited for use on horseback ; hence perhaps the persistence in the use of the short classical bow by Eastern nations.

Neither the long-bow nor the cross-bow constituted the complete armament of the soldier. The long-bowman carried a mace or mallet with which to kill those whom he had disabled with his arrows ; sometimes he was furnished with a pike, which, stuck into the earth in a slanting direction, afforded some slight protection from a cavalry charge. He, like the cross-bowman, was sometimes attended by a *paviser*—that is, a page or varlet—who bore a huge shield, behind which he and his master could shelter from the arrows of the enemy. In the illustration the cross-bowman is taken from the " Chronique d'Engleterre," and the paviser from a copy of the " Romaun de la Rose."

The cross-bowmen usually carried a sword, and it is not to be supposed that they and other archers were the only warriors who sought the shelter and aid of the paviser : even the knights not infrequently put that bulwark as one more thickness of iron between themselves and the missiles they so much dreaded.

The methods of warfare were not greatly changed by the bow ; the knights still fought the single combat when they could, and the ordinary rank and file of an army did not count for very much.   It is recorded that Richard I., with

Cross-bowman and his Paviser.

seventeen knights and three hundred archers, once sustained the charge of the whole of the combined Turkish and Saracen army, some thousands strong. It is also recorded that *four* English archers landed near a besieged town on the French coast, changed the fortunes of battle, and brought about the rout of the French army. But if the bow was bad, the hand-gun was much worse. Henry VIII., who was erratic in legislation, granted a charter to the Guild of St. George in 1537 authorising its members to practise with every kind of artillery—bows, cross-bows, and hand-guns alike—almost the same year that he forbade guns entirely, and made the possession of a cross-bow a finable offence. In the reign of Queen Elizabeth Sir John Smith, a general of much experience, stated that the bow was the superior of the hand-gun, and although he was taken up sharply by Mr. W. Barwick, Gent., he stuck to his contention. " I will never doubt to adventure my life," he writes, " or many lives (if I had them), amongst 8,000 archers, complete, well chosen and appointed, and therewithal provided and furnished with great store of sheaves of arrows, as also a good overplus of bows and bow-strings, against 20,000 of the best harquebusiers and musketeers there are in Christendom."

Several trials between the gun and the bow are on record, the results generally showing military advantages to the latter. A reliable match decided at Pacton Green, Cumberland, in August, 1792, resulted in a grand victory for the bow. The distance was 100 yards, the bow placing sixteen arrows out of twenty into the target, and the ordinary musket twelve balls only. A similar match took place the same year with very similar results.

Perceiving such results as these so late as the eighteenth century, it is not surprising that in its earlier days the gun proved an inferior weapon to the bow in the hands of a good archer.

There is no record of the muskets used at the trials above quoted, but in all probability the " Brown Bess " would be the one chosen, it being the standard military arm at that period.

CHAPTER II.
THE INVENTION OF GUNPOWDER.

THERE seems little doubt that the composition of gunpowder has been known in the East from times of dimmest antiquity. The Chinese and Hindus contemporary with Moses are thought to have known of even the more recondite properties of the compound. The Gentoo code, which, if not as old as was first declared, was certainly compiled long before the Christian era, contains the following passage :—

"The magistrate shall not make war with any deceitful machine, or with poisoned weapons, or with cannons or guns, or any kind of fire-arms, nor shall he slay in war any person born an eunuch, nor any person who, putting his arms together, supplicates for quarter, nor any person who has no means of escape."

Gunpowder has been known in India and China far beyond all periods of investigation; and if this account be considered true, it is very possible that Alexander the Great *did* absolutely meet with fire-weapons in India, which a passage in Quintus Curtius seems to indicate. There are many ancient Indian and Chinese words signifying weapons of fire, heaven's-thunder, devouring-fire, ball containing terrestrial fire, and such-like expressions.

Dutens in his work gives a most remarkable quotation from the life of Apollonius Tyanæus, written by Philostratus, which, if true, proves that Alexander's conquests in India were arrested by the use of gunpowder. This oft-cited paragraph is deserving of further repetition :—

"These truly wise men (the Oxydracæ) dwell between the rivers of Hyphasis and Ganges. Their country Alexander never entered, deterred not by fear of the inhabitants, but, as I suppose, by religious motives, for had he passed the Hyphasis he might doubtless have made himself master of all the country round them; but their cities he never could have taken, though he had led a thousand as brave as Achilles, or three thousand such as Ajax, to the assault; for they come not out to the field to fight those who attack them, but these holy men, beloved of the gods, overthrew their enemies with tempests and thunderbolts shot from their walls. It is said that the Egyptian Hercules and Bacchus, when they invaded India, invaded this people also, and, having prepared warlike engines, attempted to conquer them; they in the meantime made no show of resistance, appearing perfectly quiet and secure, but upon the enemy's near approach they were repulsed with storms of lightning and thunderbolts hurled upon them from above."

Although Philostratus is not considered the most veracious of ancient authors other evidence corroborates the truth of this account, and it is now generally acknowledged that the ancient Hindoos possessed a knowledge of gunpowder-making. They made great use of explosives, including gunpowder, in pyrotechnical displays, and it is not improbable that they may have discovered (perhaps accidentally) the most recondite of its properties, that of projecting heavy bodies, and practically applied the discovery by inventing and using cannon. The most ingenious theory respecting the invention of gunpowder is that of the late Henry Wilkinson :—

"It has always appeared to me highly probable that the first discovery of gunpowder might originate from the primæval method of cooking food by means of wood fires on a soil strongly impregnated with nitre, as it is in many parts of India and China. It is certain that from the moment when the aborigines of these countries ceased to devour their food in a crude state, recourse must have been had to such means of preparing it; and when the fires became extinguished some portions of the wood partially converted into charcoal would remain, thus accidentally bringing into contact two of the principal and most active ingredients of this composition under such circumstances as could hardly fail to produce some slight deflagration whenever fires were rekindled on the same spot. . . . . . It is certain that such a combination of favourable circumstances might lead to the discovery, although the period of its application to any useful purpose may be very remote from that of its origin."

The introduction of explosives into Europe followed the Mahomedan invasion. Greek fire, into the composition of which nitre and sulphur entered, was used prior to the fall of the Western Roman Empire. In 275 A.D. Julius Africanus mentions "shooting powder." Gunpowder, or some mixture closely resembling it, was used at the siege of Constantinople in 668. The Arabs or Saracens are reputed to have used it at the siege of Mecca in 690; some writers even affirm that it was known to Mahomet. Marcus Græcus described in "Liber ignium" an explosive composed of six parts saltpetre and two parts each of charcoal and sulphur. The MS. copy of this author in the National Library at Paris is said to be of much later date than 846, inscribed upon it; the recipe given is nearly akin to the formula still employed for mixing the ingredients of gunpowder.

Other early uses of gunpowder recorded are: by the Saracens at Thessalonica in 904; by Salômon, King of Hungary, at the siege of Belgrade, 1073; in a sea conflict between the Greeks and Pisanians the former had fire-tubes fixed at the prows of their boats (1098), and in 1147 the Arabs used fire-arms against the Iberians. In 1218 there was artillery at Toulouse. In the Escurial collection there is a treatise on gunpowder, written, it is supposed, in 1249, and it is from this treatise that Roger Bacon is presumed to have obtained his knowledge of gunpowder; he died

Its manufacture in England, as an industry, dates back to the reign of Elizabeth, when mills were first established in Kent, and the monopoly conferred upon the Evelyn family.

As to what was known of the origin of gunpowder by authorities living prior to the Commonwealth, the following extract from Robert Norton's "Gunner," published in 1628, shows exactly :—

"I hold it needeful for compiling of the whole worke as compleate as I can, to declare by whom and how this so dieullish an invention was first brought to light. *Vffano* reporteth, that the invention and vse as well of Ordnances as of Gunnepowder, was in the 85 yeere of our Lord, made knowe and practized in the great and ingenious Kingdom of *China*, and that in the Maratym Provinces thereof, there yet remaine certaine Peeces of *Ordnance*, both of Iron and *Brasse*, with the memory of their yeeres of Foundings ingraued vpon them, and the Arms of King *Vitey*, who, he saith, was their inventor. And it well appearethe also in ancient and credible Historyes that the said King Vitey was a great Enchanter and Nigromancer, whom one Sune (being vexed with cruell warres by the Tartarians) coniured an euill spirit that shewed him the vse and making of *Gunnes* and *Powder ;* the which hee put in Warlike practise in the Realme of *Pegu*, and in the conquest of the *East Indies*, and thereby quieted the Tartars. The same being confirmed by certain *Portingales* that have trauelled and Nauigated those quarters, and also affirmed by a letter sent from Captain *Artred*, written to the King of Spaine, wherein recounting very diligently all the particulars of *Chyna*, sayd, that they long since used there both Ordnance and Powder; and affirming farther that there hee found ancient ill shapen pieces, and that those of later Foundings are of farre better fashion and metall than their ancient were."

CHAPTER III.

EARLY ARTILLERY.

THE FIRST FIRE-ARMS.

FIRE-ARMS of various kinds were well known to the ancients; the accounts given of them are so incomprehensible, exaggerated and generally unreliable, that from them little beyond the fact of the existence of fire-arms can be learned. The development of fire-arms will therefore be traced from their introduction into Europe.

Seville is said to have been defended in 1247 by "cannon throwing stones." On a cannon in the castle of Coucy is "Fait le 6 Mars, 1258, Raoul, Roi de Coucy"; the dates are in Arabic figures. In 1259 Melilla was defended by a machine which, from the description, must be a cannon or like fire-arm. In 1273 Abou Yuesof used canon, firing stone shot, at the siege of Sidgil-messa. In 1301 a "fire mouth" was made at Amberg. In 1308 Ferdinando IV. of Castille employed guns (marquenas de Trueñas) at the siege of Gibraltar. A cannon was found in 1560 among the ruins of the castle of Heyer, on the Rhine, which was destroyed in 1308. In 1311 Ismail attacked Bazas, in Granada, with machines "throwing balls of fire, with a noise like thunder." In the archives of the town of Ghent it is stated that in 1313 the town was possessed of a small cannon; and in the records of the Florentine Republic it is stated that in 1325 two officers were ordered to manufacture cannon and iron bullets for the defence of the castles and villages belonging to the republic. From this date references to their use on the Continent are frequent.

Fire-arms are said to have been possessed by the English in 1310, and to have been used by them at the siege of D'Eu in that year. The first mention in a *contemporary* record is in an indenture dated 1338, between John Starlyng and Helmyng Leget, which mentions, as part of the equipment of the King's ship, "*Bernard de la Tour*," "ij. canons de ferr sanz estuff; un canon de ferr ove ii. chambers, un autre de bras ove une chambre, un ketell," etc.; also for the ship "*X'ofre de la Tour*" "iij. canons de ferr ove v. chambres, un handgone," also "un petit barell de gonpouder, le quart plein." In 1346 John Cooke, a clerk of the

King's wardrobe, to which department the arms and munitions of war belonged, states that 912 lbs. of saltpetre and 846 lbs. of sulphur were provided for the use of the army in France; later in the year, before Calais, he obtained a further supply. That fire-arms were used by the English at Creçy in 1346 is a well-ascertained fact. In 1347 the words "gunnis" and "bombarde" first appear in the

Fire-arms in War Chariot: Fifteenth Century.

State records. When Chaucer wrote his "House of Fame" (about 1373) the use of fire-arms must have been widely known, since he draws a simile for speed from the firing of an engine filled with an explosive :—

> "Swift as a pillet out of a gonne
> When fire is in the pouder ronne."
>> "House of Fame," b. iii.

In 1344 the household of Edward III. comprised : "Ingyners, lvij.; artillers, vj.; gonners, vj." Their pay was sixpence a day in time of war. John Barbour wrote in 1375 that in 1327, at the battle of Werewater, the Scotch first saw fire-arms :—

> "Twa noweltys that dai thai saw,
> That forouth in Scotland had bene nane

> Tymris for helmys war the tane
> That thaim thoucht than off grete bewte ;
> And alsua wondre for to se
> The tothyr crakys war off wer,
> That thai befor herd nevir er."

An inventory of Baynard Castell in 1388 includes "j. petit gonne de feer." In the records of Henry IV., for 1400, there are mentioned payments for "quarrel gonnes, saltpetre and wadding"; in 1428 entries for "bastons à feu" (fire-sticks —that is, hand-guns).

Early fire-arms were variously named in Europe, hence much confusion as to the dates at which fire-arms were used. Valturius, who wrote in the fifteenth century, terms both cross-bows and cannon "balistæ." Before gunpowder was used to propel missiles it was employed *in* or upon projectiles, sometimes affixed to lance-heads made tubular for the purpose ; hence, it is argued, the name "cannones" or tubes. Robert Norton has the following with reference to the naming of fire-arms :—

> "*Beraldus* saith that at the first invention of Ordnance they were called by the name of *Bombards* (a word compounded of the verbes *Bombo*, which signifieth to sound, and of *Ardeo*, to burne), and they that used them they called Bombardeer, which name is yet partly retained. After which, as Bertholdus saith, they were called *Turacio* and *Turrafragi*, of the breaking-down of towers and walls : and by *John de Monte Reggio* they were called *Tormenti*, their shot *Sphæra tormentaria*, and the gunners *Magistri* tormentorum. But now [1628] Ordnance are eyther named at the will of the inventor, either according to his own name (as the Canon was) or by the names of birds and beasts of prey, for their swiftness or their cruelty; as the Faulconet, Faulcon, Saker, and Culvering, etc., for swiftnesse of flying ; as the Basiliske, Serpentine, Aspitic, Dragon, Syrene, etc., for cruelty."

The Germans called their early arms "buchsen," or fire-boxes ; the Netherlanders "vogheleer" or "veugliares." The name "gun" is supposed to be derived from "maguinale" or "mangonel," an engine of war like the "balista."

EARLY CANNON.

The earliest arms were small ; usually they were of iron forged, and shot arrows weighing about half a pound, and were charged with about a third of an ounce of powder. The fire-arm at Rouen in 1388 was of this description. With it were forty-eight bolts—feathered iron arrows : these were put in from the muzzle. The charge of gunpowder was usually put in a separate movable breech-block or

Early Cannon. (*After Grose.*)

chamber. Each cannon was usually supplied with two or more extra chambers. The first mention of cast cannon relates to thirty made by a founder named Aran at Augsburg, Germany, in 1378. These were of copper and tin. Another variety

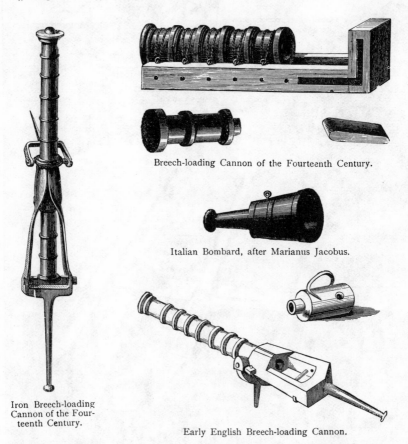

Breech-loading Cannon of the Fourteenth Century.

Italian Bombard, after Marianus Jacobus.

Iron Breech-loading Cannon of the Fourteenth Century.

Early English Breech-loading Cannon.

of the same early breech-loading cannon for use on ship-board differs only from the foregoing in having a wooden frame. These cannon were built up of iron strips surrounded by iron rings—a method which continued for several centuries. The cannon often had trunnions, and were mounted as wall pieces, or, attached to wooden frames, were used as in the illustration from Grose's "Military Antiquities."

The smallest among the early fire-arms were the Italian bombards, one of which is here shown. These bombards were muzzle-loading, and had the powder chamber of much smaller calibre than the forward portion of the weapon—this fore part was usually more or less taper both inside and out so that shot of different diameters might be fired from them.

There is little doubt that at first the chief advantage supposed to be possessed by fire-arms was the terror and confusion produced by their use ; as fighting men

Italian Cerbotain of the Fourteenth Century mounted upon a Semi-portable Carriage.

became more accustomed to them they were as far as possible improved, their range and calibre both increased, and they were employed for new purposes—as, for instance, at sieges in lieu of battering-rams. An arm of this description, mounted upon a semi-portable carriage, and so placed as to afford some protection to the gunner, is shown next. The illustration is after a manuscript decoration, and has no pretence to accuracy of detail either in the construction of the carriage or the

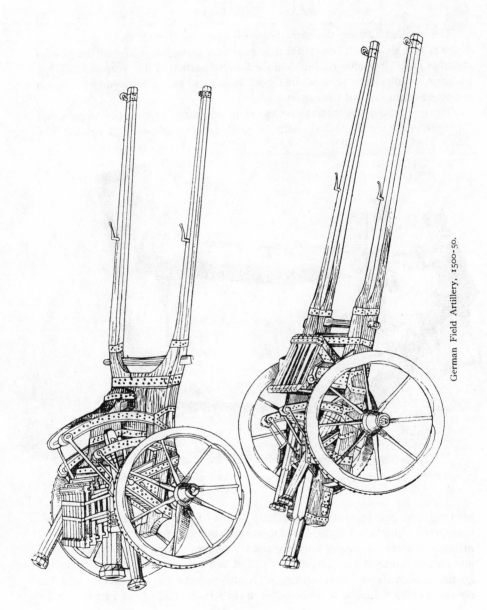

German Field Artillery, 1500-50.

supports to the gun.   This particular style of fire-arm is referred to by the name of
"blow tube," or cerbotain.   Another early weapon was the "bombardo cubito," or
"elbow-joint gun."   In this, the tube of the cannon was fixed at right angles to
the powder chamber, A, an aperture in the side of B permitting its introduction ;
it was held in position by a wedge driven between a cross-piece of the frame and
the rear of the powder-box.   The angle of firing was adjusted by means of the
prop, C.

The difficulty in discharging fire-arms quickly was attempted to be met by
making several cannons and uniting them on one carriage; sometimes they were
arranged like the spokes of a wheel, the breech ends towards the centre, at

The Elbow-joint Bombard.

which point the revolving table was pivoted vertically to a suitable stand.   Sometimes it appears to have been suggested that the cannon should be arranged as the
felloes of the wheel ; in this case the disc turns on a horizontal pivot.   Illustrations
of such arms appear in old treatises, particularly in various editions of the military
writings of Robert Walther (Valturius), but, like many of the drawings of this
date, are presumably ideal sketches, and not copied from weapons actually in use.
The bombards arranged on a vertically pivoted disc or table were frequently
used, the principle being adhered to until quite recently, as will afterwards be
demonstrated.

Large cannon were made at a very early date, even if they were never used.
The fact that such a weapon was possessed by a town possibly terrorised opponents.   If so small a cannon as may be lifted by one man has wrought such havoc,
how can any number of men stand before such fire-arms as these people possess?

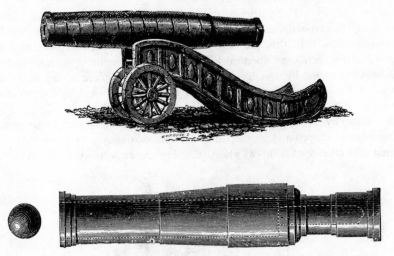

The "Mons Meg" of Edinburgh Castle, as it is, and as restored by M. Louis Figuier.

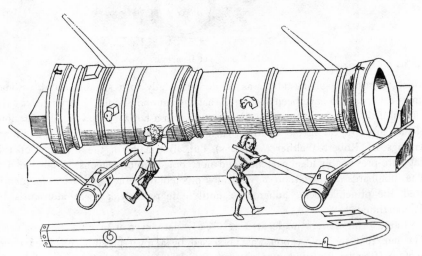

Fifteenth-century German Cast Cannon.

In 1413 Mahomet II. had one of these huge weapons at the siege of
Constantinople. It is reported to have been forty-eight inches in diameter, and
to have fired a stone bullet of 600 lbs. weight. Froissart states that the people
of Ghent made a large cannon which was used by D'Ardevelde at the siege
of Oudenarde : " Therefore to terrify the garrison he caused to be made a
marvellous great bombard ; which was forty feet long, and threw great heavy stones
of wonderful bigness."

At the middle of the fifteenth century the production of large cannon became
quite common in Germany ; several of these huge weapons are often referred to
by name, and have repeatedly figured in local chronicles. The " Foulenette "

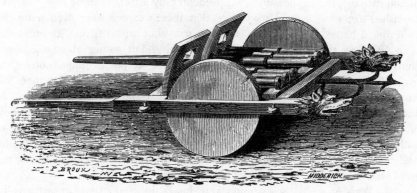

French "Orgue des Bombardes."

was one, the " Helfant " another, the " Endorfferen " made for Sigismund of
Tyrol in 1487, and was a pair with " Bassina " of the Paris Museum. A still
larger cannon was the " Faust bucleæ " of Frankfort, made in 1399 and used
at the siege of Tannenburg Castle. Its bullet is said to have weighed 8½ cwt.
The " Mons Meg " of Edinburgh Castle is supposed to have been of the same
general construction as the cannon which in 1460 killed James II. of
Scotland. " Mons Meg " was made at Mons, from which town it takes its name ;
it is now badly broken. It weighs nearly four tons, and its stone shot is calculated
to have weighed over 350 pounds. The touch-hole is placed a little in front of the
powder chamber, and runs in an oblique direction. These large cannon all appear
to have been muzzle-loaders ; ordinarily the powder chamber was of about one-third

the diameter of the bore of the cannon, and the usual method of construction was of iron strips and rings welded together as already described. These cannon were for the most part used in the defence of fortified towns or for besieging strongholds ; it was not unusual for them to be made where they were to be used and, having served their purpose, they were broken up or retained for further use, since their removal was almost impossible.

Small cannon were used at Creçy, the first credited employment of them on the field of battle. Such weapons were of a semi-portable character, were removed in carts or carried by hand from battle-field to battle-field with the camp baggage. The only pieces designed specially for field use were the " ribeaudequins " or "orgues des bombardes," which consisted of a number of small cannon on a common carriage, the cannon often supplemented by a " chevaux de frise," or pikes were lashed to the carriage. It was rare that these weapons were fired more than once during a battle. Most of the early fire-arms shot arrows, stone, and iron shot, and in Germany the mortars were filled up with small stones about the size of walnuts—the first form of what was afterwards long known as grape-shot. Other German States forbade the use of "hail shot" entirely. Monro, writing in 1626, with reference to early cannon states : " It is thought that the invention of cannon was found first at Nuremberg for the ruin of man, being at first used for battering down of walls of cities . . . . till at last they were used in the field to break the squadrons of foot and horse, some carrying pieces called spingards of four foot and a half long, and shot many bullets at once no greater than walnuts, which were carried on the fields on little chariots behind the troopers."

In the Wars of the Roses cannon were but little used ; the Lancastrians had them in the field at Northampton, but, owing to the heavy rain, could not use them. At the taking of Bamborough Castle several were employed, and these were of different sizes—some of iron, others of brass—but the Yorkists did not wish to destroy the castle, but to take it whole and keep it for King Edward. For the siege of Harlech Castle a large cannon was requisitioned. It was brought specially from Calais, and had done good service in France, but it burst at Harlech —probably because overloaded in order to obtain the range required.

Very little more is known respecting these cannon except that each was separately named, as "The King's Daughter," " King Edward," " Bombartel," etc. ; that they were painted either bright red or black, or, if of brass, were brightly polished. They were the property of the King ; of the nobles ; or of the towns ; sometimes of humble individuals, who held their weapons and their own services for hire.

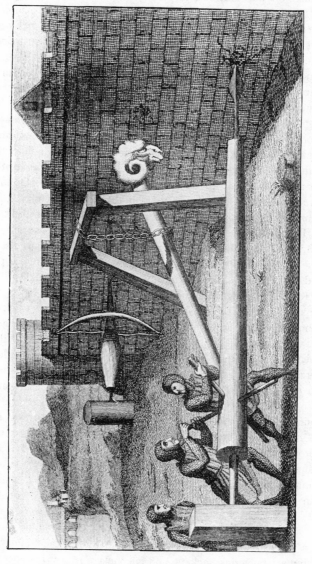

Mediæval Battering-ram and Engines of War. (*After Grose.*)

The battering-ram was the most important engine of war at sieges until the middle of the fifteenth century. Some of the larger rams were far more powerful than the largest of the early cannon : it has been computed that one worked by a thousand men had a force equal only to that from a 36-pounder at close range. In the Middle Ages the rams used were smaller, and other engines were used in conjunction with them to make breaches in the walls ; some of these are shown in the accompanying illustration from Grose's " Military Antiquities."

To the improved cannon must be attributed the losses of the English in France during the reign of Henry VI. ; the artillery of Charles VII. was greatly superior to that possessed by any of the English garrisons, and fortress after fortress, impregnable with the earlier conditions of warfare, fell to the French artillery. At the siege of Orleans Metz lent the beleaguered town a gigantic cannon, and when Joan of Arc went to raise the siege she had with her an immense quantity of fire-arms. The few cannon then in the possession of the English in France are enumerated in a contemporary record cited in Stevenson's " Wars of the English in France."

It was in Italy and Germany that cannon were manufactured and the early fire-arms developed ; and it was from these countries that the French were supplied with guns larger and in every way superior to any possessed by the English. After the Wars of the Roses the English remedied the defect. King Henry VIII. was particularly anxious to add to his store, and sometimes, as in 1522, he levied princely blackmail of fire-arms from the Venetian galleys trading to Flanders ; yet as early as 1513 the Venetian Ambassador had reported to the Doge that Henry had " cannon enough to conquer hell." A visitor to the Tower of London in 1515 states that there were then in the Tower about 400 cannon, and that most of them were mounted on wheels. It was in the reign of Henry VIII. that cannon were first cast in England. Peter Bawde, a Frenchman, was the artificer ; he cast brass cannon in Houndsditch in 1525. Later, about 1535, John O'Ewen was engaged in the work, and by 1543 the industry was flourishing at Uckfield, Sussex, then the centre of the iron trade in Britain.

About this period also so numerous and divers were the pieces in use that they were divided into classes and arranged and named according to the calibre, length, or weight. In France in the reign of Charles V. cannon were mounted upon carriages, and had trunnions and handles, and the touch-holes were covered with hinged flaps. The cannon of the French army then consisted of mortars, four sizes of cannon throwing bullets weighing from 6 to 40 lbs. each, and were called respectively, cannons, culverins, sackers, and falconets. In 1551, under Francis I., the artillery of the French army consisted of six pieces, and as they included the leading styles of cannon of this period, a full description will not be out of place.

The "cannon" was nearly 9 feet 10 inches long, weighed 5,300 lbs., carried a bullet 33¼ lbs., and was drawn upon a carriage by twenty-one horses.

The "great culverin" was nearly 10 feet long, weighed 4,000 lbs., carried a bullet 15 lbs. 2 ozs., and was drawn by seventeen horses.

The "bastard culverin" was 9 feet long, weighed 2,500 lbs., and carried a bullet weighing 7 lbs. 2 ozs. ; it was drawn by eleven horses.

The "small culverin" weighed 1,200 lbs., and carried a bullet weighing 2 lbs. The "falcon" weighed 700 lbs., and carried a bullet of 1 lb. 10 ozs. ; and the "falconet," which was 6 feet 4 inches long, weighed 410 lbs., and carried a 14-oz. bullet.

These cannon were of a bronze alloy, formed by mixing nine parts of copper to one part of tin.

The following is an account of names, dimensions, weight of cannon, shot, and powder of the ancient English ordnance. (Time, Elizabeth and James I. ; but properly applicable to latter period.)

Names.	Bore of Cannon.	Weight of Metal.	Weight of Shot.	Weight of Powder.
	inches.	lbs.	lbs.	lbs.
Cannon royal	8½	8,000	66	30
Cannon	8	6,000	60	27
Cannon serpentine	7	5,500	53½	25
Bastard cannon	7	4,500	41	20
Demi-cannon	6¾	4,000	33½	18
Cannon petro	6	4,000	24½	14
Culverin	5½	4,500	17½	12
Basilisk	5	4,000	15	10
Demi-culverin	4	3,400	9½	3
Bastard culverin	4	3,000	5	5¾
Sacar	3½	1,400	5½	5½
Minion	3½	1,000	4	4
Falcon	2½	660	2	3½
Falconet	2	500	1⅓	3
Serpentine	1½	400	¾	1½
Rabinet	1	300	½	¾

NOTE.—The weight of spherical lead shot of the diameter of the bore is often less than the weight of shot given in the table ; probably the weights indicate the safe limit of the load for grape, bar, spherical, or double shot.

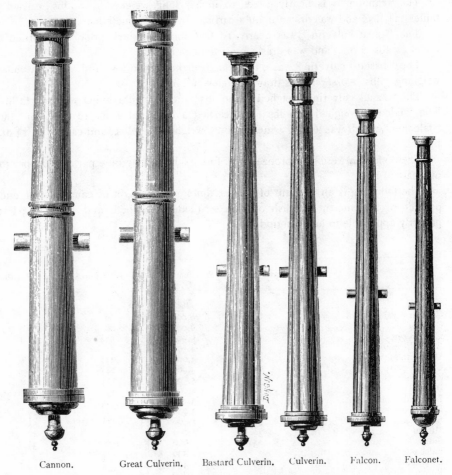

Cannon.   Great Culverin.   Bastard Culverin.   Culverin.   Falcon.   Falconet.

The Cannon of France under Francis I. (1515-47).

Bas-relief from the Church of Genouillac : Sixteenth Century.

A carving on an old French church shows a gun mounted without trunnions ; apparently fixed to the frame underneath by a loop, through which passes a transverse pin, so that the gun is capable of being elevated from the breech end.

EARLY MORTARS.

The first fire-arms, being made with a powder chamber of smaller diameter than the remainder of the short barrel, were therefore constructed upon the principle of the mortar. The touch-hole was usually placed in the front of the powder chamber. Mortars were classed separately from the cannon by Charles V. ; but they appear to have thrown stones or solid metal bullets, not shells. It is stated that red-hot iron shot were fired in defence of Cherbourg in 1418, at the siege of La Fère in 1580, just as at Gibraltar in 1782. The early gunners usually fired their guns with a red-hot iron rod heated in a charcoal fire made for the purpose on the battle-field.

Paul Jove, a historian contemporary with Charles VIII., and who chronicles the campaign of that monarch in Italy, says that the falcons and cannon of smaller calibre fired leaden bullets containing " bloqueraulx," or thimbles of iron. Explosive bombs, or " grenades," appear to have been first used by the Germans. They consisted of hollow metal balls filled with fine gunpowder ; the ball was surrounded by a slow-burning coat, and the whole contained in a case, the inflammable coat being ignited immediately before throwing the bomb. To the Netherlanders, however, is due the honour of successfully applying the explosive shell to fire-arms. This nation appears to have greatly improved the cannon and mortars and other fire-arms during the fifteenth, sixteenth, and seventeenth centuries. In the sixteenth century they successfully employed the explosive shell in conjunction with other missiles fired from their mortars. The accompanying illustration represents the mode of firing a mortar and bomb-shell, or, as they were then called, explosive bullets or grenades.

The bomb, after being filled and a slow match placed in the aperture, was put into the mortar with the match projecting from the mouth of the mortar. This was first lit and afterwards the charge ignited. This system was found to be dangerous

Soldier firing a Mortar and Bomb-shell requiring Double Ignition.

to the users, as in case of a misfire of the charge in the mortar, there was every probability of the shell bursting before the priming could be replaced or the shell extracted. The Germans improved upon this plan by the bomb with a single ignition. Senfftenberg of Dantzic, in his book written in 1580, describes the new invention as consisting of a slow match composed of two different materials. The tube was capped on the outside of the shell by a coil of highly inflammable vegetable composition. The bomb was placed in the mortar, as shown, with the coiled cap of the shell projecting into the powder chamber. Upon the discharge of the mortar the powder ignited the cap, which fired the slow-match in the tube

The Partridge Mortar. (*From Grose's "Military Antiquities."*)

leading to the interior of the shell.   Senfftenberg states that there was one
drawback to this shell, viz. in making night attacks the burning tow on the
shell lit up the surrounding country and showed to the enemy the position of
the besiegers.   Shortly afterwards oval bombs were successfully used, and shells
made in two or more pieces and bolted together.   Mortars were affixed to stands
capable of firing a bullet at any elevation between 40 degrees and the perpendicular.

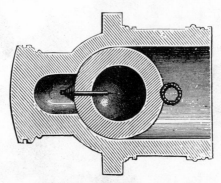

Mortar and Shell requiring Single Ignition only.

Numerous weapons of a compound character were made in the fifteenth
century; for instance, one large cannon with one of smaller bore on each side,
or above or below.   In mortars the most notable are those which fire three or
more projectiles at the same time ; these were fired simultaneously by means of
a common touch-hole communicating with each chamber.   One of nine chambers
is in the Tower, and another of thirteen is illustrated by Grose.

Gun-carriage and Team of Horse : Sixteenth Century.

EARLY BREECH-LOADING CANNON.

In addition to the primitive breech-loaders, in which the charge of powder was loaded into a separate breech-box and wedged up to the cannon, there were numerous methods employed for closing the breech of the cannon after inserting the charge. One of these is shown in the annexed illustration. The intercepted screw was used about the same time ; but in the seventeenth century, when cannon of greater strength were designed and grained gunpowder was used, it was found impossible to prevent the escape of gas at the breech, and the muzzle-loading

German Breech-loading Cannon of the Sixteenth Century.

cannon quickly superseded all methods of breech-loading for ordnance ; and have but recently disappeared in favour of the perfected breech-loaders fitted with effective gas checks.

EARLY SHIP CANNON.

The use of fire-arms on shipboard dates to the latter part of the fourteenth century, but the weapons had no distinctive feature. At the end of the following century it was usual for trading vessels to carry two or more bombards. The war vessels of the early sixteenth century were furnished with small cannon which were fired from the taffrail, and others which were fixed to the decks and fired through ports, as shown in the pictures still extant of the *Great Harry.*

The *Mary Rose*, an English vessel, was wrecked in the reign of Henry VIII., about 1545, while standing along the coast.   During a distant firing from the French

Warship carrying Cannon. (*After Valturius*, 1470-1500.)

fleet, under Admiral Annebout, she was overpowered by the weight of her ordnance, and sank, together with her commander and 600 men.   Owing to the praiseworthy exertions of Mr. Dean, several brass and iron cannon were recovered from the wreck about fifty years ago, and these relics throw some light upon the manner in which the English vessels were armed in the sixteenth century.

The gun shown is composed of a tube of iron, its joint overlapping and running the entire length of the barrel. Upon this tube is a succession of hoops composed of iron three inches square, being, in fact, immense rings. These were driven on whilst red-hot, and by their contraction formed a much stronger gun than would at first

Breech-loading Cannon of the *Mary Rose*.

appear probable. It was affixed to a large beam of timber by means of iron bolts, similar to the manner in which an iron musket-barrel is fastened to its stock. The loading was effected by removing a breech-block, inserting the charge, replacing the block, and wedging it into the barrel from behind, as shown on page 22. The recoil was prevented by means of a "bitt," or large beam, fixed perpendicularly in the deck.

Similar cannon were found in the Tyne whilst dredging, and are still in the old castle at Newcastle-on-Tyne.

The Venetians were among the first to use cannon on shipboard. In 1380 one of their vessels was taken at Sluies ; on board was a master gunner, "divers greate gunnes, and a quantitie of powder." This last is recorded by the chronicler to have been worth more than all the rest.

MISCELLANEOUS EARLY ARMS.

Cannon of three and more barrels were made in the fifteenth century ; a curious breech-loading cannon of this description is shown in the annexed illustration ; a different method of arranging the three barrels is also illustrated.

The bore of the cannon was not always circular ; an oval-bore cannon was made in Germany in 1625. A weapon of still greater elliptical bore is shown on the opposite page. This peculiarly shaped mortar was sometimes used to make breaches in barricades at close quarters, when it was charged to the muzzle, and bars of iron fired from it. It was also used for firing bar-shot.

Wooden Cannon of Cochin China.

The petard was a peculiar arm used for affixing to doors or walls in order to effect a breach. It consisted of a short gun, or rather cannon, loaded to the muzzle, and fixed in a peculiar manner against the surface to be blown apart, so that when fired the door or wall should receive the shock, and not the petard. Their use has long been discontinued, bags of gunpowder hung against barricades answering the purpose just as well.

Various substitutes for metal have been used for constructing cannon and mortars. Leather was probably the most successful ; it was often used by the Venetians, sometimes in conjunction with hempen rope, sometimes alone. A leather cannon was fired three times at King's Park, Edinburgh, in October, 1788. Cannon of paper, brought from Syria by the Crusaders, are preserved at Malta, and considered great curiosities. According to Nathaniel Nye, who wrote in 1640, an artificer of Bromsgrove, near Worcester, was very successful in making fire-arms or paper and leather, and they were recommended by Nye, as master gunner of Worcester, because of their lightness and strength.

Wooden cannon do not appear to have been at all common in Europe ; several have been brought from China and the East, where they seem to have been in general use. The one illustrated is still in the Paris Museum, and, as shown, is

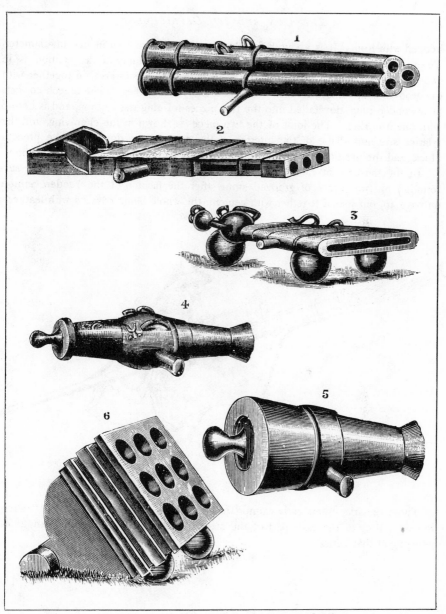

Old Cannon, Mortars, etc., from the Tower of London.

hooped with iron.   It is about 8 feet long, and the bore is 6 inches in diameter. The wood used is of light colour, but very hard.   The body of the cannon is in two pieces, each having a groove in its centre ; the two pieces are laid together with the grooves coinciding with each other, and hooped together.   The breech consists of a wooden plug, dovetailed into the two pieces forming the cannon, and is bound with one iron ring.   The joint of the two pieces is shown in the engraving, and the relative size and shape of the interior of the cannon, the dovetail of the breech-block, and the position and shape of the touch-hole, are shown by the dotted lines

In the museum at Zürich is a cannon made of a thin iron coil or tube sur-rounded by two pieces of grooved stone after the fashion of the wooden cannon on page 40, but joined together with cement, the whole being covered with leather.

Soldier Firing Semi-portable Gun (from an early MS.).

These remarks upon early cannon may be aptly concluded by an illustration from a painting of the early part of the sixteenth century, showing the manner of besieging at that period.

Besieging a Fortified Castle : Sixteenth Century.

CHAPTER IV.

EARLY HAND FIRE-ARMS.

CANNON AS HAND-GUNS.

No distinction can be drawn between the small cannon or "crash-guns" of the fourteenth century and the earliest hand fire-arms. A pyrotechnical piece developed into a variety of hand weapon, and used for military purposes—especially for causing disturbances among troops, frightening horses and stampeding cattle—was employed by Eastern nations and by the Arabs in Northern Africa. The following description of this weapon is from the "Dictionnaire Mobilier Français," and, according to that work, it was also used by incendiaries, pillagers, and outlaws. In the illustration B shows the exterior of the gun; A is an end elevation, and C a sectional view showing the construction. The gun consisted of an iron tube about six feet long, covered with two hollowed pieces of wood, and bound round with

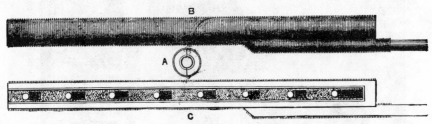

Pyrotechnical Hand-weapon.

hair, hemp, hide, or other suitable substance. The charge was composed of, first, a bed of fine gunpowder, four fingers in thickness, then a bullet made of hempen stuff mixed with powder, wax, etc., then a layer of coarse powder, composed of powdered glass, Grecian wax, steel filings and saltpetre, then two fingers of fine powder and bullet alternately, until loaded to the muzzle; it will thus be seen that the weapon greatly resembled a *Roman candle* or *pump*, throwing successively burning wax and inflammable balls. The weapon was, of course, fired from the muzzle, and the whole tube bound upon a stick, to handle it during the discharge.

it is said that such weapons were in use amongst the Arabs during the fifteenth century.

The "hand-cannon," as first used by the French, Italians, and Netherlanders, consisted of a small bombarde (*bombardello*) affixed to a straight piece of wood, and fired from the shoulder by means of a match, as shown in the accompanying illustration. A slight modification of this weapon rendered it applicable for use upon horseback. Instead of being fastened to a stock, the bombarde was welded on to an iron rod about 30 inches long ; the extremity of the rod was pierced, and a cord passed through, and thus suspended from the neck of the soldier.

Foot Soldier firing Hand-cannon : Fourteenth Century.

The bombarde was supported by a forked rest projecting from the saddle-bow, and pointed by the left hand, the right serving to apply the fire to the touch-hole. Both illustrations are from the MS. of Marianus Jacobus, written in 1449.

The first account of hand-cannon being used in Germany was in 1381, when the town of Augsburg supplied thirty men armed with them to the contingent of the Suabian towns in their war against the South German nobles.

The exact construction of these early cannon is shown by the annexed illustration. The powder chamber was of smaller internal diameter than the bore of the gun, but externally larger ; the mount was sometimes a staff forced into the ferrule at the base of the chamber ; more often a spike from the breech of the gun was driven into the staff. These cannon were known as *bastons-à-feu* or " fire-sticks," and were common in the Netherlands in the fifteenth and sixteenth centuries.

These fire-arms were sometimes so fashioned as to be capable of use as clubs or battle-axes. The club pistol shown on page 48 is about two feet in length, the touch-hole is on the top, and the pistol was held in one hand and fired by application of a

Cavalier Firing Petronel. (*After Marianus Jacobus.*)

slow-match from the other. The next figure represents a pistol battle-axe in the Dresden Museum ; dotted lines show the position of the touch-hole. For use as a fire-arm the grip of the axe had to be reversed, and it was grasped near the head ; later pistols had the axe-head fixed upon the muzzle end of the barrel. The two weapons here illustrated are both of fifteenth century manufacture.

The ordinary hand-culverin consisted of a small cannon affixed to a stock by iron bands, as represented. The barrel was of forged iron ; the stock of rough wood, nearly straight; the barrel being fastened to it by the five iron bands, and the two side bridles fastening the trunnion or swivel band to the butt. These culverins were of small bore (about ½ or ¾ inch), and were extensively used towards the close of the fifteenth century; for at the battle of Morat, in 1476, the Swiss army counted not less than 6,000 culveriners. The hand culverin required two

Early Hand-guns, showing Methods of handling them, as illustrated in contemporary MS. ; and a Sectional View of Gun, showing its Construction.

men to manipulate it. It was fired from a rest, sometimes forked (*fourquine*), and sharpened at its lower extremity to obtain a firm hold in the soil, and served also as a ramrod. One man (the culveriner) levelled and held the weapon during discharge, whilst his companion (the *gougat*) applied the priming and the match, and assisted in loading and carrying the weapon. The culverin was improved at a later date by having the bore enlarged, the stock more bent, and affixed to the barrel by entering into a recess in its breech-end, as shown in the accompanying illustration by the dotted lines. The internal bore of the barrel and the position of the touch-hole are also shown by the dotted lines. A forked rest was used with this

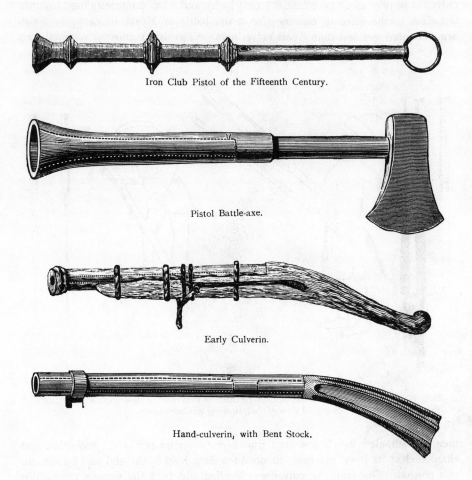

Iron Club Pistol of the Fifteenth Century.

Pistol Battle-axe.

Early Culverin.

Hand-culverin, with Bent Stock.

culverin, and in some instances the stock was ornamented with grooves of various sizes. The culverin was afterwards improved by placing the touch-hole upon the side, with a flash-pan for the powder, as shown. The barrels were made of bronze, and cast in octagonal or hexagonal form ; the stock was lengthened, fitting under the arm, and shaped like the butts of modern punt-guns. Several good specimens of these early culverins are to be seen in the Musée des Invalides at Paris. The culverins varied greatly in their dimensions and weight ; the smallest for horseback use, and similar to, or identical with, the pétrinal, were about 4 feet long, and weighed from 10 to 15 lbs. ; the larger culverins were from 4 to 8 feet long, and weighed from 12 to 60 lbs. By the end of the fifteenth century hand-cannon were in use throughout Europe as military weapons. Charles VII. had a corps of horse-culveriners, and the hand-culveriners of Charles VIII. played an important part in Italy during his campaign in 1494. Hand-cannon were also used by the Emperor

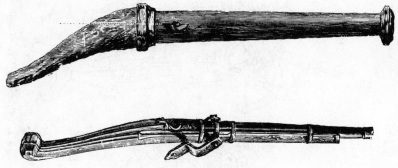

Culverins with side Flash-pans.

Sigismund, who led 500 men armed with "rest-guns," in his Roman campaign in 1430, when they created a great sensation, although similar guns had been made at Padua as early as 1386. Hand-guns figured conspicuously in the Hussite wars, and at the siege of Lucca by the Florentines in 1431. All these early hand-guns were, however, roughly constructed, for their accuracy in hitting was as small as the trouble of loading was great, and their imperfections as numerous as those of the gunpowder with which they were fired, which was veritably powder, resembling dust —powder not being granulated till the sixteenth century.

The first English illustration of a hand-gun appears in the Royal MS. 18 E. fol. xxxiv., written in 1473. On page 51 is reproduced the illustration, which, however, has already appeared in "Hewitt's Ancient Arms and Armour." The drawing is not an explicit one ; it fails to show the position of the touch-hole, or to explain in which way the gun was fired. As the bearer carries neither flask nor pouch, he must have been accompanied by an attendant, who carried the accessories and applied

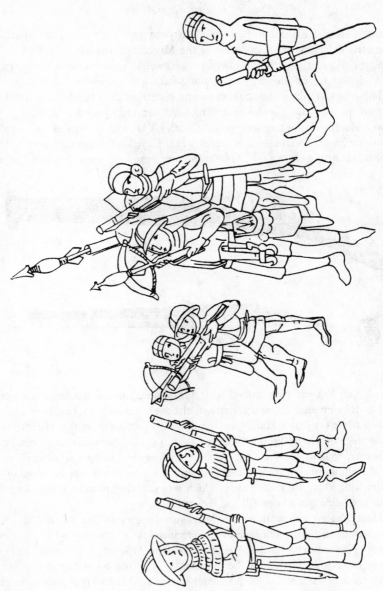

German Gunners and Cross-bow Men of 1430.

the ignition to the arm. The position of the man is very peculiar, and one not well calculated to withstand the recoil. The manner of grasping the gun is also original, and from the general appearance of the drawing it appears to represent a

Soldier Firing Hand-gun : Fifteenth Century

soldier shooting a weapon of precision at a dead mark. Much allowance must, of course, be made for the rude drawing of the time—a point still more emphasised in the preceding group, which is reproduced from a German MS. of 1430--40, now in Vienna.

THE MATCHLOCK.

The development of the matchlock is shown in the following illustrations, all taken from German MSS. of 1460–80, now in the Royal University Library at Erlangen. The pointed protuberance at the muzzle is, of course, the sight, the corresponding jagged disc at the breech of the middle gun of the group may be a back-sight, or simply points upon which to fasten the prepared tow which served as a slow-match ; more probably the former, since in the third figure the disc to

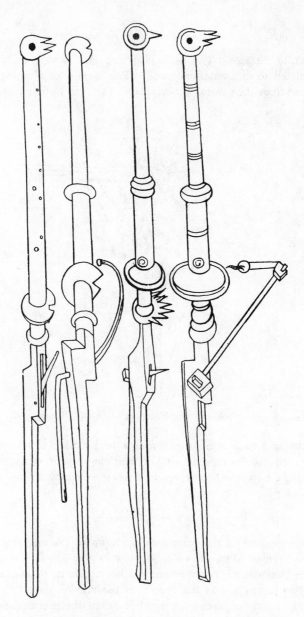

The Development of the " Matchlock.

protect the hand of the firer from being burnt by the powder in the flash-pan is undoubtedly notched in order to serve as a back-sight.

THE FIRST MATCHLOCKS.

The main feature of the invention consists of the "serpentin," or cock for holding the match. In later models the arrangement was as in the following illustration.

Gun with Serpentin.

The slow-match is kept burning in a holder on the top of the barrel; the flash-pan and touch-hole are at the side. The serpentin is hung upon a pivot passing through the stock and continued past the pivot, forming a lever for the hand. To discharge the piece the match in the serpentin is first brought into contact with the burning match on the barrel until ignited : then, by raising the lever and moving it to one side, the serpentin is brought into the priming in the touch-hole, and the gun discharged—though it is highly probable the first arquebuses did not carry the fire in a holder on the barrel, but only the match in the serpentin.

The advantages of the matchlock were at once appreciated, and its adoption was general. Its improvement was rapid ; in great measure due to the adaptation of the releasing trigger mechanism of the cross-bow to the fire-arm.

In a few years it was found advantageous to place the serpentin the reverse way, and to provide a spring to hold the match—away from the touch-hole ; pressure upon the lever caused the serpentin with the lighted match to fall into the flash-pan. This is the mechanism shown in the illustration of the lock. The same general arrangement will be noticed in the matchlock fire-arms carried by the soldiers elsewhere illustrated in this chapter.   Particularly the simple arquebus, as

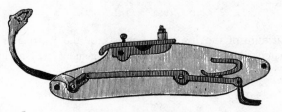

Mechanism of the Matchlock.

used by the Spaniards in 1527, when they captured Francis I. at Pavia, which had a trigger matchlock, to which mechanism the success of that battle has been attributed.   This weapon was also used by the Spaniards in the conquest of Mexico (1519) and Peru (1530-40).

Spanish Arquebusier of the Sixteenth Century.

OPPOSITION TO THE USE OF FIRE-ARMS.

Guns upon their introduction, and more especially hand-guns, met with great opposition.

The French were perhaps the most bitter against them. One old French author says :—

" On ne faisoit point encore usage en France, en 1547, de cette arme terrible contre les hommes; les François s'en étoient bien servis en 1338, pour l'attaque de quelques châteaux mais ils rougissoient de l'employer contre leurs semblables. Les Anglais, moins humains, sans doute, nous devancèrent et s'en servirent à la célèbre bataille de Creçi, qui eut lieu entre ces troupes du Roi d'Angleterre, Edouard III., qui fut si méchant, si perfide, qui donna tant de fil à retordre à Philippe de Valois et aux troupes de ce dernier; et ce fut en majeure partie à la frayeur et à la confusion qu'occasionnèrent les canons, dont les Anglois se servoient pour la première fois, qu'ils avoient postés sur une colline proche le village de Creçi, que les François derent leur route."

[Translation.]

" No use has yet been made in France, in 1547, of that terrible weapon against men. The French used it with good effect against some castles in 1338, but they would blush to employ it against their fellow-creatures. The English, less humane, without doubt outstripped us, and made use of some at the celebrated battle of Creçy, which took place against the troops of King Edward III. of England, who was so spiteful and treacherous that he plagued Philip de Valois and his troops to the last; and the greater part of the terror and confusion was occasioned by the cannon, which the English used for the first time, and had placed upon a knoll near the village of Creçy, and to which the French assign their defeat."

When the celebrated Montluc made his first appearance in the field under Francis I. fire-arms were less esteemed than the cross-bow, and the characteristic remark made by him in " *Michaud et Poujoulat* " clearly shows his opinion of these new weapons :—

" I must observe," says Montluc, " that the troops which I commanded consisted of cross-bow men only; since at that time there were in our nation no soldiers armed with guns. Only three or four days before, six Gascon arquebusiers, deserters, came over from the enemy's camp to our army, and these men I kept with me, as I had the good fortune on that day to be on duty at the gate of the town. One of these men was from the Montluc estates. I wonder, however, that it could have been the will of Providence that this unlucky instrument should have been invented. I myself still bear about me the marks that it has left, which even now cause me to suffer much weakness; and have seen brave and valiant men killed with it in such sad numbers, and it generally happened that they were struck down to the ground by those abominable bullets, which had been discharged by cowardly and base knaves, who would never have dared to have met true soldiers face to face and hand to hand. All this is very clearly one of those artifices which the devil employs to induce us human beings to kill one another "

Fire-arms were greatly dreaded by all classes, and Shakespeare humorously alludes to this fact in *King Henry IV.* :—

> " And that it was a great pity, so it was,
> That villainous saltpetre should be digg'd
> Out of the bowels of the harmless earth,
> Which many a good tall fellow had destroyed
> So cowardly ; and, but for those vile guns,
> He would himself have been a soldier."
>
> *Henry IV.*, act i. scene iii.

Most loudly did the armoured knights clamour against the use of fire-arms, for even their thick armour could not be made proof against the heavy bullets, and it was not a usual thing for a well-armoured knight to be killed. A good suit of armour would generally repel the blow of an arrow or quarrel; although the horses, not so fortunate, and driven mad by the rage and pain caused by the thrusts of the rough barbed missiles, would rear and throw their riders; then the doughty warriors would roll about for a time upon the earth, to retire with only a few bruises, and ready to engage in the tilting match another day. In several battles about this time not a single knight was slain ; even when unhorsed, it was difficult to administer the *coup de grâce* to the valiant cavalier, for the *miséricorde,* or dagger of mercy, refused to penetrate the chinks of a closely jointed suit.

At the battle of Fournoüe a number of Italian knights, being unhorsed, could only be killed after they and their armour had been broken up, like so many lobsters, with wood-cutters' axes. Well might James I. remark that defensive armour was a double protection, preventing the bearer from being injured or from injuring others.

Gunshot wounds in these early days were considered to be all but necessarily mortal, which may be accounted for by the unskilful surgery of the times. Some of the recipes for the cure of gunshot wounds were, however, much more likely to prove mortal than the wound itself. The following is one given, but the precise details are wanting :—Take of oil and wine equal parts, inject them into a living dog, well boil the animal ; its flesh, together with the oil, wine, and other ingredients, form the application.

It was clear that the armour could never be so increased in strength as to withstand the missiles from field artillery, even if successful against the handguns. The gunners improved in marksmanship, and then weapons were more carefully made, so that they at length became formidable, and, as they were

Group of Harquebusiers. (*From the Treatise by Jacob de Gheyn.*)

numerous in every army by the middle of the sixteenth century, the heavily mailed knights bowed to the inevitable, and protective armour gradually decayed, after having been so increased in weight that the horses could barely sustain their burden.

THE HARQUEBUSIERS.

The harquebusier or culveriner—the man who carried and fired a hand-gun— was usually also conversant with its manufacture, sometimes was the actual maker of the weapon; hence the application of the name to gun-makers. The great difficulty with which he had to contend in the field of battle was obtaining fire with which to ignite his gun or, when armed with a matchlock, to keep the match aglow. The weapons were very heavy, most unwieldy, tiresome to load, and continually missing fire.

Having discharged their weapons, a body of culveriners would be for the time defenceless. To remedy this, the culveriner was supplied with a sword, or the rest was converted into a defensive weapon, by adjoining a dagger, which was released by a spring. Such rests received the name of swines, or Swedish feathers.

The sword was too much for the early culveriner, for he had already too many encumbrances. Grose says that "he had, in addition to the unwieldy weapon itself, his coarse powder, for loading, in a flask; his fine powder, for priming, in a touch-box; his bullets in a leather bag, with strings to draw to get at them; whilst in his hand were his musket-rest and his burning match."

The French culveriners, too, generally carried their lighted fuse at the girdle, until about firing, when it was wound round the right arm. With all these encumbrances, it is not surprising to find that the bow was for many years considered a superior weapon.

The culveriner was generally accompanied by an attendant, called a "varlet" or *gougat*, to carry the rests and keep the fire going—a difficult matter in a shower of rain, unless, as was once the custom, the matches were carried in the hat. History states that great difficulty in retaining the fire was experienced by the English musketeers in the battle of Dunbar (1650), which was fought during a dense fog, and a heavy fall of rain took place the night previous, to which the troops were exposed.

An extract from an old military work will give some idea of the powder, matches, and arms of the sixteenth and early seventeenth centuries. It is from the " Military Fireworks," by Kabel, published in 1619. The author says :—

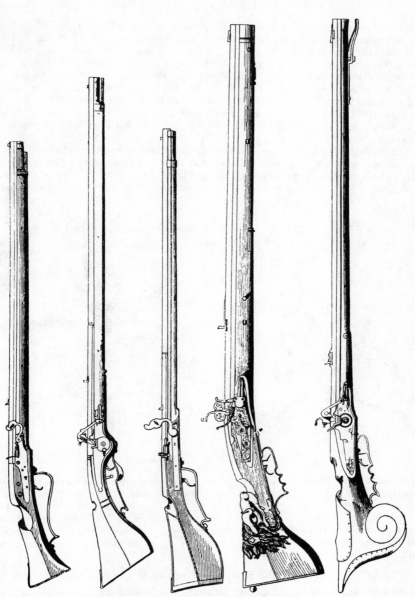

Early Arquebuses, illustrating the Development of the Gun stock.

" One of the greatest helpes consist in the pouther and match. For a souldier must ever buy his pouther sharpe in taste, well incorporate with saltpetre, and not full of coal-dust (raw charcoal). Let him accustome to drie his powder, if he can, in the sunne, just sprinkling it over with *aqua vitæ* or strong claret wine. Let him make his tutch powder, being finely sarsed and sifted, with quick-pale, which is to be bought at the powder-maker's or apothecarie's ; and let his match be boyled in ashes-lie and powder, that it may bothe burn well and carry a long coale, and that will not falle off with touch of his finger. This preparation will at first touch give fire, and procure a violent, speedy, and thundering discharge. Some use brimstone, finely powdered, in their touch powder, but that furs and stops up your breech and tutchole.

" The bullet of a souldier's piece must be of a just bignesse with the mouth of the same, so that, falling in smoothly, it drive down and close up the mouth of the powder. If the stock of his piece be crooked, he ought to place the end just before the right papp ; if long and straight, as the Spaniards use them, then upon the point of his right shoulder, using a stately upright

Horseman using Hand-cannon.

pace in discharge. The musquet is to be used in all respects like the harqabuse, save that in respect it carries a double bullet, and is much more weightie. The souldier useth a staffe breaste high, in the one end a pike to pitch on the ground, and in the other an iron forke to rest his piece upon, and a hole a little beneath the same in the staffe, whereunto he doth adde a string, which tied and wrapped about his wrest, yealdes him commodity to train his forke or staffe after him, whilst he in skirmish doth charge his musquet afresh with powder and bullet."

The difference between the musket and arquebus is here defined. At a later period, the light for igniting the matches was carried by a slow-burning fuse contained in a metal case perforated with small holes to afford egress for the smoke.

The Holy-water Sprinkle.

These fire-holders were usually attached to the girdle. All the early fire-arms were so slow to load that as late as the battle of Kuisyingen, in 1636, the slowest soldiers

Gun *v.* Lance. (*From a Sixteenth Century German Treatise on Military Exercises.*)

managed to fire seven shots only during eight hours; and in 1638, at Wittenmergen, the musketeers of the Duke of Weimar shot seven times only during the action that lasted from noon to eight o'clock in the evening.

METHODS OF USING EARLY FIRE-ARMS.

The object of the early gunner was to frighten; guns were made expressly for the purpose of the report caused by firing them —"crakys of war" they were termed—and, indeed, this appears to have been the most valuable and satisfactory performance of the early guns; for Montaigne wrote in 1585, when numerous improvements had been made, that

German Shooter, 1545.

" the effect of fire-arms, apart from the shock caused by the report, to which one does not easily get accustomed," was so insignificant that he hoped they would be discarded.

To add to the terror of the knights, and for unexpected use at close quarters, a variety of peculiar fire-arms were produced. The repeating arm was advantageous when the enemy, having seen the gun discharged, came boldly up and was fired

Methods of Shooting in the Sixteenth Century.

upon again and again at very close range. So the pistol battle-axes and clubs already described were a species of secret or surprise weapon. The " Holy-water Sprinkle," a fire-arm much favoured by the English of the early sixteenth century, consisted of a strong mace, the head of which was formed by four or more barrels joined and arranged in the same manner as the chamber of a modern revolver, and having upon the outside one or more spike-studded collars. There was usually but one flash-pan having connection with all the barrels ; the powder was placed in and fired by a match from the hand.

For use on horseback the fire-arm appears to have been considered as supplementary to lance and sword until the middle of the sixteenth century. Old drawings show that it was of secondary importance. Books of military exercises instruct the gunner how to use his weapons to best advantage against infantry, but the fact that the fire-arms could be used by cavalry as an offensive weapon against foot soldiers was not soon discovered.

The German cavalry called Ritters were the first to use the pistol with signal success. At the battle of Renty, fought in 1544, they charged the French in squadrons fifteen to twenty ranks deep, and halted immediately on coming

South German Harquebusiers, 1500-10.

within range, each rank firing in turn and wheeling to the right or left, falling in again at the rear and reloading the pistols. The manœuvre, called " caracole," was entirely new, and was at once adopted in the French army; and occasioned lances to be gradually but surely replaced by pistols.

The methods of holding the gun whilst firing were as various as the weapons used. From the illustration on page 62 it will be seen that many shots were made with the butt of the gun against the hips or against the breastbone. Short guns appear to have been held against the cheek, and, as already shown, the earliest hand-cannon were fired whilst the butt rested upon the shoulder—a method confirmed by the shape of gun stocks of very much later date.

METHODS OF SHOOTING IN SIXTEENTH CENTURY.

The group of shooters is from a picture by M. Ferelen, and is dated 1533; the shooter kneeling is from a wood-cut of 1545. It was usual to shoot with both eyes open at this date, but from a drawing of 1500–10 in the Munich State Library the habit of closing one eye was also practised; this drawing is here reproduced (page 63), and shows the intention of the shooter unmistakably.

THE WHEEL-LOCK.

To obviate the difficulty of retaining fire in the matchlock, it was sought in Germany, early in the sixteenth century, to fix a flint and steel to the side of the gun, the powder in the flash-pan serving the purpose of the tinder in the box of the domestic strike-fires. In the Dresden Museum the " Monk's Gun," as it is called,

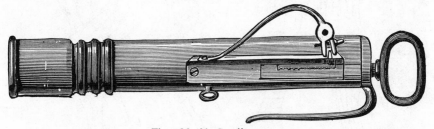

The "Monk's Gun," 1510-15.

is still preserved, and, as will be seen by the illustration, the friction necessary to the production of the sparks is obtained by drawing out and pushing in the roughened steel, or file, against the flake of flint which presses down upon it near the flash-hole. The pyrites is held in the jaws of the serpentin so shaped as to form a strong spring upon the side of the weapon; there is a guard underneath to assist the hand whilst gripping the pistol. The ring at the breech is attached to a bar of steel with a serrated edge against which the pyrites presses: the touch-hole is immediately in front of the pyrites; by drawing the ring sharply the serrated edges move past the pyrites, and the required stream of sparks is thus obtained and the priming ignited.

The wheel-lock proper was invented in 1515 at Nuremberg, and its mechanism was entirely different to anything constructed up to that date. Its parts were a grooved steel wheel with serrated edge, which worked partly in the flash-pan, and was connected to the lock-plate by means of chain and strong spring, after the fashion of a watch-drum. The spring power was stored by winding the wheel up with a key or "spanner." In front of the pan a catch was placed, moved by a strong spring, and holding a pyrite with its jaws. When ready for firing, the wheel was wound up, the flash-pan lid pushed back, and the pyrites held in the cock allowed to come in contact with the wheel. By pressure on the trigger a stop-pin was drawn back out of the wheel, and the latter, turning round its pivot at a considerable speed, produced sparks by the friction against the pyrites, and thus ignited the priming.

The improvements in the application of the flint for the purpose of igniting fire-arms were made by Kehfuss, of Nuremberg, in 1517, further improvements of note being made in 1573 and 1632 at Nuremberg and in Venice about 1584.

The next illustration shows the mechanism of the ordinary German wheel-lock ; AA, is the lock-plate ; BB, the wheel-drum ; C, the axle ; D, the serpentin holding

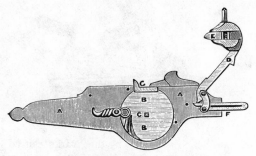

The German Wheel-lock.

the pyrite, E, and kept pressing against the edge of the wheel, B, in the flash-pan, G, by means of the spring, F. The scear and scear-spring are arranged upon the opposite side of the plate. At first the scear simply withdrew from a notch in the wheel, but later various complicated mechanisms were affixed ; but they are not of sufficient utility to require a description. The scear was acted upon by a trigger in the usual way.

The wheel-lock gun was most expensive to manufacture, and was therefore confined in a great measure to sporting purposes and for use upon horseback, where it offered great advantages over the clumsy, but far less expensive, matchlock arquebus. With the introduction of the wheel-lock the fire-arm came into more general use for sporting purposes : with the old-fashioned culverins, or hand-cannon, game could only be shot upon rare opportunities, or by waiting *caché* until the unwary animals passed the sportsman, and it was altogether impossible to take a fine aim ; with the wheel-lock a steady aim could be obtained ; the guns were made lighter, and leaden bullets used.

The use of fire-arms for sporting and other purposes became so general towards the middle of the sixteenth century that a prohibition appeared in the State Papers of the Elector Augustus of Saxony, dated the 10th October, 1555, and in it the following passage occurs :—"Whereas the carrying of fire-arms in our dominions has become so general that not only travellers, but peasants and shepherds, are found to use them."

THE FLINT-LOCK GUN.

In the flint-lock the hammer, or *cover plate* to the *flash-pan*, is knocked backwards by the blow of the flint screwed in the jaws of the *cock*, and uncovers the

Spanish Flint-lock.

priming in the flash-pan, which is ignited by the sparks caused by the flint coming into contact with the steel face of the hammer.

The most reliable accounts state the flint-lock to have been of Spanish origin, and invented early in the seventeenth century, and prior to 1630. Immediately upon its introduction it was styled the Lock à la Miquelet, and so named, it is said, from a Spanish regiment composed of marauders (Miquelitos) of the Pyrenees ; in which case the account of its invention will correspond somewhat with that given by Grose and other English writers, who state the flint-lock to have been of Dutch origin, and first used by robbers, or rather poultry stealers (*snaap-hans*), who, it is said, invented the flint-lock from a study of the wheel-lock, the use of the matchlock exposing them, on their marauding expeditions, to great inconvenience from the light of the priming-match showing their position, and they being unable to provide themselves with wheel-locks on account of their heavy cost. The flint-lock was called after them the Snaphaunce, under which name it certainly was known for many years in the Netherlands. Soon after their introduction the flint-lock guns were called fusils, from the flints (*fucile*), by a very common abuse of language, which consists in giving to an entire object a name taken from one of its parts. The flint-lock is so well known that it is almost unnecessary to describe its mechanism.

Many years elapsed before the lock assumed even the shape and arrangement generally known, but it consisted of a mainspring upon the outside of the lock-plate that answered also for the hammer-spring, and had no swivel ; the scear and the piece of metal answering to what afterwards became the tumblers were fixed upon the inside of the lock-plate. The illustration represents an early Spanish flint-lock taken from a gun in the royal collection at Dresden, and which, from the ornamentation upon it, appears to be intended for a sporting weapon.

The flint-lock was not readily adopted either in England or France. In the latter country the generals of Louis XIII. raised numerous objections to its use, saying—as was indeed true—that the sparks caused by the flint striking the hammer were not always sufficient to fire the charge, the stream of sparks going on either side of the pan, and failing to enter it. To remedy this fault *musket* fusils were constructed, which consisted of guns having a combination of both the flint and the matchlock.

In the year 1653, by an ordinance of Louis XIV., soldiers were forbidden to use flint-lock guns, and by another, later in the same year, the use of these guns by soldiers was made a crime punishable with death. They were introduced into England in the reign of William III., and from that time gradually increased in favour till they became the general weapons of this country. They remained in use in the British army until 1840, flint guns being manufactured in Birmingham for the English Government as late as 1842.

EARLY SPORTING FIRE-ARMS.

As a sporting weapon, the gun dates from the invention of the wheel-lock ; before that period the long-bow in England and the cross-bow on the Continent were the usual weapons of the chase. In the fifteenth century fire-arms were used for sporting purposes in Italy, Spain, Germany, and to a lesser extent in France. In Great Britain little use appears to have been made of them for game-shooting until the latter half of the seventeenth century, and at that time the arms used for the purpose were entirely of foreign make.

The large, long, heavy hand-cannon used for military purposes were quite unsuited to the chase, but from certain references in mediæval manuscripts it appears that they were occasionally so used. The earliest gun at all suited to purposes of sport is the short matchlock here shown ; but it may have been intended to serve primarily as a weapon of defence.

The invention of rifling at Nuremberg in the fifteenth century leading to the production of arms giving greater accuracy, and the invention of the wheel-lock

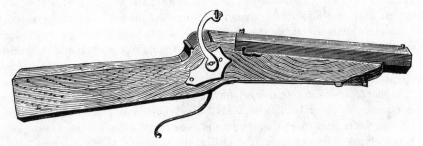

German Matchlock Gun.

permitting fire-arms to be used for stalking, for which the matchlock with its ever-burning torch could not be used, led to the acceptance of fire-arms by sportsmen. These arms, being evidently expensive and highly valued, have been so well preserved that numerous specimens still exist. Some few well deserve fuller description than space permits, but the illustrations will doubtless convey a better idea of their finish than would any verbal enumeration of their dimensions and construction.

EARLY GERMAN SPORTING FIRE-ARMS.

The first weapon illustrated is a German rifle of the first half of the seventeenth century. This beautiful weapon is one of several equally valuable found in the Birmingham collection. It is a wheel-lock musket, of which the serpentin resembles the head of a griffin. The stock is richly carved with scroll designs, and the engraving upon the weapon, especially that of the lock-plate, is worthy of the highest commendation, representing a hunting party in chase of a stag. The barrel bears the stamp and name of the maker, I. Georg Dax in München.

The wheel is inside the lock-plate and the pressing of the trigger causes the flash-pan (*couvré bassinet*) to slide back ; a safety-bolt is also attached to this gun, which is actuated by a small pointed stud descending from the stock immediately in front of the trigger. A bead-sight is affixed upon the muzzle, and a back wind-gauge peep-elevating sight is placed upon the stock in front of the grip. This sight is exactly similar in construction to the one used during the first half of the present century by the late Mr. J. Purdey and other English gun-makers.

Ornamental German Wheel-lock Musquetoon.

The next arm illustrated is of a similar type and character, but the workmanship is of better quality. The stock is inlaid with ivory and ebony in fanciful designs.

The engraving upon the lock-plate represents an army encamped. It is of a little later date than the preceding gun. The barrel is rifled, and the weapon appears to be of German manufacture, and probably was made about the end of the seventeenth century.

The next to be illustrated are four "handbüchse," taken promiscuously from a case in the Dresden Museum. The upper one is a German rifle, the wheel-lock and hammer artfully concealed by the stag; the back sight is silver, the stock artistically inlaid with sporting and scroll designs, of a shape prevalent in Germany in the seventeenth and early eighteenth centuries.

The next is a wheel-lock sporting carbine, the well-curved stock being profusely ornamented by silver and ivory inlaying. The third rifle has the stock wholly of buck-horn, and doubtless was so constructed by way of novelty. It, as well as the two preceding, is of Saxon make. Saxon pistols, too, of same date and style, are in the Museum; the stock of one, some 18 inches in length, being carved from one horn, and without a join—a rare sample of man's ingenuity. It would be tedious to enumerate the various materials of which gun-stocks have been constructed. Woods of almost every known kind, steel, iron, copper, silver, whalebone, ivory, leather, paper,

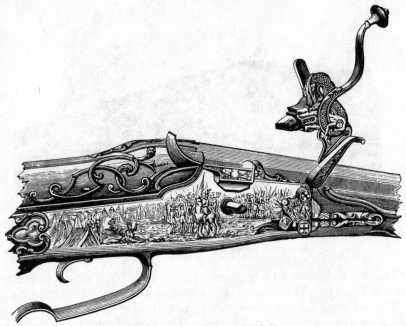

Ornamental Musket: Seventeenth Century.

and even straw, have each in their turn been used for the purpose of stocking. A remarkable weapon—the stock composed of many-coloured plaited straws—is in the Dresden Museum. The weight of the arm—a ball gun, the barrel 34 inches long—is barely 6½ pounds; the effect of the brightly-dyed straws is pleasing, and the numerous plaits are fixed and the stock made rigid by a strong glue.

The last arm figuring in the illustration is an early South German wheel-lock, the stock and lock both presenting ornamentation of a superior kind and worthy of

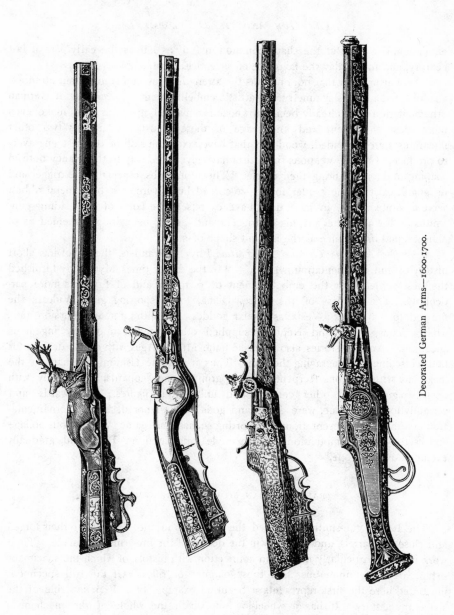

Decorated German Arms—1600-1700.

emulation, the stock of the shape common in Italy as late as the early part of last century, and to this day the favourite of several Eastern peoples.

These arms show that not only was the strength of the gun studied, but attention also directed towards symmetry and artistic embellishment. Specimens of German ornamentation have already been shown and remarked upon ; but to make even more clear the talent and knowledge of these industrious artisans two other illustrations are appended, wood-cuts that have taxed the skill of the best engravers to produce. In these weapons the artists have given free play to their fancy both in shaping and ornamenting their stocks. The utile limbs, especially the trigger and its guard, exist in the cruder forms—a curved bit of wire or a bent metal ribbon serve as limbs which, in later days, have exercised the fancy of the leading gun-smiths of Europe : the shaping of triggers and guard being now esteemed as of almost equal importance as the lay and shape of stock.

In " *Die Moderne Gewehr Fabrikation*," by F. Brandeis, the following short history of gun ornamentation is given :—" In the earlier times Mythology furnished the best subjects for the embellishment of weapons, and of fire-arms more par-ticularly. The goddess of the chase, Diana, for a sporting gun ; Vulcan, the fire-god, for a fire-lock ; Vesta, as tutelar goddess of smiths, for a percussion gun ; whilst Venus, Mars, and Neptune supplied other needful and very ingenious allegories. Ancient stories also furnished the Middle Ages with ample designs for both chiselling and engraving the gun. Thus it was the fashion to ornament the lock-plate with dragons, serpents, tigers, griffins, and leopards, and finally with devils, pigmies, and other comical and unbeautiful figures. Afterwards, and certainly for a long time, were devils and gods wholly ignored, and the ornamenta-tion confined to representations of sporting scenes and game with various foliage and scroll-work combinations, which style originated in Paris and gradually extended over Europe."

EARLY ITALIAN SPORTING FIRE-ARMS.

The Italian gun-smiths surpassed the Germans in the elegance of their forged and chiselled barrels, and generally in the design of the fire-arms they made. Their work is more particularly noticed in connection with pistols, of which the specimens extant are more numerous than those of guns or rifles. Of the two specimens illustrated here the first represents a beautiful example of a Venetian rifle of the sixteenth century. It has a wheel-lock in which the whole of the mechanism is arranged upon the exterior of the lock-plate, and may be easily understood by a

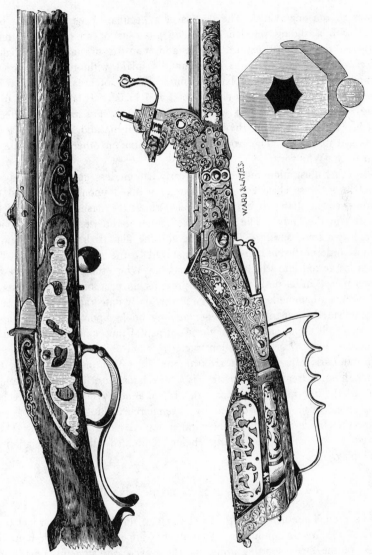

Flint-lock Hammerless Gun.   Venetian Rifle.

reference to the engraving. The butt is of a peculiar shape, and has a box-trap covered with a sliding wooden lid. The guard is of an original pattern, but the trigger, the plainest feature in the gun, consists of simply a straight piece of wire. The stock, which is of walnut, is inlaid with gold, mosaic, filigree, and mother-of-pearl, and is probably as fine a sample of ornamentation as any extant. The barrel is beautifully damascened and inlaid. It is bell-nosed upon the outside. The bore of the rifle, which is hexagonal, is very small, five-sixteenths of an inch. An end view of the muzzle is also given, and shows the enormous thickness at that part. The grooves are straight, but in other respects the bore is similar to the Whitworth.

The other illustration represents an early hammerless gun. The body of this weapon is of brass chiselled. The hammer is fixed upon a hinge, and kept in position over the flash-pan by means of a spring ; the flash-pan is at the base of the barrel in the body. The flint is fixed upon a rod working in the body, and actuated by a spiral spring. To cock the gun the flint is drawn back by means of the knob underneath the barrel, which is affixed to the rod in the body. There is a notch in the rod into which a scear engages. When the gun is cocked, and the hammer placed in its position, the gun presents no protuberances whatever, but is to all intents a hammerless gun. Even at this early date the advantages of having no complicated mechanism or ever-entangling hooks upon the exterior appear to have been well appreciated, for in the Continental museums are preserved several high-class specimens of guns so constructed.

In the Paris Museum there are two, one differing in no respect from the one illustrated, but better made ; the other is a breech-loader of Portuguese manufacture, and bears the inscription " Fabrica-real, Lisboa, anno 1779." It is a breech-loader, all the mechanism being covered by a semicircular hinged lid. The mode of igniting the charge is by a flint and spiral spring, as already described. The barrel is fixed to the stock, the charge being ignited by the manipulation of the breech-plug.

EARLY FRENCH SPORTING FIRE-ARMS.

The French gun-makers of St. Etienne claim for their town that it is the oldest centre of the fire-arms industry. They do not appear to have made more than the barrels of the finest sporting arms, and these even were sometimes made in Paris. The production of fire-arms by the artists of Paris reached its zenith about the middle of the seventeenth century. The annexed illustrations represent French arms in the Paris Museum. In the first figure will be found an example of the excessive ornamentation produced by carving in relief, the deeply sunk hollows interspersed amongst the raised work having anything but a pleasing effect. In the figure representing a musquetoon with a double wheel-lock the ornamentation consists of inlaying the stock with metals, mother-of-pearl, and ivory. The devices

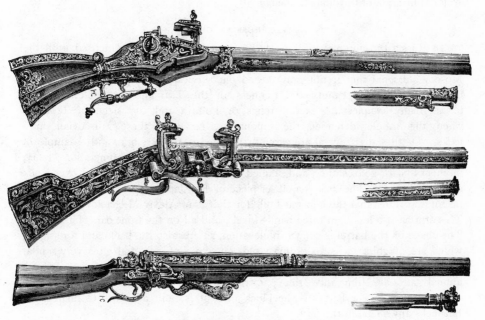

French Arms in the Musée des Invalides, Paris.

consist of an odd medley of human figures, animals, foliage and scroll, but the general effect is much more pleasing than that shown in the preceding. The last figure represents a matchlock musket that formerly belonged to the celebrated Cardinal Richelieu, and this curiously shaped and remarkable weapon is best described in the expressive words used by M. L'Haridon in the catalogue of the Museum :—"The barrel cut and squared towards the base, chased and gilt, exhibits three oval medallions, representing in relief warriors in ancient armour. The sight is formed of two rams' heads coupled together. The upper part of the barrel, formed like a fluted column, supports a capital in which are introduced four caryatides in full relief.   The lock, decorated throughout with chasing on gold, has a head of Medusa in high relief.   Beneath the gun-stock, which is of cherry-wood, is a boldly sculptured figure of a dolphin.   Above—where the barrel joins the stock—is a beautiful mask of a man's face surmounted by a shell; and on the shoulder-plate of the butt may be seen the three chevrons with a cardinal's hat, the armorial insignia of Cardinal Richelieu."

EARLY RUSSIAN GUNS.

In Russia the gun-maker's art—as most arts—was scarcely practised until the day of Peter the Great.   This enterprising monarch so developed the resources of Moscow's arsenal that it not only turned out serviceable weapons for the troops, but arms of passing beauty and richness for the Tsar and his nobles.   Of the former many samples are extant, relics of Poltava and the siege of Troitska, when the monks defended their monastery by using these Muscovian flint-locks.   Of the latter several are carefully guarded in the Kremlin, and a sample of these is here shown.   Its profuse ornament forbids detailed enumeration ; ivory, mother-of-pearl, gold, stones, and stained wood are lavishly bespattered over stock and barrel alike.   The lock is a clever piece of Russian fretwork, and a queerly cut inscription states that the gun was built for the Tsar Alexis Michaelovski in 1654.   This arm has no less than three band-swivels, and all on the front part of the stock.   The shape of the barrel is shown in elevation, as are also the back- and fore-sights, which are of gold.   B is an ordinary old Russian flint-lock, and guns very similar may still be bought as usable commodities in the rag markets of Moscow, or the annual fairs at Nijni and Irbite; c represents a more elaborate weapon of Muscovian make—a Russian wheel-lock rifle—it is built after the German style, but lacks any shape in the butt.

Arms with locks on the principle shown in A, but with an octagonal stock slightly bent, are still largely in use amongst the Tartars, and are common enough at Oranienburg, Russia being far behind Western countries in this respect.   Nevertheless, the arms museums of Russia are without equal for completeness and diverse systems both of cannon and small-arms.   The Kremlin at Moscow, the Monastery of Troitska, the Museum at Tula, and the royal collections of St. Petersburg and the Zarskoe Seloe, contain more devices in arms mechanisms than would seem conceivable.   They have never been properly catalogued, though a certain arrangement has been followed.   The St. Petersburg collections are rich in combined arms and revolving and repeating guns and cannon, all of which however, appear to have a greater antiquity than they in reality possess.

Arms made in Moscow Arsenal.

EARLY REPEATING ARMS.

The hand-gun to fire more than one shot at different times appears to have been contemporary with the introduction of fire-arms into Europe ; or, at any rate, was in use at the same period as the *orgues des bombardes* already described.

The first specimens were simply three- or more barrelled hand-cannon—the author has never seen a two-barrelled specimen—and of these two varieties are

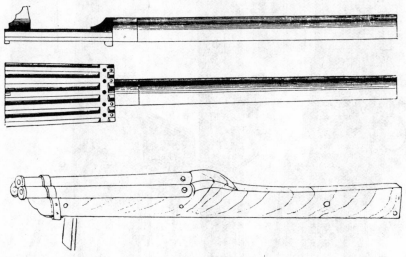

Multi-barrelled Hand-cannon.

shown in the above illustration. The three-barrelled weapon has a wooden stock, and was intended for use from ramparts. Its date is about 1500, and the original drawing is preserved in the Munich State Library. The same MS. shows similar arms with four and with six barrels, all with barrels side by side, and one with three barrels, two of which are side by side, the third superposed between them.

The five-barrelled gun shown is of about the same date ; the barrels, instead of being forged are all cast in one mould, and are of bronze. The fore-sight on the middle barrel has a corresponding back-sight immediately behind the touch-hole of that barrel, but this is likely to escape notice in the drawing. The same principle of construction for the same class of weapon was long continued. In the French

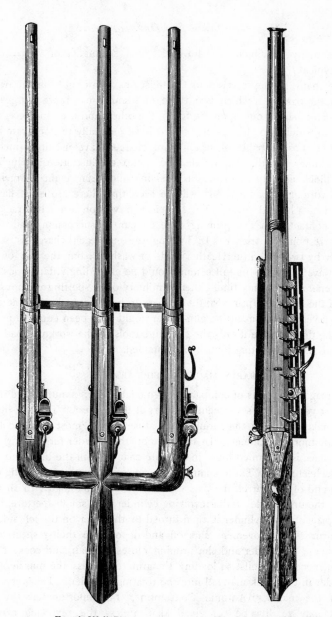

French Wall Piece.   The Repeating Matchlock Rifle.

museums are many specimens of flint-lock guns so made, of which the one illustrated is typical.

There are many guns preserved in the museums with double match, wheel, or flint locks, in the barrels of which two, three, and sometimes more charges are inserted in the same barrel, one upon the top of the other, and fired in succession.

The guns in which two charges are placed have generally two separate locks or touch-holes, but those capable of firing more charges have usually a mechanical arrangement similar to that shown in the annexed illustration ; which represents a matchlock arquebus capable of receiving and firing eight charges in the same barrel without reloading.   It will be seen that there are eight flash-pans, each protected by a hinged cover.   The serpentin travels on a notched rack, and is brought into contact with the priming of each pan in succession, and fired by pressing a corresponding trigger.   In loading the gun, each charge is separated from the other by two well-fitting leather wads or washers ; but the use of such a weapon, if always loaded to its full extent, would be exceedingly dangerous.   They were not in general use at any time either as military or as sporting weapons.   The advantages of the repeating principle thus appear to have been observed at an early date, and the inventive genius of the gun-maker would have been equal to producing weapons of the desired type if only the skill and tools of the workman had allowed of a perfect mechanically-fitting joint being obtained.

EARLY MAGAZINE FIRE-ARMS.

The first magazine gun is of comparatively modern date, manufactured undoubtedly in the first years of the seventeenth century at the earliest.   The one illustrated is of Italian make, and is in the Birmingham Museum, but most public collections include one or more specimens.   In this weapon the powder for priming and for charging the piece is contained loose in separate chambers in the butt, and inserted by raising the heel-plate.   These chambers communicate with a revolving cylinder at the breech-end of the barrel, the axis of which is at right angles to that of the barrels.   On the under-side of the revolving cylinder is a small aperture, in which the bullet is placed ; the cylinder is then turned by the lever on the left side almost a complete turn.   This movement cuts off and deposits in their respective places the proper charge of powder and the priming, closes the pan, and cocks the lock.   It is, however, necessary whilst so loading the arm, to depress the muzzle, in order that the powder in the stock may fall into the rotating cylinder.   This weapon bears the name of the maker, "Antonio Constantine," but unfortunately the date is wanting.   It may readily be conceived that, unless the revolving cylinder is accurately fitted, the danger of using such a weapon must be great, the powder in the butt (sufficient for six charges) only being separated from the barrel by the revolving cylinder, which also acts as a false breech for the barrel; indeed, the late W. Greener states that a pistol of similar construction blew up whilst being experimented with. A weapon of like construction to the above is in the Paris Museum; but the bullets, instead of having to be inserted each time by the hand, are contained in a recess under the breech-end of the barrel, and forced into the cylinder by a spiral spring.

Italian Magazine Gun.

In another specimen there are two tubes in the stock for the powder, and it is forty shot, instead of six, as in the one shown; the lever forms the trigger guard, and by being moved to the right loads and also cocks the weapon.

The makers of these weapons appear to have been foreign without exception, and chiefly to have issued from Amsterdam, Hanover, and Liège. The peculiar complication of the various mechanisms, and the general inutility of the weapons themselves, render a detailed description of little value to the inventor or the general reader; but the connoisseur will find several varieties in the Paris Museum; these are comprehensively described in the valuable catalogue of the collection.

EARLY REVOLVING GUNS.

Revolving cannon—some of large calibre—are described in mediæval manuscripts, but these bear little resemblance to that type of arm which has become known throughout the civilised world by the name of revolver.

Before the introduction of the flint-lock various revolving matchlock guns were in use. The earliest description is an arquebus with four chambers, a specimen of which is to be seen in the Tower collection, and is supposed to have belonged to King Henry VIII. It appears to be of the first half of the sixteenth century. The barrel is 2 feet 9 inches long, and the chamber $7\frac{1}{2}$ inches, bore about half an inch. There is a separate flash-pan for each chamber, covered with a sliding lid, and they are moved in succession underneath the serpentin. An end view of the chambers is also given. The barrel is fastened to the spindle, and strengthened by a rod fastened to its top, with the other extremity fixed to the butt of the gun. The lock

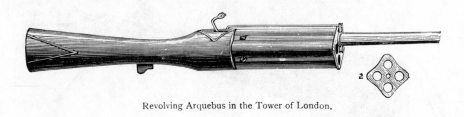

Revolving Arquebus in the Tower of London.

mechanism is exceedingly simple, consisting of a serpentin pivoted in the stock, and extended below and behind the pivot to form a trigger. By pressing up the trigger the serpentin falls into the flash-pan, the weight of the trigger serving to bring it back into its place. Several similar weapons of a later date of French and German manufacture are to be found in the Paris Museum. In one a spring is attached to the barrel which engages in a stop in the chamber immediately it is in the proper position for firing. The chambers in all cases are moved round by hand. One has eight, and another three, and the rest have five chambers.

In one arquebus of the middle of the seventeenth century the fire is communicated to the chambers by one flash-pan only, which requires repriming after each discharge.

In the Paris Museum a three-chambered wheel-lock revolving gun is preserved. There is but one flash-pan, and the chambers are moved round by the hand after each discharge, and are kept in position at the time of firing by a spring button placed upon the tail-piece of the barrel. The date of these weapons is about the latter end of the seventeenth century. A six-chambered *flint-lock* pistol of the first half of the eighteenth century is also to be found in the same museum. The mechanism is similar to that of the preceding weapon, but it is self-priming, the magazine being fixed to the hammer or striking-piece, and, upon being closed after each discharge, deposits the priming in the flash-pan. The stock is finely carved, and ornamented with copper and filigree work. The lock bears the name "A. Leotien."

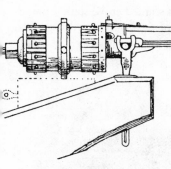

Double-chambered Revolving Gun.

The German double-chambered revolving gun illustrated is probably unique in principle. In addition to the increased speed in firing which would result from the

Revolving Arms, Russian.

ten chambers, the chambers, by being made long enough to contain two charges, one in front of the other, and fired by separate touch-holes, allowed two shots to be fired in very quick succession. As the touch-holes were not covered, it was necessary to prime afresh each time the chamber was partly revolved. The first rotating gun with touch-holes and flash-pans covered by a sliding lid was made about 1570; the gun shown was probably made at the end of the sixteenth century, and certainly prior to 1650.

In Russia revolving arms of the kind long since discarded in Western Europe were used in the last century. The close likeness of the short-barrelled gun to

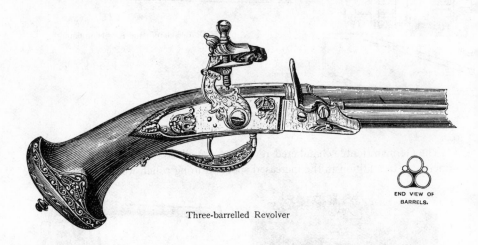

END VIEW OF BARRELS.

Three-barrelled Revolver

the weapons described by Valturius in the fifteenth century, and already referred to, will be at once noticed. The other revolving gun resembles the German weapon above described; but some of these Russian guns were made at so late a date as to be provided with nipples for ignition by means of the well-known percussion cap of the present period.

In the Birmingham Museum there is an Italian three-barrelled flint pistol of the latter end of the seventeenth century. In this pistol, the three barrels turn round upon one common axis, and are brought opposite the flash-pan by the hand. The barrels are arranged as shown in the muzzle elevation, which also shows the position of the wooden ramrod.

The pistol is well made, and by an ingenious contrivance the hammer or striking-plate closes whilst in the act of cocking. The spring catch for retaining the barrels in position at the moment of firing is released by pressing the trigger with the cock down. The pistol is neatly ornamented and mounted in chiselled steel, which, together with the shape of the stock, seems to indicate that it is of Italian manufacture. In the same museum there is also a revolving gun having two barrels, rotating upon a common axis, and each having its own flash-pan and hammer. One lock, cock and trigger, however, serves to discharge both barrels, they being turned in succession until opposite the cock and in the proper position for firing, in which position they are retained by a small spring bolt, moved by a stud fixed and working upon the fore-part of the trigger bow. This gun has a gold

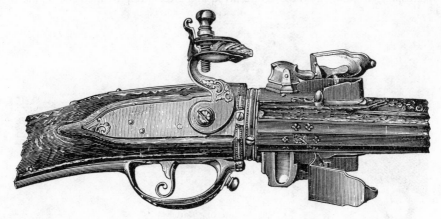

Double Revolving Gun.

stamp upon the barrels, a fine scroll trigger, and the stock is beautifully finished and carved. From the shape and ornamentation of the gun the date of its manufacture can be fixed as early in the eighteenth century; it is probably of Milanese origin. Several weapons of similar construction are to be found amongst the various Continental collections, both private and public. In the Paris Museum there is a similar gun, but with four barrels, and two locks and triggers.

Revolving carbines were made upon the same principle, or with slight modifications, during the latter part of the eighteenth century, and various specimens are preserved in different English and Continental museums. About 1810 a revolving carbine of unique description was manufactured in England by E. H. Collier. It will be seen by the engraving that the lock is placed nearly in the centre of the stock, the flash-pan and hammer upon the strap which connects the top of the barrel with the butt of the pistol, the touch-hole passing through the strap and into the chambers in an oblique direction. The breech is formed as a cap to the chambers, and in which their breech-ends revolve. This cap, by being always in contact with the outside of the chamber, prevents any escape of powder at the touch-holes. The chambers are revolved by the hand, but before turning they must be drawn backward about one-eighth of an inch, the chambers being slightly enlarged at their mouths, and fitting over the taper breech-end of the barrel; this ensures the axis of the chamber being true with that of the barrel during the discharge. The chambers are forced over the tapered barrel by a flat spiral spring working upon the centre pivot, and are held up to their position at the

Collier's Revolving Carbine.

moment of discharge by a small horizontal sliding bolt or lever, actuated by the trigger immediately it is pulled to fire the weapon. The arm is well made apparently, the only weak part being the lever holding the chamber up to the barrel during the discharge, which is too small to withstand the constant wear and strain of firing. The weapon represented has two barrels, interchangeable, one a rifle and the other a shot barrel: both are about 24-bore, and 28 inches in length. Weapons of similar construction by the same maker are preserved in various museums, and this system appears to be the last of note before the introduction of percussion weapons. In fact, a few years later specimens of this same weapon with self-priming mechanism for percussion ignition are to be found.

COMBINED FIRE-ARMS.

As already stated, it was usual when fire-arms were first introduced to combine with the fire-arm some other warlike weapon. These combined arms are most varied, and appear to have been made in large numbers. That the idea of combining a fire-arm with a lethal weapon possesses many attractions to persons of inventive genius, if not proved by the many examples of such arms still extant, is exemplified by its persistent reiteration in the records of the Patent Office, whence a patent for a combined dagger and pistol has just been issued, and by the modern advocacy of a pistol-lance as the most suitable German cavalry weapon.

The fire-arm with axe is the commonest of the combinations and the one most widely spread; for the battle-axe here shown is almost identical with the one already described and illustrated, which was made in Europe in the fifteenth

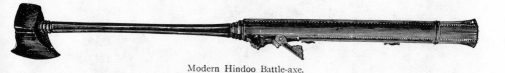

Modern Hindoo Battle-axe.

century. The particulars of this battle-axe have been furnished by E. A. Elliott, Esq., to whose courtesy the author is indebted for the illustration. The axe was taken from the Santals, one of the hill-tribes of India. The thickness of metal at muzzle is only one-fifth inch, and the weight 1 lb. ; its length over all is $16\frac{1}{2}$ inches, of which the pistol-barrel takes $8\frac{1}{2}$ inches. A primitive type of combined axe and pistol is shown in the next illustration. This arm is of German manufacture. The barrel is 6 inches long and is well concealed by the head of the axe and the handle, nearly 2 feet 6 inches long. The weapon is fired by a wheel-lock, and the

Pistol Battle-axe.

trigger is fixed near the extremity of the handle farthest from the lock. This weapon was probably intended for horseback use, and manufactured at the commencement of the seventeenth century. The pistol battle-axes on the plate are of a later date and of a higher class workmanship: all are from the Dresden

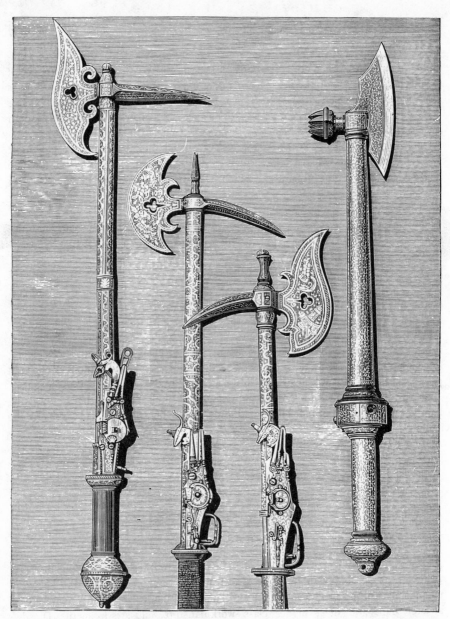

German Battle-axes in the Dresden Museum.

collection, which is particularly rich in arms of this kind and of this period—perhaps no better collection of wheel-lock arms has yet been brought together.

The combination of pistol with dagger is by no means rare, and several specimens are in the Birmingham collection ; the two illustrated show the chief principles employed in effecting the combination. In the earliest, the barrel is in the centre of the blade, a muzzle stopper being removed whilst loading and

Wheel-lock Dagger-Pistol.

shooting the weapon. The muzzle stopper, upon being replaced, forms the point of the dagger. The pistol has a beautiful wheel-lock and an ingenious safety-bolt, working upon the left side of the handle ; the lock is discharged by pressing a small stud on the handle. The whole pistol is of steel, artistically ornamented, and the mechanism neatly and cleverly arranged, as may be seen upon reference to the illustration ; the barrel is of Damascus iron.

The other of these curious weapons represented has the barrel, about 4 inches in

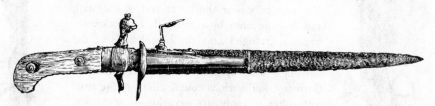

Dagger-Pistol, Seventeenth Century.

length, along the side of the dagger blade and is discharged by pressing a small trigger in the handle of the weapon. The lock is a modification of the common flint-lock, the cock, hammer, and trigger-guard forming the cross of the dagger. Similar weapons with pistol on each side of blade are preserved in the same collection.

Another and still later form of the same weapon is also
shown ; in this last type it will be observed that of the two weapons
combined in one the pistol is the superior, and the dagger
blade subordinated to its requirements ; whilst in
the earlier models the blade was of first importance, and the fire-arm but subsidiary thereto.

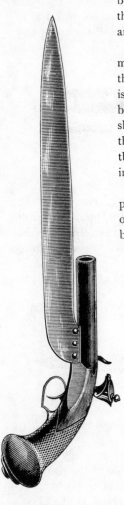

Sword-pistols of various forms are found in
most collections, the best, possibly, being that in
the Berlin Museum. In the Paris Museum there
is, combined with a 20-inch damascened sword
blade—curved somewhat like that of a sabre—a
short wheel-lock arquebus, the barrel of which forms
the backbone of the sword ; the lock is placed upon
the cross-hilt, and the gun is discharged by pressing a small stud in the handle.

Pistol-pikes are not uncommon ; a musket-
pike, like the one shown, is more rare. This is
of the first half of the sixteenth century, and the
blade affixed to its muzzle is available for both
thrusting and hacking.   In the Tower collection
there is a " thief-taker " with the usual pike-staff
and two pistol-barrels, one on each side, projecting
at an angle of 45°, about midway on the staff.
The trigger is near the lower end of the staff,
and is connected by a rod with the lockwork,
which is arranged near the breech ends of the
pistol-barrels. A combination of gun and
cross-bow was by no means uncommon in
Germany, and various combinations of fire-arms
with other weapons are occasionally met with,
but they were not made in sufficient quantities
to become general, which, indeed, would have
defeated the object they were constructed for ;
and although they will always be regarded as
great curiosities, the subject is not of sufficient
importance to render further details of any
practical utility.

German Pistol-Dagger,
Eighteenth Century.

Musket-Pike.

CONCEALED ARMS.

Before the introduction of fire-arms, concealed arms for projecting missiles were extremely rare, but in the Museum of Arms at Birmingham there is a small curious cross-bow of the early part of the fifteenth century intended so to be used. It is about 10 inches in length, and constructed wholly of iron ; the bow is double and set by a fast-travelling screw ; it is released by a small stud, which acts in the same manner as the triggers of a large arbalist. This singular weapon, when not armed, lies in a sufficiently small compass to be easily concealed in the folds of a cloak or tunic. Its range cannot have been very great, and it was probably constructed to serve the ends of some private assassin. With the introduction of portable fire-arms, concealed weapons became more numerous ; the surprise occasioned by the sudden discharge of a volley of unknown weapons caused more consternation and confusion than could have been gained by the actual killing or wounding power of the weapons themselves.

A purse, or sporran, of peculiar construction is preserved in the Museum of Edinburgh. It consists of an ingenious combination of the ordinary Highland sporran with a small flint-lock pistol hidden in the interior of the purse ; by turning a succession of metal studs and buttons, when closing the purse, the trigger of the pistol is brought into connection with the clasp, so that anyone unacquainted with the mechanical arrangement endeavouring to open the purse would cause the pistol to fire, with the possibility of wounding the intermeddler, or at any rate of considerably startling him, and perhaps causing him to relinquish the purse entirely, as a remarkably "uncanny" article. The connection between the clasp of the sporran and the pistol-trigger is broken by reversing the action of the mountings, but which would appear bewildering to any person unaware of their purport. The date of this sporran is placed about the seventeenth century, but Sir Walter Scott, in "Rob Roy," makes his hero the possessor of a similar sporran ; the idea it is said having originated upon Sir Walter Scott seeing the above weapon in the Museum during a visit. The following extract from "Rob Roy" gives a good description of this purse :—

"A tall, strong mountaineer, who seemed to act as Macgregor's lieutenant, brought from some place of safety a large leather pouch, such as Highlanders of rank wear before them when in full dress, made of the skin of the sea-otter, richly garnished with silver ornaments and studs.

" ' I advise no man to attempt opening this sporran till he has my secret,' said Rob Roy ; and then twisting one button in one direction, and another in another, pulling one stud upward and pressing another downward, the mouth of the purse, which was bound with massive silver plate, opened and gave admittance to his hand. He made me remark, as if to break short the subject on which Bailie Jarvie had spoken, that a small steel pistol was concealed within the purse, the trigger of which was connected with the mounting, and made part of the machinery; so that the weapon would certainly be discharged, and in all probability its contents lodged in the person of anyone who, being unacquainted with the secret, should tamper with the lock which secured his treasure. ' This,' said he, touching the pistol, ' is the keeper of my privy purse.' "

A weapon of unique character is the pistol-shield preserved in the Tower. It is known that these were made in the reign of Henry VIII., and twenty-one specimens, all identical, still remain. They are circular in form, and have a breech-loading, matchlock pistol fixed in or near the centre; the system adopted for loading

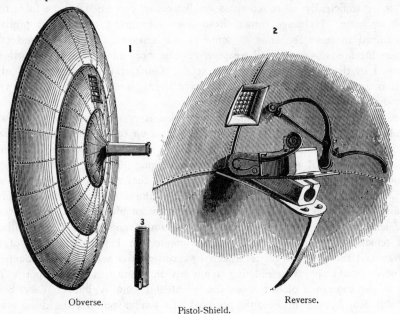

Obverse.   Reverse.
Pistol-Shield.

consists of a block hinged upon each side of the barrel: it is raised up for the insertion of a loaded thimble or steel chamber. The match was affixed to a serpentin attached to a rod stapled to the interior of the shield, which was depressed by the hand into the flash-pan upon the top to ignite the charge. The mechanism will be more readily understood by a reference to the illustration 2, which shows the breech of the barrel; 1 is the exterior view of the shield; and 3, the steel thimble or chamber. According to Hentzner, who noticed these shield-pistols during his visit to England in 1598, each pistol possessed four movable thimbles or chambers for loading and inserting in the barrel. There is a small barred aperture near the top of each shield through which an aim may be taken, and being bullet-proof, they afford ample protection to the shooter from the missiles of his adversaries. These shields are enumerated in the inventory of King Edward VI. as target-shields with guns, and this, combined with their shape and size, should betoken that they were made about the first half of the sixteenth century.

Another species of concealed arm is a whip-pistol, of which there is a fine

Brigand's Whip-Pistol.

specimen in the Birmingham Museum, having formerly belonged to a notorious Neapolitan brigand. The barrel is concealed in the whip stock, and runs its whole length, about 12 inches. The lock, a small flint and hammer one, is concealed by the ornamental tassels or fringe in front of the handle; it has a secret trigger.

The use of such weapons, however, was not confined to brigands and outlaws, for during the seventeenth and eighteenth centuries the postillions of the French mail coaches travelling south of Lyons were all supplied with similar whip-pistols, specimens of which are preserved in the Paris Museum.

CURIOUS AND NOTABLE FIRE-ARMS.

The early gun-makers, when constructing guns for notable personages, frequently tried to produce weapons quite different to the ordinary type; for instance, the

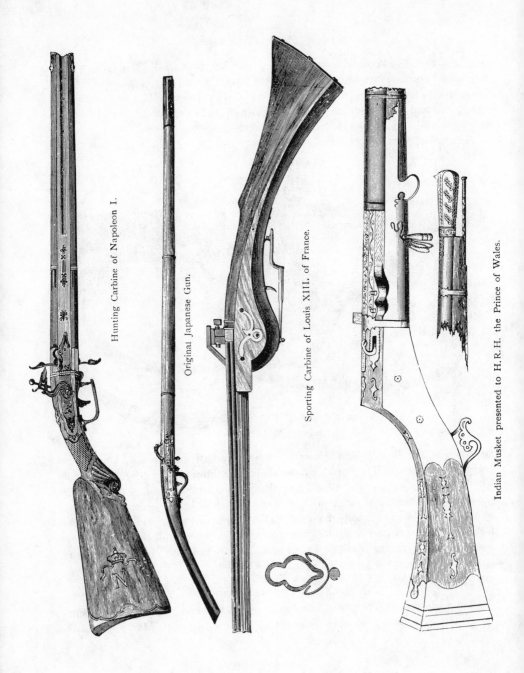

Hunting Carbine of Napoleon I.

Original Japanese Gun.

Sporting Carbine of Louis XIII. of France.

Indian Musket presented to H.R.H. the Prince of Wales.

peculiarly shaped barrel of the hunting carbine of Louis XIII. As shown in the illustration, the barrel is apparently composed of irregular tubes joined together. The object of so forming the barrel—which form is intended to represent the *fleur-de-lys* of France—was meant as a delicate flattery to Louis. The bore is about ¾-inch from groove to groove, and the length of barrel about 4 feet 6 inches.

Several extraordinary weapons were made for the first Napoleon. The one

Nock's Seven-barrelled Carbine.

illustrated is a poly-grooved sporting carbine, double-barrelled, the barrels revolving on a common centre, and each carrying its own flash-pan and hammer. The shape of the butt is peculiar, and the ornamentation only ordinary. The barrel is considerably shorter than that of the carbine of Louis XIII., although heavier; the bore is about ⅞-inch.

The Indian musket is the weapon presented to King George, when Prince of Wales, by an Indian Rajah; a very fine specimen of Eastern workmanship, heavily jewelled and highly decorated. This gun has been exhibited in most of the art galleries of the United Kingdom, and may be taken as fairly representing the Eastern sportsman's idea of what a gun should be.

The Chinese and Japanese—more particularly the latter—are now manufacturing fire-arms resembling the models purchased in Europe. An original weapon is illustrated for comparison with early European fire-arms. The similarity may be taken either as convincing proof that fire-arms originated in the East or as further

Ornamented Saxon Daggs.

evidence of the fact that most ideas are common to the human race, and not to any particular nation.

Many people may be surprised that so recently as 1807 J. Nock, the renowned London gun-maker, made for the British Government a shoulder gun of the same principle as the multi-barrelled cannon of the fourteenth century. It consisted, as shown, of seven round barrels brazed together, and fired from the same touch-hole, all the barrels being fired, practically simultaneously, but actually in very rapid succession. The bore is 20, length of barrels 28 inches; the weapon is very heavy and unwieldy. It is fitted with sights and top-ribs, but the barrels are not rifled.

PISTOLS.

Pistols, as distinct from the smallest of hand-cannon, are understood to have been made for the first time at Pistoia, Italy, from which town they receive their name. Caminelleo Vitelli is the accredited inventor, and he flourished in 1540.

As at first manufactured, the true pistols had short barrels and heavy, clumsy butts, nearly at right angles with the barrel, and surmounted by enormous balls or

Italian Dagg.

caps. In a short time, however, the pattern changed, the butts being lengthened out, and almost in a line with the barrels. To all these early pistols the wheel-lock was the most applicable, and consequently the majority of the pistols of the sixteenth and seventeenth centuries are found so fitted. Short, heavy pistols, called " daggs," were in common use about the middle of the seventeenth century. In some cases the butts were of ivory, bone, or hard wood, in others of iron or metal. There were various patterns in use, but the one illustrated will convey an idea of

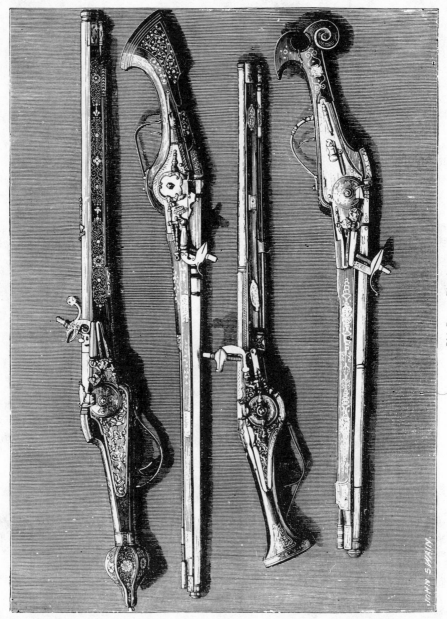

Old Saxon Pistol.

the general appearance of this weapon ; a chiselled Italian dagg manufactured by one of the Comminazzo family about 1650. The barrel is slightly bell-nosed, about eight inches in length, and 14-bore. There is also a safety-bolt affixed on the right-hand side of the weapon, which is entirely of metal.

The wheel-lock pistols of German manufacture were used also for military purposes by the Ritters ; these, with their balled stocks, so well known to frequenters of arms museums, were apparently built for Grafs and Dukes, and ornamented so profusely that photography alone can adequately reproduce the beauty of their intricate details. For chiselling, carving, and *Schnittwerke* they cannot be surpassed : the designs are originally conceived and admirably executed. The interior work is likewise good, especially that of the smiths, but the finish would now be considered rough.

Duelling, whenever and wherever in vogue, has caused the production of weapons most accurately made and reliable at twenty paces, good specimens of the gun-makers' craft at their date of manufacture. The pattern of pistol seldom varied, and for exterior appearance and handling the duelling pistol of to-day is the same as that of last century. The specimen shown on page 100, a very good one of its class, was recently in the author's hands. It has figured in several memorable contests, the best-known encounter being that between His Royal Highness the Duke of York and the Honourable Colonel Lennox in 1789. The little meeting took place on Wimbledon Common, and His Royal Highness, who did not fire, lost a curl by his adversary's shot. The accuracy of this pistol is equal to that of more modern ones, the same principle of a heavy bullet and a small charge of powder being employed.

Pistols with metal hafts were common in the seventeenth and eighteenth centuries ; some very beautiful specimens were made in Edinburgh, Highlanders preferring them to those of the ordinary type, as, with the blue metallic stock and silver mountings, they matched better the ornaments of the Highland costume.

In the double pistol with barrels under and over, the trigger mechanism is the chief peculiarity, as it serves to discharge both locks. The trigger is pivoted vertically ; an inclined plane on the right tumbler forces the trigger under the left scear, when the right tumbler has been let down ; on the tumbler being raised, a spring forces the trigger beneath the right scear. It is necessary to remove the pressure of the finger upon the trigger before the second barrel can be discharged, in the same manner as with a double-action revolver, but the pistol trigger does not require so much travel. This method of constructing guns is advocated in a German book on gun-making.

A Notable Duelling Pistol.

Saw-handle Duelling Pistol by Smith.

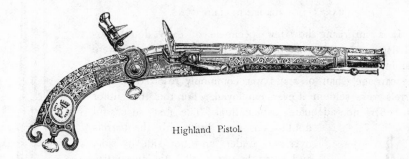

Highland Pistol.

Double Pistol with Single Trigger.

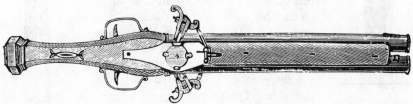

Double Horse-pistol of the Sixteenth Century

EARLY DOUBLE-BARRELLED GUNS.

It is surprising how few specimens of early double-barrelled guns are known. It seems that when fire-arms were first introduced, although the multiplication of cannon upon one carriage, shaft, or stand was commonly resorted to, two barrels were seldom, if ever, employed. For this the author can offer no adequate explanation. The first successful

double-guns were built with the barrels over and under, and not side by side, and certainly not until after the introduction of the wheel-lock into Italy. The first inventor of this double gun appears to be one Giuliano Bossi, of Rome, who in 1616 wrote describing the qualities and advantages of the double arms of his design.

The pistol illustrated fully explains itself, as the weapon was so formed as to shoot with either barrel uppermost, and was only the crude idea of a double-barrelled fire-arm. Towards the middle of the sixteenth century, wheel-lock carbines with two barrels, one over the other, were made in Germany. The barrels turned upon a common axis, and were fired by a separate or common lock, as already illustrated : this was the invention of Bossi.

In the Tower of London there is preserved an early double fire-arm of the commencement of the seventeenth century. It is a long double pistol, in which the barrels are placed side by side. It is an early specimen of the wheel-lock, and the shape of the stock or handle is remarkable. The weapon appears to have been intended for sporting purposes. It

Double Pistol of the
Seventeenth Century.

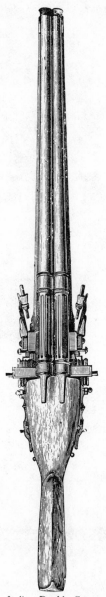

Italian Double Gun.

is ornamented with brass, and has barrels about eighteen inches in length. These two weapons are clumsily made, and unwieldy ; not so, however, is the pretty little Italian arquebus illustrated on page 102. This handy little weapon appears to have been manufactured for solely sporting purposes, and is undoubtedly one of the earliest double sporting guns with the barrels side by side. It is a wheel-lock arquebus of about the middle of the seventeenth century. It is beautifully ornamented with chiselled copper mountings : the barrels are nicely finished, both at the breech and muzzles, and the flash-pans are also of copper. The barrels are about twenty-two inches long and half-inch bore, but the name of the maker is wanting. A similar gun, but of a considerably later date, is preserved in the Paris Museum, and bears the name of Berch.

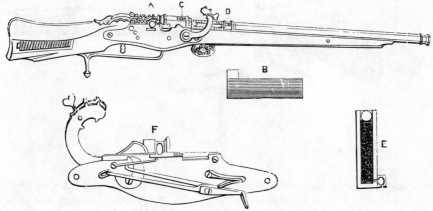

Breech-loading Arquebus of King Henry VIII.

Double shot-guns do not appear to have been in general use until the present century. In 1784 they were so new that Dr. Aikins deemed it worth while to write and publish a description of them. Joseph Manton is thought to have been the first man to unite the barrels with a rib ; but the success of the double gun was more directly due to the lighter weight which better material and higher class workman-ship made possible.

EARLY BREECH-LOADERS.

One of the earliest breech-loading hand-guns is to be found in the Tower of London, in the specimen cherished as the hunting arquebus of Henry VIII. The above illustration represents this curious weapon. It is a matchlock arquebus,

and bears the letters " H. R." and the date 1537. The system of loading is similar
to the Snider breech-action. The breech-block is, however, hinged on the left side,
and opens from the right to left. The charge is put in a small steel thimble or
chamber, which has a false flash-pan and touch-hole in one side that fits into the
flash-pan upon being placed in the chamber. The shape and comparative size of
the movable chamber are shown in the engraving at B, and in section at E. A is the
breech-block, C the Royal arms, D the King's initials, and F shows the mechanism
of the lock. It will be seen that a rod actuating a lever to the flash-pan cover is
affixed to the scear, so that upon the scear being raised the cover slides from over
the flash-pan. This weapon is probably of French manufacture. The armourer's

Early German Breech-loader.

mark is a *fleur-de-lys* surmounted by the letters " W. H." It has also stamped on the
breech a crowned rose supported by two lions. The barrel is fluted and about
3 ft. 6 in. in length.

Another breech-loading arquebus was in common use in Germany during the
earlier half of the sixteenth century. In this gun, represented with its movable
chamber, the barrel is enlarged to take a steel thimble and breech-block in one ;
the thimble having an elongated tail or handle to allow of its being easily moved
in or out of the chamber. The thimble is retained in the barrel during the
discharge by a cotter pin passing through the barrel, the base of the thimble, and
the stock, firmly wedging the whole together, and similar to the German breech-
loading cannon shown on page 37.

Henry IV. of France is said to have invented a similar breech-loader, with
which some of the French troops were armed during his reign.

The next distinct type of breech-loading arm was of French invention and made about the middle of the seventeenth century; it was called the "*Amusette du Maréchal de Saxe.*" It was usually made as a wall-piece, but a few were also manufactured as carbines for use by the dragoons. By turning the trigger-guard the breech-plug was caused to open, the block consisting of a cylindrical plug. The charge was placed in loose, cartridges not being employed by the French at that time. It was soon discarded, on account of the great danger in manipulating the weapon, for the friction was so great that the gun frequently went off before the breech-plug was returned to its place.

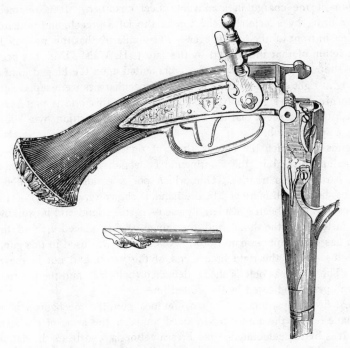

Early Breech-loading Flint-lock Pistol.

During the seventeenth and eighteenth centuries breech-loading arms were very numerous and of greatly diversified mechanism; it will therefore be in the compass of this work to describe and illustrate a few of them only. Wheel-lock arquebuses on the drop-down system were manufactured in the second half of the sixteenth century, but in most of these early arms breech-plugs and fixed barrels were employed. In many instances the charge is placed in the breech-block, and not in the barrel itself.

For sporting weapons breech-loaders of curious forms have been made, and generally on the drop-down system. It was not until after the introduction of the flint-lock that any inventions now valuable were produced. Amongst these early arms the one on the drop-down plan, as shown, is most worthy of detailed description.

It is a very long-barrelled pistol, probably of Italian manufacture about the middle of the sixteenth century. The barrel drops on a hinged joint, to allow of the insertion of the charge in a movable steel chamber. It is retained in its position for firing by a catch on the top of the false breech, and actuated by a spring trigger in front of the lock trigger. The similarity that this weapon bears to the breech-action of that introduced by the late J. H. Walsh, Esq., has been noted by some of the readers of the *Field*, who commented upon the hinged joint and the barrel falling at right angles to the stock, which peculiarities were supposed to have belonged to Mr. Walsh's gun only. A gun similar to this one is preserved in the Edinburgh Museum, except that the barrel is retained in position by a sliding bolt, and not by a spring catch.

Such guns—in which the barrels drop at right angles to the stock—are not rare. There are several in the Continental collections, and some are illustrated in various parts of this treatise. One, which possesses also an extended top rib and top cross-bolt which is moved by the hand, is shown on page 107. This gun—which appears to have been considerably used—is still sound and in working order. Both the fastenings—the hook and the hinge—being placed behind the joint, the breech has been kept close and firm. No cartridge was used in this gun, but the charge was inserted in the rigid breech-end of the barrel, and not in the movable fore-part. The top cross-bolt is shown detached (half-size), and the position of the barrel when open is indicated by the dotted lines.

The next figure illustrates an Italian flint-lock gun, the mechanism of which is the best made of any the author has noticed amongst the arms of the seventeenth century. It is by the celebrated Aqua Fresca à Borgia, and bears the date of 1694.

By pressing the guard a catch under the barrel is released, and, the barrel being pivoted vertically, a lateral motion may be given to the barrel, which swings open horizontally, as shown in the illustration. The charge, contained in a steel tube, may then be introduced, and the barrel returned to its position. By a system of wheels the gun primes itself, the powder being placed in the magazine affixed to the hammer. The butt is hollowed to contain a bullet-mould, and the whole weapon is nicely finished, the mountings being of chiselled steel.

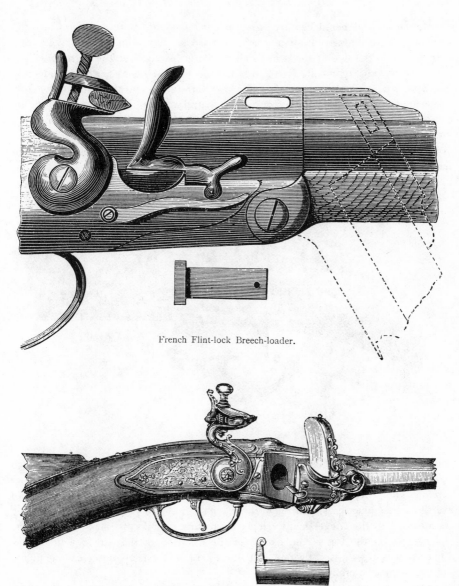

French Flint-lock Breech-loader.

Italian Flint-lock Breech-loader.

During the eighteenth century breech-loading flint-guns were made in which the barrel or barrels revolved on a common axis, as shown on page 85, a space being cut from the side of the arm to allow of the insertion of the cartridges. In single-barrelled weapons the barrel was usually pivoted on a centre considerably below the axis of the barrel, so that upon the barrel being turned over to the right or left it was thrown clear of the stock. The barrel was kept in position for firing by means of a spring stud or catch entering into the barrel from the false breech.

A breech-loading carbine, known as the Fergusson rifle, was used in the American War of Independence, and is here illustrated. It is the first breech-loading carbine ever used by a regularly organised British corps, and is the

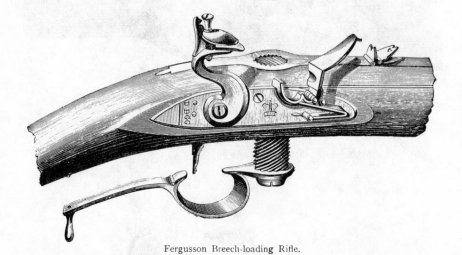

Fergusson Breech-loading Rifle.

invention of Patrick Fergusson, Major, 2nd Batt. 71st Regt. Highlanders, who constructed it some time previous to 1776. It is a flint-lock, and sighted from 100 to 500 yards. The breech mechanism consists of a three- to twelve-thread vertical screw plug, passing through the breech-end of the barrel. This screw plug is attached to the trigger-guard, which, when turned, sinks the screw plug, leaving an aperture in the top of the barrel for the insertion of the cartridge or charge. The screw is then raised by replacing the guard, and the aperture leading to the barrel chamber thereby closed.

Another type of breech-loader is that of Mr. Theiss, of Nuremberg. In this arm the stock is hollowed immediately behind the breech of the barrel to admit of the charge being introduced, the barrel being closed by a vertically sliding breech-block, actuated by a button attached to a lever under the barrel in front of the guard. When pushed upwards by the button, a hole in the breech-block is in a

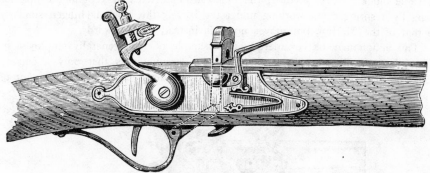

The Theiss Breech-loading Gun.

line with the axis of the barrel. Through this aperture the cartridge is pushed into the chamber of the barrel, which is closed by knocking down the breech-block.

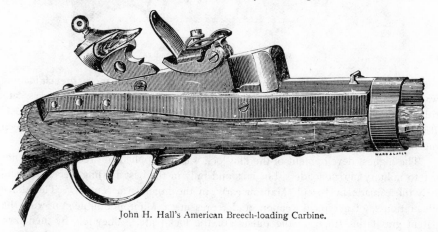

John H. Hall's American Breech-loading Carbine.

The weapon is a flint-lock, and was manufactured in Germany about 1804, but was discontinued owing to the large escape of gas at the breech.

Another type of flint lock breech-loading arm is the next illustrated on page 109. It was the invention of an American, who afterwards made arms on the interchangeable system for the United States Government.   In this arm the breech-block itself is loaded, the flash-pan, hammer, and cock all being arranged in or upon the movable block.   After loading, the block is depressed and kept in position for firing by a spring catch working under the barrel; the block is hinged similarly to that of the Martini, but moves upwards instead of downwards.

This action may be considered a fair sample of that generally employed in old wall-pieces, though the modifications are so numerous that only a cursory notice of them would fill a volume.   As muzzle-loaders, wall-pieces, on account of

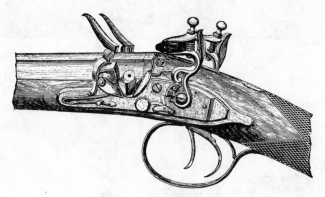

Manton's Flint-lock Muzzle-loader.

the length of their barrels, were most difficult to load, so that more breech-loading wall-pieces than early breech-loading small-arms were made.   In some cases cartridges were used which were placed in the barrel itself or in the breech-block. Rigid barrels and movable blocks appear to have been the principle on which most of them were constructed.

The highest development of the flint-lock was not applied to breech-loaders, nor yet to military muzzle-loaders, but is found only in the best fowling-pieces, particularly those made by Joseph Manton early in the nineteenth century.   The above illustration is of a typical weapon, and represents a Manton double-gun with the patent gravitating stops on the outside of the lock-plate.   They fell, by their own weight, whenever the gun was in a perpendicular position, and locked the hammers automatically, securing them whilst the gun was being loaded and the charges rammed down.

CHAPTER V.

THE PERCUSSION SYSTEM.

HISTORICAL NOTE ON FULMINATES.

THE main appreciable difference between ordinary explosive and a fulminate consists in the amount of percussion required to produce explosion and the difference in the rapidity of the explosion. Ordinary black gunpowder and some nitro-compounds may be ignited by percussion between steel or other metal faces, but the explosion so produced is not appreciably more rapid or violent than if ignition is produced by the simple application of fire. A fulminate, on the contrary, is most readily ignited by percussion, and so exploded exerts greater force in less time than if fired by other means. The qualities of the fulminates and various mixtures used in connection with fire-arms are briefly enumerated in the chapter on " Modern Explosives "; here an attempt is made to show how certain of them came to be employed for igniting the powder charges in fire-arms, and in what way the fulminate has been applied to the purpose.

Chlorate of potash is probably the best-known fulminate ; mixed with powdered glass, it is one of the most sensitive detonating mixtures used in connection with fire-arms. Used as a substitute for the nitrate of potash in gunpowder, or as an additional ingredient, it changes the product into fulminating powder—a much more violent and dangerous explosive, and an unstable one. In England no *mixture* containing chlorate of potash and sulphur is now allowed to be manufactured, although the Patent Office continues to afford protection to numerous explosive mixtures into the composition of which these ingredients enter. Many accidents occurred during the eighteenth and nineteenth centuries with gunpowders so made —notably in 1788 to Berthollet, the famous French chemist. Other percussion powders are derived from the fulminates of mercury, silver, gold, platinum, etc.

The first researches for these powders appear to have been made by Peter Bolduc, a Frenchman, at a date anterior to 1700. In the reports of the Royal Academy of Sciences from 1712 to 1714 notices are given of the experiments of Nicholas Lemery in the same direction. Nothing of great importance appears to have been arrived at by either of these personages, but in 1774 Bayen, chief army physician to Louis XV., discovered *fulminate of mercury*, and made known its explosive properties; but there was no idea, even at that time, of applying fulminates in any way whatever to fire-arms; indeed, it was not until after the discoveries of Fourcroy in 1785, of Vauquelin in 1787, and of Berthollet in 1788, that an attempt was made to provide a substitute for saltpetre in gunpowder by the use of chlorate of potash.

Berthollet, the famous chemist and experimentalist, essayed in vain to effect this; and, after two successive explosions—cruel evidences of the terrible force of the new salts—he desisted, although not entirely relinquishing his researches, as he studied the fulminates, and discovered *fulminate of silver*. Immediately this fulminate became known, endeavours were made to use it in pyrotechnical displays, and after a few trials it was applied to fire-arms, but did not answer effectually; its extreme sensitiveness, and the great care required in handling and using it, rendered it most unsuitable for pyrotechnical purposes.

Scientific persons then endeavoured to combine with the fulminate of silver other combustible ingredients that would render it less sensitive, such as a mixture of chlorate of silver and sulphur, iodate of potass with sulphur, ammoniates of gold, platinum, silver, etc.

In 1800 an Englishman named Howard, after a study of the experiments of Vauquelin and Fourcroy, essayed to manufacture a fulminate composed of fulminate of mercury and saltpetre. This powder was extremely sensitive, possessed all the requisite qualities of a priming powder, and was for years known as Howard's powder.

The most notable invention in connection with the application of fulminates to fire-arms was then discovered. According to the Patent Office Records, the Rev. Alexander John Forsyth, LL.D., a Scotch clergyman, and for fifty-two years minister of Belhelvie, Aberdeenshire, is the person to whom the honour of inventing the percussion system is awarded; his letters patent, dated April 11th, 1807, describe the *application* of the detonating principle for exploding gunpowder in fire-arms, etc. Various modes of applying the same to ordnance are shown. The validity of this patent was disputed in the case of " Forsyth *v.* Reveiere," tried in the King's Bench, June 4th, 1819, in which it transpired that other persons had privately used a similar invention before the date of the patent—which, however, was established; the Judge (Abbot, L.C.J.) ruling that if several persons simultaneously discover the same thing, the party first communicating it to the public is the legal inventor, and entitled to the protection of letters patent. When Lord Moira was Master-General of Ordnance (1806), Mr. Forsyth, at his request, carried out some experiments in the Tower of London, with a view to the application of the detonating system to existing arms; but the experiments did not culminate in the immediate adoption of the invention, and, after a few months, Mr. Forsyth returned to Belhelvie and resumed his pastoral duties, not further engaging with gunnery. His inactivity with respect to his clever invention led to his patent being evaded by many persons. The fulminating mixtures he made use of are thus described in the specification of his patent:—

> "I do make use of some one of the compounds of combustible matter, such as sulphur or sulphur and charcoal, with an oxymuriatic salt; for example, the salt formed of dephlogisticated marine acid and potash (oxymuriatic of potassium), or of fulminating metallic compounds, as fulminate of mercury or of common gunpowder, mixed in due quantity with any of the afore-mentioned substances, or with an oxymuriatic salt as aforesaid."

With regard to the manner of ignition the specification reads:—

> "Instead of permitting the touch-hole, or vent, of the species of artillery, fire-arms, mines, etc., to communicate with the open air, and instead of giving fire by a lighted match, or flint or steel, or by any other matter in a state of actual combustion, applied to a priming in an open pan, I do so close the touch-hole or vent by means of a plug or sliding-piece as to exclude the open air, and to prevent any sensible escape of the blast, or explosive gas or vapour, outwards, or from the priming or charge; and, as much as it is possible, to force the said priming to go in the direction of the charge, and to set fire to the same, and not to be wasted in the open air."

The charge was fired by a plunger working in a hole having communication with the charge, at the bottom of which a small quantity of the detonating mixture had been previously placed. The rod was struck by a cock, or, in artillery, by means of a hammer.

The success of the principle was soon observed, notwithstanding the clumsy and often inefficient inventions which were adopted in order to apply it to existing types of guns. Nor can the value of the invention be too highly appreciated, since to it is due the modern method of igniting powder charges in all small-arms.

DETONATORS AND THE COPPER CAP.

The mechanical means by which Forsyth's system of ignition was utilised were very numerous; a few only need be mentioned. The original patent specified a magazine turning on a roller or tube screwed into the breech of the gun; the fulminating powder was deposited in the roller, the magazine was restored to its position, and the cock struck on a pin with a spiral spring attached, which pin reached and ignited the powder. Various improvements were made by those engaged by the patentee to produce for him; the gun-makers also adopted the principle, whilst varying the mechanism by which it was applied, and when the patent had been in use some years many makers had their own particular mechanisms licensed by the patentee.

In 1808 a Genevan gun-maker named Pauly, practising in Paris, invented a percussion breech-loading gun, in which a fulminating paper cap was affixed to the breech of the cartridge. Upon pulling a trigger, a needle pierced the cap, and thus ignited the charge. It was from this gun that the Lefaucheux breech-loader was subsequently developed.

In 1812 this same Pauly invented a percussion gun, in which the hammer,

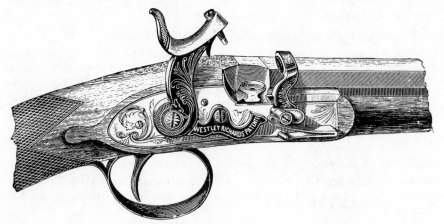

The Westley-Richards Detonating Gun.

cock, and flash-pan were dispensed with, all being replaced by a small piston, actuated by a spiral spring, striking a nipple upon which a few grains of fulminate were placed.

Numerous inventions between 1807 and 1825 relate to self-priming guns, and the systems are greatly varied; sometimes the fulminate was enveloped in paper or metallic covers, and in others the powder was simply rolled into small pills or pellets. In 1821 Westley-Richards invented a percussion gun which ignited with either the simple detonating powder, the paper caps, the pellets, or the balls.

The cock strikes into the flash-pan, which is covered with a pivoted lid actuated by a spring. The falling of the hammer causes the cover to move from over the pan by its breast pressing against an extremity of a pivoted lever, whose other extremity is connected with and actuates the pan-cover. The touch- or communication-hole is situated in the bottom of the pan, and enters the barrel in an oblique direction. A small peg is screwed through the cock-nose so that the point of the peg falls into the centre of the pan, which is concave, and thus renders the percussion more certain.

Many similar systems were used and patented between 1812 and 1825. The chief systems were those of Egg, Wilkinson, Lancaster, Lang, and Westley-Richards. The accompanying illustration shows a few of the numerous detonators ; many others existed but a very short time, and were not extensively used. No. 1 represents the paper cap, the fulminate being placed between two small pieces of paper. No. 2 is a priming-tube, the one end being inserted in the touch-hole and the other

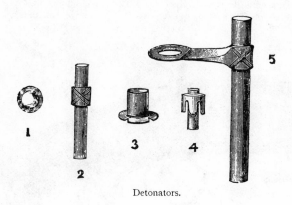

Detonators.

struck by the cock. No. 3 is a musket percussion-cap. No. 4 is the Westley-Richards primer. This consisted of a priming-tube with flanges affixed to it. The tube was inserted in the nipple, the flanges preventing it being driven in altogether when struck by the cock. No. 5 is a friction-tube, as used for firing cannon. It is placed in the touch-hole and by pulling a string attached to the ring in the cross-arm the required friction to ignite the fulminate within the tube is obtained.

The copper cap was the latest and best form of percussion ignition. Many persons claim to have invented it ; among them the gun-makers Egg and Manton. Wilkinson states that Egg purchased it of Roantree, a gun-maker of Barnard Castle but that it was actually first used in 1814 by a Mr. Joshua Shaw, of Philadelphia, who, at that time, put the fulminate in a steel cap, which, after use, he kept for the purpose of repriming. The next year he employed a pewter cap, which he threw away after using, and in 1816 used a similar cap of copper, exactly as used on percussion muzzle-loaders forty years later.

Colonel Hawker says respecting it :—

"The copper cap is now in general use all over the world, and therefore many gun-makers attempt to claim its invention as their own. I do not mean to say that I was the inventor of it —probably not ; but this I must beg leave to state :—When Joe (Manton) first brought out his detonator in Davies Street, he made the most perfect gun I ever saw; and doubting whether such another could be got, I set my wits to work in order to simplify the invention. At last the plan of a perforated nipple, and the detonating powder in the crown of a small cap, occurred to me. I made a drawing of it, and took it to Joe. After having explained it, he said he would show me something in a few weeks' time, when, lo and behold ! there was a rough gun altered to precisely my own plan—his factotum, poor old Asell, informing me that the whole job was done from my drawing. Thus Joe, who led the fashion for all the world, sent out a few copper-cap guns, and I know with some degree of reluctance. The trade, finding he had then deviated from his own patent, adopted this plan, and it proved to answer so well that we now see it in general circulation."

Joseph Manton's "Tube" Detonating Gun.

The reason for Manton's reluctance appears to be that he wished to push his own patent tube-gun. In this a metal primer was placed in the touch-hole and held there by a spring catch, and exploded by the blow of the cock on the *side* of the tube—the fired tube being blown out of the gun by the force of the explosion.

The late W. Greener used tinned iron caps. Another plan deserving mention was that of Baron Heurteloup, who, discovering that a fulminating powder enclosed in a tube of soft metal could be cut through without ignition yet detonated if struck by a blunt instrument, designed a self-priming gun in which a long tube of detonating powder was contained in the stock and moved forward into position by each fall of the hammer; the fall also cutting off the fragment of tube required and then instantly detonating it by continuing its blow.

The detonating mixtures used in copper caps and the methods of manufacture are described in the chapter on " Explosives."

THE PERCUSSION MUZZLE-LOADER.

The percussion principle of ignition was applied to muzzle- and to breech-loading guns. It succeeded first with the muzzle-loader, and it was to this principle that the English gun-makers confined their attention. Percussion guns were not quickly accepted as military weapons; the British Government was very slow to adopt the principle, and at first many sportsmen would not use the copper-cap gun. Old sportsmen chiefly adhered to the flint-lock; notably that great authority, Colonel P. Hawker. When first made, it was a common fault to overload the cap; an error which resulted in numerous accidents and serious injuries to sportsmen. The metal of the cap was not always of the best quality, was often too thin, and had a dangerous way of flying into fragments and scattering in all directions when exploded. There was also an idea prevalent that the flint gun shot stronger; a wrong conclusion was formed, but it took years to reverse it in the public judgment.

The ignition given to the charge is certainly more rapid, and there is not the violent escape of gas at the nipple as there is at the touch-hole of a *flint gun*. The penetration and recoil are therefore proportionately increased. Colonel Hawker made several trials between flint and detonating guns, the results showing the advantage of the flint system. He thus addressed Joe Manton after this trial :—

" From the result of very many experiments, Colonel Hawker is of opinion that for neat shooting in the field or covert, and also for killing single shots at wildfowl rapidly flying, and particularly by night, there is not a question in favour of the detonating system, as its trifling inferiority to the flint gun is tenfold repaid by the wonderful accuracy it gives in so readily obeying the eye. But in firing a heavy charge among a large flock of birds the flint has the decided advantage.

" Moreover, the sudden and additional recoil of a detonator with the full charge for duck-gun is apt, if the shooter be not careful, to strike the hand back and give him a severe blow on the nose."

With the flint-lock in a heavy shower of rain, or a continuous drizzle, it was a matter of impossibility to keep the priming-powder dry. With detonating paper caps and pellets the same difficulty was experienced, and it was not until the introduction of the copper cap that the percussion gun could be considered in every way superior to the flint, although the tube detonating gun of Westley-

Richards, already described, had considerable vogue, and was in use for many years.   The extreme quickness of fulminate powder, the combustion of which is so rapid that its unchecked flame may pass through gunpowder without igniting it, brought into general requisition various forms of nipple and the patent breech. The latter was invented by Nock in 1787, with the object of getting a front ignition of the powder charge.   Prior to that date barrels had been made with a plain hut or breech-plug, screwed in the end ; by hollowing out this plug so that part at least of the charge of powder should be behind the touch-hole, Nock expected to obtain

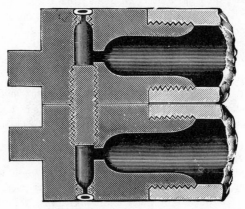

Nock's Patent Breech.

stronger shootin3 and avoid the blowing out of the grains of powder by the explosion of the rear part of the charge.   Sporting guns in those days were of small bore—24 or less—and the Nock patent breech was advantageous.   With the early percussion guns there were often misfires, owing to the extreme quickness of the fulminate used.   Sometimes, too, the charge was started up the barrel by the detonator before the powder charge ignited.   Much was gained by improvements in the fulminate employed, and by diminishing the quantity used.   Still more by altering the position of the nipple and contracting the flash-hole, so that the flames of the cap impinged at that point, and this brief check caused greater heat to be generated and secured the immediate firing of the charge.   The touch-hole removed from the side and then placed upon the top of the breech-plug was a great improvement, so far as the performance of the gun was concerned, and, in time, the shape and arrangement of nipple, breech and break-off were altered, until in 1850 the muzzle-loading percussion gun was a truly elegant weapon. No one did more towards effecting this development of type than the late W. Greener; a facsimile of one of his latest pattern guns is here reproduced, and it may be said, with truth, that it accurately represents the highest form of the muzzle-loading sporting shot gun.

W. Greener's Double Muzzle-loader, 1858.

To facilitate the manipulation of the percussion muzzle-loader various mechanisms were subsequently added to the lock mechanism. For instance, guns have been fitted with an ingenious arrangement for automatically conveying caps from a magazine and placing them in position *upon* the nipple by the motion of raising the hammer to full cock. In the event of a cap missing fire it was necessary only to raise the hammer again and pull the trigger. The invention obviated the troublesome fumbling with small caps, but even an invention so ingenious could not maintain the popularity of the muzzle-loading principle.

The sportsman of the twentieth century equipped with a modern gun has but a slight conception of the difficulties under which his forefathers laboured when shooting with a muzzle-loader, and it is interesting to note the many points of superiority possessed by *all* breech-loaders of to-day, over even the best of the percussion muzzle-loading guns.

A frequent and ever present danger connected with the use of the muzzle-loading gun was that of accidental discharge when loading. Then, again, there was the risk, with a double-barrelled gun, of over-loading—it was no uncommon thing for the sportsman to put both charges of powder into the same barrel, sometimes with disastrous results, at least to the gun, if not to the user or his friends.   Another serious objection was that the ramming down of the charge carried with it the damp fouling, and this being forced on to the new load had considerable effect upon the powder, which naturally gave but indifferent and irregular results.

The ramrod was a constant worry, frequently breaking, and at times, when occasion arose for a rapid shot, it would be left in the barrel and fired from it by an excited sportsman.

The nipple was undoubtedly the *bête noire* of the shooter of that time.   If too hard it broke off, if too soft the point quickly become dubbed up and useless; added to this, misfires were constantly caused through the nipple getting rusty or becoming fouled by the previous shots.   This was especially the case with guns of poor quality.

The cleaning of the barrels was a troublesome and dirty job.   They became so fouled that it was frequently necessary to scour them out with boiling water, while the passing of the ramrod, when charging or cleaning, up and down the barrels dirtied the shooter's hands and clothes.

Caps were also a regular source of trouble.   Many sportsmen would use the cheapest caps procurable; these often failed to explode, or split and flew about in a most dangerous fashion, and many were the shooters whose eyes were injured by this false economy.

The breeches soon became fouled and rusted, and could not be removed by the sportsmen; in fact, the only way in which the gun-maker could manage to unscrew a thoroughly fouled breech was by pouring oil down the barrel, allowing it to stand a while, and then placing it in the fire.   Some nasty accidents occurred when doing this, through omitting to properly withdraw the charge.

This fixed breech-end permitted careless workmanship to pass undetected.   It was impossible for the inside of the barrels to be examined, and even in guns of medium quality but little attention was given to the boring; in fact, many of the barrels were left with the rough borer's rings in them : they naturally became leaded up, and were quickly rendered useless for good shooting.   The advent of the breech-loader, permitting of closer examination of the interior of the barrels, quickly changed this, and the cheapest breech-loader of to-day is superior in this respect to many of the best muzzle-loading guns.

It is a curious fact that nearly all muzzle-loading barrels were made too light at the breech (the ramrod weighed from 4 to 5 ounces, and this additional weight has been utilised in strengthening the breech-ends of modern gun-barrels).   Accidents from this unnecessary weakness were of frequent occurrence, but it is worthy of note that during the author's sixty years' experience only two accidents with *breech-loaders* have resulted in injury to the users of the guns—in one case the sportsman's thumb was injured, and, in the other, his face. Both these guns were made in the early 'sixties; and when one considers that—in spite of the great increase in the number of guns now used, and the irregularity of, and excessive force exerted by, many of the modern smokeless powders—serious accidents are but rare, one is struck by the great improvement in the manufacture of the modern shot gun, which is theoretically and practically perfect.

The author recalls two serious accidents, in what is now the city of Birmingham, with muzzle-loading guns. Both occurred through the falling out of the fore-end

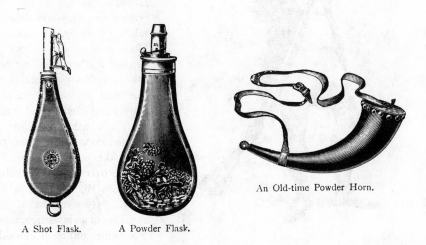

A Shot Flask.   A Powder Flask.   An Old-time Powder Horn.

bolt, which permitted the barrels to drop down; the weight of the breech-ends caused them to fall nipples downwards, and in both instances the charges were exploded with fatal results.

The sportsman of to-day, with his gun and cartridges, is easily and quickly equipped: not so the sportsman of the 'thirties. The nipples of his gun being properly cleaned, he had to remember his ramrod, shot pouch or belt, powder flask, caps, cap-charger, paper for his wadding, spare nipples and a nipple-key, although the latter was useless if the nipples were rusted in.

The illustration on page 122 shows an old-time sportsman in a typical loading position, and the following instructions on how to load a gun are extracted from

W. Greener's book, "The Gun" : "Place the butt on the ground or on your foot, and incline the muzzle well outwards.   When you have to load one barrel only, let the loaded barrel be that farthest away.   Do not grasp the ramrod with the hand, but with the thumb and forefinger only.   Both locks should be at half-cock when loading.   Muzzle-loading caps should fit the nipples accurately, so as not to burst in putting on ; they may then be taken off easily, but are not likely to drop off.   If water-proofed and capsuled, no fulminate is likely to adhere to the head of the nipple and cause an accidental discharge."

Correct Position for charging a
Muzzle-loading Gun.

There was unanimity of opinion among the early writers as to the superiority of the muzzle- over the breech-loader. The late W. Greener, in his book, "Gunnery in 1858," speaking of an invention, says : "Notwithstanding all the skill and ingenuity brought to bear upon it, it is, we think, sufficient to prove that breech-loading guns cannot be made sufficiently durable to yield any reasonable return for the extra expense and trouble attending their fabrication."

Colonel Hawker was of the same opinion, and it was only in the last edition of his book (1859), which was edited by his son, that the breech-loader received true recognition.

The drawbacks of the muzzle-loading system were increased a hundredfold when applied to rifles, owing to the difficulty of getting a tight-fitting bullet into the bore.

The muzzle-loading rifle may be said to have reached its zenith in 1859, although it is curious that at the *Field* Trials of that year the shooting of the rifles then tested was, even when judged by the standard of that day, exceedingly bad, and it is to be regretted that the Whitworth rifle was not entered at these trials, the mean deviation with this rifle at the Hythe Trials of 1857 being but $4\frac{1}{2}$ inches at 500 yards.

The winning rifle at the *Field* Trials was shot with but two drams of powder and a conical ball weighing 1 oz 7 drams. This light load of powder was necessary with the old system of rifling, as an increased charge would cause the bullet to strip and, of course, keyhole.

The second rifle was made by Smith upon Mr. Purdey's two-grooved plan, and it seems probable that if this rifle had been correctly loaded and shot it would have secured first place.

The 200 yards targets used at the *Field* Trials measured 22 inches by 19 inches, and at 100 yards 22 inches by 18 inches, and the average deviation from the centre made with the winning rifle at 200 yards was $7\frac{3}{8}$ inches, and at 100 yards $2\frac{1}{2}$ inches.

At this time the author was occupied with the manufacture of the Cape Rifles, more fully described elsewhere (rifled upon a similar principle to the Purdey Express), with which it was no uncommon thing to put six shots in a 3-inch circle at 100 yards. Unfortunately, as these rifles were being made for another firm, the author was not permitted to enter them at the trial.

Mr. Jernigan, in his interesting book on China, says:

"The Miaotzu sportsman generally makes or helps to make such a gun as he wished to use, not only the lock, stock and barrel, but his ammunition as well. He first provides the necessary quantity of good scrap iron and charcoal, builds a forge near his house and erects a light shed of mats or branches over it, and then invites some famous smith of the district to come and forge the barrels for the intended gun. This is done by welding the scrap iron into several bars, each about 1-in. broad and $\frac{1}{4}$-in. thick. Each of these bars is then coiled spirally on a small mandril and afterwards welded into as many cylinders or tubes, each about one foot long. These tubes are joined together by welding end to end, and thus united form the barrel of the gun, which is a twist barrel of good material and manufacture.

"The barrel is now fastened by wedging into a log of timber, the muzzle end downwards, and bored out by hand with square steel rimmers. These rimmers are made of different lengths and diameters, and have a wood cross-bar at the top which is turned slowly and steadily until the whole length of the gun-barrel has been bored out in a uniform and satisfactory manner. The work may occupy months of the shooter's spare time, but when finished the long barrel has been bored true and straight and smooth, and he has the satisfaction of knowing that his gun was built directly under his own supervision and materially with his own hands. The breech is closed by welding a prepared plug of iron therein.

"The barrel is mounted on a pistol stock, fitted with a spring cock and trigger, and fastened on the outside of the stock near the breech, the barrel being fastened to the stock by movable thin silver bands, each from a half to one inch in width."

One can well understand the backwardness of these sportsmen when reading later that—

"The Chinese sportsman of the present day is in every essential equipment as far behind the Western sportsman as China is behind Western nations in civilisation. He shoots with an old pattern muzzle-loading matchlock gun, which he calls Niao-Chiang. The barrels may be from 4 to 6 feet long, sometimes longer. . . . The gun barrels are usually round, except in Kweichow, where the barrel is generally octagon in shape and from 5 to 7 feet long. All occupations in China are classified, and the son invariably follows the occupation of his father; the sportsman or the shooter is therefore a professional, especially in Western China, where many of them are pious men. There they worship Loa Tien Yah, the old heavenly sire, and beseech him to

A Chinese Sportsman, from Jernigan's Book on China.

preserve them from all harm and grant them success in their perilous undertakings among the beasts of the forests."

It is entirely due to the intelligent division of labour, combined with practical supervision of every detail, that the modern gun has reached so high a state of perfection in England, and until John Chinaman is prepared to adopt similar conditions, so long will he be content with his monstrous, unwieldy and unserviceable gun.

THE PERCUSSION BREECH-LOADER.

The percussion method of ignition was early applied to breech-loaders : in some the fulminating powder was attached, more or less effectually, to a paper cartridge case; in others it was placed in the gun in the shape of powder, pellet, paper cap, or tube; in others, later, the copper cap was used, it being found that its flash was strong enough to pierce the paper of the cartridge and ignite the charge.

A breech-loader, consisting of a hinged breech-block, pulled upward from the breech end of the barrels by a hand-lever, was invented early in the century by Robert, a gun-maker of Paris, and had a certain local popularity. Pauly, to whom reference has already been made, invented several, including one on the drop-down principle from which the Lefaucheux gun was developed. Potet, Bastin Lepage, and other Parisian and Continental makers had breech-loading mechanisms for sporting guns.

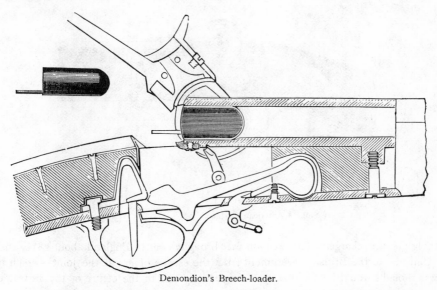

Demondion's Breech-loader.

In 1831 M. Demondion patented the breech-loading percussion gun illustrated. In this arm the breech-block is raised for loading by means of a lever attached to it, and lying along the top of the grip when in position; the act of raising the breech-block depresses the mainspring hammer, situated beneath the barrel, until it engages with the spring trigger, in shape similar to a door-catch. The cartridge has a small percussion tube projecting from the base, against which the flattened end of the mainspring strikes to discharge the gun, the base of the breech-block acting as an anvil on which to strike the tube.

The lock mechanism will easily be understood by referring to the illustration, and the cartridge case was self-consuming, so that no extractor was needed. This arm is one of the first in which cartridges containing their own ignition were used.

GILBERT SMITH'S AMERICAN RIFLE.

In this arm the barrel drops for the insertion of the cartridge, which is of india-rubber, with a perforated cardboard base. The barrel breaks off in the middle of the chamber, and falls at nearly right angles to the stock, as shown by the dotted lines. The cartridge being flexible, it readily accommodates itself to the fixed portion of the chamber, and, the base being perforated, an ordinary cap is sufficient

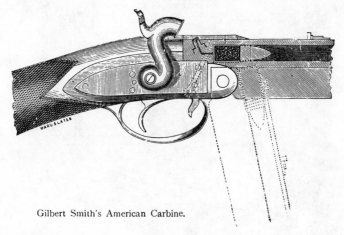

Gilbert Smith's American Carbine.

to ignite the charge. This weapon was brought over to England about 1838, and submitted to the British Government; but the escape of gas at the joint—which it was thought would be avoided by having the breach in the centre of the cartridge—was sufficient to condemn it. This gun is fastened at the top by means of a horizontally sliding bar actuated by a small trigger-lever in front of the lock-trigger the whole action being very similar in mechanism to that of the French flint-lock drop-down breech-loader described and illustrated in the chapter on "Early Breech-loading Mechanisms."

THE NORWEGIAN CARBINE.

A large number of the percussion breech-loaders were designed for military arms. No arm of the kind was generally adopted for use by the British, and their use has been so long discontinued that the author has not deemed it advisable to include any in the chapters devoted to military rifles. A few of the most inclusive type are therefore shown here. The first to be illustrated is the Norwegian military arm of 1842. The action is different from any yet described, the hollow breech-block being pivoted upon a strong pin, and worked by a side-lever which works upon an eccentric affixed to it. By depressing the lever the breech-block is withdrawn from the barrel and raised, as shown in the illustration, and the cock situated beneath the barrel must be depressed to force it into full-cock. The charge is placed in the breech-block, and the cap placed on the nipple, which, when returned to its proper

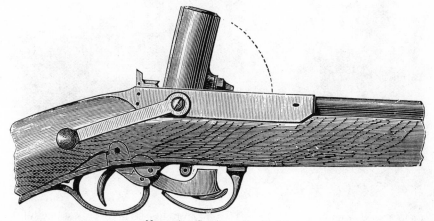

Norwegian Carbine : 1842 Model.

position for firing, is in a vertical position, projecting from underneath the barrel. The mainspring is fixed to the fore-part of the stock, and works along the back of the cock. There is a small stud projecting from the breech-block as a safeguard against the premature ignition of the cap. It must be moved from position by the hand before firing.

The sight is placed on the break-off immediately behind the base of the breech-block. The weapon is about 500 bore, and rifled with six grooves.

In 1851 Karl d'Abezz, of Zürich, invented the percussion breech-loading carbine next illustrated. This gun is loaded in the breech-block, which is capable of moving horizontally in a frame connecting the barrel with the stock. The movement is communicated to the breech-block by an eccentric pivot actuated by a quarter-turn of the lever under the guard. A forward motion is given to the block by the eccentric pivot when returning it to its place, so as to insert the projecting neck on the breech-block into the barrel itself.

Thus the greater portion of the strain was sustained by the eccentric pivot attached to the lever. The lever moved to the left to open the gun-block, and an ordinary cap, cartridge, and lock were employed.

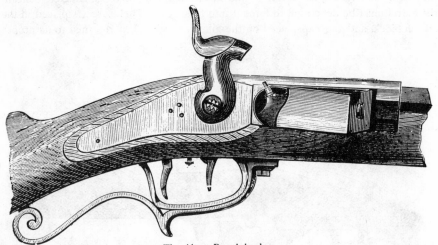

The Abezz Breech-loader.

The Calesher and Terry Capping Carbine, introduced in 1853, was one of the most generally successful arms of this type. The action was on the bolt principle, the shoe being closed by a plug held up to the breech by an intercepted screw. To open the gun a locking piece was raised, and when at right angles to the barrel it formed a handle by which to turn and withdraw the breech-plug. The paper cartridge was inserted through a hole in the side of the shoe; the plug thrust forward, the lever-handle turned down, and when in its place, pressed quite home along the shoe, it covered the hole by which the cartridge was inserted.

WESTLEY-RICHARDS CAPPING BREECH-LOADER.

This was adopted as a cavalry arm in 1861. The principle resembles several which preceded it. The breech-bolt slides to and fro on a flap hinged above the breech end of the barrel; this flap is raised to admit the cartridge D, and, in closing the movable head A to the breech-bolt, pressed forward by its rear extremity C pressing against the back of the breech-shoe or standing breech, F forces the cart-ridge into the chamber of the barrel and wedges the bolt securely between the face of the barrel and the standing breech. The bolt A together with the breech-block is withdrawn from the barrel, an opening by the catch C engaging the bottom of the breech-shoe E. As a 52- or ·450-bore, the arm is still used in South Africa, where

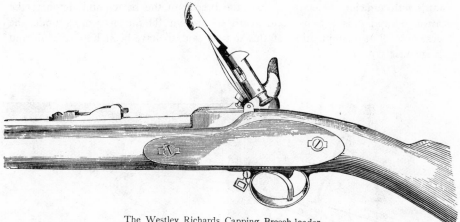

The Westley Richards Capping Breech-loader.

for many years it was most popular. It was fired by the ordinary military cap and nipple, the flash passing through the paper of the cartridge case and so igniting the charge; the arm could be converted to a muzzle-loader by inserting a metal plug and a couple of wads. The wad at the base of the cartridge

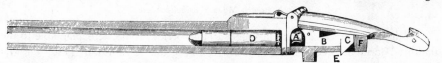

Mechanism of theCapping Carbine.

by its expansion practically stops escape of gas at breech, and the wad is pushed forward by the next cartridge inserted and shot out in front of the bullet.

THE FRENCH *MOUSQUETON.*

The "*Mousqueton des Cent Gardes*" was invented in France shortly afterwards; its mechanism and cartridge is the next illustrated. The pin A for the cap is placed under the base of the cartridge, and projects barely $\frac{1}{8}$-inch. The long pin, F, on the top of the case is to withdraw it from the chamber after discharge. The stock is

hollowed behind the breech to allow of the cartridge being pushed into the barrel A.
The breech-block B carries a small stud b, which strikes the cap of the cartridge C
when the gun is fired.   Affixed to the block B is a scear D, forming part of the
trigger-guard, the other part being composed of the scear and trigger-spring F, one
end acting upon the trigger E, and the other causing the breech-block D to fly upwards with sufficient velocity to close the breech of the barrel and detonate the
cartridge cap ; G is a swivel and guard, to prevent the finger coming under the
scear tail.   The manipulation of this arm is said to have been both difficult and
dangerous.

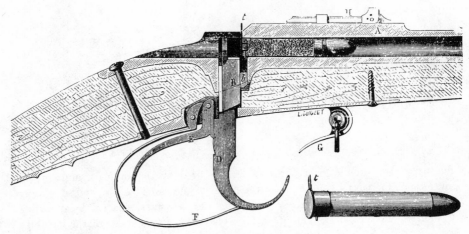

Early French Military Breech-loader.

Of the other breech-actions invented at this period, some were adaptable to the
improved form of breech-loading cartridge, and in the new form are better known ;
a few may be still in use, but the majority have fallen into desuetude.   With the
single exception of the Westley Richards capping carbine, the percussion breech-
loader may be pronounced to have failed.   It united the disadvantages of ignition
on the outside : requiring the fixing of a cap in addition to the manipulations of
the breech mechanism necessary to loading, and the raising of the cock for firing, it
is not surprising that it was quickly superseded as a weapon of war, and as a sporting
arm was never able to compete with arms firing cartridges containing their own
means of ignition.   In but few instances, and in but few points, was the percussion
breech-loader preferred to the muzzle-loader.

CHAPTER VI.

MODERN SHOT GUNS.

HISTORY OF THE BREECH-LOADING SYSTEM.

THE modern sporting breech-loader may be said to have originated with the invention of the cartridge case containing its own ignition; though the breech-loading mechanism of the gun antedated the cartridge by many years, being, in fact, a slow but continuous development of the earliest type of breech-loader already described. The cartridge—that is to say, a charge of powder and bullet in a paper envelope—dates from 1586, and, on the authority of Capo Bianco, such articles were in general use in Europe at the close of the sixteenth century. They were used ordinarily with muzzle-loaders, the base being ripped or bitten off by the soldier before placing in the barrel. At the same time, many attempts were made to use cartridges in breech-loaders. As stated in the section on Ancient Arms, some of these cartridge cases were strong and heavy, and were made of metal; it was not until the detonating cap came into use that the paper cartridge was made to answer well in breech-loading arms. These cases were consumed or were blown out of the barrel; they were not extracted and refilled as were the heavy metal ones in use with wheel, flint, and even matchlock breech-loaders. The flash of the copper cap was sufficient to penetrate the thin paper of the cartridge case and fire the charge; as instanced in the Westley Richards capping carbine already described. Sometimes, as in Demondion's breech-loader, the case contained its own ignition—a detonating pellet or other primer, projecting from the case at or near its base. Bastin Lepage, of Paris, produced a cartridge case, about 1840, in which a copper cap, enclosing its anvil, projected from the base of the cartridge; he claimed that by doing away with the nipple there was no escape of gas at the breech, for he not only did away with the nipple, but provided a stout wad, which, affixed to the base of the cartridge, served the double purpose of supporting the cap and anvil which projected beyond it, but also, by expanding, sealed the breech at the moment of discharge. Presumably there were difficulties in the extraction of the unconsumed remnant of the cartridge and cap, and the idea seems to have been originally intended as applicable chiefly to very small bores and to pistols. Houiller, another

Paris gunsmith, in 1847 patented the pin-fire cartridge as now used. Instead of putting the nipple and cap, or their equivalent, projecting from the base of the cartridge case, he placed the detonating cap, or a detonating pellet, or primer, within wads at the base of the cartridge, and allowed the anvil only to project beyond. As another method, he specified the rim-fire cartridge, and a variety of the central-fire case ; in these, as in the pin-fire, the cap or priming mixture was in the wad base of the cartridge case, and the whole was covered by a thin metal capsule, as at present used.

Some fifteen years previous to this Lefaucheux, a gunsmith of Paris, had improved the Pauly system of breech-loading. The Pauly mechanism was not unlike the Gilbert Smith American rifle, but resembled in other points some of the still earlier breech-loaders. Lefaucheux specified a hinge joint at greater distance from the breech, and the holding down of the barrels at the breech, where they rested upon the prolonged portion of the fore-part of the standing breech, by an interrupted screw. The screw had only one thread, and was practically identical with the double-grip mechanism, later to be described. Later, he still further simplified this grip by doing away with one-half of the half-thread of the interrupted screw, and thus a projection on the head of the lever engaging with a corresponding notch in the lump affixed to the barrels for the purpose of hinging them to the standing breech, became the best known type of Lefaucheux gun. The Houiller pin-fire cartridge was quickly accepted by both Lefaucheux and Lepage, and in a short time its use became general.

The pin-fire cartridge and the modern breech-loader, even in this form, were not the outcome of any one great invention, but resulted from one improvement after another, each later form differing but slightly from the one which immediately preceded it. By the modification and combination of details a principle of breech-loading was gradually evolved, and although that principle has never since been departed from with success, the breech-loading gun, in all its minor details, has been radically changed. The chief alterations have been in the breech-action and the lock mechanism, and it is by tracing these changes that the best idea of the development of the modern gun is to be obtained, and it is by describing them that the history of the gun will be unfolded.

The essential feature of the modern principle of breech-loading is the prevention of all escape of gas at the breech when the gun is fired by the employment of an expansive cartridge case containing its own means of ignition. In the earlier breech-loaders there was an escape of gas through the joints of the breech mechanism, however well fitted, because the metal expanded at the moment of firing and the cartridges were formed of a consumable case, or the load was put in a strong non-expansive breech-plug. In those arms in which the ignition was by cap, or other flash from the outside of the barrel, there was, of course, always a considerable escape back through the vent, or touch-hole, in addition. In the earliest efficient modern cartridge case—the pin-fire—the cap, or detonator, is placed within the case; an anvil, or striking-pin, projects through the rim of the case, and, when struck by the hammer, explodes the priming and ignites the charge of powder. The thin, weak shell is then expanded, by the force of the explosion, until it fits perfectly in the barrel, bears hard against the standing breech, closes tightly round the striking-pin, and thus forms a complete and efficient gas check. Further, the cartridge case is a fresh lining to the breech, every shot, forming, as it were, a second breech, which relieves the permanent breech of much wear and prevents its corrosion.

Probably no invention connected with fire-arms has wrought such changes in the principle of gun construction as the invention of the expansive cartridge case. It has been used for every description of small fire-arm, and has been applied with success even to cannon. It has completely revolutionised the art of gun-making, and has called into being a new and now important industry—that of cartridge manufacture.

The whole of the advantages of the breech-loading system were not immediately apparent, for the original type of gun and cartridge had both to be greatly improved upon before some of its benefits were realised, but the principle involved is of too great importance to be easily overrated.

THE LEFAUCHEUX BREECH-LOADER.

The breech action of the Lefaucheux gun is a crude mechanism. Through a lump fastened beneath the barrels a pin passes, and on this pin the barrels turn. A slot is cut at the opposite end of the lump and in this slot a projection upon the vertical pivot of the action lever grips to hold the breech end of the barrels close down to the bed of the breech-action body. The "grip" is required only to hold the barrels in position; the hinge-pin has to keep the breech ends of the barrels firmly up to the standing breech and prevent the barrels from moving forward when the gun is fired. The face of the standing breech, against which the base of the cartridge presses, has to bear the force of the explosion. The thickness of the breech, and the strength of the metal of which it is made, are supposed to be sufficient to enable it to maintain its position; actually, when the gun is fired, the force of the explosion causes the standing breech to spring back and the joint to gape. A like result is produced by wear, and can be produced at any time by forcing in a very tight cartridge and using the power of the lever to screw down the barrels to their place. This lever, when " home," lies parallel with the barrels and extends to the extremity of the fore-end ; which, originally, was not detachable, but formed the hinge on which the barrel lumps were hooked, and to which the barrels were secured by a fore-end bolt. In other patterns the lump is hooked on to the joint-pin as shown in the illustration. Large numbers of pin-fire guns, closely resembling the original model, are still made in Belgium and France. The

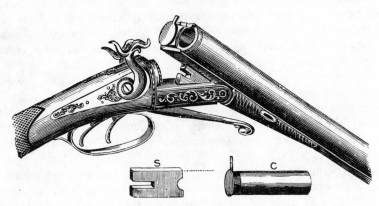

The Original Lefaucheux Breech-loader : 1836.

first cartridges were without rims, and the gun had no extractor, the fired cases being withdrawn by the striking-pin. The great fault of the gun is the weakness of the breech action and the clumsy and inefficient method of securing the barrels thereto ; defects which English gun-makers were quick to observe and remedy.

THE DOUBLE-GRIP BREECH MECHANISM.

This gun—the invention of a Birmingham gun-maker—is substantially the same mechanism as the original Lefaucheux. It differs in the lever, which fits over the bow of the trigger-guard, instead of along the fore-end beneath the barrels, and has two grips, engaging, each with its own particular slot, in the double lump. An inclined plane on the cylindrical head of the lever works against the barrel lump, and forces the breech ends of the barrels upward, when the lever is turned from the trigger-guard. When it is returned to its place the two flanges on the cylindrical head of the lever enter the notches on the barrel lump, and draw down the barrels, securing them firmly to the breech-action body. The lever, L, is held in position by the screw, s, and washer, w, to a pivot passing through the head of the lever, the pivot being solid with the action body ; a stop on the washer allows the lever to travel one quarter of a circle only. A modified form was made in which the lever was returned by a spring ; the idea being to convert the mechanism to that of a snap-action gun. This double-grip lever mechanism is very simple ; all

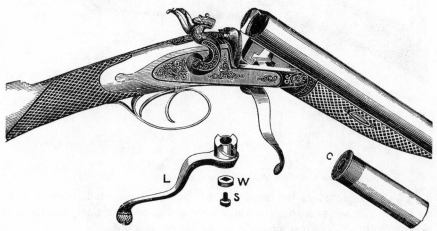

The Double-grip Bar-lock Gun, and Central-fire Cartridge.

the parts are strong, and, with back-action locks, it is a form of breech action which but for the time required to manipulate might still find favour with sportsmen.

From the fact that the screw-like grip with its long lever is capable of binding down the barrels very tightly to the breech-action body it is sometimes inferred that the double-grip is a stronger form of breech mechanism than some snap mechanisms which will not work automatically when the action is foul or a too thick rimmed cartridge case is put in the chamber. As will subsequently be shown, this inference is wrong, since the strain exerted by the force of the explosion is in a line with the axis of the barrels ; to support this strain the double grip affords no power whatever. The work it actually does requires no particular strength ; for the barrels may be held to the bed of the breech-action body by the thumb and fore-finger, even though a full charge be fired.

THE SLIDING BARREL BREECH MECHANISM.

In Bastin Lepage's breech-loader the barrels are not hinged, but slide to and fro on the fore-part of the stock. They are actuated by a lever linked to the fore-end, moving forward just sufficiently to receive the cartridge. A catch upon

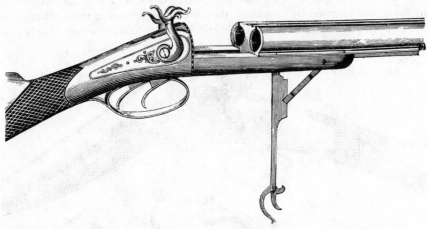

The Bastin Lepage Breech-loader.

the lever bolts, or wedges, the barrels against the face of the standing breech when the lever is returned to its place, but this was found to be insufficient, and, the plan being proved faulty in other ways, the mechanism fell into disuse.

COMBINED SLIDING AND HINGED BREECH MECHANISM.

The sliding barrel of the Bastin and the hinged barrel of the Lefaucheux are combined in the Dougall lock-fast breech mechanism. The hinge-pin is eccentric, and is turned by the lever attached to it. The barrels not only turn upon this hinge-pin, but are moved by it in a line parallel with their axis sufficiently far to clear, and engage with, projecting discs upon the face of the standing breech.

To open the barrels for loading, the lever is depressed; this turns the eccentric hinge-pin, and moves the barrels forward about one-eighth of an inch, when the breech ends are clear of the discs and the barrels drop, as in the ordinary Lefaucheux gun. When the cartridges have been inserted the barrels are brought up and held in position until the lever is turned, and the barrels forced back by the eccentric until the discs on the face of the standing breech enter the chambers behind the cartridges and prevent the barrels from turning on the hinge-pin.

These discs were advocated as a remedy for side motion of the barrels when the breech mechanism became worn. Now two wings or side clips projecting, one on each side, from the face of the standing breech are extolled as effecting the same

Dougall's Lock-fast Breech-action.

purpose. It is surprising that first-class gun-makers should continue to make these unsightly protuberances, which are useless for any purpose for which, presumably, they have been designed. A well-fitting top extension is a safer and more sightly remedy for a fault which ought not to exist, and one that will rarely, if ever, be found in a soundly made gun constructed on any reliable system.

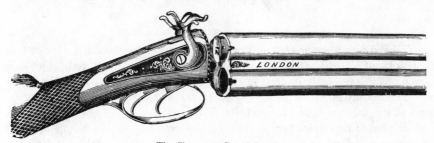

The Turn-over Breech-loader.

THE TURN-OVER BREECH MECHANISM.

Another form of breech mechanism tried repeatedly without success is the turn-over action. In this the barrels are secured to the standing breech by a screw-pin entering the barrel lump just below the extreme breech-ends. This screw-pin is the pivot on which the barrels turn for loading. By turning the barrels to the right the breech-ends will be exposed sufficiently to admit of the cartridges being inserted. They are then returned to the firing position, and secured there by a bolt entering the rib. The turn-over is the simplest of all the principles of breech-loading described, but it has not been generally employed; it is suitable only for the pin-fire cartridge, and in the event of the case bursting or the action jamming from other causes there is very little leverage obtainable for forcing the gun open. It requires also back-action locks, to which there are several objections.

Jeffries' Side-motion Breech-loader.

THE SIDE-MOTION BREECH MECHANISM.

Of the side-motion breech mechanisms the best known is that invented by Mr. Jeffries, of Norwich, about 1862. The barrels are turned on a vertical pivot by a lever pivoted vertically under the breech-action body, and having a projection fixed eccentrically upon the turning head of the lever, which projection engages with a slot in the barrels and moves them.

This plan of breech-loading is probably the next best to the "drop-down" or Lefaucheux principle for sporting guns; but its inventor, after making it for many years, finally abandoned it; and the Fox gun, constructed upon the same principle, but dispensing with the lever, was strenuously pushed in the United States without greater success. Gun-makers and sportsmen seem agreed that the drop-down principle has greater advantages and is the most convenient for all sporting purposes.

THE SELF HALF-COCKING MECHANISM.

With the pin-fire cartridge it is necessary, after firing the gun, to raise the hammers to half-cock before the breech action can be opened. In order to effect this half-cocking of the locks automatically the author produced in 1864 a snap-action breech mechanism which presented several novel features.

It was one of the first guns on the drop-down principle in which the barrels were bolted to the top of the standing breech. This locking-bolt works in the top of the standing breech, between the hammers and in a line with the barrels, with which it engages by entering a slot immediately below the top rib. The lever placed over the trigger-guard turned the pin which served as its pivot, and upon this

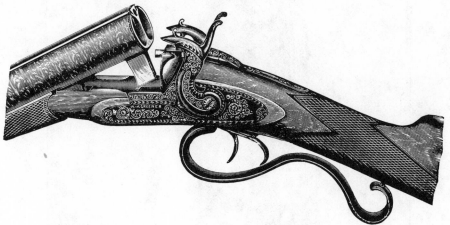

W. W. Greener's Self Half-cocking Gun, and First Top Bolt Breech-action.

pin were two arms which raised the hammers to half-cock before the action bolt was withdrawn, and the barrels left free to open. This breech mechanism, simple and fragile as it may appear, withstood a great amount of hard work, especially upon the large-bore rifles used in India, and is here illustrated for comparison with later mechanisms, which demonstrate the great improvement made in gun construction since this mechanism was introduced.

NEEDHAM'S SIDE-LEVER BREECH MECHANISM.

Like the foregoing, the Needham side-lever breech-action has for its first object the self half-cocking of the locks by depressing the lever for opening the gun. This

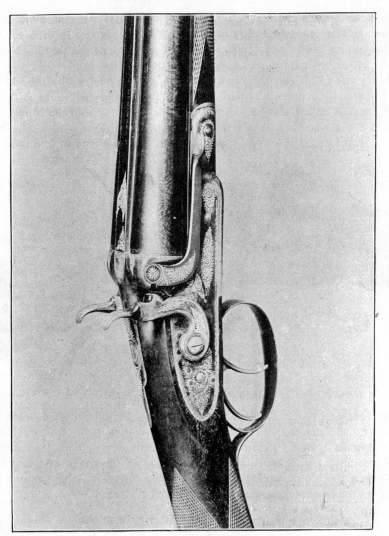

Needham's Snap-action Mechanism.

gun is noteworthy on other accounts ; it was the first modern breech mechanism on the snap-action principle, and it was the first of which an illustrated advertisement appeared in a newspaper. The advertisement appeared in the *Field* in 1862, shortly after the introduction of the gun.

The mechanism proved to be a good one ; some of the guns constructed on this system have seen much hard work and are still in use, whilst the snap-action principle is that now generally employed by gun-makers for all sporting guns. The locking-bolt, or holding-down bolt, which secures the barrels upon the breech-action body, is forced into the slots by a spring when the gun is closed, instead of requiring the lever to be moved by hand.

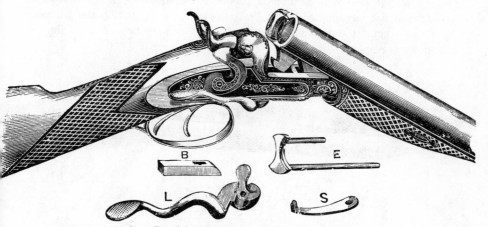

Side-lever Breech-loader with Bar, or Front-action, Locks.

THE SIDE-LEVER BREECH MECHANISM.

One of the earliest snap breech-actions is the side-lever, which for a long time remained the favourite of American sportsmen and some London gun-makers. The lever is bent round from underneath the breech-action body so as to lie on the lock-plate ; its thumb-piece conveniently placed immediately behind the hammer. The lever, L, is pivoted beneath the barrels ; an arm continued upwards engages in a slot in a steel holding-down bolt, B, working to and fro in a slot in the breech-action body, being forced forward by a spring, s, and moved backward by depressing the lever. The spring is sometimes fixed in the breech-action body, forward of the lever, and is uncovered ; it should be placed on the trigger-plate and connected to the lever by an S-swivel. Such guns work more pleasantly especially if the holding-down bolt is kept constantly pressing against the back of the fore-lug of the barrel lump, and allows the gun to be closed without appreciable snap or jerk. The principal objection to the side-lever is, that in some circumstances the position of the lever renders it difficult to raise the left-hand hammer to full-cock—an objection which was well met by placing the lever on the left side of the gun.

THE CENTRAL-FIRE SYSTEM.

The early central-fire guns were used with consumable cartridge cases, and the difficulty to be overcome was the escape of gas at the breech joint at the time of firing. In 1838 Dreyse, of Sommerda, produced a central-fire gun of this type. A modification of it was adopted by the Prussian army in 1842, and became famous as the "needle gun," the breech mechanism being a combination of the sliding and drop-down principles.

Dreyse's Gun.

To open the Dreyse gun the lever is depressed; by this motion the barrels are forced forward, clear of the discs, and allowed to rise beyond the level of the standing breech. The lever has an arm extended upwards beyond the point which engages with the tumblers, and cocks the locks by forcing the hammers back, as shown. The gun was without outside hammers, and the chief drawback to its use was the fouling of the lock mechanism, but more particularly the needles, which had to pierce the soft cartridge case and force through the powder charge to strike the cap, which was fixed to the wad separating the powder from the load of shot.

NEEDHAM'S NEEDLE GUNS.

A somewhat similar cartridge, but having the cap at the base, was used in the central-fire gun introduced by Needham about 1850. The gun is of a very different type, having barrels fixed to the stock like those of a muzzle-loader and in double-guns, a separate action for each barrel. The only well-known gun at all resembling

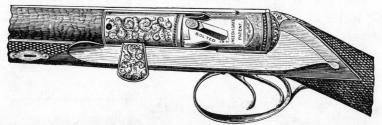

Needham's Central-fire Needle Gun.

it in principle is the almost forgotten Bacon breech-loader or some hybrid weapon like the double-barrelled Remington. This gun is loaded by turning the finger-piece towards the top of the barrel, and pulling outward the "action" or breech-block pivoted vertically upon the pin, B; the cartridge is inserted in the recess left vacant by the "action" and pushed into the barrel, the breech-block is then returned to its place, locked there by depressing the finger-piece, and is ready for firing, the lock contained

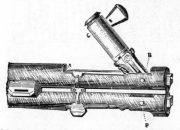

Mechanism of Needham's Needle Gun.

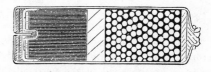

Needham's Central-fire Cartridge.

in the "action" having been automatically cocked by the turning up of the finger-piece. The cartridge consists of two cardboard wads for the base (as shown), the cylinder of ordinary cartridge paper, and the cap is placed on the inner side of the two wads, its cup towards the base. The striking-needle passes through the outer envelope of the cartridge and through holes pierced in the wad forming the base, and strikes into the cap.   The base is stiffened by a zinc washer or cap, and the case is not extracted after firing, but the base, pushed forward by the next cartridge inserted, acts as a top-wad.   The gun had considerable success, but was soon superseded by higher developments of the central-fire system.

THE LANCASTER CENTRAL-FIRE SYSTEM.

This system was introduced by the late Mr. Lancaster in 1852.   It differed from the needle guns in the construction both of breech mechanism and the form

The Lancaster Central-fire Breech-loader and Cartridge.

of the cartridge used.   The barrels, like those of the Dreyse gun, slide forward before turning on the hinge-pin ; the forward motion is conveyed by means of an eccentric on the head of the vertically pivoted under-lever.   A projection of the under-lump engaging below the standing breech takes the place of the disc for holding down the barrels.   The cartridge case is not consumed, but is withdrawn by an extractor after firing.   It differs from later central-fire cases in the mode of effecting the ignition of the charge.   At the base of the cartridge case is a copper disc perforated with four holes ; on the disc the detonating mixture is spread.   The whole of the base is then covered with a copper capsule, which is then in the centre, and there receives the blow from a striking-pin having a flattened head. It is stouter at the edge, where it is somewhat wider than the diameter of the cartridge, and forms a slight rim by which it is withdrawn. It will be noticed that the gun differs but slightly from the ordinary central-fire gun in general use since 1860—so much so, in fact, that in some languages the term " system Lancaster" is a synonym for central-fire breech-loader.

THE DAW CENTRAL-FIRE SYSTEM.

The central-fire cartridge, practically as now in use, was introduced into this country in 1861 by Mr. Daw. It is said to have been the invention of M. Pottet,

Daw's Central-fire Breech-loader.

Daw's Central-fire Cartridge.

of Paris, and was improved upon by a M. Schneider, and gave rise to considerable litigation with reference to patent rights. Mr. Daw, who controlled the English patents, was defeated by Messrs. Eley Bros., owing, it is understood, to the fact that the patent had not been kept in force in France, where the invention was originally protected. Mr. Daw was the only exhibitor of central-fire guns and cartridges at the International Exhibition in 1862 ; the system with which his name is intimately connected is shown here. The bottom lever withdraws the holding-down bolt ; the cartridge is of the modern type, the cap detonated by a striker passing from the outside of the standing breech to the inner face ; and, after firing, the cartridge case is withdrawn in the ordinary way by a sliding extractor fitted to the breech ends of the barrels.

SOME ADVANTAGES OF THE CENTRAL-FIRE PRINCIPLE.

The pin-fire cartridge, however well made, is found to occasionally permit an escape of gas at the pin-hole.   Especially is this the case when the breech ends of the barrels become worn, or the chamber is so large as not to properly support the case, thus allowing too great expansion.   The cartridges are not so handy to carry, on account of the projecting pin, as the central-fire.   The central-fire gun has no pin-hole in the barrels to admit wet, nor is it needful to note that the cartridges are put in the right side uppermost.   The central-fire gun is much more rapidly loaded ; the extraction is automatically performed, and its advantages are so apparent that it is surprising the system encountered any serious opposition when first introduced.   The chief objection raised by sportsmen was that the gun did not show at a glance whether or not it was loaded.   Gun-makers, therefore, fitted indicators, or small pins, which protruded through the action when a cartridge case, fired or unfired, was in the chamber ; experience proved them to be unnecessary. Eighteen or more years later the same objection was advanced against hammerless guns.   They, too, have been fitted with indicators to show when the gun is cocked, whilst one maker provides a small window in each lock-plate, so that the shooter may, when he desires, inspect the mechanism and ascertain which barrel has been fired.   With the facility for opening and closing the gun modern snap-actions afford, the best and simplest way is to open the gun and look at the cartridge.   Everyone should observe the rule of treating a gun as loaded—accidents would then be rare. There cannot now be the slightest excuse for leaving a breech-loader with a cartridge in it, and doing so should be considered a grave offence.   One of the great advantages possessed by the breech-loader is that it can be so readily loaded and unloaded ; so that if only a little trouble be taken accidents with loaded guns would be rare indeed.

TOP-LEVER ACTIONS AND OTHERS.

There are two distinct types of top-lever mechanisms ; in one the lever swings upon a horizontal pivot on the standing breech, and is either raised or is depressed to withdraw the holding-down bolt and open the gun.   This type is not generally used.   In the other the lever turns upon a vertical pivot, and actuates various mechanisms, used to bolt the breech-action body and the barrels together.

The first top-lever mechanism is said to have been that of a Birmingham gunsmith named Matthews.   His production was a crude one, but the principle was improved upon and adopted ; a better form of it was introduced by Westley Richards about 1860, and was applied to pin-fire guns. The chief advantages of the breech-action lever being placed upon the top of the gun are : first, it is possible to carry the gun in any position without catching or displacing the lever ; second, the shooter can at once detect whether or not the action is securely fastened, the position of the lever being noticeable as the gun is raised to the shoulder for firing ; third, it is easier to manipulate than any other, and, length for length, allows of greater leverage than if placed elsewhere ; the power the manipulator has to control the lever fixed in this position is very great, it being possible with even a short top-lever to raise both locks to full-cock as well as withdraw the holding-down bolts and overcome the weight of the spring which drives them home. Another advantage is that the hand, after firing the gun, can work the lever without losing its grip of the stock.

Top-lever Gun with Back-action Locks.

A variety of bolts have been used with the top-lever, the most common being the double holding-down bolt shown in the illustrations of the " Top-lever Gun with Back-action Locks." Single, treble, and even quadruple grip-bolts have been made. The double bolt is preferable, as the single bolt, being short, is liable to spring—a contingency provided against in the double bolt by giving it a longer bearing surface ; this also causes the gun to close more evenly. The treble-bite bolt cuts away so much metal from the under lump and the action under the barrels as to weaken them, and is of less service than a well-fitted double bolt.

In addition to the levers already described, the holding-down bolts have been actuated by other devices, or by modifications of one or other of the levers noticed A favourite at one time was the " Purdey," a short lever in front of the trigger-guard, the bow of which was pierced to allow the thumb to reach the lever and

force it forward.   Other levers in this position, instead of being pushed forward, or
from the gun, to open the mechanism, were pressed towards it—a plan favoured by
"Stonehenge," and still in use on a modern French gun, and but recently discarded
by a well-known firm of manufacturers in America.   In some cases the lever,
instead of being moved by thumb or finger, is worked by the hand, as in the
"comb-lever," which extends from the breech to the comb of the gun-stock, and is
depressed to withdraw the holding-down bolts.

LOCKS AND MINOR MECHANISMS.

In the lock of the muzzle-loader it was important that the hammer should
continue to press upon the cap until after the gun had been fired.   To a lesser
extent this was advisable with the pin-fire gun, but, as shown, gun-makers tried to

Comb-lever Treble-grip Gun.

devise efficient mechanism to automatically raise the hammers to half-cock as the
lever drew back the holding-down bolts.   With the central-fire gun it was of still
greater importance that the hammers should be at half-cock before opening the
gun, and also that the strikers should not project beyond the face of the standing
breech ; if they do so, by snapping the gun up sharply it is possible to discharge
the cartridge prematurely.

Prior, therefore, to the central-fire system, the main difference existing in
ordinary gun-locks was the arrangement of the work upon the lock-plates.   If the
mainspring is placed behind the tumbler, the lock is a back-work lock ; if it is
placed before the tumbler, it is "front-action" or "bar."   With the muzzle-loader
one was as good as another, the preference being given to the bar-lock on the score
of appearance.

With the breech-loader the case is not the same ; for the bar-lock more metal
has to be cut away from the breech-action body, where it is badly needed.   With

back-action locks this metal is left, but the stock is weakened at the point where it is most liable to fracture. The sportsmen of Cape Colony, most particularly, object to the back-action lock, for, subjecting their guns to much rough usage, the stocks are often broken unless very strong in the grip and furnished with front-action locks.

About 1866, the rebounding lock was introduced, and was further improved in 1869. In this lock the mainspring, by a species of overdraft, reacts upon the tumbler, and automatically raises it to half-cock, as will be found fully detailed in that part of this book treating of Gunmaking.

Other inventions of minor importance have in their time served a useful purpose and led to valuable improvements in the sporting gun. For instance, the springless.

Greener's Patent Self-acting Striker Gun.

striker, which obviated much jamming in guns with nipples; the patent "striker" invented by the author, which was carried from the base of the cartridge by a stud on the hammer engaging with a projection on the head of the striker; the through lump, which, with "circle jointing," removed much of the strain from the hinge-pin at the moment of firing, and has lengthened the life of the gun. The spring fore-end fastener has saved sportsmen time and trouble; the one-legged extractor (first used by the author) obviated the weakening of the barrel at a point where faulty workmanship is fraught with peril, and permits of the barrels being left sound and whole. Details respecting some other minor inventions will be given later; attention is drawn to these now in order to make clear to the reader that the modern gun has been gradually perfected: one piece of mechanism here, a useless limb discarded there, metal added in one place, wood diminished in another, but on the whole tending towards simpler mechanism, although designed for harder work, and to perform mechanically what originally the shooter had to do less effectually by his own effort.

WESTLEY RICHARDS' BREECH-LOADER.

This gun is one of the first, if not the first, of the top breech-bolt mechanisms, and was patented in 1862. In addition to the lump underneath the barrels, upon which they turn, there is a lump projecting from the breech ends at the top of the barrels. This lump is of dovetail shape and has a hook; the projection fits into a correspondingly shaped slot in the top of the standing breech, and is secured there by a holding-down bolt sliding to and fro in the line of the barrels. This bolt is

Westley Richards' Patent Breech-loader.

pushed forward by a spring behind it, and is withdrawn by pressing the lever lying between the hammers to the right. The object of this particular arrangement is to prevent the standing breech from springing back at the moment of firing, and was undoubtedly a step in the right direction. In 1865 the author invented a top cross-bolt, which passed through an extension of the top rib, thus wedging the barrels to the standing breech. Both of these mechanisms were suitable for pin- and central-fire guns; indeed, many of the Westley Richards guns, by an ingenious arrangement of the strikers and hammers, were made to answer equally well for firing pin- and central-fire cartridges.

THE DOLL'S-HEAD GUN.

In this breech mechanism the barrels have an extension of the top rib—or a separate steel lump equal thereto—which extension is let into a correspondingly shaped hole in the top of the standing breech.

The belief is that this head keeps the standing breech from springing back at the moment of discharge, and consequently increases the solidity of the weapon. It has been demonstrated that unless the " doll's-head " is bolted fast to the

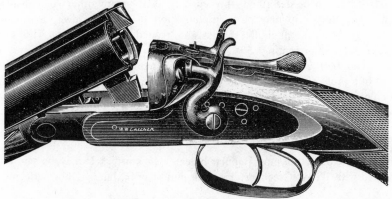

The Doll's-head Gun, with Bar Locks.

standing breech by a strong grip, either on the top-lever or an efficient separate bolt, it gives little or no appreciable increase of strength.

TREBLE-GRIP GUNS.

When, in addition to the usual double holding-down bolt, a gun is furnished with a bolt, engaging with the extension of the top rib, it is called a treble-grip gun.

The Treble-grip Gun.

The ordinary doll's-head gun is sometimes so styled, but wrongly so. The crude idea of the ordinary treble-grip gun would seem to have originated from a

combination of the well-known Westley Richards top-grip breech action with the
double holding-down bolt ; but, strange to say, this is almost the last form the
treble-grip gun has taken.   The well-known and very much superior treble
wedge-fast gun—to be described—preceded it, as did many others of considerable
worth.   The third grip may be a prolongation of the top lever, a small bolt
actuated by it, or a fancifully shaped and named head engaging with slots or
V-grooves in the projecting rib.   The treble-grip gun illustrated is one of the
simplest and best of the many forms now common.   The third grip is a plain
bearing of a prolongation of the top lever upon the projecting rib, and, if well fitted,
it not only materially lessens the strain upon the under bolts, but also keeps the
projecting rib, which is dovetailed into the standing breech, up to its work.

THE TREBLE WEDGE-FAST MECHANISM.

This is decidedly the most popular breech mechanism.   It may be said to have
originated with W. W. Greener's cross-bolt gun of 1865, but was not perfected until

W. W. Greener's Patent Treble Wedge-fast Gun.

1873, when the top cross-bolt was united with the double holding-down bolt, and a
mechanism evolved which effectually, and by the simplest means, locked barrels
and breech-action body together with a treble wedge.   It consists of a steel projection from the top rib, which fits into a slot in the standing breech.   A round
steel bolt, actuated by an arm of the top lever, works transversely in the standing
breech, and passes through the steel projection, binding the top of the barrels
securely to the breech, so that any gaping or wear at the joint is impossible.
Nothing more simple nor so efficient can be imagined.   This top bolt is in itself

fully equal to the strain of firing heavy charges, but in connection with the double holding-down bolt it works smoothly, and forms the strongest mechanical contrivance applicable to guns on the drop-down principle.

The mechanism is equally applicable to front- and back-action locks, and is made on both plans, and is also applied to various hammerless guns. This gun is more expensive to produce than treble-grip guns, and, if well made, it is certainly without any equal for strength or beauty. So far from adding to the weight of the gun, it diminishes it, for guns made on this principle, being stronger, may be built lighter.

In 1874, an editorial notice of this gun appeared in the *Field*, from which the following is extracted :—

" We have previously noticed the guns of Mr. W. W. Greener, of St. Mary's Works, Birmingham, the strength of which, at the time of our former notice, mainly rested in the cross-bolt, which is driven into the projecting rib, as shown in the annexed diagrams. The present guns vary only in the levers by which this cross-bolt and the additional double-grip are moved, and in the locks employed. Having always contended for the advantages accruing from this top connection between the barrels and the false breech (which Mr. W. W. Greener's action possesses in common with that of Mr. Westley Richards), we need not refer to it further than to remark that the double-grip now employed forms, with the cross-bolt, the strongest development of the Lefaucheux action with which we are acquainted."

Many gun-makers, jealous of the great success this gun achieved, brought out numerous imitations of the system, but to avoid the patent were obliged to omit particular points on which the main strength and efficiency of the invention depended. Most of these would-be treble wedge-fast guns have well-sounding names—"giant grip-fast," "treble lock-fast," "climax grip," etc., all mechanisms inferior to the original of which they are a weak copy. Since it is now open to every gun-maker to build a treble wedge-fast cross-bolt gun as he likes, the chief fault made is the weakness of the parts constituting the mechanism ; in some the extension of the top rib is but a sham, and the top fastening but an apology for a bolt.

In order to demonstrate the advantage of a secure top fastening it is necessary to point out the weakest part of the breech-action. The accompanying illustration shows in section an ordinary 12-gauge breech-action body (actual size), the bar-locks and furniture being removed. It is cut through at that point where the greatest strain is exerted, the junction of the standing breech with the end of the breech-action body. The metal shaded is all that there is to withstand the great strain of continued firing with heavy charges.

To remedy this fault gun-makers sometimes leave more metal in the breech-action body between the barrels and the locks, which requires also more metal to be left where it can be of no use, and not only spoils the appearance of the gun, but adds considerably to its dead weight. By using back-action locks a stronger breech-action body results, but to these locks many objections are raised. The best, easiest, and simplest way is to affix an efficient bolt uniting the top of the standing breech and the upper portion of the barrels. None is so strong and thorough as the Greener cross-bolt, which has been proved by actual experiment to add enormously to the safety and wear of a gun. Occasionally the barrels part from the stock when there is no top connection between barrels and standing breech : the author has known it occur with a back-action double-bolt gun, the breech-action breaking through completely.

Section of Bar-lock Breech-action.

The experiments detailed below were made by the editor of the *Field* immediately at the close of the Explosives Trial of 1878, from the report of which the extract is taken.

"THE BREAKING STRAIN OF POWDERS ON GUN ACTIONS, ETC.

" Among our various remarks referring to the then proposed trial of explosives, etc., we stated that we intended to show the superior strength of the top connection between the barrels and break-off of hinged breech-loading guns over the bolt at the base. Mr. Greener's action happening to combine these two bolts in such a way as to allow of their separate use, we had a 10-bore so constructed by him that the top cross-bolt (d) could be readily removed from its hole (c) or applied at will. This allowed of one barrel being first fired with the bolt in position, and then, after removing the bolt, firing the other. To this action we had a little apparatus fixed, as shown in the accompanying engraving.

" By this arrangement a piece of silver paper can be strained between the hook (b) on the break-off and the screw-clip (a a) attached to the barrels, so that when any separation takes place during an explosion, the paper breaks. To prevent the possibility of any doubt as to this being caused by the jar of the explosion, both barrels are loaded equally, after which one is fired with the bolt in, and then, supposing no breakage occurs, the bolt is removed and the other barrel discharged.

" Experimenting in this way, we found that in Mr. Greener's action no breakage occurred, either with the bolt in or out, using any charge of powder which the cartridge case could be made to hold, until we charged it with sixty grains of the ' Blissett '* sample of Schultze powder, considerably compressed, a thin felt wad, and two ounces of shot, when the discharge of the first barrel (with the bolt in) produced no effect on the paper, but on removing the bolt the second discharge broke it up completely. Repeating this experiment, the same result again occurred, which we considered conclusive as to this powder. After this we confined our experiments to the Schultze of 1877-8, that of 1878-9 used at the recent trial, and Nos. 3 and 6

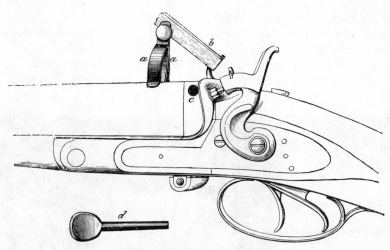

Experimental Breech-action.

of Curtiss and Harvey's black powder, as follows: the shot in each case being 2 oz. No. 6 introduced from the muzzle after charging the cartridge case with powder and an ordinary felt wad. In each case the bolt was in position with the firing of the first barrel, and was removed afterwards; but with the bolt in position the paper remained intact up to the last.

	Powder.	Result.
1.	5 drachms Curtiss and Harvey No. 6	No breakage.
2.	,, ,, ,, No. 3	Ditto.
3.	55 grains Schultze 1877-8	Ditto.
4.	,, ,, 1878-9	Ditto.
5.	6 drachms Curtiss and Harvey No. 3	Ditto.
7.	65 grains Schultze 1877-8	Ditto.
8.	,, ,, 1878-9	Slight breakage.

* This was a special issue of powder made to the order of Mr. Blissett for use in pigeon guns. It was used in guns having ordinary breech-actions and light barrels, and the results were so disastrous that this make of powder has not been again issued above the normal strength.

Powder.	Result.
9. 7 drachms Curtiss and Harvey No. 3	Slight breakage.
10. 75 grains Schultze 1877-8	Complete breakage.
,, ,, 1878-9	Ditto.

"In the last case there was not only complete breakage of paper, but such a permanent opening of the breech of the gun as to stop the experiment."

Had the cross-bolt been kept in during the whole trial, it is evident no breakage of the paper could have occurred. This shows conclusively the great strength and advantage of the top connection.

Mr. J. H. Walsh, in his work on the " Modern Sportsman's Gun and Rifle," Vol. I., writes in flattering terms of this action, whose advantages he was one of the

Greener's Improved Wedge-fast Grip.

first to demonstrate, and even contemporary gun-makers now acknowledge its merits, for the patent has expired, and in many districts it is very difficult to sell a gun not possessing the Greener cross-bolt. Such guns are therefore made, both in Birmingham and on the Continent, by manufacturers who cater for the wholesale market. Unfortunately, many of these guns are far from fulfilling requirements, as the cross-bolt demands accurate workmanship and very carefully fitting if it is to bear its proper share of the work in holding action and barrels together. The treble wedge-fast cross-bolt gun is far superior in strength and lasting power to the double-grip action. A double 4-bore and a double 8-bore were made on this, the top cross-bolt, principle in 1874, for the late Mr. G. P. Sanderson, superintendent of the Government Elephant Keddahs, Decca. They were in continual use by him until his death, firing 2-oz. bullets with 12 drams and 4-oz. bullets with 16 drams of powder, "hundreds of times," and, to quote Mr. Sanderson, "the breech-actions are as sound and close as when they left the factory nearly ten years ago." These rifles are still doing excellent service.

For large-bore guns and rifles it has been found desirable to provide still greater gripping power at the top; for this purpose the cross-bolt mechanism has been modified by doubling the extension; the one cross-bolt passing through both prolongations of the top lump. An increased bearing surface has also been obtained by enlarging the extension at its furthest extremity, the cross-bolt engaging with it just in front of the dovetail or doll's-head. This form of the mechanism is by no means clumsy upon guns of large bore, but the ordinary form is all sufficient for those of usual calibre, and using full sporting charges of ordinary explosives. The special form renders even the largest shoulder gun absolutely unbreakable with the heaviest charges which can be fired, and ensures free working of the mechanism even when nitro-explosives giving greatly increased pressures are employed.

Instead of a round cross-bolt, a square bolt is used by some makers, but the form has no advantage, and its use is detrimental, as the extension of the top rib is weakened more by a square hole than by a round one of the same area. Breech actions in which the extensions have been too light for the work required of them have shown weakness first between the hole and the junction of the extension with the breech ends of the barrels, but the tendency to break there is lessened by having the hole round. With a sharp angle, as needed for a square bolt, the extension needs to be much thicker and broader to give equal strength, and this makes the action clumsy, as it also widens the slot-way which the cross-bolt has to bridge; the bolt, too, must be made larger to give equal strength, since the bearings supporting it are farther asunder. Added to these disadvantages is the extra trouble of fitting a square bolt accurately.

CHAPTER VII.

HAMMERLESS GUNS.

HISTORICAL NOTE ON HAMMERLESS MECHANISM.

HAMMERLESS guns are those in which the mechanism for firing is placed within the gun. As previously stated, the advantage of having guns without lock mechanism upon the exterior was appreciated long ago, flint-lock guns having been so made early in the last century (*vide* p. 73). The hammerless breech-loader of modern times dates from the invention of those early central-fire guns in which consumable cartridge cases were used; but the development of the hammerless principle was retarded by the success of the pin-fire gun, to which external hammers were a necessity.

The Dreyse, the Chateauvillier, and even the much earlier Demondion, breech-loaders were hammerless; but no particular claim to advantage on this score appears to have been advanced. The arrangement of the parts in the manner best suited to the firing of the special cartridge used and the principle of breech-loading employed happened to secure that the firing mechanism should be within the gun : there is no evidence that it was specially designed in order to obviate the disadvantages of exterior hammers. The vogue obtained by the pin-fire system used sportsmen to the large external hammers, to which of course, the older among them were accustomed in the days of the muzzle-loader—so much so that the hammers, by their size and position, had obtained a fictitious value, and were supposed to be advantageous to the firer when aiming the gun.

As already stated, the automatic half-cocking of the hammer of the pin-fire gun by the movement of the action lever to open the gun was decidedly advantageous. The self half-cocking of the central-fire gun was obtained by using the rebounding lock ; but later the idea occurred that it would be still better to raise the hammer to full-cock by the simple movement of opening the gun.

Self-cocking guns with hammers on the outside of the lock-plates were made about forty years ago, but were not well received. Later, about 1876, when the hammerless gun was becoming popular, an attempt was made to substitute the self-cocking hammer gun for the hammerless, but the attempt signally failed. At that time the most was made of the argument that the hammers acted as a sort of back-sight and facilitated the alignment of the gun—an argument which had been discounted by the great success of the gun with "hammers below the line of sight"—an arrangement of the lockwork produced by the author some years before.

Another compromise was the semi-hammerless gun, in which fingerless hammers were placed upon the outside of the lock-plate, for which arrangement it was claimed

The Semi-hammerless Gun.

that there could be no mistake as to whether or not the gun was at full-cock. The makers forgot that there was nothing to show when the gun was loaded, and as it was not more safe, but was certainly more complicated, than the true hammerless, it found few supporters.

If the reader will turn back to the illustrations of the Greener and the Needham self half-cocking pin-fire guns, the principle of the self-cocking gun will be seen at once. Further travel of the under lever used to open the gun would result in the hammers being raised to full- instead of half-cock. It was on this principle of cocking by the under lever that the first English hammerless guns were constructed. Later, about 1870, Needham used a projection from the under lever to force up the breech ends of the barrels and utilised the weight of the fore-parts in dropping to assist in raising the hammers to full-cock. Five years later the Anson and Deeley principle was produced; the barrels, or rather the fore-end attached to them and turning upon the same centre, being used to cock the locks. It is upon one or other of these systems that every variety of successful modern hammerless gun has been constructed. The action lever moved by the hand to open the gun was the earlier, more primitive, and least successful form of cocking mechanism; the

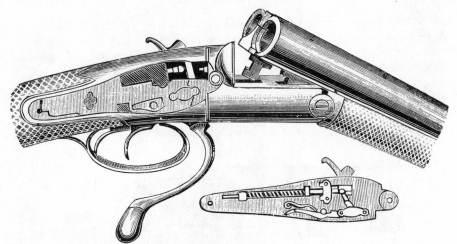

Lang's Self-cocking Gun, with Dummy Hammers.

The Lefever American Hammerless Gun.

barrels, used as a lever, whether in opening, or closing, or in both, is the later, and more generally followed, method of obtaining the same result with less labour.

There are guns which cannot be relegated to either class : for instance, that primitive weapon in which a separate lever moved by the hand is used to cock the locks ; and guns—to be described in detail—in which the locks rebound to full-cock and the action of the mainspring is reversed by pressure put upon it by the barrels in closing the gun. The history of the development of the principle of constructing the cocking mechanism of hammerless guns ends with the "barrel cocker" in the latest and most simple form.

HAMMERLESS GUNS COCKED BY THE ACTION-LEVER.

DREYSE'S HAMMERLESS GUN.

In this gun the breech mechanism is actuated by a lever similar to that of the original Lefaucheux ; the barrels, however, do not drop, but are first pushed forward, then turned to the right by an eccentric, as in the Jeffries gun already described. The same motion cocks the locks, which are furnished with spiral

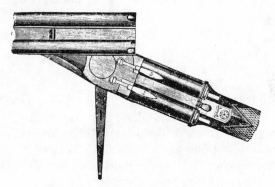

Dreyse's Hammerless Gun.

springs fixed round strikers similar to those used in the "needle" gun. When the gun is cocked, the near extremities of these "needles," or strikers, project beyond the breech and act as indicators. Between them a safety-bolt is fitted which, when pressed down, is made to take the weight of both mainsprings. The gun is central-fire ; the empty case is extracted by two small spring clips fixed upon the top of the standing breech; they slip over the rim of the cartridges when the barrels are closed after loading, and retain the cartridges as the barrels slide forward in opening, until the lateral motion commences, when they lose their grip, and the cases are removed by hand when the barrels are clear of the breech.

DAW'S HAMMERLESS GUN.

This gun was introduced about 1862 by Mr. Daw; but it never attained the popularity of the central-fire hammer gun he invented at the same period.

Daw's Hammerless Gun.

In this gun the lock mechanism is fixed on the trigger-plate, somewhat in the manner of the gun next to be described. The strikers project behind the breech when the gun is at cock, just as in Dreyse's gun. The cocking is effected by the lever, which, in addition to the force required, is still more difficult to manipulate owing to its great travel. A flat spring under the trigger-plate causes the lever to snap home when the gun is closed.

Compared with the Daw hammer gun, this arm was clumsy; was apparently more complicated, and certainly more expensive to produce; therefore the preference was given to the hammer gun, which, with its central-fire cartridge, was a great novelty. The safety-bolt usedt in he hammerless gun is simply a sliding bar working laterally across the standing breech, and is pulled outward to block the holes through which the strikers have to pass to reach the caps in the base of the cartridges.

GREEN'S HAMMERLESS GUN.

This gun, the invention of an English gun-maker, was first produced in 1866, and its mechanism in whole or in part, has been used in many later and better known varieties of the hammerless gun. The lock mechanism is arranged on the trigger-plate; it differs from the Daw in having the centre-pivot of the lever

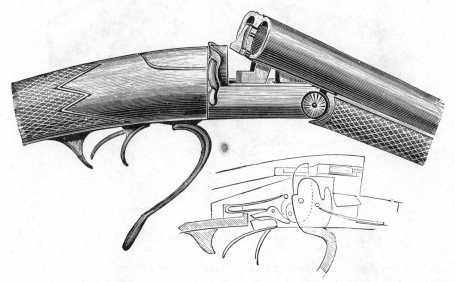

Green's Hammerless Gun.

identical with the axis of the tumblers—a matter of moment in obviating friction during the process of cocking. The strikers do not project beyond the breech at the rear; the action-lever requires a shorter travel, and by shaping it to serve as the bow of the trigger-guard greater length, therefore leverage, is obtained without clumsiness of construction. The safety-bolt is a half-round rod placed in the standing breech, and when moved one-fourth turn by the thumb-lever on the right-hand side, bolts the strikers. This gun was never a commercial success, but the Gibbs and Pitt, which was produced soon after it, and of very similar construction, had a considerable sale.

THE MURCOTT HAMMERLESS GUN.

This gun, patented by the late Mr. T. Murcott in 1871, was the first hammerless gun to achieve distinct success, and was the first in which the ordinary type of

Mechanism of Murcott's Hammerless Gun.

side-lock was used.   The illustration represents the gun with the right lock removed
and the stock part broken away, thus exposing section of left lock.   The lever
A has drawn back the bolt B, and raised the tumbler C, to which is attached the

Lock of Murcott's Hammerless Gun.

striker D, accomplished by one motion of the lever A. In the next illustration the lock mechanism is shown; the loose striker affixed to the tumbler or hammer, which has a propelling stud C, with which the upper arm of the action-lever engages; this stud also prevents the gun from being fired unless the breech-action is properly closed. Mr. Murcott was an indefatigable advocate of the hammerless principle, and it was owing to his perseverance that the system so early obtained trial in the hands of practical sportsmen.

ALLPORT'S HAMMERLESS GUN.

The hammerless guns so far described—excepting the first—have possessed a common feature; they all have the same type of lever, which is placed under the

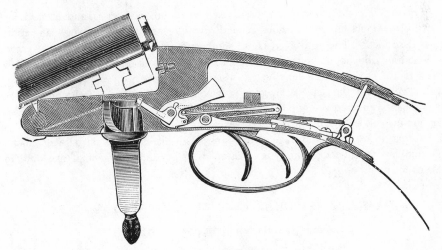

Allport's Double-grip Hammerless Gun.

trigger-guard, and is depressed to open the gun and cock the locks. Another type is the German gun first described, in which the lever is turned to right on a vertical pivot instead of downwards turning on a horizontal pivot. In the Allport gun the usual double-grip bottom lever is utilised as a means of cocking the locks.

For convenience of manufacture, the lock mechanism, consisting of tumbler, scear, and mainspring, is fixed to the trigger-plate. The tumblers and cocking-lever are pivoted on a common centre; an arm from the cocking-lever projects under each tumbler forward of the centre. The other end of this lever is furnished with a friction-roller, and travels up a helical curve on the vertical cylindrical head of the breech-action lever.

The action of the parts is as follows :—On opening the gun, the under lever is made to describe the quadrant of a circle ; the cocking cam, by travelling up the curved plane of the action-lever, becomes a powerful lever of the second order, and without any appreciable strain raises both locks into full bent. On closing the gun, the cocking-lever descends, and the gun may be fired. The preference given by many to the double-grip lever, and this ready method of utilising it in a hammerless gun, promised to make the system popular for double and single rifles and guns.

OTHER LEVERS.

The ordinary side-lever is sometimes used in hammerless guns, and utilised for cocking the locks upon the same general principle as the under lever snap-action guns described. The top lever, being short, and providing but sufficient leverage to withdraw the action-bolts, is not equal to the increased work of raising both locks to full-cock—unless lengthened, when it interferes with the proper grasping of the gun, and then needs so great a travel as to lose some of the advantages which have rendered the top-lever breech mechanism popular. The principle of the gun cocked by means of the action-lever is decidedly inferior to other principles of cocking, in which the leverage of the barrels is utilised for the purpose of raising the tumblers to full-cock—the type of hammerless gun now in general use both in this country and abroad.

HAMMERLESS GUNS COCKED BY THE BARRELS.

THE ANSON AND DEELEY GUN, 1875.

The first gun in which the weight of the barrels falling as they turn on the hinge-pin on opening the gun is utilised to cock the locks is the Needham gun, which is remarkable for a mechanism of equally great importance embodying a new principle of extraction, and the gun is later to be described in that connection (v. Ejector Guns). The next mechanism was that of the Anson and Deeley gun, patented in 1875, which quickly became popular, and may be regarded as the first really successful hammerless gun.

The lock mechanism is elsewhere described in detail. The adjoined illustration shows the arrangement of the limbs and the means by which the gun is cocked. The tumbler, or striker, has an arm projecting forward beneath the body of the breech-action, and under its foremost extremity is one arm of the cocking-lever, or "dog." This dog is pivoted concentric with the hinge-pin, and has its opposite extremity projecting through the joint of the breech-action body, and entering a slot in the fore-end ; upon the barrels being dropped for loading, the fore-end is depressed and carries with it the fore-arm of the cocking-dog ; the after-arm is consequently raised, and the tumbler, by projecting over the extremity of this arm, is raised by it until it reaches full bent, and is retained there by the scear.

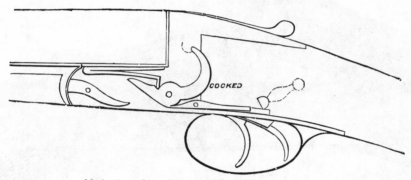

Mechanism of the Anson and Deeley Hammerless Gun.

The great safety of the lock-work is owing to the breadth of the scear and tumbler, which is double that of an ordinary gun lock, and the depth of the bent itself, which necessitates a better hold by the scear.

The lock mechanism has stood tests sufficiently severe, but it is no longer the easiest to manipulate, and a great drawback is the square and clumsy appearance given to the gun, especially just underneath the breech-ends of the barrels, as will be seen by referring to the next illustration, which represents the Westley-Richards hammerless gun with the Anson and Deeley lock-work, and the Anson patent Automatic Trigger-Bolting Safety, which last is also shown detached.

The method of making the barrels fast to the stock is the well-known Westley-Richards doll's-head top-lump and top-lever. The safety has the disadvantage of cutting away the wood in the narrowest, and consequently the weakest, part of the stock. It is automatic in action, the spindle of the top-lever action spring forcing the arm backward, upon the lever being moved to open the gun.

As made by Messrs. Westley-Richards the gun is undoubtedly serviceable, but the Anson and Deeley gun, as made by some firms in this country and abroad, now that the patent rights have lapsed, is far from equalling the original type from whatever point of view it may be regarded.   In order to cheapen the cost of production and cut down the prices, guns are made with loose hinge-pins, sham top-fastenings, and even, in many cases, without any top connection whatever.   As may be

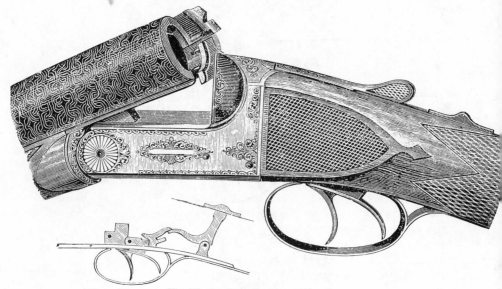

The Westley-Richards Hammerless Gun.

expected, these guns do not stand continual wear ; not only does the lock-action prove faulty, but even the breech mechanisms, after firing but a few shots, are found to gape at the breech joint, thus proving that, however good the principle of a hammerless mechanism may be, good workmanship is essential to the production of a safe and durable gun.

NECESSITY FOR A TOP CONNECTION IN HAMMERLESS GUNS.

Since the Anson and Deeley Hammerless Gun has been introduced, the distance from the face of the breech-action to the hinge-pin has been considerably shortened, to allow of greater leverage being obtained to cock the locks.   On account of the breech-action being so much shorter, the top connection to the barrels is of greater importance, the gun being more liable to gape at the joint than ordinary guns with greater length of breech-action: in fact, this gun cannot be made to stand continual firing unless strengthened with a good top fastening.

In the spring of 1878 an opportunity of submitting treble wedge-fast hammerless guns to a severe test presented itself, by supplying Dr. W. F. Carver with one of these guns for his exhibition shooting. In his hands this gun was shot upwards of

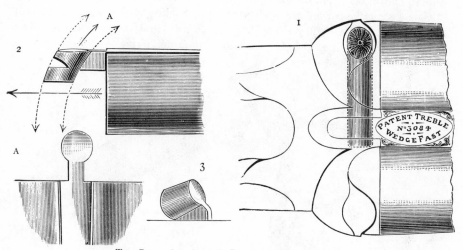

Top Connections between Barrels and Breech-loaders.

200 consecutive days, during which upwards of 40,000 shots were discharged from it, many of them being large charges of either black or Schultze wood powder. This was done without either the locks or breech-action being stripped for cleaning or repairs. The action stood remarkably well, and was not tightened up during the whole period. This gun was used continually by Dr. Carver for two years, upwards of 130,000 shots being fired from it. This test was the most severe a gun could possibly be submitted to, and as a wear-and-tear trial it is of the greatest value, being equal to the wear experienced by an ordinary gun during forty years' game-shooting; and in all probability no other breech-action on the drop-down system would have stood the great continued strain.

Any gun with a *well-fitting* bolted top connection is vastly superior to those with bottom-bolts only, or with extension of the rib without any bolt fastening into it. Many guns are still made with top-levers and single or double bottom-bolts only. The top extension is in the shape of Nos. 2 and 3, and is known as a "doll's head"; it fits into a mortice in the top of standing-breech. The intention of this extended rib is to prevent the springing back of the standing-breech at the moment of discharge; when made as No. 3 it is proved by experiment to be utterly useless, having no bite whatever. No. 2, an accurately fitting head in a circular mortise, should only loosen from its bearing when moved in the direction of the arrow in the arc A A; if the barrels are firmly secured by holding-down bolts, the hook and sides of the doll's head will assist slightly in taking the strain of the discharge, which is crosswise in the direction of the dotted arrow; but, owing to the expansion of

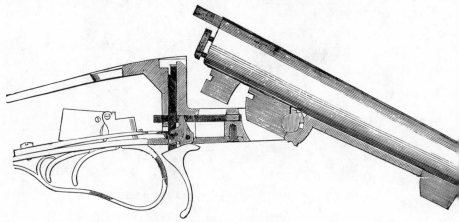

The Abbey Breech-loader.

the metal of the barrels, the doll's head is lifted in some measure from its bearing, and its value as a holding bolt is therefore lost; a doll's head with a bolt in it is preferable to one without such bolt, but both varieties fall a long way short in gripping quality when compared with the through cross-bolt, known originally as Greener's Wedge-fast, which is shown in No. 1.

Sometimes it is advisable to make the cross-bolt grip a double extension of the top-rib or engage a dove-tail, or doll's head extension; this method is used chiefly for large-bore guns and rifles, and is of especial service when nitro-explosives are used in such weapons. This variety of the cross-bolt is illustrated on page 151.

Another form of top bolting revived by the late Editor of the *Field* and by Mr. Rigby in their hammerless guns is shown in the Abbey breech-loader, an American invention of some twenty years ago.   It is a sliding bolt, binding vertically to the breech action a flat extension of the top-rib.   It is probably more secure than the ordinary doll's head, for the expansion of the barrels being upward and the strain on the breech-action backward, the bearing of the bolt remains unaltered at time of the explosion.

GREENER'S TREBLE WEDGE-FAST HAMMERLESS GUN, THE " FACILE PRINCEPS."

From the annexed illustration it will be seen that the shape of this breech action is neater than the Anson and Deeley hammerless gun.   This is due to an

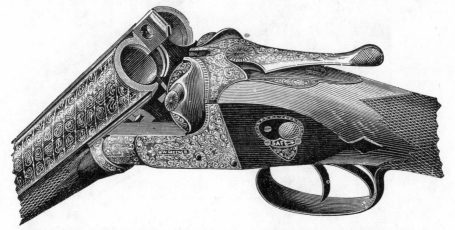

The Treble Wedge-fast Hammerless Gun, with Greener's Patent Locks.

entire change in the lock-mechanism and method of cocking the gun; by this change of principle a strong screw joint-pin is substituted for the solid hinge-pin; the holes through the breech-action joint and fore-end are not required, and the lifting-cams, or " dogs," are dispensed with.   This allows of a round-shouldered body being substituted for the objectionable square Anson and Deeley pattern body, and greatly increases the handiness and solidity besides adding to the appearance of the gun.

The cocking is effected by a sliding rod working in the under lump; the tumblers are arranged similarly to those of the Anson and Deeley, but have their fore extremities turned in so as to engage with the cocking rod.   Upon the barrels being dropped for loading, the cocking rod is raised with the lump and lifts the tumblers at the same time, and so effects the cocking. The shape and arrangement of the tumblers and cocking rod are shown in the following illustrations, the first of which is a sectional view of the mechanism, and the second shows the gun as exposed underneath when the cover-plate has been removed.

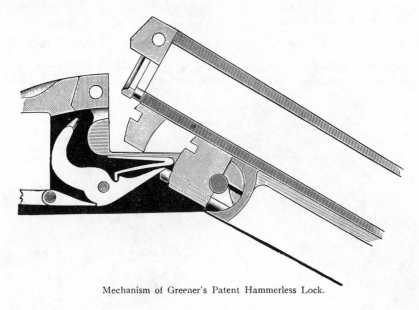

Mechanism of Greener's Patent Hammerless Lock.

To dismount the gun the fore-end is taken off, and the sliding cocking-rod is then free to slip forward past the tumblers, instead of carrying them upward, as the barrels swing; on putting the gun together the placing of the fore-end upon the gun presses the cocking rod into position and holds it to its work there.

This mechanism was at first made with a cocking swivel hooked in the lump and kept in position by a sliding rod; it has now been further simplified by sub-stituting the cocking slide for the swivel and rod. During the past twenty years thousands of guns have been made upon this principle, which has been found to possess decided advantages and proved as effectual as it is simple. It is the plan used by the author for hammerless guns and rifles of all bores, and the general arrangement of the lock-work having been found the best suited to all requirements, is followed in the later patterns of self-ejecting guns, which will be described later.

BARREL-COCKING MECHANISMS COMPARED.

The leverage obtained by the falling of the barrels to open the gun was first used for the purpose of effecting the cocking of the locks by J. Need am in his ejector gun, which is elsewhere described. Later the Anson and Deeley mechanism was produced, and in this the same leverage was utilised, but by different means. This was followed by the author's hammerless mechanism, in which use was also made of the leverage of the barrels, but in a different manner. The common use of the principle led to considerable litigation with reference to the rights of the various patentees. In the suit of Couchman *v.* Greener, which was carried to

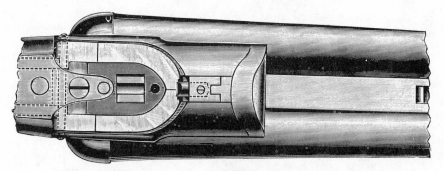

Greener's Patent Hammerless Lock Mechanism, with Cover Plate removed.

the House of Lords, it was shown that at the time of the Anson and Deeley patent it was not new to effect the cocking by means of the leverage which is brought into play on tilting the barrels to open the breech, and Mr. Needham's gun was put in to show this ; and that, this being so, all that the plaintiffs had protected by their patent was that part of the cocking mechanism which was combined with the leverage afforded by the barrels. This, according to their own specification, is a lever formed by the prolongation backwards of the fore-end beyond the hinge-pin of the barrels, such lever working in a groove in the lump, the long arm being the fore-end, the short arm being the prolonged part of it, and the fulcrum being the same as that on which the barrels turn. It was pointed out that the mechanism which Mr. Greener had combined with the leverage afforded by the barrels was not a lever at all, but a to-and-fro movement in a horizontal plane ; and that, although the sliding stem might possibly be considered as a prolongation backwards of the fore-end, it was not a lever, but merely an abutment to give rigidity to the hook attached to the lump. That there was an essential difference between the Anson and Deeley mechanism and that of the Greener " Facile Princeps " was the view taken by all the three courts in which the case was successively heard. The Master of the Rolls in the Court of Appeal said—

" The essential part of the combination of the lock mechanism—the Anson and Deeley— claimed by the plaintiff, was not only that the fore-arm should be used for the purpose of cocking, but that the forward part of it should be the long-arm of the lever. But, although that part of the defendant's gun was used for the purpose of cocking, yet it was not used as the long-arm of the lever, and was therefore not part of the combination claimed by the plaintiff."

Lord Justice Lindley remarked—

" The scheme is different, the idea is different : that is to my mind so plain, when you look at the guns and mechanism, that it presents to me no difficulty in the matter ; in other words, I say the two guns are worked upon different ideas altogether."

Lord Justice Bowen also remarked—

" Juries sometimes are apt to be led away more hastily by similarities which are not similarities in principle. Treating the question as one of fact : do the defendants, with the gun as made, use the fore-end as a lever ? That is a question of fact. Lord Justice Lindley has expressed my views most fully, and I agree entirely in the views expressed by him upon that point."

HAMMERLESS GUNS COCKED BY THE MAINSPRING.

To ease the strain of cocking hammerless guns when opening or closing the gun, several plans have been devised. Possibly the ordinary rebound principle—to half-bent only—was employed in hammerless guns with this intent. If so the notion was false, as a stronger mainspring had ultimately to be overcome. More successful from this standpoint are systems in which the alteration of the position of the mainspring or its fulcrum is a basis to ease the hand-strain of cocking. To date of writing, four systems employing one or other of these principles are known.

The first is Tolley's Patent (Specification No. 461, 1877). The principle here employed is the use of a sliding mainspring, and a narrowing or > tumbler ; the tumbler-pivot is situate between the mouth and inner extremity of the > ; each arm of the mainspring is provided with a roller, and the mainspring itself is in connection with the barrels, from which, by means of cam, connecting-rod, or other gear, it receives a longitudinal motion ; on opening the gun the mainspring is drawn away from the tumbler, and immediately its arm is past the tumbler-pivot it presses up the incline and thus cocks the lock ; on closing the barrels the mainspring is pushed toward the tumbler and past its centre pivot. This is the first system in which the *closing* of the barrels cramps the mainspring after the lock has been cocked. Three other systems are worthy of greater detail.

PURDEY'S HAMMERLESS GUN, 1880.

This gun has the ingenious cocking mechanism of Beesley's Patent (No. 31, 1880), and is here illustrated. The principle employed is a spring having two arms, one of which is stronger than the other, the stronger cocking the lock, the weaker

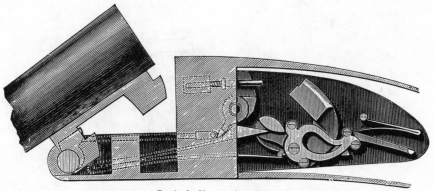

Purdey's Hammerless Gun.

firing it ; the stronger arm being thrown out of gear by a cam when closing the barrels, and remaining thus disconnected from the lock so long as the gun is closed.

As shown in the illustration, the upper limb of the **V** mainspring is much heavier and stronger than the lower ; its extremity bears against a prolongation of the tumbler, and acts upon it as does the upper arm of the mainspring in an ordinary rebounding gun-lock. This arm is ungeared from the lock-tumbler by depression. On closing the barrels, the cam projecting through the breech-action bed is forced downward and backward on its centre, and by eccentric movement depresses the mainspring. The mainspring is thus further cramped, and additional strength thereby transferred to its lower arm. On opening the gun the stronger arm overcomes the lower, and forces the tumbler into full bent, whilst it exerts further strength on the action cams, and so greatly tends to open the gun and withdraw the extractor.

THE WALKER HAMMERLESS GUN, 1881.

This system resembles the preceding so far as the cramping of the mainspring goes, but the arrangement of the parts is as illustrated ; the **V** mainspring is placed vertically behind the breech-action body, whilst by simply prolonging backwards the horizontal striking-pin and notching it, it does duty as a tumbler.

The mainspring, when the gun is open, is extended ; and by pressure against the central resistance of the vertical cramping-lever and striking-pin, the latter is

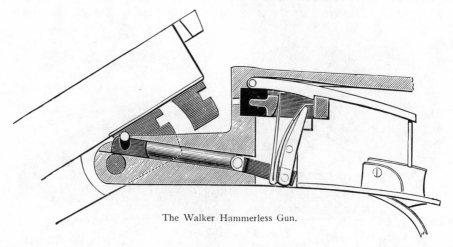

The Walker Hammerless Gun.

thereby withdrawn from the face of the breech until it is past a reversed scear pivoted over the striking-pin and spring. On closing the gun, the vertical cramping-lever has its lower arm pressed backward by the connecting-rod running through the body of the breech-action to the under-flats of the barrels. The upper arm of the cramping-lever compresses the mainspring, the entire force of which then reverts to the forward bearing on the striking-pin, and its whole energy is available for driving the striker against the cartridge-cap. The scear lies under the tang of the breech-action, and is lifted by a deep-bladed trigger.

GREENER's " EMPEROR " HAMMERLESS GUN.

In this action quite a different system is employed. The lock, instead of being cocked by a lever which compresses the spring as the hammer goes into bent, is actuated by a flat mainspring, which is in itself both lever and spring. This spring-lever is pivoted near the centre, the hinder end fitting into a slot in the tumbler while the other is carried through the knuckle into the fore-end iron. It will be observed that the mechanism is of the simplest description, only three pieces being required to the lock.

The action is as follows : On opening the gun, the fore-end being dropped carries down the mainspring, which acts as a lever and cocks the gun (Fig. 1). On

Fig. 1.   Fig. 2.

Greener's " Emperor " Hammerless Gun.

closing the gun the fore-end acts in the same way to bring the tumbler back to its original position, but on account of that being held fast by the scear it cannot do so, and the lever is consequently bent and converted into a mainspring (*see* Fig. 2). The spring is compressed along all its length, on both sides of the pivot, so that a very strong blow is given.

OTHER HAMMERLESS MECHANISMS.

As already stated, the leverage of the short top-lever is alone insufficient to do this work with ease to the shooter ; by various mechanisms, therefore, it has been

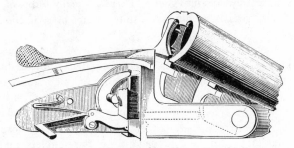

Combined Lever and Barrel-cocking Hammerless Mechanism.

sought to supplement the action of the top-lever by utilising the weight of the barrels. The readiest way is so to shape the back of the lump under the barrels, against which the holding-down bolt presses, that on opening the gun the bolt is forced back. Arms on the back of the bolt engage by projection or otherwise with the tumblers, so that less force is required to be exerted on the lever. One such gun is here shown, but of this plan there are many modifications, all embodying the same principle, and none equal in ease of working or efficiency of action to the true barrel-cocking mechanisms already described.

Another plan, much favoured by American gun-makers, consists in arranging a pivoted lever so that one arm engages with the barrel lump and is raised by it, and

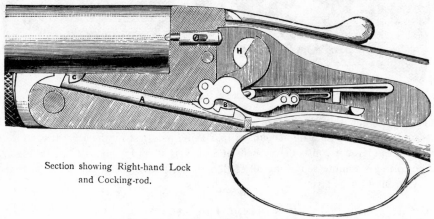

Section showing Right-hand Lock
and Cocking-rod.

Mechanism of Scott's Hammerless Gun.

the other presses the tumblers into cock. There are many forms of lever, and the arrangement of the parts is modified to suit various breech-action mechanisms in use.

The Scott hammerless mechanism was patented in 1878, and illustrates another method of cocking. It will be seen that there are rods, A, moving diagonally in the body of the breech-action, and having a notch in their fore extremity with which two studs, C, fixed upon the flats of the barrels are made to engage, their opposite extremities engaging with the tumblers at B. Upon the barrels being raised for loading, their leverage draws forward the horizontal cocking-rods, which communicate a like motion to the extended arms of the tumblers, and so raise them

into full cock.   The lock mechanism employed is affixed to side lock-plates, and is
similar in construction to that generally used in modern hammerless guns, and the
lock-plates may have crystal apertures, H, which expose to view the position of
the tumblers, and obviate the use of indicators.

Many improvements, some covered by recent patents, have been made upon this
mechanism since first introduced.   The principle is not generally adopted, although
several gun-makers of high reputation prefer it to other mechanisms ; and some
recent inventions are based upon the same general principle of cocking and lock
arrangement.

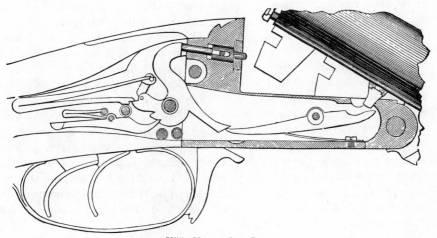

Hill's Hammerless Gun.

Messrs. Scott have special safeties and checks applicable to this and other guns,
and these mechanisms will be described subsequently.

From the fact that the opening of the gun could be used to effect the cocking,
it was clear that by a rearrangement of the lock mechanism the closing of the gun
could effect the same purpose.   The advantage of doing so has never been evident ;
it is claimed that the force required to withdraw the cartridge cases is an all-sufficient
drag upon the barrels in opening the gun, and therefore that the extra work of
cocking the locks should be done in closing the gun.   Advocates of the principle
appear to overlook the fact that the force required to press new cartridges into the
chamber is usually equal to that needed to extract them.   The weight of the barrels

falling by gravity is all in favour of cocking the gun whilst it is being opened; for when the operation is effected during the closing, the barrels have to be lifted, and their weight is increased by just that force necessary to raise the tumblers to full cock. The first, and perhaps the simplest of the guns on this principle, was introduced in 1879 by Mr. Hill, a Birmingham gunsmith, and its mechanism is here shown.

The lock-work is affixed to a side-plate in the usual manner, but the cocking-lever is fixed in the body of the breech-action. This cocking-lever is hung upon a pivot; one extremity engages with an extended arm of the tumbler, and the other is acted upon by a studded rod working transversely through the fore lump under the barrels. The two studs upon this rod, on the barrels being closed, come into contact with and press downward the fore extremity of the cocking-levers, and so raise the tumblers into full cock, and hold them in this position until moved transversely to the left by a finger of the left hand. It thus acts as a safety bolt, which must be moved when the gun is raised to the shoulder for firing.

It would be futile to attempt to enumerate, much less to describe, in this limited space the numerous modifications of the various principles of lock mechanism already referred to. Many of them do not depart widely from the original type, others are modifications made to suit particular guns: the Rogers system, for instance, which resembles generally the Anson and Deeley, but has the cocking-levers bearing directly against the barrels and turning upon another centre than that upon which the barrels hinge. This permits of detachable locks of the ordinary type being used, and is consequently much employed by those gun-makers who prefer the lock mechanism when arranged upon a side-plate than when fitted into the breech-action body as in the Anson and Deeley gun.

Of the other mechanisms, some of which were illustrated in earlier editions of this book, a few yet survive and have been adapted to guns of later type, and will be noticed subsequently. The majority have fallen into desuetude.

ADVANTAGES OF HAMMERLESS GUNS.

When the hammerless gun was first introduced in its present modern form it encountered much opposition from both sportsmen and gun-makers, but the advantages the hammerless possesses over every variety of gun with hammers have won for it the general approval of experienced sportsmen. The late Mr. Walsh, editor of the *Field*, quickly found that the hammerless principle was preferable; he wrote, " The hammerless gun is the superior in point of safety and efficiency. . . . The hammerless gun is, I think, to be preferred." The writers of the Badminton volumes on shooting were divided in their opinion as to the merits of hammer and hammerless guns.

As Mr. Walsh wrote, the hammerless is superior; as a sportsman's weapon it is safer and more efficient. No more has been claimed for it; so much has been proved over and over again. The following are extracts from the published opinions of some notable experts which appeared at the time when the controversy raged most keenly; they are still of interest :—

"The absence of hammers makes the gun very convenient, especially for covert shooting, to which I cannot speak too highly of its superiority, combined with safety and ease of manipulation.   "GERALD L. GOODLAKE, Col."

"The hammerless guns you made for me about four years ago have stood remarkably well. They have never been out of order; the locks have never been taken off; neither has the safety-bolt been taken out or cleaned.   "GRANARD."

"With reference to the safety of hammerless guns, I agree with you that a safety-bolt, to be of any value, ought to be reliable, and to illustrate my meaning, the following may interest your readers:—When grouse driving on the Berwyn Mountains, in Montgomeryshire, some ten days since, and using a Greener ejecting gun, with safety-bolt, the rain commenced descending in torrents, and, as a fog seemed imminent, the order was given for home. Instead of following the downward track adopted by the keepers and beaters, I decided on a shorter line of country, and decided to make my way along the face of a steep hill scantily covered with fern. Placing my gun, which was loaded, at 'safe,' I made the attempt, and got on fairly well for a hundred yards, when I suddenly slipped and began rapidly to descend. After going some forty feet, and finding the pace increasing, I was forced to let my gun go. Slipping and swinging round, presenting its stock and muzzle alternately at my head, it shot rapidly down the hill and disappeared over the cliff, towards which I unwillingly followed. My sensations at that moment I keep to myself. Luckily some friendly ferns checked my pace, and I brought up a few yards from the edge. Regaining my feet, I cautiously proceeded till I got on a sheep track, and succeeded by the aid of a boulder in gaining such a foothold as to enable me to approach the edge and attract the attention of the men, then hundreds of feet below me. Indicating that I had lost my gun, one of them with great difficulty climbed up the face of the hill, and after some time uttered a shout. Then, far below me, and embedded half way up the barrels, with the stock sticking straight up, I perceived the gun. A mossy spring between two rocks had received it in its fall; a couple of yards to the right or left, and it would have been smashed to atoms. Twenty minutes later it was restored to me, the barrels plugged up for some inches, but apparently having received no external injuries, save a few scratches, and a piece chipped off the heelplate. The trigger-guard was, however, a study; bits of fern and rushes were twisted round the triggers, which caught in everything in the downward course; but the safety-bolt had done its work, and the cartridges were intact. While I write there hangs above me an old and valued servant, a Greener gun with rebounding locks. Nearly 100,000 shots have been fired out of that gun; had it, however, been with me on the hills that day, a different sequel might have been told. I always considered hammer guns with rebounding locks required care, not only in crossing fences and in covert, and from the liability to explode when dropped, but from the tendency of the hammers to catch in buttonholes and watch-chains, as has frequently happened to me. Sportsmen have every reason to be thankful that science has invented such a boon as hammerless guns with reliable safety-bolts—in my opinion the safest and pleasantest gun anyone can desire—provided gentlemen recognise the fact that a cheap gun on that principle is one of the most dangerous things out, and, when they decide to go in for a hammerless gun, select a first-class gun-maker for the purpose.''

ON THE CHOICE OF A HAMMERLESS SYSTEM.

The hammerless gun of inferior quality is as dangerous as the inferior hammered gun, if not more so; and in the choice of a hammerless gun the sportsman will be guided by, first, the simplicity of the mechanism; secondly, the efficiency of the mechanical parts introduced to effect that hitherto performed by hand.

It has been shown that a hammerless breech-loader can be constructed with fewer parts than a hammered breech-loader. The sportsman must choose a gun so constructed. If a special lever is desired—as under, side, or the double-grip lever—good guns have been devised on each of these plans. The top-lever will doubtless have the preference, and here there is abundant choice. Any gun cocking by means of mechanism geared or in any way connected with or dependent upon the motion of the top breech-action lever for effecting the cocking of the gun will be at once rejected; because it is liable to miss-fires if the lever does not snap "home," and because it is *generally* fitted with weak mainsprings, and often requires great force to open.

Of those guns cocked by the falling of the barrels, or closing of the gun, will be rejected all that, first, do not permit of the barrels being placed readily upon the stock; secondly, that may be wrongly put together and so cause a breakage; thirdly, that require a jerk to open or shut; because all such guns will be an annoyance to the owner, and in the case of the last objection will cause undue wear at the hinge-joint and need early repairs.

There are several guns which will fulfil every requirement of the sportsman so far as mechanism goes. The hammer gun, notwithstanding the use of the rebounding locks, which saved the many accidents that resulted from the half cocking of the locks, cannot be so safe as hammerless, as hammer guns have been known to go off unexpectedly owing to a twig wedging in between the hammer at half-cock and the striker, and many more owing to wear or faulty construction have exploded when at the rebound by means of an accidental blow upon the hammer. The most common cause of accidental discharge in the hammer gun is when placing the gun at full-cock from half-cock, or the reverse, the hammer is likely to slip from the thumb and explode the cartridge. With some hammerless guns, nothing short of pulling the trigger can fire the gun.

However expert he may become in manipulating the locks and loading the gun, a sportsman armed with a weapon of the ordinary type is heavily handicapped against the sportsman provided with an arm in which, without any trouble or extra exertion on his part, such processes as cocking the locks and taking out the fired cases are performed for him more quickly and more surely than they could be were he the most expert manipulator.

The Anson and Deeley type of lock gives quicker ignition than the ordinary lock, for the blow is much shorter and the mainspring stronger. The side-lock hammerless guns have not this advantage. Some of them, also, are liable to miss-fire, especially the lower-priced ones—for the tumblers and other lock mechanism, being placed so far from the joint-piece of the breech-action, require long bolts and levers to effect the working of the locks, and, leverage being lost by the distance from the fulcrum, the tendency is to make the mainspring very light, in order that the cocking of the gun may seem easy and not cause the barrels to drag too heavily when the gun is opened. The advantage they possess is the ease with which the locks may be removed and the lock-work inspected. This is not a matter of importance, since a well-made " box-lock " is so placed as to be efficiently protected from the intrusion of dust, dirt, or wet, and will work well for years without attention. The oiling and cleaning of the locks and other parts, so far as in all probability will ever be required, may be easily accomplished, as indicated in the paragraph on gun cleaning, and thus the inferiority of the enclosed lock in this particular is not appreciable. The great advantages the principle possesses over those in which side-locks are used should determine the sportsman in his choice, for, in addition to the disadvantages already mentioned, side-lock guns are found to be more liable to accidental discharge ; the weaker lock mechanism more readily " jarring off," and this, as recently proved, notwithstanding the safeguard of automatic intercepting locking bolts to scears, tumblers or triggers.

CHAPTER VIII.

EJECTOR GUNS.

NOTE ON EJECTING MECHANISMS.

THE ejector gun is one which by suitable mechanism automatically ejects from the chamber of the barrel the fired cartridge case as the gun is opened. This principle had for very many years been used in single rifles, but its application to double guns is due to Mr. J. Needham, who, in 1874, produced a shot gun on the drop-down principle furnished with a separate extractor for each barrel. The extractors were independent of each other, save that both were thrust out together by the fore-end to the same extent as in ordinary guns ; then, if the one barrel had been fired, the lock mechanism was made to act—in the manner as will later be described—in giving a further forward movement to the right extractor, which movement results in the cartridge case being thrown clear of the gun. Mr. Needham used the main-spring of the lock to provide the necessary force to effect the resulting expulsion. It was clear that by duplicating the lock mechanism, and employing the ordinary lock merely to gear with the extra lock, which might be so provided for the purpose, the extraction could be just as effectually done. Mr. Needham preferred the simpler mechanism, and, as his use of a separate extractor for each barrel—an essential part of his invention—was protected by his patent, the ejecting mechanism was not widely departed from until the expiry of his patent. The author was the first to adapt the Needham ejector to a gun of modern type, and from this modifica-tion very little departure has been made ; but gun-makers and inventors, quick to notice that two-lock mechanisms could be employed to do the work performed by one in the Needham ejector, have produced a large number of variants upon the original type of a separate lock for each extractor and a separate lock for each barrel.

Though seemingly numerous, the varieties of the ejecting mechanisms in actual use are few. The Needham principle, with one or two important modifications, constitutes one type of gun, the chief varieties of which will be described. The ejecting mechanisms which are separate from the lock mechanisms permit of greater variation. There is a possible difference in principle, as between ejecting mechanisms which are cocked by closing the gun and those cocked by opening it, and again between both and those in which the ejecting cock is normally at cock and pressure is brought to set the mainspring, etc. The mechanism itself, its shape and arrangement, may be modified in many ways. The mechanism may be still more elaborate and complex than the Deeley, as is Maleham's, or it may be simplified to the two or three limbs of the Southgate, but the chief modifications are only such alterations of detail as will enable the separate mechanism to be applied to guns having breech-actions, locks, etc., of a special type favoured by certain gun-makers and sportsmen, unless it may be some have been produced with a view of evading the claims made

The Needham Ejector Gun.

by earlier inventors or as improvements upon the first types. For instance, taking the Deeley as the type of early separate mechanism, modifications have been made either in the means by which connection is established between the ejecting mechanism and the firing mechanism, or in the method of cocking the ejecting locks.

NEEDHAM'S HAMMERLESS EJECTOR GUN.

In this gun the extractor is in two halves; one half for each barrel. The tumblers have arms projecting forward and engaging with the barrel lump, and upon the gun being opened the lump raises the tumblers just as in some of the hammerless guns which have been described. When the barrels have dropped far enough to permit the cartridges to pass out of the gun without catching against the top of the standing breech, the tumblers are not quite at full cock, and the stud by which they are raised is so adjusted that at this point they slip past it, and their fore-arms fall upon the lower extremities of two levers pivoted in the lump. The upper ends of these levers engage the legs of the extractors and force the extractors sharply to continue the movement of extraction, and the fired cases are thrown quite clear of the gun.

The fore-extremities of the tumblers then have to be raised again by the further opening of the gun. As each lock and extractor works independently of the other lock and extractor, and as the ejection depends upon the fore-extremity of the fallen tumbler engaging the tripping stud and falling upon the ejecting levers, it follows that if the gun is not fired the tumblers remain at cock and loaded cartridges are not ejected ; but if only one barrel is fired, that the tumbler corresponding to the barrel falls, and on opening the gun the ejection of the fired case, and of the fired case only, is effected.

In the gun as originally made the barrels were forced upward by an arm on the action lever pressing against the under lump, and this lever by forcing the barrels open to the widest possible extent ensured the cocking of the locks after the ejection of the cases had been accomplished. A modification of the gun with top lever breech-action was also made some years ago, and varieties of this type are still occasionally found.

PERKES'S EJECTOR MECHANISM.

In 1878 Mr. Perkes, a London gun-maker, patented a mechanism based upon the principle of ejecting the cartridge cases by a separate mechanism situated in the fore-part of the gun. The cocking mechanism has nothing whatever to do with the ejecting mechanism, nor has the lock mechanism, only in so far as the ejection cannot take place, although the ejecting mechanism functions, until the tumbler, by falling, withdraws a cartridge stop projecting above the standing breech. As in ordinary guns, there is one extractor for the two barrels ; the extractor is actuated by a lifting lever, pivoted near the hinge-pin, pressing upon the extractor leg as the gun opens. When the barrels have fallen so far that the cartridges will clear the standing breech —but not the stop-pins projecting above it—the extractor lever, actuated by a spring, gives a final flip to the extractor, and the cartridges, instead of being withdrawn only as far as permits of their withdrawal by hand, are thrown against the "stops," or, if these no longer project, are completely ejected. In its crude form the mechanism can offer no advantage over that of the ordinary non-ejecting gun, and the importance of the invention is entirely due to its having been the first separate ejecting mechanism patented. It has been several times improved upon by Mr. Perkes, and, the original patent having lapsed, the principle has been adopted by other gun-makers for various ejecting mechanisms of an improved form ; all, on the lapse of the Needham patent, using separate extractors for each barrel, and duplicating the lock and ejecting mechanism.

THE DEELEY EJECTOR GUN.

This mechanism, patented in 1886, is one of the earliest of the fore-end or separate ejector type, and is much more elaborate than the Perkes. In the illustration only one lock and one extractor are shown—the right lock and barrel are similarly fitted and the ejecting lock mechanism in the fore-end is in duplicate. This fore-end ejecting mechanism closely resembles that of an ordinary lock ; there is a hammer or tumbler worked by a spring attached to it with a swivel, and held at

The Deeley Ejector Gun.

cock by a scear engaging in the bent. This ejector tumbler is cocked by the extractor leg, which forces it back into bent as the gun is closed (and it is understood that this is the method of cocking employed in the following patents unless other-wise stated), although the extractor cam usually assists the movement, and has even been constructed to execute it alone. The trigger by which the scear is actuated is a sliding bar or rod attached to or moved by the mainspring. As already pointed out, it is a peculiarity of this form of lock that the mainspring works to and fro in the body as it is in turn compressed by the cocking of the tumbler and liberated by the release of the tumbler from bent ; this motion is utilised to liberate the scear of the ejecting lock, for when the firing tumbler is down the connecting slide is pushed forward into engagement with the hooked scear of the ejecting lock, so that the action of opening the gun puts this scear out of bent, and, the tumbler falling, the empty case is ejected.

TRULOCK'S EJECTOR.

In all guns with separate mechanisms for the two actions of firing and ejecting, the method of connecting them is of great importance, and it is also subject to much variation. In order to secure the ejection of the fired case only, it is obvious that the ejector lock must be connected in some way with the tumbler of the firing lock. In the Deeley, as already described, it is an extension of the main-

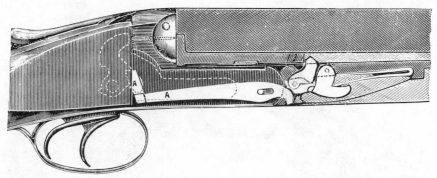

Trulock's Ejecting Mechanism.

spring which serves to liberate the ejector scear; but in the Trulock ejector gun, which was patented in 1890, it is a rod or bar, pushed forward by the fall of the tumbler till it engages with the scear of the ejecting lock, as is shown in the accompanying illustration.

The sliding rod A, by the mechanism shown, has a to-and-fro motion in the body, and projects beyond the joint of the fore-end when the tumbler falls; if the tumbler does not fall, it maintains its position, and the ejecting mechanism does not come into play. On opening the gun after firing, the projecting part raises the front and depresses the rear of the scear, so that the tumbler slips past the back of the scear and strikes against a "kicker," which communicates the blow to the extractor leg. This sliding rod is common to other ejectors than the Trulock; it is, perhaps, the means of connection most generally used.

BAKER'S EJECTING MECHANISMS.

In the ejecting mechanisms patented by Mr. Baker, of Birmingham, the sliding rod is also employed, and can be arranged to work in either of two distinct ways. The first figure shows it pushed forward by the fall of the tumbler, but in the second the rod is pushed forward by the tumbler being raised by the opening of the gun. In this gun the ejecting mechanism, which consists of a tumbler and spiral spring only, is contained in a case or "box," which is pivoted in the fore-end, and lifted into position at the time of ejecting. The ejecting locks are cocked by the extractor cam on closing the gun. The action is as follows :—The

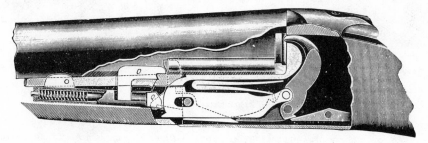

Baker's Ejecting Mechanism.

fall of the tumbler having pushed the rod c under the end of the ejector box Q, the act of opening the gun raises the ejector box, which is pivoted just above the coiled spring, till the nose of the bent arm o of .the tumbler Q is clear of the retaining notch or bent formed in the fore-end iron, when it is free to strike upon the legs of the extractor, and so eject the cases.

The second figure shows the shape of the split sliding rod, of which the action is as follows :—Assuming the gun to have been fired, the slide c is wholly within the action body ; as the gun opens, it is pushed forward by a projection on the tumbler as the Anson and Deeley cocking dog raises the tumblers into cock, and at once engages with the ejecting tumbler Q, which it puts out of bent. As there is no obstruction to the free sliding of the rod, the projecting stud simply pushes the rod forward without entering the recess formed by the spring ends. On closing the gun, the fore-end forces the slide within the action body, and pressure being now brought on the hinder part of the slide, where it bears against the stud on the tumbler, the split ends come into play and the stud enters the recess in the slide.

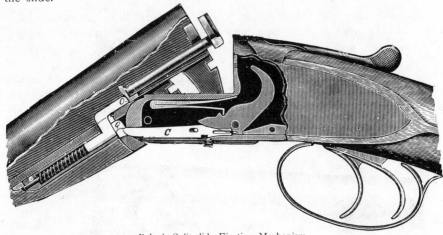

Baker's Split-slide Ejecting Mechanism.

ROSS'S EJECTING MECHANISM.

The sliding bar to bring the tumbler within range of the ejecting mechanism is, of course, an essential feature in all guns in which the locks are arranged upon side-lock plates instead of within the action. In some guns this long sliding bar

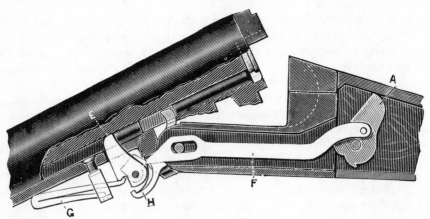

Ross's Ejector Gun.

has been an admitted source of trouble, and numerous are the attempts which have been made to ensure its working. Sometimes it is used to cock the gun, as in Ross's ejector (1891), this mechanism—a later development of a pivoted cocking lever—serving the double purpose of cocking lever and ejector trigger, which was the subject of an earlier patent.

The essential feature is the combined tilting and sliding motion of the cocking bar. The action of the parts is somewhat as follows:—On opening the gun, the cocked ejector hammer is prevented from moving by a slant on F engaging with another on E, and, E being unable to move farther back, the rod F is forced backward by the action of the inclined planes engaging, then the bar F cocks the

Maleham's Ejector Gun.

tumbler A. The point of F having now passed by E, the ejecting mechanism is free to act; the spring forcing the hammer forward and against the extractor leg in the usual manner. When the fore-end is removed a secondary scear, H, is requisite to retain the ejecting mechanism in the cocked position and facilitate the putting together of the gun.

MALEHAM'S EJECTOR.

In guns furnished with a separate ejecting mechanism in the fore-end, the cocking of the ejecting mainspring, as already stated, is ordinarily accomplished by the forcing home of the extractors in closing the gun. This plan has disadvantages;

consequently it has been sought to provide other mechanisms for setting the ejecting levers and cramping the springs which actuate them. One plan, patented by Mr. Maleham in 1891, is here shown.

The general arrangement of the parts is as in the Deeley gun, but a stud on the lower part of the joint *releases* the ejecting scear, and the sliding mainspring of the lock is only used to put the ejecting scear *into* bent; the arrangement so specified being no part of the invention. The mainspring of the ejector H, instead of being cramped by the closing of the gun, is compressed by the levers K and the link K2, pressing against the knuckle when the gun is opened. The arrangement is such that the spring is compressed only just at the time required for the purpose of actuating the extractor; both of the firing locks and both of the ejecting locks are in this gun cocked whilst opening the gun.

HARRISON'S EJECTOR.

In Mr. Harrison's ejector, instead of using the ordinary **V** spring and tumbler, the mechanism is simplified and rendered more compact by employing spiral

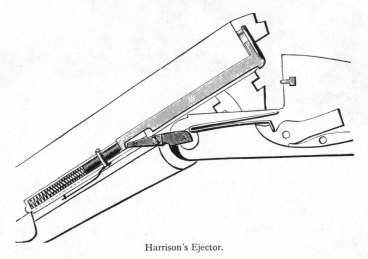

Harrison's Ejector.

springs, which act directly upon the extractors, so that the ejecting locks are cocked every time the gun is closed. The scear, which is actuated by the end of the mainspring, has its bent formed in the extractor leg, and it enters this bent only when firing the gun. The action is as follows:—When the firing tumbler falls the mainspring is pushed forward, slightly depressing A, whilst B enters the bent in the extractor leg D, which is thus retained at full cock. Upon the opening of the gun, the end A of the lever A B travels down a slot until near the finish of the drop of the barrels, when A comes against the bottom of the slot (shown in black) and the further opening of the gun elevates A and depresses B. The extractor is thus impelled by the spiral spring, and so ejects the fired case. When the gun has not been fired the retaining scear does not come into play. The ordinary cartridge lifter is not shown in the drawing, but acts in the ordinary way in bringing out a tight cartridge the usual distance.

PERKES'S EJECTOR.

Mr. Perkes, whose early ejecting gun has been already referred to, has more recently (1892) produced mechanisms of a more complex character. The essential feature of the one here shown is the method of cocking the ejecting locks. Instead of compressing the mainspring by direct pressure of the extractors in closing the gun, or by mechanical means set in motion by opening the gun, as in Maleham's mechanism, the arrangement is as follows :—The usual sliding rod or the end of

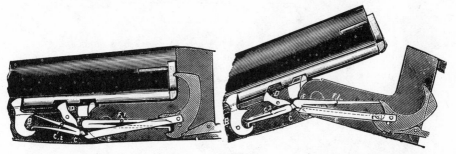

<table>
<tr><td>Perkes's Ejector—Gun fired.</td><td>Perkes's Ejector—Spring compressed.</td></tr>
</table>

the mainspring projects, and engages with the rear end of the ejector spring, which spring is pivoted about the middle of its upper arm. On opening the gun, the piece projecting through the knuckle joint of the action forces upwards the rear end of the ejecting spring (thus compressing it), until it engages a suitable scear acting on the extractor leg, which it puts out of bent, and, the leg being released, the spring is free to expand by acting upon the lever, and so eject the cartridge. On closing the gun, the projecting mainspring is gradually lowered so that the rear end of the ejecting spring can rotate down, and in doing so cocks the ejecting hammer. In this mechanism, also, the ejecting spring is only compressed at the time required to eject the case.

HOLLAND'S EJECTOR.

The essential feature covered by Mr. Holland's patent (No. 800 of 1893) is the utilisation of the ordinary cocking arm C to put the ejector mechanism into operation, thereby dispensing with any additional limb to connect the ejector mechanism with the locks, and reducing the working parts to two limbs only.

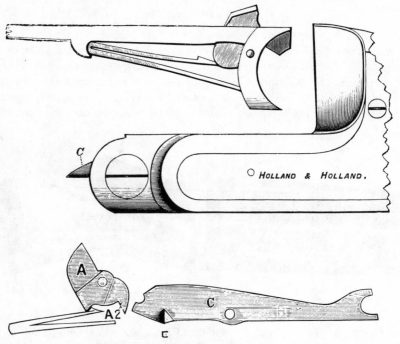

Holland's Ejecting Mechanism and Separate Limbs.

A is the ejecting tumbler, which is engaged by the projection E on the cocking-dog C at A 2. The upper figure shows the tumblers holding the springs compressed; the lower one, the position when ejecting. As the gun is opened the barrels are depressed, and the ejector tumbler is pushed round by the projection E on the lever c until it is in such a position (over centre) that the short arm of the ejector spring A acts upon the tumbler B and flicks it sharply round against the end of the extractor at the moment the gun has been opened sufficiently to allow of the cartridge case clearing the face of the action. On closing the gun, the ejector springs are again compressed, and the tumblers return to the cocked position.

SOUTHGATE'S EJECTING MECHANISM.

In Messrs. Southgate's mechanism (Patent No. 8,239 of 1893) the arrangement of the ejecting parts is the same as that of the last-mentioned patent, but a different means of connection between the locks is employed from that of Messrs. Holland, as shown.

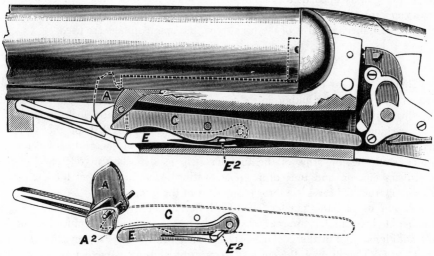

Southgate's Ejecting Mechanism and Separate Limbs.

In the illustration c is the cocking dog, and E the connecting rod pivoted at its extremity and having a projection, E^2, lying under the cocking lever. The fall of the tumbler has depressed the cocking-lever and forced down the connecting-rod, which now projects through the knuckle and bears against the tumbler A at A^2.

On opening the gun the action is the same as Messrs. Holland's ejector, and in both the above mechanisms the closing of the gun forces in the extractors and compresses the ejector springs, and brings the ejector tumblers or "kickers" into position to act upon the extractor legs ; but they are not free to do so until, the gun having been fired and reopened, the respective connecting parts are in a position to trip up the kickers and release them at the moment the gun is open to its widest.

GRANT'S EJECTING MECHANISM.

The chief feature of the mechanism patented by Mr. Grant in 1893 is the arrangement and form of the connecting rod. On firing the gun, the tumbler strikes the tail of the cocking lever or connecting rod and raises it so far as to engage a projection on the scear of the ejecting lock and bring that scear *into position* to engage a proper projection on the action body as the barrels are opened ; then, when the gun is opened, the scear so acted upon comes into contact with the releasing projection, and the extractors, thus freed, shoot out the fired cases. The ejecting lock mechanism is of the usual type, but spiral springs are used.

W. W. GREENER'S SELF-ACTING EJECTOR GUN.

Simpler than any of the preceding, and working upon a different principle, is the ejector gun which the author introduced nearly thirty years ago by adapting the Needham principle of ejecting to his own form of breech and lock mechanism. The cocking mechanism of this ejector gun differs from that of the Greener hammerless in so far as it includes the addition of a stud on the cocking lever, over which stud the fore-arms of the tumblers trip as described in reference to the Needham ejector, and thus drop upon ejecting levers and propel the extractors so sharply that the cases are thrown out clear of the gun.

Presuming that the gun has been fired, the action is as follows :—On opening the barrels, the tumblers are raised by their turned-in forward extremities bearing on the additional stud of the cocking swivel ; when nearly to cock, they slip past the stud and fall sharply upon the ejectors' lower arms, and the extractors, already forced partly out by a lever in the fore-end in the usual manner, are violently propelled to their full extent by the blow, and flip out the fired cases. If one cartridge only is fired, the other lock, remaining at cock, does not engage with the cocking swivel or ejector lever ; consequently, unfired cartridges are simply withdrawn to the ordinary extent.

The power available for ejecting the cases is only that of the mainspring falling about one-eighth of an inch, with an initial force of 18 lb., slightly increased by leverage gained in pivoting the ejecting cam. This force alone would not extract a

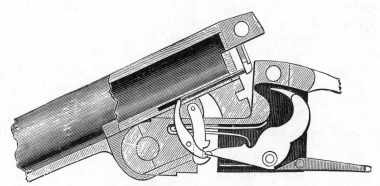

Greener's Self-acting Hammerless Ejector Gun.

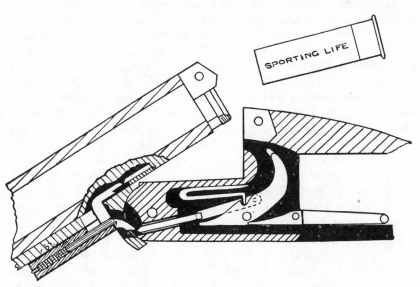

The Fore-end Ejector adapted to the Greener "Facile Princeps' Hammerless Mechanism.

case; but, owing to the case being partly withdrawn by the powerful extracting leverage of the fore-end cam engaging with the extractor legs, and the cases being contracted after firing, the ejecting is effected perfectly.

There is no doubt as to the strength and reliability of this mechanism. Its simplicity is a strong point in its favour, as, although the parts require to be accurately placed with respect to each other, they can neither twist nor wear, so that the gun does the work required of it as well when much worn as when new; and from the principle of its construction it throws out the cases with less friction and with as much strength as if a separate extracting lock, the mainspring of which has to be cocked or cramped each time the gun is opened or closed, were provided for the purpose.

W. W. GREENER'S "UNIQUE" EJECTOR GUN.

In addition to the modifications of the two chief principles of ejecting—the Needham and the Deeley—there is a third principle, found only in one gun, the "Unique" hammerless gun. This gun closely resembles the Needham in the form and arrangement of the lock-work, and in the fact that, instead of a separate lock to work the ejectors, the expulsion of the case is effected by the ordinary mainspring; it differs from the Needham, and all varieties of that mechanism, in principle; the ejection of the fired cases being brought about after the gun is cocked, instead of before that operation is completed. Compared with the W. W. Greener ejector of 1880, the essential difference consists in the tumbler, which, instead of being of one piece, is jointed, the fore-arm by which it is raised to cock being pivoted in the tumbler instead of solid with it. The parts are then so adjusted that the action is as follows:—On the gun being opened after firing, the tumbler is raised, both parts moving substantially together until the scear nose is beyond the bent; the gun is at that time opened to quite its full extent; at this moment the point of the fore-arm slips past the tripping point on the cocking swivel, and by the power of the mainspring is driven down upon the projecting ends of the ejector levers and the fired cases are thrown out. This action is most sharply brought about, owing to the great strength of the mainspring and the sudden stop to the blow by the fore-arms of the tumbler driving the lower ends of the ejecting levers until they are stopped by abutting against the cocking swivel. The gun may then be loaded without any further opening of the barrels. As it is closed, the back or striking part of the tumbler descends until retained in bent by the scear, and remains there at full cock until the scear is released; the fore-arm, carried down on its pivot, becomes shorter as it descends. When the upper part of the tumbler falls to fire the gun, the fore-arm is thrust forward until its extremity again engages with the tripping stud on the cocking swivel, and thus is ready to perform the like motions of cocking and ejecting upon the gun being reopened.

Upon comparison with the systems already described, the advantages possessed by this gun will be at once perceived: first, the result obtained is precisely that of a gun having extra locks for the specific purposes of ejecting, yet in this gun there is no extra mechanism. The gun opens no wider than is requisite to insert the loaded cartridges, and it is cocked before it can be opened even so far as that. As

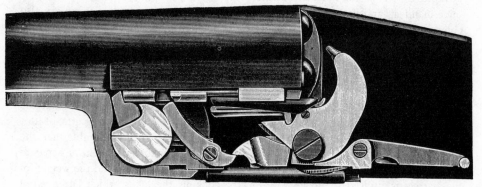

W. W. Greener's "Unique" Hammerless Ejector.

there is but one mainspring, and that so adjusted that only a slight travel is required of it, the gun is easy and pleasant to manipulate, the whole of the mechanism working smoothly without any appreciable jerk, and even if the barrels are thrown open with a sharp movement, the adjustment and position of the ejector levers and mainspring automatically act to check any violent stoppage of the barrels by being brought suddenly against the stop—a plan which absolutely prevents jar or strain upon the hinge joint, and thus adds to the durability of the gun as well as renders its manipulation much more pleasant. This point is thought much of by American experts, who for many years have sought to devise an efficient "check hook" to prevent a strain the arrangement of the "Unique" ejecting mechanism entirely obviates.

EJECTING MECHANISMS COMPARED.

The ejecting mechanisms which have been described are divisible into three classes: the original Needham, to which class the Greener self-acting gun also belongs ; the guns which have separate locks to effect the ejecting, of which type the Deeley mechanism is the most representative ; and the Greener "Unique," in which the one lock serves both as an ejecting and ordinary lock, but performs each function independently.

In all ejecting guns accurate adjustment of the parts is indispensable to the successful working of the ejecting mechanism. With accurate adjustment and good workmanship the expulsion of the fired cases is equally well performed by guns of each class, so that upon this one point neither principle exhibits any marked advantage. When the mechanisms are compared for simplicity, great disparity is at once manifest, and if the size and strength of the parts of each mechanism are also compared the guns of the first class —those having but one lock—are seen to be decidedly superior to each and every gun in which a separate lock mechanism is added for the purpose of throwing out the fired case. It has been advanced against the Needham principle that the double work of firing the gun and ejecting the cartridge-case, being thrown upon the one lock, causes greater wear of the parts; but in practice there is found to be no appreciable increase of friction, so that the objection is purely academic. Indeed, the greater strength of the parts of this mechanism, together with its extreme simplicity, renders it far more durable than the mechanisms of all guns constructed upon the more complicated system of separate locks. There is really much less friction, the gun closes easily, and the weight of the barrels is utilised to do all the work of cocking the locks, which latter is not usual with guns having separate extracting locks, these being in most guns cocked by the forcing in of the extractors—a motion producing much friction, as the extractors grate upon the face of the standing breech during the whole of the process.

The only disadvantage of the Needham principle is the wide opening of the gun ; the barrels have not only to drop sufficiently to allow of the cartridges being thrown out clear of the standing breech, but still farther in order to effect the cocking of the locks *after* the ejection has been completed. In Greener's " Unique" ejector this disadvantage is overcome, since the movement of the barrels in opening the gun first cocks the locks ; *then*, the cocking being subsidiary to the primary object of opening the barrels, which is, of course, in order to reload, the gun has to be opened sufficiently wide to allow of the cartridges being inserted, *but no farther.* Taking into consideration the fact that the ejecting of the fired cases and the cocking of the locks are accomplished by one mechanism, and that only the simplest form of gun-lock, this last gun stands out pre-eminently as the highest and latest development of the sporting gun, and as possessing advantages not found in any other hammerless principle, whether ejecting or otherwise. It proves, if further demonstration of the point be necessary, that separate ejecting locks are wholly unnecessary complications of the mechanism necessary to the most modern and perfect type of sporting gun ; it is as simple as it is effective, as apt as it is strong.

Apart from the merits and the disadvantages of the various mechanisms viewed simply as means for ejecting the fired cases, the lock-work of each type must be considered as firing mechanism. The advantages of the Anson and Deeley lock over the various side-lock mechanisms used with hammerless non-ejecting guns are increased by the addition of the ejector work. The sharp quick blow of the Anson and Deeley tumbler, with its short travel, ensures speedy and certain ignition. The side-lock, with its longer travel, its weaker mainspring, and its interposed striking pin, has its action still further retarded by having to set the scear of the ejecting locks, or perform some equivalent mechanical function. The time required to fire the charge after pulling the trigger is therefore still further increased ; not unfrequently miss-fires result owing to the clogging, stiff working, or other stoppage of the separate ejecting mechanism or its gear acting as a drag upon the firing mechanism. This tendency to miss-fire is the objection most often raised by sportsmen to the side-lock ejector gun; it most often fails in the striking mechanism, which is unequal to the extra work required of it. It is true that some of the leading gun-makers have adopted the principle of a separate ejecting mechanism ; its weaknesses they admit, but contend that by excellent workmanship and accurate construction the liability to miss-fire is greatly lessened ; it is true, too, that the best guns on this principle function fairly well. Their faults are not, in practice, found to be of the greatest importance in England, for the gun can be at once sent to the makers if the mechanism should fail, but for service abroad or far from a gun-making centre the side-lock ejectors cannot be recommended. Their construction is too complex for the ordinary mechanic to satisfactorily repair in the event of a breakdown, and they are ill suited to the rough usage, hard work, and frequent neglect to which most guns are subjected.

An enthusiastic advocate of ejector guns, the author has never lost an oppor- tunity of pointing out the advantages they possess ; yet, great as the convenience of ejecting is, if it be secured by sacrificing the efficiency of the gun in more important particulars, the cost is too great, and the author considers that the present tendency is to produce guns with intricate mechanisms in order to effect a function of minor importance. As already shown, an ejecting mechanism may be effective without being either intricate or complex. So much the Needham principle alone has long definitely demonstrated.   That this principle has proved trustworthy also the author has had ample opportunities of ascertaining in the thirty years since it was introduced.

It is for the sportsman to judge whether the single lock-work or the principle of the separate ejecting mechanism is preferable.   If the more complex type is deemed superior, it does not follow that the simplest mechanism is the best ; for an efficient lock mechanism must consist of several limbs properly constructed and arranged. Doubtless each of the separate ejecting mechanisms which have been illustrated and described possesses some advantageous point which another lacks.

The sportsman can be cautioned ; he should not buy a gun having complicated lock mechanisms at a lower price than he would expect to give for a high-class simple hammerless gun.   As already pointed out, with ejector guns so much depends upon the fine workmanship and accurate adjustment that it is futile to expect efficiency in low-priced guns.   As a matter of fact, such guns cause their users endless trouble and annoyance, and disgust their owners with ejector guns generally, when really it is only the particular mechanism that is in fault.   With ejector guns, if with none other, the best is always the cheapest ; and the best, no matter of what form the ejecting mechanism, is at present, and is long likely to be, a high-priced weapon, wherever bought.

ADVANTAGES OF THE EJECTING MECHANISM.

The self-cocking of the locks is in itself an immense advantage, and the self-ejecting of the fired cases, by reducing the number of movements to be made by the hands when loading, is decidedly worthy of support.   The ejecting mechanism as made by the author has been tested in every quarter of the globe and under all possible conditions ; it has been found thoroughly reliable in every climate, and is consequently recommended by all who have made use of it ; at the present time it stands at the head of sporting guns, the nearest to perfection.

For speed, the self-ejecting gun is ahead of all magazine or repeating shot-guns, and not only can it be fired more quickly, but it is free from any liability to "jam" when rapidly manipulated, whilst the repeating mechanism of shot-guns is more prone to "jam" than the mechanism of a magazine rifle, since paper cartridge-cases, which vary in size more than metal cartridges and do not expand so uniformly, are generally used with shot-guns of every kind.

Compared with ordinary hammerless guns, the ejector is superior, because it performs automatically and effectually the total withdrawal of the fired cartridge-cases much more quickly and easily than even the best-drilled expert can do by hand. As described, the ejecting mechanism is simply the utilisation of the force of the mainspring, or of another spring, for the special purpose of throwing out the cases. The fired cases are first withdrawn a short distance by a cam on the fore-end, and the weight and leverage of the barrels are available to effect the partial withdrawal just as in ordinary hammer and hammerless guns. The case being taper and the cartridge chamber also being taper, when the case, even if tight-fitting or "jammed," has been withdrawn the usual fourth of an inch, it is usually quite loose and free, and requires only a flip of the cartridge extractor to throw it clear of the gun. This motion the ejecting mechanism produces, and nothing more; there is therefore no increased leverage, and no extra strain upon the breech-loading mechanism; nor even upon the lock mechanism, provided that the ejecting mechanism is upon the most approved principle, as the Needham or the "Unique." Sportsmen, however, should remember that, although the ejecting mechanism can throw out the cartridges in a small fraction of the time required to remove them by hand, yet *some* time is required for the mechanism to function, and that it is quite possible by a too violent jerk in opening the gun to prevent the ejection of the cases, the mainspring or its equivalent not being given the necessary fraction of a second it requires to act upon the ejecting levers. This is no failure upon the part of the gun or its mechanism, but is due to the too great haste of the person manipulating it. The ejector enables the quick shot to reload in less than half the time possible with an ordinary gun, and by a little practice even the quickest manipulator of the gun can acquire the habit of opening the gun evenly and, in reality, with less loss of time than results from violently jerking the gun in order to raise the breech end of the barrels.

The testimony in favour of the ejector gun is overwhelming. Here, as in the case of hammerless guns, the extracts from the opinions of experts are taken from reports published at a time when the advantages of the ejector were not so generally admitted as at present.

"I like the gun very much indeed, and find it very handy. The action, too, is very neat, and an improvement on the older pattern of hammerless."

"I do not see that there is anything in the ejecting action which will make them wear out sooner than other guns; at any rate, mine work as smoothly and perfectly now as they did the first day I used them."

"I received the ejector last autumn. I returned it three weeks since. It was never in that time out of my possession, was never out of gear in any way. It had done lots of work before it came into my hands, and is as ready to go through as much more. . . . Its three advantages appear to me to be *celerity*, *comfort*, and *economy*. An ejector gun *will* do the work of *two* guns."

"The ejector gun is a step in the right direction; it throws out the empty cases perfectly. This ejecting is a great convenience in a hot corner."

Another sportsman has found that by carrying a spare cartridge conveniently between the fingers of the left hand, he can obtain a *third* shot at a bird or covey if he uses the ejector gun ; but this only after he has practised the manœuvre and become expert in the manipulation of the gun. The benefits derivable from the self-extracting mechanism are so considerable that all who use guns will find it to their advantage to learn how to handle the gun so as to obtain the utmost value from the additional mechanism.

SAFETIES AND SAFETY BOLTS.

Hammerless guns, and some hammer guns, are provided with safety-bolts. The object of these mechanisms is to protect the shooter and others from the consequences which might result from an accidental or premature discharge of the gun. Safeties are of various kinds ; some act automatically, others require to be moved to " safe " by the hand of the shooter. The bolts have been used to lock the tumblers, the scears, and the triggers. A well-made hammerless gun is safer

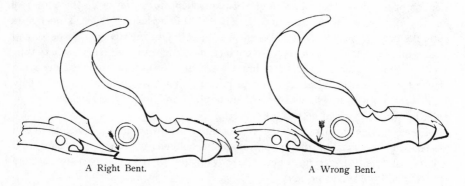

A Right Bent.   A Wrong Bent.

than a gun with hammers ; it is not so liable to accidental discharge as is the hammer gun—consequently, the necessity for safeties upon hammerless guns is not so apparent, although all, or nearly all, of them are so fitted. To a hammerless gun, with well-made locks, and of mechanism sufficiently strong and simple not to get out of order, an external automatic safety-bolt is of use only to take the place of the half-cock. In shooting dangerous game, and usually in all shooting, the gun is carried at full cock, whether it be hammerless or not ; therefore the locks must be efficient, so that they will remain at full cock until disengaged by the trigger. It is evident, then, that a trigger-bolting safety is all that is required, and the simpler it is the better. There is no safety more simple than the side safety shown with the lock mechanism of the Anson and Deeley lock on page 269.

The safety and durability of a lock are dependent on the shape of the bent. Taking for an instance the tumbler and scear of the Greener "Facile Princeps" or self-acting ejector mechanism, the sketches on page 204 show the bearing of the scear rightly and wrongly. A bent shaped as shown, if of such depth, and with the centres of both tumbler and scear in proper relation, will never jar off; the work, however, is so fine that many guns on Anson and Deeley, and other systems, are made as in the second figure, the body as well as nose of the scear in contact with the tumbler. Any gun-locks in which scear and tumbler are so shaped or arranged as to permit of contact of anything but the nose of the scear in the tumbler-bent are liable to be jarred off by extraneous blows or the firing of one barrel. When the Anson and Deeley, or other guns of like mechanism, have gone off unawares, or both barrels together, it is probably due to this fault; it is certain that such accidents arise from defective workmanship rather than from any fault of the principle of this type of hammerless lock.

TRIGGER-BOLTING SAFETIES.

The hammerless gun cannot be considered complete unless fitted with an efficient external safety; and although many forms of intercepting bolts fitted to

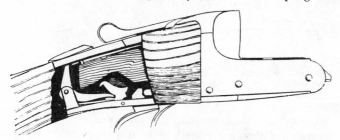

Automatic Top Safety, showing the amount of woodwork cut away to accommodate the mechanism.

the inside mechanism and operated automatically have been devised, but little alteration has been made in the design of the hand-operated external safety since its adoption for hammerless guns over thirty years ago.

When the author commenced the manufacture of the Anson and Deeley hammerless gun in 1875 he considered the top safety with which it was then fitted too complicated, and utilised the simple side safety, which is still used with complete success on Greener guns.

The trigger-bolting safeties are usually fixed on the top of the grip of the gun, and the opening of the gun forces the bolt backward, so as to bring the mechanism into contact with the trigger blades and secure them, preventing them from engaging the scears until the bolt has been moved forward by the shooter.

The automatic top safety fitted to nearly all hammerless guns other than those made by the author is undoubtedly a relic of the old half-cocking hammer in that it necessitates an additional movement on the part of the shooter before the trigger can be pulled; it weakens the stock considerably just where it is least calculated to withstand the strain, a large portion of the "hand" being cut away to accommodate its mechanism; it is liable to be pushed on uncon-

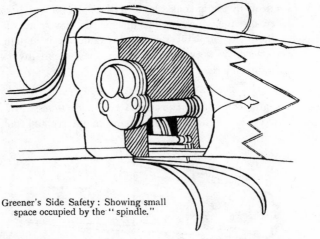

Greener's Side Safety : Showing small
space occupied by the " spindle."

sciously when carrying the gun on the shoulder, and many a bird has been lost through the shooter omitting to push it off "safe" in the excitement of shooting.   The side safety is a distinctive feature of Greener hammerless and ejector guns.   It is placed where there is more wood, and it cuts away very little more than the ordinary lock-pin or "side-nail"; it has the further advantage of being so placed as to be within convenient reach of the thumb, but at the same time where it cannot be thrown out of safety unconsciously or accidentally by the grip of the right hand on the stock.   It may be made either independent in action or to bolt automatically.   This safe may be locked—for pigeon-shooting or other purposes—by plugging the space between the safety-lever and its plate with a small piece of cork, or a small metal plate may be screwed in.

The top safety is used on so many guns of all qualities that one can only suppose that use has accustomed the sportsman to it, and further, that few, unless their attention is particularly drawn to this point, really give the matter consideration, but accept what the gun-maker gives them without due regard to its personal convenience; yet although the top safety is a "London fashion" it is probable that the author has supplied a larger number of guns fitted with the side safety than the London makers have turned out with the automatic top safety mechanism.

The old "grip safety," placed behind the trigger-guard, was known and used more than a hundred years ago; it is of little use, because the gun, when carried, is usually gripped on the safe—the triggers consequently are unbolted. This form of safety has recently been applied to hammerless guns, and in several forms is still used. The "Silver" safety is constructed upon the same principle, but with the

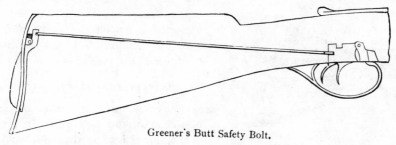

Greener's Butt Safety Bolt.

gearing so modified that not only are the triggers bolted, but the scears and tumblers also; they are all usually unbolted immediately the gun is grasped.

With the muzzle-loaders also a safety-bolt was used, which was held by a spring, to bolt the triggers, and was automatically released when the gun was put to the shoulder by gearing attached to a movable heel-plate or a movable projection therein. As soon as the gun was pressed to the shoulder the triggers, etc., were released; but, as this was also the case when the gun was placed on the ground for loading and ramming home the charge, it was of little use as a safety. In 1879 the author introduced a certain modification for use in hammerless guns. The general arrangement is here shown, and the bolt referred to, because several patents for similar bolts have since been granted, both in this country and abroad. It was objected to it that the gun was not safe when left on the ground muzzle upward; but this is not a serious objection, since, if the gun fell or was knocked down, the bolts would automatically engage the tumblers or triggers befcre the

locks could jar off. The movable heel-plate was not liked ; to this cause most
probably the failure of the principle may be attributed with greater truth.

There are many instances on record of the automatic safety proving dangerous ;
one may be recorded.   A party in India were elephant-hunting.   One, a well-tried
sportsman and known elephant killer, with a gun by an eminent maker, had a splen-

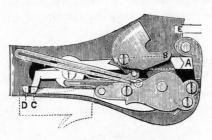

did chance of dropping a wounded tusker.
He aimed, and the elephant, seeing him,
charged.   To the surprise of his brother-
sportsmen—who were hastening to the
finish—he dropped his rifle without firing,
and beat an ignominious retreat behind a
friendly boulder, dodging the elephant
until the others arrived to his assistance.
The result proved that he, a cool and
expert hunter of dangerous game, had
neglected to unbolt the safety, and he
acknowledged that it had been an element
of danger to him instead of security.

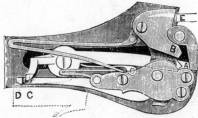

INTERCEPTING SAFETY BOLTS.

Sometimes the safety takes the form
of an intercepting bolt, which by means
of a spring is held so that it blocks the
tumbler or hammer, should it be jarred
from full cock. When the trigger is pressed,
a lever or other gear moves this intercepting bolt from its position in the path of
travel of the hammer, which is then free
to reach the cap of the cartridge.   The
principle is very old (it was used in a
modified form before the middle of the
last century), but in its more modern and

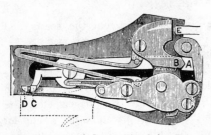

Scott's Automatic Intercepting Safety Bolt.

most popular form it is found in the mechanism known as the "Scott" safety.   In
this a lever is pivoted so that its one extremity, c, comes into contact with the
trigger exactly as does the scear, d.   A projection, a, on the other extremity of this
lever will, under certain conditions, block the tumbler, b, so as to prevent its
reaching the exploding pin, e.   In the three figures, the lock is shown cocked and

ready for firing in the first; in the second, the trigger has been pulled, and the tumbler released and struck the striker, E. In the last, it is supposed that the tumbler has been liberated by some means other than the pulling of the trigger, and the tumbler has consequently failed to reach E, being effectually blocked by the stud A. This safety, as made, is not strong enough to be relied on implicitly.

A second scear, working just as the ordinary scear, but not engaging with the tumbler unless the tumbler falls from the position in which it is held by the primary scear, is sometimes used as an automatic intercepting bolt; but this in common with other—many other—so-called self-acting bolts is found in practice to be a cause of much annoyance by occasionally blocking the tumbler when the trigger is pulled.

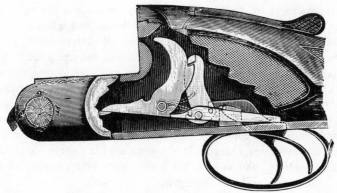

Greener's Automatic Intercepting Safety Bolt.

Nevertheless, the ejector gun should be provided with some such mechanism, or its equivalent ; for the ordinary ejector gun, as already explained, depends entirely upon the accurate adjustment of various mechanisms to act conjointly and simultaneously. If by reason of hasty manipulation, the undue straining, clogging, or breakage of a limb, the various parts of the mechanism do not act in unison, it may be that the cartridge-case is ejected before the lock is cocked, and upon the gun being reloaded and hastily closed the tumbler, if not fitted with a bolting mechanism, would fall upon the cap of the cartridge, and possibly with such force as to explode it.

A secondary scear, intercepting safety, or catch bolt would prevent an accident of this kind; hence such bolts are fitted to some lock mechanisms of ejector guns. It also acts to prevent the premature explosion of the second barrel if the tumbler is jarred from bent as a result of firing the first barrel or from any jarring of the gun, and should, in fact, prevent the striker coming into contact with the cartridge until after the trigger has been pressed.

With so many and diverse forms of lock and ejecting mechanisms it is not surprising that the safety bolts are of different types; practically all are of the same principle modified to suit the particular mechanism, arrangement, or size of gun to which the bolts are fitted. In the one illustrated the trigger acts directly upon the lower arm of the horizontally pivoted vertical blocking bolt to withdraw the upper arm from a position intercepting the path of the tumbler. If, from any cause other than pressure on the trigger, the tumbler escapes from full cock, it is caught by the hook of the catch bolt before it can reach the cap ; in like manner, if the cocking mechanism should fail to lift the tumbler to full bent, or from the snapping of its spring the scear should fail to catch it there, or by breakage or fouling of the scear point fail to retain it, the catch block will prevent the tumbler falling.

As shown, the catch bolt is strong, and is so placed as to effectually control and block the tumbler on its fall. Consisting practically of but one piece, it is unlikely to jam or fail to act, and it is readily fitted to any lock. Of course, this safety, as all others of the same type, may never be required; it is never brought into requisition until some other portion of the mechanism is broken, weakened, or worn out, though every time the gun is opened and fired it acts automatically, blocking and freeing the tumbler alternately, in the same manner as, but quite independent of, the ordinary scear. It is a piece held in reserve—a precautionary mechanism safeguarding the shooter, but acting quite independently of the parts necessary to the proper working of the gun.

These remarks apply more particularly to hammerless and ejector guns having locks of the "box" or Anson and Deeley pattern. Side-lock hammerless guns, being neither so rigid nor so strong as those of the box pattern, are more readily "jarred off" ; a smart rap on the stock is often sufficient to free both locks from full-cock. This liability is due to the wrong centring of the tumblers and scears, and to the less breadth, and consequently weaker grip, of the scear. A further mistake in side-lock guns is to fix automatic intercepting safety bolts similar to second scears, and so arrange them that a jar which will liberate the scear from bent will, at the same time, produce a corresponding movement, but of greater degree, to the safety-bolt, and thus prevent its action at the very moment it is required. In the author's opinion the box-lock, constructed as here specified, is more trustworthy, without any safety-bolt, than is the ordinary hammerless side-lock with any of the intercepting automatic bolts commonly used ; it has greater wear, and no ordinary blow or shock will jar its scears from bent.

CHAPTER IX.

GUN-MAKING.

THE HISTORY OF THE FIRE-ARMS INDUSTRY.

FIRE-ARMS, as weapons of war, upon their introduction into Europe were produced under the immediate supervision of military commanders   In the case of large cannon it was not unusual to construct the weapon on the field of battle, as such "engines" were used only for the besieging of fortified towns.   When the weapon had served its turn —the town having fallen or the siege been raised—it was sold for old metal, if too cumbrous to be readily removed. In the circumstances, therefore, a knowledge of fire-arms construction came to be regarded as necessary to the education of the warrior, and the military treatises, from that of Robertus Valturius in 1472, were incomplete unless containing references to "military fireworks" and instructions as to the manufacture of fire-arms.

It is known that 500 hand cannon, wholly of metal, the barrels about four inches in length, were made at Perugia in 1364.   These were probably forged by the smiths—and it was the smiths' guild which subsequently monopolised the fire-arms trade on the Continent.

The centres of the gun-making industry were either

Martin Merz—Gun-maker of Amberg, died 1501.

arsenals, as at St. Etienne, Brescia, etc., or the industry became localised in the country of the smiths, particularly of the nail forgers, as at Bilboa and Eibar in Spain, Liége in the Netherlands, and Suhl in Germany.

The Suhl gunsmiths obtained incorporation as a distinct craft in 1463, but it was not until the seventeenth century that the barrel-welders of Liége founded their society, and then only as a division of the older guild of smiths.   In Liége the mounting of the barrels was the privilege of the carpenters, and anyone not

belonging to their guild found to have stocked a musket was fined three golden
florins and his work confiscated.

The tyranny of the guilds caused many who had learned the craft to seek employment and liberty abroad.   In 1545, Henry VIII. had in his service a number
of Hainaulters who knew how to use, repair, and make the arquebus.   These men
were stationed in the Tower of London, and formed the nucleus of a craft which
has been carried on continuously in that neighbourhood ever since.   In the reign of
Elizabeth there were thirty-seven accredited gunsmiths plying their trade in the
Minories; in 1590, Henricke, a Dutchman, was the acknowledged head of the craft.
King James I. repealed an Act of Queen Mary, and bestowed the monopoly of gun-
making upon Edmund Nicholson; so that the trade dwindled until, in 1607, only
five members remained, and they prayed to Parliament for the abolition of the
monopoly which threatened the extinction of the "mystery" of gun-making.   Their
grievance was redressed, but no important forward movement was made until 1637,
when the London gun-makers obtained their charter of incorporation, the provisions
of which were enlarged and the privileges referring to the proof of arms re-bestowed
in 1672.   The London gun-makers henceforth appear frequently in past annals,
chiefly as petitioners to Parliament for orders ; for powers to restrict or prohibit the
importation of fire-arms (1680); and later (1710) for payment—they being creditors
to the extent of more than thirty thousand pounds—for arms supplied, of which sum
they could "not get a farthing," although 10,000 arms could be "bought up in
Holland and ready money remitted to the Dutch."   The purchase of weapons
abroad has been a standing grievance, and was expressed most emphatically in the
petitions of 1680, 1706, 1710, and after the large purchases in 1793, and the
attempt to buy up all obtainable in 1803.   It has also frequently reappeared in the
Parliamentary debates of more recent periods.   Another lasting trouble of the
London gun-makers was the competition of Birmingham manufacturers.

The first cannon foundry was established by John O'Ewen about 1535.   Cannon
were cast at Uckfield in 1543, and a century later, if not at an earlier date,
culverins were made by the smiths of Deriton, Birmingham.   Nathaniel Nye,
master-gunner of Worcester during the Commonwealth, states the fact, also, that
fire-arms, of a sort, were made at Bromsgrove, a town midway between Birmingham
and Worcester.

The gun-making industry of Birmingham more properly dates from 1683, when
Sir Richard Newdigate, the then member for Warwickshire, procured from the
Government an order for muskets which he prevailed upon the Birmingham smiths
to accept, rendering them financial assistance in order to fulfil the contract.   These

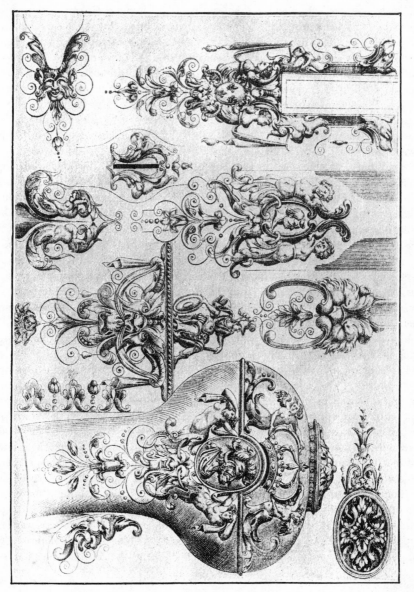

Specimens of Ornamental Gun Work. *Jacquinet, 1660.*

weapons were approved, much to the chagrin of the London Company, who complained to Parliament, and the Board was recommended to "compose the matter
in dispute." The Birmingham smiths were able to furnish more guns than required,
and turned out two hundred muskets a month. In 1692 they presented Sir Richard
Newdigate with a testimonial and the first gun made in Birmingham, which quaint
weapon is still preserved at Arbury, the Warwickshire seat of the Newdigate
family.

In 1693 the guns made at Birmingham were proved there; in 1698 the English
industry received an impetus from the opening of the African trade. The rivalry
between Birmingham and London makers became acute. J. Goodwin, F.S.A.,
writes: "There is too much reason for believing that the London smiths had
recourse to very questionable expedients in the hope of driving their Midland rivals
from the field." In February, 1707, four hundred Birmingham makers petitioned
Parliament that, unless the persecution of the London Company was stopped, they
should have to emigrate to a foreign nation. They decided to remain, and have
since held their ground. At the close of last century the Government instituted a
branch "tower" at Birmingham for the examination and proof of arms purchased in
the neighbourhood. Birmingham supplied enormous quantities, not only of finished
arms, but of barrels, locks, and parts, and has almost uninterruptedly supplied the
Government since. In 1813, in addition to the Government testing establishment, a
general proof-house was provided for the use of the trade and the protection of the
public; at it there were proved 1,388,725 gun barrels and 292,245 pistol barrels
during the first twelve years of its existence.

The subsequent development of the fire-arms industry in Birmingham is well-
known history. The enormous output resulting from the improved methods of
making gun-barrels by machinery was not injured by the withdrawal of all Government orders for ten years (1817-29); but the military branch of the trade was
checked at a later date by the establishment of fire-arms manufactories by the
Government at Lewisham and Enfield, and was almost extirpated when this lead was
followed by the foreign Powers generally. The Birmingham gun-makers, adapting
themselves to the changed conditions with praiseworthy promptitude, turned their
attention more particularly to the manufacture of sporting arms; wresting supremacy
from other centres by the cheapness and thoroughness of their work, and the rapid
improvements in the mechanisms of breech-loading arms. This progress was only
temporarily checked by the revival of the military trade during the American Civil
War, and it is upon the sporting trade chiefly that the Birmingham industry
still depends.

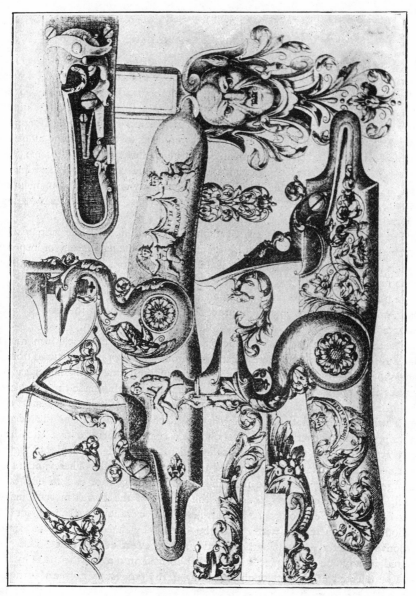

Parisian Work. Early Seventeenth Century.

GUN-MAKING IN BYGONE DAYS.

Of the actual practice pursued by the artisans of the Middle Ages very little is known.　What the skilled workman learns by long years of toil at his craft he could not impart by verbal description, even had he the mind to do so.　The guilds, moreover, most jealously guarded what they considered to be their trade secrets ; but from the many specimens of mediæval gun-making which are still extant it is apparent that there was less of mystery than of art required to make a competent gunsmith.　It is possible, but hardly probable, that in the lost treatise of Cataneo, *"Arte de fare le Arme e i Fucili,"* the methods of manufacture current at Brescia in 1577 were explained in detail ; but we do know, from Cotty and others who mentioned the treatise when in the Paris Library, that it described some processes of manufacture.

The works of Fucar (1535), N. Spadoni, V. Bonfadini, and other writers of the seventeenth century, supplemented by the information obtainable from an inspection of arms made in Spain and Italy, enable an expert to form a fairly approximate idea of the methods followed.

In the first place, the forging is the most remarkable :　close work, correct in shape, and often elegant in design, proves the early gunsmiths to have been able craftsmen.

The method of making barrels prior to the introduction of Damascus iron from the East was to forge them from plates or strips of iron—this iron manufactured from old horse-shoe nails—not perhaps so much because of the virtue in the metal as from the fact that nail forgers were the particular smiths who made the gun barrels. The method of the Spanish forgers was to weld a number of nails into a short strip, which strip was curled into a cylinder, six inches or so in length, and the edges of the strip, instead of overlapping slightly, made a complete turn, so that each barrel was practically double throughout.　The cylinders when welded were pieced together end to end, until a barrel of the required length was produced.　The cylinders were so forged that the grain of the iron, instead of running from end to end of the barrel, is disposed circularly, following the round of the barrel in such manner as to give the effect of a *twist* barrel.　The advantages claimed for this method of manufacture were that the metal by being forged in smaller portions was better wrought and purified ; in the event of any defect being discovered in any one of the pieces after being formed into a cylinder, that cylinder could be rejected and a perfect one substituted ; by proportioning the thickness of each part to the part of the barrel in which it was to be placed, very little filing of

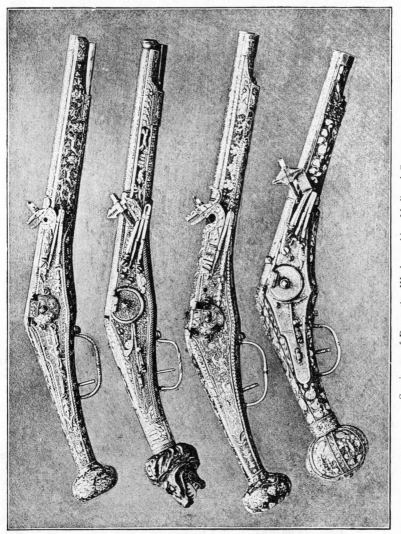

Specimens of Decorative Workmanship: Mediæval German.

the barrel was necessary.   About forty-five pounds of nails were required to make a barrel of six pounds ; the bore of the barrel was generally twenty-four or twenty-two, and if three feet long it was sometimes as light as three pounds.   Martinez del Espinar, the gun-bearer of Philip IV., was of opinion that the barrel forty inches long should weigh four and a half pounds.   These barrels were expensive, costing sometimes £12 when filed and bored, and they were used only on fine sporting guns.

The method of manufacturing the celebrated *canons à ruban* current in France at the end of last century is stated by Marolles to be as follows :—With a strip of much less thickness than is required for an ordinary barrel, a tube is formed as though a barrel were to be made.   On this *chemise* is rolled a strip three or four lines in thickness, an inch broad, and chamfered to a point on each side.   The whole is put into the fire and heated a few inches at a time.   This strip is called the *ruban*.   To roll it round the chemise they use a pair of tongs, of which one beak is flat and short and the other rounded and very long.   This long arm serves first to turn and press the strip of metal on the chemise.   It is worthy of note that the twist-barrel is not made all in one piece like other barrels, owing to the difficulty of rolling a piece sufficiently long to form a barrel of the usual length—that is to say, about 3 ft.   It is made in three pieces, which are afterwards welded together. Five feet of *ruban* are required for each foot of barrel.   When the *ruban* is thus spirally turned the whole length of the chemise, and made to overlap, edge to edge, they give a few heats to forge the whole together, as in an ordinary barrel.   The barrel is at once passed to the boring shop, and bored until the lining, or chemise, is for the most part taken out by the boring bits, and there remains little but the strip with which it is covered.   One cannot deny that the barrel made in this manner possesses a strength superior to that of the ordinary barrels, insomuch as it has not, so to say, a weld, or at any rate the weld is almost transversal, and in this way better placed to resist the force of the explosion than if it were straight along, or even if it were spiral, as in the barrels which are simply twisted tubes.

Of the other methods of welding, the simplest and most primitive was to take a strip the length of the barrel, bend it into a cylinder with the edges abutting for a butt weld, but usually slightly overlapping, and then weld the joint throughout the length of the barrel.   Sometimes a barrel so made, after being heated, was twisted upon itself in order to make the grain of the iron take a spiral direction round the barrel, instead of longitudinally from end to end : this plan was said to produce a stronger barrel.   The method of detecting it from a genuine twist was to touch either extremity with *aqua fortis* and note the direction of the grain.   To avoid this

French Arquebusiers of the Seventeenth Century. (*From Jacquinet.*)

detection the smiths then made the barrel longer than required, and cut off the extremities which they could not turn.

Other methods may be briefly described. Instead of one plain strip the length of the barrel, two shorter ones were sometimes used; a thick one for the breech end, a thinner one for the muzzle, the two cylinders joined. The muzzle-piece, instead of being of iron or steel, was sometimes of brass or bell-metal, and brazed on —a common plan for the bell-mouthed blunderbuses. Plain iron barrels were drawn, just as other tubes, in 1808, by Benjamin Cook, of Birmingham. His method was to roll a block of iron, drill a hole through it, fix a mandrel within the hole of the block previously made red-hot, and pass between rolls with taper grooves, repeating the process until a barrel of the required length was obtained. This plan was discontinued in a few years. The method adopted in its stead was to roll the barrel out of a short strip of iron; the strip was then turned round a mandrel and passed between rolls, the edges being welded as the barrel passed between the rolls; the mandrel, however, was used merely to start the barrel, and did not pass through the rolls with it. These methods were strenuously opposed by the welders; serious riots resulted from their introduction, but the plan was so advantageous for musket barrels that it was persisted in, and is even now employed in the production of barrels of the cheapest grade, for slave-trade and other muskets.

The wire twist barrels—not an imitation of the figure of coiled wire—were made by Barrois of Paris at the end of last century. On a chemise, wire was coiled and welded, or soldered, then at the breech end another coil, until the requisite thickness was attained. The barrels when browned were said to have had a very pleasing appearance, and Marolles, who tried them, says they were very strong.

In England the development of the twist barrels appears to have been worked out without knowledge of the processes current in France and Spain as detailed in the book of Marolles, of which an English translation was published in 1789. William Dupein obtained a patent in 1798 for a twist gun-barrel of iron and steel. His method was to wind round a rod of iron a strip of steel, then a coating of iron or "iron and steel mixed"; the whole was then welded together, and the iron cores bored away so as to leave the barrel of steel, or steel and iron, as desired. In 1806 J. Jones patented a method of making barrels from scelps or strips coiled round a mandrel so that the edges overlapped, and then welded together at the edges of the strips. Stub barrels, made from old horse-shoe nails, were greatly in vogue at the commencement of this century. The nails were welded together into a straight or taper bar, which was turned over a mandrel and welded into a tube by uniting the edges; a different process from that current in Spain and France.

Highly-decorated Belgian Gun on the Percussion System.

These barrels are easily distinguished, being figured; the figure runs longitudinally, the nails being light, with dark lines at the weld where they are joined to each other. The horse-shoe nail stub barrel was the first attempt to produce a figured barrel in England. When the twist or scelp method was introduced, it soon gained favour. Scelp or plain rods were first twisted, afterwards the strips of horse-shoe nail iron were twisted in like manner; and the introduction of the Damascus iron followed shortly afterwards (1820). The Damascus iron as first manufactured in England by Mr. Wiswould, of Birmingham, and Mr. Adams, of Birmingham, differed but little in composition from that now used, except that it was made wholly of scrap metal. This was gathered into a bloom and welded under tilt hammers, then drawn out to the required thickness by rolling, as will be afterwards described.

Wire twist, often made from a scelp of iron and steel scrap, had a certain vogue. It was also a custom of unscrupulous manufacturers to "paint" a plain iron barrel with the lap weld as described, in order to make it resemble a barrel manufactured of iron and steel, that is, of the more expensive Damascus iron. This practice continues for cheap muzzle-loaders; it has never been used on breech-loaders. The manufacture of gun iron barrels from scrap has now almost, if not entirely, died out. In the middle of this century no other metal was considered its equal, and from 1845 to 1855 John Clive's mill at Birmingham turned out very large quantities of high-class figured barrels.

In London the barrel-welding industry was never of great importance; since 1844 no gun-barrel welder has practised in the Metropolis. The last maker was W. Fullard, of Clerkenwell, who enjoyed a high reputation for all kinds of sporting gun barrels. The military barrels were obtained from the Midlands, whence, or from foreign centres, the figured barrels used by London makers are now imported. In the Midlands the barrel welders are not so numerous as they were, the demand for twisted barrels not being so great as formerly.

Cold-drawn steel barrels were made in 1865, and for the few years following. They were much superior to the plain iron lap-welded and other rolled barrels in use at that period. These barrels were made by forcing blocks of steel through dies by means of hydraulic pressure. Owing to the slowness of the process, and the great wear upon the machinery and tools necessary to their production, the company were unable to compete with barrels made on other methods, and they have long been unobtainable. The other processes of gun-making in past periods call for no special comment; the work done depended upon the skill of the artisan with hammer, file, drill, and burin, and the methods are so closely allied to the modern practice that the description of modern methods will apply equally to those

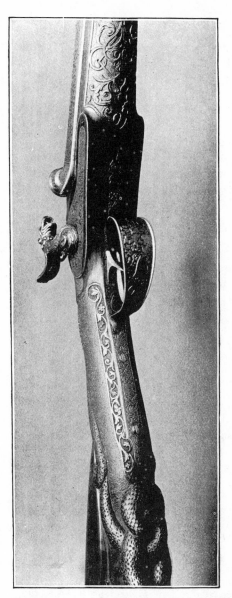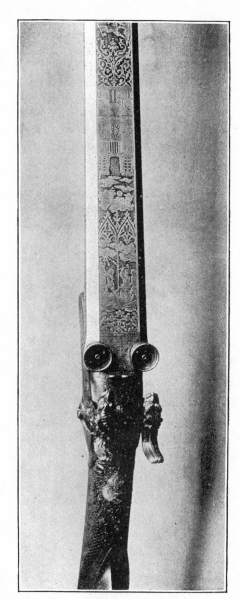

Percussion Belgian Gun, showing Ornamentation.

of other times, due allowance being made for the improvements in tools, and the aid which machinery has lent to do quickly what formerly was accomplished only by the expenditure of much time and labour.

The craftsmen of the old guilds, like their present-day equals, the trade unionists, made their mistakes. The result of one, as stated, was the loss to the Liége industry of the wheel-lock gun ; a more common result was the perpetuation of mediocrity. The men whose names are known were artists and inventors, rather than craftsmen. Chief among them was Lazarin Comminazo, a master among many fine workmen of Northern Italy in the seventeenth century. This school is renowned for the beauty in design and accurate execution of the ornamentation upon wheel-lock pistols.

In the production of fine barrels for fowling-pieces the Spanish smiths were long unexcelled and rivalled only by their contemporaries in Northern Italy. Nicolas Bis, the goldsmith to Philip V., enjoyed an enviable reputation, and his

Nicolas Bis.

Migona.
Gun-makers' Marks.

Gabriel del Algora.

barrels were sold at prices equalling £40 in the present coinage. He did not mount his barrels. Juan Sanchez de Mirvena, gun-maker to Philip III., is accredited the ablest artist of his day. Gabriel del Algora and Migona of Pistoja were also gunsmiths of the first rank, and of whose work specimens are still in request by collectors. Appended are facsimiles of the marks found on their arms.

Camillio Vittelli of Pistoja, the inventor of the pistol (1540), and Bossi of Rome, the inventor of the double barrel wheel-lock arquebus (1623), did more than any guild in developing fire-arms.

In Germany the wheel-lock was very popular. The workmanship of German arms of the seventeenth and eighteenth centuries—particularly in the ornamentation —is far inferior to the best work of Milan, Paris, and Madrid at corresponding periods ; but in Germany the progress, if slow, was general, and the best known

The late W. Greener shooting Wild Cattle in Chillingham Park.

names are famous rather on account ot the new mechanisms invented than by reason of the workmanship they displayed.

The ornamentation of fire-arms was an art apart from that of the gunsmith, although certain artists devoted their energies entirely to beautifying the work of the gunsmith. Jacquinet of Paris has left a book of the designs in use by the gun-makers of his day (1660), some specimens of which are reproduced from Mr. Quaritch's reprint.

The productions of Milan enjoyed the widest reputation; even in France a Milan piece was thought of as highly as in England. Pepys in his Diary (1667) mentions that French guns had a vogue among English gentry, also that a London gunsmith named Truelock possessed considerable reputation. F. Page, the gunsmith of Norwich, whose treatise on the art of shooting flying was the first of its kind produced in English, praises the Spanish barrel and the Milan fowling-piece, giving the results of some curious experiments made with barrels of different lengths in 1766—a date at which the English gunsmiths had barely commenced to compete seriously with the Continental manufacturers.

Liège has always been famous for the quantity rather than the quality of its productions. The makers there had much to contend against. Not only were the guilds all powerful until swept away by the French Revolution in 1789, but restrictions of varicus kinds were from time to time imposed, and under so many rulers it is surprising that the trade thrived. More than once the production of arms was altogether forbidden; then none were to be produced for one country; then none sent to another; now one kind of arm was prohibited, anon another variety, and even so late as during Napoleon's rule no guns other than fowling-pieces of less than 22 calibre could be made except to the order of his own Government or for his allies.

Lisbon, Copenhagen, Cracow, and Prague have all reared talented gun-makers of more than local reputation, and the gunsmiths of Bohemia during the first half of the present century obtained a reputation for workmanship and knowledge of technique which they have not outlived.

At the end of last century the Napoleonic wars afforded the English gun-makers an opportunity of wresting from their Continental competitors the supremacy traditionally theirs. By strenuous effort and directing their genius towards developing fire-arms as efficient weapons they ultimately succeeded. English makers sought to reduce the weight, improve the shooting powers, and perfect the lock mechanism of the sporting gun, and increase the range of the rifle and render it an efficient military arm.

In this connection much is due to the encouragement given by the Society of Arts, and in the published " Proceedings " of that admirable institution many proofs will be found of the early recognition of meritorious inventions connected with fire-arms.   It was from this society that Western Europe learned the secret of Damascus iron, a metal which had been used for many years as the material for gun-barrels— a gun dated 1613 with a browned Damascus barrel is in the Paris Museum—and the early employment of which by the English makers in its improved form probably did more than anything else to promote the popularity of English sporting guns.

The name best remembered among the gun-makers of this period is that of Joseph Manton, who was not only a clever and talented gunsmith, but an inventor not devoid of genius.   His guns were deservedly popular, and extraordinarily high prices were given for them, seventy guineas being his usual price.   He produced the best of flint-locks, and fitted them with numerous improvements.   The gravitating stops, to prevent accidental discharge whilst loading, were probably more highly esteemed than any of his inventions relating to self-priming and water-tight flash-pans.   Like all men of genius, he was occasionally absurd ; one particularly fatuous invention of his was a vent-hole which allowed the air to escape but not to enter.   He lost much money in litigation, and died poor at the age of sixty-nine.   This was in 1835, when Colonel Peter Hawker was at the zenith of his popularity.   This genial sportsman rendered Manton excellent service, and repeatedly eulogises Manton's work, both as practical gun-maker and inventor, in his " Instructions to Young Sportsmen."

Ezekiel Baker made many improvements in locks, sights, and bullet-moulds, and was an enthusiastic advocate of the rifle.   Other makers—as Nock, Durs, Egg, Wilkinson, and Smith—did much at this time to enhance the reputation of London as a centre of gun-making ; for they did not confine themselves wholly to one type of gun, but, by oft-repeated experiments, evolved improvements, not only in guns and gun parts, but in articles quite foreign to the business of gun-making.

The late W. Greener, of Newcastle and Birmingham, was one of this class.   Some of his more notable inventions relating to fire-arms are elsewhere noted ; he was also the patentee of the first electric light publicly used in England (1846), he improved the miner's safety lamp, invented a lifeboat which was self-righting by the use of water ballast, and gained a prize for a mechanical contrivance by which the four gates at railway crossings are worked simultaneously.   He was instrumental in improving the reputation of Birmingham as a gun-making centre, though his denunciations of "trash" made him many enemies, and his whole-hearted attacks upon the wardens of the Proof House were deeply resented, notwithstanding that they led to better administration, improved methods of proving, and the passing of the present Gun-Barrel Proof Act, which has done much to protect the public, and greatly advanced the interests of English gun-makers.

Good material and good workmanship he regarded as the secrets of successful gun-making. Regarding his own muzzle-loading percussion guns as near perfection as it was possible for arms to be, he was a strong opponent of all breech-loading systems. In this conservatism he was equalled by the majority of the London gun-makers, who, proud of the reputation achieved by Manton, Egg, and others,

Flint-lock made by Moorish Gunsmiths at the Author's Factory in 1885.

were content to adhere to the type of gun those masters of the craft had been so successful in making. One notable exception was the late Mr. Lang, who was among the first to adopt the Lefaucheux drop-down principle of breech-loading, and who saw clearly its good points and its possibilities. With reference to the opposition of noted makers, it should be stated that the breech-loaders when first introduced were badly made, they shot abominably, and the breech mechanisms were not only flimsily constructed, but the workmanship was poor; so poor indeed were they that much of the criticism written by W. Greener was in itself commendable. Mr. Greener wrote several treatises on fire-arms and their manufacture, the chief being "The Gun" (1835), "The Science of Gunnery" (1841), and "Gunnery in 1858." He died in 1869.

CHAPTER X.

MODERN METHODS OF GUN-MAKING.

THE MANUFACTURE OF IRON FOR GUN BARRELS.

GUN barrels may be made of plain iron, as described in the history of gun-making. As shot-gun barrels they are worthless with modern explosives. They may be made from solid steel, as are rifle barrels; or they may be made of figured iron —that is, of a mixture of iron and steel.

The method of producing this special material is as follows : Pig-iron obtained from a mixture of the best ores is placed in a furnace, melted, and cleansed from all dross by puddling—the dross, being much lighter than the iron, rises to the surface, and is skimmed off. When sufficiently cleansed, the draw-plates of the furnace are lowered, the heat reduced thereby, and the liquid iron whilst cooling gathered and worked into blooms of about 1 cwt. each. The puddler takes the bloom with a pair of tongs, runs with it to the tilt hammer and hands it over to the shingler, who, by dexterously turning the metal under the hammer, forms it into a square block and passes it to the roller; it is then passed through the various rolls until of the required size, and drawn out into a bar of about ten feet in length. The hammering under the heavy tilt condenses the metal, and causes the dross and scale to fly off. The rolling increases its ductility and tenacity by elongating the fibre.

If scrap steel is used, it is treated in the same way. But if new metal is employed, the finest qualities of rolled bars are chosen; the steels suitable are open hearth and ingot steels produced by modern methods, if low in carbon. On account of its purity and uniformity, best Swedish steel is most usually preferred. Steel is *not improved* by puddling.

Iron is improved—that is to say, purified—by the process of puddling; so it is usual to take bars of puddled iron, cut them into short lengths, and pile them into faggots. These faggots are heated in the draught furnace, welded under the tilt hammer, and the block of metal is reheated and hammered for the manufacture of the best barrels, to condense the fibre of the metal and increase the specific gravity. After being hammered, the blocks are rolled out into bars; these bars are again cut into equal lengths, laid and fastened into faggots, heated in the furnace, and welded together and rolled into thin, narrow strips. In the above processes the ends of the bloom, or extremities of the rods, are cut off and thrown aside, being less dense, and consequently useless for gun-iron.

The loss in the puddling is about 15 per cent., in the shingling and rolling about 14 per cent.; in reheating the metal it also loses considerably, making a loss of about 40 per cent.. in those three processes alone; and there are successions of similar losses in each further stage of the manufacture of iron. The proportionate amounts of the different descriptions of metals in a barrel determine its quality. The old-fashioned laminated steel was composed of nearly three parts of steel; best English Damascus and modern laminated steel contain over 60 per cent. of steel; and the best silver-steel Damascus contains nearly 75 per cent. of the best worked steel. The amount of steel is determined upon before making the metal into faggots for the last time; if for scelp barrels, the strips of iron are twice the thickness of the steel, the faggots being formed of alternate layers of iron and steel. In single iron Damascus barrels the proportion of iron used is not much less than the steel, but the metal for these common barrels does not pass through quite so many processes as that for the best barrels, and, although far superior in quality to ordinary iron, its tenacity and specific gravity is not so great as that of the very best gun-iron. In best Damascus barrels the iron and steel are mixed together systematically.

In the piling of the iron and steel, it is possible to so arrange the metals that many different figures—that is to say, direction of the grain of the metal—result. In the best silver-steel Damascus, used by the author, the exact proportions of iron and steel used are such as have been found by experiment to give the greatest strength; the figure is fine and uniform. By using more iron than steel, and keeping to the same arrangement of the metals, a very inferior barrel would result. The tenacity, durability, and beautiful figure of the barrels depend almost entirely on the proportions and arrangement of the steel and iron, the desiderata being the placing of the iron in the best position to give the regular and fine figure of the finished barrel.

In piling the iron for the ordinary Damascus twist strips of iron and steel are laid upon each other alternately. In another figure the iron, in lieu of being in strips, is in rods, which are arranged so that in cross section they resemble a chequer-board.

In producing chain twist, diamond twist, and irregular-figured and fancy-figured barrels the iron rods are differently piled. They may be of hexagonal section, or rhomboidal, or some square and others parallelopipedonical. Combinations of strips and squares are common on the Continent, where also, instead of plain rods or bars, the iron and steel used for piling is sometimes of v, l, t and other sections, or combinations of various figures. There seems to be no limit to the varieties of figure obtainable by the arrangement of the iron and steel in the faggot, and afterwards suitably working the metal.

The next process is to heat and weld the faggot of piled iron and steel and roll them into rods of the sizes required by the welder.

The welder may, for a common barrel, have the metal in the shape of a strip about ¾ inch wide and of rhomboidal section. For a figured barrel it is necessary to have the rods of square section, and to heat them and twist them upon themselves —a process which turns the grain of the alternate strips of iron and steel running longitudinally from end to end of the rod in a spiral direction.

In twisting the rods care is taken to keep the edges of the iron and steel strips to the outside, for it is the twisting of the different metals that gives the various figures in the finished barrel. The steel, being hard, resists the acids, and retains a white or light brown hue, whilst the iron, or softer metal, is so acted upon by the acid as to be changed into a dark brown or black colour. The manner in which the strips are laid and welded together will be found described in the chapter on "Barrel Welding."

Eighteen pounds of prepared gun-iron are required to weld an ordinary pair of 12-gauge barrels, which, when finished, weigh, with the ribs, lumps, and loops, but little over 3½ lbs. After bearing in mind this fact, and considering the great expense and loss of expensive steel and iron attending the manufacture of the metal, and the cost of welding of best barrels, it will no longer be a matter of wonderment that best guns are expensive to produce.

GUN BARREL WELDING.

The methods practised in manufacturing Damascus barrels differ but in unimportant details from each other. The welding of barrels by hand is still carried on in the author's factory, and the various processes of barrel-making as employed there will be first described and illustrated.

The square rods of prepared iron are first twisted to give the Damascus figure. The rods are about four feet long, and are placed in the forge fire until about eighteen inches of the rod is brought to a red heat, when one end is thrust into a

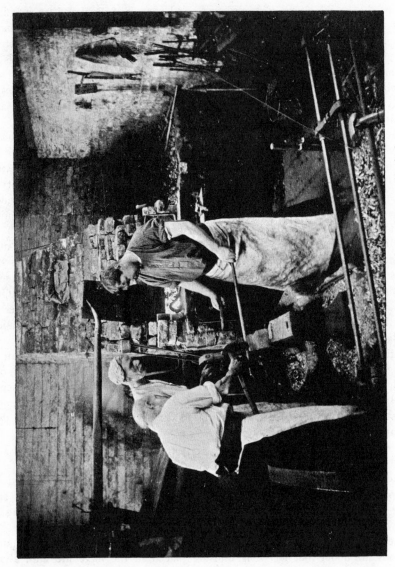

Gun Barrel Welding at W. W. Greener's Gun Factory, Birmingham.

square hole in a block made fast to a frame, and the other end fixed into a movable head at the other end of the frame; a rotary motion is then given to the movable head by means of a winch-handle and cog-wheels; the rod, being square, cannot turn round with the head, so is twisted in itself. The rod is carefully watched whilst twisting, and should one part commence to twist more rapidly than another, a man is ready with a pair of tongs to hold that part of the rod, so that it is prevented from twisting. This process is repeated until the whole rod is perfectly twisted, and a regular figure in the barrel insured.

When finished twisting, the rod will be round, except the squares at each end where held in the block and head, and the four-feet rod will have become shortened to about three feet three inches, and have about eight turns to the inch. All Damascus barrels must be made of twisted rods, whilst plain twist or scelp barrels are made from plain straight rods or ribands.

Without this twisting of the rod the finished barrel would have the appearance of a wire twist barrel, or it might be of a plain barrel if the top or bottom of the rod, instead of one of the sides, was kept to the outside of the barrel. By twisting the metal the grain is so arranged that it appears on the outside of the finished barrel in the form of a number of irregular links or circles.

The rod prepared, it is either joined to other rods or coiled and welded into a barrel singly.

The cheapest Damascus barrels (single-iron stub Damascus) are made from a single twisted bar, rolled out into a riband $\frac{7}{8}$ of an inch by $\frac{1}{8}$ for the fore-end of the barrel, and $\frac{7}{8}$ by $\frac{1}{4}$ for the breech-end.

Two-iron stub Damascus barrels are made from two twisted rods, each $\frac{3}{8}$ square, and welded together and rolled into a riband $\frac{5}{8}$ by $\frac{1}{16}$ for the fore-part, and $\frac{5}{8}$ by $\frac{3}{16}$ for the breech-end, with the twisted spirals in opposite directions.

Three-iron stub Damascus barrels are made from three twisted rods, each $\frac{3}{8}$ by $\frac{7}{16}$, and laid and rolled together with the spirals, as shown in the illustration; forming a riband of $\frac{1}{2}$ an inch by $\frac{7}{16}$ for the breech-ends, and $\frac{1}{2}$ an inch by $\frac{3}{16}$ for the muzzle-piece.

Best laminated steel barrels are twisted, and the rods welded in the same manner as the stub Damascus, but the rods are composed of superior metal containing a larger percentage of steel.

In laminated steel and stub Damascus barrels it is not usual to use more than three rods in their manufacture. Fine Damascus barrels, as manufactured by the Belgians, are occasionally made from four or six rods together, but three are sufficient to give a very fine figure.

Gun-barrel Iron, Twisted, and Laid into a Riband.

Two-Iron Damascus Barrel.

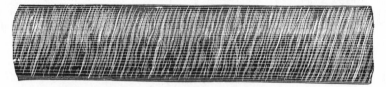

Scelp Gun-barrel.

Three-Iron Stub Damascus Barrel.

Single-Iron Damascus Barrel.

The true English Damascus barrel is prepared from three rods, twisted as described and put together as shown in the twisted riband, and is known technically as three-iron Damascus ; the silver-steel Damascus is similarly made, but of different metal piled in a different order.

The rods having been twisted, and the required number welded together, they are sent to the iron-mill and rolled at a red heat into ribands, which have both edges bevelled the same way. There are usually two ribands required for each barrel, one riband or strip to form the breech-end, and another, slightly thinner, to form the fore, or muzzle, part of the barrel.

Silver-steel Damascus Barrel.

Upon receiving the ribands of twisted iron, the welder first proceeds to twist them into a spiral form. This is done upon a machine of simple construction, consisting simply of two iron bars, one fixed and the other loose ; in the latter there is a notch or slot to receive one end of the riband. When inserted, the bar is turned round by a winch-handle. The fixed bar prevents the riband from going round, so that it is bent and twisted over the movable rod like the pieces of leather round a whip-stock. The loose bar is removed, the spiral taken from it, and the same process repeated with another riband.

The ribands are usually twisted cold, but the breech-ends, if heavy, have to be brought to a red heat before it is possible to twist them, no cogs being used. When very heavy barrels are required, three ribands are used—one for the breech-end, one for the centre, and one for the muzzle-piece.

The ends of the ribands, after being twisted into spirals, are drawn out taper and coiled round with the spiral until the extremity is lost, as shown in the representation of a coiled breech-piece of Damascus iron.

The coiled riband is next heated, a steel mandrel inserted in the muzzle end, and the coil is welded by hammering. Three men are required—one to hold and turn the coil upon the grooved anvil, and two to strike. The foreman, or the one who holds the coil, has also a small hammer with which he strikes the coil, to show the others in which place to strike. When taken from the fire the coil is first beaten upon an iron plate fixed in the floor, and the end opened upon a swage, or the pene of the anvil, to admit of the mandrel being inserted.

When the muzzle or fore-coil has been heated, jumped up, and hammered until thoroughly welded, the breech-end or coil, usually about six inches long, is joined to it. The breech-coil is first welded in the same manner, and a piece is cut out of each coil; the two ribands are welded together and the two coils are joined into one, and form a barrel. The two coils being joined, and all the welds made perfect, the barrels are heated, and the surplus metal removed with a float; the barrels are then hammered until they are black or nearly cold, which finishes the process.

This hammering greatly increases the density and tenacity of the metal, and the wear of the barrel depends in a great measure upon its being properly performed.

When the barrels are for breech-loaders, the flats are formed on the undersides of the breech-ends. If an octagon barrel is required, it is forged in this form upon

Portion of Gun-barrel Coil.

a properly shaped anvil; in rifles the barrels are welded from thicker ribands and welded upon smaller mandrels.

Another method of making twist barrels is practised in Birmingham, and may be shortly described.

The iron is twisted in much the same way as that already described, but steam-power is used to turn the winch instead of hand-power. The forge-fires are blown by a steam-fan, instead of the old-fashioned bellows, and the welding is done by one man instead of three. This is accompanied by having a tilt-hammer close to the forge regulated to give sharp, quick, short blows, and capable of being thrown in and out of gear with the foot. The welder is also provided with an anvil, swages, mandrels, etc. When he removes the coil from the fire, he has only to knock in a mandrel, straighten the coil on the anvil, jump it close by striking it on the floor in the usual manner, and place it under the tilt, reheating the coil, and repeating the process until the barrel is properly finished. The appearance of barrels so welded is not so good as that of those hammered by hand, but they are strong and sound, and, on account of less care and labour being bestowed on their production, they are cheaper than hand-forged barrels.

The latest method of making the plainer twist barrels is to treat the iron for twisting, and the coils, in a furnace instead of a breeze fire. The theory is that the metal is less liable to be burned, the heat being uniform, and freedom from greys and faulty welds thereby ensured. Experience does not fully bear out the theory. Possibly more can yet be done in this line towards producing a perfectly welded and clear barrel.

FOREIGN TWIST BARRELS.

Damascus iron barrels are forged in Belgium and at other gun-making centres of the Continent by the same methods as practised in England. The chief difference between English and foreign welded barrels exists in the quality of the materials; iron of local manufacture being that generally employed. Another difference is that barrels of a smaller figure and barrels of fancy figures, already alluded to in the paragraph on iron-making, are frequently produced by French, Belgian, and German welders.

Softness is the characteristic of Belgian iron; it is found in all their iron manu-factures, and is particularly noticeable and objectionable in their barrels. The welders prefer the soft metal, as being easier to manipulate, welding more freely, and containing fewer surface flaws than hard metal, into the composition of which steel largely enters. There is, comparatively, little steel in the Belgian barrel; there are even barrels in which there is no steel, two different qualities of iron serving to produce that distinction which is necessary to produce figure in the finished barrel.

The barrel-welders of Belgium are chiefly located at or near Liège. The very best barrel-makers who manufacture for the London, Berlin, and Vienna markets are to be found at Chaudfontaine or Nessonvaux, both places a few miles from Liège. Their method of welding is much the same as that practised by the best English welders, but they work at a smaller forge, and, instead of breeze, use a mixture of coal-dust and clay. The fires being much smaller, the barrels are heated only a few inches at a time, so that greater labour has to be bestowed upon their manufacture.

The greatest care is taken to keep the anvils and tools perfectly clean and free from scale, so that no foreign matter can get between the coils and thus affect the soundness of the welds.

The type of barrel, which is peculiarly their own, is the fine figured or six-stripe Damascus; in this the figure is very minute, as shown in the illustration, and is produced in the following manner:—The welders take thirty-two alternate bars of iron and steel, and have them rolled into a sheet $\frac{3}{16}$th of an inch in thickness;

the sheet is then split by a machine into square rods. These rods are then twisted after the method of the English welders already described; but to such an extent that the rods resemble the threads of a fine screw, there being as many as eighteen complete turns to the inch. Six of these rods are then welded to each other side by side and rolled into a riband, and the result is a figure so fine

Fine Stripe Belgian Damascus Barrel.

that it appears no larger than the eye of a needle, and requires special care in browning to obtain markings which can be distinguished.

For these fine barrels and for some others the old plan of welding on a chemise is still in use. The other old plan of plating or welding a thin coating of Damascus iron upon a barrel of plain iron has been abandoned, save for very heavy barrels for

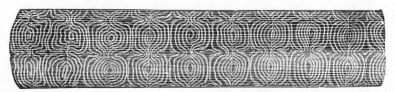

Two-Iron or "Boston" Damascus Barrel.

duck-guns, etc., which are still not infrequently welded of the cheaper scelp, or plain twist iron, then coated with fine figured iron.

The regular Belgian barrel of commerce is the double-iron Damascus, "two-iron," or "Boston"—the same barrel by whichever designation known. It differs from the English two-iron Damascus in showing fewer white or light-coloured streaks, and being usually of coarser figure, obtained by piling larger rods in the faggot and again not rolling them to so small a section as is the practice of the English masters.

At St. Etienne in France, where a manufactory for sporting fire-arms was founded early in the fifteenth century, the Belgian models are followed and the iron of the district is soft and ductile. One plan much used in this district, but by no means original, is the forming of barrels of two twisted rods to one untwisted ; the appearance is that of a " barber's pole," a distinct broad stripe of straight-grained metal running spirally round the barrel from end to end between a broader band of curled Damascus figuring.

The only centres at which Damascus barrels are made are, in addition to those already cited, Brescia in northern Italy, and Suhl in Prussia.

VARIETIES AND QUALITIES OF TWIST BARRELS.

In the foregoing descriptions of the methods of manufacturing twist barrels it is stated incidentally that some kinds are superior to others. The comparative strength of gun barrels and of the material employed in their manufacture, the merits and disadvantages of chosen varieties, will be found stated in detail later, but as the method of manufacture, as well as the material employed, affect the quality of the barrel, it is advisable to state here that, so far as known, the strongest forged or twist barrel is the laminated steel now usually termed " stub-Damascus," made of three twisted rods to the riband.

The word laminated, as the designation of a gun barrel, arose from the fact that early in the last century thin strips, plates, or *laminæ* of steel, piled alternately with iron strips or plates, formed the composite metal from which they were made. They differ from Damascus in so far as the iron and steel are differently arranged in the pile, so that instead of a decided curl in the figure there is only what may be termed " herring-bone" lines running spirally round the barrel from end to end. Technically, laminated steel is a name metallurgists apply to faulty steel. It has been used in the gun trade for more than half a century in quite a different sense, as here stated.

By rolling the rods too fine before twisting, by twisting too much, or by twisting to a degree the particular metal so treated will not bear, the material of the finished barrel is weakened. This, apart from any possible faults in the forming—that is, welding and shaping—of the barrel itself.

Over-twisting, over-heating, and the endeavour to produce a fine-looking barrel at a low price result in weakened material.

In the twist barrel the iron and steel must be so arranged that perfect welds may be easily made ; and so disposed that the fibres of steel and iron intermingled shall support each other when the strain of the explosion has to be borne by the barrel. Steel of the hardness—that is to say, steel as high in carbon—employed in the manufacture of Damascus iron would be too brittle to withstand the shock of the explosion if used alone ; on the other hand, the iron alone would be too soft and the barrel would bulge. By combining the two metals in the best manner, so that neither loses its character, they together give to the twist barrel sufficient hardness to withstand bulging ; sufficient elasticity to ensure that the barrel, after the expansion produced by the force of the explosion, shall return to its previous calibre and that high tenacity which prevents the bursting of the barrel by the sudden shock.

The mechanical structure of the twist-barrel, not less than the purity of the metals employed, enhances the strength.

Some barrels of good material may have their strength lessened by faulty arrangement of that material, whilst barrels made of much inferior material will yet be stronger because of the better use made of that material by arranging it with judgment. So far as can be explained, without too greatly indulging in technical minutiæ, the best proportions of iron and steel can be arranged to best advantage in what is known as the three-iron barrels whether the iron be piled to give a curly figure when twisted, or to give the plain, straight, short-lined figure of the "laminated" steel, is quite immaterial. One is as good as the other. Four-stripe barrels are not so good, unless the barrel is heavier, thicker, and larger than ordinary, when, of course, a point would be reached when the four-stripe would equal the other. In like manner the two-stripe is inferior, though, perhaps, not to the same extent. The Belgian six-stripe barrels, apart from the softness of the material of which they are made, are over-twisted. Many of the fancy-figured barrels are not improved by the manner in which the iron and steel are combined, but the reverse. The advantage claimed for the St. Etienne barrel, that by the combination of the Damascus with the plain twist greater tenacity in both directions is obtainable, is yet to be proved, whilst the method is decidedly disadvantageous on other grounds.

In the trials of barrels by the Birmingham Proof House—barrels of thirty-nine different varieties obtainable by the Birmingham trade—the first place is given to the group of English "laminated" steel barrels of three strips. The next best of the twist-barrel groups is the "English Damascus" in two strips ; the next best "English hand-forged Damascus" in four strips ; then "English two-strip Damascus" ; and then "English Damascus" in three strips ; then English laminated steel in two strips. The first group of foreign-made twist-barrels is the "Pointillé" (a fancy figure), eighteenth down on the list in order of merit ; foreign "Damascus

Crollé," in three and in four strips, come next, and have the same figure of merit, both being placed twenty-fifth on the list. At the same trials, when individual barrels were tested to bursting or bulging to the extent of ·01 inch, the first place in the order of merit was occupied by "English variegated Damascus," two-strip; "English Damascus," three-strip; and "English Damascus," two-strip again, all three barrels withstanding exactly the same test. The foreign "Damascus" two-strip, and the same in three-strip, passed equally to the seventh place, whilst last in order of merit were the foreign fancy figured "Pointillé" and the foreign "Crollé Damascus" four-strip barrels.

This report issued in 1891 only confirms what the author wrote in earlier editions of this book with respect to the relative strengths of twist-barrels, and has now repeated more concisely.

A figured barrel, notwithstanding the fineness of the figure and the apparently high quality of workmanship, is no indication of trustworthiness, much less of excellence and unusual strength. To obtain barrels combining the utmost strength with lightness and beauty, the best way is to purchase or order from a gun-maker of repute and leave the choice to him. It is not always that the type of barrel best suited to one calibre or weight will prove so advantageous when used in the construction of guns of other calibres or weights. There is only one wide difference in the practice of the English gun-maker and his Continental competitor when choosing a barrel for a particular purpose : with the English maker the figure of the barrel is the last thing to be considered when determining the type most fit for the particular purpose, whereas with the foreign manufacturer it is usually the first, and often the only, consideration. The English maker takes a barrel that will do best ; the foreign maker the barrel that will look best.

The decline of the English trade in Damascus barrels is undoubtedly due to the introduction of choke-boring. Prior to 1875 Belgian-made Damascus barrels, owing to their handsome appearance, were used by many English gun-makers, amongst whom were some of the best London makers. These barrels proved quite satisfactory for cylinder-bored guns, but were incapable of withstanding the heavier strain of the choke, and numerous complaints were made of such barrels bulging at the muzzle. English Damascus barrels contained a larger percentage of steel, consequently they were harder and withstood this strain better, but as London gunmakers were then dependent upon the Midlands for their supplies it became exceedingly difficult to obtain sufficient of these barrels to meet their requirements, and as at this time Whitworth steel was giving great satisfaction for rifle barrels, a leading London gun-maker decided to adopt it for shot-gun barrels. As their merits became better known steel barrels gradually supplanted those of Damascus and laminated steel, until to-day nearly all the best guns are fitted with steel barrels ; these can be made lighter than Damascus, and offer greater resistance to the heavier pressures exerted by modern nitros ; they do not bend or dent so easily as Damascus barrels, and the trade in the latter has dwindled away until it is now exceedingly difficult to procure reliable English barrels of either Damascus or laminated steel suitable for best-quality guns.

WELDLESS BARRELS.

In addition to the seemingly large variety of figured barrels, there is now an even greater assortment of weldless barrels available for shot-guns. These are, for the most part, of steel ; some drilled, some drawn, some forged, of steels of many qualities and made by different processes.

First as to the history of the weldless barrel, and its increasing popularity.

One of the greatest difficulties with which a gun-maker has to contend is the "grey" in gun barrels. The "grey" is a defect of small actual importance, but decidedly a blemish on a fine weapon and an eyesore in every description of gun barrel.

The numerous twistings and weldings of gun-iron rods and ribands are fully detailed in the description of the barrel-welding processes, and it must have occurred to the reader that the Damascus barrel is one mass of welds from breech to muzzle. This is so. Unfortunately a certain amount of burnt metal, or scale, is imbedded within some of these welds, and in the finished barrel this fragment of scale forms a "grey," or small speck of useless material, which will not colour in harmony with the other part of the barrel, but is made more apparent by the finishing processes of polishing and browning. These "greys" may appear some time after the gun has been in use, the hard metal composing the barrel being eaten into by rust, or the thin coating over the "grey" being worn away. They are developed in the inside by the chemical action of the powder gases, and are practically ineradicable. Sportsmen must not imagine that "greys" weaken a barrel to any appreciable extent, and their development in a gun, after some months' or some years' wear, in no way reflects upon the reputation of the gun-maker.

A barrel eaten right through with rust, at or near the muzzle, may be fired with perfect safety ; consequently a "grey" is not to be regarded as an element of danger ; and barrels after thirty years' wear, or after firing upwards of 100,000 shots, are safe to use, providing they are free from dents, bruises, and rust inside.

Best quality barrels can be ruined—and many have been—in a couple of seasons by rough, careless usage, firing when dented, and being allowed to rust inside and out.

A welded barrel will not stand a blow given sideways. A knock against a hard substance will dent one barrel and frequently break the other in the weld. Many more guns are ruined by hard knocks than by hard wear.

Owing to the great difficulty in procuring perfectly welded barrels, gun-makers are now discarding tubes of the Damascus variety for those of solid steel which are free from greys and blemishes, and if carefully chosen and tested will fill every requirement of the sportsman; in fact, guns of every quality, from the cheapest to the best, are being fitted with barrels made from one or another of the numerous brands of steel available. The harder the Damascus barrel the greater the liability to "greys," and a soft barrel will not make a fine shooting gun.

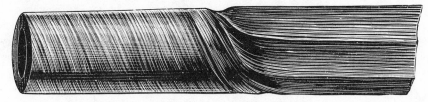

Greener's Solid-Weldless-Twist Gun Barrel.

It is possible to have a twisted weldless barrel. Some years ago the author produced his "solid weldless twist," a figured barrel which is admirably adapted for sporting and other rifles and in every way suitable for shot-guns. The grain runs spirally and the figure is similar to that of the wire twist. The illustration shows clearly the method of manufacture from ordinary gun-barrel iron. The twisting closes the grain of the iron, making it more dense towards the centre, thus presenting an even solid surface for rifling; outside the grain runs spirally from end to end.

Of the steels used for shot-gun barrels, the best known is Whitworth's fluid compressed steel. This is a cast steel; the ingot whilst in a liquid or a semi-liquid state is submitted to pressure, with a view to eliminating blow-holes. The top and bottom of the ingot are cut off and thrown aside as usual. Eminent metallurgists contend that in the process of cooling the contraction of the ingot is so great that no pressure which can be brought to act upon it by mechanical means can affect the metal—at any rate, beyond a few inches from the surface. The process is therefore by some regarded as quite superfluous. On the other hand, it is generally allowed that the Whitworth steel is of excellent quality, and it has been used for barrels for so many years that its superiority for that purpose may be taken as fully proven.

The Whitworth steel is to be ordinarily distinguished from other steels by its brand, and by that alone. This mark is a " wheatsheaf," and London gun-makers who have sold guns with these barrels for many years now have their barrels with this registered trade mark stamped on the under side and the ordinary lettering " Whitworth's steel," etc., on the top of the barrel or the top rib. Whitworth steel is higher in carbon than many steels used for gun barrels, but it is sufficiently ductile to allow of drilling.

Steel made by the Siemens-Martin process has been used successfully for shot-gun barrels as well as rifles. So, too, tubes of basic open hearth steel, made from hematite pig and scrap, and carburized by Darby's filtration process, were tested at the Birmingham Proof House in the trials already referred to and obtained a high figure of merit.

Steel barrels may be made by drilling them from the ordinary rolled bar ; they may be drawn by rolling out pierced blanks ; they may even be rolled hollow by the Mannesmann process, or they may be forged, then drilled.

The quality of the barrel depends less upon the method of forming the barrel than the quality of the metal used—the reverse of the twist-barrel, where manipulation is all important.

In the choice of a suitable steel, actual experience is a surer guide than the indications of theory as to the composition which ought to be the best for the purpose.

The author uses a brand of metal to which the name of Greener's "Wrought Steel" has been given, which steel he has found specially suited to the requirements of the gun-maker for shot-gun barrels : in this steel the metal is not drawn, but is forged out of a solid bar, and drilled its whole length. Barrels so made are of close metal, stronger and denser than any obtainable by other means.

The "Wrought Steel" recommended is made of a homogeneous metal, of very fine quality, and admirably adapted by its great tenacity, or tensile strength, for use in gun barrels. It has been thoroughly tested by the author, as well as at the Government Proof House, with very heavy charges, viz. 28 drams of powder and $4\frac{1}{2}$ ounces of shot, this charge being equal to nine ordinary charges of powder and four charges of shot. This test and many others it withstands perfectly.

Unlike "cast-steel" barrels of the old type, "Wrought Steel" barrels bulge instead of breaking, and increased strain produces an open burst similar to that of a welded barrel, instead of a sharp break or a longitudinal rip, as is found to result with imperfect steel barrels. The quality of the metal is such that it will stand successively more than double the strain to which a sportsman can submit his gun with fair usage. And it will not "rip" or "crack," however sharp may be the explosive used.

The author has made many experiments with various explosives, in order to test thoroughly the fitness of this steel for gun barrels, and the results prove that there is no material which will excel it, and, as the illustration shows, when tested to a bursting strain, the break which follows the bulging of the barrel is similar in character to the failure of Damascus under like circumstances.

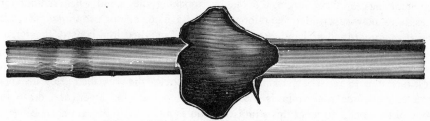

Bulges and Burst in a Barrel of "Wrought Steel."

The bulges were caused by placing a small charge of shot between two felt wads (first a thick felt, then the shot, then the thin felt) at the spot where the bulges are, and firing an ordinary charge from the gun.

The burst was effected by increasing the charge of shot between the wads; the bulges appeared about fifteen inches from the breech end after firing.

As many as five thick wads may be placed in any part of the barrel, and the gun fired without causing a bulge, but experiments prove that even the small quantity of $\frac{1}{8}$ oz. shot placed between wads at any place in the barrel will cause a bulge even as near as nine inches from the breech. The different sizes of the bulges in the illustration were caused by different charges of shot. The shape of the burst indicates the extent of bulging before bursting. The illustration is reduced to half-size.

In choosing steel for gun barrels, many things have to be considered. The author attaches much more importance to the iron from which the steel is made than the amount of carbon contained in it. "Wrought Steel" is made from the very toughest iron that can be procured, and as much carbon is used as can be allowed to admit of the drilling and boring of the barrel, so that the barrel is both hard and tough. These "Wrought Steel" barrels will stand being heated for brazing, without deterioration. Messrs. Krupp have introduced a steel which has many excellent qualities, and there are several other brands of equally suitable steel available for gun barrels.

OTHER METALS USED IN GUN MANUFACTURE.

The furniture of the gun was formerly made of swaff iron—that is, chippings, filings, borings, etc., of the iron barrels and other parts, collected, re-welded and forged. The material now most used is either puddled iron, ingot iron, or mild steel, containing 0·15 of carbon. The ingot iron is preferred as being clearer than puddled iron. Mild steel, when case-hardened, is quite suitable for breech-action bodies. The bolts are usually of cast steel.

Stampings, or drop forgings, made by knocking the metal when red-hot into dies, have now superseded hand-forged parts, save for one or two minor pieces, as the trigger-guard. For hand-forging "best best" puddled iron is used, the forging performed in much the same manner as in the ordinary blacksmith's shop.

The desideratum of good forging is to get the grain of the iron to run in the best direction to resist the strain given to the article when finished ; for instance, in a gun hammer the strain is along the nose, across the finger, and down the body of the cock ; to meet this strain the iron is bent with the grain running up the body of the cock, and split at the top, one half being bent at an acute angle to form the finger.

Stamping is accomplished in the following manner : A model of the article to be stamped is first made, and one half let into a steel block called a die, the other half into another steel block or die, one die forming the bottom, the other the top. Die-sinking, as it is called, is a business of itself, and is applicable to many trades besides that of gun-making.

The dies when finished are hardened, and fixed in a stamp worked by hand and foot for small work, and by steam for bodies, fore-ends, and other heavy forgings. The top die is worked by fastening it into a hammer of wrought or cast iron ; this hammer is carried up between two perpendicular rods to the height of 6 or 7 feet, by the aid of a belt or rope over a pulley. The top die is raised, and let fall on the bottom die, just at the moment that the forger places the iron to form the article, at a welding heat, over the bottom die, and the great weight forces the iron into the top and bottom die, forming the articles to the shape made in the dies. The man working the stamp hammer has it perfectly under his control, and can give a light blow or a heavy one as required.

Stamped work is especially advantageous where the articles have to be machined afterwards, as, all being the same size, they fit evenly into the holders.

GUN-MAKING PROCESSES.

As in the ordinary breech-loading hammer gun there are ninety-five separate pieces, it is evident that to construct the gun economically there must be considerable division of labour. It would be tedious, in a book not intended for the instruction of the master gun-maker in his craft, to describe in detail how each piece can be best made, or how the whole can be most advantageously assembled. The processes of chief interest to those who use guns are those by which the gun is made particularly serviceable as a sporting weapon. By knowing how the gun is bored, and by learning in what manner the barrels are put together, the gun user may be able to distinguish a good gun from one of inferior quality ; will understand better how a gun should be used, and will be able to form a close estimate as to the capabilities both of the various mechanisms of which it is composed and of the completed gun as a sporting weapon. It is not to be supposed that gun-making as an art can be learned by reading how a gun is, or should be, made ; but the technicalities of gun-making may be explained, and, when understood, should enable the users of guns to choose arms likely best to fill their requirements.

BORING, STRAIGHTENING, AND GRINDING.

The gun barrel, whether forged, rolled, or drawn, is known technically as a *tube.* The first process to which the rough-forged tube is subjected is the rough boring. The rough-boring bench is similar to the fine-boring bench illustrated. The head carrying the bit revolves rapidly, and the tube, fixed in a carrier, is forced towards the head by means of a hand lever used with a rack on the bench as a fulcrum. The bit is a square rod of steel, slightly tapered at the point, and is usually about five feet in length. The process of boring is as follows :—

The barrel to be bored is fixed in the carriage, a bit of suitable size selected, and, by means of the rack and crowbar, the bit is forced right through the barrel. A bit of larger dimensions is then introduced and passed through, and others of still larger dimensions, until the whole of the scales are removed and the barrel is bored to the required size. Should the scales not be bored out' the barrel is returned to the welder, who heats it and hammers down that portion of the barrel in which the scales remain, after which it is re-bored. During the process of rough-boring, a stream of cold water is kept playing on the barrel to keep it cool.

The *setting*, or straightening, of the barrel has then to be effected—a nice process, on the proper execution of which the utility of the arm, whether shot-gun or rifle, largely depends. Previous to 1795 there was no reliable method of ascertaining when a barrel was or was not perfectly straight. The barrels of the finest ancient guns were usually far from straight. Some years ago a fine public collection of old small arms was examined by an expert barrel-maker, and it was found that in the whole collection, which includes some of the choicest specimens of the most renowned makers of mediæval times, there was but one barrel that was then, or had ever been, even approximately straight—in the sense of the perfect straightness which is now obtainable; whilst the greater portion were, and always had been, decidedly crooked.

The old way was to look along the outside, and set the barrel as straight as possible from the *outside*. About 1795, however, a barrel-maker of Birmingham, named Parsons, introduced a plan of straightening barrels from the inside. His method consisted in stretching a string or fine wire inside the barrel from end to end, and touching the side at each end. He then hammered that side of the barrel until it touched all along the string. The string was then moved to the opposite side of the barrel, and if it touched all along the string it was straight. The same process was repeated on the top and bottom sides of the barrel. A few years afterwards, the method of shading the insides of gun barrels was discovered. This simple and reliable plan has since been universally adopted as the standard.

To determine if a barrel is straight, the setter holds it a few inches from his eye, with one end pointing towards the top of a high shop-window. The rays of light being horizontal, and the barrel at a slight angle, it shows about half the bore in shadow; if the shade is irregular the barrel is crooked; if the shade is perfectly level from breech to muzzle, on the barrel being turned round, the barrel must be a perfectly straight one. To straighten a barrel, the setter should note where the swellings appear on the shade, and strike the barrel in that place, with a hammer, upon a hollow anvil. Some setters straighten from the indentations in the shade, in which case the barrel must be struck on the opposite side to the one shown on the indentation in the shade. A skilful setter can make a barrel perfectly straight with a few taps of the hammer. A simple expedient for detecting the straightness of a gun-barrel is as follows: Place the barrel at a slight angle upon two fixed stands; take a small frame and cover with tissue-paper, and place the same at about six feet distance from the muzzle of barrel with a light behind it; point the barrel towards the top edge of frame, and a dark shade will at once be seen upon the bottom side of the barrel.

Turn the barrel round upon the stands, and if the shade keeps a perfectly true edge, the barrel is straight. Place at any point between the stands, about three inches below the barrel, a lighted lamp or candle. This will cause the barrel to bend, and an irregularity in the shade line will be immediately observed ; upon the light being removed, the barrel will return to its original form, or very nearly so. If the barrel is of steel (as a rifle-barrel), and not twisted, it may be experimented upon with the candle four or five times, and the barrel will return to its original straightness.

The importance of the invention and the value of the method cannot be over-rated ; and it would be impossible to obtain the extraordinary precision of the match-rifles of England and America unless a perfectly straight barrel could be made. The first order for Government *rifles* was executed in Birmingham about 1816, at which time the art of setting barrels was so little known that many of these barrels were far from straight.

In 1892 Mr. J. Rigby, the superintendent of the Government Small Arms Factory at Enfield, produced, at the Institute of Civil Engineers, a newly-designed machine for detecting any crookedness in rifle barrels. It consisted of an accurate lathe-bed and heads, a mandrel which exactly fitted the barrel at the breech end, and at a point in or near the centre. The barrel to be tested is placed upon this mandrel, the mandrel stretched tightly between the heads of the lathe, and the barrel turned on the mandrel. A needle, pivoted on the machine, has a point pressed against the inside of the barrel, and the needle behind the pivot is extended so that the long arm acts as an indicator, or actuates a mirror or other mechanism, which, by the reflection of its light or other movement, is supposed to show whether or not the barrel is straight. The indicator, for instance, showed when the needle-point was moved by the barrel from the position it had assumed ; as it followed the barrel, it must have been that the inside of the circumference of the barrel, in lieu of describing a circle, was describing an ellipse ; therefore the barrel was not straight. The same deflection would be shown if the bore of the barrel instead of being quite circular had been slightly oval ; consequently the machine as a test failed to detect what the eye of a practised workman would at once have discovered.

When the boring and straightening is completed, the tube is placed in a lathe, the extreme breech end and the muzzle turned to the required thickness, and is next removed to the grinding shop, where, on large rough stones, revolving rapidly, the tube is ground down to the turning marks and other gauges. The grinders have a method of allowing the tube to revolve in their hands at half the rate of the stone, and have acquired such skill that many would be puzzled to say whether or not the finished tube had been turned or ground. Again and again tubes taken from the grindstone and spun between dead centres on the lathe have been found almost as true as a rod could be turned.

Great difficulty exists in turning a light tube such as used for gun barrels ; the method employed with rifle barrels fails because the lighter barrel is more easily moved from the true centre by the pressure of the cutter, so that a tube turned with the best possible appliances is often more crooked than one roughly ground by the "rule of thumb" method described, and found to be the best in practice.

The tube, after being smoothed to take out the marks of the stone, has a plug screwed on the breech, and is sent to the Proof House and submitted to the test prescribed for barrels of its size, and the charge of powder and load of lead used are given in the Scale of Proof Charges in the next chapter. This first, or provisional proof, is a gun-maker's proof ; it determines, or should determine, whether or not the barrel is flawed. If passed, the barrel-welder's liability ends.

SHOOTING.

The shooting powers of the gun depend chiefly upon the shape and finish given to the interior of the barrel by the processes of chambering, fine-boring, choke-boring, lap-polishing, etc., performed at various stages of the gun's manufacture, but described here consecutively.

It must be borne in mind that prior to the introduction of breech-loading the majority of the shot-guns and smooth-bore muskets made were very roughly bored ; the leading gun-makers certainly endeavoured to have the barrels smooth inside from end to end, but very few troubled to have them polished from end to end by hand lapping. Before 1870 next to nothing was known of the art of gun-barrel boring ; it was thus that so often the right barrels shot better than the left—being the result of accident, not design, for until choke-boring was practised there was no certain way of improving the shooting of a gun.

The shooting qualities were taken for granted. If a gun had a barrel externally of the shape found to give good results, and was free from rings and roughness inside, it was assumed that it would shoot well if the right charge was used with it ; but most often the gun was not tested for this by the maker. A few gun-makers shaped the barrels inside more or less after a premeditated plan, the most usual being to polish the gun at breech and muzzle, leaving it of slightly smaller calibre midway, as will afterwards be described.

In Birmingham, prior to 1875, the ranges available for testing guns at targets could be counted on the fingers, and London gun-makers were even worse supplied. The author's method of choke-boring, introduced in 1874, required targets upon which the results of his processes could be shown. It is not possible, even at this date, to predicate exactly what the shooting of a barrel of a given shape and size will be; it may be approximately estimated, but that is not sufficient, and each barrel must be repeatedly shot and the targets inspected and its performance

Shooting Range in W. W. Greener's Factory at Birmingham.

calculated from the averaged results of the various shots made with that barrel. In no other way is it possible to guarantee that any gun will shoot as close or as strong as the average gun.

Two iron plates at the end of a forty yards' range used to comprise the whole furniture of the testing ground, more often a single plate had to suffice; thus at least 160 yards had to be walked to inspect one shot from each barrel. The author invented folding targets closing one over the other and actuated by wires from the firing point. The plan is now generally adopted, saving much time and reducing

the heavy cost of gun testing.   At the author's range in the Birmingham factory
there are pits for firing rifles, plates for testing ball guns, and various instruments
for testing velocity, pressure, recoil, penetration, etc., but the folding targets, as
showing the shooting of the gun most readily, are always first employed.   If not
satisfactory at the target, the barrel is at once altered—and this is often done—and
the gun shot again and passed in less time than it would take some London gun-
makers to drive from their shops to the shooting ground.   It has been found that
with the author's system guns can be fired and the patterns inspected at the average
rate of thirty seconds a shot.

FINE-BORING AND CHOKING.

Of all processes through which the shot-gun passes in the course of production,
the fine-boring is the most important, as upon its proper execution the shooting of
the gun is entirely dependent.   In the term "fine-boring" is included all that is
done to the inside of the gun barrel subsequent to the preliminary rough-boring,

The Fine-boring Bit and Packing.

previously described as being done when the barrel was a roughly-forged or drilled
tube.   It includes fine-boring, choke-boring, chambering, and lapping, or final
polishing.

The fine-boring, by which the inside of the barrel is enlarged to exactly that
diameter required to give the best shooting, is done upon a similar bench to the
one used for rough-boring.   The bit, however, revolves at scarcely half the speed of
the rough-boring bit, and cuts on one edge only.   A weight and chain are used,
instead of the crowbar and rack, to force the barrel to the bit.   The bit is made to
fit the barrel by means of a spill of wood, packed with strips of paper called "liners,"
between the wooden spill and the bit, as shown in the illustration.

By using more packing or a larger "spill," the same bit may be made to bore
several sizes out of the barrel.   Usually the bit has but one sharp edge ; the other
is rounded and acts as a burnisher, whilst the two remaining edges are prevented
by the "spill" from coming into contact with the barrel.   The amount of "cut" is
regulated by the packing ; usually one paper liner is inserted between the bit and
the spill, and the thickness of that paper is bored from the barrel when the bit is

next inserted. The bit is ground quite square, and, being twenty inches or more long, it centres itself in the barrel, and has a tendency also to keep the barrel quite straight, for the barrels are fixed in a carrier which plays quite freely on the bed of the bench and the bit fits but loosely in the revolving head of the machine. The bench commonly used is of the type shown.

When bored up to the desired size, the barrels are chambered. A cutting tool

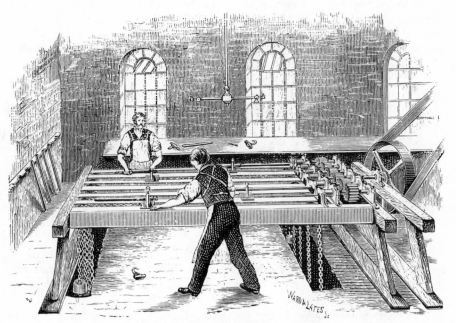

Gun-barrel Boring at W. W. Greener's Factory.

the exact size of the cartridge to be used is the reamer last to be inserted ; and this is forced in whilst slowly revolving in a lathe. The chamber must be in exact line with the bore of the barrel, so a guide projects beyond the cutting portion of the tools and centres in the bore of the barrel, which it exactly fits. It is generally requisite to again bore the barrels, as they are needed to be of different sizes, according to the charge to be used or the closeness of shooting desired ; whereas the chamber is always of one size, and the leg of the chambering tool must fit the bore of the barrel when of that size which it is deemed will be the smallest ever likely to be required.

The proper shape for the chamber where it unites with the base of the barrel is a not too abrupt cone. That shown in the illustration gives the exact dimensions of the standard 12-bore. Sometimes it is required to have the cone longer; if the barrel is larger inside, with the same sized chamber, the cone will, of course, be slightly shortened at its fore-end.

As to the shape of the interior of the finished barrel. A true cylinder from chamber to muzzle is rarely found; such a barrel does not shoot close enough to satisfy either sportsmen or gun-makers. What is known as the cylinder is a barrel which is not "choked"—that is to say, there is no point between the chamber-

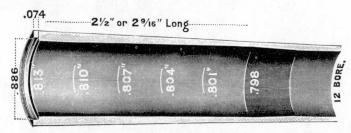

The 12-bore Cartridge Chamber.

cone and muzzle of greater or smaller diameter than comprehended in a difference of less than five-thousandths of an inch.

In the illustration, page 261, the three usual forms of "cylinder" barrels are shown. No. 1 is the true cylinder; No. 2 is slightly larger at both ends than in the middle, a style of boring known as "relief"; and No. 3 is a more or less gradual taper from breech to muzzle.

The old-fashioned way of boring was accomplished by inserting the bits in the muzzle and boring towards the breech. This was simply because it was more convenient for the borer. The introduction of the breech-loader so facilitated the inspection of the barrels that fine-boring from end to end became a necessity; yet the barrels were still bored from the muzzle ends. Before then the breech ends of muzzle-loaders could be neglected with safety. Boring from the breech end alone, it is almost an impossibility to form a perfect cylinder to within a few inches of the muzzle; the taper from the breech to that point, by wear of boring bits and compression of the liners, may reach 3,000ths of an inch. If bored from both ends alternately, from the same cause the barrel will be slightly constricted in the centre. Thus it is that the forms of old boring are as described ; the forms were the necessary result of the manner of boring ; though this, of course, does not preclude the possibility of any one form being the outcome of a preconceived design. The only method of producing a true cylinder is by lapping out after boring.

HISTORICAL NOTE ON CHOKE-BORING.

On the authority of M. de Marolles, who wrote in 1781, it is asserted that choke-boring was known to, and practised by, the gun-makers of his day. He writes : " An iron or wooden mandrel, fitting the bore, is furnished at one end with small files, which cut transversely only. This tool, put into the muzzle of a barrel and turned round by means of a cross-handle, forms a number of superficial scratches in the metal, by which the defect of scattering the shot is remedied. One effect of this plan is that of destroying the smoothness of the barrels within, rendering them liable to foul, and causing them to lead sooner, after the discharge." Deyeux, who published the " Vieux Chasseur " in 1835, writes : " I have seen these results produced by a barrel slightly opened at the muzzle, choked in the centre, and freed at the breech, such as some good smiths pretend is best to make them. I have seen the same results by a barrel choked two sizes at the muzzle, and by a perfectly cylindrical gun." Again, at page 36 : " The barrel whose muzzle is too much choked seldom makes a good pattern in the centre of the target." From these statements little more is to be learned than from the following advertisement, which appeared in the *St. James's Chronicle*, May 7th, 1789 :—

" To GENTLEMEN SPORTSMEN.—Guns matchless for shooting to be sold, or twisted barrels bored on an improved plan, that will always maintain their true velocity, and do not let the birds fly away after being shot, as they generally do with guns not properly bored. The shortest of them will shoot any common shot through a whole quire of paper at 90 yards with ease. This method of boring guns will enable every shooter to kill his bird, as they are sure of the mark at 90 yards. A Tryal of their performance, as above, may be seen at Mr. Mellor's, Greyhound Lane, near the Infirmary, Whitechapel, London, where he bores any sound barrel for two guineas, to shoot in the same manner, and makes them much stronger than before ; has also twisted double-barrel guns, famous for partridge shooting, and all double proved.

" *Note.*—No guns sent to strangers without the money, nor letters received unless the postage is paid."

It is, therefore, apparent that the gun-makers knew the need for increasing the range of their guns and concentrating the shot to the centre of the target, and, knowing this, it is probable that they sought to effect an improvement by altering the shape of the bore ; but from the statement of Deyeux—and his statements are similar to those of other writers of the time—it would seem that the methods had little success. If a gun constricted at the muzzle to the extent of two sizes did not shoot better than one cylindrically bored, or one widened at both breech and muzzle, it is evident that the secret of the modern choke was not discovered. The plan specified by M. de Marolles seems the most correct in principle, although the benefit to be derived from it would affect the first few rounds only, the scratches thrown up by the file quickly wearing away.

The invention of choke-boring has been claimed by many, and is usually attributed to the American gunsmiths. The first patent for choke-boring was granted to Roper, an American gunsmith, on April 10th, 1866, thus preceding

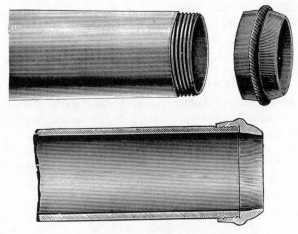

Roper's Detachable Choke-muzzle.

Pape, the English claimant, by about six weeks. Roper's invention consisted of a removable muzzle, and was applicable to single guns only; it had but little sale owing to a serious fault in the breech mechanism, which was of a revolving magazine type. The author in 1885 secured one of the original Roper guns and gave it an exhaustive trial; he found that with the attachment there was an improvement in the closeness of the patterns, but all were below the standard of a good modified choke. Mr. J. W. Long, in his book on "American Wildfowling," states : "Just when choke-boring was first practised, or who is rightfully entitled to the honour of its invention, will probably never be known. There have been scores of claimants, however, and one, Mr. Pape, of Newcastle, England, so far made good his claim as to receive recognition as the inventor from the proprietors of the

London *Field*, who appointed a committee of sportsmen to investigate and if possible determine the matter. Mr. Pape, however, is *not* the original inventor, for he dates his discovery back only to the year 1866; and though he may have found out its peculiarities by personal effort and without knowing it to have been previously practised, yet he put his revelation to little use, and, it would seem, hardly appreciated its value." Pape's claim would appear to have been attached as an afterthought to the specification of a patent for a breech-loading action, and no details are given as to how he proposed to carry out the suggestion; the bore of his gun was constricted at the muzzle from 12 to 13, and although this undoubtedly gave better shooting than a cylinder, its performance fell far behind that of a modern choke-bore. Again quoting Mr. Long: "I have most positive and reliable proof of its having been practised in this country, according to the most approved manner of the present day, over fifty years ago; the earliest person to whom I

Side and End Views of Bit for Choke-boring (from Mr. Long's book, 1879).

have been able to trace a knowledge of it being Jeremiah Smith, a gunsmith, of Southfield, R.I., who discovered its merits in 1827." The evidence was never published in detail. No other writer appears to have given so much consideration to this question as Mr. Long, and his book is full of many interesting references to the history of choke-boring. He appears to have first heard of "close shooting" guns about the fall of 1870, and his first gun, a muzzle-loader bored on the choke principle, was made in July, 1871, by Tonks, of Boston, Mass. It was a 10-bore weighing a little over 9 lbs., and some exceptionally good patterns are credited to it. At its first trial, using four drams of powder and one ounce of No. 4 shot, 151 pellets to the load, it placed 68, 73, and 76 pellets in a 1 ft. sq. at 40 yards. There appeared to be considerable difficulty in shooting straight with these guns, and it was found necessary to aim low in order to hit the game. The first *public* notice of choke-boring is stated by Mr. Long to have been contained in a circular issued in 1872 by Mr. J. L. Johnson, of Young America (Monmouth, Ill.), but the circular is nothing more than an assertion that the advertiser has discovered the secret of making guns to shoot close and carry farther, and that he will "guarantee them to put the whole charge in a 30 in. circle, or from 45 to 60 pellets No. 4 in a foot square at 40 yards ; as from 10 to 20 is the average shot for an ordinary gun, the range is increased from 20 to 30 yards." While Johnson was at work in his shop a man named Faburn endeavoured to discover the secret. He was not allowed to get the breech pin out of the gun, and from his observations of the muzzle end of the barrels he concluded that a short recess had been cut out just at the back of the muzzle ; he therefore contrived an expanding bit to do this boring, and on June 25th, 1872, secured a patent for it. This bit, which ostensibly carried with it the right to "choke-bore" barrels, had a large sale throughout the United States, and every gunsmith claimed the knowledge of choke-boring, but endeavoured to keep the method of boring a secret.

From Long's evidence one gathers that considerable trouble was caused by leading in choke-bored barrels, and he advised the continual dipping of the muzzles into water to counteract this ; this defect was confirmed by a letter written later by "Engineer" to the Editor of the London *Field.*

An American 6-bore muzzle-loading gun, the property of Fred Kimble, a companion of Long's, was sent over to England for trial, and while it shot well with large shot it did not give regular results, making but one really good pattern out of every three shots, which would point to the conclusion that although the Americans were undoubtedly the pioneers of the choke-boring system, they had not really progressed far beyond the elementary stage, and their guns still continued to lead, threw irregular patterns, and did not shoot straight.

The author's attention was first drawn to the question of " Close Shooting " guns by the *Turf, Field and Farm* trials held at New York in 1873. The representative of the Greener gun at these trials only had cylinder guns bored upon the same plan as used at the 1866 trials. Unfortunately, as he had but little knowledge of guns or shooting, the information obtained as to the system of boring then in vogue in the United States was exceedingly meagre, and although English-made guns were successful at this trial, it was openly stated that the winning guns had been re-bored in America.

The author's first intimation of the true choke formation was derived from the instructions given in a customer's letter written in the early part of 1874 ; this described the choke, but did not of course say how it was obtained ; hence numberless experiments, rendered doubly difficult by the lack of suitable tools, were necessary before regular shooting could be relied upon.

The first barrels were bored with the old-fashioned four-square bit commonly known as a reamer ; this, though a perfect instrument for the true cylinder bore, was quite unsatisfactory for choke-boring, the shape of the tool at the extreme end creating a roughness behind the shoulder of the choke ; this caused the barrel to lead, and spoilt the shooting of the gun. Having as the result of these experiments discovered the true shape of the choke and being convinced from the results obtained that guns so bored gave superior results to the ordinary cylinder, the next difficulty was to devise tools that would bore correctly and smoothly. These after much labour and expense were obtained, and a perfectly bored choke-bore gun was produced.

Mr. Teasdale Buckle, in his book " Experts on Guns and Shooting," published Sampson Low, Marston & Co., says :—

"The introduction of choke-boring may be regarded as W. W. Greener's greatest achievement ; his previous inventions had shown his cleverness ; this one made him famous throughout the world. Mechanism in a mechanical age like ours is not easy to grow famous upon. But choke-boring as brought out by Greener in 1874 altered the whole system of gun boring, and made close shooting the servant of the gun-maker, where before it had been his will-o'-the-wisp.

"Good shooting guns at that time were accidents to a great extent ; with such an accident Mr. Pape had won at a public trial with a pattern of less than 130. That is our opinion of the matter, and moreover, no English maker could guarantee any such pattern as 130 until Mr. Greener showed the way in 1874."

The author has never claimed to be the inventor of choke-boring, although it is generally attributed to him. All that he wishes to say is that the form of choke he produced, which has now been generally accepted, and the method of producing it, are of his own invention ; and the *Field* trials, reported fully in Chapter 13, conclusively proved that, in spite of the many claimants to the invention, many of whom had, according to their own statements, had knowledge of the system for years, none were able to produce guns equal in shooting powers to those bored upon the Greener system.

THE VARIOUS STYLES OF CHOKE-BORING.

The term choke-boring appears to have originated with the French—as in the writings of some old French authors choke-boring is mentioned, and called *étranglé* for want of a better name—and been adopted by the English and Americans. To an English gun-maker the terms mean simply " barrels whereof the diameter of the bore at the muzzle is less than the bore at some point behind the muzzle, other than the chamber," while any gun barrel constricted at the muzzle to the extent of

·005 inch may be termed a modified choke. A full choke may be con-stricted to the extent of ·030 to ·040 inch. Some makers constrict more, but past a certain limit this defeats its own object by diminishing the pattern, though the larger the bore the greater must be the constriction at the muzzle. The constriction of the bore, to be effective, must finish close to the extremity of the barrel ; this same constriction, if placed 3 or more inches from the muzzle, fails to throw the shots close together, but will give better penetration than a cylinder-bored barrel. There are two distinct plans of choke-boring ; the first, and probably the original method, is to bore the barrel cylinder for nearly the whole length, contracting it from $2\frac{1}{2}$ to 3 inches from the muzzle, like No. 6 in the illustration on page 261.

The other plan, similar to that patented by Faburn in 1872, is to enlarge the bore immediately behind the muzzle, and extending 3 or 4 inches towards the breech, as shown in No. 4.

A modification of the " recess choke " is shown in No. 5. In this a kind of double choke is formed by enlarging the barrel from the first choke towards the breech in a more elongated form.

There is still another modification, which consists of gradually enlarging the barrel from the breech to within 2 or 3 inches of the muzzle.

HOW THE CHOKE IS FORMED.

Barrels intended for choking are left one or two sizes smaller than the cartridges they are intended for—that is to say, the 12-bores are left 14-bore or 13-bore, and the barrels are bored up within three inches of the muzzle with a fine-boring bit, using a spill and liners as already described. The bit, however, is not allowed to pass right through the barrel, but is withdrawn before reaching the muzzle. This is a very tedious process, it being a difficult matter to get the metal from that part of the barrel nearest the muzzle. When sufficient metal has been taken from the barrel it is removed to another bench, where another bit is inserted revolving at a slower speed. This bit is of a different nature to the boring bit, it being cham-fered off towards the point in order to shape the cone of the choke and the flat, between the top of the choke and the muzzle of the barrel. By the use of this tool the choke is kept perfectly straight and true with the barrel; but it is not used by all makers—some shape the choke instead with an ordinary taper boring bit.

Instead of boring out the barrel, it is a practice with some makers to bore the barrel cylinder, or nearly so, then constrict the barrel tube from the outside by

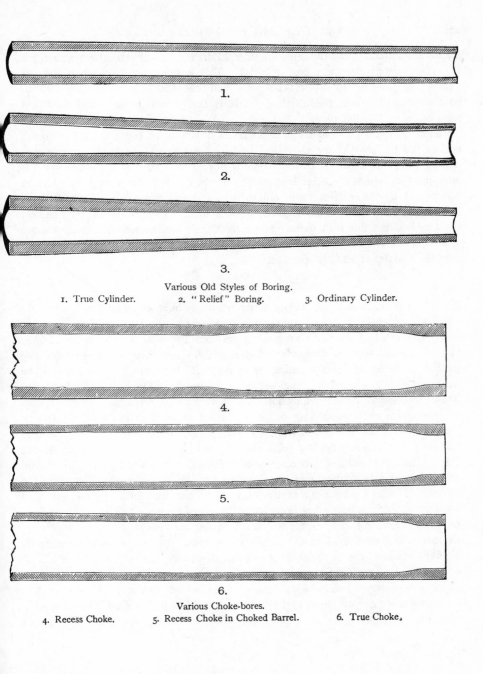

1.

2.

3.

Various Old Styles of Boring.

1. True Cylinder.   2. " Relief " Boring.   3. Ordinary Cylinder.

4.

5.

6.

Various Choke-bores.

4. Recess Choke.   5. Recess Choke in Choked Barrel.   6. True Choke.

forcing the muzzle into a die until the internal diameter at the muzzle is about two sizes smaller than elsewhere on the barrel. This is undoubtedly cheaper, and was often first resorted to by makers who had not the necessary machinery to bore out the barrel in the usual way. It is therefore regarded—and doubtless rightly—as a makeshift plan.

Some London gun-makers have followed a system of choking at the breech end of the barrel. At the chamber, the barrel is a 12 gauge; at the muzzle end, and for the greater length of the barrel, the bore is only 20. It is claimed for this principle that a gun of better balance can be constructed; an advantage which is outweighed by the inferior result obtained as a shooting weapon. The shot jams in the barrel, and the pellets lose their spherical form, taking a wider flight. The best shooting is obtainable with barrels which have their bore as near that of the calibre of the case as possible, and this size should be maintained, and the choke formed near the muzzle, as already specified.

LAPPING, OR LEAD POLISHING.

The final polish of the barrel, to which regularity of shooting is due, is a process which has not been in vogue among the gun-makers generally until the last few years. The well-known first-class gun-makers knew the value of the process, and the guns of the late Westley-Richards and the late W. Greener, which were remarkable for the closeness of their shooting, were polished by pushing to and fro in the barrel a well-fitting long lead plug, coated with fine emery powder and a lubricant. This process was called "draw-boring." The process, with the aid of modern machinery, is not now so long or so expensive, whilst it is more efficiently and thoroughly done, as the lap, as well as passing up and down the barrel from end to end, also revolves rapidly. A perfectly true and highly polished and even surface from chamber to choke is thus obtainable. The lap consists of an iron rod, around which is cast a leaden case of the same size as the diameter of the barrel to be lapped. The lead is kept constantly covered with a mixture of emery and oil.

This lap is fixed into a head revolving 650 times a minute. The barrel is fixed on a carriage upon a lathe bed, and the lap having been inserted, and set revolving, the barrel is moved backwards and forwards along the lap, in order to perfectly level the inside of the barrel and remove any slight inequalities that may have been occasioned by irregularities while boring, and also to polish it as fine as possible, which is necessary if first-class regular shooting is to be obtained. It also renders the barrel more easy to clean, and less liable to lead or foul. This process requires very great care, owing to the great speed at which the lap revolves. The barrels being bored very thin at the muzzles are likely to bend, or the rib to be loosened or twisted; so, during this process they are kept cool by the frequent application of cold water.

BARREL FILING.

After proof the gun-maker examines the tubes, and re-sets them if made crooked by the strain of the enormously heavy proof test. It is from the stock of tubes that the barrels are chosen suitable for guns of particular weights.

The workman called in the Birmingham district the "barrel-filer," and in London the "barrel-maker," takes the tubes, and for a double gun joins two together, fits top and bottom ribs, the lumps, loop, etc., required for the breech-action. The most important point is the jointing of the barrels, by filing flats on the inner sides in order to get the tubes closer together, and at such an angle to each other that the axes, if continued beyond the muzzle, will converge at sixty feet beyond. If the barrels were not closed in they would shoot "wide"— that is, the right to the right, the left to the left, of the mark at which the gun is aimed. This is due to the fact that, being in juxtaposition, the inner side of the barrel, reinforced by its neighbour, does not expand equally with the outer side; barrels placed one above the other, instead of side by side, shoot high and low instead of right and left. The breech end of the barrel being of necessity stouter than the fore-part, the gun would be unwieldy unless jointed in. One barrel being brazed to the other at the breech, the thinnest sides are practically reinforced by the metal of the neighbouring barrel, so that the inner side is in reality stronger and less likely to burst than the outer and thicker side of the barrel.

Next in importance is the fitting of the lumps: the best plan is to dovetail in the bottom lump as shown in the illustration (page 265), and then to braze the whole together for about 3 inches up the barrels from the breech-ends. When the barrels are wanted for wedge-fast guns, the top lump, or extension rib, is brazed on at the same time. The space between the barrels is packed at intervals with pieces of tinned iron. The ribs are then soft-soldered on, and the loop fitted in.

It is a common practice with foreign gun-makers to braze their barrels together from end to end, and to hard-solder the ribs to the barrels. This is most injurious, as the barrels are made crooked by the process, and cannot again be straightened effectually; this is particularly the case with twist-barrels. With steel barrels the result is even more disastrous, the heat required being more than sufficient to ruin the qualities of some steels used for barrels.

The barrels are struck up from end to end with flat strikers or oblong files, which are used like joiners' planes, and serve to take off all inequalities on the barrels and ribs. In a well-filed pair of barrels the rib will be seen to be level, straight, and nicely taper, and the barrels round and even, and free from flats.

The slope of the tubes to a large extent fixes the shape of the barrels; it is impossible in guns of usual weight to have the barrels a perfect taper from breech to muzzle. The rib is so shaped as to give the right elevation to the gun, and is made hollow, and often swamped, so that the barrels may be light and the gun balance well. These points have all to be considered before the tubes can be assembled, and any error of judgment will undoubtedly result in a gun either heavier or lighter than was required to be made, or one that is ill-balanced and clumsy to handle. The barrel-filer has practically finished his work when the tubes are put together, the lumps, etc., fixed, and the ribs shaped, soldered on, and in place ; but, as a convenience in manufacture, the finishing touches to both rib and barrels are usually deferred until the gun is practically completed. The top rib may be *grooved*, or it may be *flat ;* it may be left plain, or it may be *engine-turned*, *file-cut*, *roughened*, or *engraved*, at the choice of the sportsman.

BREECH-ACTION MAKING.

Numerous subdivisions are comprised in the branch of gun-making designated breech-action making. In the first place, it includes machining the bodies and other parts of the breech-action mechanism and locks, and of this some particulars will be found under the heading " Machine Work."

The other important divisions are jointing, filing, and fitting up. Jointing consists of fitting the barrels to the breech-action—a matter of importance, seeing that upon it depends not only the "life," but the safety of the gun. The jointer takes the body and fore-end of a breech-action in the machined state, and first proceeds to square the holes in the body, and drift them out to the proper size. He next files the lump, or lumps, on the barrels to the gauge of the holes in the body, and gradually eases the body on to the barrels, by smooth-filing the lumps on the barrels. The extractor is then fitted into the machined recess, and the face or end of the barrels squared, the joint or hinge-pin is inserted, and the hook on the bottom lump cut for it ; and the breech-ends of the barrels, by blacking and smoothing (which has to be repeated many times), brought to fit closely and bear hard against the face of the standing-breech, and the flats of the barrels firmly bedded upon the bottom of the breech-actions. The smoking, or blacking, and easing, have to be repeated until every surface fits evenly and closely against the

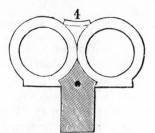

Dovetailed Barrel Lump.

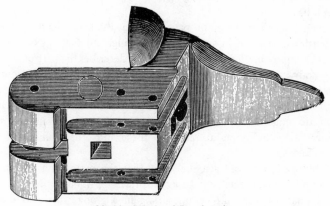

Machined Body of Breech-action.

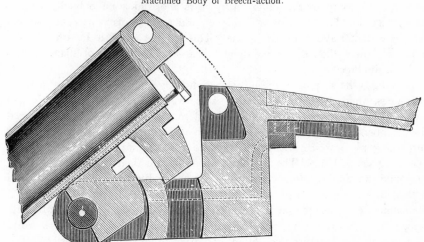

Section of Hammerless Breech-action, showing the Working and Bearing Parts.

other, and very careful and skilful workmanship is necessary in this branch to ensure perfect fitting. Unless this work is well done, and the holding-down bolts well fit, the breech-action will wear shaky with very little use. The jointer also prepares the hole for the under-bolt in top-lever guns, and in double-grip actions he fits the lever. In jointing the Anson and Deeley hammerless guns, the hinge or joint-pin being usually solid with the body of breech-action, the process of bedding down the barrels and bringing them to bear against the face of the standing-breech have to be combined.

It will be seen from the drawing on page 265 that the breech-ends of the barrels describe the portion of a circle in opening and shutting, and that the back portion of the bottom steel lump, being filed on the circle, also describes the part of a circle, and the slot in the body, being shaped to correspond with the circle on the lump fitting against the circle in the body, causes part of the strain of the discharge to be removed from the hinge-pin, and distributed over the body of breech-action. The extension rib must be accurately fitted, yet made to work in and out with perfect freedom. It is the proper attention to these and other points that adds so greatly to the cost of guns.

From the illustration it will also be seen that the extractor is in one piece, the leg being round. The extractor is kept from turning, when out of its " bed " in the barrel, by a small rounded projection sliding in a groove in the extension rib. This plan was devised by the author many years ago, and is undoubtedly the best method of guiding the extractor. The other, and general, plan is to put a second leg on the extractor above the longer one. This requires a hole to be drilled in the barrels just where they are thinnest, and has been the cause of many barrels bursting at the breech.

The filing is the shaping of the breech-action body ; in hammer guns it includes other things, when the first thing done is to drill and plug out the nipple and striker holes. The striker holes are first drilled to a centre marked by a tool fixed in the chamber. Each hole is then enlarged to admit of the shoulder of the striker or exploding pin working freely, and plugged out and tapped, to admit of the nipple being screwed in. The locks and furniture are then fitted, the fences or scroll round the nipples formed, and the body, fore-end, etc., filed into shape, and smooth-filed. The gun is then ready for the top-lever work to be fitted.

In hammerless guns the routine is slightly different. The bodies are first roughly shaped, they then go to the lock filer and have the inside work, or lock work, fitted to them, the furniture, etc., fitted, and triggers and pull-off adjusted. The action is then sent back to the filer, who finishes shaping it.

The fitting up is the making, fixing, and adjusting of all the bolts which are necessary to keep the barrels and breech-action body together. In the treble-wedge-fast and top-lever guns this branch is considerably subdivided. One man usually fits the bottom bolt, another fits the lever, another prepares the tumbler-springs, pins, etc., the whole being put together and adjusted by the master-man of the shop. Care has to be taken in this branch so to arrange the work that the top and bottom bolt commence to travel together, and immediately on the lever being moved. The bites or grip upon the bottom and top lumps must also be good, and the bolts fitted evenly and closely in the slots prepared for them, so as to equalise the strain as much as possible. A crooked, and consequently badly fitting, bottom bolt is more apt to break than one properly fitted, as it would have to stand the whole strain of the explosion, whereas in a well-fitted bolt the strain would be borne by the slot in the breech-action, as well as by the bolt itself.

With the action body jointed to the barrels, adjusted thereto, the body, fore-end, etc., filed to shape, and the holding-down bolts all fitted, the action-making may be said to be completed. Of late years, however, the hammerless locks and the self-ejecting mechanisms have brought additional work to the action filer, since the successful working of the gun depends wholly upon the accurate adjustment of the various mechanisms, and the firing and extracting mechanisms require to be fitted to, and made to work with, the particular weapon for which they are designed; they are neither interchangeable nor adaptable.

LOCK-MAKING.

Before describing the methods of constructing hammerless locks and self-extracting mechanisms, a little space may be given to describing and illustrating the manufacture of gun locks.

The various parts of a gun lock are forged by experienced hands from the best iron and steel, and handed to the lock filer, who first squares the lock-plates, and drills the holes from a pattern laid on the plate. The tumbler shank and pivot are turned or ground between two cutters, which makes the pivot and shank central with each other, and at perfect right angles to the body of the tumbler. The bridle is then filed up and fixed, the scear placed on and shaped, and the swivel fitted to the tumbler. The mainspring and scear spring have then to be shaped, filed to the requisite thickness and strength, fitted upon the lock-plate, hardened, and tempered. The bents are then cut in the tumbler with a small saw, and finished with files and smoothers until the scear works with as little friction and rubbing as possible. A very old smooth file, worn almost to a burnisher, is used to finish the bents and bearings of the lock.

In the illustration, page 269, 1 is the mainspring ; 2, the bridle and scear spring pins ; 3, the swivel ; 4, the scear ; 5, the hammer affixed to tumbler shank, showing an end elevation of tumbler ; 6 is the nipple ; and 8, the striker or exploding-pin (the two latter are not inside the lock, but are fixed into break-off of breech-action); 7 is the scear spring ; 9, the bridle ; 10, the tumbler pin ; and 11, the tumbler (side view). The bridle, hammer, and lock-plate only are of iron, the remaining parts being of steel. The springs are forged in long flat strips, and are bent into the V shape by the filers.

In the Anson and Deeley hammerless guns there are no lock-plates ; the work is fitted into slots machined underneath the body of breech-action, as shown in the illustration of the " Machined Breech-action " on page 265.

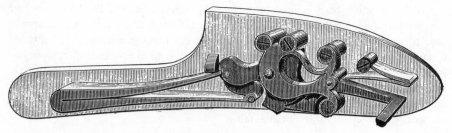

Modern Rebounding Gun-lock.

In the illustration of the lock-work itself, 1 is the mainspring ; 2, the lifting or cocking lever ; 3, the tumbler, striker and exploding pin ; 4, the scear spring ; 6, the scear ; 7 and 8 are the pivot pins passing through the body on which work the scears and cocking levers ; 5 is the pivot on which the tumblers work, and shows an end view of the tumbler in elevation ; 9 is the scear spring pin ; and 10, a safety bolt for affixing to the gun and bolting the triggers. It will be seen that there are fewer pieces in the Anson and Deeley lock, and, compared with the ordinary lock, they are all very much broader and stronger.

In W. W. Greener's hammerless lock the cocking dog, 2, is dispensed with, and a new and more simple method of cocking employed, all fully described under the heading " Hammerless Guns."

The great point in all this kind of work (action, lock and furniture filing) is to file flat and square ; proficiency in this art is only acquired after many years'

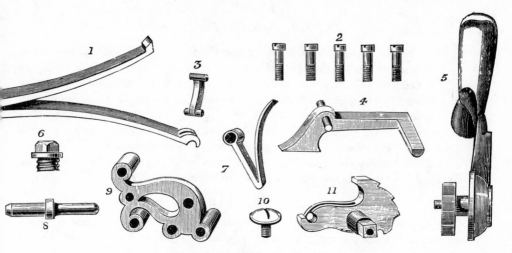

Pieces of Modern Hammer Gun-lock.

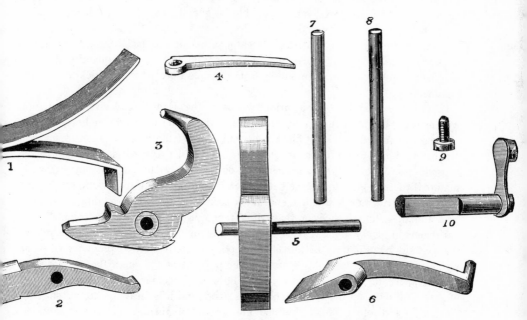

Lock-work of the Anson and Deeley Hammerless Gun.

practice, and by those who have been apprenticed to the work while young.   It is
well known that the Birmingham gun filers are unexcelled by any in their skilful use
of the file, and it is certainly extraordinary to see the beautiful shapes and close
fitting turned out by them.   It is not too much to say that their work cannot be excelled,
if equalled, by that of any artisan employed in any country at any trade.   The
above remarks are equally applicable to the gun-lock filers of the Black Country :
Darlaston, Wednesbury, and the neighbourhood of Wolverhampton have long been
famous for the excellent quality of their locks, and as good locks may still be
obtained from there as any the world can produce.

GUN STOCKS AND GUN STOCKING.

The material most generally in use for gun stocks is heart walnut (*Juglans
regia*) ; in America the indigenous variety (*Juglans nigra*) is that commonly in use.
The finest European walnut is that brought from south-eastern France and from
the forests of the Eastern principalities.   " English " walnut is the trade term used
to designate a finely-figured variety suitable for gun stocks.   It seems paradoxical to
state that it is chiefly imported.

English timber, from well-grown trees of sufficient age, lacks but one quality—
colour.   It is, however, so seldom in the market in sufficient quantity that the
merchants prefer to draw their supply from districts where it is an article of general
commerce.

As to the qualities of the various woods.   The English is heavy, very tough,
well marked, but not gaudy ; that from France is lighter in weight, richer in colour,
marked with broad streaks of black; and well veined ; in grain it is more open than
English timber.   Swiss timber is often grey, soft, and pulpy, as is also much of the
German-grown walnut, though when well cut, properly chosen, and not artificially
matured, there is little to choose between Swiss and German and the finest French
wood.   Belgian walnut is not plentiful ; it is inferior to that of meridional France.
The Italian walnut is heavier than the French, is not so bright in colour, it has
dark veins in plenty, but the background is one-hued, instead of having the yellow,
orange, and neutral tints of the finest wood.   Eastern Europe produces very fine
walnut, but it is not so well prepared for the purpose of the gun-maker as that sawn
by the experts of the Western centres.   The wood is characterised by its closeness
of grain and its exact marking, its colour is good, and it is fairly free from "shakes,"
"cracks," and other faults, but is not easily obtainable in large quantities.
Circassian walnut is exported in logs.   These are converted by the stock makers
of Europe, and furnish the finest of all gun stocks, hard in grain, full of figure,

exact in marking, bright in colour, without cracks and galls, heavy, but with qualities which quite outweigh this disadvantage. American walnut is a distinct variety, a useful wood of dark colour, varying considerably in quality, and apparently lacking the figure common to *J. regia.* It takes a poor oil polish, and is seen at its best when varnished ; for the purposes of the gun-maker it is distinctly inferior to European walnut.

The most beautifully marked stocks are cut from the portion of the tree where the roots and trunk join. The tree, therefore, requires to be grubbed up and planked when in that state. Inferior stocks are cut from the branches ; sometimes they are well marked, but they are all liable to warp.

There is a great difference in the quality of gun stocks, even amongst those cut from the same tree. Some stocks exhibit a species of cross figure, generally in a paler or yellow tint ; this is termed " fiddle," and enhances the value of the stock. A few possess hard galls which, from their unusual colour, give the stock an uncommon appearance. Good gun stocks are light, handsome, and straight in the grain at the grip and head of the gun, free from shakes or cracks, close-grained and without galls or soft places. In the best stocks the pattern is decided, and generally the black markings are large.

It is necessary that the stocks be perfectly dry before working them. Nominally the dealers, but actually the gun-makers, bear the expense of storing the wood until fit to use. The tree is sold to the sawyer, who cuts it up as soon as convenient to himself. The planks are examined and patterned out by the marker, who must have a sharp eye to detect any niceties of figure in the rough-sawn plank ; his chief object, moreover, is to get as many stocks out of the plank as possible without regard to the whereabouts of grain markings even. The stocks are kept no longer than requisite to get them dry enough to plane or polish, so that the buyer may judge their quality. The amount of really fine wood available is limited.

Of other woods which are or have been used for gun stocks, beech is the one best known ; it is heavy, and has no figure. Birch is inferior to beech. Ash, well chosen, has a pretty marking, which shows to best advantage when french-polished or varnished. Birdseye maple is too brittle. In America cherry and tulip wood have been tried, as well as Honduras walnut, but apparently with as little success as the attempt made some time ago to popularise the South African stink-wood as a material for gun stocks. The trial of Queensland honeysuckle, so much recommended, seems likely to prove as disappointing.

Walnut seems to be purposely designed for gun stocks. No other wood or material possesses qualities so admirably adapted to the requirements of the gun-maker, and for sporting weapons it is doubtful whether anything will ever supersede it. The only objection raised to it—save with respect to its great cost—is its high conductivity. Experts think that a wood of less conductivity, as maple or honeysuckle, would be more pleasant to use; the shock of the recoil would, it is argued, be less.

GREENER'S UNBREAKABLE STOCK.

The necessity for additional strength to the usual gun stock is fully proven by the numerous orders gun-makers receive for extra butts to be supplied with new guns and rifles intended for use in India, Africa, and other wild countries.

The author has designed and patented a gun stock which is practically unbreakable. The stock is fastened to the breech-action by a long butt-pin passing through the centre of the hand and screwing into the back of the breech-action (similar to the Martini), and thereby firmly securing the butt to the action, and, at the same time, strengthening the weakest part of the stock.

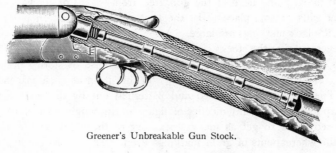

Greener's Unbreakable Gun Stock.

The diameter of the butt-pin is reduced at intervals to allow for the expansion of the wood and prevent the stock splitting.

A gun fitted with this improvement was used for several seasons, and in order to test it, it was purposely submitted to very rough treatment: such as striking it against wooden rails other obstacles, dropping it from a dog-cart, letting it fall from horseback, throwing it several times from a tree (20 ft. in height) on to the ground, and other similar tests, all of which it withstood perfectly.

Another plan adopted by the author is to place strengthening pieces along the outside of the stock, either by elongating the top strap and guard or by fitting metal plates to the back of the action, and continuing them down each side of the grip; either of these methods makes the stock practically unbreakable, and they are strongly recommended for Express and large bore rifles.

GUN STOCKING.

The stocker upon receiving the stock first roughs it into shape, or, as it is called, trims it out, with a mallet, chisel, and draw-knife. He next proceeds to fit the breech-action to the stock, first bedding the breech-action firmly against the stock, and then letting in the strap. He adjusts the bend or crook of the gun, and the amount of cast-off, partly by the angle of the joint, and partly by the shape given to the stock in trimming-out. When the required bend has been given to the stock, the gun is sent to the screwer to have the trigger-plate let in and the breech-pin fitted. The stocker then proceeds to let in the locks, or, if hammerless, the scears and tumblers only. The locks are stripped and the plates first let in, put together again, and the wood gradually removed until the lock will go into its place and work perfectly free. The head and grip of the gun are then shaped, and the wood cut away to admit of top-lever work acting. The stock is then rounded up with a draw-knife and rasp-filed over, the fore-end fitted to the barrel and shaped up, when the gun is again ready for the screwers.

This branch requires a great number of tools—chisels and gouges of different sizes and twists. A large assortment of floats and shovels are also required, to cleanly remove the wood from the locks and fore-end. In Birmingham stocking is the only branch done by one class of men (the gun stockers) ; in London and country shops the stocker also screws and sometimes even finishes the gun.

For various gun stocks designed to suit the peculiarities of the shooter, *see* "The Choice of a Gun," more particularly the paragraphs upon the "Fitting and Dimensions of the Gun Stock."

SCREWING AND FINISHING.

The screwing and finishing of a gun comprise the making and fitting of the pins by which the woodwork is held to the iron parts of the gun, the bolt which secures the fore-end to the barrels, and the fitting and fixing of all the furniture—heel-plate, trigger-guard, etc.

The screwer first lets in the trigger-plate of the gun, and fits the breech-pin, taking care so to fit it that it draws the breech-action firmly on to the stock. He receives the gun again when finished stocking, and fits the side pins to keep the locks in their place; hangs the triggers, screws in the guard and fore-end ; fits the fore-end and safety-bolts, if any, and screws on the heel-plate. The gun is then ready for the percussioner, and the barrels go to be finished in the boring, and smoothed ready for browning. When percussioned, the gun is shot at a target, and altered till it makes the required pattern, as described.

When shot and found correct the gun is sent to the finisher, who has to make the gun conform either to pattern or to the measurements given; adjust the length and bend of the stock, verify the "cast-off" and balance, shape the heel-plate, making toe and heel of right length and the inclination of the butt plate exact.

When the finisher has attended to these points, he has to file up and shape the stock and fore-end, smooth the ironwork; wet, dry, and smooth—or, as it is called, "cleanse"—all the woodwork several times, so that the stock will not become rough when wet. The whole of the woodwork is then buffed over with a leather buff-stick and pumice-stone and rotten-stone. The chequering is now done, and the gun stripped of all the ironwork, and sent for polishing and engraving. When polished and hardened, the finisher has to put the gun together again, see that all the work lies properly on the wood, and set any piece that may have warped from the heat of the fire; then oil and buff up the stock. The gun is now ready for final adjustment and inspection.

The finisher is, in short, the workman who not only does much towards completing the gun, but prepares the various parts for the final touches of action, lock, and barrel filers, and brings their work into harmony with the general scheme of construction. His work is done at intervals, but his knowledge and skill enable him to form the gun in accordance with the plan to be followed, and as no one workman touches the gun at so many different stages in the course of its manufacture, or at so many different points, the finisher requires to possess a wide knowledge of the art of gun-making, and to be acquainted with the details of most parts of every mechanism of any and every gun which may pass through his hands. The work of the finisher will be made more clear by the critical notes on gun-making at the end of this section.

PERCUSSIONING.

In the days of muzzle-loaders the percussioner's branch was a very important one, he having to fit the nipple, chamber the breech, drill and plug the vent-hole, besides shaping the fences and fitting the cocks. With the introduction of breech-loaders his trade has diminished to fitting the cocks only, and with hammerless guns he has nothing to do.

The hammers or cocks are filed from either forgings or stampings. In the illustration, *a* represents a modern-pattern central-fire cock-stamping, *b* is a forging, whilst *c* represents the forging filed up in the neatest and most approved pattern. The stampings are very tough if made from good iron, but the leading gun-makers adhere to forgings for the hammers of all their best guns. The percussioner, upon receiving the stampings or forgings, first proceeds to drill and square a hole in the hammer to admit shank of tumbler, and fit the hammer upon it ; it should fit tightly, to prevent play or liability to fly off; the hole is drifted from round to square by knocking in different-sized drifts, which condenses the iron round the hole, and so prevents the hammer from wearing loose. He then files the noses of the forgings, and adjusts them to strike evenly over the face of the nipple, and proceeds to file up

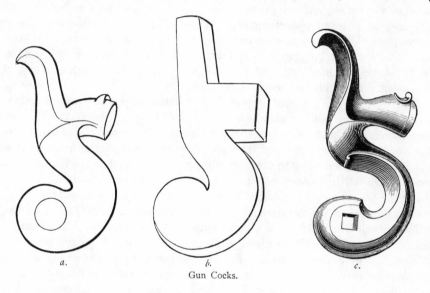

a.   b.   c.

Gun Cocks.

the cocks, the only care being to get them exactly alike, and to see that they stand the same height as each other when the cocks are at both full and half bent.

POLISHING AND CASE-HARDENING.

The object of the polisher is to remove from the ironwork of the gun all traces of the file ; this is accomplished by polishing the work on emery bobs of various degrees of fineness ; all flat parts and the grooves of the hammers are stick-polished, and finished by burnishing with a hard stick burnisher. Some parts of the lock-work are also lapped upon a revolving leaden surface plate, with emery and water, the best plan for level polishing. The bobs and laps should be driven by steam-power, as is the case in Birmingham. To obtain good results they should make about 2,500 revolutions per minute. In some London and country gun shops the bobs are run upon a foot-lathe. All ironwork intended for bluing is burnished over after it is polished; this tends to close the grain of the iron, as well as giving a deeper colour and gloss to the article when blued. The polishing bob consists of a wooden wheel or disc from 10 to 15 inches in diameter, around which is glued a tyre of buff leather; the tyre is coated with emery powder, also glued; the buffs require the emery coating to be frequently renewed. A number of bobs of various degrees of fineness and coarseness are kept at hand, so that they may be changed instantaneously. When polished, the work goes to be engraved; after the work is engraved, it is case-hardened or blued. The body, fore-end, hammers, trigger and lock-plates, bridles, triggers, escutcheons, and all the screws are hardened, and also the lever, if of iron, which is always the case in the double-grip Lefaucheux action.

The work to be hardened is placed in a cast-iron pot with animal charcoal (made by parching bone-dust), which must entirely cover all the work. The pot is then placed in a bright coal fire, where it remains till the whole is of a worm red. The fire must be a slow one, and the work will require to remain in from one to one and a half hours, according to the body of the material to be hardened. A practical hardener can tell by looking into it whether it is ready to come out. When taken out of the fire, the work is plunged into cold water. The iron when at a red heat absorbs the carbon, which causes the surface to become perfectly hard after being suddenly cooled, and also gives a nice mottled colour to the iron. The hardening does not extend beneath the surface, so that it is possible to bend and set the iron as though it were altogether soft. In Birmingham, where bone-turning is a considerable industry, bone-dust can be easily obtained in sufficient quantities, but in the country and abroad, whenever it is found necessary to case-harden, and bone-dust is not to be obtained, burnt leather is a good substitute, and old shoes are saved for this purpose. Some work is case-hardened by plunging when at red heat into a solution of prussiate of potash, but work so hardened will be found of a dead grey hue, and wanting the fine mottled colours so much admired. The blue colour is obtained by heating the work in a pan of pounded vegetable charcoal. It is necessary that the charcoal be very fine, but any amateur may blue by placing the pan of charcoal upon a fire and burying the work to be blued in it. The work must be removed occasionally, and rubbed with tow or powdered chalk, to remove any grease and keep a fine gloss upon the work.

The work will change colour repeatedly; it will first attain a pale straw-colour, afterwards a light blue, a purple, a dark blue, a red, a white, and lastly a dark deep blue, approaching a black. Bluing has a tendency to temper hardened steel, which should not be taken below a light blue; it takes a few minutes only. The dark blue takes from twenty to twenty-five minutes, according to the size of the article.

ENGRAVING AND THE ORNAMENTATION OF GUNS.

Of the few useful things which can be decorated to a high degree without spoiling their beauty or affecting their efficiency the sporting gun is one.

Engraving, as most people know, is done by cutting lines into the surface of the metal with a sharp, fine, triangular chisel called a burin or graver. A well-engraved gun should not only exhibit elegance of design in the decoration added, but the execution of the work should be by fine, firm lines, cut into, not scratched upon, the metal surface. All, of course, depends upon the artistic sense and the skill of the engraver; any design may be traced upon the metal and cut up. Very fine scroll work is the style now usually adopted, as these lines best adapt themselves to the first requisite of engraving from the gun-maker's point of view, namely, the hiding of joints, ugly straight lines, obtrusive pins, etc. etc. The engraving of game, bouquets, and other subjects, demands greater skill from the executant, and a clearer perception of artistic effect.

The prevalent idea that engraving is very expensive is entirely erroneous. It may have induced some sportsmen to prefer quite plain guns, and is therefore deserving contradiction. The gun quite devoid of engraving looks well enough when new, for the rich colours of the case-hardening supply the requisite decoration. When the gun is a little worn, the hardened surfaces assume the dirty white hue, and the rich blue on the furniture also wears to bright white metal; then the joints between the portions of the breech mechanism become too apparent, the pin heads are obtrusively to the fore, and the gun offends; whereas, by the expenditure of only a few shillings in lasting decoration, the greater the wear the more the good qualities of the engraving and the elegant form of the weapon would become apparent.

Another objection to engraving is that the weapon cannot be so readily kept clean. The lines of the engraving should be so shallow that the engraved part is as readily cleaned as the plain surface.

The real objection appears to have been the result of a practice once prevalent of making the only difference in quality and price dependent upon the amount of engraving. The natural effect of this was that, engraving being a comparatively cheap process, badly-made and inexpensively-produced guns had a few additional shillings spent upon the engraving, and were sold as, and represented to be, guns of good quality, if not of the highest grade.

In the decoration of the guns made, the author has always been guided by one rule—not to elaborately engrave, or otherwise decorate, guns which have to be sold at moderate prices. The money so expended, if it could not be laid out to better advantage in workmanship on the mechanism of the gun, could at least be so expended that attempts to misrepresent the quality of the gun, owing to its highly-decorated exterior, should be difficult. Appreciating to the fullest extent the real worth of appropriate decoration upon fire-arms, he has never preferred to make guns of really good quality so bare that when once the gloss of newness had gone, their bald appearance should prejudice the owner and user against them. Engraving and decoration have, therefore, with him at least, been used as in some measure an indication of the quality of the work.

Fine workmanship is of itself an excellent indication of quality ; and fine workmanship is more noticeable in the decoration than in many other points observable in fire-arms. The author has repeatedly been requested to produce fine guns well worth the hundred guineas offered, and has succeeded in satisfying even the most fastidious of these ardent admirers of beautiful workmanship. In only one instance was it insisted that the decoration of a gun of this type should include not a line of engraving, and, of course, no addition of precious or other decorative metals. This gun, highly decorative in other ways and beyond reproach, and all-satisfying to the purchaser whilst it was new, yet looked meagre when hard wear in a tropical climate tarnished its colouring and toned the bright figure of the stock.

Of recent years the demand for highly decorated guns has greatly increased, and the author has supplied some very beautiful specimens of decorated arms. In some instances the work consists simply of sporting subjects carved or chiselled in low relief in the metal itself; in others the decoration has taken the form of allegorical figures embossed in high relief upon the action and barrels in gold, platinum and other precious metals. Naturally this class of work greatly enhances the value of a gun, it being an easy matter to spend fifty or sixty pounds upon the decoration alone. Two beautiful examples of gun decoration are shown on the annexed plate.

Decoration need not be wholly confined to the engraving of lines. The greatest beauty of all is the elegant contour of a well-designed gun, proportionate in every part, and boldly outlined, yet gracefully turned where a too sharp angle would offend the eye of the artist. The breaking of the straight line between the breech-action body and the head of the stock not only makes a better and stronger union of wood and iron possible, but adds to the appearance of the gun. So, too, the chequering upon hand and fore-end not only enables the sportsman to obtain a surer grip, but is of itself attractive when well-designed and skilfully executed. The

AN EXAMPLE OF "CHISELLED" RELIEF DECORATION.

The Highest Development of the Sporting Gun. Designed and manufactured at Birmingham by W. W. Greener, 1907.)

A W. W. GREENER SIDE LOCK HAMMERLESS EJECTOR GUN.

(*A Specimen of Fine Scroll Engraving.*)

well-decorated gun will have every bolt, every pin, every part not only proportionate, rightly fitted, and well designed, but so placed as to be of actual service and its position utilised in the general scheme of decoration followed, so that upon close examination it would appear that without that most minute line or point the weapon itself would be incomplete.

BARREL BROWNING.

The bronzed appearance of the finished gun barrel is obtained by a process of rusting the barrels, the rust being cultivated, then stopped ; the complete oxidation of the surface renders the barrels less liable to rust by natural means.

The beautiful figure of the fine Damascus and laminated steel twist barrels is not surface-deep only ; the figure runs completely through the barrel, as will be made clear by referring to the description of the process of making the iron for, and the methods of welding, the barrels. Consequently, it is impossible to get by browning any finer or more beautiful figure than is already in the barrel ; it is possible, by inferior browning, to hide that figure, or so obscure it that recognition is barely possible. That fine gloss, seemingly the effect of lacquer or copal varnish, is nothing more than the burnished surface of the barrel, which before browning was as highly polished as a silver mirror.

" Browning," according to the statement of a technical writer, "is a dirty, a long, and a tiresome process." It should not therefore be attempted by amateurs, and the *best* results are only obtainable when there are facilities for maintaining variable temperatures for any length of time by night and day.

The method of colouring figured barrels usually followed may be shortly described. The barrels, highly polished, are plugged with tightly-fitting pegs. During the processes of browning they are handled entirely by these pegs, and are not touched by the hand. Double barrels have usually one barrel corked at the breech, the other at the muzzle ; the wooden plug projects also from each barrel about four inches. The barrels are coated with damped whiting ; this is brushed off when dry, and removes all grease. A browning mixture is then applied with a piece of flannel, and the barrels are put by in a moist atmosphere at about 50° F. This coating of mixture will rust the barrel if allowed to remain for twelve or eighteen hours. It must then be scratched off by energetically scrubbing with a brush of steel wire ; the barrels are then again coated with the browning mixture, which may remain on ten to twelve hours ; the removal of the second coating of rust is effected in the same way ; the coating and scratching processes are repeated time after time, until the barrel is completely rusted. The barrel is brought into a warmer temperature with each succeeding coating, and a shorter time allowed to elapse before it is removed, as the acid acts more quickly when once a start is obtained and the oxidation of the surface proceeds.   If the rust is not removed by the scratch-brush on every part of the barrel before it is re-coated, that untouched, or partly scoured, portion will be streaky when the browning process is completed. So, too, the barrel must be coated evenly—a thinly-spread coat ; no over-wetting so that the acid runs, or lighter patches and half-browned surfaces will appear, not to mention ugly spots where the acid has collected.   The barrel being dark enough, it is boiled for a few minutes in a trough of soft-water in which a few logwood chips and a little soda have been placed.   Sulphate of copper is sometimes preferred to soda.   The barrels are then wiped dry, and should show distinctly every curl in the figure, the grains of the steel lighter than those of the iron, the welds darker than either.

There are many recipes for browning mixtures ; a good one is as follows : —1 oz. muriate tincture of steel ; 1 oz. spirits of wine ; $\frac{1}{4}$ oz. muriate of mercury ; $\frac{1}{4}$ oz. strong nitric acid ; $\frac{1}{8}$ oz. sulphate of copper ; 1 quart of distilled water.   This mixture should be allowed to stand for some days, in order that the ingredients may properly amalgamate.

Hard barrels, those in which there is much steel, require longer time and the browning mixture should be still further diluted.   Soft barrels may be more quickly browned, and a stronger mixture used.   Where the figure is bold and the iron and steel threads are large there is less difficulty in browning.

The colours which can be obtained vary from a light yellowish-brown, through various red-browns, to a deep Vandyck-brown.   A rich plum brown is obtained if time is taken and a little black brimstone, say $\frac{1}{4}$ oz., added to the above mixture. Spirits of nitre and nitric ether are sometimes used in lieu of spirits of wine.

The black-and-white brown may be obtained by using much diluted mixture, and touching up the barrel before boiling by sponging with water in which a little muriate of steel has been stirred.   The colours can be heightened also by plunging the barrels in cold water immediately they are taken from the boiling trough.   In all fine-figured barrels the coating of rust is necessarily very thin, or the figure could not be distinguished.   This coating of brown soon wears off.   The only remedy is to have a greater body of brown, hiding the figure, or to use the black-brown, as in military rifle barrels.   This last brown is much more durable, and effectually pro-tects the barrels from rusting by salt air ; hence it is much used on ducking, punt, and wild-fowling guns.

Steel shot barrels, when black-browned, show no tendency to rust, however much exposed to atmospheric changes.   The black-brown is obtained in a shorter time, and a much stronger mixture may be used—as, for instance: $1\frac{1}{2}$ oz. spirits of wine; $1\frac{1}{2}$ oz. tincture of iron; $1\frac{1}{2}$ oz. corrosive sublimate; $1\frac{1}{2}$ oz. sweet spirits of nitre; 1 oz. sulphate of copper; $\frac{3}{4}$ oz. strong nitric acid; 1 quart of water.

Before re-browning any figured barrel it is essential that the old brown be effectually removed. The barrel must be well polished again before re-browning, if that fine sheen so much desired is required; otherwise, simply rubbing off the brown with emery cloth, with fine emery in water, or by sponging the barrel with strong vinegar, will answer the purpose.

MISCELLANEOUS MOUNTINGS.

The manufacture of gun-mountings comprises many branches. The mountings consist of sights, fore-end fasteners, safety-bolts, nipples and strikers, thumb-pieces, horn tips and heel-plates, and the screw-pins.

FORE-END FASTENERS.

Of the many fore-end fasteners introduced, the Deeley and Edge is the most in

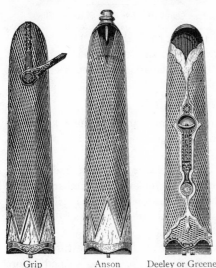

Grip Fore-end.   Anson Fore-end.   Deeley or Greener Improved Fore-end.

favour, owing to its handiness and neat appearance. The author has now introduced an improved model of the Deeley and Edge type, in which a square bolt, sliding in a groove and affording a much stronger grip, is substituted for the hook and half-circle motion of the original pattern. Outwardly both fore-ends have the same appearance. The Anson patent bolt consists of an iron rod in a tube, kept in position by a spiral spring. The grip fore-end fastener is of a similar construction to the original Lefaucheux lever used in breech-loading guns to secure the barrels. The old bolt, although the most secure, is fast falling into disuse, owing to its requiring a turn-screw to remove the fore-end.

SMALL FITTINGS.

Nipples and strikers are turned in a lathe, and are usually supplied to the trade by men who make the small work and nothing else. The old spring exploding pin, because it not unfrequently jammed, was practically superseded by the striker fitting freely and pushed back flush with the face of the standing breech by the extractor on opening and in closing the gun.   Another form of pin, with a large head to prevent dubbing up by the repeated blows of the hammer, is shown, and it, too, is worked in the same way.

Sometimes it is convenient to have a sling to the gun or rifle, in order that it may be slung across the shoulder.   For this purpose there are attachable slings

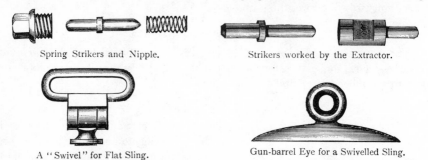

Spring Strikers and Nipple.   Strikers worked by the Extractor.

A "Swivel" for Flat Sling.   Gun-barrel Eye for a Swivelled Sling.

made, of which the one described on page 617 is probably the best, but it is neater to have soldered upon the barrel and screwed into the stock a swivel for a flat strap, or an eye ; if the latter, a swivel will have to be attached to each end of the strap used as a sling.

HORN TIPS AND HEEL-PLATES.

The heel-plates are either of buffalo horn or ebonite, and are glued, as well as screwed, to the stocks.   The tips and caps, for pistol-hand guns, are of buffalo horn, and glued to the wood.

The anti-recoil heel-plate consists of a layer of pliable vulcanised india-rubber affixed to an ebonite heel-plate, the centre of which is hollow, and together with the rubber covering forms a pneumatic pad.   The ebonite is pierced with holes to admit screws for fastening to the stock, as illustrated on the hammerless duck gun, page 399.

The wood screws and iron pins for gun-work are made from the best iron.   The wood screws are taper and smoothly finished off, and are always soaped before being turned in, to prevent their binding in the wood.   The screws are manufactured in the neighbourhood of Birmingham.   The same people also make the rifle eyes for slings, etc.

The iron pins are made from rolled bar-iron.   They are stamped upon olivers, in much the same manner as described for stamping with dies. Common iron pins are made by screw-cutting machinery.

THE USE OF MACHINERY IN GUN-MAKING.

The idea of making guns on the interchangeable system by the aid of machinery appears to have originated with the French during the latter part of the eighteenth century. The process of stamping instead of forging the various parts of the gun was the only successful result, and the honour of working out the system to a successful issue is due to the Americans.

About 1797, Eli Whitney, the owner of cotton mills in some of the Southern States, moved northwards, and was induced to try his fortunes as a gunsmith. A contract for 10,000 arms was secured for him ; these he manufactured almost entirely from stampings, and he also applied machinery to the shaping and, as far as possible, to the finishing of the several parts. He also introduced the system of gauges, by which uniformity of construction is ensured for parts made after the same model.

John H. Hall, of Harper's Ferry, was the next to improve the system. In 1812 he wrote to the United States Government, laying particular stress upon his plan of making guns. He says :—" Every similar part of my gun is so much alike that it will suit every gun." This system of interchangeability was first applied to Government service by Hall in 1818, and it has since established itself as the rule of the Government workshops.

Blanchard, of Middlebury, Massachusetts, carried the improvements a step beyond either Whitney or Hall, by the application of the lathe to the turning of the barrel and shaping of the gun stock.

Blanchard required seventeen separate machines for the shaping of his stocks, but by the combination of processes these have since been reduced to thirteen. Some idea of the extent to which the use of machinery in the making of military arms is carried may be gathered from the fact that one of the American factories has more than 1,758 machines, and can turn out each day five hundred rifles of a particular pattern. A Belgian factory constructed for an estimated output of three hundred a day has 900 machines, which cost more than three million francs before being fixed. The various processes through which the several limbs of the gun pass are technically termed " cuts." It is not unusual for 1,000 " cuts " to be made in producing a particular rifle. In some as many as 1,250 are necessary, but the general tendency is to simplify the mechanism and materially reduce the cost of the military small arm.

In England Mr. Prosser was requested by the Government to report as to the possibility of making guns on the interchangeable plan.   This was in 1850 ; in 1852 Col. Colt was examined by a Committee of the House of Commons with reference to the same subject, and upon the strength of his representations a Commission visited the United States ; the result of that visit was the founding of the Enfield factory, the purchase of American machinery and the introduction of the interchangeable system of manufacture into England at the close of the Crimean War.

The strikes of the gunmen in Birmingham during the Crimean War undoubtedly greatly influenced our Government to take this step to ensure a sufficient supply of arms in case of emergency ; for, during the war, the supply of Enfield rifles was so small that they had to be despatched after the troops, and some regiments were even armed, *pro tem.*, with the old Brown Bess.   Had the workmen of Birmingham worked during the rush, instead of immediately and continuously striking, in all probability the Government factory would never have been founded ; and the two large factories built afterwards in Birmingham for the manufacture of military arms by improved machinery would have been fully employed.

The making of military arms by machinery, however, has its drawbacks.   It impairs the value of skilled labour, for by the division of labour and the subdivision of the various branches the workman becomes a mere machine, going through the monotonous routine without interest or endeavour to render more perfect the article he assists in shaping, although, doubtless, the work itself is better done by means of such subdivision.

That improvements and changes are not desired in a large machine factory can easily be imagined, as the expense of altering the machines, gauges, and tools is so great ; therefore the tardiness in adopting a new model.   And whatever may be said in favour of machine-made arms, unless skilled labour is at hand to fall back upon, nations may sometimes be at a loss.   For instance, during the American War the machine factories at Harper's Ferry were captured by the South, and the long war was concluded before the Government could again set up machinery to turn out arms in the quantities required.   Both sides depended for their supply upon hand-made guns manufactured by the English and the Belgians.

In military arms the advantage of the interchangeable system is apparent ; but for sporting arms, where in every case individual taste has to be considered, their production must ever be fraught with formidable obstacles, and perfect as works of art they never can be.

In the production of sporting guns machinery now has an important part.   The ordinary sporting gun, not the interchangeable article, is here referred to.   Much of the labour which was formerly done by hammer, file, and foot-lathe is now more readily and cheaply performed by the judicious use of machinery. In the hammer-less gun, for instance, much work which could only be done indifferently by hand-drills, " routers," and special tools, is cleanly and squarely cut by slotting and profiling machines. Probably the gunsmiths of Bohemia are the only workmen who, at this date, could take the bars of iron and steel and the plank of wood and single-handed produce therefrom a modern shot-gun. Such a weapon would be much inferior to even the ordinary qualities produced in this and other countries at less than one-third the cost. The work which can be profitably accomplished by machining includes much of the first shaping of breech-actions and barrels, but it is only of late years that steam machinery has been considered necessary for the manufacture of sporting breech-actions, and even now those few London and country gun-makers who manufacture their own breech-actions are, with very few exceptions, under the necessity of labouring with the slow and old-fashioned foot-lathe. Those gun-makers, however, who have to produce first-rate weapons at a moderate price, as well as high-class hammerless guns, are obliged to provide themselves with machinery sufficient to carry on a light engineering business, and most of them are now able to manufacture upon the premises such tools and light machinery as may be required for general purposes.

By adopting steam machinery and the division of labour it is not only possible to reduce cost of manufacture, but the work is done much better than if one man did three or four branches. The ordinary work of the machine-shop may be shortly described.

The barrels are placed in a lathe for chambering, the tool revolving very slowly, about 120 revolutions per minute. The barrel is slowly forced towards the lathe head by the screw centre, and soap-suds are continually kept running upon the tool, to assist the cutting and keep the tool clean. The barrels are first rough-chambered, the extractors fitted, and then finished chambering. The roughing tool is generally half round, which cuts on one side only. The finishing tool cuts very fine, and has generally three or five cutting edges. The barrel, when chambered, is taken to a milling machine and the recess for the extractor cut, the hole for the leg having been drilled in the steel lump before brazing it to the barrels.

The steel lump is planed on each side to gauges, so that it may be in the centre of the barrels, and a more uniform thickness ensured.

The parts worked in this shop consist of forgings for the body or breech-action proper, the fore-end, and, when double-grip actions, the lever.

The milling machine, which does most of the work to the breech-actions, resembles a lathe head upon a short bed, in front of which is a slide rest, capable of being moved vertically as well as horizontally. The body is fixed in a holding block, and a cut taken down one side. This side then serves as a basis from which the body may be machined square and true. By moving the handles right or left, forward or backward, up or down, the body may be planed all over, and a much truer form obtained than if done by a file.

The lock holes, to receive the mainsprings, can also be cut, the slots for lump drilled ; the joint, or hinge-pin, on which the barrel turns, put in perfectly true, and the fore-end joint shaped a half-circle, of which the joint-pin is the centre.

The hollow joint in the fore-end is cut by a tool running between centres in a lathe, and is made to coincide with 'the joint formed on the breech-action. The bolt-hole, or slot in the body for the under-bolt, is generally drilled in a lathe. Besides the above, the extractors, hinge-pins, strikers, etc., are turned in this shop, and various tools and cutters made ; therefore it is necessary that the whole shop be managed by a clever engineer and tool-maker.

The wedge-fast hammerless guns are treated in the same manner, but the slots for the lock-work are cut in the bottom of the body and block of the standing-breech.

The hinge-pin also has sometimes to be left solid in the action, instead of being screwed in, as is the case with ordinary actions.

MACHINE-MADE SPORTING GUNS.

Endeavours to produce double shot-guns by machinery have not been altogether successful. The United States for years has been the best market for shot-guns, and with the Americans originated the idea of supplying the demand by cheaper production. Several firms embarked in the venture, glutting the market for a time. An enterprising Liége firm followed with similar weapons, and latterly English and German firms have also produced machine-made guns on the interchangeable plan.

These productions are of various qualities, and each successive model is an improvement on preceding ones; nevertheless—without contending that the production of a perfect machine-made double shot-gun is an impossibility—all models yet produced have defects not found in fine or medium quality hand-made guns.

Machine-made guns must be considered a production of mechanical engineering, not of gun-making, and from that standpoint may give that satisfaction which from any other point of view would not be forthcoming.

The radical error made is the assumption that one type of gun will suit, if not everyone, yet a very large number of persons. As no two persons are exactly alike, each person to be perfectly suited with a gun will require something different to that which will suit anyone else ; and the interchangeable system of manufacture precludes any change in design, or even such modifications of form as will suit a gun to differences of personal physique.

The common plan, too, is to use hand-welded barrels of differing weights, but fitting all to the same size of breech mechanism and stock. Thus some guns will be badly balanced, in fact, any slight variation from the exact original model will fail, because, in a sporting gun, if any one piece is made larger or smaller, many other pieces, if not the whole, which comprise the gun must conform proportionately, or the weapon will be imperfect.

The machine factories, however large their stock, cannot carry, because they cannot profitably make in small quantities, arms of the different lengths, weights and bores required by sportsmen. The author carries, perhaps, the largest stock of finished sporting guns of anyone in England, yet out of the thousands in his possession there are, with the exception of match pairs, probably no two guns quite alike in every particular. If the demand for sporting guns could be met like the call for military muskets, then the interchangeable method of manufacture would succeed. As long as sportsmen require so many different weapons, it can never prove profitable.

Again, the introduction of new explosives of greater or varying strengths, of which there appears to be a constant supply, and of improved mechanisms, is not only against, the manufacture of a particular type of gun by machinery in great quantities, but also militates against the accumulation of stock. Of late years the author and leading gun-makers in this country have deemed it advisable to increase the strength of the breech mechanisms of guns likely to be used with certain nitro-explosives. In like manner, at and near the breech-ends the barrels are made stouter, yet the gun is kept to the usual weight, is in some cases even lighter, and the balance is where it is always found in high-quality guns. The changes required the whole construction of the gun to be modified. So much, or so little, could not be accomplished profitably or in like time with the machine methods of production. The interchangeable guns of a few years ago are not all so well suited to modern explosives as later patterns of hand-made guns ; some of them have burst or broken when used with heavy charges of these now fashionable powders, and others may do so ; yet not only the method, but the very model is still adhered to.

In short, a machine-made sporting gun is not a higher development of the shot-gun, but rather a degenerate specimen. It is a *sine quâ non* that all be alike : no scope is given for the fancy of workman or artist, no incentive to producing a better arm than all before turned out ; and instead of being a perfectly balanced, proportionate, tastily ornamented and well-built gun, it is but the assemblage of various synoforms, neither artistic nor symmetrical ; in many instances a poor, and at best only a mediocre, production.

CHAPTER XI.

THE PROOF OF GUNS.

HISTORY OF GUN-BARREL PROVING.

THE compulsory proving of fire-arms most probably originated in the jealousy of the gun-makers' guilds. The guilds sought by enactments, ostensibly for the benefit of the public, to prevent the manufacture of fire-arms by unauthorised persons. However this may be, the compulsory proving of gun barrels has invariably been beneficial to those engaged in fire-arms manufacture.

At St. Etienne, in France, the testing of fire-arms has been carried on for many years, probably since the date of the introduction of the industry in the fifteenth century, but it has never been compulsory in France. In London, Birmingham, and Liége, before compulsory tests were required to be made, most gun-makers privately proved guns within their own factories, or at a trade proof-house, a system still in vogue in Austria, France, and probably in America.

The first Charter of Incorporation of the London Gun-makers' Company possibly did not confer the powers which rendered gun-barrel proving at the Company's house imperative, but the second charter, granted in 1672, gave powers of searching for and proving and marking all manner of hand guns, great and small, daggs and pistols, and every part thereof, whether made in London or the suburbs, or within ten miles thereof, or imported from foreign parts, or otherwise brought thither for sale; and a scale for proof was thereby established. In pursuance of their charter the Gun-makers' Company established the Proof-house near the City of London.

In Birmingham a company was formed, and an Act of Parliament obtained in the year 1813, with suitable premises for the proof of gun barrels. This Act proved insufficient, as many makers found easy means of evading it. Another Act, likewise inoperative, was passed in 1815.

After much agitation another Act was obtained in 1855, and this proving quite unsatisfactory, the agitation did not subside until the wardens of the Proof-house, and those responsible for its control, accepted a new Bill, which was passed in 1868, and remains in force. By this Bill—which is a private Act, not a Statute of the Realm—the trade elect their own guardians, and it is enacted that any person or persons making and selling any gun the barrel of which has not been proved at either this or the London Proof-house become liable to a penalty of £20. And it further enacts that any person or persons forging the stamps or marks of either of the two Proof-houses should be liable to the same penalties, and in default of payment, to a certain term of imprisonment, etc. It also orders that the barrels be proved with the quantity of powder in proportion to the various bores.

About twenty years ago, owing to an agitation by certain persons, who pointed out the inefficiency of the proof test, a Committee appointed by the London Company and the Birmingham Guardians drew up an amended scale of proof and classification of small arms. The new rules were sanctioned by her Majesty's Secretary of State, and became compulsory on the first day of April, 1888. It was provided by these rules that, on application in writing by the person sending the arm for proof, it might be tested with any nitro-compound or explosive in addition to the official test with the regulation black gunpowder. In 1893 attention was called to the fact that this supplementary proof was rarely employed, and in 1896 new rules were substituted by which the testing of all guns intended to be used with nitro-explosives is ordered to be made with treble-strong fine-grain sporting powder in addition to the ordinary test with the regulation powder, and they *may be* submitted to any further tests with other explosives, if the sender so requires. Still later, in 1904, new rules were formulated and an alteration made in the proof marks. The following extracts from the schedules and rules will be found sufficiently full to convey the meaning of the Act and to ascertain the proof charges used in provisional, definitive, and supplementary proofs of any description of fire-arm. The tests at both the London and Birmingham Proof-houses are the same, but, as will be explained, the marks differ.

SCHEDULE B.—RULES AND REGULATIONS AND SCALES APPLICABLE TO THE PROOF OF SMALL ARMS.

Classification of Small Arms.

FIRST CLASS.—Comprising Single-barrelled Muzzle-loading Arms of Smooth Bore.

SECOND CLASS.—Comprising Double-barrelled Muzzle-loading Arms of Smooth Bore.

THIRD CLASS.—Muzzle-loading Rifled Arms.

FOURTH CLASS.—Breech-loading Arms of Smooth Bore.

FIFTH CLASS.—Breech-loading Rifled Arms not being of the Sixth, Seventh, and Eighth Classes.

SIXTH CLASS.—Express Breech-loading Rifles.

SEVENTH CLASS.—Breech-loading Rifled Arms of a bore not exceeding .315 of an inch, in which a cartridge capable of containing a full Military Service Charge of Nitro-Powder is used.

EIGHTH CLASS.—Breech-loading Rifled Arms specially constructed for use with Shot and Bullet, having the whole or a portion only of their bore rifled and not being of the Fifth Class.

NINTH CLASS.—Revolving Arms and Repeating Pistols.

Rules of Proof.

1.—There shall be three kinds of Proof, viz., Provisional, Definitive, and Supplementary. Provisional proof is the first proof applied to barrels which, according to these rules, require two proofs. Definitive proof is that applied as the second proof to barrels which require two proofs, also that applied to those which require one proof only. Supplementary proof is an additional one applied after the definitive proof, according to Rules 17, 18, and 19.

2.—The descriptions of powder used in proof shall, except as provided in Rule 18, be as follows :

That known as "Tower Proof," or "T.P.," which shall be of strength equal to Waltham Abbey, "R.F.G. 2," and of a grain varying between Nos. 4 and 5.

That known as Curtis's and Harvey's "T.S. No. 2."

That known as "Col. Hawker's Duck-Gun Powder," and

The nitro-powder known as Cordite, or any other description of nitro-powder which may hereafter, from time to time, be adopted by His Majesty's War Department.

Provided, nevertheless, that, if any of the powders for the use of which this rule provides should be considered by the Two Companies unsuitable for the proof of any particular description of barrel, they shall have power to adopt such other powder as they may consider to be most suitable, having first obtained the approval of His Majesty's Principal Secretary of State for the War Department.

3.—The shot used in proof shall be that known as "soft shot," Size No. 6.

4.—The bullets used in proof shall be of pure lead, except as provided in Rules 13, 14, 16, 19, and 26, and of such forms as are hereinafter defined in the rules relating to the proof of the different classes.

5.—The wads used in proof shall be of felt or other suitable material, and shall not exceed in thickness one diameter of the bore.

6.—Barrels for arms of the First Class shall be proved once definitively, and for those of the Second, Third, Fourth, Fifth, Sixth, Seventh, and Eighth Classes provisionally and definitively, except as provided in Rule 24. Provided, nevertheless, that barrels for arms of the Second and Third Classes, and for single-barrelled arms of the Fourth and Fifth Classes, sent in a state for definitive proof, may, at the request in writing of the sender, be proved once only, according to the scale for provisional proof, and they shall receive a special definitive proof mark, denoting that they have been so proved, as hereinafter provided in Rules 39 and 46.

7.—Barrels for arms of the First Class shall be proved with T.P. Powder and a spherical bullet, according to Scale No. 1.

8.—Barrels for arms of the Second Class shall be provisionally proved with T.P. Powder and a spherical bullet, and definitively proved with T.P. Powder and shot according to Scale No. 2, or may be proved once only, as provided in Rule 6.

9.—Barrels for arms of the Third Class shall be provisionally and definitively proved with T.P. Powder and a cylindrical flat-ended bullet, according to Scale No. 3, or may be proved once only, as provided in Rule 6.

10.—Barrels for arms of the Fourth Class shall be provisionally and definitively proved with T.P. Powder and shot, according to Scale No. 4. Barrels for single-barrelled arms of this class may be proved once only, as provided in Rule 6.

11.—Barrels of arms of the Fifth Class shall be provisionally proved with T.P. Powder and a cylindrical flat-ended bullet. They shall be definitively proved with T.P. Powder and a cylindrical flat-ended or cylindro-conoidal bullet, according to Scale No. 3. Provided, nevertheless, that, should a barrel be chambered for a cartridge which cannot contain the Service Charge defined in the scale, it may receive a special definitive proof with a charge based upon the maximum Service Charge of such cartridge. Provided also that, should a barrel be intended to be used with a larger charge than the Service Charge defined in the scale, the sender shall declare the same in writing, and a special definitive proof based upon such declraed Service Charge shall be applied. In each case the proportion of Proof Charge to Service Charge shall be the same as in the scale. Barrels which have received a special definitive proof under this rule shall be marked as hereinafter provided in Rule 52. Barrels for single-barrelled arms of this class may be proved once only, as provided in Rule 6.

12.—Barrels for arms of the Sixth Class shall be provisionally proved with T.P. Powder and a cylindrical flat-ended bullet, according to Scale No. 3. They shall be definitively proved with T.S. No. 2 Powder and a flat-ended bullet, or such other form as may be, from time to time, considered to be most suitable, according to Scale No. 5. Barrels proved under this rule shall be specially marked, as hereinafter provided in Rule 53.

13.—Barrels for arms of the Sixth Class specially constructed for the use of nitro-powders, shall be so declared in writing, by the sender when presented for definitive proof. They shall be definitively proved with Cordite-powder, or such other nitro-powder as the Two Companies may, under the provisions of Rule 2, consider to be most suitable, and with a nickel-covered bullet, similar in form to that of the Service Cartridge for which the barrels are chambered, or of such other material and form as may be, from time to time, considered to be most suitable. The Service Charge shall be declared in writing by the sender, and the Proof Charge shall be such as shall give a stress not less than thirty per cent. over that of the Service Charge, as may be readily ascertainable. Barrels proved under this rule shall be specially marked, as hereinafter provided in Rule 54.

14.—Barrels for arms of the Seventh Class shall be provisionally proved with T.P. Powder and a cylindrical flat-ended bullet, according to Scale No. 3. They shall be definitively proved with Cordite-powder, or such other nitro-powder as the Two Companies may, under the provisions of Rule 2, consider to be most suitable, and a nickel-covered bullet, of a similar form to that of the Service Cartridge for which the barrels are chambered, or of such other material and form as may be, from time to time, considered to be most suitable. The Proof Charge shall be such as shall give a stress not less than twenty-five per cent., and not more than forty per cent. over that of the Service Charge, as may be readily ascertainable. Barrels proved under this rule shall be specially marked, as hereinafter provided in Rule 55.

15.—Barrels for arms of the Eighth Class shall be provisionally proved with T.P. Powder and shot, according to Scale No. 4 for the Fourth Class. They shall be declared in writing by the sender to be of the Eighth Class when presented for definitive proof, and shall be proved with T.P. Powder according to Scale No. 4, with a conical bullet one and three-quarters the weight of the Service Charge of shot of the said scale, of a diameter suitable to that of the muzzle of the barrels. In case barrels are intended to be used with larger charges of powder than the ordinary Service Charge set forth in the said Scale No. 4, they shall be so declared in writing by the sender, and a Proof Charge proportionate thereto shall be applied. Barrels proved under this rule shall be specially marked, as hereinafter provided in Rule 56.

16.—Arms of the Ninth Class shall be proved with a cartridge of the maximum size suitable thereto, and containing such a charge of powder, and such a bullet, as, in the opinion of the Two Companies, will cover the Service Charge to be used. Revolving Arms shall be proved once definitively in each chamber. Repeating Pistols shall be proved definitively, and be fired with the number of shots the magazine will contain. Arms of the Ninth Class shall be marked, as hereinafter provided in Rule 47.

17.—Barrels for arms of the Fourth and Eighth Classes, in which nitro-powders are intended to be used, shall be so declared in writing by the sender, and shall receive a supplementary proof, in addition to, and after, the definitive proof under Rules 10 and 15, with T.S. No. 2 Powder, according to Scale No. 6, which scale has been based on the ordinary Service Charges of the nitro-powders now in general use, and which, in the opinion of the Two Companies, do not exert higher pressures than those recognised as Standard. In case barrels are intended to be used with larger charges of nitro-powders than such ordinary Service Charges, then the quantities of powder and shot so intended to be used shall be declared in writing by the sender, and a Proof Charge which the Two Companies may decide to be suitable shall be applied. Barrels proved under this rule shall be specially marked, as hereinafter provided in Rule 57.

18.—Barrels for arms of the Fourth Class may, after having been definitively proved under Rule 10, and supplementarily proved under Rule 17, at the request in writing of the sender, receive a further supplementary proof with any particular description of nitro-powder, in general use, named by him, with a Proof Charge which the Two Companies may decide to be most suitable. Barrels proved under this rule shall be specially marked, as hereinafter provided in Rule 58.

19.—Barrels for arms of the Fifth and Eighth Classes may, at the request in writing of the sender, receive a supplementary proof, in addition to, and after, the definitive proof, with Cordite-powder, or such other nitro-powder as the Two Companies may, under the provisions of Rule 2, consider to be most suitable. The Service Charge shall be declared in writing by the sender, and such a Proof Charge of powder and such a bullet as the Two Companies may decide to be most suitable shall be applied. Barrels proved under this rule shall be specially marked, as hereinafter provided in Rule 59.

20.—For Barrels of all Military Arms, sent for proof, manufactured for the

British Government, the method of proof shall be the same as that employed by His Majesty's War Department.

21.—Barrels for arms of the Fourth, Fifth, and Eighth Classes of 8 Gauge having chambers of 4 inches and longer, those of 10, 12 and 14 Gauge having chambers of 3 inches and longer, and those of 16 to 32 Gauge having chambers of $2\frac{3}{4}$ inches and longer, shall be so declared in writing by the sender. They shall be definitively proved with one-sixth more powder than that used for ordinary definitive proof, and shall be marked with a special Chamber mark, as hereinafter provided in Rule 50.

22.—Barrels for arms of the Second and Fourth Classes, of a larger Gauge than 4, for which no charges are laid down in the scales applicable to such classes, shall be provisionally proved according to Scale No. 1 for the First Class.

23.—Barrels for arms of the Second and Fourth Classes, of a larger Gauge than 4, sent for definitive proof, for which no charges are laid down in the scales applicable to such classes, shall have the Service Charge declared in writing by the sender, and the Proof Charge shall be twice the weight of powder and one and one-third the weight of shot of such Service Charge. The Service Charge shall be marked upon the barrels, as hereinafter provided in Rule 60.

24.—Barrels for arms of the First, Second, and Fourth Classes of not less than 5 feet 6 inches long shall be proved once definitively with Col. Hawker's Duck-Gun Powder and shot. The Service Charge shall be declared in writing by the sender, and the Proof Charge shall be twice the weight of powder, and one and one-third the weight of shot of such Service Charge. The Service Charge shall be marked upon the barrels, as hereinafter provided in Rule 60.

25.—Barrels for arms of the First, Second, Fourth, and Fifth Classes which are Choke-bored shall be declared to be so, in writing, by the sender when presented for definitive proof. Choke-bored barrels are such as have the diameter of the bore at the muzzle less than at some point behind the muzzle other than the chamber, or the cone or lead in front of the chamber. Barrels which are choked ·004 of an inch may, at the request in writing of the sender, be marked, and those which are choked ·008 of an inch shall be marked, when proved, as hereinafter provided in Rule 51. Barrels which are choked ·008 of an inch or more, and not marked as provided in Rule 51, are required to be re-proved.

26.—A barrel of any description for which the classification and scales of proof do not provide, or to which the said scales are, in the opinion of the Two Companies, inapplicable or unsuitable, shall be proved with such a charge of powder, and such a bullet or charge of shot, as, in their opinion, is most suitable for such barrel, and they may, if they think fit, require the Service Charge to be declared by the sender. In case a barrel shall not be capable of containing such a Proof Charge, as large a charge as the barrel will contain shall be applied. Barrels proved under this rule shall be marked, as hereinafter provided in Rule 61.

27.—Whenever a barrel is sent for proof chambered for a cartridge of unusual size or of a pattern not in general use, the cartridge case required to prove such barrel shall be provided by the sender.

28.—The Two Companies will not be responsible for the proper proof or marking of, and may refuse to prove, barrels which, according to Rules 13, 17, 18, 19, 21, 23, 24, and 25, require special definitive proof, supplementary proof, or special marking, unless such barrels are accompanied by the necessary requests or declarations, defined in the said rules, when presented for proof. Provided always that the Two Companies may prove and mark barrels unaccompanied by any request or declaration in such a manner as, in their opinion, such barrels should be proved and marked.

29.—Should a barrel be presented for any special or supplementary proof, which, though it may belong to a class to which such proof may be applicable, is unsuited to such proof, the Proof Master of the Company to which it is presented may refuse to prove it. He may also refuse to prove a barrel declared to be of a certain class. which is not of such class, except for the class to which it should belong.

30.—If a barrel which has already been proved and marked with the definitive proof and view marks be again presented for definitive or supplementary proof, and shall fail to stand proof, the person or persons respectively, who is or are entitled to impress the proof and view marks, shall efface the existing marks of definitive and supplementary proof therefrom. Should a barrel which has obviously been weakened after definitive proof be brought to the notice of the Proof Master of either of the Two Companies, it may be re-proved definitively without the consent of the owner. Should a barrel be brought to the notice of the Proof Master of either of the Two Companies which is in such a condition that it would be impossible to re-prove it, or to properly view it, the marks of definitive and supplementary proof may be effaced therefrom by the before-mentioned person or persons.

31.—Any barrel which may have been enlarged in the bore after definitive proof, so that the bore mark impressed upon it at proof is not a true representation of the diameter, shall be required to be re-proved definitively, and if it shall have received a supplementary proof, it shall be required to be re-proved supplementarily ; such, for example, as an enlargement from $\frac{9}{2}$ to 8 or $\frac{13}{1}$ to 12, as set forth in Scale No. 4.

32.—The various powders used in proof shall, at all times, be open to the inspection, without notice, of any officer authorised for the purpose by the Secretary of State for War, who may take samples of the same for examination or trial.

Conditions Precedent to Proof.

33.—Barrels for arms of the First Class sent for proof shall be bored and ground and in a proper state for setting up, with the squares set off, looped and the proper breeches in, with the thread of the screws sound and full. Barrels for percussioned arms shall be percussioned and have nipples in. Twisted barrels shall be fine bored and struck up.

34.—Barrels for arms of the Second, Third, Fourth, Fifth, Sixth, Seventh, and Eighth Classes :—

For Provisional Proof.—Barrels of plain metal shall be fine bored and turned or ground, and those of twisted metal shall be struck up in addition. They shall have plugs attached with touchholes drilled in the plugs of a diameter not exceeding one-sixteenth of an inch.

For Definitive Proof.—All barrels shall be struck up and smoothed, the insides shall be clean, the ribs fairly struck up, and such as are Muzzle-loading shall have breeches properly percussioned, huts filed up, the proper breeches and nipples attached, with the thread of the screw sound and full. Barrels for rifled arms shall be rifled.

35.—Barrels for Breech-loading arms shall be definitively and supplementarily proved with the action attached. The action shall be finished or in the finished filed state.

36.—Revolving arms shall have the cylinder or chambers with the revolving action and firing work complete and in working order. Repeating pistols shall be complete and in working order with the magazine attached.

Marks of Proof.

The Marks denoting Provisional Proof shall be as follows:

As to the Gun-makers' Company (London):

The Letters " G P " interlaced in a Cypher surmounted by a Lion rampant.

As to the Guardians (Birmingham):

The Letters "B P" interlaced in a Cypher surmounted by a Crown, thus:

The Marks denoting Definitive Proof shall be as follows:

As to the Gun-makers' Company:
The Proof Mark being the letters "G P" interlaced in a Cypher surmounted by a Crown, and the View Mark being the letter V surmounted by a Crown, thus:

As to the Guardians:
The Proof Mark being the Letters B P surmounted by a Crown, and the View Mark being the Letters B V surmounted by a Crown, thus:

The Mark denoting the special Definitive Proof of barrels proved once only, according to Rule 6, shall be as follows:

As to the Gun-makers' Company:
The Letters "V G P" interlaced in a Cypher surmounted by a Lion rampant, thus:

As to the Guardians:
The Letters "V B P" interlaced in a Cypher surmounted by a Crown:

The Special Proof Mark applied to barrels proved for use with nitro powders according to Rules 13, 14, 17, 18, and 19 shall be as follow:

As to the Gun-makers' Company:
The Letters "N P" surmounted by an arm Dexter in Armour embowed, holding a Scimitar.

As to the Guardians:
The Letters "N P" surmounted by a Crown, thus:

Mode of affixing Proof Marks.

The proof marks are stamped upon the under-side of each barrel, within three inches of the breech—the provisional proof mark on the round part and the definitive proof mark on the flat—and the mark of definitive proof (*vide ante*) is also stamped upon the breech-action body, and in rifles with movable breech-block, upon the breech-block also. If a gun is double proved, both proof marks are on the flats. Revolvers are marked upon each chamber, upon the barrel, and upon the frame.

The gauge size is impressed on all guns at the definitive proof, and on guns and choke-bored rifles it is enclosed with the letter "C" in a device as shown and explained below.

In gun barrels from 4- to 10-gauge, the gauge is divided into three parts, and is marked accordingly—for example, 8, $\frac{8}{1}$, $\frac{8}{2}$; from 11 to 17 it is divided into two, as 12, $\frac{12}{1}$. In breech-loading guns the gauge size is taken at a point nine inches from the breech end; in rifles and muzzle-loading guns it is taken at the muzzle. On choke-bored barrels the word "choke" is added to the proof-marks following the gauge size, and to choke-bored rifles "R. Choke" is added.

The following illustrations show the marks put upon ordinary weapons:

The marks of the Birmingham Proof House, indicating a simple proof of a 12-bore gun.

Marks of the London Proof House, signifying that the barrel has been twice proved, that the diameter of the barrel is ·740 of an inch, that the chamber is more than three inches long, that the barrel is rifled and choke-bored, and has been proved as required for that description of boring.

 ·577 EX.

Marks of the London Proof House for a ·577 Express Rifle.

 ·500 EX.

Marks of Birmingham Proof for ·500 Express Rifle.

Proof Marks indicating a 400 Bore High Velocity Rifle.   Birmingham Proof.

Barrels proved with T.S.2 fine-grain black gunpowder, as a supplementary test, are marked in addition, "Nitro Proof, ...oz. Maximum," indicating the weight of shot to be used; as:—

NITRO PROOF 1½ OZ. MAXIMUM.

The marks of the London Proof House upon a barrel intended for use with nitro-explosives, and tested with fine-grain black gunpowder; the load of shot to be used not to exceed 1½ oz.

Barrels proved with a nitro-explosive as a supplementary test to that made for ordinary definitive proof are further marked with the name or abbreviation of the name of the explosive used in the test, together with numbers showing the maximum service charges of powder in grains, and shot in ounces, that may be used, as for example :—

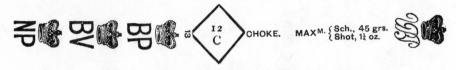

The marks of the Birmingham Proof House for 12-gauge choke-bored shot-gun, tested for use with a maximum charge of 45 grains of Schultze powder and 1¼ oz. of shot.

In like manner, the barrels of punt guns and other large bores have the service charge marked in drams and ounces, following the proof and view marks of the ordinary kind.

On barrels for arms of the Eighth Class, definitively proved according to rule 15, which are rifled through their full length, the letters "S & B," signifying Shot and Bullet, shall be impressed, following the definitive proof mark or chamber mark, thus—

"S. & B."

SCALE OF PROOF FOR BREECH-LOADING ARMS OF SMOOTH BORE.
(Fourth Class.)

Number of Bore.	Diameter of Bore by Calculation.	Provisional Proof.			Definitive Proof.				Service Charge.			
		Powder T. P.		Shot.	Powder T. P.		Shot.		Powder.		Shot.	
		grains.	drs.	grains.	grains.	drs.	grains.	ozs.	grains.	drs.	grains.	ozs.
5/2	1·026	740	27	1421	492	18	1912	4⅜	246	9	1421	3¼
5/1	1·001											
5	·976											
6/2	·957											
6/1	·938	649	23¾	......								
6	·919											

SCALE OF PROOF FOR BREECH-LOADING ARMS OF SMOOTH BORE (*Continued*).

Number of Bore.	Diameter of Bore by Calculation.	Provisional Proof.			Definitive Proof.				Service Charge.			
		Powder T. P.		Shot.	Powder T. P.		Shot.		Powder.		Shot.	
		grains.	drs.	grains.	grains.	drs.	grains.	ozs.	grains.	drs.	grains.	ozs.
$\frac{7}{2}$	·903	567	20¾	984								
$\frac{7}{1}$	·888											
7	·873											
8	·860				328	12	1312	3	164	6	984	2¼
$\frac{8}{1}$	·847	492	18	984								
8	·835											
$\frac{9}{2}$	·824											
$\frac{9}{1}$	·813	417	15¼	984								
9	·803											
$\frac{10}{2}$	·793											
$\frac{10}{1}$	·784	348	12¾	711	232	8½	930	2⅛	116	4¼	711	1⅝
10	·775											
$\frac{11}{1}$	·763	294	10¾	711								
11	·751											
$\frac{12}{1}$	·740	266	9¾									
12	·729			547	178	6½	738	1 11/16	89	3¼	547	1¼
$\frac{13}{1}$	·719	260	9½									
13	·710											
$\frac{14}{1}$	·701	246	9									
14	·693			492	164	6	656	1½	82	3	492	1⅛
$\frac{15}{1}$	·685	.. ...	......									
15	·677	239	8¾									

SCALE OF PROOF FOR BREECH-LOADING ARMS OF SMOOTH BORE (*Continued*).

Number of Bore.	Diameter of Bore by Calculation.	Provisional Proof.			Definitive Proof.				Service Charge.			
		Powder T. P.		Shot.	Powder T. P.		Shot.		Powder.		Shot.	
		grains.	drs.	grains.	grains.	drs.	grains.	ozs.	grains.	drs.	grains.	ozs.
16/1	·669	226	8¼									
16	·662											
17/1	·655	218	8	437	150	5½	574	1 5/16	75	2¾	437	1
17	·649											
18	·637	211	7¾									
19	·626	205	7½									
20	·615			383	136	5	520	1 3/16	68	2½	383	7/8
21	·605	198	7¼									
22	·596											
23	·587	191	7									
24	·579	184	6¾	355	123	4½	465	1 1/16	62	2¼	355	13/16
25	·571	184	6¾									
26	·563	178	6½									
27	·556	171	6¼									
28	·550	164	6	328	109	4	437	1	55	2	328	¾
29	·543	150	5½									
30	·537	144	5¼									
31	·531											
32	·526	137	5									
33	·520			246	82	3	328	¾	41	1½	246	9/16
34	·515											
35	·510	130	4¾									
36	·506											
37	·501	123	4½									
38	·497											

SCALE OF SUPPLEMENTARY PROOF, WITH POWDER "T.S.2," OF ARMS OF THE FOURTH CLASS IN WHICH NITRO-POWDERS ARE TO BE USED.

See Rule 17.

No. of Gauge.	Charge of Powder, T.S.2.		Charge of Shot.		Shot Service Charge.
	Grains.	Drams.	Grains.	Ounces.	Ounces.
4	301	11	1,805	$4\frac{1}{8}$	3
8	218	8	1,312	3	2
10	150	$5\frac{1}{2}$	903	$2\frac{1}{16}$	$1\frac{1}{2}$
12	116	$4\frac{1}{4}$	711	$1\frac{5}{8}$	$1\frac{3}{8}$
12 extra *	137	5	738	$1\frac{11}{16}$	$1\frac{1}{4}$
14	109	4	656	$1\frac{1}{2}$	$1\frac{1}{16}$
16	102	$3\frac{3}{4}$	602	$1\frac{3}{8}$	1
20	95	$3\frac{1}{2}$	574	$1\frac{5}{16}$	$\frac{7}{8}$
24	89	$3\frac{1}{4}$	520	$1\frac{3}{16}$	$\frac{3}{4}$
28	82	3	492	$1\frac{1}{8}$	$\frac{5}{8}$
32	62	$2\frac{1}{4}$	355	$\frac{13}{16}$	$\frac{9}{16}$
·410	34	$1\frac{1}{4}$	246	$\frac{9}{16}$	$\frac{3}{8}$

* Extra-long cartridge chambers.

The marks of the Birmingham Proof House, which were in use prior to August 1st, 1904, are as follows :—

These marks were applied in the same way as those at present in use, and arms bearing such marks may be legally dealt with. Further information, together with full scales for all classes of arms, may be obtained from the "Schedule" issued by the Combined Proof Houses.

MODE OF PROVING.

A description of the *modus operandi* in the proof of gun barrels may be interesting to sportsmen and gun-makers in those countries in which no proof-house exists. The system of proving at both the Birmingham and London proof-houses is identical. Each barrel passes through the proof-house with a number attached to it, so that the name of the owner or maker is not known to the workmen, who therefore have no opportunity, if they were so willed, of spoiling the article from spite or malice against the maker. Before the barrel is sent into the loading-room it is gauged by plugs and stamped with a number. The workman whose duty it is to stamp the barrels stands at a bench upon which fifty or sixty numbered steel punches are arranged in order. Corresponding to these are numbered gauging-plugs, varying in size from that of a pea up to two inches. Having ascertained the exact bore of the barrel by means of one of these plugs, he takes up a punch, bearing a similar number to the plug, and stamps that number upon the barrel—say seventeen. The man whose duty it is to load the barrel, seeing the number, is able to judge of the proper amount of loading to put in it. Leaving this room and following a short tramway, along which the barrels are conveyed, we come to the "Loading-Room." Here everything is done by rule and measure, every precaution taken to ensure safety, and every means used to prevent fraud. The room is divided into three compartments by strong brick walls, so that, should an explosion occur in either, the injury would be confined to the division in which it took place. The floors of these rooms are always kept damp and well swept. In the first compartment the barrels are loaded by one man, who has the barrels arranged round the room. In front of him is a rack of copper measures numbered successively from one to about fifty; upon ascertaining the number stamped upon the barrel by the man in the receiving-room, he takes up one of the measures bearing a corresponding number, and having filled it with gunpowder from a bowl by its side, he places the charge in the barrel; he next takes a proper-sized felt wad from a numbered box corresponding with the bores, and afterwards a second felt wad, with which he loads the barrel.

Thus loaded, the barrels are passed into the next compartment, where the charge is duly rammed home with copper rods prepared for the purpose. The barrel is then passed on to the third compartment, where it is primed, and then transported into the firing-room. The firing-room is a large lofty building lined throughout with sheet iron, and has ventilators; in the roof and the windows are apertures, capable of being immediately closed, with iron shutters arranged upon the same principle as the Venetian blind. The barrels are arranged upon a grooved rack, and fired by a train of gunpowder which connects the breech vents with each other. The train is fired by a percussion cap, which is detonated by a hammer working on a pivot and pulled from the outside; the door is of iron, and it and the

Proving Gun Barrels at Birmingham.

shutter are closed before firing. After the train is fired the doors and shutters are opened, the smoke allowed to clear off, and the barrels may be seen then partially buried in a sand heap behind the rack; the bullets are shot into the sand heap on the other side of the room. The barrels are then collected, and those that have through any cause missed fire are re-primed and again placed on the rack; the other barrels are conveyed to the inspecting rooms, where they are washed out, inspected, and, if found perfect, marked according to the Proof Act.

The hot water test is not now used, but in case of doubt as to a crack the barrel is tested in a machine by hydraulic pressure up to 600 lbs.

Common barrels have to stand for twenty-four hours before being cleaned or looked over, so that if any flaws are in the barrels the action of the acid residue from the powder will eat into them and make the flaws more apparent.

The plan of proving described and illustrated is provisional proof, when the barrels are in tubes: when the tubes stand proof, they recoil straight into the bank ; those that burst fly about in all directions. For definitive proof, when the barrels are together and have the breech-actions attached, each barrel is fired separately. The guns when loaded are taken to the lobby of the firing-room, and one gun is taken into the room and proved at a time ; the barrels and breech-actions are fixed upon and fastened to a travelling block of the required shape, and fired by means of hammers dropping upon a striker which strikes the cap in the cartridge. The hammer is pulled by a cord passing through a hole in the wall. Various-shaped blocks are provided to suit the various-sized and differently constructed single-rifle breech-actions. Should any flaws or defects be discovered after proving the barrels, they are returned to the maker, who remedies them as best he can, and returns them for proof. Best barrels are frequently burst at proof, but they are more often bulged, in which case the bulges are knocked down by the maker, and the barrel re-proved until it either bursts or stands proof. It is said that in one case a barrel was proved and bulged eight times, but that it stood all right after being proved the ninth time. In the definitive proof the weak breech-actions are frequently blown to pieces, or else made to gape at breech, in which case the maker hammers the false breech till close and case-hardens it, and when again proved it generally stands. The proving of breech-actions is very necessary, as it prevents, in a great measure, dangerous common breech-actions being sold.

THE WORK OF AN ENGLISH PROOF-HOUSE.

Apart from the fact that the tests of provisional and definitive proof are of use to the gun-maker, they are, or can be made, of much service to the public by preventing the issue of unsound guns. In this connection it may be of use to cite a few figures with reference to some of the work done by the Birmingham Proof House in the past. It is known that Birmingham gunsmiths at the beginning of the last century (1804–1815) supplied to the Government no less than 3,037,644 barrels, including 32,582 rifles, and 1,743,382 finished arms, including 14,695 rifles. When tested at the Proof House the bursts or breaks averaged only two per thousand. An ordinary year's work at the Birmingham Proof House means about half a million proof tests.

Taking a return of a recent year, it shows upon analysis that common barrels are the most often rejected—"African" barrels, for instance. Of these, out of 209,765 received, 6,851 were broken in proof, 1,168 rejected with split breech plugs, and 5,828 for unsound breeching. Of twisted tubes, etc., rejected at the first proof, 2,930 were cracked, 856 broken, 2,807 bulged, 297 breech plugs blown out, 232 with unsound breeching, 22 with blown nipples. Of steel and plain iron tubes, 1,420 were broken and 390 rejected for other faults. Of common saddle pistols, 98 were broken.

With reference to the definitive proof, which is the more important as protecting the public rather than as guiding the gun-maker to throw away imperfect barrels before working upon them, fuller details may be of interest.

Of twisted muzzle-loading barrels, 645 were cracked, 373 broken, 488 bulged, 97 had nipples blown out, 271 were rejected for unsound breeches, 38 for faulty insides. Of plain iron and steel barrels, 252 were rejected.

Of the breech-loading guns: cylinder shot-guns, 409 rejected with cracked barrels, 174 with broken barrels, 407 with bulged barrels, 474 with faulty breech-actions, 67 with faulty insides. The chokes numbered 41,000 against 52,000 cylinders, and of these only 50 were rejected with cracked barrels, 33 with broken barrels, 145 with bulged barrels, 97 with unsound breech-actions, none had faulty insides. Of the large-bore barrels only 1 bulged, and 4 had faulty actions.

It is to be regretted that the Gun Barrel Proof Act does not apply to the English Colonies; the colonial authorities might with advantage to themselves pass a measure excluding unproved arms and recognise only the marks of those Proof Houses in which the gun-barrel tests are compulsory, and, as in England, the scale of charges directly in the control of the Government.

FOREIGN PROOF-HOUSES AND PROOF MARKS.

The proving of gun barrels has been compulsory in Belgium since 1672, the date at which it became compulsory in England. Three proofs are required on breech-loaders—the first two, like the provisional proof in England, being intended to safeguard the gun-maker; the third to protect the public.

The tests now approximate those current at the English Proof Houses ; until 1892 they were inferior, but in that year Germany made gun-barrel proving compulsory, and adopted the English tests with slight alterations ; accepting, too, arms proved at the English Proof Houses without further tests on importation, but rejecting those proved in Belgium. The Belgian Proof-house authorities then promptly adopted the higher standard.

There are Proof Houses at St. Etienne in France, at Wiepert and Ferlach in Austria, at Buda-Pesth and possibly at other towns ; but in those countries the proving is not compulsory, and the tests imposed do not command the recognition given to those of England, Germany, and Belgium.

For purposes of reference and guidance, the marks of the establishments known as public Proof Houses are reproduced in facsimile. It is customary to mark all barrels at or near the breech end.

AN EFFICIENT PROOF TEST.

It would seem best in testing guns for safety to use a stronger powder than that likely to be used for sporting purposes, or to increase the load—not the charge —thereby increasing the pressure in the chamber. Nitro-compounds do not produce the same kind of stress when fired with different charges, nor is the increase of pressure with increase of powder charge regular, so to test with them is not all-sufficient. It is quite possible that a proof charge of such explosive would ruin a gun which in all circumstances of ordinary sporting use would have proved a safe and effectual weapon. On the other hand, a gun which may stand the proof test with a nitro-explosive successfully may give way when fired with an ordinary sporting charge of some other nitro-explosive, or with the same nitro-explosive under different conditions.

FOREIGN PROOF MARKS.

FRANCE (PARIS).

(ST. ETIENNE).

On the Barrel.   On the Action.   Foreign arms proved in France.   French arms made elsewhere than at St. Etienne.

FOREIGN PROOF MARKS (*Continued*).

	On the Barrel.				On the Action.	Rifles and Revolvers.	Nitro Proof

BELGIUM.   The No. of Calibre in Millimetres.   R

PV

GERMANY.

First Proof.	Second Proof.				Double Proof

   U and

B

U

The No. of Calibre as	Cylinder Barrels.	Choke Barrels.	Rifles.	Choke-bore Rifles.

S W G

AUSTRIA-HUNGARY.

	First Proof.	Second Proof.	Third Proof.		First Proof.	Second Proof.	Third Proof.

FERLACH. | PRAGUE.

WIEPERT. | VIENNA.

HUNGARY (BUDA-PESTH).

Definite Proof.	Single Barrels	Double Barrels.

CHAPTER XII.
TESTS AND TEST-RECORDING INSTRUMENTS.

CLASSIFICATION OF TESTS.

THE chief tests to which sporting fire-arms are submitted are : first, those to determine the soundness and strength of the weapon ; second, those to ascertain the shooting capabilities—either of the gun with the standard charge, or of various charges in any particular gun.

To the first division belong the ordinary proof tests, which consist of the firing of very heavy charges. The pressure exerted by the charges used for proving and the pressures produced by ordinary sporting charges of various powders have been ascertained relatively by means of the crusher gauge.

To the second class belong the chronographs, for measuring the time occupied in the flight of a projectile or pellets between two or more points; the various devices for ascertaining penetration ; and the force-gauge, designed by the late J. H. Walsh, to record the striking force at impact of the shot pellets. There is also the rotating target, used by Mr. R. W. S. Griffith, of the Schultze Company, to show the order of the pellets during flight and ascertain the velocity of individual pellets.

The machine-rest designed by the late editor of *The Field* is used for the purpose of recording the recoil of guns and rifles, and there are various instruments for ascertaining the relative strength of explosives, and one for testing the force of percussion caps, which merit more than the brief mention that can be here accorded.

THE CRUSHER GAUGE.

The crusher gauge is, as is shown, a gun barrel fitted with means for firing at the breech, and having holes bored through the thick barrel at various points between breech and muzzle. Perfectly fitting stoppers are placed in these holes, and they are kept in position by a lead or copper plug or disc, which in turn is supported by a steel screw. The internal pressure at the time of firing acts upon the stoppers, and they, being driven outward by the pressure, squeeze the lead or copper plugs against the steel screws holding them in position. The plugs being of uniform density, and of exactly the same size and thickness, this reduction of their thickness is used as a basis for calculating the force exerted; but the

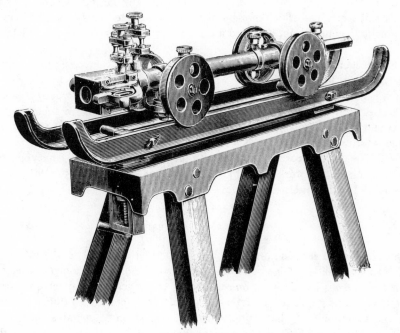

The Crusher Gauge.

deductions, in whatever terms they may be expressed, must be regarded as comparative only.

In a modification used by Mr. Borland, of the "E.C." Powder Company, two crusher plugs are used and the reading taken over a much larger area than the twenty-fifth of an inch usually represented. The pistons are fitted opposite each other in the barrel and connected by a strong metal ring. One of the pistons has an area exceeding that of the other by ·o1 of a square inch, so that upon the explosion taking place, although the ring moves as though actuated by a very small piston, the motion is really the result of the average pressure on the area of the two plugs.   The advantage of a record produced from a greater area is obvious, and by taking the pressure from opposite sides of the barrels at the same time some of the effects of wave pressures have been eliminated.

Instead of computing the force from measurements of lead or copper discs subjected to that force, Mr. Borland has employed the raising of a dead-weight. The piston bears a load which may be so adjusted that the limits of weight between which motion is and is not recorded are an index to the pressure exerted by the powder.

The crusher gauge is of chief use for determining the strength of various explosives, and for ascertaining at what point in the length of the barrel the pressure is greatest, and to what extent it diminishes as the muzzle is approached. It has also been of use in showing to what extent variations in the charges of powder and load of shot affect the pressure, and how the pressure is increased by different obstructions in the barrel.

Particulars of the records registered with the crusher gauge, and some comments upon the value of the work done by the instrument, are given in the chapters on " Explosives " and " Internal Ballistics."

THE BORLAND CAP TESTER.

Until the use of various nitro-explosives in sporting guns led to the differences due to various qualities of ignition being observed, the only test thought necessary to apply to percussion caps of breech-loading cartridges was the relation to the strength of blow requisite to detonate them.   In shooting, so much depends upon the uniformity of the ignition that the cap-testing apparatus devised by Mr. Borland, of the " E.C." Powder Company, is a distinct boon, and more than anything else will lead to the standardising of caps for various arms and special explosives.

Mr. Borland regarded the cap as an explosive charge, and produced instruments to measure the work it is capable of performing, the time in which the work was done, and the variations due to alterations in the strength of the blow used to produce the detonation.   The details of the early experiments to determine the best methods of ascertaining and recording the strength of the caps are too full to be given here ; they, as well as descriptions and illustrations of the machines, are contained in the *Sporting Goods Review*, Vol. IV.

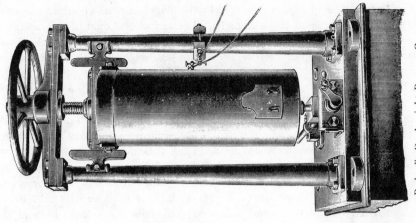

Borland's Dead-weight Pressure Gauge.

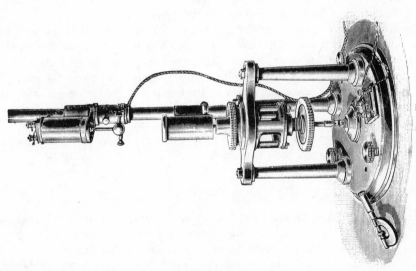

Borland's Cap Tester.

The sensitiveness of caps is measured by the height from which a dead-weight of 2 oz. must fall to detonate them properly. Twelve inches should be sufficient, but some caps require a 30-inch fall. The shape of the striker affects the issue considerably ; the ogival head will detonate with less weight than the hemispherical point.

Three methods of observation are usual to determine whether the detonation is efficient. The sound of the explosion—there is no probability of mistaking a miss-fire or fizzle. The flash may be received on paper, and the extent of the charring and residue afford the required indication. The explosive result may be measured. After various experiments, the means decided upon as being the best for the purpose consist of a steel bolt which, by the force of the explosion of the cap, is driven to compress or cut off soft lead plugs. The bolt, or plunger, carries a knife or chisel, which rests upon a plug or small cylinder of lead, the 2 oz. weight is held by an electric magnet, and on the current being severed, falls upon the striker in the hinged cap over the cylinder in which the cartridge case, or cap, in a suitable holder is placed. The explosion acts upon a piston connected with the bolt or plunger, the chisel edge of which is driven into the lead plug placed in the anvil below. With the help of the chronograph the machine may be made to measure the time elapsing between the fall of the weight upon the cap and the movement of the piston, thus giving the time occupied by the explosion of the fulminate.

To determine the weight of the blow given by the gun-striker, Irvine's gun-lock tester is used. It is based on the principle of notching lead discs, the blow of the striker acting in lieu of a weight and driving the piston against the lead disc. The leads are contained in a dummy cartridge case, the piston occupying the place of the cap ; a micrometer screw gauge fits into the fore part of the instrument, and the readings of the depth of the notch. produced by the fall of the hammer, may be read as foot-ounces, since the drop is calculated as three-fourths of an inch, which is a sixteenth part of a foot : 2 lbs. dropped $\frac{3}{4}$ inch gives ·028 indentation ; 10 lbs., same distance, ·060 ; and 14 lbs., ·070 of an inch.

CHRONOGRAPHS.

The chronograph is an electrical instrument by which the time occupied by the flight of a projectile from one point to another may be so recorded that by calculation its speed is ascertainable in feet per second. The first instrument of the kind was the Navez-Leurs chronoscope, which consisted of two pendulums suspended in identical axes, and so arranged that they could be retained at either

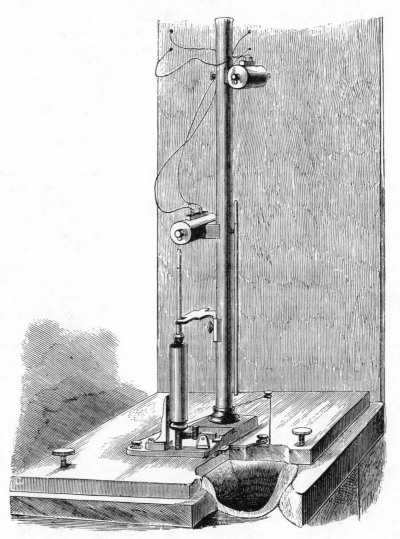

Boulengé's Chronograph.

end of their swing by magnets. The circuit of one magnet was connected by wires with a screen some distance in front of the gun, the other by wires to a screen 120 feet distant from the first screen. When the projectile passed through the first screen, the current was interrupted and the pendulum fell; on the second screen being reached by the projectile the second pendulum fell. By a clamping device and an index needle, the distance one pendulum was behind the other was recorded, and served as an accurate time basis for calculating the speed of the projectile. Professor Bashforth's chronograph consists of a vertical paper-covered drum, with a heavy fly-wheel on the arbor, to prevent unequal motion. This is rotated by clockwork. The registering apparatus consists of two electro-magnets actuating separate pens, the one recording the vibrations of a half-seconds' pendulum, the other the passage of the projectile through each screen. The next instrument is the revolving drum invented by Colonel Schultze. The drum is driven at a high speed by clockwork, and on the surface, covered with lamp-black, a true record is made by a tuning-fork kept in vibration electrically. This and the preceding instrument, with later improvements, are still used, but chiefly for recording the velocities inside large cannon.

The Boulengé was made when velocities higher than 1,000 feet per second were uncommon; now that velocities are much higher the instrument has needed important modification, and at present, chiefly through the improvements of Colonel Holden, it is possible with it to ascertain differences in velocity as little as two feet per second.

This chronograph consists of a heavy brass pillar supporting two electro-magnets. From the upper one a long rod hangs; around the rod is a soft cartouche. When the shot passes the first screen, or leaves the muzzle, as the case may be, the electric circuit is interrupted and the rod falls. A shorter rod hangs from the lower magnet; it is released when the projectile reaches the next screen. It falls upon a trigger, which releases a marking knife; this knife then comes sharply into contact with the cartouche on the longer rod whilst falling from the upper magnet. The distance the rod falls before being struck is accurately measured by means of a Vernier rule, reading in 1,000ths of an inch; the distance is convertible into time, and the time occupied by the flight of the shot thus ascertained. Numerous safeguards and checks are used to ensure the right strength of current and uniformity of action of every part of the instrument. The wire is now usually attached to the muzzle of the rifle or gun, and the chronographs are used in pairs, so that there may be less chance of passing an erroneous record.

PENETRATION TESTS.

The Pettitt Pad.

For rifles the penetration of solid pine, beech, oak, or other woods; one-inch or three-inch planks; thin steel plates; sand; untamped clay; masonry and other materials are used. For shot-guns the old way was the penetration of a number of pieces of brown paper. Usually these were cut into squares $9\frac{1}{2} \times 10\frac{1}{2}$, and piled on each other, making a compact, solid, and almost impenetrable pad. The Pettitt pad, as it was named, afforded a ready but an inefficient test; for it is susceptible to every change of weather, and it is very difficult to get any large number of pads, even if all are made at about the same date, to be equal in resisting qualities. For this reason they have been generally discarded. It was usual to count as penetration the largest number of sheets through which three pellets had passed.

The Copper and Water Tests.

Thin copper plates, superposed, have been used for the purpose of registering the penetration of pellets from shot-guns. They are expensive, and in no way superior to the strawboards hereafter described. Another plan is to fire into a trough of water, the face being a penetrable gelatinous sheet, which closes immediately the pellets have passed, thus preventing the leakage of the water. A tray divided into half-inch divisions lies at the bottom of the trough; it is raised after the gun has been fired, and the position of the shot pellets in the various divisions of the tray forms a basis for calculating the penetration or striking force of the shot.

THE CARD RACK PENETRATION REGISTER.

For any sportsman wishing to make a private trial of a gun the easiest plan is to follow that used at the Chicago Gun Trial of 1879; and the readiest, most simple, and certain way of registering the force or penetration of the shot is by an apparatus similar to the one there used and illustrated here. It consists of a wooden frame about 30 in. in length, 6 in. wide, and 7 in. deep, made of deal 1 in. thick, strengthened by an angle-iron facing. Sheets of strawboard are slid into the rack, and kept $\frac{3}{4}$-in. from each other by slips of wood nailed to the inner sides of the rack. The rack is placed upon a stand, so as to raise it about 4 ft. from the ground.

The strawboard is of common quality, of an uniform texture, and not of a fibrous nature. Sheets cut suitable for the rack weigh 25 to the lb., and are not half so expensive as the Pettitt pad. Usually, 25 to 30 sheets are ample for testing the penetration of each shot, but the rack is constructed for 40 sheets.   The same sheets may be used several times by turning or marking off with pencil, so that each shot can cost but little over a penny to test.

For gun-makers and gentlemen—especially those who are not used to finely-adjusted and fragile machines—this *simple*, *ready*, and *efficient* means of testing the striking force offers many advantages over the one used at the London Trials of

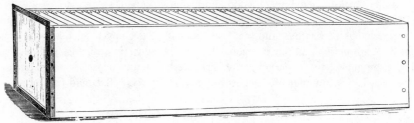

Rack for Testing Penetration.

1879.   As the holes are punched clean through by the shot, no dispute can be raised, and there is no fine adjustment and reading of the machine.

The atmosphere will cause the resisting power of the strawboard to vary to a very slight extent, but all charges fired on the same day may be compared (and to be strictly correct, all guns at any trial should be fired on the same day), so that the slight variation in the cardboard need not enter into any calculation, but larger size shot penetrating an equal number of sheets will, of course, show slightly more penetrative force than the smaller.

In the notes in Chapter XIV., relating to the performances of average guns with different charges and sizes of shot, the penetration of strawboards is given ; the figures recorded were all obtained by means of the rack and boards used as specified here.

THE *FIELD* FORCE GAUGE.

This instrument was invented by the late J. H. Walsh ("Stonehenge"), and was used at the London Gun and Explosives Trials of 1879.   It is based upon the principle of the old-fashioned *balista*, or pendulum, but in lieu of moving a dead weight, the resistance to the force of the shot at impact is supplied by a spring.   The value of the "striking force" is computed from the known value of a blow from a hammer of a given weight falling from a given height ; such a hammer is still used to regulate the tension of the spring, as shown.

It will be seen that the face-plate, *a a*, is a 10-in. steel target, from which the force of the pellets striking it is registered. It is fastened to the platform and swung from the frame of the machine, *d d*, by four parallel rods, *c c* (two on each

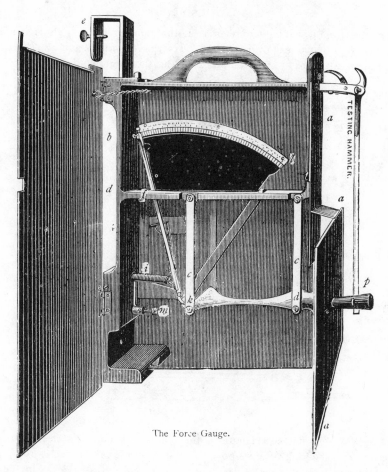

The Force Gauge.

side). Upon the target, *a a*, being struck by the shots, it is forced back on the short arm of the lever, *f*, the friction being minimised by the roller, *k*. The long arm, *g*, is shaped at the top to receive a vulcanite pointer, which bears upon the enamelled glass plate and traverses it from end to end ; *l l*, is the scale ; *i* and *j* are springs for registering the force of the blow, which is marked by the vulcanite pointer upon the enamelled glass plate.

THE MACHINE REST.

The rest from which guns were fired at the London Gun Trials is not widely different in principle from some used years ago for rifle shooting. Such rests record the result more or less accurately, but, as shown at the London *Field* Rifle

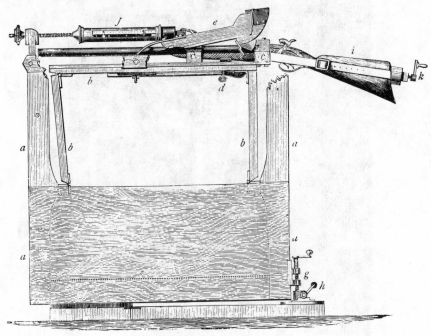

The *Field* Machine Gun Rest.

Trials of 1883, are not so accurate as the ordinary gun-maker's or rifleman's rest for testing the shooting of a weapon. In the illustration the frame, *a a a a*, of ash and mahogany, is cut away. The frame being made of ash yields to the force of the explosion, and imitates the human shoulder far better than any iron or perfectly rigid machine rest ; *b b b* is a platform supported on two hinged parallel uprights ; the gun is affixed to this platform or slide by the blocks, *c c*, which are cut out to receive the barrels, which are further embraced by a padded clip adjusted by the thumbscrews; *e* is a double wedge dropping down to catch shoulder of *c* when gun recoils. The recoil is registered by an ordinary steam locomotive gauge, *f*, adjusted by a screw, and having a travelling indicator. In this trial the gauge was set at 80 lbs. In setting the machine a correct aim may be taken, as the rest is capable of being moved perpendicularly by the adjusting screw, *g*, and transversely by the screw *h*—of course, a wheel-plate is necessary in the fore-part, to admit of these movements—*i*, the stock of gun fixed ready for firing, and held firmly by the leather breeching, tightened by means of a screw-pad, *k*, on the principle of the surgical instrument known as the tourniquet; when once set, the gun was supposed not to require any readjustment, but experience proves that the recoil of each shot affects the machine, or the position of the weapon in it, to such a degree that after each shot a re-alignment of the weapon is necessary to obtain accurate shooting. The gun is discharged by a cord being brought to press against the triggers.

The *Field* Gun-rest and Recoil-gauge—New Model.

A new mechanical rest was devised for the use of the *Field* tests in 1890, chiefly because by the machine designed by Mr. Walsh "no definite dynamic value could be assigned to recoil records based on the static 'pounds' marked on the scale of the spring balance, as the resistance of the spring is not constant, but increases with each notch on the scale. Consequently, no absolute comparison could be made between the amount of energy indicated by the velocity of a shot-charge and that exhibited by the recoil of the gun from which the charge had been fired."

" In the new mechanical rest, an endeavour has been made to remedy these imperfections. The apparatus is constructed almost entirely of iron, and thus is rendered comparatively light and portable ; and, inasmuch as the energy of the gun's recoil is indicated by definite weights being lifted or moved through measured amounts of space, the records thus obtained are convertible into ' foot-pounds ' of work done."

A is an iron frame placed near to the ground, and resting on three small standards or feet.   B, immediately under the gun, is a fixed platform supported by the iron tripod CCC.   This platform limits the travel of the recoiling portion of the rest, and also carries the scale, K, by which the recoil is measured.   D is the recoiling platform, to which the gun is attached, at E, by a universal joint.   At F the barrels of the gun are supported by a V-shaped groove ; and the barrels are held in position before firing by a strong indiarubber band shown in front of the groove.   The elasticity of this band allows the gun, on being fired, to behave in just the same manner as it would do if it were fired from the shoulder.   The recoiling platform, D, is supported by the parallel motion GG, moving on centres at the top and bottom of the rods.

H is a spring balance connected with the parallel motion by the toggle-joint I. The toggle-joint is an important feature in this gun-rest, as the varying strength of the spring is equalised by its means, and the gun therefore recoils against a constant resistance.

J is an oil reservoir containing a cylinder and piston, which automatically bring the gun slowly back to the firing position after it has been discharged.   This arrangement is very convenient for ordinary target work ; but when, for experimental purposes, it is desired to ascertain the recoil with great exactness, the oil reservoir is detached and a ratchet and pawl are used instead ; but, of course, their use gives some little additional trouble.

K is the marker, which records on the scale the extent of recoil, as measured in inches, with tenths and hundredths of an inch.

" Under ordinary conditions of use, the machine stands on the ground, in the position shown in the illustration, and the gun is fired in a horizontal direction. For the purpose, however, of ascertaining definitely what the work performed in the recoil movement actually amounts to, a number of experiments have been carried out with the machine suspended vertically, a few yards above ground—the gun being fired with the muzzle pointing downwards.   In such case the recoil must necessarily take an upward direction; and (the spring having been temporarily detached) the gun, in its recoil, has to lift up its own weight, together with the operative weight of the movable portion of the machine. The space through which this combined weight is raised is registered on the scale of the machine; and from these data, of weight lifted and height of lift, the amount of work done can be readily calculated."

THE CONVERSION OF MEASUREMENTS.

All the instruments are alike in recording of the results the tests by lineal measure; but for convenience these figures are sometimes converted into others denoting the nature as well as the amount of work done.

For instance, the chronograph indicates distance, and the figures are read as speed. The recording rod, dropped the instant the bullet leaves the muzzle, is marked instantly the bullet reaches the screen; the distance the rod has fallen in this interval is ascertained, but since the speed at which the rod fell is known, as is also the distance the bullet traversed, the distance has to be multiplied by the time, in order to get the average speed per second of the bullet. If the rod falls only 12 inches at the ascertained rate of 16 feet per second, whilst the bullet traverses 120 feet, the average velocity of the bullet is computed as 1,920 feet per second; but of course it left the muzzle at a higher velocity and reached the target at a lower one.

The conversion of distance into time is much more satisfactory than the conversion of the measurements of the crushings of lead or copper—or the motion given to dead-weights, as in the recoil rest and force gauge—into terms of kinetic energy, because the work is done in varying periods of time, which differences the instruments fail to record.

For instance, the cap-testing machine indicates the strength exerted by caps by cuts of various depths notched in a leaden plug. The cuts may be gauged in micrometer callipers, and the results are most accurately expressed by the actual measurements obtained, and from them a satisfactory curve may be constructed, showing the relative " notching strength " of caps of different values or exploded under varying conditions, but to express the results in terms of energy, as foot-pounds, can be only an approximation to the truth, for notches of equal depth might be produced by heavy weights falling from a low height, light weights from a greater height, or the continued pressure of a still heavier weight simply resting upon the chisel.

In the same way the translating of crushings of lead and copper plugs to figures purporting to express the values in tons per square inch, although relatively correct to scale, may not be the absolutely equivalent readings of the energy the compression of any one plug recorded.

According to Captain Noble, although "the crusher-gauges may give approximately the pressures that actually existed during an infinitesimal portion of time, such pressures must not be taken as correctly indicating the pressure due to the density and temperature of the explosion."

To obtain even approximately accurate registration by the crusher it is necessary that the cylinder crushed shall be capable of supporting without motion pressures very near to those which it is desired to measure. If the compression of the plug or cylinder is large, part of it must be due to the energy impressed upon the cylinder during its motion, and consequently will be in excess of the actual local pressure within the barrel.

Captain Noble says further :—"Although I do not deny that crusher-gauges placed in the chamber of a gun may give valuable indications, I still consider that unless confirmed by independent means the accuracy of these results is not to be relied upon. Where gases and other products of combustion are in extremely rapid motion there is always a probability of a portion being forced into the gauge at a high velocity, and so affecting the record."

Another way of ascertaining pressures at different parts of the bore is to use barrels of different lengths, fire them under the same conditions, and from the calculated muzzle velocities compute the pressure. It is not possible by this method to ascertain, even approximately, the minimum local pressure at any point within the bore ; it permits only of the pressure on the base of the bullet being computed.

Foot-pounds, tons per square inch, striking force, etc., etc., are terms used more or less exactly as denoting the energy as computed by various formulæ, from *lineal* measures shown upon some recording instrument. The terms, if convertible, may not be rightly converted by the formulæ at present used for their translation ; in all probability these calculations will be corrected and modified in the light of further research, and, in truth, the recoil gauges seem to show that the doctrine, "action and reaction are equal and opposite," is hardly correct in the restricted sense in which it is employed in the formulæ used by musketry experts.

On the other hand, the many experiments made with the various instruments prove that their action is correct ; the simple readings give figures of relative value, and from these curves may be constructed to demonstrate differences recorded— beyond much is conjecture, for by whatever names the results derived from the recorded results are known, it must not be forgotten that the instruments themselves are limited to the expression of lineal measures.

This will explain why some series of experiments give results widely different from others of similar character and made in like conditions ; why it is pressures are stated in some instances to be only a thousand pounds or so to the square inch, and others expressed in figures denoting tons to the square inch. If the values of each series be shown in curves the resemblance will be seen, and as in each case the zero differs and is arbitrarily and probably erroneously constructed, the wide disparity between one series and another will disappear.

Less diverse results might be obtained if the same bore of barrel, and particularly the same size of plugs and crusher pistons, were used. It is suggested that Eley's standard plugs should be generally employed. The following table gives the equivalent tons of pressure to the square inch for respective crushings of their leads of ·325 diameter and half-inch thickness by pistons ·225 inch in diameter.

REMAINING LENGTH IN INCHES.

Inches.	Tons.	Inches.	Tons.	Inches.	Tons.	Inches.	Tons.
·500		·470	2·75	·438	3·60	·406	4·39
·499	1·00	·469	2·78	·437	3·63	·405	4·41
·498	1·32	·468	2·81	·436	3·65	·404	4·44
·497	1·50	·467	2·84	·435	3·68	·403	4·46
·496	1·63	·466	2·87	·434	3·70	·402	4·48
·495	1·74	·465	2·90	·433	3·72	·401	4·50
·494	1·83	·464	2·92	·432	3·75	·400	4·52
·493	1·89	·463	2·95	·431	3·78	·399	4·55
·492	1·95	·462	2·98	·430	3·80	·398	4·57
·491	2·01	·461	3·00	·429	3·83	·397	4·59
·490	2·06	·460	3·03	·428	3·85	·396	4·61
·489	2·11	·459	3·06	·427	3·88	·395	4·63
·488	2·16	·458	3·09	·426	3·90	·394	4·65
·487	2·21	·457	3·11	·425	3·92	·393	4·67
·486	2·25	·456	3·14	·424	3·95	·392	4·69
·485	2·29	·455	3·17	·423	3·98	·391	4·71
·484	2·32	·454	3·20	·422	4·00	·390	4·73
·483	2·36	·453	3·22	·421	4·02	·389	4·75
·482	2·40	·452	3·25	·420	4·05	·388	4·78
·481	2·43	·451	3·28	·419	4·07	·387	4·80
·480	2·46	·450	3·30	·418	4·10	·386	4·82
·479	2·50	·449	3·33	·417	4·13	·385	4·84
·478	2·53	·448	3·35	·416	4·15	·384	4·86
·477	2·56	·447	3·38	·415	4·18	·383	4·88
·476	2·58	·446	3·41	·414	4·20	·382	4·90
·475	2·61	·445	3·43	·413	4·23	·381	4·92
·474	2·64	·444	3·46	·412	4·25	·380	4·94
·473	2·67	·443	3·48	·411	4·27	·379	4·96
·472	2·70	·442	3·50	·410	4·30	·378	4·98
·471	2·73	·441	3·53	·409	4·32	·377	5·00
		·440	3·55	·408	4·35		
		·439	3·58	·407	4·37		

CHAPTER XIII.

PUBLIC GUN TRIALS.

THE GUN TRIALS OF 1858–59–66.

Breech-loaders v. *Muzzle-loaders.*

Mr. J. H. Walsh.

(Reproduced from " British Rural Sports," by permission of Warne & Co.)

THE circumstances which led to the first of the long series of gun trials instituted by the *Field* newspaper were briefly stated by the late editor, Mr. J. H. Walsh ("Stonehenge"), in the following paragraph :—

"At the close of 1857, in undertaking the editorship of the department of the *Field* connected with shooting, I found its columns deluged with an angry correspondence on the comparative merits of the breech-loader and muzzle-loader. Statements and counter-statements were made, week after week, all of which could not possibly be true, since many of them were in direct opposition to each other; theories were propounded of the most visionary kind; yet, as generally happens, their inventors expected them to be received as conclusive of the opinion to support which they were brought forward. The battle had raged for several months, but after all this 'bubble, bubble, toil and trouble,' no one was convinced, and the question was left exactly where it was when the correspondence commenced. But as numerous good sportsmen seemed really desirous of ascertaining with something like exactness the real merits of these guns, it was determined to give them a public trial, and the task of making the arrangements was undertaken by myself. The two Gun Trials of 1858 and 1859 were carried out with great care and trouble, and the real pretensions of Muzzle-loaders and Breech-loaders have been settled for the time to the satisfaction of all reasonable men."

Only those who were intimately acquainted with the work done by Mr. Walsh in connection with these early trials can form a true conception of his wonderful ability for organisation and indefatigable energy in carrying to the utmost limit of utility the many suggestions emanating from his own resourceful brain, or suggested by his *confrères*.

Writing in the *Field* of April 17th, 1858, he says that "a trial in the ordinary way, as practised by gun-makers, was worth a whole cartload of reasoning upon a subject where the data are almost always liable to exception from depending upon the evidence of the disputant himself." He did not hold a very high opinion of gun-makers as a class, and the loss of the thumb and forefinger of his left hand through the bursting of a gun in his early manhood, for which accident he failed to obtain any compensation, did not tend to develop a kindly feeling towards guns or their makers ; yet, looking back over a period of forty or more years, one cannot help but think that neither the gun trade nor sportsmen have fully realised how much they really owe to Mr. Walsh. By his convincing and absolutely impartial testimony he undoubtedly accelerated the use of the breech-loader and convinced a doubting generation of the merits and importance of choke-bore guns, and to him also may be attributed the standardisation of results obtained by the counting of the pellets on the target.

The tests made at the 1858 trials were indecisive, and may be looked upon merely as a preliminary canter to the more pretentious trials of 1859.

The target selected on the score of economy, 28 inches × 11 inches, was altogether unsuitable for testing the pattern of a gun ; further, only one shot was fired from each barrel at the three ranges, 40, 50, and 60 yards, and although the same procedure was followed in the 1859 trials, later experience proved that it was an entirely unsatisfactory method of testing the gun's performance. Again quoting Mr. Walsh : "The great guns stood aloof, having everything to lose and nothing to gain by a competition with their provincial brethren, but perhaps next time they may see they suffer more in reputation by their absence than they could possibly by their being present."

The **records obtained with** the highest and lowest gun in Class I. at the 1858 trials are of interest, particularly as prior to that time no gun-maker of renown had looked upon these results as of importance; they are not referred to by Col. Hawker, W. Greener, or other early writers on Gunnery, neither did any gun-maker habitually test his guns for pattern at a target.

THE *FIELD* GUN TRIAL, 1858.

Name of maker.	Kind of Gun.	Charge of Powder	Charge of shot.	No. of marks on face of target.						No. of shots through targets.						Total on face of 6 targets.	Total thro' 6 targets.	Weight.
				40 yds.		50 yds.		60 yds.		40 yds.		50 yds.		60 yds.				
Prince ...	Muzzle-loader 12-bore.	2¾ dr.	1¼ oz.	51	60	39	51	21	9	1	0	4	3	6	3	231	17	7¼lbs.
Lancaster	Breech-loader used with Lancaster cartridges.	2¾ dr.	1⅛ oz	18	25	23	14	14	23	0	0	0	0	4	6	122	10	7-7½ „

The *Field* Gun Trial of 1859 was tried at targets made of double bag cap paper, 90 lbs. to the ream, all circular, 30 inches in diameter, with a centre 12 inches square, and nailed against a smooth surface of deal boards. This centre was composed of 40 thicknesses for the 40 yards, and 20 at 60 yards, the squares, which were cut evenly at the edges, weighing 18 oz. and 9 oz. respectively, on the average, with a slight variation, which will always occur in brown paper. Powder— Laurence's No. 2, which was selected because it gave satisfaction the previous year. Shot No. 6 (290 pellets per ounce). Charges weighed in every instance. There were twenty-nine entries. The following table summarises the results obtained with the three best muzzle-loaders and the three best breech-loaders :—

THE *FIELD* GUN TRIAL, 1859.

Name of Maker.	Kind of Gun.	Charge of Powder.	Charge of Shot.	Pattern at 40 yards.		Penetration.		Weight.
				Barrel.		Barrel.		
				1st.	2nd.	1st.	2nd.	
Pape	Muzzle-loader (12-bore).	2¾ drams	1¼ oz.	118	158	33	28	6 lbs. 11 oz.
Prince & Green	Muzzle-loader (12-bore).	2¾ drams	1¼ oz.	98	148	22	28	6 lbs.
Pape	Muzzle-loader (12-bore).	2¾ drams	1¼ oz.	116	129	28	25	6 lbs. 8 oz.
Egan	Breech-loader (12-bore).	3 drams	1¼ oz.	90	144	30	28	7 lbs. 8 oz.
Prince & Green	Breech-loader (12-bore).	3 drams	1¼ oz.	93	103	31	24	7 lbs. 2 oz.
Pape	Breech-loader (12-bore).	3 drams	1¼ oz.	93	132	33	26	7 lbs.
Joe Manton ...	Muzzle-loader (16-bore).	2¼ drams	1 oz.	86	122	28	27	6 lbs. 12 oz.

Remarks.—At 60 yards the best muzzle-loading gun in this trial made a pattern of sixty with the first and sixty-three with the second barrel ; it penetrated twenty sheets with two pellets with the first and twenty sheets with five pellets with the second barrel at the same distance.

The performance of the Manton above recorded was not extraordinary ; the barrels were in first-rate condition.

The great contest was as between muzzle- and breech-loaders, and it will be seen that in each class the old-fashioned gun carried the day, though very closely pressed by its rival. The main point deserving notice at this later date is the irregular shooting of all the guns tried. The best breech-loader made a pattern of 144 with one barrel, but only 90 with the other ; a difference of the same kind and of almost equal degree is observable in the records of the two best muzzle-loaders, and the performance of the Manton muzzle-loader was not in any way superior in this respect.

In comparing this record with that of the cylinder guns in the great trial of 1875, it must be borne in mind that the shot contained in $1\frac{1}{4}$ oz. was about 370 pellets, against 305 in the $1\frac{1}{8}$ oz. used at the later trial ; consequently the improvement in shooting in 1875 is greater than apparent upon cursory examination of the tables of results.

THE LONDON GUN TRIALS OF 1866.

Breech-loaders.

The *Field* Gun Trial of 1866 took place at the " Lillie Arms," Old Brompton, on the 22nd and 23rd of May, 1866. All the shots were made with the foremost foot of the shooter 40 yards from the target—a circular plate of iron, 30 inches in diameter, having a square of paper suspended in the middle of its face and close to it. This central square was composed of forty thicknesses of double-imperial brown paper, 140 lbs. per ream, procured from Messrs. Pettitt, of Frith Street, Soho, by whom it was cut and tied up at each corner, the size being $10\frac{1}{2}$ inches by $9\frac{1}{2}$ inches—in round numbers, 10 inches square. In counting the pattern the hits on the iron were added to those on the paper, and in counting the penetration the number of sheets broken by any one shot was scored. The shot used was Walker, Parker and Co.'s No. 6, London size, 280 pellets per ounce. Powder—Curtis and Harvey's No. 3, 5 or 6, at the discretion of the shooter, who was allowed any charge he pleased. The eight guns highest on the list used No. 5 or 6, and the seven lowest [No. 3—a fact telling strongly in favour of coarse powder.

There were thirty-two guns entered in the chief class—that for 12-bores. The performances of the three best guns, as well as of the lowest, are given in the table.

TABLE OF RESULTS.

Maker, Description and Weight of Gun.	PATTERN. (Six shots from each barrel.)						Average of six shots.	Mean of two barrels.	PENETRATION. (Six shots from each barrel.)						Average of six shots.	Mean of two barrels.	TOTAL FIGURE OF MERIT.
	1	2	3	4	5	6			1	2	3	4	5	6			
1 Pape, Lefaucheux Breech-loader, with pin cartridge; 7¼ lb.	Right...140	146	130	132	135	104	131·1 }	127·1	Right...23	27	27	26	31	27	26·5 }	25·4	305·4
	Left ...158	144	47	106	159	126	123·2		Left ...24	25	20	23	27	27	24·2		
2 Pape, Lefaucheux Breech-loader, with pin cartridge; 7 lb. 1 oz.	Right...134	94	138	165	110	163	134 }	125·3	Right...24	23	23	26	22	26	24 }	24	299
	Left ... 52	156	129	157	73	135	117		Left ...20	32	23	27	20	22	24		
3 W.W.Greener, his Patent Wedge-fast Breech-loader, with pin cartridge; 7¼ lb.	Right...114	124	115	110	158	125	124·2 }	121·4	Right...26	19	31	18	26	28	24·4 }	25·3	294·2
	Left ...130	80	127	137	118	122	119		Left ...23	30	26	27	26	26	26·2		
			Average.	Highest.	Lowest.						Average.	Highest.	Lowest				
32 Hast. Central	Right ...	...	67	87	43				Right ...		20	32	15				164
	Left ...	...	57	78	34				Left ...		19	24	15				

In the first two guns 3 drms. No. 6, in the third 3 drms. No. 5, and in the last 3½ drms. of powder were used. Shot 1¼ ounce in all guns.

Remarks.—In comparing these results with later trials, it must be remembered that smaller shot was used at this trial, viz., 280 instead of 270 to the oz. ; this will make about twelve more pellets to the load used, which would equal an average increase of pattern of five shots ; thus the best gun would average about 122 instead of 127·1. In class 2, for 16-bores, the best gun made an average pattern of 109·4, an average penetration of 22·5 ; an ounce of shot only was used.

The three lowest scores made by 12-bores were 69·4, 62·1, 75·5.

At this trial an 8-bore, 36 inches, 14½ lbs., double gun was also shot; it made the extraordinarily low average pattern of 108·2 with 6 drs. of No. 3 powder and 1½ oz. of shot. Of the thirty-two 12-bores shot at the trial, 19 failed to score an average pattern of 100. These figures prove that very poor shooting was generally obtainable, but few makers being able to produce guns which would give even a fairly close pattern. Gun-makers can now make cheap guns which surpass in shooting qualities the best gun shot at this or any previous trial. Soft shot was used at this date, and choke-boring was not known to English gun-makers.

THE GREAT GUN TRIAL OF 1875.

Choke-bores v. *Cylinders.*

This was undoubtedly the greatest, not only of the London gun trials, but of every public trial or test of shot-guns in this or any other country. The results completely revolutionised gun-making and demonstrated the unmistakable advantages of a new method of boring gun barrels : a method the author was instrumental in producing and bringing into general use. In the spring of 1874 the author made his first experiments in choke-boring, and was so far successful in increasing the shooting power of the shot-gun that the Editor of the *Field*, in noticing a new breech-mechanism (W. W. Greener's treble-wedge-fast gun) submitted for his inspection, thought the statement of the author with reference to the shooting power of the gun deserving mention. The following excerpt from the *Field* of December 5, 1874, is also of interest as being the first public notice of what a choke-bore gun could accomplish :—

"We have not ourselves tested these guns, but Mr. W. W. Greener is now prepared to execute orders for 12-bores warranted to average 210 pellets of No. 6 shot in a 30-in. circle, with three drams of powder, the weight of the gun being 7¼ lb. With larger bores and heavier charges, he states that an average pattern of 240 will be gained. As we have always found Mr. W. W. Greener's statements of what his guns would do borne out by our experience, we are fully prepared to accept those now made."

The statement attracted considerable attention ; the performance was so far in advance of any record that neither gun-makers nor sportsmen would credit its possibility. In the next issue of the paper the following letter appeared from E. O. Partridge, Esq. :—

"Your article in last week's *Field* on the 'improvement' of breech-loaders by Mr. Greener, of Birmingham, in my estimation scarcely does justice to the gravity of the question. The 'improvement' would have been better rendered by the word 'revolution,' for I do not hesitate to assert that it is a revolution as complete, and, alas ! as sad to those of us who thought we possessed the best guns that science and skill were ever likely to produce, as was he change from flint and steel to percussion (which I am old enough to remember), or from that again to breech-loaders. It is with the hope of inducing brother sportsmen who are thinking of buying new guns to pause and see the results of this change before they do so that I now write.

"My experience in guns and makers has been pretty wide, ranging from old Joe Manton (my first love) down to the first makers of the present day. Two months since I thought I was the owner of guns second to none for pattern and hard hitting ; the illusion has been rudely dispelled, as will be, I guarantee, those of thousands of others who think as I did. A few weeks back I received a circular from Mr. Greener, descriptive of the improvements he had made, accompanied by a note intimating that he had (I fancy by some new system of boring) attained pattern and penetration which would throw the performances of any gun I had into the shade. Of this I took no notice, but on going to the dog show I took with me a gun by one of the most eminent makers of the day, inwardly chuckling with a certainty of the result of any trial in its favour. The Greener selected was put into the scales, and proved to be a trifle under the weight of my own 7lb., both of 12-bore. The range was forty yards, the target 30 inches diameter, the test first for pattern. Steadily, shot after shot, the Greener beat my gun by never less than 60 pellets, and with a regularity of pattern which astounded me. Nor was the trial for penetration less remarkable in its results. The target in that case was the ordinary field pad of tough brown paper, thirty-six sheets. The Greener in every instance nearly put pellets through the whole thirty-six; the best performance of my gun was twenty-five. Reverting to pattern, I think with the Greener gun, at forty yards, it would have been almost impossible for a snipe to escape. I omitted to say we were using No. 6 shot, the charge being 3 drs. and 1⅛ shot.

"Whilst I was there, an entire stranger to me came to try a 10-bore he had just bought. I stayed to witness it. I did not enquire what charge was used; I only know that the 30-inch target was literally smothered. I think it would have been difficult for even a humming-bird to escape.

"I returned (in one sense) a sadder and poorer man to the extent of two new guns.

"EDWARD OTTO PARTRIDGE.

"*Easton Court, Herefordshire.*"

The same issue of the *Field* also contained the author's first advertisement of the choke-bore, and this is now of such historical interest as to warrant reproduction,

It read as follows : "W. W. G. is now prepared to manufacture guns to order, that will put on an average of 210 pellets with 12-bores weighing under 7¼ lbs. with a charge of 3 dr. powder, and 1⅛ oz. of No. 6 shot, and over that weight 220 pellets; 10-bore guns weighing 9 to 9½ lbs., with a charge of only 4 dr. powder and 1¼ oz. No. 6 shot, an average of 240 pellets; closer shooting may be obtained if desired, and the penetration is also one-third greater. By using only 2¼ dr. of powder, better pattern and penetration can be obtained than from other guns with 3 dr. of powder, and with much less recoil."

Target Illustration used in W. W. Greener's First Choke-bore Advertisement.

The readers of the *Field* still refused to credit such extraordinary shooting. A special commissioner from the office of the *Field* newspaper visited the author's factory, witnessed the shooting of the new guns, and verified the results. Even this was deemed insufficient, and many arguments were advanced for, and against the new system, probably the most ridiculous being that formulated by Mr. Pape, who claimed that owing to the construction of the range on which the author's gun was fired, a considerable number of the shots would ricochet on to the target, and further, that on account of the lightness of the Chilled shot, similar patterns could not be procured on an open range ; and so serious did these objections appear to some, that later trials on an unprotected range—where better patterns were obtained—were considered necessary to satisfy the doubters, and the results but confirmed how little this man, in spite of his pre-tensions, actually knew of the principle of choke-boring.   In January of the same year a "minute trial" of the author's gun was made by "Peverill" of *Bell's Life*. This painstaking and skilful writer gave longer time to his trial than that given by the *Field* representatives to both their preliminary trials at the author's range, and the results, although obtained in a different way, fully confirmed the report of the *Field* commissioner—in fact, they were really more favourable to the author's guns than either of the preliminary trials conducted by the *Field* newspaper.

The Editor of the *Field* himself, accompanied by Mr. Rigby—then a rival gun-maker—next visited the author's open-air testing ground, and satisfied them-selves that the shooting obtainable was equal to that claimed. As a matter of fact, the performance was better; the patterns averaged 220, with high penetration and great regularity.   Other gun-makers, amongst whom may be mentioned Scott and Dougall, having claimed to produce equal results, the Editor of the *Field* also decided to give their guns a private trial, and commenting upon the first, he says : "We cordially congratulate both Mr. Greener and Messrs. Scott on the result of their labours, and whether or not they can fairly claim any improvements upon the American system they, and especially Mr. Greener, are entitled to the thanks of English sportsmen for bringing it prominently forward." Some went still further and claimed to possess a knowledge of the system of boring the author used ; some deemed it an unsatisfactory method of boring, others declared for choke-boring, so, after a lengthy discussion, it was determined by the proprietors of the *Field* to carry out such tests as would settle the matter in dispute and prove which maker could produce the strongest and closest-shooting gun.

As a further inducement a Cup, value forty guineas, was offered for the best shooting 12-bore gun bored on any system, as the secret of the choke was claimed by several ; and a Cup of smaller value for the best shooting gun bored on any system other than the choke.

At the previous gun trials, as well as at all the demonstrations the author made before the Editor of the *Field* and others, the load of shot used was 1¼ oz.

This load the author knew to be the one best suited to the 12-bore choked gun. Some correspondents of the *Field* suggested that the load should be restricted to 1⅛ oz. by weight, and this load was decided upon as one of a sporting character; it did not bring out the best qualities of the choke, as the author pointed out at the time, but he was compelled to agree to the conditions imposed.

The author fortunately discovered that special boring was requisite in order to obtain the best results with this reduced charge, and although the time at his disposal was short, he immediately set to work on new guns for the trials, and his success was, in a great measure, due to his foresight in thus making special guns for this charge.

Experience has confirmed his first opinion and shows that the addition of 34 pellets to the standard load of 1⅛ oz. No. 6 shot, 270 to the ounce, will generally give an increase of from 20 to 30 pellets in the 30-inch circle at 40 yards.

The gun-makers both of London and the provinces freely entered into the contest. The result demonstrated the superiority of the author's method of boring, the choke-bore guns he entered winning every class; and the advantages of the new system of boring were at once apparent. The details of the shooting will be found in the following tables and summaries.

Classification.—The guns were divided into four classes.

Class 1.—For 8- and 10-bores of any weight or any kind of boring, and used with any charge. Class 2.—For guns of any kind not exceeding 12-bore or over 7¼ lbs. weight. Class 3.—For 12-gauges and smaller of English (cylinder) boring, and not over 7¼ lbs. weight. Class 4.—For 20-bores and under of any kind of boring. No gun over 6 lbs. weight. The charge of shot for 12-bores was 1⅛ oz. No. 6; for 20-bores ¾ to 1 oz. of No. 6.

Conditions.—" The entries to be confined to gun-makers, and in each class no gun-maker to enter more than three guns. The Editor of the *Field* to be the manager, and his decision on all points to be final, subject only to the committee, who are to be chosen by the proprietors of the *Field*. No entrance-fee to be charged for the guns.

" The competition to be at the ground of the All England Croquet Club, near the Wimbledon Station, commencing at ten o'clock on Monday, April 26, and continuing daily from the same hour till completed. The guns to be shot in the order of their entry, from the usual gun-maker's adjustable rest, by the competitor or his representative.

" The guns in each class to be tried twice—the first round at 40 yards, with a Pettitt pad of 45 sheets in the centre of a 30-in. circle, six shots each barrel. The greatest number of pellets within the circle to be added to six times the number of sheets penetrated by three pellets, in order to give the figure of merit; the counting to be done in the presence of the competitors at the conclusion of each set of 12 shots. If this round in any one class is completed in one day, then the guns giving the six highest figures to be selected for the second round; but if not, then a proportionate number, making up together the required six, to be taken from each day's score.

" For the second round, these six guns are to be shot at a target 4 ft. square, having a Pettitt pad in the centre for penetration, and a selected group included in a 30-in. circle, to be drawn from a centre fixed on by the competitor, or his representative, for pattern. First time,

6 shots from each barrel, at 40 yards; second time, ditto, ditto, at 60 yards. The figure of merit to be computed the same way, and the gun making the highest score from both distances combined to be adjudged the winner of the cup or prize.

" The distances to be measured from the butt of the gun.

" The shot to be either Lane and Nesham's or the Newcastle Chilled Shot, No. 6, about 270 pellets per oz. ; each charge to be weighed."

' NOTE —There were 33 competitors, who entered 114 guns ; the greatest number ever entered at a public gun trial.

RESULTS.—Class 1.   Large Bores, any boring.

Only nine guns competed, four makers withdrawing their weapons. The first gun was the W. W. Greener 8-bore, with an average pattern of 321, with 2½ oz. No. 6 chilled shot. The author was also first and second with two 10-bores, guns which obtained a higher figure of merit than two of the 8-bores shot against them. One 8-bore by a London gun-maker of high reputation made an average pattern of 163·9 only, which was far behind the author's 12-bore gun. In the second round, with a selected group, the W. W. Greener 8-bore made an average pattern of 358·9, and the Greener 10-bore 241·2, with the same charge as used in the first round, 1¾ oz. of No. 6.

REMARKS.

The manager of the trial (J. H. Walsh) stated, concerning the performance of the W. W. Greener 8-bore gun—

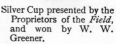

Silver Cup presented by the Proprietors of the *Field*, and won by W. W. Greener.

" With regard to the performances of the guns in Class 1, Mr. Greener's 8-bore certainly did wonders at 40 yards, both in pattern and penetration ; but beyond this distance the enormous charge of shot (2½ oz.) did not seem to be of much service, and it evidently requires a larger size than No. 6 to do justice to these ' cannons,' which, of course, are only to be treated as duck guns. The ' choke' is with them an immense advantage, and will no doubt be largely used for the above purpose."

RESULTS.—Class 2.   Choke-bores, 12-gauge.

In this class there were sixty-eight guns and thirty-three competitors. The first prize (a Silver Cup, valued 40 guineas) was taken by W. W. Greener, the gun making an average pattern of 214 and a penetration of 206·5. The second gun, by a provincial maker, made an average pattern of 182·2, and penetration of 200·5. The two worst choke-bores in this class made average patterns of 109·6 and 93, which were much worse than many of the cylinders. The remaining sixty-four guns averaged every pattern between these extremes.

EXTRACT FROM THE "FIELD" REPORT.

Of the guns entered for the principal prize we give the averages made by the first thirty. These averages represent the mean results of twelve rounds, six from each barrel, fired for pattern and penetration. The penetration is represented by the average number of sheets pierced by three pellets being multiplied by six, so that if thirty sheets were pierced the number registered would be 180. When in the following table the letter P is put after the number of the powder it indicates that it was made by Pigou, in all other cases the powder was made by Curtis & Harvey. In two instances the weight and length were not recorded.

FIELD GUN TRIALS, 1875.

	Weight.	Length.	Powder.	Pattern (30 in.)	Penet. (× by 6)	Figure of Merit.
	lb. oz.	inches.				
Greener	7 4	30	3¼ drs. No. 4 P	199 ...	206	405
Pape	7 4	30	3¼ " No. 6	182 ...	200	382
Davison	7 3	30	3 " No. 6	179 ...	197	376
Baker	7 1	30	3⅛ " No. 4	175 ...	196	371
Baker	7 4	30	3⅛ " No. 4	176 ...	188	364
Green	7 0	30	3¼ " No. 6	172 ...	189	361
Maleham	6 15	30	3 " No. 6	174 ...	186	360
Green	7 3	30	3¼ " No. 6	170 ...	188	358
Greener	6 13	30	3½ " No. 4 P	161 ...	194	355
Jones	7 0	30	3 " No. 6	163 ...	191	354
Rigby	6 13	30	3 " No. 4 P	182 ...	170	352
Davison	7 2	29	3 " No. 6	166 ...	186	352
Gates	6 10½	28	3 " No. 6	174 ...	177	351
Maleham	7 3	30	3 " No. 6	166 ...	183	349
Tisdall	7 3	30	3 " No. 5	166 ...	183	349
Holland	—	—	3¼ " No. 6	185 ...	164	349
Green	7 2	30	3 " No. 6	169 ...	178	347
Jeffries	7 0	30	3¼ " No. 5	153 ...	192	345
Wales	7 0	30	3 " No. 6	172 ...	173	345
Thomson	7 3	30	3 " No. 4 P	171 ...	173	344
Maleham	7 2	30	3 " No. 6	158 ...	185	343
Tisdall	7 4	30	3 " No. 5	158 ...	185	343
Thomson	7 3	30	3 " No. 4 P	166 ...	173	339
Wilson	7 4	30	3 " No. 4	151 ...	186	337
Crane	7 3	30	3 " No. 6	168 ...	168	336
Jeffries	7 2	30	3 " No. 5	146 ...	190	336
Tolley	7 4	30	3 " No. 6	159 ...	172	331
Holland	—	—	3¼ " No, 6	168 ...	161	329
Davison	7 3	31	3 " No. 6	143 ...	185	328
Gates	6 14	29½	3 " No. 6	149 ...	178	327

CLASS II.—Round 2. (Same charges as before, with selected group of 30 in. circle at both distances.)

	40 YARDS.				60 YARDS.			Final
	Pattern.	Penet.	Figure of Merit.		Pattern.	Penet.	Figure of Merit.	average.
Greener	214 ...	188 ...	402	.. ...	92 ...	100 ...	192 =	297
Davison... ...	176 ...	191 ...	367	......	108 ...	97 ..	205 =	286
Pape	173 ...	194 ...	367	......	91 ...	93 ...	184 =	275
Baker	170 ...	192 ...	362	......	85 ...	87 ...	172 =	267
Baker	177 ...	190 ...	367	......	76 ...	85 ...	161 =	264
Davison... ...	174 ...	171 ...	345	......	84 ...	89 ...	173 =	259

Accordingly, Mr. Greener became the winner of the forty-guinea Silver Cup.

REMARKS.

This was extraordinary shooting; nothing equal to it having been attained in the gun trials of New York, 1873, or Chicago, 1874; the best 12-bore at the New York trials made an average pattern of 150·5 only, with paper shells. At the Chicago trials the highest average pattern with a 12-bore was 166·5. It is impossible to draw comparisons in penetration, as at the American trials a different system of scoring was adopted. There is, however, no reliable evidence to show that previous to 1874 the Americans were able to bore guns to shoot as close as the best of those shot at the 1875 trials, and it is the author's opinion that they had not worked out the choke-bore system to its utmost capability; then this opinion is supported by the fact that at the Chicago trial of 1879 the best 12-bore choke registered an average pattern 170 pellets only, with 3 drs. and 1⅛ oz., the ounce containing about twenty pellets more than there are in the English No. 6. Comparing the results with those of the earlier English trials the advance is remarkable, especially when the difference in the shot is considered; for in this trial, in this and the next class, the load contained from 40 to 50 pellets less than that used in 1866 and about 60 pellets less than at the trials of 1859.

RESULTS.—*Class 3. For Guns of English Boring or Cylinders.*

This was won by a slightly modified choke-bore, the muzzle being contracted nearly 5,000ths of an inch. This gun made an average pattern of 148·5 and penetration of 165. The second gun, a true cylinder, made an average pattern of 129 only, and penetration of 168·5. The lowest average pattern was 82.

REMARKS.

In comparing the results with the trial of 1866, a little improvement in the penetration is noticeable, but the average patterns were hardly equal to those obtained in 1866; this is accounted for by the difference in the shot, as already explained; also the cartridges were loaded by weight instead of by measure. Chilled shot, which was first brought prominently before the public at this trial, was used in all the choke-bores, whose performances were among the best.

RESULTS.—Class 4.   Small gauges, any boring.

Seven guns only competed in this class, and all were 20-gauge and choked.   These little guns beat all the 12-bore cylinders at 40 yards, both in pattern and penetration.

At the longer range of 60 yards the reduced charges told against these light guns, and they were well beaten by the cylinder twelves, both for pattern and penetration.   The author's 20-bore, weighing only 5½ lbs., came out the winner by several points.   A charge of 2⅛ drs. and 1 oz. of No. 6 chilled shot was used.   The average pattern at 40 yards was 145·3, penetration 141 ; at 60 yards average pattern 50·1, penetration 54.   The second gun made an average pattern at 40 yards of 135·5, penetration 129 ; the lowest average pattern recorded at this distance was 71.   In all except the winning gun a charge from 2⅛ to 2½ drs. was used, and some of the guns were as heavy as 6 lbs.

REMARKS.

The only 16-bore shot at this trial was in Class 2.   It made an average pattern of 129·3 and penetration of 166·5 at 40 yards (not shot at sixty yards). It weighed 6 lbs. 4 oz., and was shot with 2½ drs. and 1⅛ oz. chilled shot.

THE WEAR-AND-TEAR TRIAL OF 1875.

The victory of choke-bore guns was so complete, and the performances so thoroughly in advance of everything ever before attempted, that the only chance left the opponents of the author's method of boring was to raise the contention that the choke would not last ; that the barrel would in a short time revert to the shape of a bad cylinder, and the shooting not only fall off but become worse than that of an ordinary gun.   Whether or not these views were entertained generally it would be hard to decide, but at the close of the great gun trial it was determined by the <i>Field</i> Committee to institute a " Wear-and-Tear Trial, " in order to prove whether or not the contention was baseless.

Conditions.—Three guns to be chosen to go through a series of firing for six weeks, one gun to be supplied by W. W. Greener, the winner of the preceding trials, and two guns by other competitors in the trial.   Two hundred shots to be fired into a pit, gun to be wiped out, and 200 more shots fired the next morning ; the gun again to be wiped out, 12 rounds fired at a target after each 200 shots.   Gun to be then cleaned and laid aside until the following week.   The firing to be repeated each week until at least 2,500 shots should have been fired by each gun.

The guns to be kept under lock and key. The pit shots to be made at the rate of 60 shots per hour.

The W. W. Greener gun came out first in both pattern and penetration, the average of 244 rounds being—pattern, 185, penetration, 151·5, figure of merit, 336·5; the second competitor averaged a pattern, 182·3, penetration, 135, figure of merit, 318. The W. W. Greener gun shot in this trial was not the gun that won the 40-guinea cup in the previous trial; the paper pads used were made of considerably thicker paper than those used in the former trial, hence a lower figure of merit was obtained. The result of the trial proved highly satisfactory to the choke-bores, it being clearly demonstrated that there was no falling-off whatever in the quality of the shooting.

A Wear-and-Tear Trial in which upwards of 80,000 rounds were fired without deterioration, and others extending over a much longer period of time, will be referred to later.

The Fifty Guinea Cup presented by Mr. J Purdey.

THE GUN TRIALS OF 1876 AND 1877 AT PIGEONS.

Completely and ignominiously beaten in 1875, the opponents of the choke, unable to prove the cylinder gun its equal at the target, and equally powerless to substantiate their contention that the choke wore out, declared it unfit for use at game, and inferior to the cylinder as a trap gun. It was proposed to test the two systems by trials at pigeons; two teams firing under the usual conditions.

The 1876 Trial was shot off at the Gun Club, Notting Hill, on July 21, 1876. The cylinder-bores scored 59 at 27 yards rise, and 47 at 33 yards rise; the choke-bores scored 57 at 27 yards and 40 at 33 yards. In this match concentrators were used in the cylindrical barrels; this made them about equal to the modified chokes. Besides this, the majority of the best shots used cylinders, being as 7 to 4; had the sides been equal it is probable that the choke-bores would have been victorious. The following year a return match was made, the sides were more equal, and concentrators were excluded. There were nine guns on each side, at five birds each at 30 yards, and five each at 40 yards, for a sweepstake and a silver cup presented by Mr. J. Purdey.

The choke-bores won the first day by 4 birds. The best score was made by Mr. H. C. Pennell, who killed 5 birds at 30 and 3 birds at 40 yards. " It was noticed that Mr. Pennell with his Greener gun brought his birds down in splendid style at from 60 to 70 yards distance ; he also used but 3¼ drs. powder, whilst 3½ drs. were used by some of the other competitors." Only one gun used in this match was made by the author ; that was in the hands of the winner of the cup, Mr. Pennell. There were fourteen guns by the first London makers and three by provincial makers. The next day a sweepstake was shot for, the same sides competing. The choke-bores were first by 14 birds. This trial fully proved that choke-bores were the best weapons for this shooting, and they have since been generally used at all the gun clubs.

THE "FIELD" TRIAL OF EXPLOSIVES, 1878.

The object of this trial was to compare the relative merits of the black and Schultze powders, and incidentally to ascertain if the Schultze powder could be relied upon for sporting purposes. The trial was of the most exhaustive nature, over 2,000 rounds being recorded. There were six chokes (of which three were by W. W. Greener), and six cylinders (one by W. W. Greener). The result of the trial showed that the most uniform and regular patterns could be obtained from the black powder, whereas the Schultze had the advantage of penetration. This is the first trial in which the recoil was registered since 1859. The guns were fired from a machine rest designed by the Editor of the the *Field ;* and by means of a Salter's spring balance the recoil of each shot was accurately recorded. The penetration was obtained from paper pads (40 sheets), 9½ in. by 10½ in., with a black square of 4 inches marked on its centre. The figure of merit was made up as follows :—

Average penetration of three shots, multiplied by six, as in previous trials, say		180
Deduct difference between lowest pattern made and average pattern, say ...	45·3	
Ditto average recoil in pounds above 50	35·5	84·3
Ditto between highest and lowest recoil	3·5	
		95·7

SUMMARY OF AVERAGES.
Choke-bores with Black Powder.

Six guns, 450 shots, mean average pattern		192·53
,, ,, ,, ,, penetration		140·00
,, ,, ,, difference of pattern		71·59
,, ,, ,, ,, recoil above 50		37·29
,, ,, ,, differences recoil		5·03
,, ,, ,, figure of merit		26·09

Choke-bores with the Schultze Wood Powder.

Six guns, 450 shots, mean average pattern		...	...	...	188·25
,,	,,	,,	,, penetration	... ...	159·08
,,	,,	,,	difference of pattern	... ...	107·66
,,	,,	average recoil above 50		... ...	36·40
,,	,,	average difference in recoil		... ...	7·25
,,	,,	average figure of merit		... ...	19·73

The W. W. Greener three choke-bores came out first, second, and third in the trial. The average of mean three with the black powder was—

Mean average pattern	...	...	...	...	...	192·60
Mean average penetration	...	...	..	...	...	146·22
Mean average merit	...	...	...	...	...	48·86

And with the Schultze wood powder—

Mean average pattern	...	...	...	...	...	191·90
Mean average penetration	...	...	...	...	...	160·45
Mean average figure of merit		...	...	...	...	41·90

The summary of this trial shows that there was very little difference in the merits of the three black powders tested—namely, that of the well-known makers, Messrs. Curtis and Harvey, Messrs. Hall, and Messrs. Pigou, Wilks and Laurence —the total variation not being beyond the range of chance, whilst the individual scores were still more up and down. The Schultze powder, however, came out much better than was anticipated, the penetration being superior to the black, and very good patterns were also made with it; but the difference between the lowest shot and average pattern was so great as to lower its figure of merit below those obtained by the black powder. As a natural result of this trial, the sporting public placed confidence in the Schultze powder, and many who had previously been afraid of using it adopted it readily.

The highest individual score was made with the black powder fired from a full choke-bore gun by W. W. Greener. It made the most wonderful shooting on record, the average pattern of twenty-five shots being 220·8; average penetration, 154·32; difference in pattern, 24·08 only; average recoil above 50 lbs., 36·88; difference in recoil, 5·00; figure of merit, 88·36, being the highest ever obtained under the same conditions. The greatest difference in pattern occurred in shooting black powder from the gun of a provincial maker, the patterns varying from 42 to 216. The figure of merit obtained by this gun was 43·06 *minus*, being 131·42 points below the winning gun. This, however, was not quite the lowest figure obtained by this maker.

Some of the cylinder guns fired in this trial showed a decided improvement upon the scores made by cylinders at the 1875 trial, the highest average pattern being 139·40, and the average penetration of this gun was 137·76. In recoil the Schultze powder showed a decided advantage, the average recoil of black powder in the chokes being 87·29, in the cylinders 87·23 ; the average of the Schultze being, in the chokes 86·40, and in the cylinders 83·29 : but there is more variation in recoil with the Schultze than with the black, the average difference with the Schultze powder being 7·25 against 5·3 with the black, in the chokes. And in cylinders the difference was even more marked.

Many sportsmen hold the opinion that the recoil of choke-bores is very much greater than that of the cylinder bores. This trial proves, however, that there is only a very slight difference between them—viz., ·09 of a lb., taking the average of 900 shots with the black powder.

FURTHER EXPERIMENTS WITH THE GUNS AT DIFFERENT RANGES.

It having been suggested by an old subscriber of the *Field* to take the pattern of each gun on a 4-inch square centre, each pad was marked with a 4-inch square bull's-eye. The author's gun scored in this centre—

At 40 yards, with black powder :—Left barrel, 9, 9, 10, 12, 13, 9, 9, 11, 7, 8, 10, 13, 16 ; Right barrel, 9, 21, 8, 10, 7, 7, 11, 7, 5, 7, 12, 7. Average 10 pellets.

At 50 yards the same gun averaged, with No. 6 shot :—Left barrel, 5 ; right barrel, 5·40. With No. 5 shot the averages were :—Left, 3·75 ; right, 3·76.

At 60 yards it obtained an average of 2·32 with the left and 2·83 with the right—3¼ drams and 1¼ oz. of No. 6 shot. With No. 5 shot and 3⅛ drams powder, the averages were :—Left, 2·32 ; right, 2·32.

The best cylinder averaged 5·5 at 40 yards. It failed on one occasion, with Schultze powder, to throw even a single pellet into a 4-inch centre, and in several cases only one shot ; at 50 yards it averaged 2·18. As the cylinder failed in several instances with this centre at 50 yards, it was considered advisable to try W. W. Greener's choke only at 60 yards, it being clear that the cylinders were useless at that distance. From these figures it is evident that at 60 yards, even with a choke, a 4-inch square may occasionally escape ; whilst with a cylinder such an escape is by no means uncommon, even at 40 yards, and at 50 it is common enough, and at 60 the rule rather than the exception.

The choke-bore gun at 50 yards made an average pattern in a 30-inch circle of 153, with 3¼ drams of No. 4 powder and 1⅛ oz. No. 6 shot.

At 60 yards, with 3¼ drams and 1¼ oz. No. 5 shot, an average pattern of 88 ; with 45 grains of Schultze gunpowder and 1⅛ oz. of No. 6 shot, an average pattern of 110 was obtained.

THE LONDON GUN TRIALS OF 1879.

LARGE *v.* SMALL BORES.

The object of these trials was to ascertain the relative merits of guns of different calibres—the 12-, 16-, and 20-bores—as game guns. The conditions were somewhat onerous, and a great point was that the pattern of a gun was not counted as a factor in computing the figure of merit, save as it departed from the pattern which had been previously declared as its average.

There were 25 rounds fired from each gun at 40 yards, and the two best guns in each day's performance were shot at 60 yards. The average pattern of each gun had to be declared before it was shot, and the figure of merit was made up as follows :—The penetration computed according to the force per pellet indicated on the force-gauge. The pattern computed according to the average deviation of the twenty-five patterns from the declared pattern, which average deviation is to be deducted from the penetration. At 60 yards the deviation to be computed from the average pattern, the average recoil above 80 lbs. to be deducted, and also the difference in recoil.

The final figure of merit to be computed from the totals of the two figures made respectively at 40 and 60 yards.

There were twelve entries in each class. The guns were fired from a machine-rest designed by the Editor of the *Field*, of which an illustration is given in the chapter on "Testing Instruments ;" and the penetration was registered by a force-gauge also invented by the Editor of the *Field*, and this is described and illustrated in the same chapter. How far the ostensible object of the trial was secured by the results obtained the following summary of the report will prove :—

RECORD OF PERFORMANCE OF THE BEST GUNS AT THE LONDON GUN TRIALS OF 1879.

TWELVE-BORES.

	40 *yards.*		60 *yards.*	
The best gun made—				
Average force per pellet...	231·20			104·40
(Average pattern, 204·20)	...		(97·52)	
Average of the deviation of pattern from declared pattern	21·32 ⎫		10·88 ⎫	
Average recoil above 80 lbs.	31·24 ⎬ 58·56		27·92 ⎬ 42·80	
Difference between highest and lowest recoils ...	6·00 ⎭		4·00 ⎭	
Figure of merit		172·64		61·60
Final figure of merit ... . 234·24				

The second best 12-bore gun made—

	40 *yards.*		60 *yards.*	
Average force per pellet		238·72		109·20
(Average pattern, 209·60)	...	...	(98·72)	
Average of the deviation of pattern from declared pattern	26·64 ⎫		14·76 ⎫	
Average recoil above 80 lbs.	31·64 ⎬ 67·28		29·64 ⎬ 49·20	
Difference between highest and lowest recoils ...	9·00 ⎭		5·00 ⎭	

Figure of merit ... ...   171·44   59·80

Final figure of merit ... ...   231·24.

Sixteen-Bores.

The best gun made—

	40 *yards.*		60 *yards.*	
Average force per pellet		224·44		111·24
(Average pattern, 170·36)	...	...	(80·80)	
Average of the deviation of pattern from declared pattern	15·36 ⎫		10·28 ⎫	
Average recoil above 80 lbs.	19·24 ⎬ 39·60		15·28 ⎬ 29·56	
Difference between highest and lowest recoils ...	5·00 ⎭		4·00 ⎭	

Figure of merit ... ...   184·84   81·68

Final figure of merit ... ...   266·52.

The second best gun made—

	40 *yards.*		60 *yards.*	
Average force per pellet		217·76		96·88
(Average pattern, 166·16)	...	...	(70·28)	
Average of the deviation of pattern from declared pattern	15·92 ⎫		13·72 ⎫	
Average recoil above 80 lbs.	26·72 ⎬ 46·44		22·84 ⎬ 40·56	
Difference between highest and lowest recoils ...	4·00 ⎭		4·00 ⎭	

Figure of merit .. ..   171·12   56·32

Final figure of merit ... ...   227·44

Twenty-Bores.

The best 20-bore made—

	40 *yards.*		60 *yaras*	
Average force per pellet...		224·48		80·16
(Average pattern, 150·72)	...	...	(67·28)	
Average of the deviation of pattern from declared pattern	14·84 ⎫		9·32 ⎫	
Average recoil above 80 lbs.	15·32 ⎬ 37·16		14·24 ⎬ 31·56	
Difference between highest and lowest recoils ...	7·00 ⎭		8·00 ⎭	

Figure of merit ... ...   187·32   48·60

Final figure of merit .. ..   235·92

The second best gun made—		40 *yards.*		60 *yards.*	
Average force per pellet		223·88			70·36
(Average pattern, 152·20)		...		(68·44)	
Average of the deviation of pattern from declared pattern	20·24			14·36	
Average recoil above 80 lbs.	21·60	50·84		21·00	43·36
Difference between highest and lowest recoils ...	9·00			8·00	
Figure of merit		173·04			27·00
Final figure of merit		200·04.			

REMARKS.

This trial, although carried out with an elaboration of detail, and, if possible, with greater care than any of the preceding, failed to be of actual service. In the first place, the figure of merit was made up in a manner that gave value to what the gun-maker knew his gun would do ; if the pattern was stated too high, the figure of merit was reduced. Again, pattern did not enter directly into the computation of the figure of merit ; regularity of pattern did, and this last was its best feature. The method of estimating the force per pellet, instead of taking the exact penetration, was not wholly satisfactory ; it certainly gave a fictitious value to small-bore guns, their figure of merit being out of all proportion to the actual value of the guns as weapons—a conclusion sportsmen have corroborated by relegating the small-bores to a lower place even than they occupied prior to the trial. Another result of the mode of computing the figure of merit was the sending of low shooting guns to the trial. The author had at the time several guns which shot closer and stronger than those he entered, but by careful experiment he ascertained that, with such conditions, guns having other qualities would come out ahead of the better performers ; therefore he entered those which he thought would win, and the result —first—fully justified this choice.

THE "CHICAGO FIELD" GUN TRIAL OF 1879.

LARGE *v.* SMALL BORES.

The trial commenced Oct. 20, and continued for five days ; in many instances the conditions were widely different from the great London *Field* Trials, and the conclusions arrived at were also different. In the first place, all the guns but one, viz. 10-, 12-, 16-, and 20-gauge breech-loaders, were supplied by the same maker; in addition one 6-gauge muzzle-loader was lent for the occasion, for the purpose of comparison. The shot used was Tatham's No. 7 (291 pellets to the ounce). The charges, both of powder and shot, were measured, not weighed. A variety of charges were also used in the same guns. The method of testing the penetration was also different; instead of paper pads of forty sheets tied at each corner, the following contrivance was used:—A *rack* slotted at intervals of ¾ of an inch; in the said slots were placed sheets of straw-board of uniform texture and thickness; at each discharge the number of sheets perforated by any one pellet was noted, and this constituted the record of force for that particular shot. The patterns counted in a 30-inch circle.

The following tables record the performances with No. 7 shot:—

AVERAGES WITH DIFFERENT CHARGES OF POWDER.

Distance, 40 yards; 6 shots from each barrel.

Charge.	Pattern.		Force.		Recoil.	
	R.B.	L.B.	R.B.	L.B.	R.B.	L.B.
No 7 Shot, 2 drs. 1 oz., 20-gauge	119	128	10⅔	11½	76⅔	77½
2½ drs. 1 oz.	106	138	12⅓	13½	80⅔	80⅚
2¾ drs. 1 oz.	113	120	13⅔	13½	81⅚	82⅓
No. 7 C* shot, 4 drs. 1¼ oz., 10-gauge	156	200	14½	15	93⅚	94⅔
4½ drs. 1¼ oz.	146	170	15	15½	97⅚	99⅓
5 drs. 1¼ oz.	157	191	16	16⅓	104½	103
No. 7 Shot, 3 drs. 1⅛ oz., 12-gauge	126	170	13⅓	13⅔	87⅓	86⅔
3½ drs. 1⅛ oz.	147	170	14½	14½	92	90⅔
4 drs. 1⅛ oz.	134	170	15½	16	96⅙	94½
2½ drs. 1 oz. No. 7 Shot, 16-gauge	119	163	13	13⅙	82½	84⅙
3 drs. 1 oz.	120	149	13⅚	14⅙	85⅚	80
3½ drs. 1 oz.	118	146	15	14⅔	89⅙	89

The 20-gauge gun with 2½ drams and 1 oz. (Tatham Bros.' No. 3 shot), 106 pellets to the oz. at 40 yards, made a pattern of 42 right, 48 left; penetration, right, 27¼; left, 26¾.

The 16-gauge gun with 3 drams and 1 oz. (No. 3 shot), pattern of 56 right, 59 left; penetration, right, 29; left, 28½.

The 12-gauge, 3¼ drams and 1¼ oz., 57 right, 85 left; penetration, right, 28½, left, 27½.

The 10-gauge, 4 drams and 1¼ oz., 68 right, 73 left; penetration, right, 30¾; left, 31.

The 6-gauge muzzle-loader, 5 drams and 1¾ oz. (B shot), made a pattern of 93; penetration, 40⅓.

60 *Yards Test.*

The 20-gauge gun, 2½ drams and 1 oz. (No. 3 shot), pattern, 16 right, 20 left, at 60 yards; penetration, right, 18; left, 20.

The 16-gauge gun, 3 drams and 1⅛ oz. (No. 3 shot), pattern, 25 right, 28 left, at 60 yards; penetration, right, 21, left, 20¼.

The 12-gauge gun, 3½ drams and 1¼ oz. (No. 3 shot), pattern, 28 right, 29 left, at 60 yards; penetration, right, 17¾; left, 20¼.

The 10-gauge gun, 4½ drams and 1½ oz. (No. 3 shot), pattern, 30 right, 28 left, at 60 yards; penetration, right, 19⅓; left, 19¼.

The 6-gauge muzzle-loader (No. 3 shot), 6 drams and 1¾ oz., pattern, 69, at 60 yards; penetration, 22 5-6.

80 *Yards Test.*

The performances of the small-gauge guns are not worth recording at this long range.

The 10-gauge gun with 4½ drams and 1⅜ oz. (No. 3 shot), pattern, 13 right, 20 left ; penetration, right, 10½ ; left, 11½.

The 6-gauge muzzle-loader, 6 drams and 1¾ oz. (No. 3 shot), pattern, 47 ; penetration, 14 5-6.

100 *Yards Test.*

The 6-gauge muzzle-loader, 5 drams and 1¾ oz. (No. 3), pattern, 13 ; penetration, 8½.

REMARKS.

It will be noticed that the large sizes of shot gave very superior penetration to the smaller sizes.

The 6-gauge single muzzle-loader shot at this trial made an average pattern of (six shots) 227 pellets with a charge of 7 drams of powder and 1½ oz. of No. 7 shot, containing about 440 in the charge. This is considered by the owner and others to be a wonderfully close shooter, but as compared with the best 10-bores in the London Gun Trial of 1875 it is far inferior. W. W. Greener's winning 10-bore guns in that trial gave an average of 241-2 with a charge of 1½ oz. of No. 6 containing 405 pellets. The author has since exceeded this last pattern with only 1¼ oz. of shot ; and again, with a 12-bore pigeon gun and a charge of 1¼ oz. of No. 6 shot, has succeeded in making the extraordinary pattern of 264·95.

The foregoing tables show that the patterns made by the 10-, 12-, 16-, and 20-gauges were not so uniform, nor were they so high, as those recorded at the London Gun Trials. With regard to the penetration, the method adopted for its registration is an excellent one, for whenever the charge of powder is increased, a corresponding increase is found in the record of the penetration. It also clearly demonstrates the great superiority of large shot over small shot for penetration.

During the trial several pigeons were shot at—distance 40 yards—with a gun of 10-gauge, for which the cartridges were loaded respectively with Nos. 7, 8, and 9 shot, as in the tests of those sizes at the target. On dissection of the pigeons after being killed, it was found that, although No. 8 shot striking in the body gave sufficient penetration to kill, No. 7 was the smallest size that could be driven through the bird when the side with wings down was presented, and from these results it was agreed that any force strong enough to perforate from twelve to fourteen sheets of the pasteboard used in this test was sufficient to kill such game as pigeons or ducks when struck fairly. It is also apparent that full chokes are absolutely necessary to kill game at 70 or 80 yards, and that the 10-bores are capable of shooting large-sized shot much closer, and with far greater effect, than the smaller bores, and in the 8-bore the capabilities may be still further developed, as larger charges may be used and a denser pattern and larger killing circle obtained.

NOTES ON GUN TRIALS.

The " Field " Trials.—The methods adopted by Mr. Walsh were not always the best that could have been devised for the purpose he had in view, which was to determine the shooting qualities of guns and explosives. For instance, the 12-bore choke requires, to show the utmost of which it is capable, a load of 1¼ ounce by weight of No. 6 shot. It was with this load that the author showed the remarkable shooting which led to the trial of 1875, but at the trial itself his guns and chokes generally were handicapped by the load allowed being limited to 1⅛ ounce. In like manner, at the 1879 trial 12-bores were handicapped in relation to small bores by the same conditions, the load for which the gauge is best suited not being allowed.

Nor was the apparatus always perfect. Of the force-gauge many complaints were made. Its action favoured the gun that strung the pellets, *i.e.* sent them up one after the other, instead of as nearly simultaneously as the gun can be made to send them. Perhaps the worst feature was the use of the machine rest in the 1879 trial and the shooting counted upon a fixed central target. This is not the way in which to arrive at a correct estimate of a gun's shooting; but the selected circle, that is, from a centre obviously in the middle of the pattern, should be taken. It is not by any means difficult to make a gun shoot straight; it is not easy to ensure that the shooter shall invariably hit the mark, and with no machine rest the author has yet seen is it possible to obtain unvarying accuracy with guns of different bores.

Before the production of the choke-bore the accuracy of the shot-gun was not questioned; at 40 yards the pattern of the cylinder is so wide that the true centre is not easily found in a small target, and at short ranges the occasional deflection is so slight as to be rarely noticed. Many of the old muzzle-loaders shot out—that is, the right barrel to the right and the left to the left—although the late W. Greener in his books gave precise directions for so placing the barrels as to avoid this fault. When the breech-loader came into use, heavier breech-ends were required and the two barrels were set wider apart at the breech, so that the shots from either would strike the centre at 40 yards.

In the matter of machine rests, it may be added that, in addition to the criticism (page 322) passed upon Mr. Walsh's "*Field* Trial" rest, no one rest, or no one adjustment, will do for varying loads, or for guns of different bores. As the recoil recorded must therefore in each instance be reached from a different base, absolutely correct comparisons cannot be made. Probably no machine can indicate the variations in recoil in such manner as to be translated into "appreciable effect of recoil." A heavy recoil as shown on a machine may be scarcely felt when the gun is fired from the shoulder; and, as demonstrated by more recent experiments, the recoil of a light gun when sufficient to injure the shooter was well within the usual maximum limit when tested on the machine.

The great achievement of the trials contested at London since 1875 was the demonstration of the powers and qualities of the choke-bore. There can be no doubt that much prejudice against them existed. Some bias may still linger; but in every trial, and subjected to every test conceivable, the choke-bore invariably came out ahead of all older fashioned systems of gun-making; with large shot or small, heavy loads or light loads, the chokes proved the best of all. The system of boring the author introduced in the year 1874—a system which was all-successful and quite revolutionised the principle of gun-making—has never been surpassed, probably has not been equalled, and still maintains its position and has substantiated every claim the author made for it.

The Winning Guns.—At most of these gun trials, more particularly at and since the great trials of 1875, the author's guns were particularly successful, beating all comers in the chief classes; yet the guns with which he competed were not invariably exceptionally good. Many that he has since made would give much better results than those recorded by his winning guns; in short, there should be no difficulty in producing guns which shoot quite as close and strong under similar conditions.

Tricks at Gun Trials.—Needless to say that, under the management of the late Mr. J. H. Walsh, every care was taken to guard against trickery and an honest attempt made to place every gun according to its merits. The decisions were not seriously questioned, and it may safely be assumed that the conditions were fairly observed. At the 1875 trial, however, one gun was noticed to ball the shot to such an extent that the charge, instead of spreading over the target, pierced the thin iron plate of which it was composed, and the gun was at once disqualified and withdrawn from the competition. The balling aroused suspicion and led to an investigation. On the ground near the target a felt wad was picked up. It had been severed laterally, the inside hollowed out large enough to hold 16 pellets or more, then the edges were pasted together again. The extra charge of shot, 16 or more pellets, would greatly increase the pattern at that range, providing, as was doubtless generally the case, the wad opened and allowed the shot to escape. At this 1875 trial the committee supplied the powder and shot only, the gun-makers furnishing cases and wadding.

At a Continental trial some years ago a rival gun-maker, during an adjournment, and after the author's guns had been shot, induced the attendants to shorten the range a few yards by advancing the target, stand, etc.; the rival gun, of course, did remarkably well, so well, in fact, that the distance was challenged, and the trick discovered. At another Continental trial the system was altogether so loose, the counting and examination of the targets so long delayed, thus affording many opportunities for tampering with them, that the author and other writers have refrained from quoting any of the official returns.

TABLES OF THE PATTERNS MADE BY THE BEST GUNS IN THE LONDON GUN TRIALS OF 1859, 1866, 1875, 1878, 1879, AND THE AMERICAN GUN TRIALS OF 1873, 1874, 1879.

		drams. oz. shot.	Chilled shot.	Pattern. Right. Left.
LONDON GUN TRIAL, 1859—				
Muzzle-loader	12-bore	$2\frac{3}{4}$ × $1\frac{1}{4}$ No. 6	290 pellets to oz.	158 118
Breech-loader	12-bore	3 × $1\frac{1}{4}$ No. 6		144 90
LONDON GUN TRIAL, 1866—				
Breech-loader	12 bore	3 × $1\frac{1}{8}$ No. 6	280 pellets to oz.	131 123
Breech-loader	16-bore	$2\frac{1}{2}$ × 1 No. 5		100^3 118^4
LONDON GUN TRIAL, 1875—				Average.
*Breech-loader	12-bore	$3\frac{1}{4}$ × $1\frac{1}{8}$ No. 6	270 pellets to oz.	214·5
*Breech-loader	10-bore	4 × $1\frac{1}{2}$ No. 6		241·02
*Breech-loader	20-bore	$2\frac{1}{8}$ × 1 No. 6		145·03
*Breech-loader	8-bore	6 × $2\frac{1}{2}$ No. 6		358·09
LONDON GUN TRIAL OF EXPLO- SIVES, 1878—				
Breech-loader	12-bore	$3\frac{1}{4}$ × $1\frac{1}{8}$ No. 6		220·08
LONDON GUN TRIAL, 1879—				
Breech-loader	12-bore	$3\frac{1}{4}$ × — No. 6	270 pellets to oz.	223·12
Breech-loader	16-bore	$2\frac{3}{4}$ × — No. 6		174·00
Breech-loader	20-bore	$2\frac{1}{4}$ × — No. 6		174·00
NEW YORK GUN TRIAL, 1873—				
Breech-loader	12-bore	3 × $1\frac{1}{8}$ No. 6	Shot with paper shell	150-$\frac{1}{2}$
Breech-loader	12-bore	$3\frac{1}{2}$ × $1\frac{1}{8}$ No. 6	Shot with metal shell	211-$\frac{1}{2}$
Breech-loader	10-bore	$4\frac{1}{2}$ × $1\frac{1}{4}$ No. 6	Shot with paper shell	211
CHICAGO GUN TRIAL, 1874—				
Breech-loader	12-bore	4 × 1 No. 7	309 pellets to oz.	180·04
Breech-loader	10-bore	$4\frac{1}{2}$ × 1 No. 7		191-$\frac{1}{8}$
CHICAGO GUN TRIAL, 1879—				
Breech-loader	12-bore	$3\frac{1}{2}$ × $1\frac{1}{8}$ —	291 pellets to oz.	170
Breech-loader	10-bore	4 × $1\frac{1}{4}$ —		200
Breech-loader	16-bore	$2\frac{1}{8}$ × 1 —		163
Breech-loader	20-bore	$2\frac{1}{2}$ × 1 —		138

* These four guns were shot in the selected circle, and with chilled shot.

Detailed accounts of these trials will be found in the author's book, "The History and Shooting of Choke-bore Guns."

CHAPTER XIV.

THE SHOOTING CAPABILITIES OF SHOT-GUNS.

THE FLIGHT OF A CHARGE OF SHOT.

THE pellets loaded into a cartridge or gun barrel leave the barrel in the same order as they occupied when in the chamber, and continue in the same direction, more or less compactly, until they are arrested by striking some object, or, their velocity exhausted, they fall to the ground. The distance from the gun to the point at which the pellet having greatest muzzle velocity falls to the ground is its extreme range; the limit of the killing range is the point at which several of the pellets have sufficient proximity to each other to hit, and enough velocity to penetrate, the game it is sought to bring to bag. The *pattern* is a diagram which, taken at any point short of the extreme range, will show the *lateral* deviation from a common centre of every pellet passing the point at which the pattern is taken. It will not show the *stringing* of the charge—that is, the distance between the first and last pellets in the direction of the flight of the charge. The distance between the widest apart pellets in a line transverse to the line of flight will be less at all sporting ranges than the distance between the first and last pellets measured in the line of flight. This fact needs to be remembered when examining the pattern as shown on a flat target. The distance between two pellets, as seen on the target, may be less than half an inch; in reality it may have been that one was six or more feet distant from the other, but both having approximately the same line of flight are, when arrested by the target, shown almost touching.

Pattern is the shown shooting of a gun, the only visible proof of a gun's capabilities. The gun which shoots best must make the closest pattern, and a pattern which reveals the least deviation of the pellets from the common centre supposes also that individual pellets have been less in advance, and in rear, of the main body of shot during flight than would have been the case had the spread upon the target been larger. For this reason, the patterns recorded at the London Gun Trials are invaluable for reference, and the tabulated summary added to the condensed report the author has made will render reference easy.

Velocity is the next important test applicable to shooting. Velocity generally means a good pattern. Penetration is still more the result of high velocity.

The author will now attempt to set forth, in as few words as possible, what patterns and what velocities have been recorded, with various explosives, in guns of different calibre, and how by alterations in the quantities of powder and shot used, the size of the pellets, etc., different results have been obtained.

The following diagrams will give at a glance an approximate idea of the difference in the flight of a charge of shot from a choke-bore and a cylinder gun, and also the difference caused by an increased charge of powder in the choke, but as the velocity varies at the different ranges, the diagrams do not show accurately the approximate divergence at all ranges. On the 40-yard diagram one inch is equal to eight feet horizontally, and to two feet only measured perpendicularly. It should be borne in mind that these diagrams were made with an acknowledged good gun, and with cartridges most carefully loaded, by Mr. R. W. S. Griffith, of the "Schultze Powder Co.," for certain experiments. The results here reproduced, and several others, will be found in the sixty-ninth volume of the *Field*, similar diagrams having previously appeared in *Land and Water*.

A few further particulars respecting the flight of a charge of shot may be of use to the sportsman. With the usual charge of 3 drams to $1\frac{1}{8}$ ozs. of No. 6, the spread of the shot at 5 yards from the muzzle of a choke-bored gun will be about 5 inches, at 10 about 8, at 15 yards 12 inches; with No. 2 shot the spread will be about $1\frac{3}{4}$ inches less at each range; and with No. 8 shot will be very little more than with No. 6 at 5 yards, but $2\frac{1}{2}$ inches more at 10 yards, and 4 inches more at 15 yards. If the charge of *powder* is increased, the spread of the shot at these ranges is increased. In a 12-bore gun charges of more than $3\frac{1}{4}$ drams do not generally give greater penetration to the majority of the pellets, although a *few* pellets of the charge have a greater velocity. No. 6 shot, having a velocity of 500 feet per second, should penetrate 18 sheets of a "Pettitt" pad, and will be equal to an energy of 0·90 foot-pounds. No. 3 shot at the same velocity should penetrate 23 sheets, and will equal 1·76 foot-pounds; whilst No. 8 shot at same velocity will penetrate but 16 sheets, and have an energy equal to 0·56 foot-pounds. A velocity of 700 is equal to a penetration of 36 sheets with No. 6, of 39 sheets with No. 5, of 47 sheets with No. 2, of 31 sheets with No. 8.

Obtained with a Choke-bore Gun loaded with 42 grains of Schultze Gunpowder and 1⅛ oz. No. 6 Chilled Shot (304 pellets).

FIXED TARGET
(4 FT. DIAMETER).

MOVING TARGET
(1/25 SCALE).

DISTRIBUTION OF THE 304 PELLETS.

At 10 yards.—All in the 30-in. circle.

At 20 yards.—Ditto.

At 30 yards.—278 in the 30-in. circle; 24 in the 30–48-in. belt; and 2 outside the 4-ft. circle.

At 40 yards.—233 in the 30-in. circle; 65 in the 30–48-in. belt; and 6 outside the 4ft. circle.

At 50 yards.—160 in the 30-in. circle; 90 in the 30–48-in. belt; and 54 outside the 4-ft. circle.

At 60 yards.—100 in the 30-in. circle; 95 in the 30–48-in. belt; and 109 outside the 4-ft. circle.

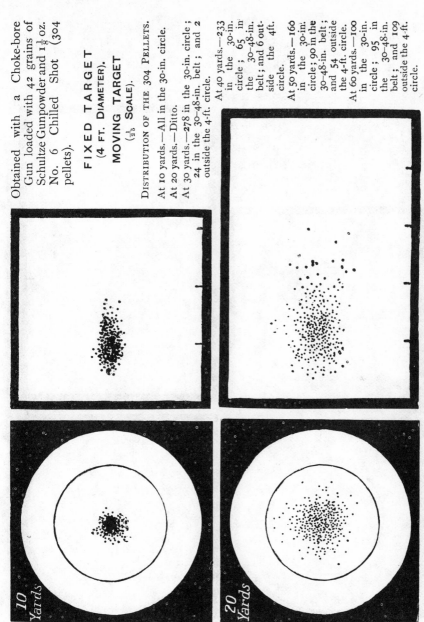

Facsimiles of Patterns showing both Lateral Deviation and Stringing of the same Pellets.

Obtained with a Cylinder Gun loaded with 42 grains of Schultze Gunpowder and 1⅛ oz. of No. 6 Chilled Shot (304 pellets).

FIXED TARGET
(4 FT. DIAMETER).

MOVING TARGET
(⅕₂ SCALE).

DISTRIBUTION OF THE 304 PELLETS.

At 10 yards.—All in the 30-in. circle.

At 20 yards.—264 in the 30-in. circle; 38 in the 30-48-in. belt; and 2 outside the 4-ft. circle.

At 30 yards.—172 in the 30-in. circle; 90 in the 30-48-in. belt; and 42 outside the 4-ft. circle.

At 40 yards.—130 in the 30-in. circle; 103 in the 30-48-in. belt; and 71 outside the 4-ft. circle.

At 50 yards.—76 in the 30-in. circle; 86 in the 30-48-in. belt; and 142 outside the 4-ft. circle.

At 60 yards.—61 in the 30-in. circle; 57 in the 30-48-in. belt; and 186 outside the 4-ft. circle.

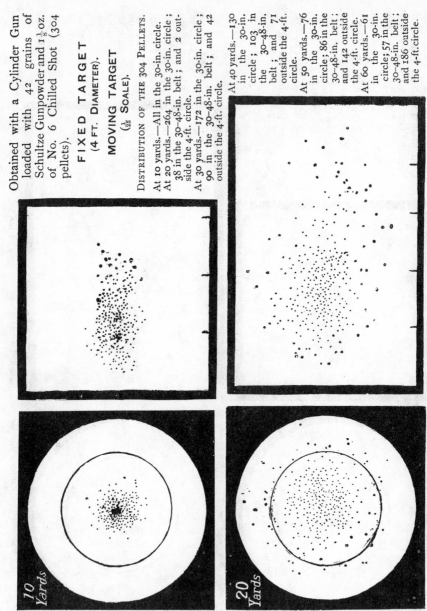

10 Yards

20 Yards

Facsimiles of Patterns showing both Lateral Deviation and Stringing of the same Pellets.

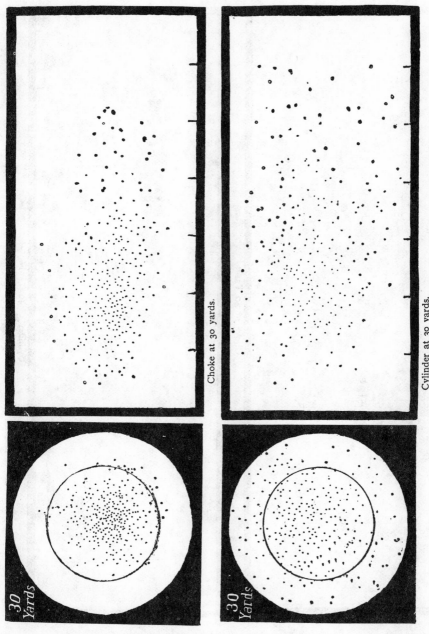

Choke at 30 yards.

Cylinder at 30 yards.

Facsimiles of Patterns showing both Lateral Deviation and Stringing of the same Pellets.

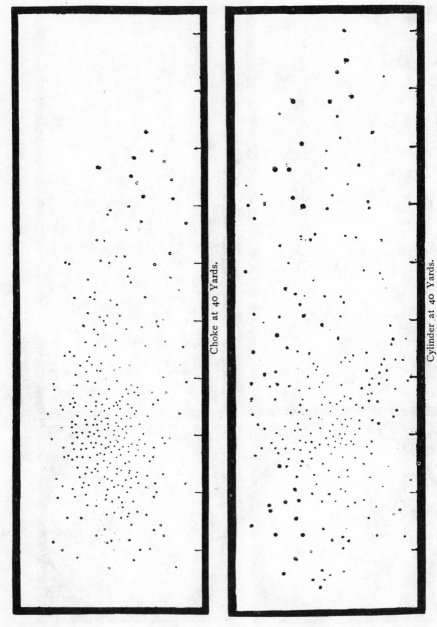

Choke at 40 Yards.

Cylinder at 40 Yards.

Facsimiles of Patterns showing Stringing of the same Pellets as shown on opposite page.

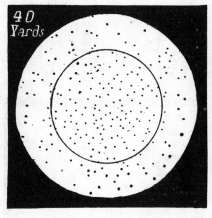

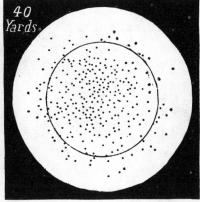

Pattern of the Cylinder Gun at
40 Yards.

Pattern of CHOKE-BORED Gun at
40 Yards.

(The stringing of the pellets of these patterns is shown on opposite page.)

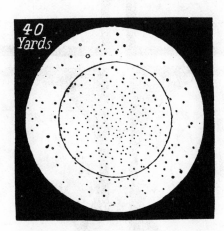

Pattern of the same CHOKE-BORED Gun at 40 Yards, with 49 grains of Schultze Powder
and 1⅛ oz. No. 6 Chilled Shot. (For stringing see page 359.)

Obtained with a Choke-bore Gun loaded with 49 grains of Schultze Gunpowder and 1⅛ oz. of No. 6 Chilled Shot (304 pellets).

FIXED TARGET
(4 FT. DIAMETER).

[MOVING TARGET (1/25 SCALE).

DISTRIBUTION OF THE 304 PELLETS.

At 10 yards.—All in the 30-in. circle.

At 20 yards.—287 in the 30-in. circle; and 17 in the 30-48-in. belt.

At 30 yards.—259 in the 30-in. circle; 40 in the 30-48-in. belt; and 5 outside the 4-ft. circle.

At 40 yards.—199 in the 30-in. circle; 89 in the 30-48-in. belt; and 16 outside the 4-ft. circle.

At 50 yards.—135 in the 30-in. circle; 108 in the 30-48-in. belt; and 61 outside the 4-ft. circle.

At 60 yards.—93 in the 30-in. circle; 92 in the 30-48-in. belt; and 119 outside the 4-ft. circle.

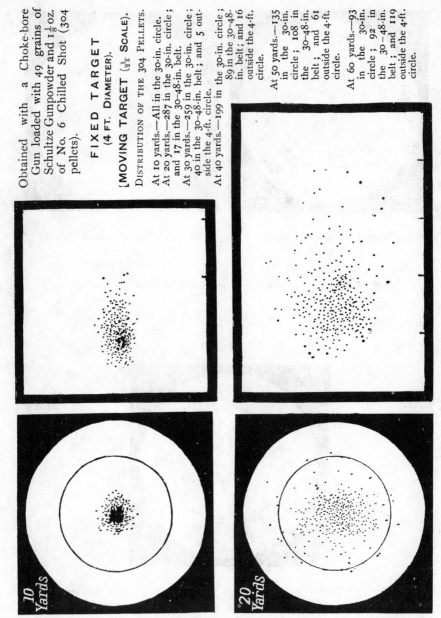

Facsimiles of Patterns showing lateral Deviation and Stringing of the same Pellets. Effects on stringing of heavy charge of powder.

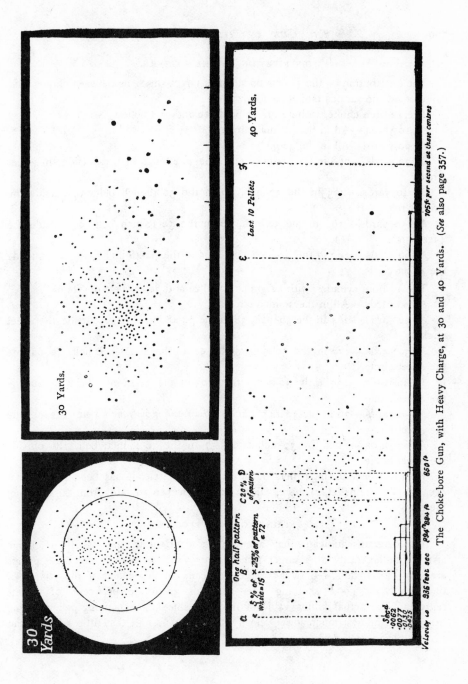

The Choke-bore Gun, with Heavy Charge, at 30 and 40 Yards. (*See also* page 357.)

DISTRIBUTION OF THE PATTERN.

The distribution of the pellets on a 4-feet target varies, as between chokes and cylinders at the various ranges, as follows :—

The 12-bore choke, with 42 grains Schultze and 304 pellets, No. 6—

At 10 yards.—All in the 30-inch circle.

At 20 yards.—All in the 30-inch circle.

At 30 yards.—278 in the 30-inch, 24 in the 30-48-inch belt, 2 outside the 4-feet circle.

At 40 yards.—233 in the 30-inch, 90 in the 30-48-inch belt, 54 outside the 4-feet circle.

At 50 yards.—160 in the 30-inch, 90 in the 30-48-inch belt, 54 outside the 4-feet circle.

At 60 yards.—100 in the 30-inch circle, 95 in the 30-48-inch belt, 109 outside the 4-feet circle.

The 12-bore cylinder, with 42 grains Schultze and 304 pellets of No. 6—

At 10 yards.—All in the 30-inch circle.

At 20 yards.—264 in the 30-inch, 38 in the 30-48-inch belt, 2 outside the 4-feet circle.

At 30 yards.—172 in the 30-inch circle, 90 in the 30-48-inch belt, 42 outside the 4-feet circle.

At 40 yards.—130 in the 30-inch circle, 103 in the 30-48-inch belt, 71 outside the 4-feet circle.

At 50 yards.—76 in the 30-inch circle, 86 in the 30-48-inch belt, 142 outside the 4-feet circle.

At 60 yards.—61 in the 30-inch circle, 57 in the 30-48-inch belt, 186 outside the 4-feet circle.

With reference to the pellets outside the 4-feet circle, it has been proved that occasionally one pellet, or more, will be 10, 15, or even 20 yards from the centre of the charge.

STRINGING AND VELOCITY.

The diagrams indicate that about 5 per cent. of the pellets of the charge arrive simultaneously at a target placed forty yards from the gun ; these pellets are very closely followed by 25 to 30 per cent. of the pellets if the charge of the gun be a good shooting one, and this 30 to 40 per cent. of pellets represents the actual killing value of the shot, since the remaining pellets, flying irregularly, and at a much lower velocity, tail off so rapidly that little reliance can be placed upon them. These differences will be at once recognised by examining the divided diagram on page 359. From it those particularly interested will be enabled to calculate the approximate distances between the pellets as shown in the other diagrams, and also between the pellets at any other distance.

The facsimile targets shown exhibit the usual pattern faithfully, being a photographic reduction of the actual diagrams; but to show accurately, and on the same scale, the side-view illustrating the pellets in flight at sixty yards from a cylinder gun, would require a diagram nearly five feet in length.

With a cylinder gun, with 42 grains of "Schultze" and 304 pellets of No. 6 shot, the first pellets reach the target at forty yards' distance in ·138 second, whereas the last pellets do not reach it until ·187 second; consequently, whilst the first pellets may strike a bird at forty yards, the slower pellets have not reached a distance of thirty yards from the muzzle of the gun.

TABLE SHOWING THE VARIOUS VELOCITIES ATTAINED BY THE PELLETS OF A CHARGE.

Gun and Load.	Range yards.	First cluster of pellets reach the target.		25 pr. cent. pattern lag behind.	Total time for the range.	Equivalent velocity.
		Chronograph velocity.	Equivalent time.			
		Ft.-Sec.	Sec.	Sec.	Sec.	Ft.-Sec.
First Series. W. W. GREENER CHOKE-BORE, with 1⅛ oz. No. 6 shot, and 42 grains of "Schultze" powder.	10	1132	·0265	·0010	·0275	1091
	20	1073	·0559	·0020	·0579	1036
	30	976	·0923	·0035	·0958	939
	40	884	·1357	·0055	·1412	850
	50	802	·1871	·0077	·1948	770
	60	675	·2668	·0102	·2770	650
Second Series. W. W. GREENER CHOKE-BORE, with 1⅛ oz. No. 6 shot, and 49 grains of "Schultze" powder. * This one is marked on photograph to show method of calculating.	10	1209	·0248	·0012	·0260	1153
	20	1124	·0534	·0022	·0556	1079
	30	1031	·0873	·0040	·0913	986
	40*	938	·1280	·0062	·1342	894
	50	855	·1754	·0090	·1844	814
	60	756	·2381	·0112	·2493	722
Third Series. W. W. GREENER CYLINDER, with 1⅛ oz. No. 6 shot, and 42 grains of "Schultze" powder.	10	1128	·0266	·0015	·0281	1067
	20	1062	·0565	·0030	·0595	1008
	30	963	·0935	·0050	·0985	914
	40	870	·1380	·0080	·1460	823
	50	784	·1915	·0102	·2017	743
	60	667	·2700	·0120	·2820	638

VARIATIONS IN VELOCITY.

It is impossible, in the space at the author's disposal, to show the many variations in the velocity of the flight of a charge of shot, but in the following table a few figures are given showing how the difference in the size of the pellets and the charge of explosive used affects the velocity at different ranges. Unlike the results in the foregoing table, which are muzzle velocities, the figures in this table give the actual velocity in feet per second of the average of the pellets over the range indicated, and were measured by Mr. R. W. S. Griffith. All were obtained with a choke-bore gun of 12-gauge, of the author's manufacture, and the explosive used was the Schultze nitro-powder.

ACTUAL VELOCITIES OVER DIFFERENT RANGES.

Charge.			5 Yds.	10 Yds.	15 Yds.	20 Yds.	25 Yds.	30 Yds.	35 Yds.	40 Yds.	45 Yds.	50 Yds.	55 Yds.	60 Yds.
drms.	oz.													
2½	1	No. 1	1039	1022	1001	979	951	929	904	880	856	829	802	780
3	1	,, 1	1185	1168	1150	1120	1076	1039	992	939	919	880	852	831
3	1⅛	,, 1	1169	1140	1126	1089	1054	1003	962	935	914	891	861	825
3½	1⅛	,, 1	1220	1198	1175	1143	1103	1060	1012	966	938	914	890	876
3½	1¼	,, 1	1172	1151	1130	1111	1073	1029	989	949	908	867	835	799
4	1¼	,, 1	1239	1221	1205	1181	1144	1106	1066	1022	976	936	909	863
2½	1	,, 5	996	975	953	924	886	850	831	792	771	744	710	684
3	1	,, 5	1160	1133	1106	1066	1021	969	922	879	840	801	764	729
3	1⅛	,, 5	1127	1034	1070	1047	1014	970	914	875	835	790	741	672
3½	1⅛	,, 5	1182	1164	1136	1088	1045	1002	950	907	875	838	799	757
3½	1¼	,, 5	1130	1111	1088	1058	1026	979	931	880	834	790	741	689
4	1¼	,, 5	1207	1190	1171	1134	1094	1051	994	932	892	853	810	764
2½	1	,, 6	990	963	941	905	863	829	804	776	752	722	690	651
3	1	,, 6	1154	1130	1100	1061	1012	950	904	862	826	770	730	694
3	1⅛	,, 6	1119	1091	1063	1035	999	942	890	850	808	769	717	652
3½	1⅛	,, 6	1175	1153	1120	1079	1032	986	940	894	861	825	780	723
3½	1¼	,, 6	1121	1100	1081	1050	1015	970	912	858	810	762	714	663
4	1¼	,, 6	1199	1177	1159	1122	1082	1034	977	907	850	816	774	734
2½	1	,, 10	922	892	872	841	802	760	703	670	622	551	465	370
3	1	,, 10	1120	1094	1071	1029	959	891	809	751	704	630	559	440
3	1⅛	,, 10	1076	1041	999	941	886	831	775	710	540	465	430	375
3½	1⅛	,, 10	1126	1096	1060	1012	965	892	830	781	711	630	550	460
3½	1¼	,, 10	1066	1041	1017	980	940	896	834	760	706	620	540	446
4	1¼	,, 10	1145	1115	1090	1045	987	927	964	792	720	642	551	495

"In connection with the general question of measuring the velocity of shot-guns, it may be interesting to point out that the records show a gradual improvement during the past twenty years. In 1878 the acknowledged standard velocity was 845 foot-seconds. In 1886 it had risen to 855 foot-seconds, and now an average of 870 to 880 foot-seconds can be relied upon at 40 yards with No. 6 shot. From this, there appears to be every prospect of reaching a muzzle velocity of 900 foot-seconds without disturbing the excellent patterns given with the lower values at present in use."—R. W. S. Griffith, Lecture to the Gun-makers' Association, 1896.

CALIBRE AS ALTERING VELOCITY.

The bore of the gun affects velocity as follows :—

20-bore gun, with 2¼ drams and 1 oz. No. 6 shot, average velocity 725 ft. ; with same charge, but No. 5 shot, average velocity 738·8 ft. per second.

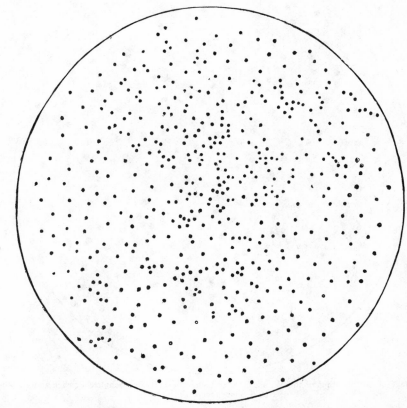

The Winning Pattern at the Leavenworth Trial, made with a W. W. Greener Gun and "Quick Shot" Powder, and 1¼ ounce of No. 8 Shot.

16-bore gun, with 2½ drams and 1 oz. No. 6 shot, average velocity 780 ft. ; with same charge, but No. 5 shot, 791 ft.

12-bore gun, with 3½ drams and 1⅛ oz. No. 6 shot, average velocity 842·171 ft.

10-bore gun, with $4\frac{1}{2}$ drams and $1\frac{1}{2}$ oz. No. 6 shot, average velocity 890 ft. ; with same charge, but No. 4 shot, 936 ft. ; with $1\frac{1}{2}$ oz. No. 1 shot and 5 drams of powder, 943 ft.

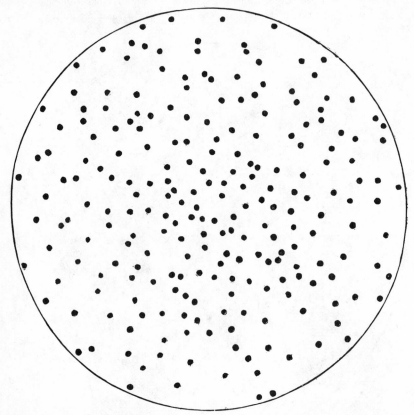

Facsimile of the Shooting of the W. W. Greener Gun with 42 grains Schultze Powder and $1\frac{1}{8}$ ounce No. 6 Shot, 270 to the ounce.

8-bore gun, with 6 drams of powder, paper case, and $2\frac{1}{4}$ ozs. No. 1 shot, average velocity 907 ft. ; with 7 drams No. 4 powder and $2\frac{1}{4}$ ozs. No. 1 shot, and brass case, average velocity 984 ft. ; with same load, but finer-grained powder, 945 ft. ; with same load, but with ducking powder, *expressly manufactured for 8- and 4-bore duck guns*, average velocity *only* 904 ft.

With 3 drams and 1 oz. of No. 6 the average velocities should be—with 12-bore, about 870 ft. per second; with 16-bore, about 885 ft. per second; with 20-bore, about 920 ft. per second.

PATTERN.

The diagram made by the pellets fired at a sheet of paper, or an iron or other target, is the *pattern* of the gun's shooting. In order to ascertain a gun's shooting power, all the expert needs to do is to fire it at a large sheet of paper with the standard charge for its gauge. For comparison with other results, the number of pellets striking within a 30-inch circle may be taken as the shooting of the gun. A good close pattern is a guarantee that the gun has sufficient force to kill; for the greater the velocity of the mass of the pellets the closer is the pattern. No close-shooting gun has inferior penetration; and, speaking generally, the nearer each pellet mark is to the common centre the less distant will the first and last pellets of the charge be to each other : a close pattern means, therefore, that there is no-great difference in the velocity of the individual pellets. Occasional bad patterns, or patchy patterns, prove the gun to be improperly bored; the closer the pattern at forty yards the longer the killing range of the gun with that load. As a pattern of a gun's shooting is easily ascertained, and is easily understandable, some space may be devoted profitably to facsimile reproductions of good average patterns and tables of loads, showing how with different bores and charges these same patterns and "killing circles" may be approximated.

A gun made by the author for the Schultze Gunpowder Company has been used for many years to test different batches of powder, and many important trials made with it, and the results made public. The following table gives the average of a thousand shots from each barrel each year—the left barrel is ordinary full-choke, the right modified choke :—

Average of 1,000 Shots per Year.

				Left barrel.				Right barrel.
1878	...	...	...	175	...	...	...	184
1879	...	...	...	202	...	...	...	196
1880	...	...	...	208	...	...	...	206
1881	...	...	...	207	..	...	...	201
1882	...	...	...	210	...	...	...	195
1883	...	...	...	214	...	...	...	194
1884	...	...	...	224	...	...	...	196
1885	...	...	...	239	...	...	...	201

These figures clearly prove that a choke will stand all fair wear and tear, and further that Schultze powder has no deleterious effect upon good gun barrels.

It is not to be supposed from these figures that guns improve in shooting to any marked extent by use, but rather as indicating a gradual improvement in the quality of the powder, and that the shooting of a gun does not deteriorate by proper use.

After 80,000 shots had been fired from the gun, it was tried, and the pattern here reproduced was then obtained with 42 grains of Schultze powder and $1\frac{1}{8}$ oz. of shot of 270 pellets to the ounce.

LEFT BARREL.		LEFT BARREL	
Patterns made on 2nd July,	273	Patterns made with same Gun	259
1885, with this gun and W. W.	276	on 30th July, 1885. W. W.	251
GREENER's Loaded Cartridges,	255	GREENER's specially Loaded	241
42 grains of Schultze Powder,	276	Cartridges, 42 grains of Schultze	235
and $1\frac{1}{8}$ oz. of No. 6 Chilled	260	Powder, and $1\frac{1}{8}$ oz. of No. 6	240
Shot (305 pellets counted in).	252	Chilled Shot (305 pellets	260
		counted in).	
Average	265·3	Average	247·4

Average obtained before two Gentlemen of the " Field " Staff, Aug. 8th, 1885—255.

Any gun, if a good one, should shoot all good powders well; it may, of course, be slightly better with one than another, but with good powder and a suitable charge it should always shoot well. The author tries all guns with the best explosives readily obtainable in England, and his guns, when shooting close and well with English powder, perform equally satisfactorily with the powders obtainable abroad.

At a gun trial held at Leavenworth in 1886, a Greener 12-bore gun was shot at forty yards with "King's Quick Shot" powder—an explosive the author had never had an opportunity of trying. The gun beat all its opponents easily—some were much heavier guns and of larger calibre—and made a target of which the diagram shown on page 363 is a facsimile.

Similar diagrams can be produced at any time, under equal conditions, so it is unnecessary to reproduce further reduced facsimiles, and it is needless to adduce proof that the diagrams were actually made—and the proof that they were so made is overwhelming—nor can the fidelity with which they have been reproduced by photographic process be doubted.

The next diagrams are *actual* size, and show exactly the positions of the pellets on the paper target, and will give the reader an idea of the actual closeness of pattern in the centre of the target. The one with No. 6 shot is equal to a pattern of 230 in a 30-inch circle; the one with No. 8 is equal to a pattern of 300 in the 30-inch circle.

Pattern of 12-bore Choke, with 1⅛ oz. No. 6 Shot, at 40 yards.

Diagram of 12-bore Full Choke, and No. 8 Shot, at 40 yards.

KILLING CIRCLES.

The term "Killing circle" is used to designate the extent of the spread of the pellets in a lateral direction, so long as the "pattern" is not too wide to allow of the escape of the game.

At 40 yards from the muzzle of a gun it has been proved that on frequent occasions a few pellets of the charge will be found 10, 15, and even 20 yards from the centre of the body of the charge; thus, at 40 yards a gun may, whilst putting the greater number of its pellets into a 30-inch circle, scatter some 40 yards asunder.

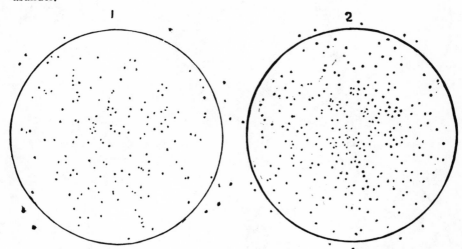

Facsimile No. 1.—Circle, 30 in. diameter.   Facsimile No. 2.—Circle, 30 in. diameter.

The facsimile reproduction of targets made by the author will enable the sportsman to see at a glance the comparative density of patterns, and the approximate killing spread of the gun. These targets, obtained with guns of different gauges, may be approximated by guns of any gauge by altering the load or the range, or both.

No. 1.—Number of pellets in circle, 163. Killing circle, about 26 in. Diagram represents the shooting of a 28-bore gun, full choked, at 40 yards, with 1½ dram of powder and $\frac{7}{8}$ oz. No. 7 shot.

A similar pattern would be made with a 20-bore and 1 oz. No. 6 shot, or a 20-bore with 1⅛ oz. No. 5 should be no closer, but a killing circle two inches larger.

No. 2.—Number of pellets in circle, 285.   Killing circle, 30 in.   This diagram represents the shooting of a 28-bore cylinder gun, at 20 yards, with 1½ dram and ⅞ oz. No. 7 shot.

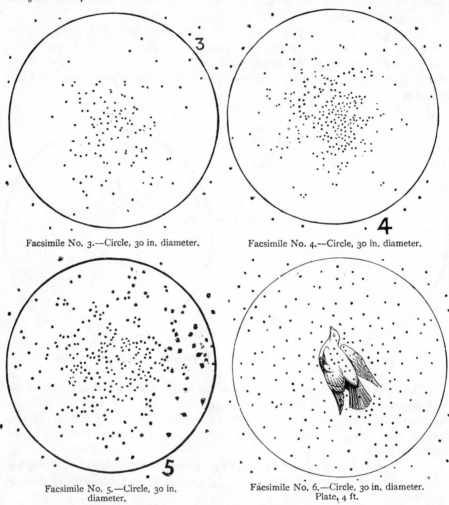

Facsimile No. 3.--Circle, 30 in. diameter.   Facsimile No. 4.--Circle, 30 in. diameter.

Facsimile No. 5.—Circle, 30 in.   Fácsimile No. 6.—Circle, 30 in. diameter.
diameter.   Plate, 4 ft.

A similar result is obtainable from a 20-bore cylinder with ¾ oz. No. 8 shot.

No. 3.—Number of pellets in circle, 131.   Killing circle, about 18 in.   This diagram represents the shooting of a 28-bore gun, choke-bored, at 20 yards' distance; charge, 1½ dram and ¾ oz. of No. 6 shot.

A similar pattern results from using a 20-bore with 1 oz. No. 5 shot at 18 yards; with ⅞ oz. No. 6 a 20-bore at 20 yards makes a killing circle about two inches larger.

No. 4.—Number of pellets in circle, 292. Killing circle, about 25 in. This diagram represents the shooting of a 12-bore gun, choke-bored; distance, 20 yards; charge, 3 drams and 1⅛ oz. No. 6 shot.

A similar pattern results with a 20-bore at 20 yards with 1 oz. No. 8 shot, but with the 20-bore the killing circle is a little less.

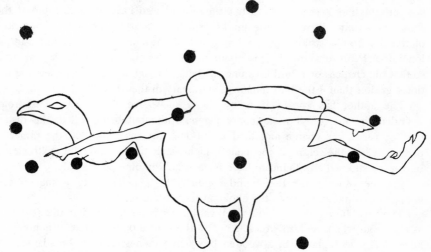

Reduced Facsimile of the "Pattern" of a Choke upon a Pigeon.

No. 5.—Number of pellets in circle, 288. Killing circle, 30 in. This diagram represents the shooting of 12-bore cylinder gun at 20 yards; charge, 3 drams and 1⅛ oz. No. 6.

The same result is obtainable from a choke at 20 yards, by using 1 oz. No. 6 and *scatter charge*, or by using a brass case gun at 40 yards with 1¼ oz. No. 7, or with 1⅛ oz. No. 8 at 40 yards.

No. 6.—Number of pellets in circle, 250. Killing circle, about 35 inches. This diagram represents the shooting of a pigeon gun, 12-bore, with 4 drams and 1¼ oz. No. 6 shot.

The boring for a gun to shoot as No. 6 facsimile is of a special kind, designed to produce a regular pattern, not too thick in centre, but sufficiently thick to kill in a circle of 35 inches.

The instructions for approximating any other gun to one of the depicted patterns are based upon several series of experiments made at different times, and the data are sufficient to permit of reliable conclusions.

The illustration shows the pattern of a 12-bore choke gun upon a pigeon ; the rough outlines of the bird's body (exact size) flying crosswise, to and away from, the shooter, were sketched in the centre of a large sheet before shooting, and the illustration is an exact reproduction of the resulting target. Had the birds been in motion, and flying rapidly enough, it is possible that they might have fled into the line of other pellets, but they would also have escaped some of those shown as striking them, for the marks were *in situ* from the time of the arrival of the first to the striking of the last pellet of the charge on the target, and the longitudinal spread at 40 yards is about three times greater than the lateral spread, so that the chances of a bird escaping by flying through a string of pellets are three times greater than if the bird remained stationary in their line of flight.

The author has known as many as six successive shots to be fired from a cylinder 12-bore gun at a stationary pigeon without it being killed, the distance only 35 yards, the charge and load a full one, and, as shown on the target, the pigeon well in the centre of the pellets' flight each time. After the sixth shot the bird was examined and found to have been struck by nine pellets only.

On the other hand, the cylinder gun put 54 pellets into a pigeon at 15 yards' range, and at 20 yards the choke averaged but 40.

The small-bore gun will kill as well as the larger bore, provided the pattern be as close, but when the bird struck is not in the centre of the pellets it is not always killed. A pigeon placed in a wooden box 6 by 7 inches, with its broadside to the gun and a piece of thin paper only between the bird and the gun, was fired at with a 21-bore gun, with the following results at different ranges :—

Charge.	Pattern on 7 by 6.	Result.
No. 1 Pigeon, 40 yards, 1½ dram, ¾ oz. No. 6	13	Bird struck in body, but not in any way disabled.
No. 2 Pigeon, 40 yards, 1¾ dram, ¾ oz. No. 6	12	Leg broken; one pellet in breast; not disabled from flying.
No. 3 Pigeon, 35 yards, 1 dram, ¾ oz. No. 6	18	Shot in body, but not disabled.
No. 4 Pigeon, 35 yards, 1½ dram, ¾ oz. No. 6	18	Shot in body, but not disabled.
No. 5 Pigeon, 30 yards, 1½ dram, ¾ oz. No. 6	23	Killed dead.
No. 6 Pigeon, 30 yards, 1 dram, ¾ oz. No. 6	35	Killed dead.

A study of these results and the loads used reveals the truth of the assertion the author has so many times made as to the relative values of pattern and penetration ; 1 dram with ¾ oz. of No. 6 gives a denser pattern than when 1½ dram is used, and kills the bird equally well ; but in all cases where the pattern was not dense enough to strike the bird in several places, although the penetration and velocity were great, the bird was not killed.

As to the amount of penetration, striking force, or velocity requisite to kill, experiments were made at the Chicago Gun Trial in 1879 to determine what penetration of straw-boards was equal to penetration of a pigeon, when it was agreed that any force strong enough to pierce twelve to fourteen sheets of straw-board was sufficient to kill such birds as pigeons or ducks. The loads and gauges which will accomplish this amount of penetration are given in detail in the next chapter. It remains only to remark that large-sized shot is more deadly : shot of 270 to the ounce penetrated and proved deadly in birds which shot of 375 to the ounce at the same velocity failed to kill. A penetration of seven straw-boards entered the body of a duck.

The reason feathers are knocked out of birds is not because the gun lacks penetration power, for the pellets striking the bird at an oblique angle cut, injure, and root out the feathers ; the bird escapes because the pattern is not close enough to ensure at least one pellet striking a vital part.

To ascertain correctly the closest pattern the gun is capable of making with a certain load, a *selected circle* must be taken, the centre of which circle may or may not exactly coincide with the fixed centre of the target. The deviation is due to faulty aiming, and the shooting quality of the *gun* must not be held dependent upon such personal errors when testing it for best results.

Numerous trials have been made by the technical staff of the *Field* newspaper to determine the relative value of guns of different calibres with various loads, and to discover the calibre which with the least powder would impart the requisite velocity to a load of shot. Roughly the results were as follows :—

" With 1 oz. of shot, 33 grs. in the 20-bore, and 35 grs. in the 16-bore, gave the same impetus as 38 grs. in the 12-bore; for, with the diminution of gauge, the length of the shot-charge increases; and the greater amount of frictional resistance to the movement of the shot causes a larger development of explosive force in the powder."

As to the most suitable loading, speaking generally—

" Under ordinary conditions, with the older varieties of nitro-powders (which are about one-half the specific weight of black powders), the proportion of powder to lead is near about 1 to 12. Thus, 41 grains of the nitro-powder are one-twelfth the weight of 1⅛ oz. or 492 grains of shot ; and 36 or 37 grains of powder are proportionate to an ounce of shot. When the proportion of shot much exceeds 12 to 1, the velocity does not come up to the standard; as is especially shown in the case of the 32-bore, where the shot-charge was rather more than 20 times the weight of the powder, and the speed of the shot was consequently very low.

CHAPTER XV.

VARIETIES OF SHOT-GUNS AND THEIR SHOOTING POWERS.

THE CALIBRE OF SHOT-GUNS.

THE varieties of the shot-gun are almost as numerous as the purposes for which guns are required. There is no actual limit, perhaps, to be set upon the capabilities of any weapon until trial has been made—a customer of the author's once shot a couple of snipe with an 8-bore elephant rifle—but ordinarily a gun is made for some special purpose, and in size and weight will conform to the shooting required of it. The collector who requires humming-birds, and the wild-fowler who thinks of getting wild geese, will arm themselves very differently.

Again, some guns have to be carried throughout a long day's walk; in other sports the gun is only in the hand the couple of seconds requisite to aim and fire. It is, therefore, evident that what is desired for one sport is of little importance in a gun desired for another sport.

The capabilities of the shot-gun as a shooting weapon are determined by its size; the smaller calibres do not do so well with the large-sized shot as the large-bores; the capabilities of each calibre, each length of barrel, and each charge suitable thereto, will now be specified, in order that the sportsman may know which variety of gun will best suit his purpose.

There are certain essentials which should be possessed by all varieties of guns. Amongst the chief of them are—Facility in loading at the breech, freedom from danger to the user or his companions, simplicity of mechanism, speed in manipulation, handiness, lasting power.

The chief purposes for which shot-guns are required are—For game shooting, for trap shooting at pigeons, for wild-fowling.

The game gun may be of any bore from 28 to 10, although it is rare that the 12-gauge is exceeded.

THE SMALL-BORE GAME GUN.

The small-bore gun is not the toy some suppose it to be. True, it has not taken the position it was thought to have gained by those who championed it at the

London *Field* Trials of 1879, but it is indisputable that, in the hands of good shots, the small-bore is a really efficient weapon.

A few instances of the use made of the 28-bore will be of interest.

"Young Nimrod," when 11 years of age, shot with a 28-bore of the author's make, and did remarkably well. In public pigeon matches he was placed at 27 yards, and at that distance upon more than one occasion has killed his 38 out of 50 best Blue Rocks. Sometimes he would grass many birds in succession, several strings of 17, 11, and 13 having been scored to him, which is evidence not only of his skill as a marksman, but of the killing powers of his gun. His score of 88-100 at clay pigeons with ¾ oz. shot also deserves recording.

A nobleman, well known in sporting circles, wrote the author the following in November, 1884 :—

" I had the 28-bore out for a few shots at pheasants yesterday, and I am much pleased with it, killing eight birds in succession, and four of them at least thirty-five yards off, flying away low, and one with the choke-barrel a very long shot—we measured it—fifty-three yards, and the bird was flying away within three yards from the ground ; it fell stone dead to the gun. I shot a hare with the right—not choked—barrel at thirty-four yards as dead as a nail. (Charge used, 1½ dram black powder, ¾ oz. No. 6)."

Again, on February 4, 1885 :—

" I can only say your 28-bore gun cannot be improved upon ; its shooting is quite first-class. I have given it a capital trial, and find it shoots as strong as a 12-bore. Of course you have to lay on straight, *then* I defy any gun to shoot harder ; it has had a really good and heavy trial.'

Another good shot writes :—

" I have tried the little gun, have made some very long dead shots at rabbits, and am confident of success at game."

A single 24-bore gun, made for a lady, and weighing but a trifle over three pounds, is a first-class all-round game gun ; partridges, pheasants, hares, and rabbits are shot regularly. The efficiency of the gun, however, is better demonstrated by the fact that it is preferred by the owner's brothers to their own 12-bore guns for shooting at the wood pigeons as they come home to roost in the high elms in the park, and on one occasion a fallow doe was shot dead with it at 25 yards' distance with seven-eighths of an ounce of No. 7 shot.

The small-bores may therefore be ranked as serviceable weapons, whilst for boys about to commence shooting, the 28- or 24-bore double is to be preferred to the single gun. They are, of course, more expensive ; to build them well requires more care and a greater outlay than the building of a gun of ordinary sporting gauge. The author does not recommend either of these bores, especially the latter, unless for use by a first-rate shot or a boy beginning to practise ; the ideal gun for ladies is of larger bore.

THE 20-BORE has been strenuously advocated by writers in the sporting papers, but there are very few sold—the proportion is perhaps one 20-bore to twenty of 16-bore. The 20-bore should not have barrels longer than 28 in., nor should it be heavier than $5\frac{1}{4}$ lbs., and the full standard load is $2\frac{1}{4}$ drams and 1 oz. of shot. They can also be made—28 in. barrels, 5 lbs. ; 27 in., $4\frac{3}{4}$ lbs., ; 25 in., $4\frac{1}{2}$ lbs. ; and so on in proportion.

In the 1875 Gun Trials, W. W. Greener's gun was first in the class for 20-bores with a gun using only $2\frac{1}{8}$ drams of powder and 1 oz. of shot, beating in both pattern and penetration heavier guns shooting larger charges. A frequent error, and one which is of importance, is the overloading of small-bore guns, for sportsmen overlook the point that the gun does not fail to kill owing to a lack of penetrative force, but because the pattern is not sufficiently close. With moderate charges the penetration of any well-bored gun is sufficient.

The following testimony proves what can be done with this calibre :—

" In trying some experiments with the 20-bore (Greener) at paper targets, I found that with 32 grains of Schultze, and thin card, felt, and *Field* wad, with 1 oz. No. 5 or 4 shot, the gun made a very good pattern, and in the month of February I did some very good work with it on big pheasants, also shot a barking deer at 56 paces with ball. I am very pleased with the gun."

THE 16-BORE GUN was at one time a favourite with Continental sportsmen, who now for the most part prefer the 12-bore ; for use in England probably not one gun in five hundred is made 16-bore. This size of gun shoots as strongly as does the 12, but the killing circle is less. The standard weight for the 16-bore was $6\frac{1}{2}$ lbs. ; the barrel was 30 inches in length and regulated to shoot best with $2\frac{3}{4}$ drams of powder and 1 oz. of shot, or with 28 in. barrels $6\frac{1}{4}$ lbs., but 6 lbs. is now considered to be quite heavy enough for any 16-bore with 28 in. barrels. The one advantage of the 16-bore is its lightness, and, when built in the same fashion as the miniature 12-bores, the 16 may be $5\frac{1}{2}$ lbs. with 28 in. barrels, $5\frac{1}{4}$ lbs. with 27 in. barrels, and about 5 lbs. with barrels as short as 26 in. The lightest 16-bore the author ever made had 25 in. barrels, and weighed 4 lbs. 11 ozs. only.

The following letter, addressed to the author by a prominent sportsman, proves that in the right hands the 16-bore possesses qualities of which much can be made :—

"The little 16-bore ejector gun I ordered came to hand, and I have had a good opportunity of testing it, and must say I am very much pleased with it.

" I killed some geese at 50 to 55 yards with it, using 3 drs. E.C. and 1 oz. No. 1 shot, but of course it is not a goose gun."

THE 14-BORE breech-loader is rarely made and possesses no distinct advantages, and has the serious disadvantage of being a size for which cartridges are not easily procurable. It was a convenient size to which to convert muzzle-loaders to breech-loaders, as few of the old 13-bore muzzle-loaders were made sufficiently stout at the breech to allow of being chambered for 12-gauge cartridge cases.

THE STANDARD CALIBRE GAME GUN.

The 12-bore gun is the standard calibre for game and pigeon guns, and is made in greater varieties and weights than any gun of other calibre. The usual weight of the double-barrelled gun is from $6\frac{1}{4}$ to $6\frac{3}{4}$ lbs., the barrels are 30 inches long, chambered for the usual cartridge case, which is $2\frac{9}{16}$ inches in length ; it will shoot well with the standard charge of 3 drams and $1\frac{1}{8}$ oz. of No. 5 or 6, but for use early in the season a lighter load may be used with advantage.

The ordinary game gun should have a killing circle of 30 inches at thirty yards with the first barrel, and at forty yards with the second.

The gun for covert shooting will give a 30-inch killing circle at twenty yards with the first and at thirty with the second.

The gun for grouse-driving will be bored to give a killing circle of thirty inches in diameter at the longest possible range ; the gun not to be more than 7 lbs. weight. The tendency, however, is to build guns still lighter, and with shorter barrels than 28 inches, as they serve equally well the purposes of general sport.

Longer barrels than 30 inches are sometimes made, but experiments have proved that no advantage is gained either in pattern or penetration by so doing. In South Africa, where much shooting is done from the saddle, the barrels of the 12-bores are often 36 inches in length. This extra length is necessary to get the muzzles clear of the horse ; from the gun-maker's point of view nothing is gained by making any gun with barrels more than 40 diameters in length.

MINIATURE 12-BORE GUNS.

The principle upon which the very light game guns of standard gauge are constructed is that of reducing the 12-bore gun in length and bore of barrel to the exact capacity required by the sporting charge of 3 drams and $1\frac{1}{8}$ ounce. From numerous experiments the author has arrived at the conclusion that a barrel of 25

inches long, choke-bored, will satisfactorily burn 3 drams of powder, and propel
1⅛ ounce of shot at a high velocity; in fact, that for ordinary game shooting the
12-bore with 25 inches will shoot this charge as well as it need be shot.   By carefully
reducing the 12-bore gun, in barrels, breech-action, locks, and stock, a miniature gun
is produced from one to one and a half pounds lighter than the normal 12-bore, and
shooting the standard 12-bore charge nearly as well as the ordinary 12-bore choke
gun does.   These miniature guns require great care and considerable skill to be
exercised in their manufacture; it is quite impossible for any maker without
practical experience to produce perfect weapons of this kind.   The 27-inch barrels
will be found to permit of better marksmanship than shorter barrels, and, consequently, unless there is a good reason for doing so, guns should not be made
with barrels shorter than 27 inches.   Although they are sometimes made lighter
than 5½ lbs., it is only at a sacrifice of strength.   A reliable gun, with breech ends
of the barrels of the ordinary thickness, can be made as light as 5¾ lbs., below which
it is inadvisable to go.

A miniature 12-bore gun, therefore, will always command a fair price, and can
never be made in the cheapest grades.   It must fire 3 drams and 1⅛ ounce to
perfection, and without appreciable recoil—a larger charge cannot be used with
comfort; balance and handle perfectly—*every part* being reduced from the ordinary
12-bore gun size; it must stand the heavy wear and tear of the hardest season, and
yet be perfectly safe.

This is the weapon Birmingham has produced, and its many advantages will
commend it to those sportsmen whose work is not such as lies beyond the
capabilities of 3 drams of powder and 1⅛ ounce of shot.

The following letters will convey some idea of the power and range of miniature
shot guns :—

"In 1878 I had a 12-gauge gun with 24-in. barrels, made by W. W. Greener, of Birmingham,
which I have shot ever since, and which, for handiness and getting quick sight upon the object
aimed at, I think cannot be excelled; in fact, you may call it a one-handed gun.

"With regard to its killing powers I cannot find any perceptible difference up to 40 yards.
I have just tried it at the target at 40 yards, and the shooting has not gone off to any extent,
considering the wear it has had.   The right barrel averages 150, and the left 170, the shots
striking very hard.

"F. LYTHALL" (in the *County Gentleman*).

"My 12-bore, by W. W. Greener, has 25-inch barrels, weighs a small fraction over 5¾ lbs.,
and is as handy and well-balanced as a gun can be.   Both barrels are 'full-choked,' and were
regulated for No. 5 shot.   The load I use is—42 grains of Schultze, 1 card wad, 1 pink edge,
1 soft thick felt, 1¼ oz. of No. 5 hard shot, 1 card wad on top.   With this load the average

(both barrels) is 200 at 40 yards, 150 at 50, and 100 at 60 yards. The patterns are always beautifully even, but at 40 yards a little close in the centre. The best shot I ever got with it at 60 yards was a pattern of 116 pellets, with a penetration of 28 sheets Pettitt's pads. . . . I have frequently killed both birds and pheasants up to 70 and 75 stepped yards. Your correspondent, Mr. F. Lythall, is perfectly right in everything he says as to short barrels, and the rapidity with which they may be aligned as compared with the conventional 30-inch. I could as well carry a long 7 lb. or 7½ lb. gun now as I could thirty years ago, but, as I can find no tittle of advantage in doing so, I much prefer to only load myself with a short, light, small-bore, with which all the ordinary work of a season is just as *well done*.

"One who has Fired 20,000 Shots at Marks."

THE SPORTSWOMAN'S GUN.

The gun for use by sportswomen should be purposely constructed; not only must the stock be differently shaped and of very different measures to the ordinary gun, but the barrels will require modification if the best possible results are to be obtained.

There are some sportswomen who can shoot well with almost any gun, just as there are men who use guns of divers bends and weights indifferently, but to most ladies the question of recoil is an important one. The author, having had more experience in the building of guns for ladies' use than perhaps any other English gun-maker, can confidently assert that the gun possessing the essentials he is about to enumerate will prove more effectual than the light small-bore guns usually recommended.

The bore 12, the barrels 27 inches long, the weight 5¾ lbs., making with the right barrel a killing circle of 30 inches at 30 yards, with the left a similar pattern at 35 yards; the charges to be used being in the right 2¾ drams of black or 36 grains of "Schultze" powder, or equivalent charge of other suitable smokeless powder, and 1 oz. of No. 7 shot, and in the left barely 3 drams by measure of black or 40 grains of "Schultze" powder, and 1⅛ oz. of No. 6 shot. The stock to be suitably shaped, well bent, and well cast off; the gun to be perfectly balanced; and not butt-heavy. A 12-bore gun cannot be made satisfactorily to weigh less than 5¾ lbs.; if a lighter gun be required a more serviceable weapon will be obtained by choosing a smaller bore, viz. 16 or even 20.

THE PIGEON, OR TRAP, GUN.

This is the most powerful variety of the 12-bore gun; it must be so built as to meet the rules of the chief clubs; in England the bore must not be larger than 12, nor the gun heavier than 8 lbs.; the charge to be used must not exceed 4 drams of powder and 1¼ ounce of shot. On the Continent and in America 10-bores are allowed, but there is usually some restriction as to charge. The pigeon-gun may be made with hammers or hammerless, preferably the latter. It should *not* have a trigger-bolting safety; and an automatic trigger safety for this species of gun is the greatest mistake that can be made.

The shooting required will in some measure depend upon the distance at which the user is generally placed, it being required to have the largest possible killing circle at one yard beyond the trap with the first barrel, and at five yards with the second. In no class of gun is uniformity and regularity of shooting more essential than in the trap-gun. The weight may be from ½ to ¾ of a pound greater than in the gun carried for game-shooting, but it is important that the balance be perfect.

An ideal pigeon-gun will balance at about 3 inches from the breech, weigh only 7½ lbs., and fire the full charge of shot (1¼ ounce) with the greatest uniformity; the gun will be hammerless without any safety bolt; it must have a strong breech-action and be fitted with the Greener cross-bolt. It is usual for the barrels to be chambered for the 2¾-inch case, and the gun is heavy enough to fire even 50 or more grains of Schultze without excessive recoil, but trap-shooters are now finding it advantageous to use smaller charges than has hitherto been the practice, so 3-inch chambers are rarely demanded, although 2⅞-inch is a length in considerable request. Many shots prefer that the gun shoot six or more inches above the mark at 40 yards, and good marksmen require that the gun shoot well—that is, very close —in the centre of the 30-inch circle. Other shots, standing nearer the traps, do not require extra elevation, and wish to avail themselves of the largest possible killing circle which can be obtained at 30 yards, or such distance as will serve them best according to the number of yards' rise at which they are most frequently handi-capped. With 1¼ ounce of shot this killing circle is about 30 inches in diameter, and means a close shooting gun, even for a choke-bore. If at 40 yards the killing circle will not greatly exceed 30 inches, and 250 is a good average pattern for a full-choke pigeon gun.

In choosing a trap-gun it must be remembered that the gun is required to shoot its best at, or just beyond, the trap; for the bird must be shot quickly, and the nearer it is grassed the safer. Uniformity of shooting is of still greater importance, and this quality can be obtained only by great care in the fine boring and choking of the barrel; a gun that makes an occasional bad shot would allow of the pigeon escaping, however true the aim; therefore the pigeon-shooter's gun should never shoot wildly, but be always good alike. Some particulars of the shooting of special pigeon guns are given in the chapter on "Trap Shooting"; here it will only be needful to say that, as some trap shooters may doubt absolute regularity of shooting being within the range of possibility, the records made by notable trap shots prove entirely what the author has advanced. A notable case was that in the series of matches between Captain Brewer and Mr. Fulford, when one of the author's guns was used, and with it the score was 199 out of 200 birds shot at, the 200th bird falling dead out of bounds.

The highest patterns the author has obtained with " original E.C." and Schultze gunpowders; using 47 grains and 1¼ oz. No 6, 270 to the ounce, with 11¾ calibre wads, it is not unusual to get patterns averaging 270 in the 30-inch circle at 40 yards, and average patterns as high as 280 are sometimes obtained. It must not be forgotten that there is a slight variation in all nitro-explosives, so that with them a gun will rarely shoot quite the same, even when using the same loads. If the charge of powder be increased the pattern will decrease, but in a good pigeon gun as much as 52 grains of either of the nitro-explosives above mentioned may be employed without the pattern being materially lowered. The high patterns are obtained with the 11¾ calibre wad over powder in some guns, in others the Swedish cup wad gives the highest pattern. For 25 yards' rise, if a larger killing circle be required the best way is to increase the load of shot beyond 1¼ oz., if the rules permit; if not, smaller sized shot may be used. A good pigeon gun with No. 8 shot will make an average pattern of 375 pellets, all well distributed. For shooters placed at 32 yards' rise No. 5 shot in the second barrel will be found advantageous : the velocity is higher, though the killing circle is smaller. With No. 5 shot the gun should give an average pattern of about 200, if the full load of 1¼ oz. is used and the shot is 218 pellets to the ounce.

The Swedish " Cup " wad, above mentioned and elsewhere described, is useful for small loads in guns specially regulated for heavy charges, as are pigeon guns. For instance, the author obtained with one of his pigeon guns, and 3 drams and 1⅛ oz., an average pattern on a first trial of 226 pellets in the 30-inch circle at 40 yards ; the second trial gave an average of 223 ; the third, one of 230. With 42 grains of Schultze gunpowder the average was 243; on a second trial, 248; with 40 grains, 232. An average of 246 was obtained with 42 grains of " E.C. No. 2 " powder. Using both black and nitro-explosives, 42 shots from one barrel gave an average pattern of 236. This gun, with 3¾ drams of black gunpowder and 1¼ oz. No. 6 shot, using also 48 grains of Schultze and " E.C. No. 2," the powders indiscriminately through the series of 30 shots from one barrel gave an average pattern of 262 for the whole series.

The best scores made with special pigeon guns will be found in the chapter on " Trap Shooting." Three noteworthy instances of one hundred birds without a miss in public matches are the scores of Messrs. Brewer, Elliott, and Fulford, all of whom accomplished this feat with guns made by the author.

THE BEST LOAD FOR A PIGEON GUN.

The two essentials are pattern and penetration.   Care must be taken not to overload with powder, and long experience has proved that 47 grains of Schultze or other suitable powder gives the best pattern.   An increase in the powder charge of 5 grains—52 grains being at one time a favourite pigeon load—actually reduces the pattern and shows but little improvement in penetration.   Shooters do not attach sufficient importance to the size of shot used; the many variations in the sizes of different makers cause much confusion, and it should be clearly understood that, in England at least, No. 6 of 270 to the ounce is the acknowledged standard.   There are other sizes described as No. 6 in England, viz.: London size, counting 285 to the ounce, and 6*, counting 300 to the ounce; while Continental and American sizes of the same number range in count from 69 to 328 pellets to the ounce.   It will be readily seen that such irregularities create difficulties between the gun-maker and his customer, unless the standard size be clearly understood ; quite recently a customer abroad complained that his gun did not make the pattern he required and which he stated his old gun did.   He required a pattern of 340 with No. 6 at 33 yards; the gun as shot in England averaged 260 with a load of 338 pellets or 1¼ oz. of No. 6 shot at 40 yards.   It was obviously impossible to obtain the pattern demanded with such a load, but a request for a sample of the customer's own shot resulted in the discovery that it counted 405 to the 1¼ oz., with which patterns averaging 320 at 40 yards were easily obtained.   It should be noted that in this instance the addition of 67 pellets to the load resulted in an improvement of 60 pellets on the target.

To obtain uniform results it is absolutely essential that the shot be counted into the cartridge case, and the sportsman's attention is directed to the shot-counting trowel described and illustrated on page 601.

If such a method be impossible, the correct weight and count should be ascertained, and the measure carefully adjusted to accommodate such load, the shot being carefully struck off for each charge.

Tables of shot sizes are given on page 612, and sportsmen abroad are advised to order small quantities of shot to be sent out with their guns if they wish to test the shooting accurately, and compare the patterns with those given by the maker.

The question, " Which is the best nitro ? " is often asked, and the multiplicity of powders from which a selection may be made has not tended to make it easier to reply.   Most are equally unstable ; from the same batch of powder one may get a falling-off of from 80 to 100 pellets in the pattern, while pressures may rise from a normal 2½ or 3 tons to 5 tons, which, as shown by a recent report in the *Field*, is capable of producing a disastrous burst. The illustration, reproduced by permission of the Editor of the *Field*, was, so far as could be ascertained, caused by cartridges exerting a pressure "in the neighbourhood of 4 tons," and it is no uncommon thing for the author to find ordinary nitros exerting pressure of from 4 to 5 tons. The reader's attention is directed to the paragraph on page 564, which, although written some years ago, in spite of the much-vaunted improvements in modern smokeless powder, still holds good. Unfortunately, foreign powders are still worse, and many strong, well-made guns are burst by the excessive pressures exerted by such powders.

Another point to be noted when testing a gun at the target: at the *Field* and other public trials the range

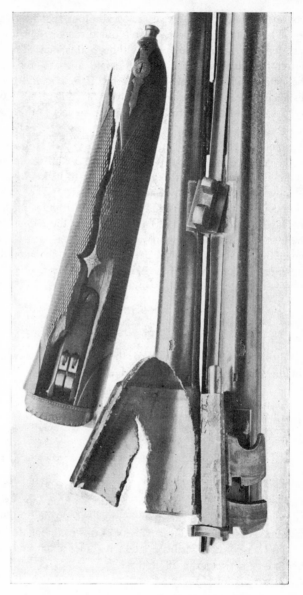

has always been *measured* as 40 yards from the butt of the gun; a rough-and-ready way is for the shooter to step this distance ; but it will be found that few men can correctly step a yard, and, although this may appear a simple matter, a yard nearer the target is sufficient, with some guns, to cause a difference of 5 pellets in the pattern with a 1¼-oz. load, so that if one man steps two yards short of the distance, and another two yards over, the difference between the results obtained by these two shooters would be about 20 pellets in the 30-inch circle.

EXTRA LONG CARTRIDGES FOR PIGEON SHOOTING.

Experience proves that 3-inch 12-bore cartridges do not give such good results as the 2¾-inch, and it is a decided mistake to make a gun with 28-inch barrels with 3-inch chambers for large charges of powder. The extra length in the case tends to encourage overloading, and no appreciable advantage is obtained. The slight increase in velocity does not compensate for the reduction in pattern, and most of the best pigeon-shooting guns are made with 2¾-inch chambers. It is exceedingly dangerous to use a 3-inch cartridge in a gun chambered for the 2½-inch case, the pressure in such circumstances rising to 5 tons or over, according to the powder used.

THE SHOOTING POWERS OF GAME GUNS.

Small Bores.

THE 28-BORE should have 25- or 27-inch barrels, which will require but little choking, and average :—

Charge powder.		30-inch pattern.	Cardboard penetration.	Mean velocity.	Force at impact.
1½ dram	¾ oz. No. 8	150	13	705	0·67
*32 grs. Schultze	¾ oz. No. 6	124	22	940	1·96
1½ dram	¾ oz. No. 6	130	17	720	1·87

* Overloaded. This charge has been too frequently used ; 26 grains does better.

The weight should not be less than 4, nor more than 4¾ lbs. Recoil 60 lbs. The 28-bore must not be loaded with 1 oz. of shot, as is too often done. This calibre especially is too frequently much overloaded. The 28-bore must be used with brass cases if the full capability of this calibre is desired.

THE 24-BORE is but little used ; it comes about midway in pattern, penetration, recoil, etc., between the 28- and 20-bore.

THE 20-BORE is the smallest bore usually sought by the general sportsman ; a gun of 5¼ lbs. weight, and with 28-inch barrels, may be taken as representing fairly the 20-calibre class, and it should average—

AT FORTY YARDS.

Charge.		Pattern. 30-inch circle.	Penetration of Strawboards.	Mean Velocity.	Force at Impact.
Drams of powder.	Oz. of shot.				
2¼	1 No. 8	230	13	756	0·67
2¼	1 No. 6	180	18	772	1·37
2½	⅞ No. 6	160	19	849	1·94
2½	⅞ No. 5	120	22	890	2·37
2½	⅞ No. 1	65	29	950	2·72
32 grs. Schultze.	¾ No. 6	150	20	820	2·00

AT SIXTY YARDS.

2¼	1 No. 6	60	9	650	0·76
2¼	1 No. 5	35	18	684	0·89

Weight not less than 5 nor more than 6 lbs.

THE 16-BORE FULL-CHOKE, with barrels 30 inches in length, and the gun weighing 6¼ lbs., should average—

AT FORTY YARDS.

Charge.		Pattern. 30-inch circle.	Penetration of Strawboards.	Mean Velocity.	Force at Impact.
Drams of powder.	Oz. of shot.				
2	1 No. 5	160	22	763	0·98
2½	1 No. 6	190	19	814	1·35
2½	1 No. 5	155	23	847	2·49
2¾	1 No. 6	180	21	833	2·27
3	1 No. 6	174	22	858	2·33
2¾	1 No. 5	155	25	856	2·48
2½	1 No. 1	85	29	936	3·00

AT SIXTY YARDS.

2¾	1 No. 6	95	9	635	1·10
2¾	1 No. 5	85	12	675	1·26
2½	1 No. 1	45	19	830	1·52

Weight from 5¾ to 6½ lbs.

THE 12-BORE GAME GUN.

Standard Gauge.

The best all-round gun for sporting purposes is the 12-bore with 30-inch barrels, weighing about 7 lbs., providing the sportsman can carry and handle a weapon of this weight.

Twelve-bores much under 7 lbs. will not shoot a heavier charge than $3\frac{1}{4}$ drams and $1\frac{1}{8}$ oz. with comfort to the shooter. If $7\frac{1}{4}$ lbs., $3\frac{1}{4}$ drams and $1\frac{1}{4}$ oz. If $7\frac{1}{2}$ lbs., the charge may be $3\frac{1}{2}$ drams and $1\frac{1}{4}$ oz.; over $7\frac{1}{2}$ lbs., guns are usually built for extra long cartridge-cases and special charges.

For the shooting of 12-bore guns with large charges see under the heading, "Pigeon Guns." The shooting of 10, 8, 4, and other large-gauge guns is given under the heading "Duck Guns." Light guns and guns with short barrels will shoot 3 drams and $1\frac{1}{8}$ ounce of shot, and an average pattern of 200 with No. 6 shot may be obtained.

The usual full-choked 12-calibre gun, with 30-inch barrels and weighing 7 lbs., should average—

AT FORTY YARDS.

Charge.		Pattern.		Penetration of Strawboards	Mean Velocity.	Force at Impact.
Drams of Powder	Oz. of shot.	Square 10-in. centre.	30-in. circle.		—	
$3\frac{1}{4}$	$1\frac{1}{8}$ No. 8	92	320	15	800	0·80
3	$1\frac{1}{8}$ No. 6	55	215	20	839	1·80
$3\frac{1}{4}$	$1\frac{1}{8}$ No. 6	51	210	21	857	1·83
$3\frac{1}{2}$	$1\frac{1}{8}$ No. 6	39	200	22	912	1·87
$3\frac{1}{4}$	$1\frac{1}{4}$ No. 6	58	240	21	864	1·85
3	$1\frac{1}{8}$ No. 5	35	175	22	878	1·89
$3\frac{1}{4}$	$1\frac{1}{4}$ No. 5	45	190	23	882	1·91
$3\frac{1}{4}$	$1\frac{1}{4}$ No. 4	40	160	24	900	2·81
$3\frac{1}{4}$	$1\frac{1}{4}$ No. 3	38	135	25	950	3·16
$3\frac{1}{4}$	$1\frac{1}{4}$ No. 1	35	105	26	980	4·18
$3\frac{1}{2}$	$1\frac{1}{4}$ No. 1	33	100	30	988	5·30

AT SIXTY YARDS.

3	$1\frac{1}{8}$ No. 6	29	110	10	652	0·93
$3\frac{1}{2}$	$1\frac{1}{8}$ No. 6	36	100	11	723	1·28
$3\frac{1}{2}$	$1\frac{1}{8}$ No. 5	28	89	14	757	1·47
$3\frac{1}{2}$	$1\frac{1}{4}$ No. 4	17	70	18	786	2·00
$3\frac{1}{4}$	$1\frac{1}{4}$ No. 1	15	50	21	799	2·46

GUNS OF REDUCED CALIBRE.

In addition to the reduction of the bore by "choking," as already described, attempts have been made at different times to give a greatly enlarged powder chamber to the shot-gun, just as in cannon and in some rifles. The latest serious production in this direction is the so-called "*vena contracta*" barrel, which consists of a 20-calibre barrel enlarged at its breech end sufficiently to allow of being chambered for the 12-gauge case. The advantages claimed for this barrel include better balance, but if a gun be required very light forward it is more advantageous to use a shorter barrel of 12-bore. The 12-bore charge is not fired to best advantage from a 20-bore barrel; and in the "*vena contracta*" there is increased strain on the barrel at the breech-end, greater compression of the shot, and the killing circle, instead of being that of a 12-bore, is that of a 20 only.

GUNS OF ODD SIZE.

Guns of 24- and 32-bore are but rarely used in this country, where they would be of but little utility, and may be dismissed with the merest mention; they are mostly exported to the Brazilian and Argentine markets, and together with the 410-bore are principally used by naturalists, or for such weapons as walking-stick guns. The 28-bore is the smallest calibre of any practical use as a game gun.

For guns of 2-bore see "Duck Guns"; a 6-bore muzzle-loader was shot at the Chicago trials, and its performance is recorded in the report.

SINGLE-BARRELLED GUNS.

The miniature gun is much to be preferred to the single gun, a species of shot-gun quickly falling into disuse. The double is now constructed so light that a single gun, if made lighter, would recoil unbearably. It is for duck guns and large-bore rifles that the single barrel is now mostly used. Two heavy barrels of 4-bore, side by side, are more than the hand can firmly grasp, so many shooters adhere to single guns for wild-fowling, preferring to lose the chances of a second shot than possess only an imperfect command of the gun.

GUNS FOR BUCKSHOT.

A special gun is preferable if the best results are to be obtained with large shot of three, four, or five to the layer, and such guns of 12-bore, if correctly constructed, will shoot at long ranges with such force and accuracy that they may with advantage be substituted for rifles for small deer shooting.

The following letter, which appeared in the *Field* on February 15th, 1887, will convey an idea of the nature and power of a true buckshot gun :—

"Mr. W. W. Greener sent me a No. 12 hammerless gun—30 in. barrels, weight 7½ lbs.—which I received last June. It has more than met my most sanguine expectations, and fully verified my opinion, not only shooting buckshot with the possibility of killing a deer from 100 to 150 yards, but also proving a remarkable shooter with small shot.

" During the past summer I only got shots at six deer, killing each shot. The longest shot was 91 yards, the deer being struck with three shot, one breaking the back, and the other two just below. I shot too high, the deer being in the act of leaping high, and the remaining six shots passed into a gum-tree above the height of the deer.

" In a number of trials at a 30-in. circle, from 100 to 150 yards, not a shot was fired that would not have killed a deer. At the distance of 150 yards a shot made by Dr. Hargrove, of Knox Point Post-office, three shots would have entered the side of a deer.

" A number of shots were fired by John A. Skannall, Money Brian, and George Conway. These gentlemen are among our most eminent planters, and distinguished for their fine shooting. At 100 yards from five to six shots were put in the target out of a possible nine at every discharge. At 125 yards never less than four shots would have entered the side of a deer.

" Last week, while hunting partridges, I inserted a shell loaded with buckshot, and gave it to Mr. Tom Barrett, a lawyer of Shreveport, to shoot at a sparrow-hawk. He killed it at the distance of 90 yards·

" At a trial made in Shreveport a number of distinguished gentlemen attended. They were sceptical as to the long range of this gun, and would not believe, unless they measured the distance and shot the gun. They brought a tape line and measured 125 yards. Among them were Hon. A. C. Blanchard, member of Congress from the Fourth District of Louisiana ; his law partner, Alexander; and Capt. Smith, superintendent of the Fair Grounds. They themselves shot my gun with results similar to what I have above stated, putting from two to three shots in less than 3 in. of the centre of a 30-in. circle at every discharge. I give the names of these gentlemen, with post-office addresses, so that, should anyone doubt my statement, they could be referred to. I would also add the names of Capt. Ike Dyer and Capt. Jas. Y. Webb, of Minden, La., who were the first to test the qualities of this gun after I received it.

" It is a very great advantage to have a breech-loader doing such extraordinary shooting with buckshot, and at the same time proving a very fine gun with small shot.

" I have no doubt that W. W. Greener, of St. Mary's Square, Birmingham, England, could duplicate this gun for anyone who may desire to get the best deer gun which has been manufactured during this century.

" Not long since, in the presence of a number of cadets of the Thatcher Military Institute, of Shreveport, I fired with buckshot at a 3-in. circle, 90 yards distant, and struck it with three shots, one grazing the centre. A deer would have been struck with eight of the possible nine shots.

" GEO. D. ALEXANDER."

Guns specially bored by the author for shooting buckshot are tested at 40 yards, and will place eight out of the nine pellets forming the charge in a 30-inch circle at this range.

In selecting buckshot, care should be taken to see that it lies in even layers in the muzzle of the gun. The illustration shows nine and three pellets

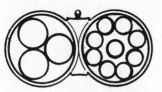

How Buckshot should fit the Muzzle of a Gun.

of A.A.A. and S.S.G. shot respectively as they should fit the muzzle of a 12-gauge choke-bore gun. If any difficulty is experienced in procuring buckshot of the correct size,

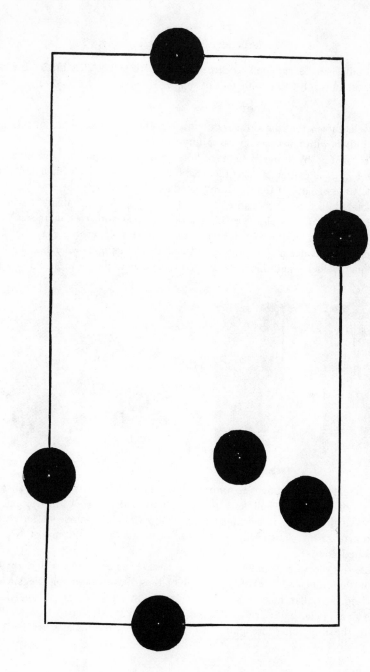

Facsimile of a Diagram made at 40 Yards' Range with a Light Full-Choke-bore Game Gun, 12-gauge, by W. W. Greener.

bullet moulds can be supplied to cast nine or twelve pellets at a time. Buckshot guns can, of course, be used with shot of smaller sizes.

SHOT-GUNS AS BALL-GUNS.

It is well known that the ordinary double-barrelled cylinder shot-gun will shoot spherical bullets with fair accuracy up to fifty yards.

The recoil felt by firing a light 12-bore gun with a spherical bullet is very considerable ; as a matter of fact, the recoil is 13 lbs. heavier with a bullet and standard charge of powder than with the standard charge of shot.

A lighter bullet was, therefore, a desideratum, and the " Mead " shell was produced. This consists simply of a hollow spherical core cast in the spherical bullet ; it is shown in the illustration below. The hollow core may be filled with an explosive if deemed advisable, and a large charge of powder may be used, and a higher velocity and lower trajectory is obtained than can be got from a

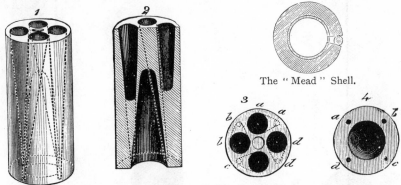

The " Mead " Shell.

Macleod's Revolving Bullet (Actual Size).

spherical bullet of the same size with a shot-gun. The ordinary game shot-gun will not shoot bullets so well as a properly built ball-gun (not rifled) ; but the accuracy is such that all bullets may be got into a 12-inch circle at forty yards by a good marksman. The charge should not be more than $2\frac{3}{4}$ drams of No. 4 or No. 6 grained powder.

For use in shot-guns, special projectiles have been invented which shall fly better than the ordinary spherical ball ; some of these have projecting wings wound spirally round the bullet, but the best known are the invention of Dr. Macleod.

In the first model holes are cast in the bullet, and it is asserted that it will be revolved by the air rushing through the eccentric holes as the bullet takes its flight,

This heavy bullet—a 12-bore, weighs $\frac{3}{4}$ oz., and is $1\frac{1}{2}$ inch in length—must not be used in a light gun, and even in a gun of 8 lbs. weight will require an india-rubber wad half an inch in thickness to be placed over the powder before the bullet can be fired without occasioning a painful recoil.

In the last model the loose revolving rudder affixed to the projectile is said to steer it a more sure course. It is open to many of the objections advanced against the first model.

In the illustration No. 1 is a longitudinal view of the bullet, and shows the exact size and direction of the perforations. No. 2 is a section showing the hollow base. No. 3 is an end elevation of the point, and No. 4 of the base.

The inherent fault of this principle of producing rotation is that the rotation is obtained at the cost of velocity ; the air resistance necessary to rotate the projectile retards it to such an extent as to impair its utility for all sporting purposes. It is recorded that a sportsman using a Macleod bullet fired at an Indian bison ; the bullet struck in the centre of the forehead, but did not penetrate even the thick skin, and but for the timely help of his companions the shooter would have lost his life. The greater the muzzle velocity, the greater the speed of rotation ; hence the higher fractional resistance and speedy retardation of the bullet.

Gun barrels, when choke-bored, may also be rifled for a few inches at the muzzle, as in the " Murphy " and the " Paradox " guns ; and these weapons, although they will not shoot shot as closely and regularly as a true choke-bore, nevertheless perform up to the average, and are accurate with bullets at short ranges. Weapons of this nature should be considered rather as rifles specially constructed for shot than as shot-guns for ball. The Government Proof-House Regulations require that such weapons be proved as rifles—that is to say, tested with ball. Fuller particulars are given in the chapter on " Rifles."

Choke-bore guns may be used as ball-guns, providing that the bullet to be fired will pass easily through the muzzle, and it may be interesting to sportsmen to know that choke-bore guns shoot ball QUITE AS WELL as guns bored ordinary cylinders. Especially is this of interest to those who use but one gun, and have often the chance of a shot or two at big game. Gunmakers and sportsmen alike have been misled by the proof marks ; on all choke-bores " Not for ball " was formerly marked.

Another point to be noticed is, that if one barrel be modified choke or cylinder, *it is only necessary to use the one-sized ball*, the larger bored barrel shooting to all intents and purposes as well as the smaller barrel for which the ball is moulded.

Any gun which is safe to use with shot would be quite as safe with ball, provided that ordinary care be taken to see that the ball be not larger than the smallest part of the barrel, and the charge of powder does not exceed the ordinary one used with shot. Further, the ring wads are not at all necessary; one card and one thick felt over the powder, the ball being fixed in either by an ordinary turnover or crimper, will give all that is needed. NEITHER WAD NOR PATCH OVER THE BALL, or the gun-barrel may be burst.

The adjoined diagram was made by a full-choke-bored light game gun, charged with $2\frac{3}{4}$ drams powder, bullet 14-bore, and 12-gauge case, distance 40 yards.

LARGE-BORE GUNS FOR WILD-FOWLING.

Guns of the largest calibre which can be fired from the shoulder are usually made single barrel and of 4-bore, the average diameter being 1·052 inch. There is a 2-bore paper case made by Messrs. Eley Brothers, Limited, but the calibre is practically that of the 4-bore thin brass case gun. The cases do not hold a larger charge, nor do the guns shoot better, if so well, and the cartridge-case has not the advantage of being so perfectly water and damp proof as that of brass; therefore, the 4-bore gun for brass cases is that recommended.

These large guns are made in four styles of breech-loading, the mechanisms being—first, the cheapest, with double-grip lever under guard, back-work lock, and outside hammers; second, the treble-wedge-fast, with top cross-bolt, top lever, bar lock, and outside hammers; third, the treble-wedge-fast top cross-bolt, hammerless mechanism; fourth, similar breech mechanism, but with the addition of self-eject-ing lock work. The gun should weigh from 15 lbs. to 18 lbs., the barrels being 42 in. to 46 in. in length, as fully choked as possible to obtain the best results with charges varying from nine to ten drams of powder and $3\frac{1}{4}$ to $3\frac{1}{2}$ ounces of shot.

Strong serviceable guns, with first-class shooting, can be had with the cheapest form of breech-actions for twenty-five guineas, and with the hammerless ejector from forty-five guineas.

Single 8-bores are made with the same styles of breech-actions as described above. The barrels are made 36 in. in length, and the guns weigh from 10 lbs. to 15 lbs., and the prices range from sixteen guineas, according to the breech-action used.

The double 8-bore is recognised as the standard wild-fowling gun. The gun is made in three distinct varieties—the "Magnum," weight 15 lbs., barrels 36 inches long, chambered for the $3\frac{3}{4}$ in. "Perfect" thin brass case. This gun fires a charge of 7 drams of powder and $2\frac{3}{4}$ to 3 ozs. of shot. This gun is best suited for boat work, shooting from a hut, a "sink," or screen, as it is too heavy to carry a long distance. It is the best shooting gun, giving 90 to 100 pellets of No. 1 shot in a

12-in. square at 40 yards, and an average of four pellets to the square foot on a four foot target at 100 yards.

The "Medium" 8-bore has 34-in. barrels, weight about 13 lbs., and shoots almost as well as the "Magnum" with 6 drams of powder and $2\frac{1}{2}$ to $2\frac{3}{4}$ ozs. of No. 1 shot. This gives an average pattern of from 80 to 90 pellets in the 12-in. square at 40 yards.

The "Light" 8-bore has 30-in. or 32-in. barrels, weighs 11 lbs. to 12 lbs., and should be chambered for the $3\frac{1}{4}$-in. "Perfect" thin brass case. The charge used is 6 drams of powder and $2\frac{1}{4}$ to $2\frac{1}{2}$ ozs. of No. 1 shot, with which the pattern in the 12-in. square at 40 yards will average 85 pellets.

Brass cartridge-cases, especially the thin brass cases called "Perfects," offer many advantages for use in these large-bore guns. The cartridges, on account of the large charges used, are necessarily cumbrous, but with brass cases there is more room for a larger charge in the same length case as the paper; escape of gas is with them an impossibility; they therefore shoot much stronger, and they will not jamb in the chambers, thus avoiding the chagrin caused by a tight shell and the loss of a second shot. Neither do changes of the atmosphere affect them. In double guns the jar caused by firing the first barrel is apt to shake out or loosen the wad in the second barrel, but this may be prevented by using an indented case, or closing in with a patent *crimper* specially made for these brass cases. (*See* page 606.)

With an 8-bore gun, fired with $6\frac{1}{2}$ drams of black powder, No. 4, or the equivalent of Schultze, and 2 ozs. of shot, the velocities will average as under:—

Size of Shot.	Velocity obtained at		
	60 Yds.	70 Yds.	80 Yds.
No. 1	892	828	748
,, 2	872	804	718
,, 3	850	775	686
,, 4	825	744	651
,, 5	798	710	612
,, 6	768	672	566

Undoubtedly the best all-round gun for shore shooting is a double 8-bore of eleven to twelve pounds weight and full-choked, bored for brass cases; this gun with No. 1 shot will have sufficient power to kill ducks at 150 yards, but its available range is practically 80 to 100 yards; at longer distances the pattern is too open, and there is great difficulty in hitting the bird. With 2½ ozs. No. 4 shot at 40 yards, the pattern should average 300 and the penetration be equal to 34 sheets of strawboard ; with No. 1 shot, pattern 220, penetration 40 sheets ; at 60 yards the penetration of No. 1 shot 34 sheets, at 80 yards 24 sheets, at 100 yards 16 sheets. The penetration of seven sheets is sufficient to kill a duck. Patterns, with same charge, at 60 yards, 130 pellets; at 80 yards, 50; at 100 yards, 18 pellets, all in 30-in. circle.

With paper cases, 5 drams and 2½ ozs. of No. 1 shot has given a pattern of 175 pellets at 40 yards ; same charge and conditions, but brass cases, the pattern was 225.

This is sufficient to prove the great benefit the shooting powers of the gun derive, when properly bored, from brass cartridge-cases.

The following results are extracted from *Land and Water* of February, 1894, and is a condensed report of experiments made by " Fleur de Lys " with a W. W. Greener, 8-calibre 36-inch double-barrelled gun of 15 lbs., chambered for 3-inch brass " Perfect " cases.

With 6½ drs. No. 4 Alliance powder, 2¾ ozs. No. 1 shot, the average pattern on a target 4 feet by 3 feet at 100 yards was 40 pellets = 3·3 to the square foot ; with 7 drs. and 3 ozs. No. 1, average 54 = 4 pellets to the square foot; with 6½ drs. and 2½ ozs. No. 4 shot, at 80 yards, 127 on target, or 10 pellets to the square foot; with 7 drs. and 3 ozs. No. 4 shot, in 30-inch circle at 80 yards, an average of 57 pellets, or 11½ to the square foot ; with 6 drs. and 2¾ ozs. No. 1 shot, at 80 yards, in the 30-inch circle, an average of 53 pellets, or 10½ to the square foot ; with 6 drs. and 2½ ozs. No. 1 shot, at 80 yards, in the 30-inch circle, an average of 48 pellets, or 9½ to the square foot; with 6 drs. and 2¾ ozs. No. 1 shot, at 60 yards, in the 30-inch circle, an average of 130 pellets ; with 6 drs. and 2½ ozs. No. 1 shot, at 40 yards, 90 to 97 pellets in a selected 12-inch square ; with 7 drs. and 3 ozs. No. 1, about 100 pellets in the 12-inch square.

With brass cases, and 7 .drs. and 2½ ozs. No. 1 shot, the pellets in the 30-in. circle averaged 224 ; average in centre 12-in. square, 90 pellets. Upon reference to the annexed diagram, which is a facsimile of a shot from one of the author's 4-bore guns, it will be seen that the pattern is sufficiently close for any purpose.

A 4-bore, at 40 yards, with 11 drs. and 3½ ozs. No. 1 shot, will average a pattern of 245, penetration 46 sheets; at 60 yards, pattern 150, penetration 34 sheets ; at 80 yards, pattern 65, penetration 24 sheets ; at 100 yards, pattern 23, penetration 16 sheets. With 12 drs. and 3 ozs. of B shot (80 to the oz.) a pattern at 40 yards of 230, penetration 54 sheets. The 30-in. circle, from which the above

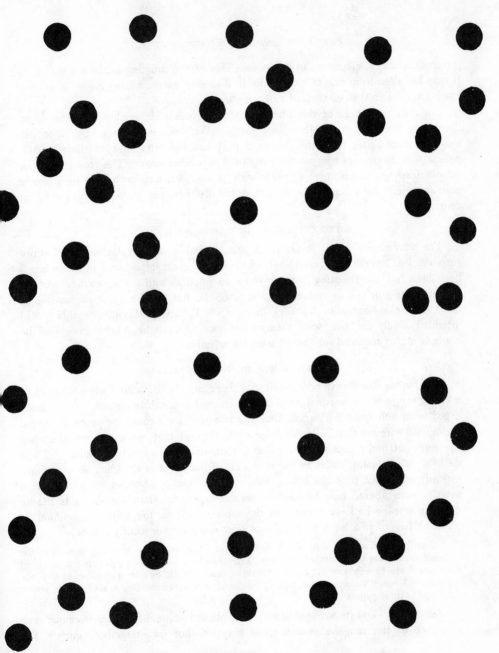

Diagram made by Greener's "Wild-fowling" Gun, 4-bore, No. 1 Shot.

patterns are taken, gives but an inadequate idea of the shooting of these large guns. It may be taken from one at least 50 in. in diameter, as the killing circle is so very much larger than that of 10- and 12-bore guns.

The only advantage of the 4-bore is that it shoots a larger charge of shot than the 8-bore, thus giving a wider killing circle. With the large shot A A, B, &c., it also performs better than the 8-bore, and it has the advantage of throwing the pellets well to the centre, as the diagram figure illustrates. The closest pattern yet obtained by the author at 40 yards with $3\frac{1}{2}$ ozs. shot was 125 pellets on a centre 12-in. square. An 8-bore, with $2\frac{1}{2}$ ozs., same distance, put 90 pellets on the 12-in. centre.

NITRO-EXPLOSIVES IN LARGE-BORE GUNS.

The advantages which result from using suitable nitro-explosives in 8-calibre guns are less smoke and less recoil, which are of great importance in these large-bore guns, but the shooting is rarely quite so good as with black powder. As the weight of the gun can be reduced if the recoil be not too heavy, it is possible to build double 8-bore guns from $1\frac{1}{2}$ lb. to 2 lb. lighter, "Magnum" calibre, and intended solely for use with nitro-explosives. The light 8-bore may also be made lighter if required for the nitro-explosive only.

KILLING RANGE OF LARGE CALIBRES.

The author has always contended that these large-bore "wild-fowling" guns had a killing range of 100 yards if properly constructed and rightly loaded. It has been urged upon him again and again that the 100-yard limit could be exceeded, but it is doubtful whether the killing of large birds beyond that range is not more often the result of lucky chance than within the capability of an ordinary gun. "Fleur de Lys," who possibly takes an extreme view of the range of the guns he so enthusiastically advocates, puts the killing range of the double 8-bore at 80 yards, but it must be remembered that he has had greater experience than has fallen to the lot of most people who have written on the subject. With the following opinion of "Fleur de Lys," in a letter to *Land and Water*, the author wholly agrees :—

"I am of opinion that with No. 1 shot a good 8-bore (equal in shooting powers to the Greener used in my trials), if held straight, is *certain* of a duck at 80 yards ; that is to say, I think ten or eleven would be bagged out of twelve shots. With the gun in question, at 80 yards, a flying duck would receive, on an average, three to four pellets of No. 1 shot, and a sitting duck two to three pellets."

Several well-known wild-fowlers have published some interesting opinions with reference to the range at which game may be shot with large-bore guns. The following extracts from letters to the *Field* will prove what is believed to be the greatest killing range and the value of the various calibres :—

Extract from a Letter written by Mr. A. G. Passingham in the "Field," February 2nd, 1895.

" As there is just now some controversy respecting the merits or demerits of 8-, 10- and 12-bore guns for wild-fowling, I think it may interest some of your readers if I mention four consecutive shots I made last week with a double 8-bore by Greener.

" Three of these shots were over 100 yards, and the other and last shot, 85 yards. The longest shot was 151 yards (measured, not stepped), at a flock of about 30 widgeon standing in some shallow water. One bird was killed; two No. 1 shot went right through the bird, in at the back and out at the breast. The next longest shot was 110 yards at two ducks, both killed. The next at a flock of teal, the two aimed at killed. The last shot at three ducks, crossing low down 85 yards, one shot dead, another fell into the sea 400 yards off. (The charges used were 6 drams of black gunpowder and 2¼ ounces of No. 1 shot; the same load of shot, and charges of 75 grains and 84 grains of Schultze.)

" I think a 10-bore is better than 12-bore, and a double 8 is the best of all shoulder guns for wild-fowling."

Extract from the "Field," January 26th, 1895.

"Mr. Chapman, in his interesting articles on ' Wild-fowling,' is, I think, unduly prejudiced against 4-bore and double 8-bore guns. The idea of 4-bores recoiling to such an extent as to capsize a single-handed punt is absurd. I have fired a good many shots from 4-bores, but never felt any unpleasant recoil, using 10 drams and 3½ ounces of shot. As to double 8-bores, I maintain they are far more useful than 10-bores; they are handy, and much more powerful than the 10-bore. I have one of Greener's double 8-bores that is as handy a gun as one need wish to have, and it is a very powerful gun. I can stop duck and widgeon going down wind when flighting at a tremendous pace, and I have shot a snipe with it.

" G. A. PASSINGHAM."

Extract from Mr. G. A. Passingham's Letter.

" You ask me how the gun handles. I am pleased to say it is simply perfect in this respect, and is a most powerful gun—by far the best shooting gun I ever had."

The gun referred to by Mr. Passingham weighs 11½ lbs. only, and has barrels of W. W. Greener's "Wrought steel," 32 inches in length and bored for brass cases.

SHOT AND WADDING RECOMMENDED.

The charges and shot recommended by " Fleur de Lys " are :—

For duck and widgeon up to 60 yards, No. 4 shot; beyond 60 yards and up to 100 yards, No. 1 or No. 2 shot. " Beyond 100 yards the chances of a successful shot are problematical, and, therefore, I believe in big shot : BB for an 8-calibre or a 4-calibre, so that if a bird be hit, it receives such a crushing blow that it is killed outright or completely crippled, and can be gathered easily."

For plover, small waders, etc., No. 4 shot up to 80 yards ; No. 1 or No. 2 beyond. Never anything bigger at these birds, as they are easily killed.

With reference to the wadding for 8-bores, it should be noted that an extra *Field* wad, or even two, between the powder and shot may be advantageously employed, if, with the usual load the charge does not fill the case to within one quarter inch, and the shooting will be improved, as the pattern will show. The No. 4 Alliance black powder gives the closest and strongest shooting ; powder of larger grain, say No. 6 or No. 7, gives less recoil, and the least recoil is obtained by using equivalent *bulk* charges of the Schultze, or " E.C." nitro-explosives.

BREECH MECHANISMS FOR WILD-FOWL GUNS.

It is only of late years that any breech mechanism other than the double-grip, with lever under-guard, as shown in the illustration of the single 4-bore wild-fowling gun, has been used in guns of large bore. The new style is hammerless, with cross-bolt and top lever, a type the author introduced with success about fifteen years ago. This style of single gun is also illustrated. The stock is fitted with Silver's anti-recoil heel-plate, and is shown in full, so that an idea may be formed of the relative size of the breech-action and other parts of the gun. The breech-end of the barrel, showing method of bolting to the breech-action, is shown in the annexed illustration.

Of the advantages of the hammerless system applied to duck guns it is almost needless to speak. Besides its greater speed, safety and strength, the ominous click caused by raising the hammer is dispensed with, and many a shot gained thereby. Its neater appearance, and the fact of all the mechanism being protected from blows and water, are also in its favour ; and they are strongly recommended by modern wild-fowlers, who also prefer double guns to single, if not larger than 8-bore, as they are not necessarily any heavier, and a second barrel is available for shooting at the flock when it is well in the air.

DUCK GUNS.

The smaller bore wild-fowl guns are often used with great success in duck shooting. It is for this sport that the 10-bore possesses its particular advantage, that of shooting large-sized shot with better effect than the 12-bore gun ; the 10- also shoots heavier loads better than the 12-bore. The diagram of the shooting of the 10-bore here given should be compared with those of the 12-bore—particularly that on page 356. This 10-bore pattern was made by a double gun, 10 lb. in weight, with 4 drams and $1\frac{1}{4}$ ounce of No. 6 shot : the highest average pattern at this distance—40 yards—with this charge is 275 pellets in the 30-inch circle.

To be really effective 10-bores should not be less than $8\frac{1}{2}$ lbs. weight ; anything

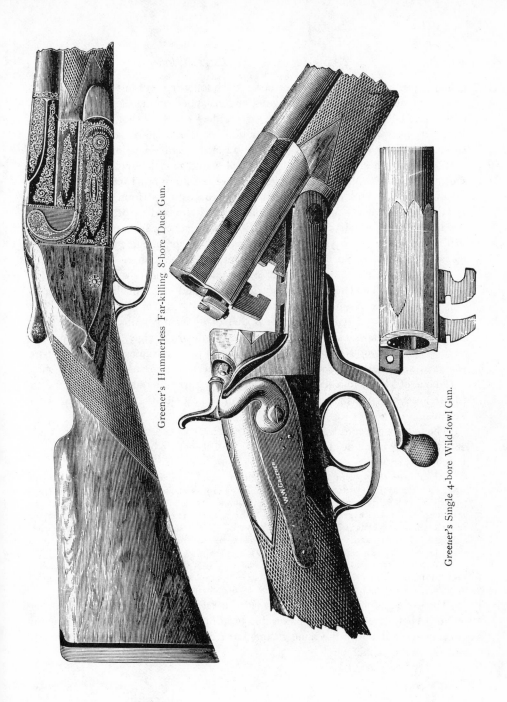

Greener's Hammerless Far-killing 8-bore Duck Gun.

Greener's Single 4-bore Wild-fowl Gun.

lighter is just as effective if made 12-bore. The following patterns and penetration have been obtained from 10-bore guns, and may be considered as exhibiting the utmost capability of 10-bores. With 4¼ drs. and 1½ oz. No. 2 shot, pattern in 30-in. circle, at 40 yards, 160 pellets, penetration 25 sheets strawboard. With same charge, but No. 1 shot, pattern 135, 50 in 12-inch square ; a 24-inch circle would have contained nearly all the pellets, as well as the 30-inch circle ; penetration 31 sheets strawboard. With same charge, BB shot, a pattern of 88 resulted.

But these patterns are far more than can be expected from the generality of 10-bores. An ordinary full-choke 10-bore, with 4¼ drs. and 1¼ oz. No. 6 shot, will average about 250 pellets; with 1½ oz. No. 4 shot, about 180 ; same charge, No 1 shot, about 110. At 60 yards, same charge, No. 4 shot, about 75, penetration 18 sheets ; same charge, No. 1 shot, about 60 pattern, penetration 26 sheets.

The old type of 10-bore was 10 lbs. or more in weight, with 32-in. barrels, and was used with a charge of 5 drams of powder and 1¼ oz. of shot : a charge in which the quantity of powder is out of proportion with that of the shot used. The most generally useful type of 10-bore is that of 8½ lbs. to 9½ lbs. in weight, firing either brass or paper cases, and using as the standard charge 4 drams of powder and 1½ to 1¾ oz. of No. 4 or larger size shot. Such advantages as the 10-bore possesses are obtained from the use of large-size shot ; for use with small shot, a 12-bore of 7½ lbs. to 8 lbs., and loading 1¼ oz. only, the smaller gun is quite its equal. 10-bore guns cost £1 1s. more than 12-bores of the corresponding styles and qualities.

The following record was published in the *Field* of February 17th, 1894 ; it was obtained by " Fleur de Lys " with a W. W. Greener 10-bore gun chambered for 3-inch brass cases.

"At 40 yards range, with a charge of 3¾ drams of No. 4 black gunpowder and 1¼ ounce No. 1 shot, the average pattern with both barrels was 119 pellets in a 30-inch circle ; the average pattern of both barrels in a selected 12-inch square, was 47·5 pellets. With 3¾ drams and 1½ ounce No. 1, the average pattern of both barrels was 112 in the 30-inch circle; in the 12-inch square 49 pellets ; with 4 drams and 1¾ ounce of No. 1 shot, the pattern with both barrels averaged 147 pellets, and 55 pellets in a selected 12-inch square ; with same charge, but No. 4 shot, the pattern was 202 in the circle.

" With Schultze powder, 54 grains and 1¾ ounce of No. 1 shot, the average pattern in a select 12-inch square was 60 pellets, in the 30-inch circle 152 pellets ; with No. 4 shot an average of 84 pellets in the 12-inch square and 220 in the 30-inch circle. Brass cases were used.

The same gun with paper cases, a charge of 54 grains of Schultze and 1¾ ounce of No. 1 shot, gave an average pattern of 57 in the 12-inch square and 141 in the circle at 40 yards ; with the same charge, but No. 4 shot, 87 in the 12-inch square and 223 in the 30-inch circle.

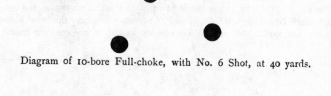

Diagram of 10-bore Full-choke, with No. 6 Shot, at 40 yards.

At 60 yards :—

Brass cases 4¼ drs. black powder and 2 oz. No. 1 shot an average pattern of 79 in the 30-in. circle.

,,	,,	54 grs. Schultze	,,	,,	2 ,,	,,	,,	,,	,,	75	,,	,,
,,	,,	55 ,,	,,	,,	,,	1¾,,	,,	,,	,,	,,	76	,,	,,
Paper cases 54 ,,	,,	,,	,,	2 ,,	,,	,,	,,	,,	70	,,	,,
,,	,,	4 drs. black	,,	,,	2 ,,	,,	,,	,,	,,	56	,,	,,
,,	,,	52 grs. Schultze	,,	,,	1¾,,	,,	,,	,,	,,	53	,,	,,
,,	,,	4 drs. black	,,	,,	1¾,,	,,	,,	,,	,,	50	,,	,,

It is apparent that a 10-bore gun should not be loaded with less than 1½ ounce of shot ; more is preferable if the gun is heavy enough to prevent recoil.

The following extracts prove what has been done with 10-bore choked guns and various charges :—

"My latest trial was with No. 1—4½ drs. 1½ oz. ; it puts the whole charge into a 2-ft. 10-in. circle at fifty yards. The size of shot seems to make no difference as regards diameter of pattern. I have tried at hares with No. 4, and have killed them dead at sixty yards, going away, which is sufficient for me. I shot three golden plover, consecutive shots, at sixty-five, seventy-five, and eighty-one yards, dead. I have purposely tried it at gulls and ducks, which I consider pretty tough ; it is a certainty at fifty yards with No. 4. I have shot two out of three snipe, with No. 6, at fifty yards. In fact, I consider your gun twenty yards better than any gun I ever tried before."

"I shot ducks with the 10-bore, killing them clean at 80 to 120 yards, using 5½ drams and 1¼ ounce ; for this charge appears to be the most desirable when using No. 4 shot."

"I have spent a few days at plover-shooting, and find that the gun shoots first-class. I killed, with one barrel at forty-five yards, twenty plover; I also killed a single plover at sixty-three yards, and two out of three that were flying at eighty yards. I killed three out of a flock of about 150 plover at 101 yards. The gun suits me in every way."

THE 12-BORE AS A WILD-FOWL GUN.

The shooting of a 12-bore gun of 7½ lbs. to 8 lbs. weight is good enough to warrant its classification as a wild-fowlers' weapon. Built specially to obtain the best possible results with 3¼ to 4 drams of powder and 1½ ounce of No. 4 shot, the 12-bore is indeed an excellent little wild-fowl gun. It should take a 3-inch case, or at least 2¾-inch, and is then a good all-round weapon, shooting even buckshot closely and well.

"Dear Sir,

"Since I have had my treble-wedge-fast 12-bore hammerless gun, 28 inches long, 7½ lbs. weight, 40-guinea quality, made by you in 1880, I have made many exceptionally long shots in duck shooting. In the month of October this fall, however, I made three shots which in justice to you are deserving of special mention. On the occasion in question my gun, which is full-choked in both barrels, was charged with 3½ drams Curtis and Harvey's No. 4 powder, with one felt and two card wads between powder and shot, and 1⅛ ounces of No. 2 chilled shot with cardboard wad. With the first shot I killed two black ducks crossing on the wing at 75 yards, the second a single blue bill (small duck) sitting at 100 yards, and the third a single black duck sitting at fully 110 yards. When the length and weight of my gun, the moderate charge of

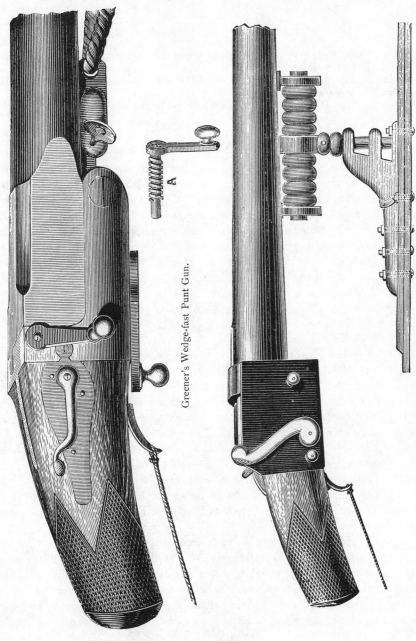

Greener's Wedge-fast Punt Gun.

Greener-Field Punt Gun, with Indiarubber Recoil-breeching.

powder and the large size of the shot used are taken into consideration, I think the three shots in question, which were all fired one after the other within an hour, are worthy of ranking as extraordinary shots. Since then I have killed another large Velvet duck—one out of four—sitting at fully 90 yards, with the same charge as mentioned above. When my little gun—which I have named Faugh-a-Ballagh—is charged right and held right, it sends the charge right to the proper place.   "Yours truly,

                                                                            " W. P. LETT."

PUNT GUNS

The best methods of using the muzzle-loading punt gun are given by Colonel P. Hawker in his well-known book ; and modern wild-fowling is treated fully by Sir R. Payne-Gallwey in "The Wild-Fowler in Ireland," and others. Breech-loading punt guns are made upon several systems, some of which will be briefly described ; the enthusiastic wild-fowler will turn to the above-mentioned, and other authorities, for details of the sport, and for fuller particulars of the weapons used.

The Snider breech-action is still used ; most wild-fowlers prefer one or other of the drop-down mechanisms illustrated here ; but the short modern stock is that now generally employed.

The London punt gun, and Greener's wedge-fast punt gun, as illustrated, have been in constant use, and fill every requirement of the sportsman, so far as breech and lock mechanism is concerned.

The punt gun is usually single barrel $1\frac{1}{2}$-inch bore, and weighs about 100 lbs. It should be chambered for the solid drawn brass case, seven inches long, taking a charge of three ounces of powder and one and a half pounds of shot. These cases may be reloaded many times, being practically indestructible. Smaller guns of $1\frac{1}{4}$-inch bore, shooting one and a quarter pounds of shot, are made occasionally. Recoil breeching of rope is the favourite, as it is the simplest gear for taking the recoil. Others in use are the Hawker coil spring, the indiarubber breeching, or the recoil box of Mr. E. T. Booth, in which indiarubber buffers are placed. A first-class punt gun, without recoil gear, is worth about £80, and is practically everlasting. The barrel may be choked or left cylinder. Double punt guns have been made ; they are very heavy and cumbrous, require a larger punt, and are not recommended.

Sportsmen who make wild-fowling their study find by experience the size and style of punt gun best suited to the locality in which they shoot ; they will certainly use any guns and punts procurable before deciding to purchase, and will then probably require a gun built to a special specification, and several months will be necessary for the construction of them. Punt guns are rarely in stock, but may sometimes be purchased second-hand.

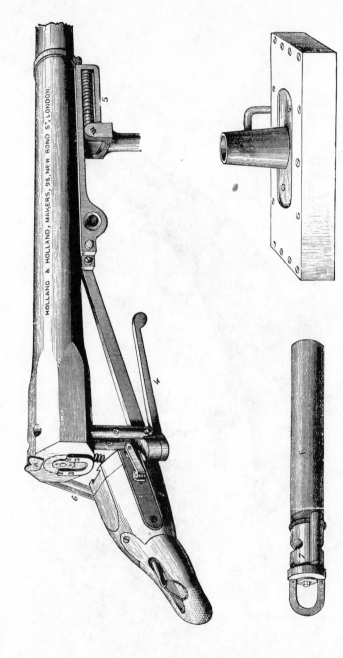

HOLLAND & HOLLAND, MAKERS, 98, NEW BOND ST., LONDON.

The London Punt Gun, and Mr. E. T. Booth's Recoil Box.

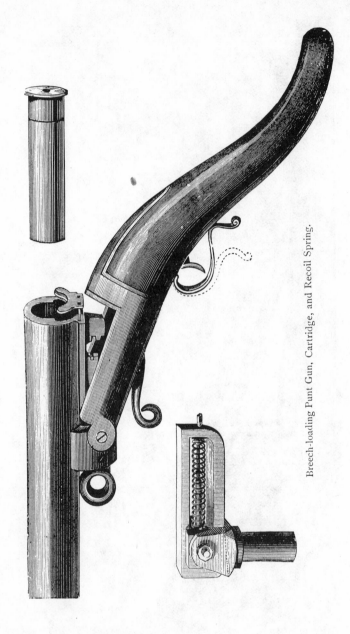

Breech-loading Punt Gun, Cartridge, and Recoil Spring.

CHAPTER XVI.

THE CHOICE OF A GUN.

SOME REMARKS ON THE COST OF GUNS.

SPORTSMEN often remark that they are unable to understand why there is so great a difference in the prices of best guns, and also that they cannot distinguish between a gun at 40 guineas and one at 20 guineas. Some makers advertise their best guns at 25 guineas, others at 50 guineas, or even 70 guineas. Why should hammerless guns cost so much more than hammered guns? and why should there be so great a difference in the price of hammered breech-loaders? A double-barrelled central-fire, 12-gauge breech-loader, proved, and a complete, usable weapon, is sold wholesale, at the present time, at thirty shillings. At that price it is at present a marketable commodity, and the tendency is downwards. A best hammered gun, 12-gauge, proved, a complete, usable weapon, is to be purchased at sixty guineas, and will not be sold for less. Is the £60 difference between the two solely for the maker's name engraved between the barrels? If not, where is the difference to be seen?

This matter should not be difficult to understand, when it is remembered how intricate and how numerous are the stages of construction through which all guns must pass.

The barrels of best guns are made from the best iron and steel, and welded into barrels by superior welders; the cheaper grades are made from inferior metal, and either welded under the tilt hammer as already described, or made into barrels by inferior workmen, who, from receiving a lower price for their work, have to weld a larger number of barrels per week. In the boring and grinding, the common barrels are done at less than half the cost of the best; this is managed by grinding them without turning and trueing them in the lathe, by being not so particular about the setting, and if a few rings are left inside from the rough-boring it is counted of no consequence.

In the filing of the barrels the difference is more marked; the common barrels are soldered together with sal-ammoniac and soft solder instead of with rosin, which is far superior, as it prevents the barrels from rusting underneath the ribs. The lumps also are plainly let in, not dovetailed, and the barrels are not struck up or planed round to remove the hills and hollows.   Commoner ribs also are used—that is, either scelp twist or plain iron, and there is not so much care taken to insure the rib being tapered, levelled, straightened, and equally placed on both barrels.

The locks also greatly vary; they may be purchased from two shillings to three guineas the pair.   In common locks the tumblers, scears and swivels are of iron, and only the springs of steel.   In medium grades the tumblers and scears are of steel, but the bridles are not so well shaped, or the bents so well cut and squared.

Breech-actions also vary greatly in quality.   Common actions may be fitted complete at nine or ten shillings each, whereas some of the best quality hammerless actions cost as much as £12 or £15 to get up.   In breech-action fitting, as in lock filing, various classes of men are employed, each working at his own quality of work, and having to get through a proportionately larger amount of work the farther it is removed from the best quality: thus, whilst it takes a good workman three days to joint a treble-wedge-fast hammerless breech-action, a common action-filer will joint, file, and fit up complete a cheap action in less than one-fourth the time.

So with the other divisions of gun-making; the prices vary according to the ability of the executant.   Gun stocks range in price from a shilling to thirty or more; the work known as finishing may be done for a few shillings; if done thoroughly, carefully, and in best style, it will cost as many sovereigns.

The polishing, the browning, etc., all vary considerably in the same manner. The engraving is a branch of the trade which is supposed by many sportsmen to add greatly to the cost of the gun, but it is inconsiderable compared with other branches.   It is now possible to completely smother a gun with cheap common engraving for a few shillings.

The very best clean-cut fine scroll engraving may cost as much as four or five guineas, or more, according to the quantity placed upon the gun.   Gold inlaying, which is often done, also adds considerably to the cost.

The workmen in every division of the gun trade are divided into classes.   The careful workman, mindful not only of his work upon the gun, but cognisant and careful in his treatment of the work of those who have gone before him—skilled, and able to do what is required and expected of him—is a *rara avis* who can command a high wage.   A staff of such men *must* be procured if the best work possible is to be obtained; and they must not only be kept fully employed, but employed upon such work as they can take an interest and pride in.   To produce a best gun, not only must every man be able, but inclined, to do his best; and above all, there must be the guiding mind, intent upon the fashioning of a weapon to its ideal.

The best gun must be tried in various stages, and must pass in each before proceeding to a succeeding stage; hence time as well as money is requisite to its production. The well-finished gun is one in which every portion is accurately shaped, rightly placed, perfectly adjusted, and with that "finish" which skill and practice alone can give. The elaborate ornamentation, either by engraving or otherwise, will not make a gun well finished; nor is such ornamentation of such use as finish. A gun made and finished in the best manner will stand more hard wear than any ordinary gun, even if the principle upon which the commoner gun is constructed be superior to that of the best gun. Common guns always give way first in the small details: a pin works loose or breaks, and as soon as it is replaced in one place it gives way in another, whereas a best gun, like "The One-Hoss Shay," breaks up altogether *when* it does go.

A great difference in cost, therefore, is due solely to workmanship. Other matters of importance in this respect depend upon the degree of excellence the maker wishes to attain. If content with producing a very ordinary gun, the expenses of so doing will be comparatively small. If a remarkably good shooting gun is required, the price may be very high, and certainly will be excessively so unless the gun-maker who essays the task has been in the habit of making very fine shooting guns. Indeed, a chief item in the cost of good guns is the regulation of the shooting, and alterations of the choking and boring; not infrequently as much money is expended in endeavours to obtain the best possible shooting, both of guns and rifles, as some makers lay out upon the whole gun—stock, lock, and barrel. This fact the author knows only too well from oft-repeated experience; for, in addition to the expense of fine-boring, occasionally large numbers of cartridges are required, and a deal of time occupied in the shooting and regulating of first-class guns. Most of the leading gun-makers try each gun in the rough as well as in the finished state. Next to safety, shooting is certainly the most important point in a gun, and great care should always be bestowed by the maker in testing his guns, so as to ensure good results when in actual work. This is a point that the makers of cheap guns never trouble about; and twenty-five years ago very few guns, either best or common, were tested, but it was left for the country dealers or the sportsmen to find out the faults or merits, as the case might be.

A gun all but finished may develop a flaw in material or workmanship that precludes it from all save the waste heap; so it is that no maker of high reputation can sell his best guns at the prices asked by a less noted maker, who sells guns of a mediocre quality produced by workmen of inferior talent, and, there being less waste, pockets greater profits.

Gun-makers who can command over £50 for one of their best guns are few, and it is a mistake to suppose they receive such prices because they are fashionable makers. The truth is, they produce an article worth the money.

A maker uses the best material, has skilled workmen, and sells his best production, which costs him—say £15, for £20. It is the best his talents and means allow. Another, out of same quality material, by sparing no pains or endeavour, produces his best at a cost of £38, which he sells for £50. Both are best guns, yet one is infinitely better than the other ; and, in all probability, a third or fourth grade gun of the latter would surpass in quality the best of the former, and sell for about the same price.

If a gun is ordered from a country maker, the maker has to come to Birmingham for his barrels and action, locks, etc., and simply stocks and finishes the same, and sends the gun to Birmingham to be polished and engraved ; or he buys a gun from Birmingham, and having put on his profit and name, sells it as a weapon of his own manufacture. A few country makers keep three or four men constantly at work, and these usually do three or four branches each ; on this account the work can neither be done so cheaply nor so well as in Birmingham.

There is no doubt useless expenditure sometimes by gun-makers of the most fashionable rank. Instead of using the simplest mechanisms they employ, for reasons, others which cost much more. They have not to meet competition in the same way as a gun-maker trading with wholesale buyers, and if by means of the finest workmanship the most elaborate mechanism can be made tolerably efficient and is their own, they all prefer it to a simpler and more easily made, therefore cheaper, mechanism the invention of someone else. At the present time this system very largely obtains, but on the other hand it must be conceded that the art of making breech-actions has advanced considerably the last fifteen years ; better work, more intelligent work, has been bestowed upon details of manufacture, and the guns of to-day, with all their shortcomings, will compare favourably with the masterpieces of long ago.

CHEAP GUNS AND THEIR RECOGNITION.

It is not always easy even for an expert to accurately appraise the value of a gun ; to the casual observer there is often no perceptible difference between a fairly good gun and a really high class weapon. It is somewhat remarkable, taking into consideration the numerous instructions which have been published for the guidance of those about to purchase guns, that so few, even of the most experienced sportsmen, are able to discriminate with certainty between " fine " and " trade " guns. As the matter is of great importance to every user of the gun, the author will endeavour to give such indications as will enable even the tyro to avoid worthless weapons should they be offered him ; by carefully observing the instructions given there should be no difficulty in purchasing a gun fully worth the estimated value.

In the first place no gun should be purchased without examination, unless from a person of whose standing there can be no doubt and who will agree to exchange the weapon or refund the money if desired to do so. The purchase of a pig in a poke is always attended with risk, which no respectable dealer or gun-maker requires a customer to run. Many advertisements of the " catch-penny " type appear in the general newspapers, and are occasionally found in the columns of the sporting press. Offers of guns at an extremely low price will not delude the common-sense man into parting with his money. Some people, in the hope of securing a bargain, get caught on the well-baited trap ; less frequently the reckless advertiser is prosecuted and convicted. The following specification, copied from a gun-maker's list, is a never-failing catch :— " 12-bore gun, laminated steel barrels, left choke-bored, top-lever, snap-action, purdey double bolt, extended rib, rebounding, and low hammers ; patent fore-end, figured walnut, half pistol-hand stock, horn heel-plate, scroll engraving. Price, 60s." The same description might be applied to a sixty-guinea gun with as much truth. Until a sportsman knows something about guns he should purchase of a respectable maker. Even "friends" will seek to benefit by a young man's inexperience more frequently than will the dealer, who wishes to secure his custom, and looks forward towards future orders as well as to present profits.

Look at the illustration on p. 412 : the cheapest gun is here depicted ; it may be known by having—1st, all the parts which should be square and flat, rounded ; 2nd, all the parts—as the barrels—which should be round, a series of flats ; 3rd, hammers which are odd, and which stand when both are at half-cock as though one were at full, and, when both are " down," one rests on the nipple, but the other will not reach it ; 4th, one lock won't " speak," the other roars ; 5th, one striker sticks out and upwards, the other is pitched as though the breast—not the head—of the hammer were to strike it ; 6th, the rib is not straight, and is very much more on one barrel than on the other—the barrels are neither straight nor round, and are generally thicker on one side than the other ; 7th, the extractor has a crooked leg, and when the gun is opened, it sticks out as though pleased to escape from its ill-shaped recess—on closing the gun, its contortions are astonishing ; 8th, the barrels are bright inside, but it is not the brightness of a silvered mirror, rather the brightness of a leaden bullet ; 9th, there is no close fitting of any part : the action body is barely touched by the barrels, the holding-down bolt is a crooked article in a crooked hole, the fore-end will drop from the gun when it is fired, or will want all your strength to get it off, and the " wide joint " may be seen wherever two pieces come together; 10th, the engraving is a series of ill-shapen, deeply-cut furrows, cross-harrowed with meaningless scratches; 11th, the balance is bad, and the gun heavy; 12th, the stock worse than that of an army musket, having traces of " file-teeth," and exhibiting that rough open grain inseparable from spongy wood, and which the oily gloss cannot hide; 13th, the butt-plate, an ornamental sporting or other design made of stamped rubber.

Such is the " export gun." If its user survives ten shots, the gun will not. On trial it may fail to go off; the striker is too short, or does not strike centrally; this

The " Export " Gun.

is rectified; then it will be found that the other striker is too long, and, after the gun has been fired, it will not open : this is altered. The mainspring is so poor its elasticity has departed, and miss-fires ensue; new mainspring fitted : this is too strong for the lock, which is only of soft iron, so the tumbler gives way; steel tumbler fit : the scear, being iron, has worn away in only trying the lock, and fails to keep lock at cock, so the gun goes off unawares; complete new lock-work fitted : hammers drop off, triggers jam, and screws drop out in an unaccountable manner. The gun is thoroughly overhauled, is kept a month at the smith's; at first shot barrels drop asunder, owing to having been soldered together with sal-ammoniac, which, from its chemical action, destroys barrels and solder. Thus the cheap gun costs more in repairs in one season than a good gun would want in twenty, and is a standing annoyance to its owner. The gun of slightly better class will *look* much the same, but the locks should be of steel, and the action fitting better. Twist barrels are a step higher; next is found close fitting, and traces of some care having been used in putting the strikers in centrally, in getting the hammers to match, in having the rib midway between the barrels. When Damascus barrels are used, the gun is up in price, and the weapon reaching a serviceable standard. Next, the barrels are straight, the stock harder and more shapable, the lines cut into the iron can be seen to follow some design—fugitive and inappropriate, it may be, but still a design. With smoothly working locks, better balanced guns, two iron Damascus barrels, usable pull off, and a well-fit action, we are rapidly approaching a grade that may be serviceable, if not high-class. When, instead of a rubber-stamped butt or heel-plate, we have an ebonite or horn *hand-chequered* one, we have reached the first grade of the artist workman, and not the turning-out machine. We find in the better grades a smoothness and flatness of the lock-plates that is easily noticeable; and, as the inside of the plate is square and flat too, the lock is cocked with an easy movement and uniform increase of pressure. Not only do the hammers match and stand alike, but nipples, triggers, and screws fit closely and tightly; and in the still higher grades every pin will be found to fit accurately, to have its slit running in a preconceived direction, and *every part*, when inspected, will be found to have had some attention paid to it, to make it as perfect as the worker's idea of it had determined. In examining a fine gun, even if it be as heavy as that of the "trade gun," it will be found to handle "like a thing of life" when compared with its "export" competitor; the bottom rib will be found as accurately shaped, as small, and as carefully put on, as though that were the rib which would receive every scrutiny; and even the butt-plate screws—which to the well-glued heel-plate are of very little service—will be found to be as well-shaped, slit, and accurately fitted as if the whole reputation of the gun and its maker were staked upon those pins alone. So must it be. Unless attention be given to *every* piece, no matter how seemingly unimportant, the gun is not well made, and may fail just where least expected.

From the first conception of the gun to the last stroke of the buffstick, there must be paramount care in the choice and fashioning of the material, and the right relation in size and position of every piece to each other and to all.

There is probably no gun without its faults of construction, but in a gun of the first quality they should be known only to the maker, and such as *he* cannot remedy nor others detect.

Then, just so much as is the talent of the maker superior or inferior to that of his competitors, will his gun be superior or inferior to their productions.

In no country are better sportsmen to be found than in the United States of America, nor does any country possess keener buyers or better men of business, yet in no country is so much of the worthless rubbish of the Continental gun-factories offered for sale. The Boers are a race of sportsmen, but it is of no use to offer them rubbish at *any* price, and the author can hardly believe that the astute American will sacrifice everything to cheapness. It is certainly a fact that the American salesmen are without equal, and have such powers of persuasion that one is half inclined to believe that the American rifle has never had its equal ; but even the ability of the salesmen could not overcome the repugnance of the buyer to the rattle-trap designated by the Suhl or Liège maker as " export guns," providing the would-be purchaser could or would discriminate between a serviceable and an unserviceable weapon. In the United States there are two classes of guns made. The machine-made trade gun, the sale of which is vigorously pushed at every opportunity. The better-class gun, made by some American-born or emigrant gunsmith, whose production is limited and sales unimportant. An American gun, at about three times the price of the American machine-made gun, will be a superior weapon in every way to the machine-made gun ; but be sure that it is of American make, for *imported* guns are sold as of any make, just as there is a demand. Of imported guns there are three classes—the real trade gun, rubbish ; the legitimate trade gun—English or foreign guns, made sound and well by a responsible maker, who will put his own name upon them, and give as good quality as the price given by the importer will allow ; the fine gun, the *bonâ fide* production of an English maker of reputation, and imported to special order, or for sale only by the special agent of the maker in question, or some honest and enterprising dealer. In America, however, dealers are very loth to keep in stock the fine guns of any maker. In England, on the Continent, especially in France, Germany, Austria, Russia, and Italy, where the sportsmen are more discriminating and exacting, there is always a choice of twenty different *grades* of guns, and—especially in France and Germany— the sportsman can appraise the additional amount spent in bettering the quality of the weapon. The American, and very many colonial sportsmen, cannot or will not discriminate between the first and second classes, and are slow even to see the difference between the second and third. Now, nothing should be more easy than to distinguish the good gun from rubbish ; the third from the first of the classes before referred to.

The worst fault of the very cheap gun is its unserviceability. It is unequal to the work required of it, and the barrels usually are unable to withstand the strain of sporting nitro-gunpowders. With a cheap gun the only possible explosive is the coarse-grained black gunpowder. The very cheap guns, again, are often dangerous because the locks used are of such quality that they not unfrequently go off unawares when the gun is carried at full cock, and, with rebounding locks, carried at half-cock, the workmanship is so bad that the hammers, by a blow from behind, may be pushed down upon the striker and so explode the cartridge. The brazing together of the barrels is untrustworthy, and the breech actions quickly wear loose, and after a few days' wear the gun is regarded—often with good reason—as highly dangerous.

THE SPURIOUS GUN, AND ITS DETECTION.

The spurious gun may be either a gun represented as being of a quality it is not, or as the production of a maker other than the real one. After taking all into consideration, it is the first class which is the most dangerous to the unwary buyer. The vapid platitudes of the salesman spread a glamour over the transaction, and the sportsman purchases a gun which will trouble him more and more as he gets to know it. Against the purchase of this class of gun the sportsman must always be on his guard.

The second class of gun is simply a forgery. Belgian guns are sent to England to be proved, or the English proof marks are imitated; "English fine twist" is engraved upon the rib, or *any* maker's name is put on to the order of the importer.

Some makers do not scruple to state in their lists that they will put upon their productions "made in London, or in Eibar, or in Brescia," or in any other town whose manufactures have a better reputation than their own. *Never* buy a gun without the maker's name upon it.

All the leading makers or their retailers now advertise, so that the exact name of the maker wished is easily obtained ; see that the gun bears this name, and rightly spelled, for the change of a letter is often made, the maker of the forgery thereby thinking that his liability is lessened, and foreign forgers make dreadful havoc with English names, whereas probably no careful maker has ever turned out a gun wrongly or incorrectly named, so far as *his* name goes. As to the more general forgeries, they will be found to be changes rung upon the name of a maker of reputation. No one would forge "Smith" or "Jones," and happy the gunmakers who possess such names; but names as "Greener" will be spelled "Greenen," "Purdey" as "Purdy," "W. C. Scott & Son" as "J. N. Scotts Son," whilst of the imitations of "Westley Richards" the name is legion. The alteration in the initials, or the Christian name, or the address is more frequent, and all "Horace

Greener," " Albert Greener," J. H., W. H., A. H., and other H. Greener guns are practically forgeries. From the affluent position most of these dealers and getters-up of spurious guns enjoy, makers of reputation prefer to suffer rather than engage in what they know must be a disagreeable and very probably a most disastrous prosecution. The author believes that he alone has instituted criminal proceedings for this species of forgery ; the result being the imprisonment of the offender. And although the method of procedure is distasteful and expensive, the author appeals to those who have been deluded into the purchase of a forged Greener gun to communicate with him at once, in order that an effort may be made to stop this nefarious trade.

There is another more subtle form of deceit commonly practised in Liège and on the Continent. It consists of engraving the gun conspicuously with the name of the patentee of one of the parts of the mechanism. The most notable instances are " Greener" upon cross-bolt guns, and "S. & W." upon the Smith and Wesson type of revolver. In a case tested before the Belgian courts the defence advanced was that the weapons were of the type associated with the plaintiff's name, and that the name was intended to refer to the system, not to the maker, of the weapon. When " Greener " is put in bold gilt letters on the top rib, and other words, if any, in small insignificant characters, the name is certainly misleading, whatever the intention ; but unfortunately there is no way of stopping the practice.

In Great Britain, under the new Merchandise Marks Act, makers of spurious guns may now be prosecuted ; and the sooner the chief clauses of this Act are made international law, the better it will be for foreign sportsmen. In the British Colonies the sportsman is fairly protected by law : but probably the most flagrant instance of trading in spurious guns occurred at Melbourne, where a Jewish firm of gun importers, in a very large way of business, selling to all the Australian colonies, had long practised a most impudent fraud. If a customer inquired for any well-known make of gun, an unnamed Belgian gun was forthwith stamped with the name of the maker demanded, and usually a sale completed. For making such unwarrantable use of the author's trade name an action was brought, in the year 1895, and the author was awarded £5,500 damages ; but it is doubtful whether this covered more than a fraction of the real injury wrought, and was, of course, no reparation to the sportsmen who had been deluded into purchasing spurious weapons. Unfortunately the defendants appealed against the verdict, and litigation proceeded for more than a year afterwards. The evidence obtained showed that many of the best-known fire-arms manufacturers had been victimised by this one firm, four members of which were subsequently prosecuted criminally and sentenced to various terms of imprisonment.

OF THE FIT OF GUNS.

The fit of a gun is a truly personal matter, for although the majority of sportsmen can shoot well with the gun which suits eighty men out of every hundred, unless the gun is liked by them they will never feel that they shoot so well with it as they should, as no two persons are alike; therefore every person, to be exactly suited with a gun, will require something different to that which will suit another, but in practice the difference is often so slight as not to be noticeable. The most important point is the weight of the weapon, for many sportsmen sadly overweight themselves with needlessly heavy weapons; the gun when put up at a mark for trial does not seem heavy, but after carrying it for a few hours or when fatigued by walking, waiting, or working, the gun will not be " put up " as it was when the sportsman was fresh. The lighter the gun the greater control the muscles have over the gun to align it properly, and the longer they retain that power. The ability to handle a gun with precision is more likely to fill the game-bag than the possession of a perfectly fitting weapon. The really good shot can shoot well with almost any gun; a perfectly fitting stock will never make a good shot out of a bad one. There is no reason, however, why the sportsman should use a gun that does not suit him. Mr. E. D. Fulford (who grassed 194 pigeons successively), Dr. Carver, Captain Brewer, Mr. J. A. R. Elliott (who killed 100 pigeons straight), making the highest possible scores—they all, when making their finest shooting, used guns built for them by the author, but for which they were never "measured." This need not be advanced as a reason why other sportsmen may not avail themselves of the best methods for getting a gun that will suit them, but it is indisputable evidence that the best marksmanship does not depend upon exact measurements by an experienced gun fitter.

OF ALIGNMENT.

Most shooters align the gun with the right eye, that eye being the stronger in most men. If the sight of the left eye is stronger than that of the right, the shooter must close his left eye when aiming; or he may shoot from the left shoulder, or have a gun so made that it is alignable with the left eye though fired from the right shoulder. If there is any doubt as to which eye directs the aim, it may be easily ascertained by proceeding as follows :—

Take a finger ring and hold it out at arm's length; look through it *with both eyes open* at some object twenty or more feet distant; close the left eye. If the right eye still sees the object through the ring—which has not been moved—the right eye will align the gun, and the sportsman may with every advantage dispense with all correcting impedimenta and shoot with both eyes open. If the left eye—being the stronger—aligns the gun, the sportsman must shut it, or shoot from the left shoulder ; or have a particularly constructed stock which shall enable him to aim with the left eye whilst shooting from the right shoulder.

Providing the sportsman be one of the minority, he should write fully to an experienced gunmaker or the nearest practical gun dealer and arrange for the building of a special gun to meet his special need.

The sight-aligner and adjustable gun, invented in 1882 by Mr. E. Oliver

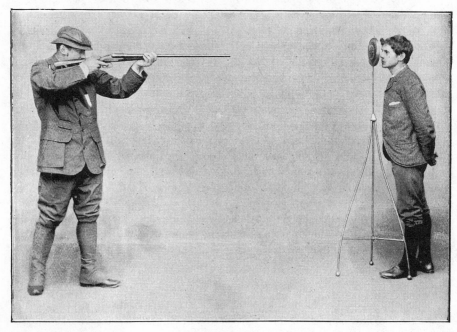

Oliver's Sight-Aligner.

(Mr. W. W. Greener's London House manager), is so contrived that an expert stands behind the sight disc, and while the aim is being taken he can discover whether both eyes of the shooter are open, and if the aim is a correct one, it is possible for him to see right down the barrels, providing there is a good light. This was used with the first try gun made, and was adopted by many gun-makers to get their customers properly fitted with guns.

TO CHOOSE A GUN WHICH WILL FIT CORRECTLY.

Take a gun, and put it up to the shoulder two or three times without aiming at anything in particular; if it seems to come up easily, and to be under perfect control, choose a mark ten or fifteen feet distant, and slightly higher than the aimer's shoulder. Fling up the gun quickly whilst looking steadily at the mark, and immediately the gun is at the shoulder close the left eye, and glance at once along the rib ; the sight on the muzzle should cover the object at which the shooter was looking as he brought up the gun. If upon this manœuvre being repeated several times, it is found that the gun each time covers the mark at which it is aimed, it should be tried in like manner at other marks at different distances and elevations. If these marks are covered in the same manner, the gun may be considered a fit, and a little practice will make the shooter quite at home with the weapon. It should then be tried at a target. Take a few snap shots at a bull's eye, and if the shots are not placed central, something is wrong with either the gun or the shooter. If a man cannot hit a fixed mark at thirty to forty yards every time with a shot gun he cannot expect to hit birds on the wing.

The sportsman who can make his choice out of a large stock of guns, or with the assistance of an experienced man to guide him, has a great advantage over the man whose trials must be made with a few weapons and without the help of an expert to correct any faulty actions which may escape the observation of the shooter. For instance, a person adept in the art of gun fitting would detect at once whether a second aim was taken in aligning the gun, and could immediately so alter a dummy try-gun as to come up in the way desired ; whereas the shooter, if alone, must note where the gun points, and calculate what amount of alteration is necessary.

If a gun is pointed much below the mark at which it is aimed, the stock of the gun is too crooked, too short, or the gun too heavy.

If it points above the mark at which it is aimed, it is too straight or has too much toe upon the stock. It is much better to use a gun that is too straight than one that is the reverse, as the author will prove in the paragraphs on the use of guns.

If it points to the right, it is cast-off too much ; if to the left, the cast-off is not sufficient. If it is not horizontal, but twisted over so that the right barrel is the higher, the stock requires to be twisted over by casting off the toe more ; if the left barrel is higher (which is very rarely the case) both the cast-off of the gun and the shape of the butt must be altered.

The straighter and longer the stock which can be manipulated with ease, the better and quicker will be the shooting, and less fatiguing the work of a heavy day's shooting. All good guns are so regulated that, aimed point-blank and dead-level along the rib, they will centre on the mark at forty yards' distance.

Some trap shots require their guns to carry as many as 6 in. high at forty yards; this is preferable to using a gun which shoots high because, being too straight in the stock, it is aimed too high. Misses with a shot-gun, as with a rifle, more frequently arise from errors in elevation than the misdirection of the aim.

The "try gun" is a gun-maker's tool, which permits of the stock being altered to any length, bend, cast-off, and shape of the butt, and is of use in fitting a sportsman who needs a gun of special build. Most of these guns are capable of

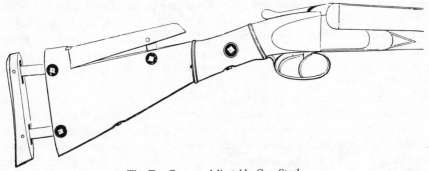

The Try Gun, or Adjustable Gun Stock.

being fired, but, as not one of them handles at all like an ordinary gun, it does not follow that, because a shooter is able to use it with success, a proper gun made with the same measurements of stock will prove quite suitable. It is a tool which can be used to good advantage only when in the hands of an experienced gun-fitter.

A short gun stock assists the shooter to get up the gun freely, but is against his holding it firmly against the shoulder; a large butt, not too flat, and with a fairly broad toe, is the best for bedding firmly against the shoulder; it should, in most cases, be slightly shorter to the left edge of the butt-plate than to the right. The better and more truly the butt fits the shoulder the more comfortable will be the gun in use, and the less appreciable will be the recoil.

The hand, or the grip of the gun, must not be so thick that it cannot be grasped with ease; it may be of oval section, or egg shape, with the smallest point at top, or, to afford a better grasp, even diamond shape in section : it must not be round, or have too fine or too flat a chequering, or feel clumsy, and the fore-end must be narrow, standing high from the barrels, and fall full into the palm of the left hand when it grips the barrels.

It is sometimes said that a sportsman cannot shoot with a gun that suits him if he varies his clothing; possibly some men cannot, but they are not good shots, nor should they pose as such, for, as before stated, the good shot, the man who knows how to handle a gun and how to aim, will shoot well with any gun. Dr. Carver has in a single exhibition shoot of less than an hour's duration shot and performed equally well with a Winchester repeating rifle of the military model, a double shot-gun of $2\frac{3}{4}$-in. bend, and a double shot-gun of 2-in. bend. The man who really means to shoot well does so irrespective of any trifling wrong dimension in the weapon he has to use, and the acquisition of the art of shooting enables one to do what the hypercritical gun-fitting faddist would not attempt with even the most favourable conditions.

OF THE SHAPE AND DIMENSIONS OF GUN-STOCKS.

There is no definite authority for the prevailing fashion in gun-stocks, and the dimensions and shape of this part of the gun have given rise to more frequent discussion amongst gun-makers and sportsmen than anything else connected with shooting.

The measures of the gun-stock include the bend, length, and cast-off. These are of great importance to the user of the gun, and must suit his particular method of handling the gun, as well as the stock being of such dimensions as the shooter's build—*i.e.*, length of arm, breadth of chest, etc.—may determine.

The measures of the gun-stock may be ascertained as follows :—

Take a piece of wood or iron, with a perfectly straight edge, sufficiently long to reach from the sight on the muzzle to the extremity of the butt; lay this straight-edge along the rib, and measure the distance from A to *heel*, and from B to *comb*. This is the *bend*. The *lengths* required will be from the centre of the fore or right-hand trigger to the *heel*, *centre*, and *toe* respectively, and the depth from the heel to the toe. The circumference of the hand may be obtained by passing a string round it *immediately* behind the trigger-guard, and measuring the string. In taking the length, measure the extreme length, and not to the edge of the heel-plate. The dimensions given on p. 422 are in due proportion, and as usually made for English and American sportsmen respectively.

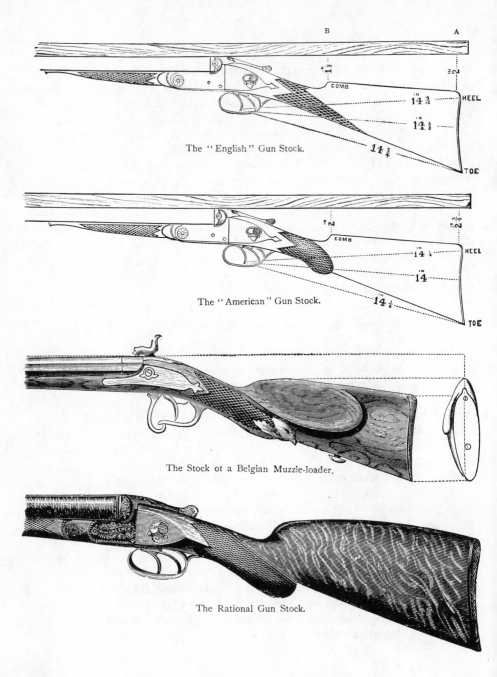

The "English" Gun Stock.

The "American" Gun Stock.

The Stock of a Belgian Muzzle-loader.

The Rational Gun Stock.

CAST-OFF is the amount the stock is thrown out of truth with the barrels in a *lateral* direction. Most gun-stocks are twisted over—that is, the toe of the butt is more "cast-off" than the heel—the usual "cast-off" is $\frac{3}{16}$ths for heel and $\frac{3}{8}$ths for toe.

Balance.—This is always to be measured from the breech-ends of the barrels. It is best to balance the gun on thin string.

A 12-bore with 30-in. barrels weighing 7 lbs. or over should balance at about 3 ins. from the breech; if with 27-in. or 28-in. barrels and $5\frac{3}{4}$ lbs. to 6 lbs., about $2\frac{5}{8}$ ins. from the breech would be considered a good balance.

The measures given in the illustration of the English gun-stock are the dimensions usually adhered to by gun-makers in this country, and guns so built are found to suit quite 80 per cent. of British sportsmen.

Americans use guns with stocks much more crooked, as, when shooting, they keep the head erect, and many English colonists follow this rule, the crooked gun-stock being quite common in South Africa and Australia.

The lengths of the gun-stock from fore-trigger to toe and heel will regulate the angle of the butt, and the *cast-off* will throw the butt over a little, so that unless the butt were rounded or chamfered, its *edge* only would touch against the shoulder. The amount of chamfer required will depend upon the amount of "cast-off" and the build of the person for whom the gun is intended. Dr. W. F. Carver always shot with a heel-plate, not only much hollowed—*i.e.*, *very much* shorter to centre than to the extremities—but also chamfered so as to fit squarely against the muscles of his shoulder. Many shooters will find it more comfortable to shoot with a gun having the butt so rounded, or sloped, than with the usual butt, which is of equal length to either edge.

Guns with stocks from 14 in. to $14\frac{3}{8}$ in. long, measuring from the fore-trigger to the centre of heel-plate and the regular "cast-off" ($\frac{3}{16}$ in. at heel and $\frac{3}{8}$ in. at toe), will be found in most gun-makers' shops. A sportsman above the average height should take a gun-stock longer than usual, and also one slightly more bent. The longest stock the author has made is 17 in., the greatest bend $4\frac{1}{4}$ in., and the straightest, a stock "set up" above the level of the rib. It rarely happens that stocks shorter than $13\frac{3}{4}$ in. are required. A shooter with sloping shoulders will find that a stock about $2\frac{3}{4}$ in. bend at heel and $1\frac{3}{8}$ in. at comb will probably suit him best.

The gun-stock must be so fashioned that the heel-plate shall be at a right angle, or nearly so, to the barrels, and the gun will stand with the barrels *almost* perpendicular. Some, however, prefer that the gun when stood upright shall be such that the sight and the centre of the butt shall be in a plumb-line.

Showing how to Balance a Gun.

The Horn before Guard Gun Stock.

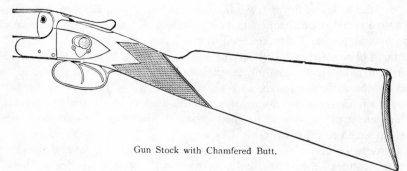

Gun Stock with Chamfered Butt.

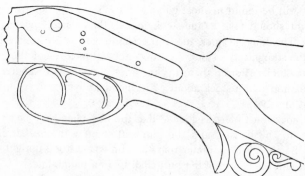

The German Horn Grip Guard.

A thin man requires but little cast off to his gun, whilst a stout man with broad shoulders may need a gun much cast-off.

The pistol-hand gun-stock, especially in that form shown in the illustration of the American gun-stock, and known technically as half pistol-hand, is the common form throughout Canada and the United States, and is also widely used by the sportsmen of Australia and South Africa.

Amongst English sportsmen the use of the pistol-grip is confined chiefly to double rifles and large-bore guns ; it permits of a firmer grip than the straight hand stock, but is not so convenient for pulling the left trigger in quick succession to the right. With the straight grip the hand may slide backwards, but with the pistol grip it is necessary to bend the trigger finger more to fire the second barrel rapidly. Some sportsmen, whether using straight or pistol-hand stocks, find it more convenient to pull the near trigger first and move the hand forward to fire a rapid second.

There are other shapes of stocks, with which many sportsmen are acquainted, but to others they will be novel, and offer certain advantages. First, there is the *horn grip guard*, equivalent to the *scroll guard* of the old-fashioned English rifle. This guard is supposed to allow a better and firmer grip of the gun to be obtained with the right hand—the same advantage as claimed for the *pistol-hand* stock, and it moreover prevents the second finger of the right hand from being bruised by the back of the trigger-guard.

The horn guard is much used by some Continental sportsmen, and the German gun-makers particularly fashion it into an ornamental fitting for either the shot-gun or rifle. Another Continental form is the *shield guard*, or horn before guard. With this style of stock, the gun is grasped just in front of the trigger-guard by the thumb and forefinger of the left hand, the palm of the left hand and the remaining fingers being firmly pressed against the guard. This style of holding the gun is not to be commended, but it must be admitted that many fine shots are to to be found who never hold their gun differently.

The rational gun-stock was introduced by the author some time ago, and it embodies qualities long sought in pistol-grip guns, and the undeniable advantage of the straight stock.

In this stock, as will be seen from the illustration, there is more than the usual bend at the *bump* or *heel*, and that the comb is not straight, but *arched* slightly ; and as the cheek touches the stock about midway between the *heel* and the *thumb*, it is there, and there only, that the stock need be straight.

With the usual English gun-stock, put up in the usual manner, it will be found that about *one-quarter* of the *butt* projects above, and has *no* bearing against the shoulder. This leaves the sharp narrow toe to steady the gun and to take the recoil. With the rational stock, the face of the shooter will be resting upon the stock when the *bump* or *heel* has reached a level of the shoulder, and the whole of the *butt* will find a bearing in the hollow of the shooter's shoulder. The bend of the gun will, with the rational stock, be about $2\frac{1}{2}$ in. at *heel*, $1\frac{1}{2}$ in. at *comb*, and $1\frac{1}{2}$ in. midway between heel and comb.

In the gun with the *cheek-piece* the cast-off of the gun is almost, and frequently quite, annulled by the projection on the left side of the stock, called the cheek-piece. From the dotted lines in the illustration indicating the full centre, it will be seen that the stock has an advantage to the right, but this advantage is compensated for by the projecting cheek-piece, which at the centre of the stock actually projects beyond the true line.

The use for and necessity of *cast-off* will at once become apparent on an examination of the next illustration, showing a gun so cast over that it may be aligned from the right shoulder with the left eye. This kind of stock serves a very useful purpose. Unfortunately, too many shooters lose the sight of the right eye from some mishap when using their guns, and to such a gun with a stock of this description is an absolute necessity. But more than one style of stock has been devised for these sportsmen, and the second model shown is, of the two, to be preferred; it is quite as handy and strong, and gives the same shaped comb at the same angle as an ordinary stock. The "Monopeian" gun comes into this same category, although the result obtained is not by bending over or so fashioning the stock that the left eye may see over to the rib and align the gun, but the sight is brought out to the left side of the left barrel, and an additional sight affixed to the breech.

THE SHAPE OF THE TOP-RIB.

The top ribs of shot-guns are usually made "hollow"—that is, grooved—and the rib follows the curvature of the outer shape of the barrels. In the illustration Fig. B is of this type; it has both its upper edges raised, as shown in section D, and is "swamped," or lower at midway between breech and muzzle than at either end: this is the lightest rib. A "flat" rib is a rib having a square cross section, as shown at C, and it may be "swamped" just as the hollow rib, and as shown in B. If it is to be level so that a straight-edge laid along it from breech to muzzle will touch at every point in its length, it is as shown in Fig. A, and is known as a "straight" rib. It is a true plane on its upper surface, and, as shown in the

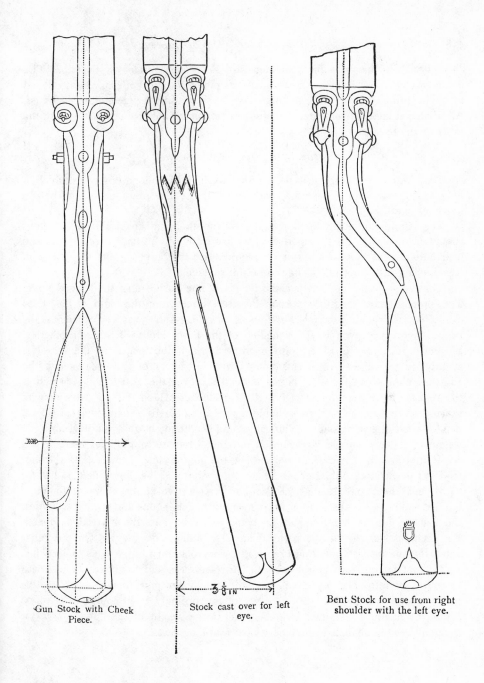

Gun Stock with Cheek
Piece.

Stock cast over for left
eye.

Bent Stock for use from right
shoulder with the left eye.

$3\tfrac{1}{8}$ IN

illustration, the line of sight coincides with the upper surface of the rib. The hollow rib may be "level" or "swamped," as preferred, and both may be deadened by engine-turning, file-cutting, or engraving—as shown in the pigeon gun illustrated. All ribs taper slightly from breech to the muzzle, narrowing proportionately with the taper of the barrels.

THE GUN THAT WILL SUIT.

The choice of a gun must be determined, first, by the purposes for which it is intended that it is to be used, and, secondly, by the physique of the person by whom it will be used.

The information given in the chapter on the shooting capabilities of shot-guns should prove ample for the sportsman to fix definitely the charge of powder and load and size of shot which will be required for his purpose, and the gauge of barrel which will shoot this charge to best advantage.

The gauge of the gun settled, the length of the barrel must be decided upon. The proportionate length will soon be ascertained from the ratio of length to calibre—40 to 1 holds good for shot-guns as for rifles—and the exact diameters of the various bores are given in the Schedule of the Proof House Tests. In practice, as good results are obtained with sporting loads if the length of the barrel is slightly less than the theoretic maximum ; with chambers of the usual length the 12-gauge choke-bore barrel is better under than over the 29·16 inches, which is theoretically its correct length. Barrels of 28 inches seldom fail to give complete satisfaction, but the short barrels should not be chambered for extra-long cartridges, neither must the light ones. The gauge and length of barrel will determine the weight of the weapon ; if its weight is not proportionate to the load used, it will recoil unpleasantly. A safe rule is to have the gun 96 times heavier than the shot load. This means a 6-lb. gun for an ounce of shot; $6\frac{3}{4}$ lbs. for $1\frac{1}{8}$ oz.; $7\frac{1}{2}$ lbs. for $1\frac{1}{4}$ oz., and these may be shot with comfort, irrespective of the gauge of the gun ; but, as made clear in the chapter on the varieties of shot-guns and their capabilities, the 12-bore gun is handicapped by being lightened and the barrels shortened. For shooting small loads the better plan is to reduce the gauge. On the other hand, the author has many times received orders to build 12-bore guns under 7 lbs. weight, yet chambered for the $2\frac{3}{4}$-inch cartridge case, and intended for use with 47 grains of nitro and $1\frac{1}{4}$ oz. of shot, and chiefly for pigeon shooting. As this heavy charge can be loaded into cases of the ordinary length nothing is to be gained by having the $2\frac{3}{4}$-inch chamber, nor is the weight of the gun suitable for such still heavier charges as may be loaded into long cases.

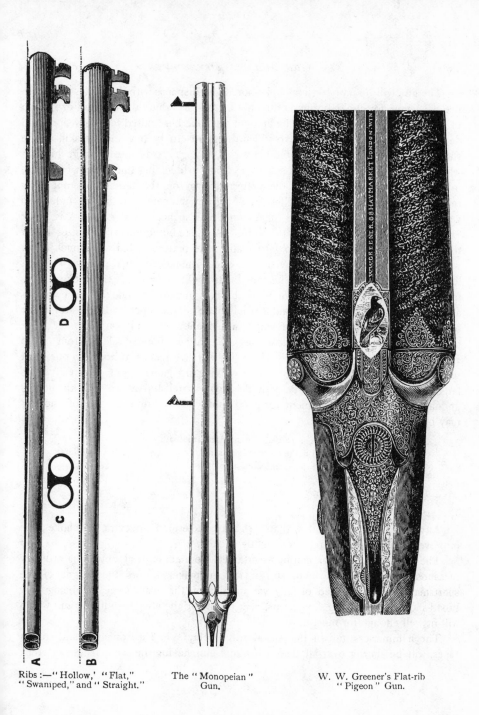

Ribs :—" Hollow,' " Flat,"   The " Monopeian "   W. W. Greener's Flat-rib
" Swamped," and " Straight."   Gun.   " Pigeon " Gun.

The gun will be more or less choke-bored; to dispense with the choke is to sacrifice efficiency, for choke-boring is the only method by which the outward expansion of the shot can be controlled. The amount of choke best suited for the weapon will depend upon the particular use to which the gun is to be put and the skill of the shooter to use it. A trap shooter placed at, say, 21 yards must change his gun when the handicapper puts him back to 28; but, in deciding the amount of choke, it must be borne in mind that the pattern shown on the target does not fairly represent the position of the pellets at any given moment, for, having individual velocities, some go ahead, others lag behind, and so actually the pattern is never exactly what the target represents it to be. A choke-bored gun is four sizes better than a cylinder; that is to say, to get equally close patterns a barrel so much larger would be needed to shoot a heavier load and so make an equal pattern, whilst at long ranges the larger barrel and heavier loads could never equal the choke. Uniformity in shooting is a quality found in the best guns only; chokes and cylinders alike, unless carefully finished, and a trial made of their performance, will make occasional bad shots, any one of which would allow of a pigeon escaping. The principal advantage a cylinder possesses is a larger killing circle at from 18 to 26 yards, or thereabouts. For this wider circle of five inches at 20 yards one must sacrifice 15 yards of killing range. For walking up game a gun which gives its largest killing circle at 30 yards with the right barrel and at 40 with the left is undoubtedly the most convenient for good shots. The various degrees of choking may be classified as:

Full-choke, which, with a 12-gauge gun, standard load, distance and conditions will make an average pattern of	215 pellets.
The half-choke (same conditions)	185 ,,
The quarter-choke ,, ...	160 ,,
The improved cylinder ,, ...	140 ,,
The old cylinder ,, ...	115 ,,

Any better *average* shooting than 215 may be termed an extra full-choke; the improved cylinder is a barrel very slightly choked.

The fit of the gun-stock can be ascertained from actual trial only; the ordinary measurements suit most men, and if the gunmaker knows the height of the sportsman, and is advised of any variation from the usual type, as being very broad-shouldered, having long arms, etc., he should be able to build a gun which will fit well enough for most men.

The hammerless gun of the Anson and Deeley, " Facile Princeps," and similar types, will be shorter over all than a hammer gun having the same length of stock and barrels, for the distance between the trigger and the head of the gun is nearly one inch less. Such guns, therefore, since they have the chief weight between the hands, may balance well—better than the hammer guns—yet indicate a fulcrum nearer the muzzle than the position three inches from the breech end of the barrels, specified as a perfect balance.

HOW TO ORDER A GUN.

It is best to order a gun personally, since it is not easy for anyone not conversant with trade technicalities to specify correctly the details of the arm required. If this is inconvenient, it is usual to supply the gun-maker with the measurement of some gun which fits the shooter for whom the new weapon is intended, or to give precise indications to enable an expert to judge of the dimensions which will probably suit best. A photograph (full-length) is often a great assistance ; any peculiarities of build should also be mentioned ; if any spaces in the usual order form cannot be filled up, some indication should be given that the points they refer to are immaterial. In using technical words, use them in the sense gun-makers understand them, or describe what is wanted in ordinary language, even though by a roundabout way, for it is better to describe a special rib at full length than to order and obtain a "flat" when a "level" one is wanted.

Instructions have already been given for measuring length and bend of the gunstock, taking circumference of the "grip" and lay of the heel-plate ; the amount of cast-off cannot be measured without special jigs or tools, and it is best not to specify the cast-off required unless it has been accurately ascertained by an expert. The weight of the pull-off of the triggers is usually 4 lbs. Any deviation from this standard should be specified if required. The method of weighing the pull is illustrated on the following page.

The author has made a series of experiments, all proving that at least four pellets of No. 6 Chilled Shot are required to kill a sitting blue rock pigeon stone dead, always excepting such fluky shots as result in one pellet striking the head or breaking the neck of the bird. If the pigeon be struck by six shots, although not one may enter a vital part, the shock of the impact is enough to drop the bird at once and allow of its being gathered. A cylinder gun will not average three shots into a pigeon at 30 yards, and must therefore be considered practically useless at that distance ; for, providing the pigeon was fairly struck, and in the centre of the charge, not more than one bird out of three would be killed outright or gathered. To ensure four pellets being put into a pigeon, a pattern of at least 200 in the 30-inch circle is necessary.

When extra barrels are required to fit the same stock, if the additional pair is widely different from the original pair, the gun will not be wholly satisfactory with either pair.   It is impossible to get a well-balanced light 12-bore gun and a heavy 10-bore wild-fowling gun simply by changing the barrels.   A heavy 12 and a light 10 may interchange, or there may be barrels of the same gauge, but differing, say, 8 ozs. in weight.   Beyond this limit it is unwise to go—the requirement is more satisfactorily met by having two guns, even if *both* be of somewhat cheaper grade.

The expense of fitting extra barrels adds quite one-half to the cost of the guns, and in cheap guns more than half the cost.   The workmanship upon the barrel and action-fitting are the heaviest items in the cost of guns, and the extra labour

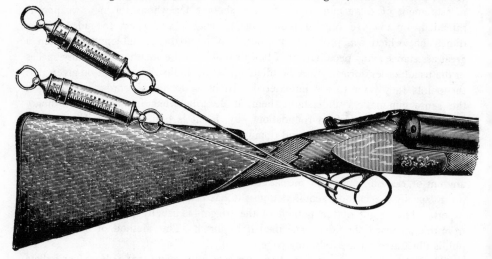

The Correct Angle to test the Weight of Trigger-pull.

entailed by having two sets of barrels instead of one accurately adjusted to breech mechanism, and geared with lock-firing and ejecting mechanisms, runs up the cost of construction enormously.

The nature of the work may be estimated from the fact that to get the same bend of stock the finest adjustment of the barrels to the action is requisite—a difference not greater than the thickness of a piece of paper on the under sides of the barrels sufficing to throw out the bend one-eighth of an inch or more.   It is evident, therefore, that it is impossible to fit a new pair of barrels to be exactly the same as the old ones unless the stock, and not the breech action only, is furnished to the gun-maker. It is also apparent that the breech-ends of barrels to fit the same stock must be of the same thickness; if one pair were thicker than the other, the striker would be above or below the cap, and, in the same way, if the barrels were not the same distance across the strikers would not be central for both pairs.

As, usually, each action is specially constructed to suit the barrels, and the gun built up in proportion to their size, no new pair of barrels can be made to fit, even approximately, unless the particular breech action, and, preferably, the whole gun, is furnished to the gun-maker.

Rifle barrels are sometimes fitted to the stock of a small-bore shot-gun, the weapon being used alternately as gun and rifle. The ·450 or ·500 " black powder " calibre is suitable for changing with a pair of 16-bore barrels, but if the action is made expressly for the rifle barrels the gun will be somewhat clumsy as a shot-gun; if it is made as a shot-gun, it cannot be expected to stand the hard wear of a double Express rifle so well as a weapon purposely constructed throughout for use with the heavier charges and greater strains. Any larger size shot barrel than 16 is unsuitable; the distance the strikers must be apart to allow of 12-gauge cartridges being used necessitates the rifle barrels being unduly large at the breech and exceedingly clumsy at the muzzle.

Another error sometimes made is in specifying the barrels of shot guns to be of a certain thickness at the breech and taper gradually to the muzzle, so that, a straight-edge being placed to the side, it shall bear evenly from breech to muzzle. No guns are so constructed. Any 12-gauge barrels with the heavy breech ends now commonly used would, if taper, weigh about 15 lbs., and the gun would balance nearly 12 inches from the breech. The barrels are *swamped*—a curve instead of a taper—the thickness of their metal being proportionate to the strain exerted by the explosion at the various points in their length.

CHAPTER XVII.

HOW TO USE THE GUN.

ON PUTTING GUNS TOGETHER.

THE purchaser of a new breech-loader should receive instructions from the seller as to the manner in which the gun is to be put together.

Putting the barrels on to the stock is a very easy matter to one used to it ; to the sportsman it is not always a simple matter, especially if the gun be of a type new to him.   The gun will generally be delivered with the barrels and stock apart. The fore-part will be upon the barrels, probably held there by the snap-bolt, which must be raised or pressed, and the fore-end at the same time lifted away from the barrels.   In cheap guns it sometimes happens that the fore-end, which is easy enough to remove when the gun is together, fits very tightly upon the barrels when the action is off.   It will come away easily if it be pressed down upon the barrels and towards the muzzle.

The gun being put together should be wiped free from dust; nothing tends more to clog the breech mechanism than dust.

There are two simple ways of putting barrels and stock together.   Take the stock in the right hand, keep the lever open with the thumb, partly draw out the extractor in the barrels ; take the latter in the left hand and hook them into the breech-action, as shown in the illustration, care being taken to pull the hook well on to the hinge-pin ; when they are down on the bed of the breech-action, let go the action-lever, turn the gun over, and put on the fore-end.   Another way is to take hold of the breech-action firmly with the left hand ; hold the barrels perpendicularly in the right, hook the breech-action on to the barrels, and press it firmly home.

In putting a Greener Ejector Gun together—

First.—Pull extractors in barrel out to their fullest extent, press back the swivel and ejectors as close to the barrel lump as possible.

Second.—Take stock in the right hand, the barrels in the left, keep both in a *horizontal* position, the left side being uppermost.

Third.—Introduce the barrels into the breech-action body, hook first, and pulling hook well down on the hinge, snap the barrels home.   No force is requisite.

Fourth.—Put on the fore-end. The bolts must be right home before affixing the fore-end, or possibly the lock mechanism will be broken if forced.

Dirt often finds its way *underneath the extractor*, and this even in a most minute quantity will frequently occasion stiffness in working, or very possibly prevent the

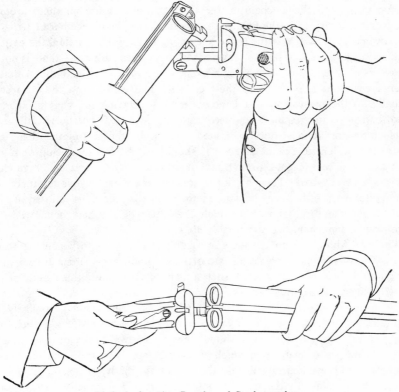

Method of putting Barrels and Stock together.

gun from closing. Oil and dust, and sometimes a little rust, will be found in the bottom holding-down bolt; this causes the gun to work stiffly. The gun must *never* be *forced* open, or unusual *force* used to close it. If the gun does not open *freely* it should be carefully examined, and on the principle that a stitch in time saves nine, it may be cleaned thoroughly, providing the cause of the stiffness is not found, and the obstruction removed. In putting a gun together, providing all the parts are clean, no stiffness will be noticed and no force requisite. In case of a *deadlock* in putting in the barrel, do not attempt to force the barrels in, but search for the *cause*. Probably, if a hammerless gun, it will require cocking; if a hammer gun, possibly the strikers are projecting through the face, and do not work freely, so that the extractor drops upon them and prevents the barrels going home. The keeping of the gun clean, and the mechanism free from grit, will ensure immunity from the annoyance of a " jam " in the field. In case of the sticking together of parts that should work freely—such as the strikers jamming in the breech-action, the extractor clogging in the barrels, or bolts or any parts becoming fast with rust—there is nothing so good as an application of petroleum; repeated applications, and the exercise of patience, will not fail to loosen the " cement," and make even the rustiest pin amenable to the persuasion of a hand turnscrew. Having the gun together, and working freely, it will require to be used carefully. It must not be let fall heavily on its butt plate; it must not be pushed underneath the seat of the dog-cart or wagonette, and left to take its chance; it should not be left muzzle-up or muzzle-down against a wall, a gate, or a tree. It should not be used as a crutch, an alpenstock, or crowbar. From a critical examination of many guns returned to the author, after very little wear, he fancies they must at times be utilised for very different purposes from those for which their makers intended them. To speak more plainly, some guns are abominably abused.

The man who means to use his gun roughly is not likely to benefit by reading any number of directions as to the care of guns; there are sportsmen who do not wish to spoil their guns, who act in such a manner as to injure them, and for them the following hints are intended :—

More breech-loaders get shaky in the action by being worked carelessly than from repeated firing or the use of heavy charges. The barrels of a breech-loader should never be jerked down, nor should they be thrown back into position with a snap. The proper manner in which to load a gun is to drop the stock under the elbow, and press it firmly against the hip or the body, unfasten the lever with the right hand, and with the left grasping the barrels a few inches in front of the fore-end, lower them easily. Close the gun in a careful manner after putting in the cartridges, bringing the stock up to the barrels.

CLEANING GUNS.

To clean a gun after a day's shooting. If the gun be wet, it should be wiped dry *at once*, but the *cleaning* of the barrels and breech-action may be left until the sportsman or his servant has time to do it properly.

To clean the barrels. Use the cleaning-rod, with tow and oil, or turpentine. To remove the fouling, put muzzles on a piece of wood, and push the rod down to within an inch of the muzzle, and draw up to the chamber. Do this two or three times; then push right through. Use the bristle brush, or the rod with plenty of flannel; finish with the mop soaked in refined neatsfoot, pure Arctic sperm oil, or vaseline.

Never half-clean the barrels; always wipe them dry and clean before finally oiling, and do not put the mop used for oiling into a foul barrel. To remove the leading from the inside of a gun barrel, soak well with turpentine; then clean well with a bristle brush, or even with a wire brush, but *never use emery* if the shooting qualities of the gun are valued.

Always wipe the *bed, face, and joint* of the breech-action with an oily rag or flannel. A *little* linseed oil may be rubbed over the stock occasionally.

Before putting the gun together, ascertain that all the bearing parts are free from dust or grit.

The *joint* may be lubricated with a mixture of half best Russian tallow and half petroleum. In most hammerless guns, if the *cover plate* underneath the breech-action *body* is taken off, the locks may be inspected, oiled, and any rust or clogged oil and dust removed from the *bent*.

The cocking-lifters of hammerless guns, the holding-down and top bolts, and the triggers, if they have a tendency to clog, may be touched with a knitting-needle dipped in petroleum. They must be lubricated, whenever they require it, with chronometer oil, Rangoon oil, or finest neatsfoot.

Do not use a feather for the purpose of putting on any lubricant; a wire knitting-needle or bodkin is much better.

To remove rust from inside or outside of a barrel, procure a tub, and with a kettle of boiling water well scald the barrels inside and out, inserting a wooden peg in one of the barrels to hold them by, wipe perfectly dry with flannel, and then oil. It is as well to do this before putting the gun aside for any length of time.

If the barrels are foul through using inferior powder, and the fouling has become hard and dry, cold water, or hot soap-suds, may be used to cleanse them. Water *boiling hot* kills rust.

Turpentine, often used successfully to clean the residue from gun barrels, will give great trouble if it gets into the fine-fitting parts of the mechanism of the breech-action and locks, and must therefore be used with care.

Rusty or tight breeches in muzzle-loading barrels may often be turned out, providing the breech-ends of the barrels have been soaked in petroleum. Very obstinate breeches may require to be well heated, as well as lubricated, before they can be turned out, but usually petroleum will be found a sufficient remedy for incipient rust of the working parts. All the parts of the mechanism may be cleaned with petroleum ; it removes clogged vegetable and animal oils well.

STRIPPING GUNS.

Some sportsmen like to take their guns all to pieces and re-arrange the parts. This is not requisite, and does not in any way add to the efficiency of the arm. The gun-maker is the proper person to take apart the locks, or strip the breech-action ; if there is not a practical man within easy reach the sportsman must, of course, himself endeavour to effect any repairs, but it is not advisable to interfere with any gun that performs properly, nor to practise upon any gun that works satisfactorily. If practicable, have a good gun examined each summer by its maker or a competent gunsmith.

To take to pieces a breech-loader for cleaning or repairs, first remove the fore-end and barrels ; then, with a strong hand turnscrew, turn out the side-pins, and remove the locks and hammers together ; next turn out the guard-pins, and remove the bow or guard ; another pin will then be seen in the rear end of the trigger-plate ; remove this pin (occasionally this "hand-pin" is placed in the reverse way; the head of this pin will then be found on the top of the grip in the tang of a long break-off). The "furniture-pin" should next be partly turned out ; this pin fastens the fore part of the trigger-plate to the body of the breech-action, and is easily distinguished. Next remove the "breech-pin" upon the top of the tang of the break-off; in top-lever action guns the breech-pin is covered by the lever, which must be held on one side whilst the pin is being turned out. Rarely a false pin is screwed into the lever, which, when removed, will leave an aperture through which the breech-pin must be extracted. After having removed the furniture-pins, the trigger-plate and triggers may be taken from the stock, after which the breech-action may be removed entire.

To strip breech-actions, if the action is a treble wedge-fast or ordinary top-lever double-bolt action, the first thing will be to remove the spring. To do this, first partly turn out the lever spring pin (under tang of break-off), and with a pair of pliers or pincers take hold of the spring and slightly grip it, and lift the spring towards the head of the pin. It will then be free from its bearing, and may be removed by completely turning out the spring pin. (This does not apply to spiral springs.) Next proceed to turn out the pin or pins connecting the top-lever tumbler with the bottom bolt, and remove the bolt by drawing straight out backwards. Next turn out the lever pin on top of lever, and by means of a small wire punch inserted in the lever pin-hole, knock out the lever tumbler. The lever may then be removed, and the top bolt, if any, will fall out. In side-lever guns, first knock out the pivot on which the lever works, then remove spring and bolt. Snap guns with lever under-guard may be stripped in much the same manner, but the spring and lever are fixed to the trigger-plate, and the spring must be removed before knocking out the pivot-pin. Owing to the numerous complicated breech-actions that are made, it is possible that the above directions will not be sufficient to enable an amateur to strip his gun; but they will be explicit enough for W. W. Greener Treble Wedge-fast and most modern guns. There are many breech-actions made that puzzle expert gunsmiths to take apart and repair, and it would be foolish for an amateur to attempt to take them apart if a gun-maker is within reasonable distance.

To strip a muzzle-loader, first remove the lock, then the barrels, then proceed to remove the furniture and break-off, as already described for breech-loaders. In military rifles, the bands fastening the barrel to the stock must be loosened by a screw underneath, and then removed by slipping over muzzle of barrel. (*Note.*—Horn heel-plates are usually glued to the stock, as well as being fastened by the screws.)

To strip a gun-lock, first remove the mainspring. This may be accomplished with a pair of lock vices, or a cramp may be made by filing a notch or slot in a narrow strip of $\frac{3}{16}$ iron or steel, the size of the breadth of mainspring when at full cock. Having cocked the lock, slip the cramp up the mainspring until it catches, then release the scear and push down the tumbler. The spring being firmly held in the cramp, it may be unhooked from the swivel and removed from the lock-plate; then unscrew the bridle-pins and remove the bridle.

The scear may then be lifted off if the tumbler is not in bent. The scear spring will then be at liberty, and may be removed by turning out the pin. Now the hammer should be removed; the tumbler-pin is first turned out, and by means of a wire punch inserted in the hole, the tumbler is knocked away from both hammers and lock-plate. If a hammer fits well, it will be impossible to remove it in any other way without injury either to the hammer or the lock. The spring must not be taken out of the cramp; it requires no cleaning except at the claw or hook. In putting a lock together, first screw on the scear spring, then the tumbler, then place on the scears, and cramp the spring with a pair of pliers or tongs, place the tumbler into half-bent. Then affix the bridle, and screw it to the lock-plate. Take the main-spring, ready cramped, hook on to the swivel in tumbler, place the stud in the hole drilled for it in the lock-plate, raise the tumbler to full bent, squeeze the main-spring down close to the plate, and remove the cramp ; the lock will be ready then for affixing the hammer, which should be knocked on after placing the lock firmly on a solid block to prevent the bridle from breaking.   (See page 268 for description of parts.)

To take apart the lock-work of the Anson and Deeley Hammerless Gun, proceed as follows :—

Having removed the barrels, snap down the hammers or tumblers, remove the cover-plate from bottom of breech-action body ; knock out with a wire punch, from the right side, the scear pivot, or the one nearest the stock, and remove the scears ; knock out the dog-pin, or the one nearest the fore-end joint, and remove the cocking levers ; partly screw on the cover-plate, and carefully knock out the centre-pivot or tumbler-pin, remove the cover-plate, and the tumblers and mainsprings will drop out upon the breech-action being reversed.   The scear springs lie along the bottom of the action, and may be removed after turning out the pins.   To put the lock-work together, first place the mainspring in the bend of the tumbler, with the stud of mainspring bearing in its proper slot, and its other extremity bearing against the under side of the nose of the tumbler ; the tumbler and spring having been placed in the slot must be forced into position with a cramp, or piece of notched wood ; knock in the tumbler-pivot half-way, insert the other tumbler and spring in the same manner ; knock the wire pivot right through the lifting-dogs, the scears must then be put in, and the whole covered with the cover-plate.   The Greener hammerless guns, which have similar tumblers and scears and mainsprings, may be taken to pieces in the same way, but there are no dogs or lifters to be removed.

The lock-work of the Greener Ejecting Guns is very similar.   Those having the lock-work in the fore-end are stripped in the manner of the Anson and Deeley, if the locks are on that principle, or like an ordinary gun if the work is affixed to ordinary side-lock plates.   The ejecting locks in the fore-part are easily stripped. The screws in the fore-end free the wood, and this removed, the box containing the mechanism is soon detached.

A difficulty is sometimes experienced in cocking the fore-end ejecting mechanism.   If the fore-end be removed while the gun is opened, it can only be replaced either when the gun is in the same position or by cramping the fore-end ejecting tumblers into bent : this may be done by pressing them against the square edge of a wooden table or bench, and, while compressing the springs, pressing downwards, thus forcing the tumblers into cock or bent ; the fore-end may then be replaced in the ordinary way.

To get the extractor from the barrels, the ejecting levers usually have first to be removed, then a stop-pin must be found and removed. It is generally on the flat in front of the hook of the barrel-lump, and in a line with the extractor-leg, or, as in the Greener gun, it is a small pin in the groove of the extension of the top rib through which the cross-bolt passes.

HOW TO REPAIR GUNS.

The following hints will be found useful to those who use guns far away from a gun-maker's shop, and need to repair broken-down guns for immediate use :—

The action or top-lever spring may break, but this need not in any way affect the utility or safety of the arm, only the lever will have to be moved home when the gun is closed, instead of it snapping there, or the spring may be roughly replaced by an elastic band suitably adjusted. The strikers of ordinary guns will become useless after continuous wear, owing to the hardened hammer flattening the head of the striker, and so shortening its travel as to make miss-fires of frequent occurrence. The nipple must then be turned out with a key or a pair of pliers, and a new spare striker inserted. In hammerless guns, the tumbler and striker being in one, and the point itself striking against the soft copper cap of the cartridge, this flattening does not occur, the strikers being of the best mild steel, carefully hardened and tempered, and so well made that breakages are of very rare occurrence.

Perhaps the most usual accident to a sportsman will be the denting or the bulging of the barrels. When a bruise is discovered, DO NOT IN ANY CASE SHOOT out of the gun until the barrels have been repaired, if the bruise is a bad one ; for firing out of a badly bruised barrel invariably causes the barrel to bulge considerably, or fracture, at the bruised part. To remove a dent, the following is the readiest expedient :—Having removed the barrel from the action or stock, insert in the barrel a solid leaden plug or bullet, or even a wooden plug, as near the size of the barrel as possible ; insert this from the chamber or breech end and pass forward, using a wooden rod for the purpose, such as a good cleaning rod with the brush removed, until the obstruction caused by the dent is reached. If the barrels be lightly hammered with a very small hammer, and the pressure on the inside maintained by forcing the plug past the bruise, the dent may be raised. It may be necessary to use various size plugs, or to beat out the leaden one, and repeat the operation until the barrel is as near normal as possible. The barrel should be warmed during the process by applying a hot iron to the outside of the bruised part. Great care will have to be taken not to get the plug jammed in the barrel. If a taper lead plug can be obtained, the process will be greatly simplified, and a slightly taper iron or brass plug is much better than a soft lead one. If the barrel is bulged a similar plug should be made, and great care will have to be taken to hammer the bruise down to the plug with a light hammer. If a hard metal plug can be obtained near the required size, it may be packed with paper until of the required diameter. The plug must be slightly longer than the bruise or dent.

Another frequent accident in wild countries is the breaking of the gun-stock. This may be securely spliced in the following manner :—First glue the stock as well as possible, then glue round the fracture several pieces of thin leather or canvas, and whilst warm tightly bind with waxed thread or a fine lace ; when the whole is dry it will be almost as sound as before. Should the break be " short " it will be necessary to glue thin pieces of cane on either side of the stock. The wood should be warmed before gluing, to enhance the chances of perfect success.

Repairs to breech-actions require great care and experience in effecting, and always when practicable the gun should be sent to the maker, as he has more interest in properly repairing it than anyone else. To tighten a breech-action, the usual way is to fit a new hinge-pin slightly larger than the old one, or by filing from the flats beneath the barrels, and hammering up the bites on the lump, which process brings the breech-ends of barrels nearer to the face of the standing-breech. When the cartridge bursts at the rim at the upper edge of the case, it is a sure sign that the gun requires to be tightened up.

THE GUN-ROOM.

Guns and shooting paraphernalia should be kept together. If a room cannot be devoted solely to them, a capacious cupboard, or a case fitted with a gun-rack and several drawers and shelves, will contain a small battery and the requisite accessories.

Guns are best kept put together and placed butt down on a gun-rack in a glass case or gun cupboard, of which a suitable pattern is shown on page 617 ; but if the case is not practically dust-proof, the guns should be first put in pliable canvas or cloth covers. Guns kept in racks in the open room should always be kept so covered.

Loaded cartridges are best kept on an open shelf, and in a current of air ; boxed up in an air-tight cupboard, they will deteriorate more quickly.

After the close of the season, inspect the guns very closely, and send those concerning which there is any doubt to the gun-maker for repairs at once.

On receiving his report, it will be as well to decide quickly whether or not new weapons must be purchased for the next season. Some wet summer day overhaul the contents of the gun-room, put the odd cartridges handy for popping at rabbits or vermin, see that the cleaning tools are complete, that the cartridge bags, game bags, etc. etc., are in good condition, and make a list of the things which will be required when the season opens.

In the season the gun-room will require frequent attention if it is made use of by more than one person. The cartridges, as soon as they arrive from the gunmaker's, should be transferred to the magazine or cartridge bags of the shooter for whom they are intended; a cleaning-rod and gear, turnscrews and extractor put in the travelling gun-case, and the oil bottle refilled.

Useful tools in the gun-room are: Full length ash, or hickory, cleaning rods; a rod with cotton-wool or fine tow kept specially for oiling barrels. It should be a standing rule never to put this oiler into a foul, dusty, rusty, or dirty barrel, but keep it for oiling only.

An oval tundish for cartridge loading, a set of turnscrews, some bristle brushes for cleaning out action slots, etc., small pliers, notched pincers for drawing out tight-fitting pins, a few steel knitting-needles, refined neatsfoot oil, vaseline, petroleum, and turpentine, may be placed near the gun-case for use as required.

THE GUN: HOW TO USE IT.

Should a man carry a gun in such a manner as to endanger his companions he will be shunned by sportsmen generally, and quite deservedly.

Sportsmen who have been allowed the use of a gun from their boyhood generally make the best and most careful shots, therefore the earlier a boy is entrusted with a gun the more likely is he to make a safe shot. The boy who shoots, or is learning to shoot, is the one who most rarely fools with firearms. The maxim that "familiarity breeds contempt" does not apply to the knowledge of weapons, for the person of the "didn't know it was loaded" order is usually someone who has had nothing to do with firearms in their proper place.

To point a gun at any person should in itself constitute a criminal offence, and all firearms must invariably be treated as if loaded; therefore in all drill, preliminary to going into the field, make a point of treating the weapon as loaded. With practice safe handling becomes habitual, and it must be habitual before any sportsman should venture to shoot in company. The man who knows in what direction the muzzle of his gun is pointed may be puzzled if it is accidentally discharged; he is rarely disconcerted, never flurried or alarmed.

The state of complete self-possession is acquired by the practice of always

Position for Loading.

Not Safe in a Crowd, but Good Position for carrying
a Gun when Front is Clear.

treating the gun as loaded.   There is time for a shooter to consider if every shot he fires is aimed in a safe direction, this without interfering with the rapidity or accuracy of the aim, provided he has previously noted in which direction he may fire with safety.

The beginner should first practise the handling of an unloaded gun until he can bring it up sharply and well to cover any point at which he is looking.   In shooting, as in other sports, ease of movement is the first requirement, and this is only attained by practice—drill.

To become proficient in the use of the gun, it is advisable to handle a gun for a few minutes every day in the shooting season, and at least once a week in spring and summer.

For this drill it is best to take a good position, such as that of a crack shot at the trap (*see* illustration on p. 462)—the left foot should be slightly in advance, the knees straight, the body bent very slightly forward from the hips, the left shoulder brought well forward, which allows a longer reach with the left hand.   The gun must be grasped firmly with the right hand, the forefinger on the trigger; the left hand must be got as far forward as will permit of the gun being quickly manipulated, the gun being held well across the body.   The left hand well forward gives a better command over the gun, especially with respect to its elevation, but if too far forward it retards a change of aim from left to right.

In taking a double rise from traps, or in making a right and left at game, it is advisable to swing the body with the gun, and sometimes to change the position of the feet also.   When time allows of this, the shooter will be always in the same position with respect to his object.   The change of position can, with practice, be accomplished without any loss of time, and the advantages are important.   There is greater certainty of aim, and the firing is easier than when the upper half of the body is swung round from the hips.

For marks use something distinctive.   A red or black seal, on a white card, is as good as anything.   These should be fixed at different heights, and if indoors two should be at least twelve feet apart.   Standing as illustration on p. 441, look at one of the marks and bring the gun quickly to the shoulder, pressing it firmly into position in doing so.   The muzzles of the barrels should cease their motion just under the mark at which you were looking.   Put up the gun similarly to other marks, changing from left to right, and high to low, at irregular intervals, until convinced that when your gun is brought to the shoulder it is directed automatically to the point desired.

To pull the trigger so as not to change the aim, let the forefinger be well bent, the first joint resting lightly on the trigger, the other joints being held free of the gun. The trigger must be pressed, not jerked, or the alignment of the gun may be altered thereby. Snapping off the gun with a fired case in the chamber will do the gun no injury (the use of "dummy" snap caps is recommended for this purpose) and will enable you to determine whether or not the pulling of the trigger affects your aim.

Next try a few shots in the open, either at a wall or a shot-proof screen. If the mark is fairly in the centre of the group of shot, practice at moving objects may be commenced.

It is also good practice to walk up to a certain distance, and upon reaching it to raise the gun and fire immediately. When this can be done well, learn to fire the gun when on the march, or nearly so—that is to say, bring the gun to the shoulder at the same time that your left foot goes forward with your body into position. This can be practised until you can be certain of the mark without breaking your regular walk, except for the very instant of firing.

Practise until both barrels can be fired with accuracy as quickly as your watch ticks "One, two."

The main point is to get a good, quick, correct aim, and to fire as the gun reaches the shoulder. This does not mean that the gun is to be fired in a hurried or haphazard manner, but when the object is in range the gun must be raised and fired in a single movement. The shooter who attempts to follow the object by following round with the game is a dangerous shot, as will be fully explained later, and cannot become an adept shot until he learns a different method.

There must be no practice at birds or other animals not in motion. Practice at the target is preferable to this sort of shooting, as from it something can be learned.

HANDLING THE GUN IN THE FIELD.

Before treating of the art of wing-shooting and its acquirement, a few words on the carrying and use of the gun in the field will not be out of place. The safest method of carrying a loaded gun in the field is to place it, top rib down, on either shoulder (*see* illustration on p. 444). Other safe positions upon suitable occasions are : Under the right arm, the muzzle down ; across the breast, muzzle high, and well to the front ; the muzzle raised, the left side of the stock against the right hip ; at the "trail" —that is, grasped in the right hand, the arm at full length, and the gun horizontal.

When standing for driven birds, expecting a shot at game in sight, take a position as recommended for trap-shooting ; when waiting, hold the gun in one of the above-mentioned positions, or take one of the positions illustrated, or vary them.

The gun should be carried at full cock, and if hammerless, with the safety off. Under ordinary conditions, it is better to unload a breech-loader when getting over a fence, crawling through a gap, or jumping a ditch. Even with hammer-guns (most top-levers will open at full-cock, and all should) it is easy to take out the cartridges. Changing the hammers from full- to half-cock is a very dangerous practice, and manipulating the safety-bolt of the hammerless lessens the risk, but does not absolutely remove it.

The author has seen a man fall in getting over a five-barred gate; luckily he had previously unloaded his gun. One may come to grief getting over a sheep hurdle or at an iron fence; the simpler the obstacle the more careless one is apt to be.

Before putting a gun out of hand, as through a fence, gate, or over a wall, or handing it to another person—unload.

Wire fencing is a great nuisance to shooters; both hands are often required to negotiate it properly. Unload the gun before attempting to cross it.

Loaded guns in boats and vehicles are an element of danger.

To load a gun, there are several safe positions which are also convenient. In closing the gun the barrels often swerve to the left. This is especially the case when tight-fitting cartridges are used or the gun is cocked by the action of closing the gun, and care must therefore be taken that the gun is not brought directly across the body. Let the left hand grasp the gun at a long distance from the breech; it gives one greater power, and facilitates both the opening and the closing of the gun. If an ejector is not used, two loaded cartridges may be taken up and held between the first and second and second and third fingers of the right hand, whilst the fired cases are withdrawn by the thumb and forefinger of the same hand.

The proper position to load a breech-loader is with muzzles pointing to the earth, for it not unfrequently happens that in dry weather and when using black gunpowder, flakes of the fouling will fall down into the breech action, when the barrels are higher than the breech, upon the gun being opened. The fouling, by lying in the angle of the action, prevents the gun from closing perfectly. This is often very annoying to the shooter, who, seeing that the bolts or the lever do not snap home, imagines the gun is broken; or if he be careless, and fire the gun in such a state, it may allow the breech action to be blown open, being but imperfectly bolted, and thereby result in a serious accident to the user and his companions.

In no case should the finger touch the trigger until the gun is in the act of being raised to the shoulder. Hammers should never be left resting on a cap or striker when the gun is loaded; let the hammers be carried at full cock. Look through the barrels before loading the first time after creeping through a fence, and after putting the gun out of hand for any purpose. If one barrel is fired repeatedly without discharging the other, it is advisable to take out the unfired cartridge occasionally, to ascertain whether the top wad has moved from position, or place the same in the barrel which is fired first. With thin brass cases the starting of the charge is more likely to occur than with paper cases having a proper turn-over.

THE ART OF WING SHOOTING.

Much is performed automatically by the nerve-compelled muscles; this intuition varies in degree with different persons. The shooter must look at the bird or other moving object, and depend upon his own muscles to correctly align the gun; his eye will correct his error, just as a boy watching a cricket-ball will put his hand where he knows the ball will be at a given moment of time, and does not need to look at his hand.

The physiology of shooting was cleverly stated by Dr. W. J. Fleming in a letter to the *Field* of February 19th, 1887—a letter which the author regrets he cannot reproduce in full, and can but summarise indifferently. He has demonstrated by actual experiment that what is known as "personal error" in the observation of objects is an important factor in calculating time or distance; astronomers, for instance, need to allow for this "personal error" in recording the time of a star's appearance at a given point. If two distinct lights are so placed that either may appear or disappear instantly, different observers vary in their ability to

Easy and Safe Position—Waiting for Driven Game.

quickly determine which light is shown, and record it by the depression of a key; the time required varied from 1-100th to 6-100ths of a second. If it be assumed that instead of light appearing a game bird is the object visible, it follows that before any person can aim his gun at it, at least 1-100th of a second of time will elapse, whilst another person, equally quick in aligning his gun, will not be cognisant of the object seen until upwards of 6-100ths of a second have passed. Consequently it follows that the allowance which one person would rightly make in order to hit the object would not be correct for another person; for, taking the two extremes, the object may have moved but 6 inches before known as seen by one, and 3 feet before known as seen by the other.　　Dr. Fleming also says :—

"Another important point in connection with this matter is the influence, noted by all ob-servers, which food, stimulants, and sedatives have in altering the figures for each individual. The effects vary in different persons, and this goes far to account for some men shooting better before, others after, lunch, for some men being unable to shoot if they smoke, others unable to shoot if they do not. I have tried to show that each must be a law to himself, and therefore, I trust, helped some men who have failed to get good results by following the rules of their mentors."

Anyone with a rudimentary knowledge of optics knows that before seeing an object that is visible several physiological processes are automatically performed by the organs of sight. Its position and its distance from the observer are estimated by the other processes, mainly by the adjustments his eyes require to make to see clearly, compared with previous experience. The principal adjustments are the amount of convergence of the two eyes required to bring their optical axis to a point at the object, and the amount of accommodation necessary to bring the image of the bird to a sharp focus in the retina. These adjustments are made by muscles both within and without the eye, and they inform of the amount by the muscular sense, that same sense which informs whether we have one ounce or a pound weight in our hands. The muscular sense may be trained; it enables sportsmen to judge accurately of distances, as letter-sorters and others judge of weights to a nicety. As it is dependent upon previous experience it does not follow that the sportsman who can tell whether a partridge is thirty or fifty yards distant will know as well as a sailor how many leagues distant is a vessel, nor can the letter-sorter estimate the weight of a bullock. Muscular sense differs in quantity and quality with individuals, and is a matter for special training. The sportsman who wishes to become a good shot must observe carefully and practise constantly. The ability to shoot well is a special gift to some, and though it may be acquired by all, it is possible only to indicate how the skilful use of the shot-gun may be developed. A sportsman may be a first-rate shot, yet unable to explain how he has acquired an unerring aim; some attribute it to one style of aiming, others to a different method. Many discussions take place amongst sportsmen and experts as to the correct method of aligning the gun, and the advocates in the sporting papers of the various styles of shooting detail circumstantially the most opposite experiences as the best.

HOLDING AHEAD.

It is not the intention of the author to enter into a long dissertation upon the various merits and disadvantages of "holding on" and "holding ahead." It must be confessed that the advocates of the last method have theoretically the best argument, as the following figures prove :—

The average speed at which game birds fly may be taken at forty miles per hour, which means that a bird flying across the shooter at that speed will have travelled about 12 inches before the quickest shooter can have brought his gun to position and pulled the trigger. The following "delays" may be assumed as unavoidable :—

> Time occupied in becoming aware of the game, 1- to 6-100ths sec.
> Time occupied in raising the gun, 25-100ths sec.
> Time occupied in pulling trigger, 1-200th sec.
> Time occupied in igniting charge, 1-200th sec.
> Time occupied in shot travelling 40 yards, 14-100ths sec.

during which the bird will have travelled 10 ft. 6 in., or thereabouts ; and to hit a mark 10 ft. 6 in. to the right or left of the mark aimed at, the muzzle of the barrel would require to be more than 3 in. to the right or left of the line of aim. As pointed out previously, if, instead of being able to pull the trigger in $\frac{1}{200}$th of a second, the shooter needs $\frac{3}{100}$ths of a second, the bird will have flown 16 in. farther than is stated above.

Even whilst the charge of shot, having left the muzzle, is on its way, sufficient time elapses for a fast-flying bird to travel a considerable distance ; for the first 15 yards or so, it may be taken that for every yard the shot advances the bird travels 2 in. The shot does not maintain its high velocity, and, providing the bird does, we have at 40 yards' range nearly 1 in. flown in the time the shot advances 1 ft., and at 60 yards $1\frac{1}{2}$ in. flown for every foot advance made by the shot.

Allowing $\frac{5}{100}$ths of a second as the time necessary for performing the involuntary and voluntary actions of seeing the mark, determining to shoot, raising the gun and firing, and also the small fraction of time required for the ignition and combustion of the powder and its passage through the barrel, we find that with the 12-bore and standard charge at fifteen yards' range, a bird flying at forty miles per hour will have traversed 5 ft. 6 in. before the shot reaches that range from the gun.

If 20 yards, then   6 ft. 6 in.
If 30 yards, then   8 ft. 9 in.
If 40 yards, then 11 ft. 5 in.
If 50 yards, then 14 ft. 8 in.
If 60 yards, then 19 ft. 4 in.

A great deal of difference is caused by the manner of bringing up the gun. Some sportsmen acquire the habit of bringing up the gun with a swing in the direction the mark is moving; others bring up the gun and follow the object; whilst the majority of good shots put up the gun and are supposed to jerk it ahead of the game, and fire it before the latter motion has ceased. Those who shoot with the gun on the swing, and intuitively increase the speed of the "swing," so that the gun races the game, and beats it, never require to "hold ahead." Those who hold on, by shooting promptly, prove the truth of the theory that it is necessary for the hand and eye to act in unison; whilst they who hold ahead, although agreeing that the hand must follow the eye, yet so shoot that the hand must point the gun in a different direction from the object on which the eye is fixed. If the hand can be entrusted intuitively to direct the gun to any required distance above or before the object upon which the shooter's gaze is fixed, well and good; perfect shooting will result.

The following hints as to aiming, etc., will be appreciated by all who have convinced themselves that they can, by practice, aim ahead of moving game :—

The young shooter, and all who desire to improve their shooting, should practise in the following manner : Commence by shooting at slow-flying birds, as pheasants (flushed, not driven), pigeons whose wings have been slightly clipped, or at rabbits frisking on the sward. Let all shots be at short range—twenty to thirty yards. When the bird gets up, the gun is to be brought quickly to the shoulder and fired whilst both eyes are looking at the bird.

Birds going straight away, and neither very high nor skimming low down, should all be killed, as the aim is the same as for a snap-shot for a fixed mark. Birds crossing may be missed, probably because the shooter fires behind them. By just how much the gun will be pointed ahead of the cross-flying birds may not be actually observed, but it must be known by the muscular sense, and if the shooter, whilst looking at a moving object in front of a wall or screen, consciously directs the gun to the right or left, according as the movement is right or left, he will quickly educate the muscles to direct the gun to any distances right or left of the object seen, and further practice will make him proficient in altering the elevation to any desired extent.

It is always necessary to keep the eyes steadily gazing upon the bird, even when the aim is into space as many as three, eight, or twenty feet ahead of moving objects. My estimate of twenty feet may differ greatly from that of another, but practice at various ranges and previous experience of similar shots will direct me, as it will everyone who follows these instructions, to aim the gun intuitively in that direction where the charge of shot and the game simultaneously bisect—the one the line of flight, the other the line of fire—so long as the bird is seen.

When practising wing-shooting there will be many misses, of course. After each miss the shooter should consider why the object was missed, and, whatsoever cause may be assigned, let him do his best to guard against it in the future ; if a cross shot, and he was behind the object, he must determine to direct his gun farther forward when another similar shot presents itself. If he does this and continues to shoot without being hurried, flustered, or disheartened, he will steadily improve in his shooting ; but to go on missing, time after time, without giving a thought as to the cause, will do no good whatever.

When a bird rises, follow its exact course with your eyes, and when it is in the best position for shooting, bring up the gun from below or behind it, and if your hands act in perfect harmony with the eye and the will, as you have schooled them to do, the gun will be aligned instinctively ; then press the trigger so as to feel recoil at the instant the object is in the position indicated in the illustrations. If you stop the gun at the moment of firing, you are sure to be behind, for your muscles have to race to get ahead, and if you stop the action at the moment you will the pull of the trigger you stop it long before the shot leaves the barrel, and much longer before it reaches the line of flight of the game.

It is a good plan to continue the swing of the weapon whilst firing ; by so doing you send the charge of shot in the direction in which the gun is moving ; but if you think you have acquired the habit of stopping the swing at the moment of firing and kill well, there is no need of changing your method. It is a mistake to bring up the gun so that it has to be lowered again in order to cover the object, or to bring it from before the object, though this latter plan is sometimes necessarily followed, as when the shooter facing No. 2 trap gets a quarterer to the left from No. 5 ; but ordinarily follow the flight of the bird, if for the fraction of a second only, then bring up the gun and fire.

The allowances which will have to be made, as already explained, can only be determined by actual experience. The following general indications may, however, be of some service :—

The straight going-away shot at birds should be point blank at any distance.

At ground game going straight away, shoot over the animal. Of approaching shots : at birds shoot dead on, unless the bird is very high, when aim well in front. If coming over at long range, but low, make less allowance, or wait until it can be shot at a pleasant angle nearer the shooter.

An approaching low shot, when a driven partridge or an "incomer" from the pigeon traps : aim under the bird rather than over it. Birds which cannot be shot as they approach, owing to the position of beaters, etc., must be allowed to pass over, and will furnish similar shots to those obtained by walking up to the birds, but their flight will probably be much quicker, and they will be higher; the bird

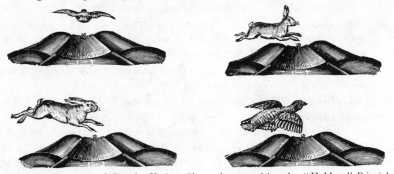

Showing the Alignment of Gun for Various Shots when practising the "Hold-on" Principle.

must, therefore, be shot well-under, *i.e.* actually in front of it. A bird that has passed and flies low is a more difficult shot ; the shooter must get ahead of it, and this is only to be done by shooting over it.

Birds crossing to the right are more difficult to hit than those crossing to the left. It is often advisable to move the position by turning one-quarter round on the right foot before raising the gun when there is a quick flyer to the right and you are shooting along or on the right extremity of a line. Longer shots may be made at crossing than at straight-away birds.

Some quartering shots are very easy, others most difficult—it depends upon the speed and angle of the flight.

Ascending shots are difficult—the most if at short range and flying quickly. Aim high.

EXPLANATION.—At the time of firing the whole of the butt-plate should be in contact with the shoulder of the shooter. When firing at ground game this is almost impossible with a straight gun stock having the usual amount of toe.

EXPLANATION.—The Rational stock at the time of firing is squarely bedded against the shoulder of the shooter, and, whether firing at ground game or at birds flying straight over, must always have a greater portion of the butt-plate in contact with the shoulder than when using the ordinary straight stock.

If the bird is well away and going straight or quartering, to get before it, *i.e.* to hit, it will probably be necessary to aim high.

Aim at the head of a pheasant rising; indeed, all game of which the head can be seen should be shot at as though the head, not the body, were the sportsman's mark. Shoot at the head of all ground game. It often happens that incoming and motionless ground game is shot over, and neither hares nor rabbits should be shot at when more than forty yards distant, nor above thirty if going straight away.

The prettiest of shots, and difficult ones to make, are the perpendicular shots. In attempting these shots bring the left hand much nearer the breech than is usual for any firing at an angle of 45° or less, and aim in front of the bird if approaching, and under it if going away.

Occasionally shots may be had at birds and hares descending, chiefly when shooting on the hillside, and these shots are difficult, the sportsman generally shooting over his game. Low flying wild-fowl, wood-pigeons coming into lofty trees, hawks, crows, and vermin, generally afford different shooting practice, by which the sportsman will profit. In order to become an expert shot, if other game is not readily available, starlings, fieldfares, larks, and even sparrows may be used as marks, and much learned from shooting at them.

To practise systematically, nothing is so handy as trap shooting—almost a separate art, but one which may be followed with beneficial results even by expert game shots.

OF HOLDING ON.

Snap-shooting and the "hold-on" principle of aiming are synonymous. Some fail to see how anyone firing a snap-shot—as they understand it—can possibly hold ahead with any amount of certainty, for the space of time which the opportunity affords in many cases is only sufficient to take in the situation and fire; it will not allow even for a mental calculation. Many favour the "hold-on" and snap-shooting system because it is prettier, safer, and, in the opinion of most, surer, and it offers, to say the least, many more chances of a full bag than the other way of aiming. First, it will be admitted that the *style* is far better in snap-shooting than in the "hold ahead" practice; secondly, it is safer, in so far that there is no tendency to "poking," which the hold ahead and slow calculating shots lean to, even though a little—a little which with young shooters is likely to become more. It must be remembered that "the man who hesitates is lost"; hesitation in firing, at any rate, means loss of game and perhaps everything else except experience to the shooter.

An instance of the danger of the "poking" aim once warned us of the dangers of the system even when practised by a sportsman and regular shooter of twenty-five years' standing who, on one occasion, allowed himself to be carried away by his excitement to the extent of " following up " a partridge at least three parts of a circle before firing. The bird rose on his left and flew low across his front, quartering to the right, until it had nearly completed the circle before it fell to the long-expected shot. The shooter had his gun to the shoulder the whole of the time the bird was on the wing, and in following up and trying to make the proper allowance his gun covered many of his companions, the beaters, and dogs, although, in the end, the bird only was shot; the attitudes of the shooter appeared extremely ludicrous to the others of the party after the muzzles of the gun were directed towards a safe quarter. Thirdly, very many more opportunities occur for snap-shots to one accustomed to take them than to one practising other methods—for instance, when shooting cover, either in line, alone, or by beaters.

After reading those paragraphs in this chapter relating to the physiology of shooting and optics, the reader will probably understand more of the reasons why some favour the " snap or hold-on " system; it is, moreover, much easier to become proficient at this style than at the other. Not much is to be said in favour of copying a good shot's style; everyone is built differently, and has different degrees of muscular sense; therefore everyone should find out for himself the method that suits him. To give one confidence there is only one necessity, and that is, that the shooter can rely on his gun coming up to the shoulder exactly to the same position every time.

OF POSITION IN SHOOTING AND THE ALIGNMENT OF THE GUN.

The accompanying illustrations show several positions in shooting and the proper alignment of the gun for game taking different directions of flight; these will be found to be pretty nearly correct, and at any rate will serve as a basis upon which young shooters may begin. The illustrations in this chapter showing positions of the gun for different shots will also be some kind of a guide for the beginner as to the fit and handling of his gun. It will be seen that the shooters follow the old style of allowing the stock of the gun at the comb to lie against the cheek; by this one is able to tell that the gun is in exact position. If the shooter has good command over it, he should fire the instant the stock touches his face; by always adopting one position for the head, shoulders, body, and feet, with the touch of the stock on the cheek as an indication for the time to fire, one will very soon make good progress in the art of snap-shooting.

Some quick shots, however, anticipate the time it takes to *fire* the gun and pull the trigger whilst raising the gun to the shoulder. This requires considerable practice to perfect, and the gun must, of course, be within an ace of the proper position ; but, however the practice may be deprecated, it is certainly *au fait* for trap- as well as general snap-shooting.

Showing Position for Ordinary Straight-away and Rising Shots.

For high overhead shots it is not advisable to shoot at a greater angle than is easy to the shooter; some men, even of fifty years old, can get back so as really to shoot game that has passed over them several yards.

For cross-shots, although in theory the gun should be held ahead, in some cases as much as 7 ft. at forty yards, yet in practice it is found that in holding

Bad Position—not to be imitated.

on to the head, as on page 454, is quite sufficient allowance to kill, though in many cross-shots at any angle not above 45 degrees the gun is always brought up from behind. It may be that the swing has the effect of throwing the muzzles more in that direction than is intended by alignment. If the gun is fired before the motion is stayed, the shot will, of course, fly in that direction in which the gun was swinging when the charge of shot left the muzzle.

Continental Style of Shooting.

The sportsmanlike use of the shot-gun implies much more than is included in good marksmanship.

The sportsman not only uses his gun, but must exercise his brains in order to use it properly. It is important to acquire an accurate judgment of distance in order to determine what is, and what is not, a sporting range at which to fire; it is also advisable to observe carefully the result of each shot, and mark where the game was struck : this may save much time in retrieving wounded birds ; but for the old-fashioned art of woodcraft there is little demand now, and good and safe marksmanship is considered a better qualification.

The modern style of shooting is the natural result of present-day methods of agriculture. The scythe and reaping machine have succeeded the sickle, and the stubbles are now shorn so close that they do not afford cover to partridges, and when partridges resort to them, as they do, to feed, at certain hours of the day, it is generally quite impossible to approach within range, either with or without dogs.

The sowing of root crops in rows has also spoiled the chance of the dogs in the turnips. The birds sneak out of the field as soon as the men and dogs enter it, as the game can see from one end of the field to the other, and cunningly escape unobserved. The sportsman who is determined to have some shooting resorts to driving, by which means he accomplishes his purpose, and also makes the game much more wild.

The sportsman who is determined to shoot over dogs and hunt his game in the old-fashioned way will find full instructions in the many books on shooting which have been published, but will need considerable experience before becoming successful. The fact that changed conditions have greatly handicapped his chances, and have forced sportsmen to other methods, may not deter him from persevering in his method, and it is quite possible, with hard work and much cunning, to out-manœuvre a few coveys by what practically amounts to tiring them out ; no one will grudge the sportsman whatever success he ultimately achieves.

The sportsman whose shoot is small and the game—not being hand-reared— scarce and wild, will be unable to practise driving to any advantage ; the best plan will be to walk up to the birds as afterwards described. The drive in the Midlands and Eastern and Southern Counties is the best manner for a proprietor or lessee to show his game, and it is generally the only way of securing a fair proportion of it.

To organise a drive upon a fairly large scale the assistance of many men as beaters will be required ; the plan is therefore only suited to a large party, and the management is a business requiring much knowledge, forethought, and preparation. The methods employed with the greatest chance of success are detailed in such a book as "Shooting," of the Badminton Series, to which the reader must refer for further information as to the management, or what may be called the "engineering," of work of this kind. The host or other responsible director, if he does what is considered to be his duty to the shooters, will have an onerous task to perform.

As to the shooters, they will learn very little of woodcraft or of the habits and habitat of the game, but they may have ample opportunities for testing their skill as marksmen and of observing the peculiarities of the flight of frightened birds ; and they may rightly enjoy the day's sport, in which they do not so much participate as—to use a Gallicism—assist.

J. A. R. Elliott's Position at the Trap.

The shooter called upon to take part in a day's sport of this kind will find, if partridges be the game sought, that the keepers or their assistants have, previous to the arrival of the guns, driven birds into convenient fields with sufficient cover to hold them—that is, with a growth which will hide the birds. The shooters are then posted behind fences, or even artificial screens, which will conceal them; they should be such as, whilst hiding the shooters, will permit them to observe the flight of the birds for from 60 to 100 yards of their nearest approach.

The shooter should be informed of the location of the other shooters and the direction in which the beaters will advance, and then go at once to his stand and

Captain Brewer's Position at the Trap.

wait quietly and expectant until the warning "mark over" of the beaters informs him that birds are on the wing.

All alert then, he will, as soon as any bird comes within range and within his circuit, be ready to fire. At all times he ought to be able to fire at the birds as they approach; successful work cannot be done if he is not. Occasionally, perhaps, two shooters will be stationed together; then one will take birds on the left and the other birds on the right—a rule which must be loyally observed, and to which the only exception is the firing at your companion's birds after he has fired both barrels and the birds are in range.

In partridge driving the stations are frequently changed. The object of driving is to break up the coveys as early as possible in the day, marking the direction of the escaped birds, and putting them over the guns again and again in successive drives, so that often a covey from which little is bagged in the morning will all be in the bag before night.

Pheasant driving is pursued, not so much of necessity for securing shots at the birds, as is the case with partridge driving, but for the object of obtaining sporting shots.

The drive is, or should be, so managed that the birds are forced to rise at some distance from the shooters, and approach at a good height, and fly faster than if put up near the guns in hedgerows or cover. Here, again, the shooter will be called upon to exercise his skill as a wing shot. There will be little walking— no hunting in the true sense—and the man who can keep cool, shoot deliberately, and observes the usual etiquette of the shooting field, will probably enjoy good sport, unspoiled by blank covers or too wary birds.

In cover shooting, some guns are usually told off to walk up with the beaters. These do not, as a rule, get so much shooting, or such pretty shooting, as those posted forward; they see more of the working of the "battue," and require to be even more careful not only as to the direction in which they shoot, but when to fire and what to fire at.

Grouse driving has become very popular with all able to rent or subscribe to a moor. The guns are stationed in batteries, butts, or shelters, especially constructed for the purpose. In Derbyshire they are occasionally posted behind the stone walls common to the country. Fifteen to fifty beaters will drive, commencing from half a mile to two miles from the guns. Driven grouse fly at great speed, and afford excellent opportunities for a display of skilful marksmanship.

The young shooter will do well to observe most punctiliously the accepted conventionalities of the shooting field. Smartness of manner is considered very bad form. A young man is not supposed to be an unerring shot, nor expected to tell good stories. If a shooting companion, older than yourself, and a shot of established reputation, fires both barrels at a bird and misses, it is better to let the bird go, even though within range, than "drop" it, to your companion's mortification. You have life before you, and may get other opportunities. Do not shoot to wound game, but to kill it. If a wounded bird struggles in front of you from a companion's gun, drop it if you can. Explain to the first shooter that you did so to save time in gathering it, or remark simply " Yours."

The compilers of books of instructions to young shooters deem it necessary to advise beginners against calling attention to the clever shots they make. It has never been the writer's luck to meet with young sportsmen guilty of this practice ; they are prone to remark " Clever shot," or " That was well done," when someone else has brought down a difficult bird, when perhaps absolute silence would have been preferable. They will talk of their performances at other times ; and so, unfortunately, will older men who ought to know better.

In order to stand well in with shooting companions, and your host, or his keepers, avoid risky shots, make yourself well acquainted with your gun's power, shoot at nothing not well within its range, and do not bang away at game too close. Learn to judge distances accurately, and you will make few mistakes on this score. Give fair play to the game and to your fellow-shooters, and if a man near you is getting more shooting than he can manage, whilst you have none, it is his place to call you to help him, not yours to edge up to him. Think of this when you have more than your full share of luck.

When walking in line up to birds, or with the beaters in covert, mind and keep to that line. It is dangerous to you and your companions to be either ahead or behind it.

When shooting with one friend, take the birds in the covey on your side, and ground game directly before you and on your own side.

To fire at low birds in covert is always very dangerous. In the same way, low birds coming towards you from the line of beaters must not be shot at unless you know that the beaters are well beyond the range of your gun.

Do not fire at anything you imagine to be a rabbit moving in covert ; this is the way dogs, foxes, and sometimes beaters, get shot.

Do not waste your time and that of your companions by insisting upon a bird you *thought* you saw fall being retrieved.

When shooting alone, or over dogs, the sportsman has greater latitude as to what, when, where, and how to shoot.

The shooting of grouse over dogs is fully treated in all old sporting works and several modern ones. The well-known authority upon sporting dogs, " H. H.," has written an excellent series of articles which appeared in *Land and Water*, and has since been published by Sampson, Low, Marston and Co., under the title of " The Scientific Education of the Dog."

To get partridges—that is, to make a bag—when not shooting over dogs, it is necessary to lose no time, and in order to avoid loss of time there should be a good dog at the service of each gun in the line. This dog preferably should be worked by the shooter, but there should be always a steady dog, not of the dashing sort, kept in reserve. The proceeding will then be as follows :—The line advances and birds drop to the gun. Do not stop the line, but as soon as it has advanced to within 30 or 40 yards of the fall of the birds, send forward the dog that belongs to, or has been allotted to, the gun that has killed. This dog will have marked the bird if he is worth his "grub," and he will have it in the keeper's or his master's hands before the line has reached its fall, and so be ready to be sent for a second bird before the ground is tainted by humanity—that is, before the fall of the bird has been crossed by the line. Sometimes the best of dogs will fail in this quick find, and it is then that the dog and man in reserve should come to a stick stuck up at the fall of the bird by the keeper in attendance on the gun who dropped the bird, whose dog should be called off, so that the line may proceed.

In the early morning the partridges are usually to be found feeding in the stubbles, and as it is next to useless to attempt to get within range of them there, it will save time if two or three men will walk the stubbles before the shooting is commenced, and thus send the birds to better cover.

A mixed line of shooters, beaters, and keepers is then formed, and if game be plentiful it is advisable to have as many retrievers as there are shooters, as better speed will be made if beaters or keepers are not occupied in going from one gun to the other for birds that ought to have been retrieved at once ; a badly broken dog will, however, prove the greatest nuisance which can be introduced into the party. The beaters should also mark as nearly as possible where each bird has fallen, and in this they can be aided by the man who shot ; when two men (beaters for choice) from different positions on the base line of the triangle mark a towered bird, and each walks his correct line towards it, the proceeding will frequently save a prolonged search by confirming accurately, or rectifying an error in, the marking, for the two lines will cut each other at the exact fall of the bird.

In turnips, partridges are always more easily approached if the party make their progress across the drills. If it is preferable to walk in a line with the drills in order to drive the partridges towards any other particular cover, each man should change frequently a few steps to the right and left of the drill in his direct line.

When there is no object to be gained by driving the birds in any particular direction, the line will wheel at the end of the field and take the next strip, otherwise the steps may be retraced over the ground already traversed, and the line re-formed so that the field may be worked uniformly in the one direction ; as the field is worked to the finish the flank men of the line will advance so as to hem in any birds which may have moved to the extremity of the field and are unwilling to leave it.

The use of kites is said to have the effect of driving the game to other ground, and should, therefore, be used rarely by proprietors. Lessors sometimes stipulate that kites shall not be used.

Shootings leased of farmers cannot be well preserved without great expense, and some farms are so badly situated that the game bred upon them frequents neighbouring lands in preference. Some lessors obtain high prices for shooting which it is almost impossible to work with satisfactory results. More game can sometimes be bagged from land the shooting rights of which are sold for sixpence an acre, than from other ground in the same locality for which five times the price is obtained. The price paid for shooting bears no relation whatever to its value.

Where the shooting is small, a couple of hundred acres or so, and the land well farmed, it is advisable to stipulate that at least a few acres shall be sown with something that will afford suitable cover to the birds late in the season. Turnips, potatoes, clover, mustard, etc., are good; but to hold the birds late in the season, if there is no natural cover on the shooting, a patch of buckwheat will afford that protection and shelter the birds prefer; grass, furze, fern, ample hedgerows, and some planted cover will attract partridges, and in order to increase the stock the birds, except cock-birds, should not be shot down close.

If an attempt is made to rear pheasants there must be a "pheasantry" and suitable plantation on the shooting, and at least a couple of men to look after the birds; a trouble when increasing the stock of pheasants on a small shooting is the greater relative expense compared with that of doing the work on a larger scale, and the difficulty of keeping the birds at home. To raise pheasants for your neighbours' shooting is often unavoidable, and if the covert frequented by pheasants is made more attractive by often placing tempting food there, a stock may be increased by birds from adjacent coverts; barley, beans, malt, raisins, etc., are used for this purpose, and it is said that a few hundred of common gooseberry-bushes planted as underwood make a first-rate cover.

Hares are becoming scarce in this country; they are always easy to hit, but not always to kill dead. They may be looked for in coverts, on fallows, grass-land, and amongst turnips. In Scotland the Alpine hare, a different variety, is plentiful, and these hares are driven owing to the nature of the ground. Good work is not so easy as some people seem to think. The gun has to keep absolutely still, and although it is easy to hit a single hare, the right time to shoot, so as to get off all your barrels with effect, is not what any novice can select with certainty.

The woodcock is, unfortunately, still more rarely found. When put up in thick cover, it is one of the most difficult birds to bag : if shot at when close, it will probably be smashed ; if the sportsman waits, it will be lost sight of in the covert, its turns to right and left being most erratic and unexpected.

Rabbit shooting is the easiest to be obtained in this country, and there are very few people fond of shooting who cannot command at least a few days' sport of a friendly farmer or landowner.

Rabbit shooting, the most generally practised of sports with the shot-gun, is the most dangerous, because the speed with which the rabbit bolts is provocative of random shooting. It is not uncommon for a rabbit to run between the shooter's legs and be shot within three yards of him by some reckless shooter on the alert for fur. In a warren or quarry a rabbit about to disappear over a ridge will be shot neatly just as the hat of a man on the other side becomes visible. When ferreting it is quite impossible to keep men from getting into places where, for their safety, they should not be. The young sportsman can more easily do irreparable damage when rabbiting than at any other sport, and must consequently use the utmost care to avoid accident. Always fire for the head of a rabbit. Shoot carefully in covert, and straight for the rabbit, or not at all.

Another dangerous practice is the division of shooters by a substantial hedge, with dogs working the hedgerows : the rabbits will run out and straight along the hedge, and then run in again. It is unadvisable to shoot towards the hedge under any pretence ; dangerous to do so unless you know exactly the position of the man, or men, on the other side of it.

If rabbits are put out properly and the shooters keep well back, good shots may be obtained when the rabbits make a run across the open for fresh cover.

The young shooter may ruin his prospects as a sportsman by a single indiscretion—the making of a risky or a dangerous shot ; he will not be an acceptable companion to shooting men unless he endeavours to kill his game in a sportsmanlike manner, avoiding the wounding of game, and not firing at quite impossible distances.

The man who may be relied upon as safe to shoot with under every condition, and who, in addition, is better pleased by killing a few birds in a clean and sportsmanlike manner than in making a heavy bag, will have opportunities for obtaining sport denied, on principle, to others.

CHAPTER XVIII.

TRAP SHOOTING.

THE HISTORY OF PIGEON SHOOTING.

THE origin of trap shooting may be traced to the ancient pastime of popinjay shooting, a game practised by the ancient Greeks and the expert bowmen of mediæval times.

The popinjay was a stuffed parrot or fowl placed upon the top of a pole, and used as a target; in some instances a living bird was used, a certain amount of liberty being given to it by the length of cord used to secure it to the pole. Homer, in the "Iliad," mentions popinjay shooting, a dove being the mark, and prizes being shot for. The Toxophilite Society during the last century held frequent meetings for popinjay shooting; the last recorded took place near Highgate, in September, 1792.

Pigeon shooting as a sport may be said to date from about the middle of this century, although there were occasional matches and contests earlier. The first handicap is said to have been shot upon Mr. Purdey's grounds at Willesden in 1856, but previous to this there had been fashionable contests at the "Old Hats" public-house, on the Uxbridge Road at Ealing, near London. The "Old Hats" obtained its name from the fact that the pigeons used for the matches were placed in holes in the ground, and covered with old hats. The "Red House," at Battersea, was afterwards the favourite metropolitan resort for wager shooting. The first *bonâ-fide* Pigeon Club was formed at Hornsey Wood House. Traps were first used here, and the fashionable pigeon gun of the period was a large-bore single gun, quickly superseded by the ordinary double-barrelled game gun. The illustration on page 470 is from a contemporary sketch of the grounds, used in "Stonehenge's" book, "Rural Sports."

Since the days of the Hornsey Wood Club live pigeon shooting has been at times exceedingly popular, and clubs for the practice of this sport have been formed in all parts of the world.

The Gun Club, London, is one of the best known, and was founded about

Pigeon Shooting at Hornsey Wood.

1861 by Sir G. East, Colonel Vansittart, and G. Battock. The rules of this Club, and of the "Hurlingham," of more recent formation, are almost identical, and are those generally adopted by the leading clubs at home and abroad. Of recent years the sport has declined in favour, both in this country and in the United States. The "Hurlingham" ground has recently been closed, while in America many of the States have entirely prohibited the trapping and subsequent shooting of pigeons.

The Blue Rock Pigeon.

The Inanimate Bird, or Clay Pigeon, has largely taken the place of the live bird, and when thrown from suitable traps it affords excellent practice, some of the newer pattern "birds" being exceptionally difficult to "kill."

PIGEONS AND APPLIANCES FOR PIGEON SHOOTING.

The pigeon generally employed for trap purposes is known as the Blue Rock. The best variety, the Lincolnshire Blue Rock, retains the wild nature of the common wild Rock Pigeon. The birds are fed in Lincolnshire by the farmers in winter time, who also raise cotes for them at a good distance from their other buildings, as the wilder the pigeons and the nearer the coast they are raised the stronger and more hardy they are. The true Blue Rock affords the best sport, and is much the hardest to kill ; being small in the body, quick in flight at starting, tough in nature, and game to the death—especially the hens.

Other Blue Rocks are bred in Oxfordshire and Yorkshire in large quantities, but are inferior to the Lincolnshire birds.

Many of the so-called Blue Rocks are also imported from Antwerp ; in fact the greater portion of the pigeons used for trap shooting are brought over from that port, and sold here as Blue Rocks.   Some years ago a number of Blue Rocks were exported to France and Belgium for breeding purposes, and it is their offspring we now import ; the foreign climate has not, however, improved them, as they possess none of that gameness peculiar to the English bird.

The real Rock is not always of the same colour and markings, but through some cross with the domestic pigeon there are white and copper-coloured Rocks, which differ only from the Blue Rocks in colour.

The next best bird to the Blue Rock is the English Skimmer, which is chiefly employed at the second-rate clubs, as are also true Antwerp pigeons.

Pigeons intended for trap shooting should not be used to being handled, and at the principal clubs several stringent rules are in force against any ill-treatment or mutilation of the birds.   The purveyor to the club should find it to his interest to supply the best, that is, the strongest, healthiest birds, and the trapper should be the servant of the purveyor, so that it is to his interest that the birds fly strongly.   The hampers used should be spacious and well ventilated, and a proper place provided for them under shelter or in the shade.   The retrieved birds should not be placed on or near the hampers containing the living pigeons.   The purveyor should provide good dogs for retrieving.   The puller should be a club servant.

Then, if the ground be properly laid out and arranged and the standard rules adhered to, any collusion as to the trapping of weak birds may be prevented, and any form of dishonesty, except the wilful missing of birds, may be guarded against.

The pulling apparatus should be of the very best.   Buss's is a very good one ; that used at Monte Carlo, and the Hurlingham pulling apparatus, are also good.   The traps must not be too small and should work smoothly, being flush with the ground when pulled over.   The cords or wires to operate them should be underground.

HURLINGHAM CLUB RULES.
Revised July, 1901.

1. The Referee's decision shall be final.

2. A miss-fire, if it occurs with first barrel, is no shot under any circumstances.

3. If the miss-fire occurs with the second barrel, the shooter having failed to kill with his first, he may claim another bird ; but he must fire off the first barrel with a blank cartridge before firing the second, and he must not pull both triggers at the same time

4. The shooter in a match or sweepstakes shall be at his shooting mark at the expiration of two minutes from the last shot, unless in the case of an accident, when the Referee shall decide what time shall be allowed to remedy the accident.

5. The shooter's feet shall be behind the shooting mark until after his gun is discharged. If, in the opinion of the Referee, the shooter is baulked by any antagonist or looker on, or by the trapper, whether by accident or otherwise, he may be allowed another bird.

6. The shooter, when he is at his mark ready to shoot, shall give the caution "Are you ready?" to the puller, and then call "Pull." Should the trap be pulled without the word being given the shooter may take the bird or not, but if he fires the bird must be deemed to be taken.

7. If, on the trap being pulled, the bird does not rise, it is at the option of the shooter to take it or not; if not, he must declare it by saying "No bird"; but should he fire after declaring, it is not to be scored for or against him.

8. If a bird once out of ground should return and fall dead within the boundary, it must be scored a lost bird.

9. If the shooter advances to the mark and orders the trap to be pulled, and does not shoot at the bird, or his gun is not properly loaded, or does not go off owing to his own negligence, that bird is to be scored lost. If the gun should break in the act of firing it is "no bird" under any circumstances.

10. A bird shot on the ground with the first barrel is "no bird," but it may be shot on the ground with the second barrel, if it has been fired at with the first barrel while on the wing; but if the shooter misses with the first and discharges his second barrel, it is to be accounted a lost bird, in case of not falling within bounds.

11. Only one person to be allowed to pick up the bird (or a dog, if the shooter will allow it), No instrument is to be used for this purpose. All birds must be gathered by the dog or trapper, and no member shall have the right to gather his own bird, or to touch it with his hand or gun.

12. In Single Shooting, if more than one bird is liberated, the shooter may call "No bird," and claim another shot; but if he shoots he must abide by the consequences.

13. The shooter must not leave the shooting mark under any pretence to follow up any bird that will not rise, nor may he return to his mark after he has once quitted it, to fire his second barrel.

14. In matches or in sweepstakes when shot is limited, any shooter found to have in his gun more shot than is allowed, is to be at once disqualified.

15. Any shooter is compelled to unload his gun on being challenged; but if the charge is found not to exceed the allowance, the challenger shall pay forthwith £1 to the shooter.

16. None but members can shoot except on the occasion of private matches.

17. No wire cartridges or concentrators allowed, or other substance to be mixed with the shot.

18. In all handicaps, sweepstakes, or matches, the standard bore of the gun is No. 12. Members shooting with less to go in at the rate of half a yard for every bore less than 12 down to 16-bore. Eleven-bore guns to stand back half a yard from the handicap distance, and no guns over 11-bore allowed.

19. The winner of a sweepstakes of the value of ten sovereigns, including his own stake, goes back two yards; under that sum, one yard, provided there be over five shooters. Members saving or dividing in an advertised event will be handicapped accordingly.

20. Should any member shoot at a distance nearer than that at which he is handicapped, it shall be scored "no bird"

21. That for the future the charge of powder is limited to four drachms   Chilled shot and "sawdust" powder may be used.   The weight of guns not to exceed 8 lbs.   Size of shot restricted to Nos. 5, 6, 7, 8.   Charge of shot limited to 1¼ oz.

22. All muzzle-loaders shall be loaded with shot from the Club bowls.

23. If any bird escapes through any opening in the paling, it shall be a "no bird," if in the Referee's opinion it could not have flown over the palings, but in no instance shall it be scored a dead bird.

24. From the 1st of May the advertised events shall begin at three o'clock, unless otherwise notified, and no shooter will be admitted after the end of the second round in any advertised event.

25. No scouting allowed on the Club premises, and no pigeon to be shot at in the shooting ground except by the shooter standing at his mark.   Anyone infringing this rule will be fined £1.

RULES FOR DOUBLE RISES.

1. In Double Shooting, when more than two traps are pulled, the shooter may call "No birds," and claim two more ; but if he shoots he must abide by the consequences.

2. If, on the traps being pulled, the birds do not rise, it is at the option of the shooter to take them or not.   If not, he must declare by saying "No birds."

3. If, on the traps being pulled, one bird does not rise, he cannot demand another double rise; but he must wait and take the bird when it flies.

4. A bird shot on the ground, if the other bird is missed, is a lost bird; but if the other bird is killed, the shooter may demand another two birds.

5. If the shooter's gun misses fire with the first barrel, it is no shot under any circumstances.   If the miss-fire occurs with the second barrel, the shooter having killed with the first, he may demand another bird, but may only use one barrel.

GUN CLUB RULES.
Revised July, 1901.

1. A miss-fire with the first barrel is no shot under any circumstances.   If the shooter miss-fire with the second barrel, he shall have another shot, but with the ordinary charge of powder and no shot in the first barrel.

2. If the gun be locked, or not cocked, or not loaded, and the bird flies away, it is a "lost bird"; if the stock or cock should break in the act of firing, it is "no bird."

3. If the trap is pulled without notice from the shooter, he has the option to take the bird or not.

4. The puller shall not pull the trap until the trapper and the dog are back in their places, even should the shooter call "Pull."

5. If, on the trap being pulled, the bird does not rise, the shooter to take it or not at his option ; but if not he must declare it by saying "No bird" before it is on the wing.   If, however, the bird rises and settles before the shooter fires, it shall be at his option to refuse it or not.

6. SINGLE SHOOTING.—If more than one bird be liberated, the shooter has the option of calling "No bird."

7. In shooting at a bird, should both barrels go off at once, it shall score the same as if they had been let off "separately."

8. A bird to be scored good must be gathered by the dog or man without the aid of a ladder or any other instrument, and all birds not gathered in the ground, or gathered inside the pavilion inclosure, having flown over the railings, to be scored lost.

9. If a bird which has been shot perches or settles on the top of the fence, or on any of the buildings in the ground higher than the fence, it is to be scored a " lost bird."

10. If a bird once out of the ground return and fall dead within the boundary, it must be scored a " lost bird."

11. If the first barrel be fired whilst the bird is on the ground, should the bird be killed by either barrel it is " no bird " ; if missed, it is lost. It may be shot on the ground with the second barrel, if it has been fired at with the first barrel while on the wing.

12. The shooter is bound at once to gather his bird, or depute some person so to do when called upon ; but in so doing he must not be assisted by any other person, or use any description of implement. Should the shooter be in any way baffled by his opponent, or by any other person or dog, he can claim another bird with the sanction of the Referee.

13. The shooter having once left the mark after shooting at the bird, cannot shoot at it again under any circumstances.

14. In matches or in sweepstakes, any shooter found to have in his gun any more shot or powder than is allowed, to be at once disqualified.

15. Any shooter is compelled to unload his gun on being challenged ; but if the charge is found not to exceed the allowance, the challenger shall pay £1 to the shooter, which must be paid before he (the challenger) shoots again.

16. Officers of the Army and Navy on full pay, provided they are *bonâ-fide* guests of a member for the day, are allowed to shoot in any sweepstakes to which the Club does not add prize or money. Members accredited from recognised Foreign clubs shall only be allowed to shoot for four weeks during the Season, after which they must be proposed and seconded as candidates if they desire to shoot.

17. Breechloaders not to be loaded until the shooter is at the mark and the trapper has returned to his place. On leaving the mark, should a cartridge not have been discharged, it is to be removed before the shooter turns his face from the traps.

18. No wire cartridges allowed ; nor is any bone-dust or other substance to be mixed with the shot.

19. Should any shooter shoot at a distance nearer than his proper distance, the bird if killed is " no bird " ; if missed, a " lost bird " ; but should he, by direction of the Referee or Scorer, shoot at any wrong distance, the bird, if missed, shall be " no bird," and the shooter shall be allowed another, which, if killed, shall be scored.

20. 1¼ oz. of shot and 4 dr. of black powder, or its equivalent in any other description of gunpowder, is the maximum charge.

21. In shooting for the principal advertised events, members can enter before the commencement of the third round, unless it shall be within the knowledge of the Referee that any member proposing to enter has been on the ground during the first round, in which case he shall not be permitted to shoot after the commencement of the second round ; for all other sweepstakes entries must be made before the commencement of the second round.

22. The sweepstakes preceding the chief event of the day shall be divided in equal proportions by those shooters who may be in at the end of the round at or after three o'clock, as the Referee may direct.

23. The baskets containing the birds for the whole day's shooting shall be numbered by paint at the back. The baskets, in the order they are to be brought out and trapped, shall be drawn for by the Referee, and the baskets so marked shall be used in the order of rotation in which they are drawn

HANDICAPPING RULES.

(From Pigeon Shooting Rules published by the " Field.")

24. That a Handicapper who does not shoot or bet on pigeon shooting be appointed by the Club.

25. That a new handicap be made previous to the commencement of each shooting season.

26. That when the handicap is made the distances shall range from twenty-two to thirty-five yards.

27. That three members of the Club be appointed as a Shooting Committee, to whom the handicapper shall submit his new handicap for approval at the commencement of each shooting season. The Committee to receive complaints of members about their handicap distances : two to form a quorum.

28. That during the season the handicapper shall alter the handicap according to his judgment previous to each shooting day.

29. That every new member shall commence at twenty-six yards, except the handicapper has special reasons to the contrary.

30. The Referee's decision shall be final.

31. In handicap sweepstakes, winners of £5 go back one yard; £10 and upwards, two yards; £20 and over, three yards, for the day. These penalties do not apply to the advertised events of the day unless they have been incurred in such advertised events.

32. In handicaps the amount of division is to be declared to the Referee, and the members dividing shall be penalised to the amount they receive. This Rule not to apply to the saving of stakes. All penalties for winning to be exclusive of the winner's stake.

33. In large sweepstakes, if the money be over £50 there shall be two prizes; if over £100, three prizes; and over £200, four prizes.

34. No shooting at birds thrown up, or other irregular practice with guns, shall be permitted on the ground at any time.

35. Should two members agree to save stakes, and one of these divide with a third person, the member so dividing shall pay the full stake to the member who does not win or divide.

36. No member to be allowed to shoot in any sweepstakes or handicap until he shall have paid the amount of his entry to the Scorer, and should he shoot without having paid his stake before firing his first shot he may be excluded from taking further part in such competition.

37. Saving of stakes shall apply to any member winning or dividing the first, second, third, or fourth prize, unless otherwise mutually agreed upon.

38. The deductions from all sweepstakes of the value of £8 and upwards in the summer season, and £5 and upwards in the winter season, is ten per cent., to go to the funds of the Club.

39. During the hours of shooting, after two o'clock cn Club shooting days, when eight members are present in summer and five in winter, no match or other shooting shall take place without the regular deduction being made from the pools for the Club prize fund.

40. No guns above 11-bore allowed.

41. Members shooting under an assumed name must have the same registered in a book by the Secretary. Only one assumed name is allowed except by special sanction of the Committee.

The following fines will be strictly enforced :

1. No bet shall be made by any member who has been called up to shoot after passing the inclosure gate, even should he have been standing there previous to his name being called. Any member infringing this Rule will be fined £5, which shall be paid before he shoots again.

2. Pointing a gun at anyone, or firing a loaded gun without permission, except at the mark, £5.

3. Any person firing at a bird after it has passed the safety flags will be fined £5, and the bird shall be scored lost.

4. A shooter calling " No bird " must not shoot at the same under a penalty of £1.

RULES OF THE MEMBERS' £100 CHALLENGE CUP.

This cup must be won three times consecutively to become the property of the winner. The minimum number of shooters is five, and the entry £5 each, but the Committee have the option of making the stakes £25 each when they consider it desirable. Distance thirty yards.

Competitions for this cup are continuous from year to year. The cup not to be shot for before the first Saturday in May in each season.

The sweepstakes for the Members' Challenge Cup shall be £25 on the Saturday in the International week, and £10 the Saturday before and the Saturday after.

Members of affiliated clubs or guests shooting by invitation can enter for the competition, and can win or divide the money in the pool, but the Cup can only be held or won by a member of the Club.

RULES OF THE TUESDAY HANDICAP CUP, VALUE £50.

This cup must be won twice consecutively, or four times in the season, to become the property of the winner. Ten per cent. is deducted every competition for the accumulative fund, until it be won. The minimum number of shooters is eight. Entry £3.

The accumulative fund can only be won by a member of the Club.

GENERAL PIGEON SHOOTING RULES.

Inclosed grounds. The wire fence erected within the inclosure is the boundary, as at the Hurlingham Club and the Gun Club.

Open boundary, 60 yards from the centre trap where obtainable, or else the fence the boundary. A line to be run out level with the shooter who stands the farthest from the trap ; and a bird falling dead behind this line cannot be scored. Traps 5 yards apart.

When a bird perches on a fence, tree, or building, and closes its wings, it is a lost bird. If it falls inside the boundary before closing its wings, it is scored to the shooter.

In the North the general rule is one trap, 21 yards rise. Gun to be held below the elbow until the bird is on the wing. 1 oz. shot ; boundary 60 yards.

In shooting from H and T traps both traps are to be filled ; only one barrel allowed ; distance from 21 to 35 yards. No spring traps permitted.

The Hurlingham Club boundary was about 90 yards in a straight line from the centre trap.

The Gun Club (Notting Hill) boundary is marked by a wire netting fence, about 2 ft. 6 in. high, erected some 30 yards from each trap.

The Monaco Boundary—a wire fence about 40 inches high, in a straight line from the centre trap.

MODIFICATIONS.

On the Continent the rules of the Cercle des Patineurs of Paris are usually adhered to; they are practically the Hurlingham rules. The charge is limited: 4 drams of powder by measure, and $1\frac{1}{4}$ ounce of shot, is the maximum; the boundary is 87 yards (80 metres) from the pavilion; 54 yards from the centre trap; the traps are five metres from each other.

> The shooter has a right to another bird if his gun miss-fires or refuses to go off through any fault not his own.
> The pigeon is lost if the shooter has neglected to cock his gun, to load it, or to place on the cap.
> If the first barrel misses fire, and the shooter fires the second, he loses his right to another pigeon, unless the second barrel also miss-fires.
> If the second barrel misses fire, the shooter having fired and missed the bird with the first, he may claim another bird; but in that case both barrels must be loaded, the first with powder only, and neither barrel must be discharged until after the trap is sprung.
> It is forbidden to shoot both barrels at the same time.

The standard gauge is twelve: any gun of larger bore than this is handicapped half a metre for each size; thus ten-bores, the maximum bore allowed, stand one metre back, fourteen-bores advance half a metre, sixteen-bores one metre; no further advantage is allowed to any smaller bore.

HINTS ON TRAP SHOOTING.

Trap shooting cannot be recommended as a profession. However good a shot a sportsman may be, he will find so many uncertainties in trap shooting that it is doubtful if any person shooting continually will make trap shooting pay expenses.

At an ordinary bird, shot at under Hurlingham rules by an average good shot, the chances are five to two in favour of the shooter. To be considered a good shot the number of kills must average more than 70 per cent. Mr. "Grace," at one time considered a reliable shot, with a Greener gun once scored a percentage of 84·3 kills in a series of International contests. Other shooters have occasionally made a higher percentage in a short series of matches.

In a series of International matches, out of 1,120 birds shot at by thirty-six different shooters, 79·9 per cent. were killed, and this is about the average in matches between first-rate shots.

"The Gun Club" Ground, Notting Hill.

The following hints may be of use to young shooters who wish to try their skill in trap shooting :—Commence at a short distance—say 18 yards—at live birds ; stand in an easy position, gripping the gun well forward with the left hand. This is a great aid in quick shooting. Do not stare at the trap which you think will give the most difficult shot to you ; and if you do not particularly regard any trap, so much the better. Do not say "Pull" until you are quite ready to shoot, and have your attention concentrated upon what you are about to do. When the bird gets up, up with the gun quickly but steadily, and the alignment should be perfect, and the trigger pulled as the gun reaches the shoulder. Some pigeon guns are so constructed that at 40 yards' range they will throw the body of the charge a few inches higher than the line of aim ; consequently, at any distance up to 45 yards, you will have the advantage over a bird rising in flight.

When shooting at 30 yards' rise this quality of the gun will be the more requisite, as to be a sure trap shot you will require generally to kill your pigeon within four or five yards of the trap, and for that distance the pigeon generally rises, and if he does not do so immediately will in all probability do so before he is out of range. The happy medium between snapping just over the trap, and "poking" after the pigeon, must be sought.

In choosing a gun, all will depend upon the rules under which it will be used, but it may be said that as a rule a gun of $7\frac{1}{2}$ lbs. will be the thing. Let it be taken from the rack just before going to the mark, and let a point be made of loading and cocking it methodically. Quite a large number of birds are scored lost every year because the shooter has forgotten to cock his gun, or to move the safety off, or from some other cause equally easy to prevent.

It is best to take no heed either of bystanders or trappers when going to the mark, and if one can be quite deaf to the shouts from the "ring" the score is likely to benefit.

In contending in a handicap it is the time spent in waiting between the rounds that tires and tries the nerve and patience. At Monte Carlo a man may have to fire but nine times, and possibly have the whole of two afternoons in which to do it. In contesting a match at 100 birds it must be remembered that the task will be trying to endurance ; and if a lighter gun can be found which suits as well as a heavy one, the use of it will enhance the shooter's chance of success. The shortest time occupied by the match will be two hours and a half, and it may drag along for double that time.

In match shooting the percentage of birds killed will be greater than in handicap shooting, and unless the shooter knows, by experience or former practice, that he can kill on the average ninety birds out of one hundred, he will do best not to contest a match with the best shots of the day.

Drive straight to the shooting-ground, so as to arrive at the time the shooting is advertised to commence. Waste no time in "plating" your gun. If the results of the shooting at the target should not please you, you will lose confidence in your gun and gain nothing. You should ascertain that the gun shoots well, and that the cartridges are suitably loaded, *before* you get to the shooting-ground. Keep yourself to the matter in hand, and pay no attention either to the remarks of the contestants or the "betting." Having won or lost, leave the ground at once. Unless the ground is one not often visited, trial shots before the serious shooting commences are not to be recommended. Upon visiting a town for the purpose of contesting the International Tournaments, it is best to lodge at some distance from the shooting-ground, and to go there only so often as the business of the contests requires it ; nothing is gained by constantly hanging about the shooting-ground and its vicinity, nor by experimenting in it.

LIVE BIRDS AND SMALL LOADS.

A modern variation of ordinary trap shooting is to use small loads of shot, thus greatly handicapping the shooter and increasing the chances of the bird. This form demands greater skill in wing shooting, perhaps, but does not require so good a gun as when a clever shot is handicapped by being put back—say to thirty yards or beyond. The sport has attained considerable popularity in the North of England, and it is usually contested at 21 yards' rise. The shooter is restricted to the use of one barrel and must not use more than one half-ounce of shot, or some other fraction, as 3, 5, or 7 eighths of an ounce, may be agreed upon. Usually No. 8 shot is chosen, and it is rare that even an expert shot, well used to this variety of trap shooting, accounts for more than half the birds. The charge of powder is proportionately reduced with the decreased load of shot—2 drams for ¾ ounce, etc. The birds are generally well trained, and fetch high prices ; they escape unhurt or are killed, few get away wounded, some are trapped a dozen times or more. Up to the present no special gun has been produced for this class of shooting.

RECORD SCORES.

When pigeon shooting first became fashionable it was considered very good shooting if the marksman grassed half his birds ; this at the short rises and with the old-fashioned wide boundaries. That it should be possible for a wing shot to kill all his birds in a match at 100 pigeons would have been doubted twenty years ago ; for when the first edition of this book was published the records made by

Captain Bogardus in 1880 were doubted by critics or attributed to good luck. Nothing is more noticeable than the great improvement since made in marksmanship.   The highest possible score at even long rises, and with the usual boundary, does not excite particular astonishment, and the killing of a hundred birds straight has now been accomplished several times in American public matches.   The improvements in guns and ammunition—particularly, perhaps, the use of the best smokeless powder—have contributed in no small degree to the higher scores which have been made.   The trap shooter is furnished with the closest-shooting gun money can buy, and usually is so sure of his aim that, as in the Brewer match, the second barrel is but rarely employed, and when this advantage is taken, it is more by way of precaution against the possible escape of a grassed bird than as making good a miss with the first barrel. When out of 200 birds shot at in succession all are killed and 199 scored, it is certainly proof that the gun shoots well and with regularity—is, in fact, absolutely trustworthy with the ammunition used—and so much may be allowed without any disparagement of the wonderful skill in wing shooting the performance of such a feat displays.

The following record scores are of undoubted interest, and may be accepted as authoritative.

PIGEON SHOOTING AND THE BEST SCORES.

One of the best scores first recorded is that of Captain A. H. Bogardus, who on July 2nd, 1880, succeeded in scoring 99 birds out of 100, the 47th bird falling dead out of bounds.   This was made in a match with Mr. Rimmell, for 250 dollars a side.   Bogardus, 30 ; Rimmell, 28 yds. : 100 birds, 5 traps, weather fair, and birds in good condition.

Other scores by Captain Bogardus are in a match with Mr. Wallace, at the Gun Club Grounds, July 19th, 1878, resulting in a tie, each shooter scoring 79 birds out of 100.   The following Wednesday the tie was shot off, resulting in a win for Mr. Wallace ; he killing 72 birds to the Captain's 61.   On July the 23rd, in the same year, the Captain shot a match with Mr. H. Cholmondeley-Pennell at the same grounds ; the scores being—Captain Bogardus, 71 ; Mr. Cholmondeley-Pennell, 69. These scores were among the best ever made in England.

On the 16th March, 1881, Dr. Carver and Mr. W. Scott shot off a match at Hendon, 100 pigeons each, 30 yards rise.   Score—Dr. Carver, 79 ; Mr. Scott, who grassed 26 in succession, scored 74.   Young Nimrod, a child of eleven, with a Greener 28-bore choked treble-wedge-fast gun, and using $1\frac{1}{2}$ drs. powder and $\frac{3}{4}$ oz. shot, in public matches, has grassed 17, 11, and 13 without a miss at 27 yards, and has, upon more than one occasion, killed 38 out of 50.

On February 7th, 1881, a match was shot off at the Welsh Harp, Hendon, between Dr. Carver and Mr. W. Scott. Dr. Carver used throughout the match a Greener choke-bore gun. Mr. Scott also used a Greener, but after the match commenced shot .with the Greener and a London gun irregularly. The score was—Dr. Carver, 66 birds; Mr. Scott, 62. The stakes amounted to £400. The birds were the finest and quickest seen during the winter, and the weather was vile : the greater part of the match being shot in a blinding snowstorm and a driving squall from the south-west.

Dr. Carver made several matches with the best trap-shots of England. He was beaten once by Mr. Heygate, of the Gun Club, in a match of 25 birds a side.

Dr. Carver tied with Mr. A. J. Stuart-Wortley in a match for £500 a side, shot at the Hendon Ground, December 8th, 1882—score, 83 each. This match was the more exciting from the fact that at the 50th bird the scores were equal, as they were again several times during the last part of the match and at the finish.

Dr. Carver's string of 50 birds killed straight off, which he accomplished at Lynchburg, Va., U.S.A., with a Greener $7\frac{1}{4}$ lb. 12-bore gun, was his best on record.

Dr. Carver shot three matches against Captain Bogardus in the United States in 1884. The following are the scores and distances :—First match (at Louisville, Ky.)—100 birds, 30 yards rise, 80 yards boundary, Hurlingham rules—Carver, 83 ; Bogardus, 82. Second match (at Chicago ; same conditions as first match)— Carver, 82 ; Bogardus, 79 ; at the 80th round scores were even, and remained so until the 90th, when Carver killed all succeeding birds, and won a well-contested match by three birds. Third match (at St. Louis ; 50 double rises at 21 yards)— Carver, 79 ; Bogardus, 81.

In a series of three matches between Mr. E. D. Fulford and Captain Brewer, in November, 1891, at New York, 100 birds each at 30 yards, Mr. Fulford, using a gun by W. W. Greener, scored the full number to his opponent's 99. The following day the scores were—Fulford, 99 ; Brewer, 98 ; the 95th bird shot at by Mr. Fulford fell dead out of bounds, thus practically 200 consecutive tries resulted in 200 kills, a truly marvellous performance, which certainly no game shot could equal. This was the highest score ever made at the trap. The third match resulted in a tie, both gentlemen scoring 94 each. The tie was immediately shot off at 25 birds each, Captain Brewer killing all his birds while Mr. Fulford scored 24, leaving Captain Brewer—who also used a Greener gun—the winner of the shoot-off by a single bird.

A final contest for the Championship of England Cup took place at Hendon on July 3rd, 1888, and resulted in a win for Captain Brewer, who killed 24 out of 25 birds, at 30 yards rise, and having thrice consecutively gained the prize against all comers, claimed the trophy as his own. Captain Brewer used a Greener gun in all contests.

In the contest for the American *Field* Champion Wing-Shot Cup, 1890, Mr. Elliott, the holder, successfully defended it with a Greener gun, scoring 59 out of 60, 48 out of 50, and 94 out of 100 birds.

The contest for the American *Field* Champion Wing-Shot Cup was decided in 1891. This resolved itself into a match between Mr. J. A. R. Elliott and Mr. E. D. Fulford. In it the largest consecutive run was made by Elliott, who grassed his last 37 birds straight. The score shows that Elliott used his second barrel more frequently than did Fulford, but on a majority of the birds this was used simply for safety. There was a large attendance of shooting men, and the victory of Elliott was well received.

" Elliott shot his Greener, weighing 7 lb. 3 oz., and Fulford used his Hammer-Greener, weighing 7 lb. 11 oz. Both men used Schultze powder in both barrels. Elliott, 46, winning the cup for the eighth time ; Fulford, 43. Conditions—50 birds each, 30 yards rise." Elliott has since won the cup for the tenth time.

In December, 1893, the same gentlemen shot a series of matches of 100 birds each a side, for $200 a match, a $1,000 bet, and $200 on a majority of the contests, usual conditions, 30 yards rise. The following were the scores made by each man : At Kansas City, Mo., Fulford, 86 ; Elliott, 85. At Indianapolis, Ind., Fulford, 96 ; Elliott, 93. At Pittsburg, Pa., Elliott, 93 ; Fulford, 90. At Williamsport, Pa., Fulford, 96 ; Elliott, 89. At Harrisburg, Pa., Fulford, 90 ; Elliott, 85. Of the 500 birds shot at in the five matches, Mr. Fulford scored 458 or $91\frac{3}{5}$ per cent., and Mr. Elliott 445, or 89 per cent.

In these matches Mr. Elliott used a Greener gun fitted with " Greener's Wrought Steel " barrels.

The killing of 100 birds and upwards without a miss has been accomplished on several notable occasions. On November 12th, 1891, in the match between Captain Brewer and Mr. Fulford. Scores : Fulford, 100 ; Brewer, 99, 80 yards boundary. This match was continued, Fulford killing 194 straight, and 199 out of 200, both competitors using Greener guns. On October 12th, 1894, in the match between Mr. Elliott and Dr. Carver. Scores : Elliott, 100 ; Carver, 99, 30 yards rise, 50 yards boundary. The winner used a Greener gun.

The greatest prize and highest honour ever shot for is the Championnat Universel, the one triennial event of the Monte Carlo International Meetings. This was won with a W. W. Greener gun, in 1886, by Mr. H. C. Pennell (who also won the Grand Prix du Casino in 1878 with his Greener gun), and again by Mr. W. Blake, in 1889, and it may interest some to know that neither of these shots was measured for his gun ; indeed, the gun used by Mr. Pennell was an ordinary weapon from stock, and a few hours before the match commenced the right or upright trigger was changed to act upon the left lock and *vice versâ.*

The winners of the Grand Prix du Casino must also be considered amongst the best of trap shooters. This match is contested by the best trap shots of all nations, and the birds are supplied by one of the most esteemed purveyors, whilst the Monaco boundary is acknowledged to be much in favour of the bird. The contest extending over several days also necessitates careful shooting over a long period, and to kill 13 consecutive birds without a miss, firing only at long intervals, is evidence of the ability of the marksman.

In several instances the killing of a dozen pigeons in succession has taken the Grand Prix, as was the case in 1887 and 1888 ; and in 1891 Count Gajoli, with his Greener, killed his 5 birds at 26 and 5 at 27 metres to win.

The following gentlemen have won the Grand Prix du Casino :—

Year.	Winner of the Grand Prix.
1872—Mr. George L. Lorillard (American).
1873—Mr. J. Jee, V.C., C.B. (English).
1874—Sir Wm. Call, Bart. (English).
1875—Captain Aubrey Patton (English).
1876—Captain Aubrey Patton (English).
1877—Mr. W. Arundel Yeo (English).
1878—Mr. H. Cholmondeley-Pennell (English).
1879—Mr. E. R. G. Hopwood (English).
1880—Count Michel Esterhazy (Hungarian).
1881—Mr. G. Camaueur (Belgian).
1882—Comte de St. Quentin (French).
1883—Mr. H. T. Roberts (English).
1884—Le Comte de Caspela (Italian).
1885—M. Leon de Dorlodot (Belgian).
1886—Signor Guidicini (Italian).
1887—Count Salina (Italian).
1888—Mr. C. Seaton (English).
1889—Mr. V. Dicks (English).
1890—Signor Guidicini (Italian).
1891—Count Gajoli (Italian).

Year.	Winner of the Grand Prix.
1892—Count Trautmannsdorf (Austrian).
1893—Signor Guidicini (Italian).
1894—Count Zichy (Austrian).
1895—Signor Benvenuti (Italian).
1896—Monsieur Journu (French).
1897—Signor G. Grasselli (Italian).
1898—Mr. Curling (English).
1899—M. R. Moncorge (French).
1900—Count O'Brien (Spanish).
1901—M. Guyot (French).
1902—Signor H. Grasselli (Italian).
1903—Mr. Pellier Johnson (English).
1904—Signor Schiannini (Italian).
1905—Signor H. Grasselli (Italian).
1906—Signor H. Grasselli (Italian).
1907—Mr. Hall (English).
1908—Count Czernin (Austrian).
1909—Signor Cacciari (Italian).
1910—Signor Vigano (Italian).

INANIMATE BIRD AND TRAP SHOOTING.

To a small extent the shooting of glass balls, etc., has long been practised in this country. About twenty years ago the apparatus used was greatly improved by American sportsmen ; and the sport, as practised there by Captain Bogardus, Mr. Ira Payne, and Dr. Carver, quickly became popular, and of late years has developed enormously. In this country the results of several attempts to popularise the sport were most disappointing, but more recently the efforts of the Clay Bird Shooting Association have achieved greater success.

Inanimate targets may be divided into two classes—balls and " pigeons." The balls are now practically obsolete. At first plain hollow spheres of colourless glass, they were afterwards made of blue or amber glass, and filled with feathers; later the spheres were chequered to prevent the shot from glancing, and this stage of development is the highest reached by the glass ball. Balls made of various resinous compositions have been tried, and have a certain sale, but as there is difficulty in getting them sufficiently brittle they have not generally supplanted the glass balls. Other plans have been tried, as bell balls, puff balls, inflated rubber bladders, explosive balls, etc., but they have not proved successes commercially.

The "Bogardus" Trap.   The Blue Rock Pigeon.   The "Carver" Revolving Trap.

The traps to throw them are numerous and varied; from the modified catapult used at the old English fairs they rapidly developed into complicated machines. The "Hatch" was like the old "Balista," the "Bogardus" was an improved form, and the "Carver," with a coiled spring instead of the flat coach-spring, better still; then came traps which were rotated and threw the ball at unknown angles—except towards the shooter—magazine traps, repeating traps, and traps to throw two balls at the one time.

The flight of a glass ball or other sphere being so widely different from that of a pigeon, and an ordinary shot being able to break most of them at usual ranges, no matter how quickly thrown, it was sought by the production of a skimming target to obtain, if not a nearer approach to bird flight, at least a more difficult target to hit.

The first to become generally known was the "Ligousky," a modified form of which remains in use. It is of baked clay, saucer-shaped, with a projection on the rim which is clamped to the throwing arm of the trap. The "Blue Rock," as illustrated, differs from the "Ligousky" in being made of a tar and ash composition, and, having no projection, it is thrown by a suitable holder attached to the arm of the trap. The essential features of this invention are, in the target—a sunk top connected to the sides by a film-like connection, permitting of a tougher material being used, as the sides and top of the target part if either is struck, though neither may break;

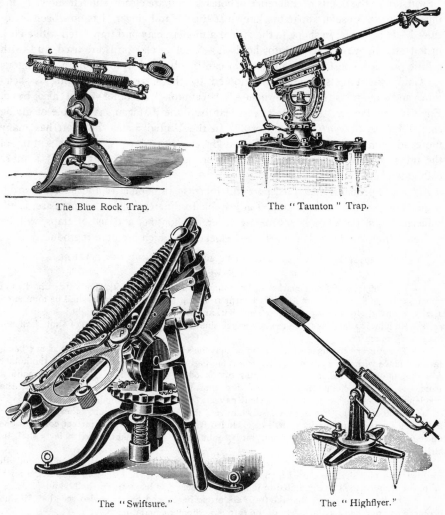

The Blue Rock Trap.

The " Taunton " Trap.

The " Swiftsure."

The " Highflyer."

and, in the trap—a holder pivoted to the throwing arm, so that the targets are not broken in the trap by the act of throwing. These principles are found in later traps and targets.   In this country favourite traps are the "Taunton," which is also satisfactorily made as a "double-rise" trap, the "Highflyer," and the "Swiftsure"; the points of difference in construction are clearly enough shown in the illustrations.   A useful apparatus, known as the "Hand-flinger," has now been introduced.   It is similar in shape to the arm of a modern clay-bird trap, fitted with a cork or felt grip by which the operator holds it.   Steel or clay birds are used, and, with a little practice, considerable amusement can be obtained with one of these flingers.

Composite targets have been adopted by the Clay Bird Shooting Association, and the traps used—"Swiftsure," "Taunton," or other—must also be of English manufacture.   The latest American trap, the "Magau," is capable of giving single, double, or *multiple* rises at will.   In the United States the sport has many more adherents; the pulling is effected by electrical devices, and the setting of the traps and arrangements for working them are totally different and of a more elaborate character.

It seems probable that the sport will increase in popularity and become world-wide.   For practice, a single trap, if adjustable to different angles, as most are, is all-sufficient; but the club arrangement, order of shooting, and set of traps, will be gathered from the official rules of the Association, which are here reproduced.

OFFICIAL RULES OF THE CLAY BIRD SHOOTING ASSOCIATION.
General Shooting Rules.

1.—Arrangement of firing marks.—There may be five firing marks, five yards apart, and shooters should stand at not less than 18 yards from the traps.   The marks shall be numbered 1, 2, 3, 4, and 5, No. 1 being on the extreme left, and No. 5 on the extreme right.

2.—No gun of a larger calibre than 12 gauge shall be used, and the charge of shot shall not exceed 1⅛ ounce.

3.—The gun or cartridges of any shooter may be challenged by a competitor as not being in accordance with Rule 2, and if found on examination to be a breach of the Rule, the holder of such gun or ammunition shall pay a fine of 10s. 6d. to the Club funds, and be disqualified from the current competition; but if the gun or ammunition be found correct, the challenger (except it be the Referee) shall pay 2s. 6d. to the Club funds.

4.—A shooter who, from any cause whatever, shall discharge his gun, otherwise than in accordance with the regulations, shall be excluded from taking part in any further competitions during the day.   All firing at passing birds, animals, or other unauthorised objects shall be strictly prohibited.

5.—If a shooter, in firing at a bird, shall let off both barrels practically at once, and kill his bird, that bird shall be scored a "no bird"; and if he misses, the bird shall be scored a miss.

6.—A Referee shall be appointed to judge all matches, and his decision shall be final.

7.—The Referee shall see that the traps are properly set, and he shall also see that all due precautions are taken for the safety of the trappers, shooters, and others.

8.—All guns must be kept open at the breech while the traps are being refilled, or while shooters are changing their marks.   Any person infringing this Rule shall be fined 1s.

9.—A shooter may refuse a " no bird " if thrown broken from the trap, or if it be not fairly thrown ; but a shooter who takes a bird or part of a bird shall be bound by the result.

10. In cases where a bird or birds are accidentally released so as to be flying in the air at the same time as the bird or birds at which the shooter is required to fire, the shooter may elect to treat it as a " no bird."

11.—If the shooter's gun, being properly loaded and cocked, fails to fire from any cause whatever, excepting through the fault of the shooter, the bird shall be counted a " no bird." If the gun misses fire with the first barrel, and 'the shooter fires the second and " breaks," the shot shall be scored a " kill " ; but if he fires the second and misses, it shall be scored a " miss " ; and if he does not fire the second it shall be " no bird." If the gun misses fire with the second barrel, the shooter shall be allowed another bird, using a cartridge primed and loaded with powder—but without a charge of shot—in the first barrel, and a loaded cartridge in the second barrel, and he shall pull the trigger of the first barrel after the trap has been released.

12.—A bird to be scored a " kill " must have a piece visibly broken from it whilst in the air. The Referee shall be the sole judge as to whether a bird is broken, and any person impugning his decision shall be disqualified from the current competition. No bird shall under any circumstances be retrieved for examination.

13.—Every club affiliated to the Association shall keep an official score book, showing in detail the results of every competition, and such score book shall always be available for examination by any person duly authorised by the Association. Broken birds or " kills " shall be indicated by the figure one (1), and missed birds by a nought (0).

14.—No betting shall be allowed.

Special Rules for Continuous Fire.

XV.—There shall be six shooters for the five marks. Five shooters shall occupy the five marks, and No. 6 shooter shall stand behind No. 1, waiting his turn. No. 1 shooter shall fire first from No. 1 mark, No. 2 shooter from No. 2 mark, and so on in rotation down the line. At, or during, the completion of the round, No. 1 shall take the place of No. 2, and No. 6 shall occupy No. 1 mark, No. 2 shooter shall occupy No. 3 mark, and so on, No. 5 becoming the shooter in waiting behind No. 1. No man shall leave his mark till the round is completed.

XVI.—When the shooters are at the mark, the puller shall call No. 1, and the first shooter shall then call " Pull," and the other shooters on the line shall call " Pull " in the order of their turn to fire without the number of their trap being called by the puller.

XVII.—If a shooter fires out of turn, he shall be scored a miss, and the shooter due to fire shall shoot again, the bird being a " no bird " notwithstanding Rule 9.

XVIII.—When the traps are set to throw at unknown angles, and there are two or more traps behind each screen, the puller should be informed by some suitable means which trap behind each screen he is to pull, so that the shooter shall be kept in ignorance of the angle at which his bird will be thrown.

Special Rules for Single Fire Competitions at Unknown Traps.

XIX.—The shooter shall stand at the centre mark and fire at five birds before leaving the line.

XX.—When the shooter is at the mark, and prepared to fire, the puller shall call " Ready," and the shooter shall then call " Pull."

XXI.—In cases where there is only one trap at each position, all five traps shall be filled before the shooter commences to shoot. The Referee may indicate to the puller, by means of a pack of five cards, each bearing the number of an individual trap (1-2-3-4-5), the order in which the traps are to be pulled. The cards shall be shuffled for each shooter, and turned up one at a time until five birds have been shot at. In the event of a "no bird" the trap throwing it shall be at once refilled, and the Referee shall re-shuffle the remaining cards, and then turn them up one at a time until five birds have been shot at.

THE BEST RECORDS.

The best records made at inanimate targets are very much higher than anything obtained from live bird shooting. There are more than fifty shooters in the United States who have broken 100 of the inanimate targets without a miss, and the score made and recorded at a public competition. Many more shooters have scored more than 90 out of 100.

In a series of twenty-five matches, at 100 clay pigeons each, at each match, between Dr. Carver and Capt. Bogardus, 2,227 were broken by Dr. Carver and 2,103 by Capt. Bogardus, at 18 yards rise. Dr. Carver made two scores of 100 each without a miss, and won nineteen matches, tied in three, and lost three. His lowest score was the first—72 ; and twenty of his scores exceeded 90 broken. Capt. Bogardus once scored 99, his highest, and three times 63, his lowest in this series of matches.

At glass balls still less skill is required ; but the best record is Mr. Scott's—700 smashed consecutively with a Greener gun. Dr. Carver, in a match with Mr. Scott, broke 9,737 out of 9,950 shot at ; Mr. Scott, 9,735 out of the same number. Out of the last 950 in this match, Dr. Carver missed two only, and Mr. Scott three.

Capt. H. Bogardus, the great American wing shot, made a match against time in December, 1879, and succeeded in breaking 5,500 glass balls in a few seconds less than 7 hours 20 minutes. The misses numbered 356. The Captain used an English gun with two pairs of barrels—one pair (10-bore) shooting 4 drams of powder and $1\frac{1}{2}$ oz. of No. 8 shot ; the 12-bore pair were loaded with $3\frac{1}{2}$ drams and 1 oz. of No. 8 shot. During the match the Captain loaded for himself, and changed the barrels no less than fifty-five times. Three miss-fires only occurred in the whole series of 5,855 shots. The balls were all sprung from spring traps.

CHAPTER XIX.

DOUBLE GUNS WITH SINGLE TRIGGERS.

EARLY MECHANISMS.

THE idea of making one trigger serve to discharge both locks of a double-barrelled gun is by no means new, for there is evidence that some two hundred years ago it had presented itself to the gunsmith.

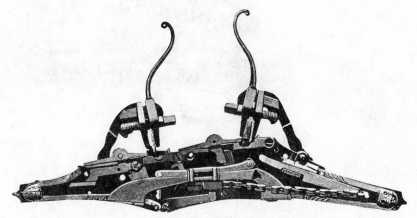

From the Collection of H. J. Jackson, Esq.

The illustration, which is taken from the collection of H. J. Jackson, Esq., represents a double wheel lock actuated by a single trigger, the scears being arranged tandem fashion and connected by a slack chain; the first pull by the trigger on the back scear releases the back wheel and tightens the chain, and a further pull releases the front wheel; this lock was in all probability made for an under and over barrelled gun or rifle.

An illustration of a flintlock pistol fitted with a single trigger will be found on page 101. In this mechanism the trigger is pivoted vertically. An inclined plane on the right tumbler forces the trigger under the left scear when the right tumbler has been let down ; on the tumbler being raised, a spring forces the trigger beneath the right scear.   It is necessary to remove the pressure upon the trigger before the second barrel can be discharged, in the same manner as with the double-action revolver, but the pistol-trigger does not require so much travel.   A gun of more modern construction was made by the author before the publication of the first edition of this book (1880), and is here illustrated.

There are various mechanical means for securing the same end ; usually the fall of the tumbler is made to gear with a connecting rod, which pushes over the trigger-blade to engage with the opposite scear and is returned to its first position by a spring.   The first gun that the author made on this principle acted admirably with

Greener's Double Gun with Single Trigger.

most shooters, but with some, both barrels went off practically simultaneously.   The advantages seemed slight, and as a possibility of firing the second barrel unawares was enough to condemn the principle, the matter remained in abeyance, but the gun was sold and gave complete satisfaction to its user.

Of recent years considerable attention has been given to this subject, particularly by inventors who have sought, by innumerable devices, to overcome the obvious difficulties of the system.   Since 1864, when the first single-trigger patent was applied for, over one hundred patents have been provisionally protected in England, there being granted, in one year alone, eighteen patents for single-trigger mechanisms.

The new devices are for the most part produced with a view to obviating the accidental or premature discharge of the second barrel.   The recoil after firing the first barrel causes the shooter involuntarily to loosen his grip on the trigger, and give a second pull; this second pull with the simple automatic mechanism sometimes frees the opposite lock, and the second barrel is at once discharged.

THE SINGLE-TRIGGER TRIAL.

During the past few years there has been much controversy as to the discovery of the principle of the three-pull mechanism. On December 15th, 1906, an action, Robertson *v.* Purdey, was brought in the Chancery Division of the High Court of Justice for infringement of a single-trigger patent. There were three claimants to the invention of the three-pull system, viz., Baker, Nobbs, and Robertson ; and it was ruled in the order named, by Mr. Justice Parker, who gave emphatic precedence to Mr. Baker as the originator of the principle, which judgment invalidated both the Nobbs and Robertson patents.

The trial extended over a period of nearly two months, during which time the question of single-trigger mechanisms was very exhaustively dealt with, and it is of interest to note the opinion expressed by one of the expert witnesses, Mr. Thorn (Charles Lancaster), who stated that he " did not consider that any single-trigger mechanism could be relied upon never to go wrong in use." This seemed to be the general opinion of the experts, and is one with which the author is in agreement. Nevertheless, from his own experience as well as that of others, he is able to testify to the reliable working of his own mechanism, in some instances for over nine years, under the most trying circumstances, without the slightest hitch.

It must be evident to everyone who will give but a moment's consideration to the question, that the single trigger, even in its simplest form, has to perform automatically the work of the human finger in changing from the first to the second trigger of an ordinary gun. This in itself necessitates the use of spring operating mechanisms, and consequently greater liability to get out of order, particularly so when it is noted that for many years past the author has made his " Facile Princeps " hammerless mechanism with the double triggers without employing any trigger-springs.

SELECTIVE MECHANISMS.

This is another phase of the single-trigger mechanism which has numerous variants. They are, however, of little value and only serve to introduce further complications in what is ofttimes an already too intricate mechanism. The selective mechanism, which claims to allow the use of either barrel at will, is nearly always actuated by a sliding finger-plate similar to that of a top safety slide, and this is usually placed on the trigger-plate in front of the right trigger. It is scarcely credible that the mechanism can be brought into action for selecting the barrel, after a bird has risen, in the same way, or so quickly, as one might decide to pull the left trigger of an ordinary gun. It would therefore appear that they are only of use when it is required to fire one barrel continuously, as would be the case in a pigeon match, in which the firing might be limited to the left barrel, and it is very evident that this slight advantage cannot compensate for the necessarily greater complication of mechanism.

ADVANTAGES OF THE SINGLE TRIGGER.

The single trigger undoubtedly possesses advantages over the two-trigger gun, principally the facility with which two barrels can be fired in rapid succession ; the same length of stock is secured—with most mechanisms—for both barrels, and there is no necessity to relax the grip of the stock. What these advantages mean to the sportsman can only be fully appreciated by a fair trial at game.

ADVICE AS TO SELECTION OF A SUITABLE MECHANISM.

Although the number of single-trigger patents is so great, there appear to be but three principles upon which the whole of the successful mechanisms are based. These are described in detail later, but may be classed as the "Three-pull system," the "Timing mechanism," and the "Recoil-regulated pendulous form." In selecting any type of single-trigger mechanism, the sportsman is strongly advised to choose that having the fewest and strongest parts, and, wherever possible, to give the system he favours an actual shooting test. It is hoped that the description given of the leading types may be of some assistance in enabling the sportsman to select out of the almost bewildering variety that best adapted for his use.

THE THREE-PULL SYSTEM.

THE JONES-BAKER SINGLE TRIGGER.

In the Jones-Baker patent (1883–1895) the principle of the intermediate pull is employed, though the mechanism specified consists of a somewhat complicated locking gear, put into motion by the fall of the right-hand tumbler, and retaining the trigger-slide until the second, or involuntary, pull on the trigger finger releases it, when the slide is free to slip under the tail of the scear of the left-hand lock, and engages that when the trigger is next pulled. The opening of the lever brings the trigger-slide back to its first position. If the locks are snapped off when the gun is unloaded, three distinct perceptible pulls are needed to free the two locks, but when the gun is fired in the ordinary way the recoil causes the shooter unwittingly to pull on the trigger and so liberate the trigger-slide from the bent into

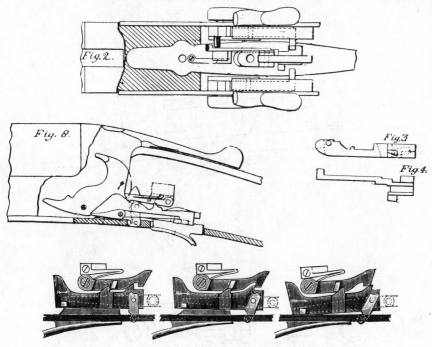

Jones' Single-trigger Mechanism (17 parts).

which the fall of the right-hand tumbler forced it. The illustrations show the position of the trigger-slide before, during, and after the intermediate pull. This patent also includes a separate mechanism for changing trigger from left to right at will.

BOSS'S SINGLE-TRIGGER GUN.

In Messrs. Boss & Co.'s single-trigger gun (Robertson's patent, 1894) the principle employed to prevent the accidental discharge of the second barrel is also that of introducing a new pull between the two necessary to discharge both barrels. This new pull is ordinarily given by the recoil of the gun, and in shooting cannot be distinguished; but if the trigger be pulled when the gun is unloaded, three distinct pulls are felt, and have to be given, before both tumblers are released. This intermediate pull is accomplished by having suitable mechanism, constituting practically a special bent and scear, upon which the trigger acts in the ordinary way.

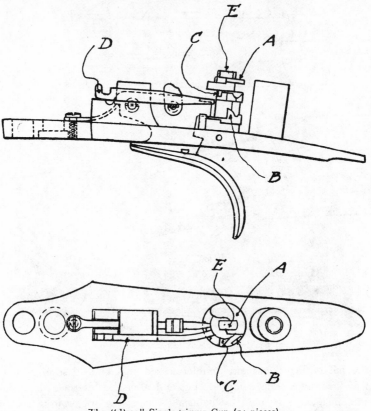

The "Boss" Single-trigger Gun (14 pieces)

The mechanism consists of a gearing wheel or drum A, pivoted vertically behind the trigger-blade; this drum is rotated by a coiled watch-spring, and has arms projecting to engage the scears. A connecting rod D, from the action or other convenient mechanism on opening the gun, turns the drum against the coiled spring, in which position the drum is retained by abutting against the end of the right-hand scare tail, when that scear is in bent. This scear rests upon the trigger, and is released in the ordinary way. When the scear tail has been raised to free the tumbler, the drum rotates, until it is stopped by a stud B on it catching against the trigger-blade. The second, or involuntary, pull upon the trigger caused by the recoil slips the trigger-blade over this stop, and the drum rotates farther, bringing the second arm immediately under the scear of the left-hand lock, and over the trigger-blade. When the trigger is next pressed it raises the drum on the vertical pivot E, and with it the left-hand scear, thus discharging that lock.

The mechanism requisite to change the pull from right to left, and *vice versâ*, at will, is quite distinct, and of a somewhat complicated character. The essential feature of this single-trigger mechanism is the automatic locking of the gearing wheel, or drum, by the trigger, and the utilisation of the involuntary pull upon the trigger to unlock it and complete the change from right to left.

The chief objection to the three-pull system is its liability to failure when the involuntary pull is not taken; it may happen through holding the gun tightly in the grasp. Under such conditions the unconscious forward movement of the finger is eliminated, and the second conscious pull is taken on the intermediate pull. The trigger is thus blocked, and it is impossible to fire the second barrel until the trigger is allowed to go forward again.

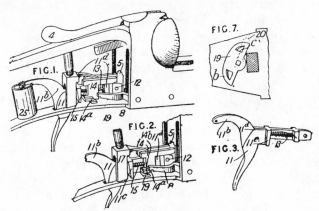

The Fulford Single-trigger Mechanism.

TIMING MECHANISMS.

THE FULFORD SINGLE-TRIGGER.

What is probably the best example to illustrate this principle is the "pneumatic trigger," and that most readily comprehensible is the Fulford patent (1904), of which a detailed description is here given.

Fig. 1 shows the parts in position for firing the left barrel. Fig. 2 shows the parts in position for firing the right barrel after the left has been fired. Fig. 3 shows the trigger-piece. The catches, 14, with shoulders, 14 A, to engage the scears, 8, slide on the rods, 13, between the projections, 11C, 11D, of the trigger-piece, 11, which is mounted on a pivot, 12, at its front end. A tooth, 14 B, on the underside of each catch, 14, is adapted to engage with the rear edge of the movable plate, 19, shown in plan, Fig. 7, when the trigger is in its lower position. The catches, 14, are forced back against the springs, 15, by the locking-bolt, 5, when the gun is broken down.

With the pivoted plate, 19, locked by the handle, 20, in the position of Fig. 7, the left-hand catch, 14, moves forward and brings the shoulder, 14A, under the scear, 8, when the bolt, 5, is withdrawn, the right-hand catch being retained by its tooth, 14B, engaging at the point B with the rear edge of the plate, 14. When the trigger has been lifted to fire the left barrel, the tooth, 14B, of the right catch moves forward until the shoulder, 14A, bears against the rear end of the scear. The return of the trigger to its lower position is checked by a piston on the arm, 11B, working in the cylinder, 25. When the trigger returns to its lower position, the tooth, 14B, on the right catch passes into the opening, C, in the plate, 19, and the shoulder, 14A, is carried forward under the scear. The hammers are so shaped as to lift the tails of the scears clear of the catches when the barrels are fired. When it is desired to fire the right barrel first, the plate, 19, is turned by means of the handle, 20, to engage the tooth, 14B, on the right-hand catch, 14.

LANCASTER'S SINGLE-TRIGGER GUN.

In the mechanism patented by Mr. H. A. A. Thorn (Charles Lancaster & Co.) (dated 1895), the end is achieved by simpler means. A switching trigger-blade is arranged in conjunction with the interceptor, or, as the patentee prefers to call it, a "time stud" (K in the illustrations). The other parts not of the usual construction are the switching blade E^1 and E^2, the single trigger and its pivot F, and a gearing lever H, pivoted upon a slide J at I. The part H^1 is actuated by a cam surface formed on the tumbler of the right-hand lock, and H^2 actuates the blade of the switching trigger F on the left-hand side. As long as the tumbler of the right-hand lock is at cock, H^2 retains the trigger-blade under the right-hand scear, but as soon as the cam surface of the lock H^1 ceases to be in contact—either by the firing of the right-hand barrel, or by the slide J being moved forward by its stud projecting in front of the trigger finger—the blade E is carried by its spring L to the position shown on the dotted lines ; that is to say, under the scear of the opposite lock. It cannot do this, however, until all pressure has been taken from the trigger finger, because the "time stud" K blocks the way. When the trigger has been released,

the spring L, pressing downward and transversely, causes the blade to dip under the "time stud" and pass to its normal position under the left scear, where it remains until the right lock is cocked or the slide moved back. When the trigger is pressed it moves the back end of the trigger switch E upwards past K. Consequently it is impossible for E to pass underneath K until all pressure has been taken off the trigger, and it is also impossible for the second lock to be released until E has passed under K.

The chief difficulty attaching to the "timing" system is the impossibility of adapting such mechanism to suit different people consequent upon the variation in recoil with different users. The mechanism is "timed" to move at a fixed

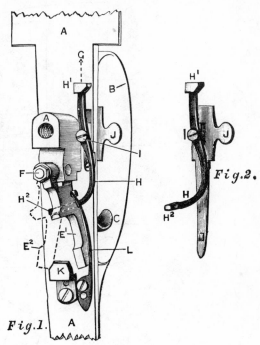

Charles Lancaster's Single-trigger Mechanism for
Double-barrel Gun (16 parts).

speed, but some people pull the trigger so rapidly that the switching blade or piston has not sufficient time to perform its function, and there is a "balk," with consequent inability to fire the second barrel.

THE "RECOIL REGULATED" OR PENDULOUS FORM.

THE GREENER SINGLE-TRIGGER GUN.

This mechanism (patented 1898) consists of a trigger of ordinary form upon the blade of which is a pivoted piece A, pressed forward by a spring B; as the scears fall into bent, the tail of the right-hand scear bears upon the sloped portion of the pivoted piece A, and holds it back. On the trigger being raised, the right-hand scear is released and fires the right barrel. The recoil throws the

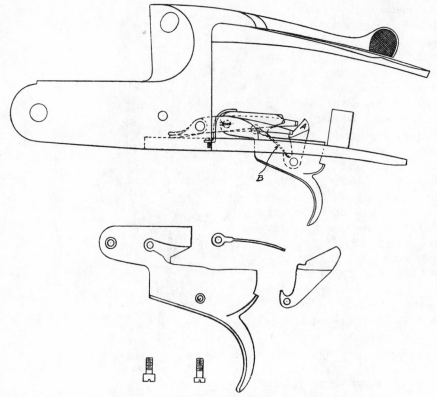

The Greener Single-trigger (5 pieces).

pivoted piece farther back on its centre, and it immediately comes forward on the action of the recoil subsiding, its flange being brought under the left scear ready to fire the second barrel. It will thus be seen that the mechanism is not dependent upon recoil to put it into action; there is no intermediate pull, and consequently there is no possibility of failure to fire the second barrel owing to the blocking of the trigger or scear, as is the case with the three-pull mechanism; whether the gun is fired or not, but two pulls are required.

The whole of the mechanism, including pins and spring, consists of but five pieces; these are strongly constructed, and it is probably the simplest and most reliable mechanism yet devised. The automatic block trigger safety, described on page 209, can be used in conjunction with this mechanism. The usual side safety, either automatic or independent, can also be employed, and a selective mechanism can, if required, be attached.

THE LARD SINGLE-TRIGGER GUN.

The Westley-Richards single-trigger (Lard's patent, 1899) consists of nineteen pieces, and may be supplied with a selective trigger arrangement, adding an additional five parts to the mechanism. The usual top safety can also be fitted in conjunction with this single-trigger, and this may be actuated automatically or by the hand.

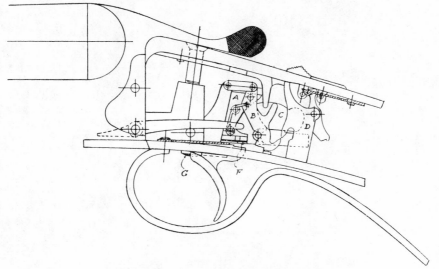

The Westley-Richards Single-trigger (24 pieces).

In the illustration the parts may be described as A the firing plate, B the safety spur or detent lever, C the weighted lever assisting the action of the detent lever.

The action of the mechanism is as follows, presuming the selective mechanism to be set for right and left. When the first trigger is pulled the firing plate A is raised and releases the right scear.   When the first barrel is fired, the toe of the detent lever B engages with the hook on the fixed pillar D, and, while in this position, prevents the involuntary pull from raising the firing plate sufficiently to fire the second barrel.

After the first barrel has been discharged the weighted lever swings back, and the firing plate is held in such a position that the second firing lug is in contact with its scear.   The second barrel is thus fired immediately upon the second conscious pull being taken.

It must not be supposed that the shooter habituated to two triggers will at once obtain all the advantages of the single trigger, but the average game shot should quickly become accustomed to it, and, providing he has been fortunate in his selection, should derive much satisfaction from its use.

CHAPTER XX.

MISCELLANEOUS.

REPEATING SHOT GUNS.

THE Repeating Shot Gun is a weapon introduced some years ago, doubtless with the intention of securing a mercantile success equal to that achieved by the Winchester and kindred magazine rifles. Let it be granted that the repeating rifle is the best mechanism for sporting rifles—a point the author will by no means concede—it does not follow that a shot gun constructed upon the same principle will fulfil the requirements of the wing shot.

Repeating shot guns may be made with an under lever travelling as in the Winchester, Marlin, Kennedy, and other well-known magazine rifles; or the mechanism may be worked by the left hand, as in the Spencer. The fore-end is furnished with a " hand-piece " sliding longitudinally, and actuating a more simple mechanism than that usually found in repeating arms. This gun can be functioned by the left hand whilst held to the shoulder, and without greatly disturbing the aim.

The well-known shot, Dr. W. F. Carver, attempted to give a " boom " to this gun. He matched himself against time, had six Spencer shot guns, and two assistants to load. Dr. Carver failed, the guns jamming—owing, it is said, to faulty shells. From what the author knows of Dr. Carver, and having supplied him with many thousands of shells and loaded cartridges, he is of opinion that this clever professional shot had cartridges and everything else as perfect as they could be made before he entered upon a trial of such importance.

A public trial of the Spencer shot gun took place in America, and the following sentences are culled from the " Official Report ":—" Defective shells were then fired. . . . Result—Slight escape of gas above and below the breech mechanism, but none towards the rear." " Considerable escape above and below, setting paper on fire in one case ; no escape of gas towards the rear."

The gun was tested for rapidity, irrespective of aim.—" Firer, expert for the Board; time, one minute; eight fired; two thrown out not fired." Magazine loaded before commencing to fire.—Firer, representative of the gun ; one minute ; rounds fired, twenty-two. Firer for the Board; time, one minute ; fired, twelve ;

thrown out not fired, three." Used as a single loader—that is, without calling upon the magazine—eighteen shots per minute could be fired. The ordinary double-barrelled ejecting shot gun can be fired upwards of thirty times per minute, and *it has* been fired and aimed twenty-six times in less than one minute, when the trial

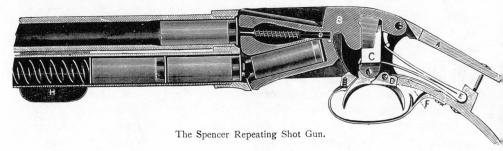

The Spencer Repeating Shot Gun.

had to be discontinued as the barrels had become too hot to hold.   The summary of the report continues : —

"In all the tests over 378 rounds have been fired from the gun.   Of these, *ten* were with defective shells and eight with excessive charges varying from 120 to 150 grains of powder, with, in several cases, double charges of buckshot.

"The gun remains in excellent condition, as far as its serviceable qualities are concerned, none of the parts being injured or out of order.   It has passed very well the various tests to which the Board has subjected it, and the Board is of opinion that the strength and endurance of the gun are entirely satisfactory.

"In the firing by the expert of the Board, Mr. R. T. Hare, seven cartridges were thrown out unexploded, six in firing rapidly at will, and one in firing for rapidity with accuracy.   In the rapid firing by the expert representatives of the gun, three unexploded cartridges were thrown out.   This does not include those thrown out because of defective primers, but those cases where the cartridges were not fired because of premature pulling on the trigger, before the primers were in position to be struck by the firing-pin.   In the firing by the members of the Board but little difficulty of this kind was experienced."

THE WINCHESTER REPEATING SHOT GUN.

This gun was introduced in the summer of 1887, and is worked by an under-lever, as in the well-known Winchester rifle, but the mechanism is more compact ; in fact, the gun is neater in appearance, and as a repeater does its work fairly well.

Another repeating shot gun, worked by a sliding fore-part, is the Burgess, for which gun it is claimed that two shots may be fired in one-eighth of a second, three shots in a second, and six in three seconds. This weapon is made with either a detachable barrel or the barrel is hinged and the gun folds until the muzzle touches the heel-plate. The magazine is a tube under the barrel.

Automatic mechanisms have been adapted to repeating shot guns, and the Patent Office records prove that several attempts have been made to produce

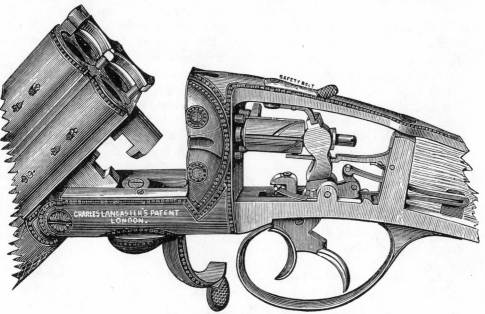

Lancaster Four-barrelled Gun.

double-barrelled repeating shot guns, but the author has had no opportunity of examining any shot gun so constructed.

A travelling representative of a firm which manufactures a repeating shot gun, and who was himself expert in the use of the gun, was challenged by a sportsman he met casually to shoot a match with him against time, the sportsman to use a Greener self-acting ejector gun, the expert his repeating shot gun. The result of the match was that the sportsman won by breaking 90 glass balls out of 100 in seven minutes ; the expert broke the same number but occupied more than ten minutes in firing. In this contest the guns became so hot that they had to be cooled by being submerged in a tub of water after every ten or fifteen shots.

Repeating shot guns have never taken in this country; they have several disadvantages. The movement of the hand and arm in reloading unsteadies the aim, and the alignment is not so easy as the double barrel with its rib to guide the eye. For rapidity of firing, too, the double-barrelled ejector is sufficient for all practical sporting purposes, as it has been already described how it is possible with it to fire three shots at one covey of partridges.

THE AUTOMATIC SHOT GUN.

The latest development of the sporting arm is the automatic shot gun. This weapon places within the reach of those who desire to "pump lead" into their birds a single-barrelled gun firing, by the simple act of pulling the trigger, five cartridges with great rapidity. The magazine holds four 12-bore cartridges, the fifth being placed in the chamber of the gun. The recoil resulting from the first shot ejects the fired case, cocks the hammer, and forces the next cartridge into the chamber, the gun being again ready for firing without being brought down from the shoulder. This type of gun has attained some popularity in the United States as well as amongst Continental sportsmen, and efforts are being made to introduce it into this country, but it scarcely seems probable that it will be so favourably accepted by English sportsmen. Like the single-barrel repeating shot gun, it is difficult to align; and further, one is compelled to fire a full-choke or a cylinder barrel, according to the boring of the barrel with which the gun is fitted, at all distances and for all classes of game—which is at times exceedingly inconvenient, even if it does not entirely spoil one's sport.

MULTI-BARRELLED GUNS.

Although the double-barrelled gun seems to have become the accepted standard for sporting weapons, some attempts have been made, even of late years, to

popularise weapons of other types. Some years ago Mr. Lancaster introduced his four-barrelled gun, which, as shown, has two pairs superposed, all four turning upon a hinge joint and secured by the usual double-grip breech mechanism. The lock mechanism is similar to that of the old Elliot pistol; it has but one mainspring, and the trigger lifts the tumbler to bent as in revolvers. The striker is a sleeve with a projecting arm, and it is rotated by a ratchet when the trigger is pulled, and so the head comes into

Muzzle of the Three-barrelled Gun.

contact with the several strikers successively. The weapon, save perhaps in 20 or smaller bores, is heavy and cumbrous; the trigger is hard to pull, and has a long travel, like that of a double-action revolver; in the last model a second trigger is furnished for the purpose of cocking.

The three-barrelled weapon, usually if not always, consists of a double shot gun,

Under and Over Wedge-fast Gun.

with a small rifle barrel placed between them and below, as shown in the illustration. Occasionally similar arms are seen having the rifle barrel on the top. It is difficult to decide which type is the more objectionable. Either arrangement interferes

Mr. J. H. Walsh's Pin-fire Gun.

with the breech mechanism, and whether with hammers or hammerless the lock and firing mechanisms are rarely satisfactory. Although the rifle barrel is of small bore and taking only a light cartridge, the extra barrel quite spoils the arm as a shot gun; necessitates a wide opening in order to insert the cartridges, and as a rifle it is rarely as accurate as a like barrel in a single or double rifle. This type of weapon is therefore not to be recommended for the general purposes of the sportsman, nor should it be chosen by any person as being equal to the two weapons it combines. Endeavours to construct them of approximate weight to shot guns have resulted in dangerously light weapons being issued, with disastrous consequences.

UNDER AND OVER GUNS.

Instead of placing the barrels of double guns side by side, they were in the earliest firearms superposed. The author has made several modern guns upon the same plan, using the drop-down principle for rifles and a vertical hinge joint for

The "Bacon" Breech-loader.

shot guns. The plan appears to possess some advantages, especially for combined rifle and shot guns; and although very few arms have been so made, a London maker has recently endeavoured to popularise this type of weapon. The one shown in the first illustration on the previous page represents a double shot gun made by the author upon his wedge-fast principle, and demonstrates how easily an important modification of that system of breech-loading may be effected.

The barrels, instead of dropping down on opening the gun, move in a lateral direction, as shown. The explosion is effected by studs on the tumblers striking exploding-pins.

Although only made as an experiment, it proved almost as handy as a single gun, and, the recoil being more in a direct line with the stock, the gun had not the tendency to throw the charge to the left or right, as is usual with guns having the barrels side by side. Other weapons built on the same principle are described and illustrated in the chapter on "Sporting Rifles."

FIXED BARREL MECHANISMS.

As stated in the introduction to the breech-loading system, the drop-down breech-loader was not at once accepted as the best form of mechanism for the shot gun.

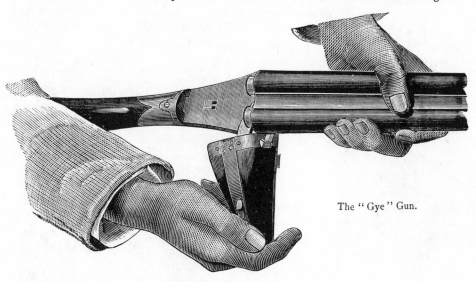

The "Gye" Gun.

At various times fixed barrel guns have been produced, but none of them attained great popularity. One of the first was the invention of the late Editor of the *Field*, Mr. J. H. Walsh, and was made for pin-fire cartridges. As shown, the locks are pivoted vertically, and open as it were on a hinge, to admit the cartridges. A reference to the engraving will make the principle appear more clear. The locks are secured in their places by a small lever turning a "button" on the inside of each lock-plate, and these engage in slots in the tang of the break-off.

Another mechanism which was ultimately adapted to the ordinary central-fire cartridge is the "Bacon," which, like the Walsh, required the separate manipulation of each lock to open the breech for loading. This gun, as illustrated, somewhat resembled the Prussian needle gun in both the breech-bolt and the lock mechanism.

The fired cases were extracted by withdrawing the bolt, and then fell through a hole in the shoe of the breech and the fore part of the stock. At one time the Bacon was thought to possess many excellent qualities; the slowness with which it was loaded, due to the separate mechanism for each barrel requiring separate manipulation, doubtless prevented its general adoption. The Remington mechanism, duplicated and slightly modified, has been employed for double shot guns and rifles. Other mechanisms may also have been so used, but have never been produced in large quantities nor received the approbation of sportsmen. Of the mechanisms purposely designed for double guns with fixed barrels, the Gye is the most modern among those generally known. Its general appearance and method of manipulation are shown in the illustration. The gun is no longer manufactured, but thirty years ago a few were sold in London by the inventor.

THE GIFFARD GUN.

This weapon, about which so much has been said and written, is a French invention. M. Giffard, whose chemical and mechanical experiments have always been regarded with interest, has long sought to utilise carbonic acid gas as a force for the propulsion of rifle projectiles. Having succeeded in liquefying the gas, and being fully conversant with its properties of expansion, he substituted a reservoir of liquefied gas for the receiver of the old and well-known air-gun. The fall of the hammer upon pulling the trigger of the lock liberates a small quantity of the liquefied gas, which, when in contact with the air, expands to its fullest extent with the force of an explosive, and propels the bullet, pellets, or whatever projectile may be placed in the barrel. When exhausted, the reservoir is detached from the gun and replaced by another. The reservoirs must be filled at the factory, and the gas specially prepared.

Much more was expected of this weapon than the principle of its construction warranted. The expansion of liquefied carbonic acid gas is many thousand volumes less than obtainable with modern high explosives. It could not therefore be substituted for them, providing they could be used in modern rifles, and there are now several explosives used in small-bore rifles which give a velocity to the bullet greater than any gas gun can equal. As a shot gun the principle is still more heavily handicapped, and after many experiments its promoters appear to have been convinced that, save for small target or saloon rifles and toy guns, the invention is practically useless.

ELECTRIC GUNS.

Very many years ago attempts were made to use electricity as a means for igniting the powder charge in firearms. A French baron had such a weapon made at Prague some forty years ago. In this muzzle-loading gun a battery in the stock generated a current, the arrangement being as shown in the illustration.

A is an ordinary bichromate battery, filled by removing the plug B in the heel-plate C. D is an induction coil, connected with A by the wire E E. This coil, when

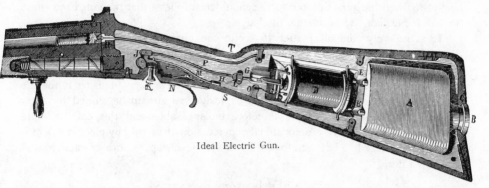

Ideal Electric Gun.

the battery is at work, vibrates most unpleasantly, so a small magnet is introduced to prevent it. To generate the spark the button K is pressed with the finger ; this causes the nut J to partly turn, withdrawing the rod H to the guide L, and come in contact with a stop at O, and, by making the circuit O P R complete, fires the gun. M is a spring depressing the button K, whilst N is a safety cover to the button K. S T is the iron framework of the stock.

The same principle, but with the advantage of modern appliances and fittings, was applied to breech-loading arms, but did not prove a commercial success. M. Pieper, of Liége, pro-duced an electric breech-loading gun which was fired by a current generated in a pocket-battery carried by the shooter. An accumulator would answer the same purpose, but, as a glance at the following illustration will show, the

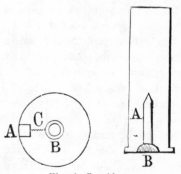

Electric Cartridge.

cartridge required is of such construction that absolutely no advantage is gained by having electric ignition.

The cartridge case is ot metal, and has extending from its base a stud, A, a wad with a metallic centre, B, and connected with a wire, C, with another stud, A, on the edge of the wad, is placed face downwards over the powder, and, on the trigger being pulled, the circuit of the current is established, the spark passing through the stud, A B, in the cartridge to the B in the wad. As the battery is carried separately from the gun, and the necessary connection is made by means of a pad and a special heel-plate when the gun is placed to the shoulder, it follows that the gun, even when loaded, is not liable to accidental discharge.

It is no very difficult matter to ignite the charges by electricity; but the disadvantages of the battery are not compensated by the extra safety possessed by the cartridge, speed, or certainty of ignition. Electricity has not yet been employed in any way as a propellant in firearms; there is no advantage in using it for the purpose of ignition, since most modern explosives require to be ignited by detonation. The fulminating cap is therefore indispensable, and this can be more quickly, readily, and surely detonated by percussion than by any electrical contrivance yet produced. The gun lock will always be cheaper, more efficacious, and probably safer.

MINOR MISCELLANEOUS INVENTIONS.

In the development of firearms numerous contrivances have been devised with a view to render arms more efficient in some particular and have, instead, proved detrimental. Some of the futile attempts to improve the gun deserve mention, if only as indications to would-be inventors.

Detachable Choked-muzzles. — The Roper detachable choke, described on page 256, is probably the earliest of these inventions. Mr. Turner, of Birmingham, tried some years ago to use a detachable muzzle upon double guns in order to convert the cylinder into a choke; later, Mr. Heath, of the same town, produced a similar contrivance. The latest plan is that of Dr. Mabberley, of Birmingham, which differs from the preceding in the mode of attachment. The detachable piece, instead of abutting against the muzzle, slips over the end of the barrels, and is secured there by a screw into the under rib. It lengthens the barrels about $2\frac{1}{2}$ inches, and is used not only for converting cylinders into choke-bores, but for lengthening short-barrelled covert-shooting guns, for making the ordinary gun better available for wild-fowling and other special purposes. The difference in balance is counterpoised by inserting a barrel-cleaner or other weight in the stock.

Grooved Shot Barrels.—Many plans have been proposed to improve the range of the shot gun; one most persistently followed is the grooving of the barrel with straight shallow channels; sometimes the grooved barrel is choked also; but the author, after repeated trials of such guns, is convinced that the shooting is in no way improved nor the value of the gun in any way increased by the process. Not only is there no gain, but in every instance the performance has been inferior to that obtained with an ordinary gun.

The illustration shows a portion of the barrels of one of these Continental oddities. Both barrels also are thickly perforated a few inches from the muzzle, as shown, the idea being to lessen the recoil thereby. A test was made of this gun

Grooved and Perforated Shot Barrel.

against one of the author's of equal weight, gauge, and length. The average recoil with the perforated gun was $11\frac{1}{4}$ lbs. in excess of the Greener, whilst the force on the *Field* gauge was less by an average of $1 \cdot 087$, and most irregular.

Wildfowler's Oval-barrelled Gun.—The oval-barrelled gun, whether smooth-bore or rifle, is no new invention, but the object of Mr. Lewis Clement in producing his oval-barrelled shot gun is quite distinct from that of the earlier makers of the elliptic calibres. Mr. Clement's design is to produce a differential spread of the shot pellets; a greater lateral deviation with the same trajectory. The amount of ellipse may be judged from the annexed diagram. There seems little advantage to be derived from a greater lateral spread, except, possibly, for punt guns. Certainly for general wing-shooting the uniform spread of the pellets is preferable; at rising birds the aim is as likely to err because of faulty elevation as at crossing shots it is on the horizontal plane; at birds crossing and rising

Wildfowler's Elliptical Shot Barrel.

the equal spread is preferable, and the cylindrical bore is so much more easily formed than the elliptical that very important advantages must be possessed by the latter if it is to displace the commoner type.

Push-down Triggers.—Instead of the ordinary trigger, a stud or other lever sunken in the head of the gun, or other convenient position, is made to serve the purpose. A quarter of a century ago a Martini so constructed as to be discharged by simply pressing down a sunken stud with the thumb of the right hand was offered to the English Government. It was claimed that finer shooting could be obtained, but the ordinary trigger was preferred by the authorities. Both guns and rifles have been and are still so made when required.

Reversed Sights.—Owing to the difficulty experienced in getting a true aim with a long-range rifle at a high elevation, an Enfield rifle was made with the elevator not only at the muzzle end of the barrel, but also on the under side of it, the

Reversely-sighted Enfield Rifle.

sight being taken through a hole in the stock, as shown by the dotted line. This device was ingenious, and a trial of the rifle convinced some experts that it had merit; but it was not so distinctly advantageous as to be generally adopted.

HARPOON GUNS.

The use of the harpoon gun is due entirely to the encouragement given by the London Society of Arts, which, during the last century, offered prizes not only for improvements in the weapon, but also to the harpooners who were most successful in using them. The whale fishery was then regarded as one of the most important of the maritime industries, and the harpoon gun not only made its practice more safe, but added also largely to the catch. Guns are carried now by all the Scotch, American, and Norwegian whalers, but the industry has decayed with the increased use of mineral oils and the hunting to extinction of the right-whale whose bone has become so valuable.

The harpoon gun is similar to a small swivel gun. It has a stock of ash or wych elm, well bent down to form a handle with which to aim it. The whole of

Whale-shooting with the Harpoon Gun.

the recoil, which is considerable, is sustained by a strong swivel pinned to the stock and barrel. The barrel is 1½ in. bore, the lock simple, being similar to that of a saddle pistol. The cap, nipples, hammer, and lock are securely protected from sea-spray or blows by a brass cover. The lock is securely bolted until a pin is removed, when the gun can be fired by pulling a cord attached to the trigger. The length of the barrel is 3 ft., and the weight of the gun complete about 75 lbs. The harpoon weighs about 10 lbs. with the shackle, and is fired with a 1-in. line attached. The charge of powder never exceeds six drams, for more doubles up the shank of the harpoon. It is rarely used at greater distances than twenty-five yards, but is fairly accurate up to forty; and the late W. Greener, whose harpoon guns were by far the best of their day, obtained in a public contest at London Dock, in 1848, an extreme range of 120 yds. Smaller harpoon guns are sometimes made for shooting white-whales, porpoises, walrus, etc., and are carried by yachts on Arctic trips.

The Norwegians use a mortar projecting an explosive ball, or bomb-lance, instead of the old-fashioned double-barbed harpoon. The illustration (page 518) shows the construction of their shell. It is often used to kill whales after harpoon-ing, the Scotch whalers adhering to the old lance for that purpose. The American harpoon lance is of slightly different pattern, as illustrated.

For the big blue whale and the Fin mark whale the harpoons now used are provided with an exploding bomb in front, and the best are fitted with a screw cap of the "Krupp" pattern. It is also now the practice to use shoulder harpoon guns; these are of the following description :—Twist barrel 20 in. long by 1¾ in. across the breech end, butt screwed on as the Martini, Silver's anti-recoil heel-plate, 14-bore, very thick muzzle. Weight 11½ lbs. ; harpoon 1½ lb. ; loose barbs to harpoon.

Another plan is to shape the front of the harpoon so as to form the bomb, or rather a small gun mitrailleuse. It is screwed on the harpoon, and the ignition is caused only when the whole harpoon has entered into the whale and the counter hooks taken hold ; when in this position the hooks act as triggers. There is a small cartridge, 300 bore, which ignites the charge, in the bottom of the shell. The charge can be finest black powder, 2 to 2½ drams. Several holes or funnels are drilled in the projectiles and are loaded with small lead bullets, which spread to all sides by the charge.

Dr. Thiercelin invented and used a shell filled with poison and burst by an explosive. Tried on ten whales, it killed all in from four to eighteen minutes ; four out of the ten were, however, lost by sinking. The poison he used was a soluble salt of strychnine and a twentieth part of curare, sixty grains of which he deems sufficient to kill the largest North Sea whale.

WALKING-STICK GUNS AND SALOON RIFLES.

Walking-stick guns, as usually made in Belgium and France and sold in quantities in London, are, like most other combination weapons, not of much use either as guns or walking-sticks. The tube inside the cane is frequently of *inferior iron or brass*, and brazed together from end to end. Several have burst with the ordinary load, and, as the mechanism is both poor in principle and quality, it is surprising that accidents with them are not more numerous.

A better article is the English pattern, as shown, made in bores ·410, 28, and even 20 bore; ·410 is the most popular. These are made entirely of iron, except the detachable stock, are proved as breech-loading guns of like gauge, and

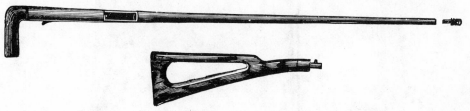

Breech-loading Walking-stick Gun.

may be regarded as trustworthy. The ·410 has a killing range of 25 yards, and the larger bores are available beyond that distance. They are in demand for naturalists, gamekeepers and others, as they are portable, and the stock can be easily hidden away out of sight in the usual convenient pocket.

Saloon rifles, incorrectly so termed, are small, smooth-bore guns with very strong, heavy barrels, and firing a bulleted breech-cap. They are made in three sizes, known as Nos. 1, 2, and 3, the diameter being 1-8th, 3-16th, and 1-4th inches. The smaller sizes generally require no breech-action, the strength of the mainspring and weight of the broad-nosed hammer being sufficient to prevent the escape of gas at the breech. The larger is pivoted on a hinge-pin similar to the side-lever rook-rifle, the bolt being actuated by a small lever on the side or underneath the breech-action.

Their range is 50 to 100 feet, and they are fairly accurate at close quarters.

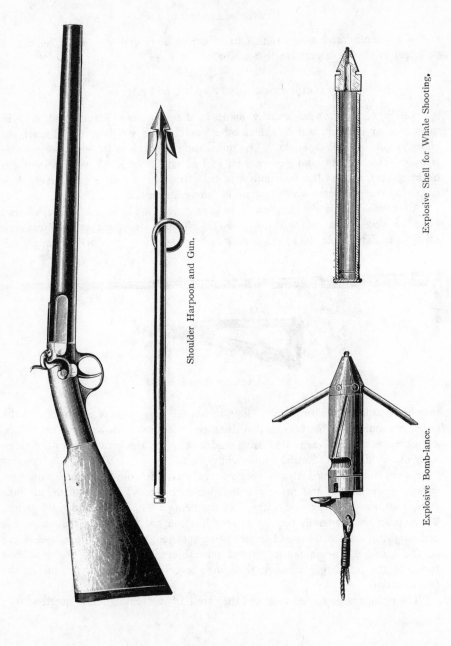

Shoulder Harpoon and Gun.

Explosive Shell for Whale Shooting.

Explosive Bomb-lance.

Pistols of the same sizes are also made on the same principle. In all saloon rifles and pistols the propellant is fulminating powder contained in a small copper case, the invention of M. Flobert, whose name is the best known in connection with these arms.

AIR CANES.

The most popular form for this is the same as the walking-stick gun (shown on page 517), though a shorter " cane," with heavy knob at end, is better for the balance. In these weapons the air is not compressed after firing by the opening of the piece, but has to be pumped into the receiver in the hand by means of a foot pump. In consequence of this, the propelling force becomes less after each shot

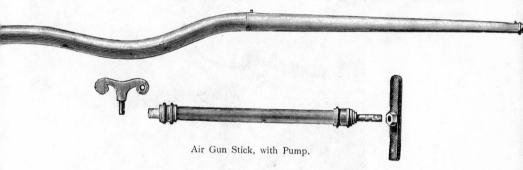

Air Gun Stick, with Pump.

fired, so that the bullet soon begins to drop. Shot is of no use in these canes beyond 15 yards, but the bullet can be relied upon up to 25 yards or more.

AIR GUNS.

Rapid strides have been made during the past few years in the manufacture of these weapons, several English gun-makers having placed some excellent "guns" upon the market. An extraordinary degree of accuracy can be obtained with a carefully sighted air gun at short ranges, and their use has become exceedingly popular for indoor target practice.

ALARM GUNS.

The principle of the alarm gun is so simple that it barely needs description. For outdoor work the alarm gun usually consists of a short cannon, with a nipple; a cap is placed upon the nipple, and over it a weight is suspended by a wire or other device, so arranged that upon the wires running from the gun being pulled the weight is released and fires the gun ; or the gun may have the nipple in the base, and be arranged to slide down an upright rod, when a peg, holding it high on the rod, is withdrawn by a pull on the wire. Various modifications to meet particular purposes will at once occur to the ingenious. The simplest gun, and probably the safest, is a short breech-loader, in which a pin-fire blank cartridge is used, and is fired by a flat spring propped over the pin by a peg, to which the string or wire is attached.

During the South African war the author supplied a special type of alarm gun to the British Government, which, in addition to the usual explosion, fired a rocket containing a magnesium light. This should be of service to gamekeepers for night use, as its ignition would instantly indicate the position of an intruder ; it would also be of value to the big game hunter as a protection against pilfering natives or wild animals.

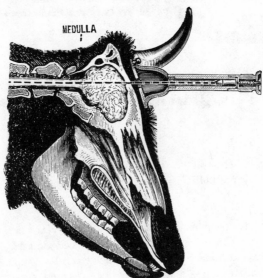

MEDULLA

The "Humane" Cattle Killer.

GREENER'S "HUMANE" CATTLE KILLER.

A modified form of pistol makes an effective form of " Cattle Killer"; the one of which most use is made is known as " Greener's Humane Cattle Killer." It consists of a short rifled barrel to which is attached a bell-shaped muzzle, the object of this device being to deaden the sound and protect the operator from the flash of the explosive. It is fired by an ordinary spring striker struck by a wooden mallet. The piece containing the striker is screwed off the barrel, a cartridge is inserted in the chamber, the top piece rescrewed firmly into its position, the safety loop is moved from over the striker, and the instrument is held firmly against the animal's forehead, and the striker slightly tapped with the mallet. The axis of the barrel should so far as possible be in a line with the spinal column ; the bullet, having sufficient force to penetrate the thickest skull, traverses the brain, pierces the medulla, entering the spinal column, so causing immediate annihilation of the sensory nerve, and consequently instant and painless death.

This instrument is suitable for killing horses, cattle, sheep, pigs, or dogs. It has been adopted by the War Office for use in the Veterinary, Remount and Butchering Departments, by the Admiralty for use in the Victualling Yards, and is rapidly becoming more popular amongst butchers and veterinary surgeons in all parts of the country.

THE "MAXIM" SILENCER.

Many attempts have been made to deaden the sound of explosion in fire-arms, the bell attached to the Greener "Cattle Killer" being one of the earliest and most effective methods, but its weight made it unsuit-able for use on a rifle barrel. The author carried out numerous experiments, some years ago, with modifica-tions of this idea, the most successful being a long tube screwed to the end of the barrel, divided into several chambers by cone-shaped walls. Considerable difficulty was experienced owing to the rapid accumu-lation of the fouling, and, as the demand at that time appeared to be but slight, the idea was not protected. In 1899 a patent was granted to J. Börrensen and S. Sigbjornsen for a similar device for "lessening sound of

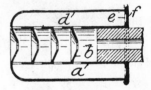

Börrensen's Silencer.

The " Maxim " Silencer.

discharge." It consisted of a perforated sleeve (a), with a series of deflectors (b), which trap the gases while permitting the bullet to pass. It fitted over the muzzle, as shown in the illustration. The "Maxim" Silencer claims many advantages from a military point of view, in that it not only kills sound but also renders the flash invisible at night.   The illustration conveys an idea of the apparatus, which is attached to the rifle muzzle off the centre.   It is made in various sizes for different types of rifle, that for the military rifles weighing about 12 ozs. and measuring 6⅜ in. long by 1½ in. diameter.

THE LINE-THROWING GUN.

A gun of novel type is used for projecting lines over buildings and establishing communication between ships and between ship and shore.   The barrel has a projecting tube at the base, over and between which and the inner sides of the barrel the canister or cop to be fired is placed.   The line is wound round the projectile as shown in the illustration; a special ring-wad is forced down upon the

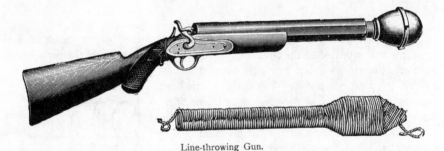

Line-throwing Gun.

small charge of powder, and the projectile inserted from the muzzle.   The line is then passed through the inner tube, and its end made fast to the gun.

The pistol, with a charge of half a dram, will throw a line 200 feet; the shoulder gun, as illustrated, has a range of 150 yards.

THE UNGE AERIAL TORPEDO.

The need for some absolutely reliable apparatus capable of throwing a line long distances in the adverse conditions under which such an apparatus is usually required has received great attention during the past few years, and in 1907 the Board of Trade appointed a sub-committee to consider the question.   Experience has shown that the ordinary rocket is unreliable in anything like a gale, while there is considerable difficulty in throwing a line 300 yards by means of a gun or cannon, the high muzzle velocity necessary to carry this distance usually breaking the line.   The Unge Aerial Torpedo was the only apparatus which successfully passed the tests imposed. The propellant used for the torpedo is a patent compound similar to black powder, so hard that it can only be fired by an electric spark or fuse. The apparatus is portable.

The torpedo line and launching tube are contained in a small box, which could if necessary be carried to and fired from the fore-top, and the apparatus is capable of throwing a 1-in. line 380 yards with absolute accuracy in a strong side-wind.

An Unge Aerial Torpedo throwing a Life-line—velocity, 150 yards per second.

CHAPTER XXI.

MODERN PISTOLS.

THE REVOLVER.

As shown in the history of early firearms, the principle of a revolving breech to one barrel is very old. The chief difference between the ancient type and the modern is that in the former the chamber was moved round by hand, as in the sixteenth-century matchlock (page 82), whilst in the modern weapon it is geared to other mechanism, and is automatically rotated when the hammer is raised or the trigger pulled; but there exists a pistol *temp.* Charles I. which is rotated automatically as the hammer is raised.

In 1814 a self-acting revolver mechanism of a crude pattern was produced in this country; four years later Collier used a separate spring to rotate the chamber.

Colonel Colt, when patenting his pistol in 1835, claimed more particularly the central-fire ignition, and details of the lock mechanism rather than the ratchet motion for moving the cylinder. Previous to this a revolver known as the " pepper-box" was largely manufactured; it resembled a revolver without a barrel, the hammer being placed either above or below the chamber, and the pulling of the trigger rotated this chamber, and also cocked and fired the weapon. Thus it possessed the trigger-action mechanism of the modern double-action revolver. The early American revolvers are single action; that is to say, the trigger is used only to fire the pistol. With single-action revolvers, favoured by Americans to this day, raising the hammer to full cock by the thumb causes the chamber to rotate. The double-action revolver was made in this country by Adams, of London, and Tranter, of Birmingham about 1855, and after these, like the Colt, were made breech-loading.

Without attempting to trace the evolution of the revolver step by step, the illustrations given show the direction the chief improvements have taken. In the illustration of the original Colt it will be seen that there is no strap or band uniting the barrel B with the breech-block G. It was muzzle-loading, the ramming being effected by the powerful lever rod, L, which forced down a very tightly-fitting bullet. This was essential, as the flash from the explosion of one chamber often penetrated

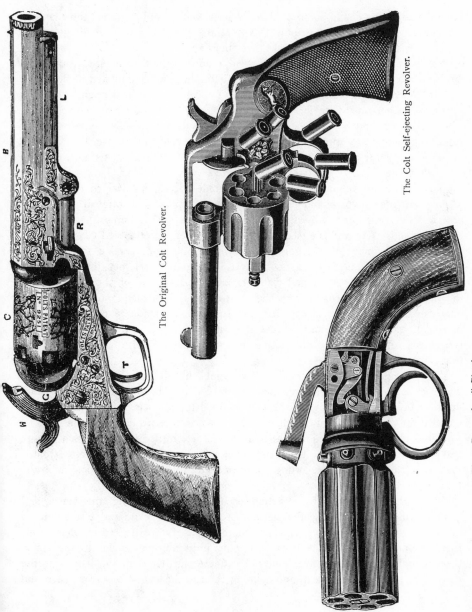

The Original Colt Revolver.

The Colt Self-ejecting Revolver.

The "Pepper-box" Pistol.

down the adjoining chambers past a loosely-fitting bullet, and exploded the charges. A noteworthy feature of the weapon is its central-fire, though the direction in which the hammer fell was far from being in the same line.

Messrs. Smith & Wesson, of Springfield, produced the first metal cartridges for revolvers. They were probably an adaptation of the Flobert bulleted breech caps used in saloon pistols ; their *rim-fire* seems to indicate clearly their origin. Pin-fire cartridges, paper and metallic, were used on the Continent for Lefaucheux and other revolvers, and when once the central-fire system proved its superiority for guns, its principle was applied to pistol cartridges—at first to the larger bores. The rim-fire and, to a less extent, the pin-fire cartridges are still much used for revolvers of small calibre.

The alterations required to adapt the muzzle-loading revolver to the breech-loading cartridge involved no decided change of type. The original Colt, as a breech-loader, was practically the same weapon as before, only the chambers were changed. As will be seen in the illustration of the R.I.C. revolver—until a short time ago the regulation arm of the finest police force in the world—the rammer is retained, its chief use being to knock out the fired cases from the chambers. A hinged flap uncovers the breech of the chamber on the right, and as each chamber reaches that point it is loaded, and at that point only can the fired cases be expelled, the frame being made to partly cover the breech of each chamber and prevent the cartridges slipping out as the chamber is rotated. This is the principle of the most general form of modern solid frame revolvers.

Many plans have been tried to overcome the difficulty of extraction. In Thomas's pattern the barrel and chamber were made to slide forward along the chamber pivot and the frame of the pistol ; the extractor being fast to the pivot, it retained the cartridges until the chamber was pushed forward clear of them.

Although ease of extraction is secured in this pattern, it is by sacrificing rigidity and strength of the frame. The plan which secures this to the greatest extent is that in which the chamber is swung out to one side to give the extraction, as in the Colt pistol illustrated.

The other principle of extracting is obtained by hinging the barrel and chamber, and, by dropping the barrel, forcing out the extractor, just as in an ordinary double gun. The five, six, or more chambers are treated as one barrel ; there is one extractor. The barrel dropping until at right angles to the stock, there is sufficient travel to force out the extractor further than the length of the cartridges, so they drop clear, and a spring returns the extractor to its place and

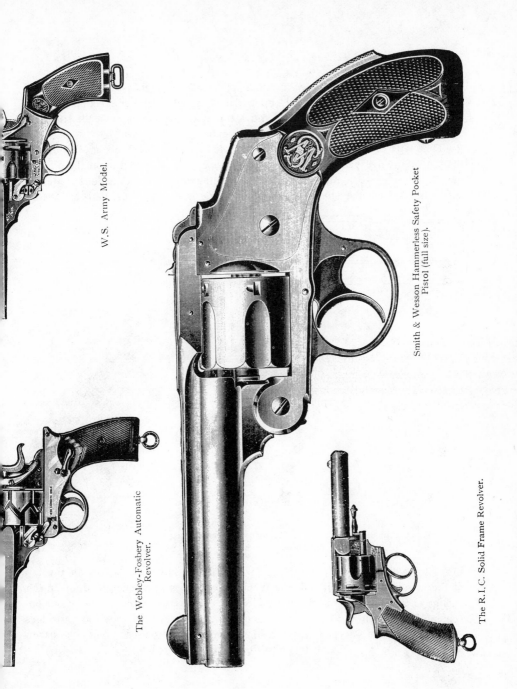

W.S. Army Model.

Smith & Wesson Hammerless Safety Pocket
Pistol (full size).

The Webley-Fosbery Automatic
Revolver.

The R.I.C. Solid Frame Revolver.

brings the barrel to an angle of about 45°, for convenience of loading. The soundness of the weapon depends upon the efficiency of the connection between the barrels and the standing breech, and a top snap bolt has proved the strongest and handiest with the pistol as with the shot gun.

This type of revolver originated with Messrs. Smith & Wesson, but during the last twenty-five years they and others have greatly improved upon the original model. Between the American pattern and the English, as made by Messrs. P. Webley & Son, the most noticeable difference is that in the Smith & Wesson

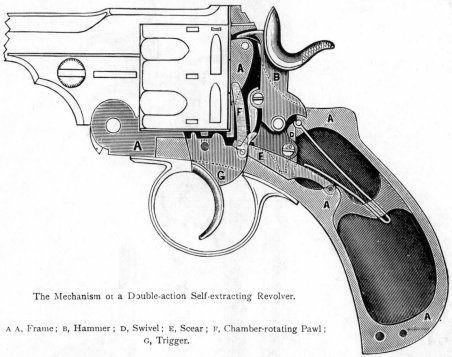

The Mechanism of a Double-action Self-extracting Revolver.

A A, Frame; B, Hammer; D, Swivel; E, Scear; F, Chamber-rotating Pawl;
G, Trigger.

the holding-down bolt or catch is upon the barrel, and it engages with the top of the standing breech, and in the Webley the bolt is upon the standing breech and grips the extremity of the hinged barrel. The latter plan is the most convenient for use on horseback, as the pistol can be opened and the cartridges extracted with the one hand; but neither plan is so strong as could be wished when heavy charges of smokeless nitro-compounds are fired.

The exact arrangement of the parts will be seen by the annexed sectional view of the British regulation army revolver. The lock-work shows an approved form of the double-action mechanism. A pull upon the trigger raises the hammer by a lifting cam; a similar cam or pawl at the same time engages the ratchet on the extractor, and rotates the chamber until the stud upon the trigger projects through the base of the frame and locks the chamber in position—that is, with the cartridge in the chamber in a direct line with the barrel; the hammer is then at full cock, retained there by the scear, with which the back of the trigger-blade is now in contact; the least additional travel of the trigger frees the scear and the hammer falls. The lever of the action is depressed by the thumb, the action jerked open, and the fired cases fall to the ground. After loading, an upward jerk brings the barrel into position, and it is locked there by the grip of the lever bolt.

THE HAMMERLESS REVOLVER.

The Smith & Wesson pocket pistol illustrated is probably the safest weapon of the size ever designed. There is no hammer or equivalent protuberance to catch as the pistol is drawn from the hip-pocket or become entangled if the weapon falls; and, to make all doubly sure, an automatic self-bolting safety blocks the action until the pistol is firmly gripped in the hand in the position usually assumed for shooting. The length of the safety-bolt, half across the palm of the hand, ensures the freeing of the block at the time of shooting.

BREECH-LOADING PISTOLS.

For many years pistols have been practically superseded by the revolver. The small pocket pistol is still made; so, too, but less frequently, is the heavy double-

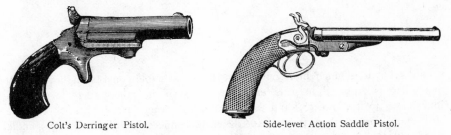

Colt's Derringer Pistol.   Side-lever Action Saddle Pistol.

barrelled horse pistol. The well-known short, large-bore pistol known as the Derringer had once a very considerable vogue; it was usually of ·41 calibre. The next illustration shows a large-bore double-barrelled horse pistol. Formerly these were much used, and took a ·577 cartridge; they are now usually made for a 20-bore case and spherical bullet, and weigh about $3\frac{1}{2}$ lbs. each. They are clumsy but very effective weapons, and will take a charge of $1\frac{3}{4}$ drm. of powder without unpleasant recoil.

Single-barrelled pistols, chambered for the ·22 or 297/230 calibre cartridges, having a barrel of from six to ten inches in length, are also made, and, if fitted with a detachable metal stock, form excellent little weapons for target practice.

THE "MITRAILLEUSE" PISTOL.

Instead of having a revolving chamber, it occurred to certain gun-makers that a more efficient weapon could be constructed on the principle of the "pepper-box" pistol, but with fixed barrels and a special striking mechanism. There is no escape of gas at the breech, as there is in a revolver, and it gives stronger

The "Mitrailleuse" Pistol (closed).

shooting, but it is much more cumbrous. The principle consists in having four or six barrels arranged in pairs, each pair lying on the other; there is a hinge-joint close to the breech, and a top-fastening; each barrel has a separate striker and spring; there is but one trigger, in connection with a vertical spindle fitted with projecting studs, so that by pulling the trigger the strikers are cocked and fired in rotation. This weapon is safe, insomuch that it can never be laid aside loaded and cocked; but it sometimes happens that the shock of the recoil prematurely discharges a second barrel, and this defect would alone prevent it coming into general use.

In all revolving pistols there is an escape of gas between the chamber and the barrel—a fault hard to remedy, and one which leads to many inconveniences, besides the loss of range and accuracy it naturally entails. The principle of the repeating rifle was therefore adapted to pistols, with a view to obtain a stronger shooting weapon. It cannot be admitted that any striking success has attended inventors who have followed the principle of actuating the feed mechanism from

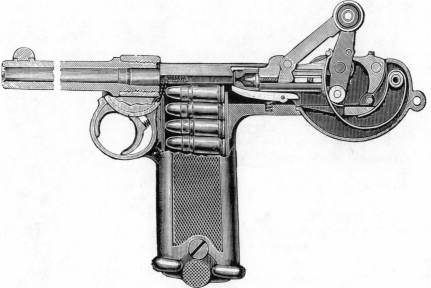

The Borchardt Automatic Magazine Pistol.

the cartridge magazine by a direct pull on the lever after the manner of the trigger of the ordinary double-action revolver. The work to be done is too great for the leverage available; often the mechanism will jam; in ordinary circumstances the strain is too great to admit of good shooting being made. Later mechanisms are so far automatic that the recoil is utilised to eject the fired cartridge and convey another from the magazine to the barrel-chamber. That the magazine pistol will supersede the revolver all experts believe, and it is hoped that the following details of a few of the principal types of automatic pistols may assist the reader in determining how far the belief of the experts is justified.

The Borchardt magazine pistol is of the automatic variety, the mechanism being actuated by the force of the recoil, and so the weapon may be fired simply by pressing the trigger and without pulling upon it, as usual in the ordinary double-action revolver and in magazine pistols of earlier types.

The pistol consists of four principal parts—the butt, in one piece with the lock mechanism case and trigger-guard ; the barrel ; the breech-bolt, with its firing piece and the toggle-joint and springs in connection working the breech-bolt. Arms continued rearward from the barrel engage projections in the breech-bolt, and the parts are so adjusted that when the pistol is fired, by the backward traverse of the barrel, produced by the recoil, the breech-bolt is stopped where shown in the illustration, and the toggle raised, and the spring working it compressed, until, the case having been ejected and a cartridge raised level with the barrel, the stop is automatically freed, and the breech-bolt forced forward by the toggle-joint, and its spring pushes

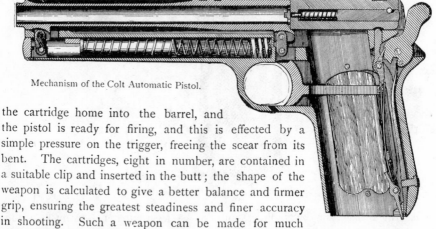

Mechanism of the Colt Automatic Pistol.

the cartridge home into the barrel, and the pistol is ready for firing, and this is effected by a simple pressure on the trigger, freeing the scear from its bent. The cartridges, eight in number, are contained in a suitable clip and inserted in the butt ; the shape of the weapon is calculated to give a better balance and firmer grip, ensuring the greatest steadiness and finer accuracy in shooting. Such a weapon can be made for much more powerful cartridges than used in the ordinary revolver ; a model made is available at 500 metres.

The automatic Colt or " Browning " pistol is made in five different models, and in ·32, ·38, and ·45 calibre. The magazine capacity is seven shots, and after its insertion in the handle the slide is drawn once to the rear by hand ; this movement cocks the hammer, and the magazine follower and spring raise the topmost cartridge so as to bring it in the path of the bolt ; the slide on being released is carried forward by the retractor-spring, and during this movement the bolt places the cartridge in the chamber. As the slide approaches its forward position the front of the bolt encounters the rear end of the barrel and forces the barrel forward. During this forward movement the barrel also swings upward on the links, and thus the

The Webley Automatic Pistol.

locking-ribs on the barrel are carried into the locking-recesses in the slide ; the barrel and slide are thereby positively interlocked, and the pistol is ready for firing.

A pull on the trigger now serves to move the scear so as to release the hammer and fire a shot. The force of the powder gases driving the bullet from the barrel is rearwardly exerted against the bolt, overcoming the inertia of the slide and the tension of the retractor-spring, and as a result the slide and the barrel recoil together. After moving rearward together for a distance, enough to ensure the bullet having passed from the barrel, the downward swinging movement of the barrel releases it from the slide, leaving the barrel in its rearmost position. Owing to its momentum the slide continues its rearward movement, thereby cocking the hammer and compressing the retractor-spring until, as the slide arrives at its rearmost position, the empty shell is ejected from the side of the pistol and another cartridge is raised in front of the bolt.   During the return or forward movement of the slide, caused by the retractor-spring, the cartridge is placed in the chamber, the slide and barrel are interlocked, thus making the pistol ready for another shot. These operations may be continued as long as there are cartridges in the magazine, each discharge requiring only the slight pull on the trigger.

The weights vary from 23 to $53\frac{1}{2}$ ozs., the length over all from seven to eleven inches, according to the model required.   The lightest, or pocket, model is made with an eight-shot magazine.

The "Mauser Self-loading Pistol" is one of the earliest of the successful automatic weapons.   It is a clip loader, the cartridges being contained in a metal clip from which they are "stripped" into the magazine.   It is usually supplied with a wooden holster, which may be attached to the grip of the pistol, and then forms a stock for the shoulder for long range shooting.

The usual type is of ·300 calibre, firing 10 shots ; weight of pistol, $2\frac{1}{2}$ lbs. ; length of barrel, $5\frac{1}{2}$ inches.   It fires an 85 grains bullet, with an initial velocity of about 1,394 f s.

It is also made as a six-loader, and with a longer barrel as a ten-loader carbine.

The "Parabellum" belongs to that class of automatic pistol in which the lock is fixed while the projectile is passing through the barrel, and its breech mechanism corresponds in principle with that of the Maxim gun.

It is of 7·65 $^{m}/_{m}$ or ·301 inch calibre, and has a magazine capacity of eight shots. Its cartridge gives a muzzle velocity of 1,150 f.s., with a maximum range of about 1,967 yards.   It is extremely rapid in action, the cartridges being contained in holders which may be quickly inserted in the grip of the pistol, from which position they are automatically fed into the chamber.

The "Webley" automatic pistol is extremely simple in construction, and can be easily dismounted without the aid of tools.   It is small, light, and may indeed be classed as a pocket pistol, its weight being but 18 oz., and length over all $6\frac{1}{4}$ inches. The pistol is constructed to fire two kinds of ammunition—the Colt 32 or the Browning 7·65 automatic—and its magazine holds eight cartridges.   A "Pocket" pattern has been recently introduced ; it is of ·25 or 6·35 calibre, and weighs 11 oz.   Its length over all is $4\frac{3}{4}$ inches, and it has a magazine capacity of six cartridges.

THE WEBLEY-FOSBERY AUTOMATIC REVOLVER.

This is an arm of a distinctly new design, in which for the first time the principle of utilising the recoil of the first shot to operate the mechanism is applied to the revolver. In appearance the weapon is very similar to the Webley Service model.

As will be seen from the illustration on p. 527, a **W**-shaped channel is cut on the surface of the cylinder, in which a large stud in the lower frame travels during the rearward movement of the frame. This causes the chamber to revolve halfway and at the same time raises the hammer ; on the return of the upper carriage the revolution is completed, and the revolver is again ready for firing.

It is made in two calibres, the ·455, six-shot, and the ·38 model, eight-shot, the weight of the former being 2 lbs. 5½ ozs., and the latter 2 lbs. 3 ozs.

THE QUALITIES OF PISTOLS.

The modern revolver is a weapon designed for quick work at close quarters and for use in one hand. The qualities of paramount importance are rapidity of fire, accuracy and penetration at short range, handiness and quick reloading. A weapon for use in a *mêlée*, the last resource in a desperate emergency, it need not have length of range ; of greater moment is the simplicity of the mechanism, which ought to make no demand upon the shooter's attention.

For this last reason, if for no other, the double-action pistol is vastly the superior of the older weapon. Self-extracting mechanism is of less importance even—save perhaps for weapons placed in the hands of cavalry—for, if after firing five or six shots at close range the danger has not passed, the time left may probably be spent to better advantage than by hastily reloading the revolver, though, of course, there may arise situations of continued peril when it may be possible, and then the self-extracting system will prove advantageous. If the weapon is chosen wholly for target practice, the solid frame pistol is preferable.

The single-trigger action gives greater accuracy than the double-action, but with practice the double-action is practically equal to the single at short ranges—say under fifteen yards—moreover, the double-action can always be used as a single-action. For smoothness of working, the trigger action of the English double-action revolvers has no equal.

The weights, lengths, bores, and other particulars of the shooting powers of modern revolvers are given in the annexed table. Many revolvers shoot different cartridges with equal precision—the English, ·450 and ·455 ; the American, long and short cartridges of different gauges and various charges, and diverse weights and lengths of bullets.

MR. WINANS' RECORD.

North London Rifle Club, June 15th, 1895.
Score : 83 out of possible 84.

Moving Target.
Bisley, July 20th, 1895.

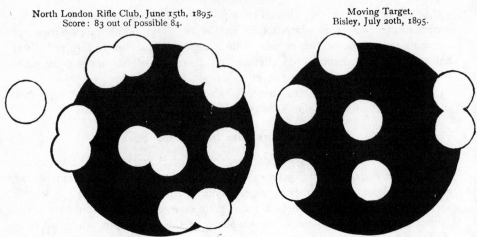

North London Rifle Club, May 29th, 1895.
Score : 42 out of possible 42.
Disappearing Target.

Target disappearing at intervals
of three seconds.
Bisley, 1896.

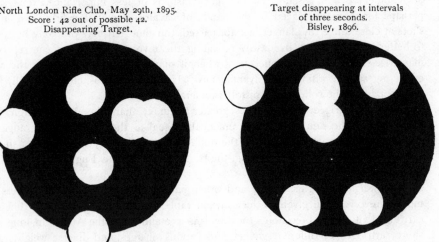

Best on Record Scores at 20 yards made by Mr. W. Winans. Diagrams full size.

VARIETIES OF THE REVOLVER.

Maker's Name.	Description of Revolver.	No. of Shots.	Calibre.	Length of Barrel. Inches.	Length over all. Inches.	Weight.		Cartridge.	
								Powder. Weight.	Bullet weight.
						lbs.	ozs.	grains	grains
Colt	New Service	6	·45	5½	10¾	2	8	40	250
,,	New Army	6	·38	4½	9¾	2	0	21	158
,,	New Police	6	·32	4	8¼	1	2	13	98
,,	New Pocket or Pocket Positive	6	·32	2½	6½	1	0	12	82
,,	Police Positive	6	·38	4	8¼	1	5½	14	150
Smith & Wesson	Double Action	5	·32	3	7½	0	12½	10	88
,,	Safety Hammerless... ...	5	·32	3	7½	0	14¼	10	88
,,	Single Action Target ...	6	·38/·44	6	12½	1	3¾	20	146
,,	,, Bisley model	6	·45	8	13½	2	9	13	226
,,	Military and Police... ...	6	·38	6½	12	1	15¼	21½	158
,,	Hand Ejector	7	·22	3	6½	0	9⅝	5	40
Webley	British Govt. Mark IV. ...	6	·455	4	9⅛	2	3	18	265
,,	"W. G." Army Model ...	6	·455	6	11¼	2	8	18	265
,,	"W. G." Target	6	·455	7½	13⅛	2	10	18	265
,,	Mark III.	6	·380	3	7⅛	1	4	3 Cor	145
,,	"W. P." Pocket Model ...	6	·320	3	7⅛	1	1	6	80
,,	R.I.C., No. 1	6	·450/·455	4½	9½	1	14	18	265

THE SHOOTING OF REVOLVERS AND PISTOLS.

The duelling pistol, as made by Gastinne Renette, of Paris, is capable of wonderfully accurate shooting. At sixteen paces there are no less than eleven persons who have put ten consecutive shots into a centre 3 centimetres in diameter, *without cutting the line.* One of the few persons who have accomplished this was the late Mr. Ira Paine, the American pistol shot. He was a gold medallist amongst the duellers, and, with such a pistol, has made the best shooting ever recorded—putting ten consecutive shots with a mean deviation of only 0·39 inch, the pistol used taking a 9-millimetre spherical bullet and about 12 grs. of powder. With his ·230 pistol he has achieved greater wonders, cutting for the author a pencil line drawn on a playing card and fixed at 20 feet distance. He could also make sure of piercing the ace of hearts at 30 feet twice out of three times, and repeatedly split the edge of a card held edgeways at 20 feet distant. Such marvellous shooting may be a special gift or the result of continuous practice, or both.

With the revolver such accuracy is impossible; the strain of the recoil is so far above the hand, and the recoil so heavy, that even moderately good shooting can be attained only with constant practice. Few, even of the New York police, could shoot sufficiently well with their revolvers to hit a man at 20 yards, but practice soon improved the score, though but few—less than one per cent.—passed into the marksman class.

Mr. Walter Winans has made some of the finest shooting with the revolver ever made by anyone in any country at any time. His best recorded scores are reproduced in facsimile (p. 536); they were made with the military model revolver, firing the usual heavy charges.

Another highest possible score made by Mr. Winans at the Bisley meeting in 1896 was at the advancing target. In this competition the target ought to have advanced at the "quick march" pace from 50 to 15 yards, but by mistake in preparing the range it advanced to within 20 yards only, thus making the performance still more remarkable, for the result was the best on record, all six shots *within* the four-inch bull's-eye. The revolver used was a Smith & Wesson ·44 calibre for the Russian pattern ammunition of U.M.C. make. As the target approaches, a different aim must be taken for each shot: high for the first and lowering the aim proportionately as the target comes closer. The other score to which attention is drawn is that made at the same meeting at a target disappearing at intervals of three seconds, range 20 yards, the revolver not to be raised from the shooting-table before each series of three seconds. The diagram was made with a ·45 calibre Smith & Wesson revolver fitted with Winans' patent fore-sight and U.M.C. ammunition with smokeless powder.

As Mr. Winans won 10 out of 12 of the revolver competitions at Bisley and divided the 11th, his opinions of the merits of revolvers and the requirements of the revolver shooter deserve the fullest consideration. He writes:—

"In my opinion revolver shooting is essentially a matter of firing rapidly at short ranges. Deliberate shooting at stationary targets, especially at long ranges, is all wrong. To begin with, the revolver is not accurate enough for such work. While with the rifle a highest possible score at twenty yards at a two-inch bull would be child's play, as also at a four-inch bull at fifty yards, in revolver shooting it is a very different matter.

"When a revolver is used practically, either in war or self-defence, the shooting is done generally at a few yards' distance and at a rapidly-moving object. Further, it often happens that a succession of shots has to be fired in a few seconds. The man who can make a possible at twenty, or even fifty, yards, but takes from one to ten minutes for each shot, would be killed long before he had time to get off his first shot, presuming, of course, his assailant is a practical revolver shot who can shoot without taking a long time over the individual shots. For instance, a man who can hit a target, say, eight inches square at five yards' range, in snap shooting is a good practical shot. It therefore seems to me that deliberate shooting at the revolver clubs and at Bisley is worse than useless, because it teaches a man to shoot in the wrong way. At Bisley the 'series four' at a twenty-yards' stationary target, and the 'series five' at a fifty-yards' stationary target, as well as the revolver pools at these distances, should be done away with; and prizes of much greater value should be given for rapid-firing competitions with, say, six shots in twelve seconds or less. Also, more prominence should be given to competitions at moving or advancing targets. The disappearing target, which is in sight for three seconds for each single shot, is too slow, in my opinion, for it is practically a stationary target.

"Another point which I think of at least equal importance to the above considerations is the trigger-pull. From the nature of its construction, a revolver is apt to vary in trigger-pull from time to time more than a rifle; and as the minimum trigger-pull allowed at Bisley is 4 lbs., the weapon has actually to be adjusted to $4\frac{1}{2}$ lbs., so as to be safe to pass the test. Now, a revolver weighs under 3 lbs., so we have the absurdity of a trigger-pull nearly double the weight of the weapon itself—a state of affairs which is equivalent to having a trigger-pull of some 16 lbs. or 18 lbs. on a rifle. Professional pistol-shots use a trigger-pull of some $1\frac{1}{2}$ lb. or less, and they could not do any of their accurate shooting with the pull which is compulsory at Bisley."

Mr. Winans thinks that a lighter pull would be *safer* instead of increasing the liability to accidents, and recommends that the minimum pull-off allowed be reduced to 3 lbs. To turn the revolver contests to a more practical purpose, the calibre also should be reduced and a minimum velocity or penetration of the bullet be fixed. Another point to be settled is the best length for the revolver barrel—the longer the barrel the easier the weapon is to aim and the clumsier to handle; the $3\frac{1}{2}$-inch barrel is too short for accuracy at the usual ranges; the $7\frac{1}{2}$-inch barrels are hardly suitable for the uses to which a revolver must be put. Mr. Winans considers that the ·38 calibre will supersede the larger bores as the Service weapon, and he recommends that the length of barrel for use in the Bisley competitions be fixed at $6\frac{1}{2}$ inches.

Revolver shooting would appear to have improved considerably since Mr. Winans' earlier records, and some extraordinary diagrams were made at the N.R.A. Bisley Meeting, 1909, the most phenomenal shooting being that of Warrant Officer Raven, R.N., who made six H.P.S. in succession. The two diagrams shown were made by the same shooter at 20 yards range, and he also established a 50-yards world's record (6 shots in a 4-inch bull) at the same meeting. Mr. Raven used a Colt revolver and Eley ·455 cartridges.

 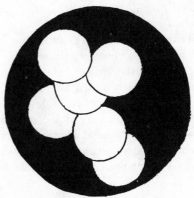

Warrant Officer Raven's Diagrams (actual size).

CHAPTER XXII.

EXPLOSIVES.

CLASSIFICATION OF EXPLOSIVES.

EXPLOSIVES may be divided into three chief classes; first, simple substances which are of themselves explosive, such as picric acid and its alkaline salts, and the fulminates of silver and of mercury; second, mechanical compounds of various substances not of themselves explosive, such as chlorate of potassium with sugar, saltpetre with charcoal and sulphur; third, chemical compounds, such as nitro-glycerine and nitro-cellulose. Sometimes the chemical compounds of the last division are used as ingredients in a mechanical compound (as nitro-glycerine with *kiesel guhr* to form dynamite).

The explosive substances of the first division are rarely used alone. They are made less readily explosive by admixture of other substances; occasionally (as with nitrate of ammonia—which also may be exploded alone if a strong detonator is employed) they are rendered more explosive when incorporated than when used alone. Generally explosives of this class do not admit of much variation, and therefore they are not suitable for use in fire-arms where gradually varying pressures and speed of ignition are all-important.

To the second division gunpowder belongs. This explosive was until recently the only one in general use, the only one the legislature needed to recognise. Other mechanical compounds (as chlorate of potassium with sugar and flour) constitute explosives which are. not nearly so stable as ordinary gunpowder, of greater strength, but in no degree trustworthy.

To the last division belong nearly all high explosives; all of the modern smokeless explosives used for shot-guns, rifles, and cannon; and many, if not all, of the patent blasting powders (as litho-fracteur, matagnite, and the like). For the most part, these explosives are nitro-compounds; their seemingly endless variety is due to the enormous number of absorbers, combustibles, and deterrents which, in different proportions, may become ingredients of patent explosives. Whatever explosive property they possess will depend chiefly upon nitric acid.

NITRO-COMPOUNDS.

The nitro-compounds are generally formed by treating suitable substances of a combustible character with nitric acid, so that by the process the hydrogen and nitrogen they contained are replaced to some extent by oxygen. An immense number of substances are more or less suitable for nitrification, such as purified cotton waste, cotton, wood pulp, the seed-pods of the *Gossypium herbaceum*, and glycerine.

Cellulose $(C_6H_{10}O_5)$ when soaked in strong nitric and sulphuric acids loses its harmless nature and becomes an explosive compound. The nitrification of the cellulose, whether this be cotton or wood fibre, varies according to the strength at which the acid is maintained during the process; mono-nitrate is but little explosive; di-nitrate is more explosive, very soluble, and upon drying becomes gelatinous; tri-nitrate is not soluble, but is much more explosive. The degree of nitrification produces other changes; mono-nitrate and penta-nitrate are very different in their character and strength. By mixing various nitrates with others—as, for instance, 1 part of di-nitrate with 2 parts of tri-nitrate—or in different proportions, it is evident that a great variety of explosives can be produced from nitro-cellulose alone.

It is usual, too, to add one or more combustibles with the oxygenator or nitrated cellulose; such substances, for instance, as sulphur and metallic sulphides; carbon —as charcoal; lamp-black, charred peat; cellulose—in the form of cotton; jute, hemp, elder pith, wood, paper, bark, straw; coal, anthracite, peat, pitch, tar, naphthalene, asphaltine, resins, camphor, wax, paraffin, spermaceti, stearin, fats; lycopodium, starches, dextrin, sugars, gall-nuts, spent tan, tannic acid, amorphous phosphorus, alkaline and earthy hypophosphates, prussiates, acetates, oxalates, tartrates; metallic antimony, iron, magnesium, zinc, copper, white arsenic, or piment and nearly every fluid oil and hydro-carbon which is readily obtainable.

As it is possible also to colour the tri-nitro cellulose with many aniline dyes, and further to render the mass more or less gelatinous before breaking it into flakes, cutting into cubes, forcing into cords, or shaking into grains, the very large variety of modern explosives is easily accounted for. It would be quite impossible, even in a volume devoted wholly to the subject, to give the components and proportions of the many mixtures which have been tried; whilst of many more the exact quantities and substances are known only to the inventors and manufacturers. The following details respecting the composition of a few of the best-known explosives may be of interest. Inventors may note with advantage that in this country, although any chemical mixture may be patented, certain ingredients preclude the compound being licensed for manufacture, importation, or sale. Such mixtures as contain both chlorate of potash and sugar or chlorate of potash and sulphur are not likely to pass the Government tests.   Nitrated glycerines and cottons to which alkalies have been added have been refused because such additions nullify the test made to determine the purity of the sample from acid.

Nitro-glycerine, as its name implies, is a mixture of nitric acid with glycerine. This violent liquid explosive is simply prepared by thoroughly impregnating glycerine with nitric acid, and allowing the compound to fall into a narrow stream of water, when the nitro-glycerine at once separates, the same chemical change taking place as in the case of gun-cotton, the hydrogen or its three equivalents being removed and replaced by the equivalents of nitric pyroxide.   The object to be obtained in the manufacture of nitro-compounds is to secure the proper portion of oxygen required to develop the maximum heat, by entirely consuming the carbon and hydrogen present.   The full explosive force of unconfined nitro-glycerine may be obtained by causing even a minute quantity of the compound to explode in contact with the charge ; that is to say, that if only the smallest quantity can be *exploded* the rest will go off as a matter of course.

Dynamite is nitro-glycerine absorbed by *kiesel guhr* (spongy earth) or other non-explosive material.   Owing to the fact that absorbers do not retain the quantity of nitro-glycerine they originally took up, and therefore leave highly dangerous deposits when stored, *dynamite* is but little used now.   The name is used in common par-lance to designate various blasting gelatines, gun-cotton cartridges, and nitro-glycerine compounds, such as nitro-glycerine, sulphur, saltpetre and clay (sometimes known as *litho-fracteur*).   The absorbers are flint-froth, or *kiesel guhr*, tripoli, alum waste, steatite, talc, asbestos, mica, gypsum, plaster of Paris, cements, shale, lime-stone, bole ochre, etc. ; sawdust, bran, meal, roots, tubers, etc. ; which, compounded with nitro-glycerine, glonorine (concentrated nitro-glycerine), dissolved gun-cotton and other materials, form the basis of nearly all high explosives used for blasting.

Gun-cotton is a nitro-compound in a solid form ; it is obtained by steeping cotton or cellulose in strong nitric acid, but more usually in a mixture of nitric and sulphuric acid.   The cellulose contains a certain amount of carbon and hydrogen. During the bath some of the latter is removed by the oxidising effect of the nitric acid, and replaced by three equivalents of nitric pyroxide, producing a substance known as tri-nitro-cellulose or gun-cotton.   This substance is of much the same appearance as when placed in the bath, but its constitution has altered.   The chemical formula for the change is :—

$$C_6H_{10}O_5 \ + \ 3(HNO_3) \ = \ C_6H_73(NO_2)O_5 \ + \ 3(H_5O)$$
cellulose + nitric acid = tri-nitro-cellulose +   water

It is next washed to cleanse it from acid and other impurities, and may be stored in that form or mixed with other ingredients. Schönbein was the first to manufacture gun-cotton, about 1846, but starch had been employed and treated in the same manner some years previously. *Cotton-powder* is merely cotton reduced to a powder, and *tonite* the same body mixed with nitrates or similar chemical bodies. Gun-cotton cannot by any process yet known be deprived of its explosive properties without destroying the compound by fire. Many years ago a large quantity of gun-cotton of extra strength was manufactured, and ordered to be made away with; some was sunk at sea, some burned, and some buried in the marshes of Faversham. The latter is occasionally met with in excavating, and upon trial has been found not to have lost in the least its fierce strength. Unconfined gun-cotton will burn quietly if ignited with a flame; if ignited by percussion the effect is as great as though confined. For submarine and war purposes gun-cotton is at present stored in a wet or damp state, and may be used and its full strength employed when in this condition. This is effected by the simple expedient of first discharging a small quantity of dry gun-cotton, called a "primer," by percussion. The primer must come into immediate contact with the wet cotton, which it will cause to explode with its full violence.

Gun-cotton as at first manufactured was so fierce and ungovernable in its action as to render it useless for military or sporting powders. The processes of taming gun-cotton, though not numerous, must be thoroughly carried out. The first samples of gun-cotton, or a like material called cotton-wool, are so rapid in action that they may be exploded in contact with ordinary gunpowder, and will not even set fire to it. By the more perfect washing of the material, and freeing it from acids (the presence of which renders it exceedingly unstable), its results have been rendered more governable. Gun-cotton as used by the British Government is reduced to a pulp, and in this state freed from all impurities; it is then pressed into slabs or moulds of any required shape, and appears in that state to resemble *papier mâché* blocks more than cotton. These blocks of compressed cotton burn freely when ignited, but do not explode with violence unless confined or fired by detonation.

The important part to be played by gun-cotton and other nitro-compounds in future wars will be watched with great interest by all scientific persons; a substance that may be stowed in a small compass and fired with the most disastrous results, either upon land or water, cannot but change the present system of warfare. For torpedo-boats, and all submarine and subterraneous works, it has a great advantage over gunpowder, on account of its not becoming deteriorated by damp or atmospheric changes. The terrific violence of a heavy charge of gun-cotton exploded under water greatly exceeds anything likely to be obtained by gunpowder.   A charge of 450 lbs. of gun-cotton sunk beneath the surface will throw a cone of water 60 feet in height, with a base of 220 feet.   No ship, even the largest ironclad, could resist the enormous force of so great a mass of surging water, and if it came within 40 feet of the charge at the time of the explosion the iron plating of the vessel would be driven into the sides, and the ship quickly submerged.   On land the gun-cotton

Submarine Explosion of 450 lbs. of Gun-cotton.

slabs will play an important part.   Cavalry skirmishers, well-mounted, and armed with these blocks, may commit great devastation in a few hours ; by their aid railway lines may be blown up, telegraphic communications cut, trees felled across forest roads, light bridges demolished, stockades razed, and infinite damage done in multifarious ways.   In future guns will be disabled by exploding in the mouth a charge of compressed cotton—the armourer's hammer and the spike being obsolete tools.   Compressed gun-cotton is second only to electricity and light in the quickness of its travel, Mr. Abel having calculated its velocity at from 17,000 to 19,000 feet per second, or 200 miles per minute.

THE COMPOSITION OF HIGH EXPLOSIVES.

E.C., No. 3, consists of nitrocellulose, very thoroughly purified and of uniform quality, with a small quantity of a suitable nitrate formed into approximately spherical granules, hardened throughout their mass by treatment with a solvent which not only renders the grain hard, but also waterproofs it without completely destroying the fibrous structure of the nitrocellulose, so that upon the surface of the granules there remains sufficient rugosity to permit a very quick ignition to be effected by the flash from the cap, and in the interior of the granules sufficient remaining porosity to ensure perfect combustion. The high quality of the nitro-cellulose used in this powder, and the great reduction of mineral constituents (as compared with the so-called 42 grain powders) produces high efficiency, the prac-tical result so far as the sportsman is concerned being increased killing power and reduced recoil and heating of the gun, together with a minimum of noise and absence of products injurious to the gun-barrels or to the eyes of the shooter.

Schultze Gunpowder is manufactured from light fibrous woods, similar to those used for making black gunpowder charcoal. The wood is pulped and then changed to nitro-lignine by treatment with nitric and sulphuric acids. The compound is then submitted to purifying and cleansing processes of an exhaustive nature, which entirely remove or destroy all acids or deleterious chemical properties. The powder is then submitted to hydraulic pressure, the cakes broken up, and the powder granulated by churning when in a moist state in revolving drums. The powder has to be dried by steam, waterproofed and hardened by chemicals, exposed to the air, and stored for some time in open cylinders.

Owing to the powder being only liable to burn and not to explode when in an unconfined state, the Government impose no stringent regulations upon the manu-facturers, except with regard to storage and to the purification, which must be com-plete, the presence of acid rendering the powder exceedingly dangerous and unstable.

There are three varieties of Schultze powder made—the original Schultze being a 42-grain powder, "Imperial Schultze," a 33-grain bulk powder, while the Standard 12-bore load for the Company's latest product, "Cube Schultze," is 30 grains.

Amberite is a mixture of di-nitro and tri-nitro cellulose with paraffin, nitrate of potassium, and barium. The mixture is granulated, hardened, and waterproofed by special processes.

"*Axite.*"—"Axite" is the name of a powder made by Kynoch, Limited, for use in military and sporting rifles. Besides the usual ingredients of Cordite, viz. gun-cotton, nitro-glycerine, and vaseline, it contains some hydro-carbons and mineral ingredients for the purpose of controlling the combustion and of lubricating the barrel. It is made up in the form of a tape, to enable higher velocities to be obtained with less pressure than is possible with strand Cordite. By keeping down the pressure and the temperature of combustion by the addition of special ingredients, combined with a scientific shape of the strip or tape, the erosion of the barrel is much diminished and its life is correspondingly increased. The lubricating effect of the slight deposit left by "Axite" has been publicly demonstrated by firing "Cordite" cartridges alternately with "Axite" cartridges, when it was shown that the Cordite cartridges gave a considerably higher velocity of about 100 f.s. than when fired by themselves. The lubricant deposited in the bore by the combustion of Axite has also a marked effect in preventing the subsequent rusting of the barrel.

Ballistite consists of nitro-cotton, combined with nitro-glycerine, with or without the addition of camphor, aniline, graphite, paraffin, mineral jelly, and carbonate of calcium or carbonate of magnesium, not exceeding one part by weight in every 100 parts by weight of the finished explosive.

Cannonite is a specially prepared nitro-cellulose, other nitrates, and resin.

Chilworth Smokeless Sporting Powder consists of gelatinised nitro-cellulose with or without nitrates.

Coopall's Powder consists of nitro-cellulose with or without other nitrate or nitrates, hydro-carbons, or resin. (*Emerald Powder* is a variety coloured with malachite green.)

Cordite consists of 37 parts of gun-cotton (as hereinafter defined) mixed and incorporated with 58 parts of nitro-glycerine and 5 parts of mineral jelly freed from acid by means of acetone or such other solvent. The gun-cotton to consist of thoroughly purified nitro-cotton (*a*) of which not more than 15 per cent. is soluble in ether alcohol, and (*b*) which contains more than 12·3 per cent. of nitrogen, and with or without carbonate of calcium.

For the rifle ·303 the threads of explosive are ·0375 in. diameter; they are made up into a faggot, and forced into the cartridge case. The next size, for use in the 12-pounder breech-loading cannon, is of cords ·05 in. in diameter, and so increasing in diameter according to the calibre of the cannon in which it is to be used, being ·2 in. thickness for the 4·7-inch gun, ·3 for the 6-inch and ·5 for heavy ordnance. The main difference between cordite and some other smokeless explosives is the shape. Instead of being in grains, pilules, flakes, squares, or cubes, it is usually issued in "threads," and is therefore somewhat inconvenient to load. It can, however, now be obtained "chopped" or granulated, in which condition it is more convenient for the sportsman to load. *Ballistite*, which preceded Cordite, was made of di-nitro-cellulose, but is now also made of tri-nitro-cellulose.

Empire powder is essentially a mixture of nitro-cotton with nitrate and hydrocarbon; the mixture, after being granulated, is hardened by a suitable solvent.

Felixite smokeless powder, *Red Star*, and "*Shot-gun Neonite.*"—The sethree powders are made by the New Explosives Company, of London and Stowmarket, the two former being pure nitro-cellulose bulk powders, containing no nitroglycerine in their compositions. Neonite is a pure nitro-cellulose gelatinised compound, smokeless and waterproof; the standard 12-bore charges for the three powders being 42 grains, 33 grains, and 28 to 30 grains respectively.

Gun Jute.—The invention of M. Mulhausen, who is also inventor of *Gun hemp.* Consists in the substitution of the fibres of *crotolaria juncea, calotrotropis gigantea,* etc., for cellulose.

Gutta-percha Explosive.—A nitrated gum, having the chemical formula $C_{10}H_{15}NO_2$, an inert substance, resulting from the action of concentrated nitric acid on gutta-percha. A weak solution or diluted acid is necessary to produce the explosive.

" K.S." is the ordinary bulk powder made by Kynoch, Limited, for shot guns, and is a gun-cotton powder containing about 15 per cent. of potassium and barium salts.

"K.S.G." is a 33 grain powder made by Kynoch, Limited, containing only about one-half per cent. of solid matter. Like most smokeless powders it is made of gun-cotton, but in the process of manufacture the grain is treated in a special manner so as to control the combustion without the addition of potassium or barium nitrates.

American Explosive Powder.—The United States Smokeless Powder Company make various explosives composed of picrate of ammonia, nitrate of ammonia, and nitro-glycerine.

Moddite.—An improved form of Cordite, introduced by Eley Bros., Limited. It is supplied in tape or strip form. While combining all the advantages of Cordite and M.D.S., it is practically unaffected by climatic variations, and is, in consequence, strongly recommended for use in tropical countries.

Mulhausen's Powder.—Dr. Mulhausen proposed an explosive of 75 parts nitrated starch to 25 parts of nitrated jute, made with acetic ether.

Normal Powder consists of thoroughly purified nitro-cellulose, gelatinised by a suitable solvent mixed or incorporated with a hydro-carbon of the paraffin series, with or without a coating of graphite, provided that the hydro-carbon has a specific gravity of not less than ·87, and a flashing point not below 300° Centigrade.

Randite.—Made by Mr. A. C. Rand, of New York. A composition of chlorate, perchlorate or permanganate of potash, with a hydro-carbon, such as nitro-benzol.

Various proportions are specified as

Nitro-benzol	20	15	13·04
Chlorate of potash ..	80	42·5	52·17
Bioxide of magnesia ...	—	42·4	34·79

Ryve's Powder.—A smokeless powder made in accordance with one or other of the following :—

Nitro-cotton	46·72	45·45	70·75
Nitro-glycerine	44·87	43·64	22·65
Oil	1·87	1·82	0·94
Carbonate of magnesia	1·87	1·82	0·94
Collodion cotton ...	4·67	7·27	4·72

Rifleite consists of nitrolignin, with or without di-nitro-toluene and di-nitro-benzol mixed with nitrates and with or without graphite.

Smokeless Diamond is a nitro-cellulose powder containing a small proportion of nitrate of barium and potassium, together, with certain other compounds which also act as moderators. It is worked up into a homogeneous plastic condition, after which it is granulated, dried, and glazed. The standard charge is 33 grains.

Smokeless Powder or " S.S." is specified as consisting of nitrolignin with a nitrate or nitrates, with or without starch or collodion or turmeric, or other colouring matter, and a substance sanctioned by the Secretary of State, but by request not made public ; also such dyeing materials as Martin's yellow and spirit-blue have been allowed.

Walsrode Powder consists of nitro-cellulose mixed with carbonate of calcium and gelatinised by a suitable process.

Von Forster's Smokeless Powder consists of nitro-cellulose, gelatinised, and with or without the addition of carbonate of calcium or graphite.

Plastomenite consists of nitro-cotton with di-nitro-toluol and nitrate of barium.

Troisdorf's Powder.—This is the powder adopted in Switzerland, and, according to Professor Gody, is composed of pure nitro-cellulose, formed into flakes and coloured.

Lewin's Forcite, also known as superior forcite. Nitro-glycerine, 70·65 ; acetic cellulose, 4·35 ; dextrine, 3·26 ; blasting powder, 21·74. Acetic cellulose is obtained by macerating cotton in a mixture of acetate of soda and sulphuric acid, and cleaning by freely washing in water.

Wetteren L3 Powder consists of deca-nitro-cellulose ($C_{24}H_{29}(O.NO_2)_{11}O$) dissolved in a volatile solvent, rolled into sheets, and cut into fragments. This powder therefore is, as far as composition goes, similar to the B French powder and the MN American powder, and to the Swedish aperite, etc. Its specific gravity is 1·479, and in the Belgian Mauser 2½ grammes, in granules of 842 to the gramme gives 600 metres initial velocity with a pressure of 2,000 atmospheres.

French Government Powders.—Since July 1st, 1892, three types of sporting smokeless powder manufactured by the State have been in the market. They are designated J, P, and S, and each class is again subdivided and known by numbers. The chief powder is said to be a nitrated cotton with which nitrate of potassium and nitrate of barium and some paraffin are incorporated. The powder is chestnut in colour, transparent, gives a pale blue smoke in small quantity, is very hygroscopic, the grains not so hard as those of military powder, and the results are variable.

An export powder is also made by the State; it is grey in colour and is known as B.N.F., and in composition it is very similar to the sporting powder already mentioned. It is hygroscopic, very sensitive to atmospheric changes, but under proper conditions gives a high average velocity, and with but little variation. It produces but very little smoke, and leaves a solid residue, and a quantity of un-burned powder in the barrel. The State are also manufacturers of another "export" smokeless powder, B.N.G., which is analogous to the Italian Nobel explosive, differing in colour, this being tinted with aniline black. The powder of which the Société des Armes Portatives are the owners is intended for military use. According to the *Moniteur Industriel* it gives, with a charge of 2 grammes in a 6·5 m/m rifle, a muzzle velocity of 740 metres to a 10-gramme bullet—that is, a ·275 calibre bullet with a velocity of 2,410 ft. per second.

PERCUSSION CAP COMPOSITIONS.

The cap composition licensed for use in Great Britain consists of chlorate of potash and sulphide of antimony, or sulphur, with or without fulminate of mercury, and ground glass. Practically, manufacturers are compelled to adhere to these ingredients, but the proportions used in various caps differ as shown in the following analysis.

CAP COMPOSITIONS.

	Eley's.	Kynoch's.	Belgian.	Mauser.
Fulminate of mercury	42·14	39·30	42·94	9.10
Sulphide of antimony	10·97	26·46	—	39·39
Chlorate of potassium	27·89	34·24	52·31	45·45
Powdered glass	19·00	—	—	3·03
Resinous matter	—	—	4·75	—
Sulphur	—	—	—	3·03

VARIETIES OF BLACK GUNPOWDER.

Gunpowder, since being granulated, has been manufactured of various sizes of grain. For large cannons the cubes of gunpowder are 1·5 in., and various sizes, from RFG to P2, are used in arms of different calibres; the size of grain being now deemed an important consideration with artillerists. Nor is it of less importance to the sportsman; for upon the size, density, and quality of his powder depends, in a great measure, his success.

Of late years it has been the rule to use a large-grain powder, as No. 4 or No. 6; only a few of the most conservative sportsmen retaining the old-fashioned fine-grained powders.

For general use in 12-bore guns the No. 6 powder is too large, and not sufficiently quick in its action.

A great deal of the quickness of the firing is doubtless due to the shape, density, and quality of the grains as well as the size. To determine the relative merits of gunpowders the *Field* Trial of explosives in 1878 was undertaken; but beyond proving the safety of Schultze wood-powder, and the merits and demerits of certain guns with various powders, nothing decisive resulted, each maker claiming the advantage for his powder. The author's experiments have convinced him that although No. 6 powder will give very regular shooting in shot-guns, it has not sufficient velocity to cope with the smaller powders. Small-grained powders, whilst giving great velocity, generally cause the pellets to scatter much more rapidly than large-grained powders. The theory for this is, that the finer powder burning more quickly has expended all its force before driving the shot as far as the muzzle; whilst the larger grain caused the shot to increase its velocity right up to the muzzle of the gun. The shape of the grain affects materially the combustion of the powder, the sharper diamond-shaped grains burning more rapidly than the rounded ones.

The various grains made by the leading manufacturers are exemplified in the illustrations of grained gunpowders chosen from the productions of Messrs. Curtis and Harvey, and of Messrs. Pigou, Wilks and Laurence, Limited.

In Duck guns of 8- and 4-bore, and in 20-bores of the lightest construction, the No. 4 Alliance Grain gives excellent results; for Punt guns the Col. Hawker punting powder, made by Curtis and Harvey, has a good reputation; a larger-grained powder, known as Col. Latour's, is made by the same firm. A well-made powder for Punt guns is Messrs. Pigou's special Punting powder, the grain coming between the sizes of Col. Hawker's and Col. Latour's.

For blasting purposes a large-grained powder is preferred in England; or a single pellet of compressed powder resembling a dynamite cartridge; this latter is made in three sizes—1, 1¼, and 1½ inches in diameter.

For export purposes the grain marked "African" is preferred. The powder marked "Brazil" is that usually exported to South America; it is highly glazed and more prized on that account, but is of very inferior quality. Travellers may note this, and not purchase this attractive powder if any other is to be obtained. For trading it is more highly prized than far more expensive powders.

A very poor quality of black gunpowder is current in all French possessions, and is one of the evil results of Government monopoly. English or foreign gunpowder of any make is not admitted into France under any conditions. The Rifle powder is of better quality, but it is not easily purchasable in a large quantity; the best brand to get is B. In Spain English powder is to be had, in many parts Spanish powder also; the quality of the latter varies according to locality. In Norway and

AMERICAN.   GERMAN.   FRENCH.

Foreign Gunpowders.

Sweden very good gunpowder is made, but almost entirely for home consumption. In Germany, also, powders of various qualities are to be obtained; some are fully equal to, if they do not surpass, our own. The grains are of various sizes, the powder being very clean, as represented, and not full of dust, like some French powders.

Messrs. Hall have introduced a mixed-grain gunpowder, which is supposed to

Hall's Mixed-grain Powder.

combine quickness of ignition with continued combustion; the results obtained have not been uniform, possibly owing to the fact that in transit the grains being of different sizes are likely to dissemble, and all, or the majority of a charge in one cartridge, being large grains, and the next small.

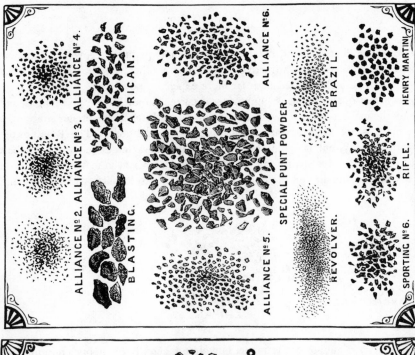

Pigou, Wilks and Laurence's Gunpowders.

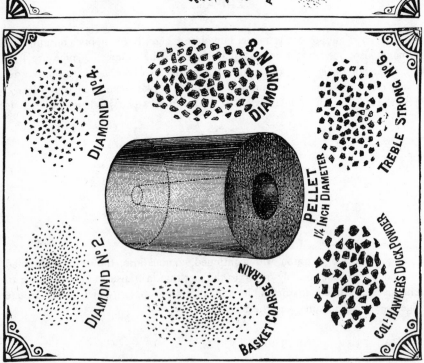

Curtis and Harvey's Gunpowders.

In the United States a large variety of gunpowders are at the option of the sportsman. They are not, as a rule, so clean as the English. American sportsmen may choose a grain resembling as near as possible the No. 4 Alliance for general purposes. The Orange Lightning and Laflin and Rands' are as good as any of American make.

For rifles a large-grained powder is essential to good shooting. No. 6, or the Martini-Henry or Snider powders will convey an idea as to size ; the grains should be sharp, angular, and hard.

MANUFACTURE OF GUNPOWDER.

As already stated in the note on the invention of gunpowder, the composition was at first made by incorporating the ingredients simply. For many years subsequent to its production in Europe the powder was made on the field of battle, where the sulphur, saltpetre and charcoal, all properly pulverised, were separately conveyed. Probably the increased use of the hand gun and the employment of light field pieces led to the manufacture—that is, the incorporation of the ingredients—at a time anterior to that when it was required. Freshly-made powder seems to have been always esteemed. It was not until the sixteenth century that the granulation of gunpowder was practised. Previous to the reign of Queen Elizabeth nearly all the gunpowder used in England was imported from abroad— Flanders, Spain, and Germany being the earliest countries to commence its manufacture upon an extensive scale. In England, in 1561, a John Tornworth was in treaty on behalf of Queen Elizabeth for the purchase of " saltpetre, sulphur, and bowstaves "; in 1588 licence was granted to some of the Evelyn family to " digg and worke for saltpeter within the realme of England and Ireland, during the term of eleven years." A few years later we find three of the same family possessed of a Government monopoly for the manufacture of gunpowder in the south of England, the mills being still in existence and producing modern powder. From 1650 the notices of English gunpowder works are of frequent occurrence, and the various mills and processes are described, including the manufacture of an explosive compound from sulphur, stones and alcohol, and the " mixing of refined sugar with the powder." According to these chronicles, corporating mills, stamping mills, corning mills, and solar stoves for drying the powder, were in use. The ingredients were mixed in various quantities; but it appears that saltpetre, sulphur, and charcoal have been almost invariably used conjointly.

In the leading mills the ingredients for the manufacture of gunpowder are now supplied in the rough state, and are there refined and prepared for use. This course has been found to be the only one by which uniformity of results and pure finished powder can be obtained. It is also a more perfect safeguard from accidents, for where the ingredients are received refined, ready for mixing, particles of grit introduced after refining may cause deplorable explosions during the corporating process.

Saltpetre, Potassium Nitrate (KNO_3), the chief ingredient of gunpowder, is a chemical compound of potassium, nitrogen, and oxygen. In some parts of the world—in India and Andalusia especially—it is formed as a natural efflorescence upon the surface of the earth, and is indeed the only source from which we derive it. In Prussia, France, Sweden, etc., the old mortar used in building the farm walls was, and perhaps still is, so treated as to produce saltpetre. Nitrate of soda (cubical nitre) is also largely imported into England for the manufacture of artificial saltpetre. The Royal Waltham mills derive their supply entirely from Bengal and Oude. The salt is collected, boiled with water, and the solution, after being concentrated by the heat of the sun and evaporated, yields impure crystals, which are packed in coarse bags and shipped to England; in this state the salt is known as "grough" saltpetre. Upon arriving at the powder-mills the saltpetre is refined by the following process:— In a large vat, capable of holding about 500 gallons of water, is placed two tons of grough saltpetre, and the fire lighted underneath, after adding about 275 gallons of pure water to it. In about two hours' time the saltpetre is in solution and boiling; the specific gravity being 1·49, and the temperature approaching 230°. The scum, containing the greater part of the organic impurities, is removed from the surface, until no more scum rises; the copper is then filled up with cold water and boiled briskly for a few minutes, and allowed to cool down to 220° Fahr., when it is pumped into filters, and the hot solution run off into shallow vats to crystallise. As the temperature falls the excess of saltpetre crystallises out, leaving a considerable quantity still in solution, which also retains the chlorides, sulphates, and other chemical impurities. Whilst in the vats the solution is continually agitated to prevent it from forming into large crystals; the salt by this means is deposited in the form of flour. The flour is then washed three times, tested, and, if pure, is ready for use.

Sulphur, another of the ingredients of gunpowder, is one of the few simple non-metallic bodies which exist in a natural state uncombined. In all volcanic countries it is very abundant. In Sicily it is found embedded in thick masses nearly pure, and it is from this island that England chiefly derives its supply. The sulphur, upon arrival at the powder-mills, is first refined. The old way is to simply fuse the sulphur, when the grosser impurities sinking to the bottom and the lighter ones rising to the surface, the intermediate sulphur is left more or less pure, and is then drawn off by a suitable contrivance. At the present day sulphur is refined by two methods, distillation and sublimation. Distilled sulphur, chiefly used in the manufacture of gunpowder, consists of masses of clear yellow crystals in the shape of rhombic octahedra, and is soluble in bisulphide of carbon. Sublimed sulphur is the common flower of sulphur, and is but seldom used in gunpowder.

The process of distillation consists of heating the grough sulphur in an iron refining-pot having two pipes leading from it—one into a subliming dome, the other into a collecting-pot—until it vaporises. The vapour at first is of a pale yellow colour, this passes into the subliming dome, and is immediately precipitated into an insoluble electro-positive form known as flower of sulphur. Upon the vapour becoming more dense and of a darker hue, the pipe to the dome is stopped and the one to the receiver opened. This pipe is surrounded by a water jacketing, and kept constantly cool by a running stream of water ; upon entering this pipe the vapour is condensed, and runs into the receiver in a liquid state, of the consistency of treacle, which it strongly resembles. When sufficiently cool it is ladled out into wooden tubs and allowed to solidify. When "set," the tubs are knocked off from the sulphur, which is broken up and placed under a mill and well ground until it will pass through a 32-mesh wire cloth—when it is ready for use.

There is, practically, no loss in refining sulphur, but care has to be taken that the temperature of the melted sulphur be not allowed to rise to 836° F., as the vapours given off at that heat are highly explosive when mixed with common air ; so that if, through the leakage of a pipe or other cause, the air is allowed to come into contact with the vapour, an explosion invariably occurs. Professor Bloxham says : " Sulphur as an ingredient of gunpowder is valuable on account of the low temperature (560° F.) at which it inflames, thus facilitating the ignition of the powder. Its oxidation by saltpetre appears also to be attended with the production of a higher temperature than is obtained with charcoal, which would have the effect of accelerating the combustion and of increasing by expansion the volume of gas evolved." Sulphur melts at a comparatively low temperature of 239°, vaporises at about 270°, and inflames at 560° F.

The third and last ingredient of gunpowder, charcoal, is manufactured from either of the following woods :—Willow (*Salix alba*), Alder (*Alnus glutinosa*), or what is known in England as Black Dogwood (*Rhamnus frangula*), although any light, soft wood may be used. In India the Grambush plant (*Cythus cajan*), Parkinsonia, and Milk-edge (*Euphorbia tiraculli*), have been found very suitable. The wood is generally cut in the spring, in order that it may be the more easily stripped of the bark; but wood felled in the fall of winter is equally as good, providing that it is carefully decorticated. The removal of the bark is compulsory, as it prevents scintillation, which would prove a very dangerous quality in gunpowder. At most of the mills large quantities of willow are grown upon the ground; but a good supply, especially of dogwood, is derived from Prussia. The following process of charcoal-burning ensures perfectly fine and pure charcoal:—The wood, in lengths of about 3 feet and from 1 to 4 inches in diameter, is placed in an iron cylinder or retort, several of which are set in the flues of a large furnace; pipes lead from the retorts to the furnace for the exit of the noxious vapours. The time taken for the proper charring of the wood depends entirely upon the heat of the furnaces and the thickness of the wood. Charcoal made at a temperature of 500°F. is readily ignited at 640° F., whilst charcoal made at 1,800° F. requires nearly double the temperature of the last to influence it; for this reason the charcoal made at a low temperature is considered the best for sporting purposes; it, if properly burnt and from the best wood, is, when powdered, of a reddish-brown hue; whilst the latter, being denser and consequently less hygroscopic, is of a black colour. When sufficiently burnt, the retorts are raised, and lowered into extinguishers, in which they remain for several hours, after which the charcoal is shot into coolers, and subsequently ground to powder and stored for use. If uniform results are required, it is essential that the retorts be kept always at the same temperature; to ensure this, pyrometers are used. Freshly-powdered charcoal is never used to make gunpowder, as it is liable to spontaneous combustion, and generates great heat. After standing ten or twelve days it loses this property, and may be safely used. The ingredients being now prepared, they are mixed in the mixing-room. The quantities are weighed out and roughly mixed with a shovel, and placed for a few minutes in a rotating drum making 40 revolutions in the minute. The bearings of the drum are hollow, to enable an axis carrying 44 arms or fliers to revolve at twice the speed of the drum in the opposite direction. The charge, consisting generally of 60 lbs., is usually made up of 75 per cent. saltpetre, 15 per cent. pure charcoal, and 10 per cent. sulphur; the saltpetre being always mixed in a damp state, 1 lb. is added to the 100 parts to cover loss in manufacture; when mixed, the compound is called a green charge; although not so inflammable as gunpowder, it is of course explosive, and when accidents do occur in the mixing-shed—happily but a rare occurrence—the victims are generally found to be more burnt than those who are killed by the explosion of gunpowder, from the slower and more lasting nature of the flame.

The process of mixing is in some mills dispensed with entirely, the incorporating mills being made to do the work of the drum, but it causes more waste. The next process, that of incorporation, consists of a long-continued trituration beneath heavy runners, by which means the mass of ingredients becomes transformed from a mere mixture of three different substances into gunpowder. This is the most important process in the manufacture, and no subsequent care can possibly improve the quality of the powder.

The incorporating is effected by grinding the mixed ingredients for several hours beneath heavy runners. The bed of the mill is of iron, or of stone with iron *tyres*. The runners weigh from three to four tons each, and vary in size from $3\frac{1}{2}$ to 7 feet in diameter, the smaller ones, creating less friction upon the bed whilst revolving round the vertical spindles, are considered the safest. Iron runners and beds were first used in Scotland in 1804; the mills, formerly turned by a horse and gear, are now worked by steam or water power. The incorporating is one of the most dangerous processes: unavoidable accidents, arising from unknown causes, frequently destroy the sheds and machinery. A cistern containing 40 gallons of water is poised upon a support immediately over the runners; the cisterns in the various mills are connected to each other, so that upon an explosion in one mill all the cisterns empty themselves automatically, thus the powder under the various runners is at once rendered non-explosive. The sheds themselves are made with strong wood frames covered with light boarding or felt, so that in the case of an explosion the damage caused is comparatively trifling. The charges are placed in the mill moist, and require watering from time to time; this is done either automatically by machinery or by the hand. The charge requires to be under the runners 10 to 12 hours for best sporting gunpowder. In the Government mills, $3\frac{1}{4}$ hours is considered sufficient for cannon powder and $5\frac{1}{2}$ for small-arm powder; with heavier runners, making eight revolutions a minute, it is not even left so long.

The greatest danger is at the moment of starting; by Act of Parliament 60 lbs. is the maximum charge allowed to be incorporated in one mill. The object, of course, is to prevent accidents if possible; but it is doubtful if a 100 lb. charge would not be more safe, as it would possibly prevent the two runners from coming into contact with the surface of the bed, which occasions considerable friction, and is the cause to which most of the accidents are assigned. After incorporation, the powder, known in this state as *mill cake*, must be reduced to a meal between rollers, in order to prepare it for pressing. This process, known as "breaking down," is not a primary operation in the manufacture, but only a preparatory measure adopted to ensure perfect pressing. The meal must not stand for any length of time, but be at once conveyed to the press-room, and subjected to hydraulic pressure. Formerly this pressure was dispensed with, and powder made in this way is still current in some parts of Great Britain, Spain, and most Eastern countries. The pressure gives consistency to the grains, increases the density of the mixture, and prevents the finished material from crumbling to dust during transit or loading. The meal is placed in the press in layers, the layers being separated by felt or canvas and gun-metal sheets. When loaded, the press is subjected to about seventy tons pressure to the square foot—more or less, according to the density of the powder required. When unloaded the powder is in slabs varying from $\frac{3}{4}$ in. to $1\frac{1}{2}$ in. in thickness. Pressing is a most important process, and it is of the greatest importance that the density obtained should be uniform. A difference of ·05 in the specific gravity of the charges may affect the velocity of a 12 lb. shot, fired with a 1 lb. charge, to the extent of about fifty feet per second. No difference between the powders may be perceptible until weighed, and therefore it has frequently happened that the fault which lay in the powder has been attributed to the weapon or projectile. After pressing, the slabs are broken up into fragments with mallets and sent to the granulating shed. The process of granulating, or corning, consists in reducing the fragments of press cake into various-shaped grains of the required sizes. In private manufactories, where all sizes of grain are required, the process is more simple than in manufacturing Government powder of one specified size ; consequently, in the latter case there is much more waste. The old corning machine consisted of a large revolving rectangular wooden frame, on which were placed a number of sieves with parchment covers, and on the axis of each was a loosely-fitting disc of *lignum vitæ*. During the rotation, the discs dashing about in the sieves broke up the cake, but created a great quantity of waste and dust, besides being highly dangerous. The Congreve machine is now almost universally employed. It is a complicated machine, the cake passing between toothed gun-metal rollers fixed at various distances from each other ; the teeth are of various shapes and sizes, and the machines are made self-feeding. The process of corning is a dangerous and dirty one ; a large amount of dust is created ; fans are at work in the shed to collect it, and blanket screens are also requisite. Even with these appliances the dust pervades the atmosphere to such an extent as to render a long stay in the shed impossible. During the process the powder is sifted to a certain extent, and the useless material and dust collected, and either re-pressed, or re-incorporated and pressed, according to the quality of the refuse.

The next process is to sort the powder by sifting, and free it from dust or minute particles of matter that may have been obtained in the corning-house. The powder is freed from dust by placing it in revolving wheels covered with cloth or wire mesh, through which the dust escapes. It is then sifted in rotating wire cylinders. The next process is to glaze or polish the individual grains ; this is accomplished by causing the grains to rub against each other in revolving wooden barrels or drums. Dense hard powder will take a higher glaze than the softer kinds, for it is clear that poorly pressed or soft gunpowder cannot stand much knocking about in the sieves or churns without becoming disintegrated and forming fresh dust. Higher-glazed and harder-grained powder will resist damp much better than soft kinds. Blacklead (graphite) is placed in the churns with the common powders to give a fine glaze in a short time, but this practice is detrimental to the quality of the powder, causing the gun barrel to foul much quicker, and leaving a greater residue. The dusting-reel is formed with twenty-four-mesh canvas, and makes about forty revolutions per minute. The glazing takes from five to eight hours, in wooden barrels revolving thirty-four times per minute. The powder is then subjected to a second dusting, same as the first, and must then be stoved. The friction in glazing necessarily engenders a good deal of heat ; some of the finer-grained powders are so hot as hardly to permit of the hand being plunged in. In every case the heat is sufficient to make the powder give off nearly all its moisture, but as there is no escape for it, it condenses in the interior of the barrels, and forms a hard coating with the powder dust. The stoving consists in subjecting the powder to a temperature of 125° or 130° Fahr. for eighteen or more hours. The powder is placed on canvas-bottomed trays, and arranged on racks in the stoving-room, which is heated by steam coils fed from a boiler some distance off. The stoving sweats the powder, and drives off any remaining moisture. After stoving, all that the powder requires is "finishing" by again revolving it in a drum ; it may then be sifted and stored in the magazines.

PROPERTIES OF EXPLOSIVES.

Captain Noble, by exploding charges—in some instances as heavy as 23 lbs.—of gunpowder in enclosed vessels, and thus confining the gaseous and other products of the explosion, was able to determine their volume and nature.

Service gunpowder (black) gave 6,500 atmospheres, or generated a pressure of 43 tons to the square inch ; 57 per cent., by weight, of the products of the explosion are non-gaseous, 43 per cent. are in the form of permanent gases, and these gases, at a temperature of 0° C. and a barometric pressure of 760 mm., occupy 280 times the volume of the unexploded powder. At the moment of the explosion the non-gaseous products are in a liquid state ; they are driven at high velocities in all directions by the gases, and as the heat generated by the explosion declines they solidify; in large cannon the solid deposit is sometimes ¾-inch thick in the chamber. The explosion of a large charge in a great cannon resembles, not the expansion of a semi-opaque gas, but the scattering, at tremendous velocity, of a load of small shot. In the bore of a shot-gun, or small calibre rifle, the same principle is involved.

The explosion generates heat and frees gases, which expand to a certain volume; for instance, 1 gramme of Curtis and Harvey's No. 6 produces 764 units of heat, and expands to 241 cubic centimetres; mining powder produces 517 units of heat, and expands to 360·3 cubic centimetres, the powders producing the largest quantity of gas evolve the least quantity of heat; there is also a large proportion of heat which escapes measurement, as its potential energy is expended in placing the solid carbon in a gaseous form when the carbon in the powder burns to carbonic oxide.

Nitro-compounds possess various advantages over black, the chief being the absence of smoke after the discharge and the small amount of residue deposited in the barrel. This is on account of the greater percentage of available gases contained in nitro-compounds to that of gunpowder. Black gunpowders usually give about 65 per cent. solid residue and 35 per cent. available gases, which of course have to drive out of the barrel the solid residue in addition to the charge of shot and wads in front of it, the major portion of the solids being in a state of fine division or smoke. The best nitro-compound will give about 30 per cent. solid residue, 70 per cent. available gases, consequently one half the charge of powder by weight is equivalent in force to a full charge of black powder. This leaves, therefore, only about 15 per cent. solid residue to be expelled from the barrel against nearly 65 parts solid from black. The solids resulting from some wood powders and some other nitro-compounds are expelled in a coherent form instead of as smoke, thus slightly lessening the recoil.

To the great difference in the density of wood and black powder may be traced the disparity between the solid residues of the respective explosives.

Black powder, generally speaking, has a real specific gravity of about 1·720, whilst the Schultze powder, pressed and granulated, has a specific gravity of ·860. Therefore, a charge measuring three drams will weigh black powder 84 grains, Schultze 42 grains. In ignition, and therefore to an extent in combustion, wood powder is slower than black. Ignition means setting each individual grain alight; combustion means the rapidity with which the grains burn. This is practically always the same with black powder, but it varies with the heat of the gas in the barrel with nitro-powders. When a greater muzzle velocity is obtained with the nitros than with black powder it is because the charge either contains more gas or because its burning evolves more latent heat. It seldom gives a greater increase in velocity than 5 per cent., although the makers affirm that it could be made to give more if desired.

Unconfined wood powder, in common with other nitro-compounds, may be ignited without obtaining a third of the available explosive force.

The " E. C." powder has many properties in common with the Schultze. Its specific gravity is about the same ; the amount of solid residue left in the gun-barrel is, if anything, less ; the smoke is less dense even than from Schultze, and the barrels do not heat so rapidly, and, strange to say, invariably heat from the muzzle to the breech, instead of from breech to muzzle, as is usual with black powder. Theoretically, nitro-cellulose is superior to nitro-lignin. In actual practice there is little difference.

Nitro-cellulose contains about 14 per cent. of nitrogen, or 46 per cent. of Nitroxyl (NO_2), when at its full strength ; but by using weaker nitric acid in the solution, a less percentage results, and ignition by detonation will be more difficult, combustion slower, and the explosion less violent.

Black gunpowder, on an average, will fire at a temperature of 539° Fahr., whilst nitro-cellulose, or "E. C." and Schultze gunpowders, fire at 370° Fahr.

The result of heat before ignition to various explosives is attended by very different results. *Nitro-glycerine* will explode with a modicum of violence when at 60° Fahr., much more strongly at 100° and 350°, and increases in violence up to 750°, but at and beyond 750° it becomes comparatively weak, and its explosiveness is more and more feeble as the temperature is raised.

Black gunpowder is much more violent if heated to 212° before igniting, and the strength of " E. C." and Schultze powders increases in a greater ratio than black, and when heated they require less to ignite them.

The strength of detonating nitro-compounds is more developed when the detonator is in actual contact with the explosive. The flash alone of an explosive cap would not develop nearly so much energy from the powder as would a detonator fired in the middle of the charge ; but the explosion would be stronger than if the charge were fired by insertion of a heated wire, or by the application of a flame.

All nitro-compounds are more violent in their action the more tightly they are confined, and the stronger the detonation by which they are exploded.

The explosion by means of a Bickford fuse of various explosives in lead cylinders 4 × 8, and bores 1 × 4 inches, capacity of 60 cubic centimetres, resulted as follows :—
1 oz. of Curtis and Harvey's No. 4 Diamond Grain increased capacity to 280 cubic

centimetres; whilst $\frac{1}{2}$ oz. of "E. C." increased it to 210, and a like charge of Schultze made the same increase.

The chemical action of the residue left in the barrel after firing "E. C." or Schultze is not more deleterious than that left after firing the best black gunpowders, and no more cleaning or preparation of the barrel is required with one explosive than with another.

Nitro-explosives, even of the same description and make, are not always of the same strength. Mention has already been made (page 155) of a specially strong issue of Schultze powder which, about 1878, was made to order and injured several guns. Much more recently another explosive was modified to suit the requirements of some ammunition makers, and the results were even worse, brought about by a long chain of coincidences, which none could foresee. In the first place, the powder was slightly stronger or more sensitive; in the second, the maker of the cap, the better to overcome a difficulty with ignition, changed the composition; a colonial gun-seller ordered an unusually heavy charge, and the special powder was used with the new cap; then the cartridges were stored in a light shed exposed to the sun's rays; when sold and used they injured the guns most seriously; after half-a-dozen weapons had been incapacitated the dealer took a new strong gun and tested the cartridges; the gun succumbed after a few shots. Such a train of circumstances might not occur again; but, to avoid like consequences, nitro-explosives for no reason whatever should be issued of any other strength than that ordinarily issued. Gun-makers, ammunition dealers, and sportsmen are at the mercy of the nitro-powder makers in most favourable circumstances; with variable powders being issued the only real safeguard would be to avoid their use entirely.

THE STRENGTH OF EXPLOSIVES.

The mean effective pressure of explosives may be obtained theoretically, when the weight of the projectile and the M. V. is known, from the following equation :—

Mean pressure in tons per square inch × 2240 × area of base of projectile in square inches × travel of projectile in feet $= \dfrac{\text{weight of projectile in lbs.} \times V^2.}{2\,g.}$

This method is purely theoretical and makes no allowance for friction. The method adopted by the gun and ammunition makers for determining the relative pressures of various explosives consists of exploding the charges in a crusher gun having pistons of uniform diameter at varying distances from the breech along the barrel. These pistons are actuated by the gas pressure of the explosion, and are made to compress lead columns of uniform shape and size called "crushers." The reduction in the length of the lead columns is called the compression, and from it the maximum pressure is calculated. The crushers generally adopted are those made by Messrs. Eley Bros.

The Eley Lead Crusher table was obtained by submitting varying loads on the lead crusher and observing the reduction in length. The load was put on by weighted lever and allowed to remain on the crusher a definite time. For all loads the time was the same, and obtained by connecting the lever to a crank fixed to a shaft, revolving at the rate of 60 revolutions per minute. The load remained on the crusher for approximately $\frac{1}{4}$ second.

The Eley table given in detail on page 325 was submitted to the investigations of the *Field* committee of experts, and they made experiments by the dropping weight system and also with a lever press, and on the latter instance the load was left on varying times. Also experiments were made in shot-gun proof barrels, using one, two, three and four lead crushers on one piston, and it was found that the sum of the pressures when using several crushers was the same as the pressure given by one crusher. This committee decided that the Eley table could not be improved, and all they did was to make slight alterations near the remaining length of ·490. In later years copper crushers have been used in shot-gun proof barrels, crushers which give a time value for pressures, independent of the time the pressure is acting. The results with copper crushers have shown that the Eley lead crusher table is substantially accurate up to 4 tons pressure.

The author has made very many tests with the crusher gauge ; one series of experiments extended over many months, and in varying conditions as to weather, temperature, etc., but the details of this one series the sportsman would find wearisome to examine, and the expert confusing. Regarding them simply as indications of the relative strengths of various explosives tried in different ways, the tests may be summarised, and show conclusively that—

1. " Alliance " No. 4 black gunpowder gives 6 per cent. less pressure than " Diamond " grain, yet with equal patterns and penetration.

2. New " Hard Grain Schultze " gives greater pressure than the old issues of Schultze, and that more or less turning down of the case affects the pressure. Wads of $11\frac{3}{4}$ gauge in the 12-bore also increase the pressure.

3. Swedish " Cup " wads give at least 25 per cent. greater pressure in the chamber; this with all the nitro-explosives with which they were tested, but not with black gunpowders.

4. Shooting long cases, as $2\frac{3}{4}$-inch case in $2\frac{5}{8}$-inch chamber, increases the pressures enormously; with 47 grains of nitro the pressures registered were double those registered with cases of the proper length.

5. The conical "pressure reducing" base to the cartridge case for nitro-explosives does not reduce the pressure.

6. No nitro-compound is trustworthy. Of late years the older explosives have become more variable, and the new ones show no improvement. It seems impossible to get successive batches of any one explosive exactly alike. Testing every batch of each explosive delivered, and having deliveries in bulk every month of the year, the author confidently asserts that sportsmen using these nitro-explosives are absolutely at the mercy of the manufacturers, who are a law unto themselves in so far as they issue the explosive of whatever strength it may happen to be. Not in one instance, but several, has the author discovered that the explosives delivered to him are far from being identical in quality with those previously delivered from the same factories. If these faulty explosives were *weaker*, it would be merely a matter of business to return them, and insist upon the right quality being delivered, but as in most instances they are stronger, and occasionally even double what is recognised as normal, so as to indicate dangerous pressures in the crusher gauge, it is a question whether or not the lot should not be at once destroyed. It is a very difficult matter indeed to re-manufacture or to manipulate in such a manner as to reduce the strength uniformly and without deteriorating other qualities—as stability—of the explosive. Possibly such explosives as may be rejected by the maker furnished with the instruments necessary to test the explosives delivered to him, are sold to persons not in a position to prove that the strength is dangerous. It is no less dangerous if shipped to a colonial buyer, and the mere possibility of such a thing occurring—even by accident—ought to awaken gun-makers and sportsmen to the need there is for a Government test being applied to gunpowders as well as to guns. For explosives of any and every strength to be in use, whilst guns are meant only for explosives of a known strength, renders the proof of guns futile in so far as the test is regarded as safeguarding the public. Who should test the powder, and to what tests it should be subjected, are matters of less concern than that *some* test should be applied at once, and by the gun-makers, if no other authority will undertake the work forthwith. For the sportsman it is sometimes a difficult matter to know when a powder is exerting an excessive strain, but very reduced patterns obtained from a gun whose shooting is known are a sure sign of increased pressure, and a trial of the cartridges should be at once instituted when such are observed.

CHAPTER XXIII.

INTERNAL BALLISTICS.

DEFINITIONS.

A *GUN* is a thermo-dynamic machine by which the potential energy of the explosive is converted into the kinetic energy of the projectile.

The *potential* of an explosive is the mechanical *equivalent* of the heat produced, acting on the increased volume of the converted charge, by the combustion of the explosive; the mechanical *effect* which may be obtained is but a part of the potential; the pressure derived is also a part only.

Internal ballistics is a term signifying the effects of the combustion of the explosive so far as they relate to the gun and to the projectile as long as it is within the gun. Therefore internal ballistics comprise—the nature and value of the stresses upon the gun-barrel and breech; friction upon the gun; the pressure upon the base of the projectile; the muzzle velocity of the projectile; erosion; fouling; recoil; jump and flip.

The *combustion* of an explosive is a gradual process, and the rise of pressure is gradual, the time varying according to the nature of the explosive and in the manner of combustion; but the explosion may be detonation, in which case ignition of individual grains is quicker than the travel of the flame, and therefore they are not ignited by flame, but are ignited by vibration.

Detonation of an explosive is a term used by Berthelot and others to signify a more than ordinarily rapid explosion; the result of particular conditions, some of which will be specified later.

Wave-pressure is a term applied to the abnormally high pressures which occasionally occur; they are the result of an unequal confinement of evolved gases.

Stresses.—The stresses upon a gun are a radial stress or "pressure"; a tangential stress, or hoop tension, which tends to split the barrel open longitudinally, being similar in its action to the force which bursts the hoops of a barrel; a longitudinal stress.

Recoil is the movement of the gun longitudinally in the reverse direction to that taken by the projectile. "Jump" and "flip" are secondary movements—vertical and lateral respectively—and are dependent both upon the charge used and the position of the shooter in firing.

THE BALLISTIC ACTION OF AN EXPLOSION.

The object of exploding a charge of gunpowder within a gun-barrel is to move a load from a condition of rest and impart to it a certain velocity; it is obtained by the gradual expansion of the explosive as it decomposes by burning. This gradual expansion, by moving the bullet and so enlarging the chamber in which the powder is exploding, reduces the mechanical effect of the combustion. Instead of the 43 tons pressure to the square inch obtained by exploding black gunpowder in a confined vessel, but a fraction results when the same powder is fired in a small arm under ordinary conditions : much of the energy is used up in producing heat which is absorbed.

There are other causes, in addition, so that comparatively little of the total latent energy—or potential—of the explosive is converted by burning into kinetic energy in the projectile; with the most favourable conditions this energy is conveyed in a manner which may be likened to a vigorous push against the base of a yielding bullet; with unfavourable conditions, is of the nature of a crushing blow.

Time for the translation of the energy is all-important ; a greater percentage of kinetic energy is derived from slow-burning powders, greater local pressure from those whose decomposition is most rapid. The nature of the work required of a gun, therefore, necessitates the use of comparatively slow-burning powders.

"Work" is the result of a force acting upon a body through a distance ; the product is termed "foot-pounds."

"The unit of work called the foot-pound is that amount which is performed in raising a weight of one pound through a distance of one foot against gravity. If one pound be raised two feet, two units of work are done; if four pounds be raised through five feet, then twenty units of work, expressed as 20 ft.-lbs. *Energy* is the expression used to define the work contained in a moving body, such as produced by falling from a certain height, and signifies its weight and velocity. Eliminating the loss of energy in overcoming frictional and other resistances, the work done by the pressure of the explosive on the bore of a gun must equal the energy contained in the projectile. The formula for ascertaining the energy is $Ps = \frac{w v^2}{2 g}$, where P is the mean thrust in pounds exerted over a length of the barrel ; s feet, on the base of the projectile; v the muzzle velocity of the projectile in feet per second ; and w its weight in pounds ; and g gravitation units. *Example.*—What is the average thrust or pressure on the base of a Martini-Henry bullet ? Length of bore = 33 inches; of powder charge, 2 inches ; the difference, 31 inches, will be the distance through which the pressure of the explosive acts on the base of the bullet. The bullet weighs 480 grains, or $\frac{480}{7000}$ lb., and its muzzle velocity is 1,315 foot-seconds, therefore $P \times \frac{31}{12} = \frac{\frac{480}{7000} \times (1315)^2}{2 \times 32 \cdot 2} = 712 \cdot 64$ lbs. *Example.*—What is the muzzle energy of the Lee-Metford bullet? Weight of bullet $= 215$ grains $= \frac{215}{7000}$ lbs., muzzle velocity, 2,000 f.s. Energy $= \frac{w\,v^2}{2\,g} = \frac{\frac{215}{7000} \times (2000)^2}{64 \cdot 4} = 1,907$ ft.-lbs. *Energy* increases as the *square* of the velocity: thus, if the weight of the bullet is constant, and its velocity doubled, the energy is four times as great. The *momentum* of a body, whose weight is w lbs., moving with a velocity v foot-seconds is $\frac{w\,v}{g}$ (seconds-pounds), and may be defined as the *quantity* of motion in a moving body. Supposing a projectile to be travelling at the rate of 1,000 feet per second, and its weight to be 1 lb., it would have the same *momentum* as a $\frac{1}{2}$-lb. shot travelling at the rate of 2,000 feet per second, but the *energy* of the $\frac{1}{2}$-lb. shot would be double that of the 1-lb. shot.''

From the formula it might be assumed that the energy is derived from constant thrust or push on the base of the bullet. Of course the action is quite different; there is *increasing* pressure upon the bullet until its inertia is overcome, but as it nears the muzzle, and its velocity increases, the pressure diminishes. As it is impossible to overcome the inertia of a mass save by the application of a force for a period of time proportionate to the weight, the *ballistic* value of an explosive depends upon the time required for the combustion, which, with black gunpowder, may be to some extent regulated by the shape, size, and density of the grains. By a proper adjustment of the powder-charge to the weight of the bullet and capacity of the barrel, such a pressure is maintained upon the base of the projectile as to increase its velocity as long as it remains within the barrel. Simple as this may seem, it constitutes a large portion of the science of gunnery; a theoretically perfect result would be obtained if the last atom of powder were converted into gas at the moment the bullet leaves the muzzle.

M. Berthelot distinguishes the variation in the rate of combustion of each kind of explosive by two classes—one, the normal explosion, as combustion; the quicker as "detonation"—but adds that "between the two there may exist a series of intermediate modes of explosion. In fact, the passage from one class to another is accompanied by violent and irregular movements of the material, during which the propagation of the combustion acts by a vibratory movement of increasing amplitude, and with more or less velocity." Black powder is computed to generate thrice the amount of radial pressure when the quicker class of combustion occurs.

Too rapid combustion produces an increase of heat and pressure, but the pressure being local—that is, confined to the cartridge chamber—it does not act upon the base of the projectile for the same *distance;* consequently the ballistic value is less, whilst the excess of pressure may prove dangerous, and is always detrimental. Means are taken to avoid a "detonation" or abnormally quick combustion of explosives when used in guns.

There are various methods by which the explosion of the charge, or a part of it, may be retarded *after* ignition. For instance, simply by granulating the powder, and proportioning the size of grain to the bore; for, supposing powder similar in all other respects, its conversion into gas depends on the rate of ignition of the *grains* and the time of combustion of each grain. The rate of ignition depends upon the facility with which the flame can penetrate the charge and its heat—that is, on the form of the grains composing it—and, further, upon the hardness of the grains, and the amount of glaze upon them ; the rate of combustion, on the bulk or size of the grains themselves, and their specific gravity. The larger and denser the grains, the slower they burn.

It has been found by experience that greater uniformity of action is secured by having all the grains of the same size. The burning of the grains first ignited produces gas, and the pressure starts the bullet; then the heat first generated causes the remainder of the charge to burn under conditions more favourable to rapid combustion, the gases are liberated more quickly, and a greater percentage of the explosive is converted into gas ; so that there is an increasing pressure upon the base of the bullet until it shall have attained a proportionate velocity.

THE CLASS OF EXPLOSION.

Ordinary nitro-powders are not readily ignited by a flame at a low temperature ; a large flame or a hot flame, as from a blow-pipe, will ignite any powder, but especially nitro-powders, more quickly.   Once ignited, the combustion of a few grains produces such heat and pressure as to cause a far more rapid explosion of the grains contiguous to them, and if the heat increases with the combustion, as with some conditions it must, then eventually a point is reached when the grains do not burn but detonate. Some years ago some experiments were carried out by Mr. Teasdale Buckell, who has long been Editor of *Land and Water;* by these he ascertained that, whereas the flash of an ordinary cap would ignite the whole of the grains of black powder farthest removed from its base in a 12-bore cartridge case, the same flash would not ignite the farthest removed grains of nitro-powder.

"When a shock sufficiently violent is produced in one part of an explosive substance, and if the pressures which result from this shock are too sudden to be propagated to the whole mass, the transformation of the *vis viva* into heat will take place chiefly in the first portion of the mass. This may thus be raised to a sufficient temperature to detonate. If the first production of gas is so rapid that the mass of material has not time to be displaced, and if the expansion of gas produces a more violent shock on the adjoining portion of the material, the *vis viva* of the new shock will be transformed to heat, and thus give rise to the detonation of a new portion of the material. This alternate action of a shock, the *vis viva* of which is transformed into heat, and a production of heat which raises the temperature of the next portion so as to produce a new detonation, transmits the reaction from portion to portion throughout the entire mass.

"The propagation of the inflammation, then, in this class of detonation may be compared to that of a wave of sound, *i.e.* it is a true wave of explosion travelling with a velocity incomparably greater than that of a simple ignition transmitted by contact from particle to particle, and when the gases freely expand as they are produced. It must also be remarked that whilst the wave of sound is generated by a periodic succession of similar waves, that of explosion is not periodic, but takes place once for all."—*Longridge.*

WAVE PRESSURE.

The maximum pressures are due to the wave action set up by the explosion. Captain Noble has determined that the *average* pressure is much less. Using pistons shielded from the effect of wave action and unprotected pistons in the same gun at the same time, the shielded crusher pistons gave pressures of 32·4, 32·0, and 33·6 tons, but the unshielded piston gave 47 tons pressure to the square inch.

Further, wave action set up in a 10-inch gun gave the same velocity as when no wave action was set up, so that the mean pressure must have been practically the same. The five crusher gauges were placed, three in the powder chamber, one in the shot chamber, and one a few inches in front; they gave—

With wave action: 63·4, 41·6, 37·0, 41·9, 25·8 tons to the square inch.
With no wave action: 28·0, 29·8, 30·0, 29·8, 19·8 ,, ,,

The theory is that the gas first produced rushes with great violence to the projectile, is checked by its inertia, and thus wave action is set up, giving irregular and local pressures in the gun, but diminishing rather than increasing the velocity.

SOME EXAMPLES AND DEDUCTIONS.

The practical value of these definitions of the two classes of explosion of black gunpowder is less than that derived from a knowledge of the conditions which induce the more violent combustion and produce pressures beyond the limit a gun-barrel can safely withstand.

The velocity of the propagation of reaction, tending towards detonation of black gunpowder, is found to increase with an increase of the initial temperature of the mass. It is well known that a gun that has been heated by firing improves slightly in its shooting; possibly this is not because the heat of the metal affects the small shot or rifle bullet, but because the barrel does not to the same extent absorb the heat generated by the burning powder, and so more *work* is got from the same charge.

It increases also with the weight of the charge, because in this case the influence of cooling is proportionately less. This is not likely to appreciably affect any variation in the charges of small arms, with which the limit of variation is comparatively slight.

It increases with the increase of pressure under which the gas is generated—that is to say, a powder has a tendency to detonate when too much work is required of it, as firing a bullet from a large powder chamber through a barrel of smaller diameter, as in the Martini, or by an obstruction in the barrel, or even by tight ramming of the powder, as too much turn-over of a paper cartridge case, or too firm fixing of the bullet in its seat.

"When the explosive is confined by 'tamping,' the pressure will rise very rapidly, and the velocity of propagation may give rise to a shock capable of detonating a portion of the mass. This is, no doubt, the case with long charges of small-grained powder ignited at the rear. The forward portion of the charge is jammed up against the projectile—for the grains at the back are consumed before those in front are ignited—the powder wedged between the burnt explosive and the projectile is crushed, and that part at least is detonated, producing enormous local pressure at the base of the bullet, which probably has not moved very far from its original position in the cartridge-chamber."

A characteristic example of this form of explosion came directly to the author's notice a few years ago with a ·450 single "Express" rifle, with "Field" breech-mechanism, and the barrel chambered for the $3\frac{1}{4}$ inch long taper solid-drawn brass case, for a charge of 125 grains of No. 6 rifle-grain gunpowder, and a bullet of 260 grains. The owner of this rifle, after using it for some months, was induced by a friend to employ a very fine-grained black gunpowder of foreign manufacture—the owner was living in the south of Europe—and to try $4\frac{1}{2}$ drams, or the full charge. After firing several shots at a target, another similar cartridge blew the rifle into fragments, as shown in the illustration. Fortunately, the shooter escaped with nothing more serious than a severe injury to his hand. The cartridges were tested, and found to give normally thrice the pressure obtained with the rifle-grain powder fired under the same conditions; the rifle was strong enough to withstand this, but was not equal to a "detonation" of the charge, and that this happened the author has little doubt.

It is unlikely that fine-grained gunpowder, similar to No. 2, would be chosen by any sportsman, having a knowledge of its qualities, for use in a rifle, and, of

"Express" Rifle burst with Fine-grain Powder.

course, in the instance cited no blame attached to the maker either of the weapon or of the powder.

If a sportsman must use fine-grained powder in an " Express " rifle, no larger grain being procurable, he runs the risk of possible detonation of the charge and the probability of a burst; but the risk may be lessened by *reducing* the charge, leaving the powder loose in the cartridge. This method is usually practised in Germany when using a ·450 Express rifle at small deer. The additional air-space behind the projectile *lessens* the pressure, and, of course, the velocity, which is the object sought.

Normally this proper ignition and combustion of the powder is obtained by using large-grained powder, the interstices between the grains affording the air-space requisite to combustion at a low temperature.

Heavy charges of black gunpowder and increased loads of shot or weightier bullets do not usually burst any well-made gun, providing the explosion is of the normal type, for there is an ample margin of strength left to safeguard the sportsman from the results of occasional over-loading. If a gun is repeatedly fired with charges producing strains it is not constructed to bear, it will bulge, crack, or burst; but the exercise of moderate care will prevent any such accident when black gunpowder only is used, and projectiles and cartridge-cases of the usual type. In fact, black gunpowder of No. 4 grain for shot-guns, and No. 6 grain for rifles, can hardly be so used with breech-loaders as to cause stresses beyond those produced by the proof charges in making the compulsory tests to which the weapon has been subjected.

" A somewhat remarkable instance of the difficulty of obtaining very high pressures with black powder in barrels of 0·303 bore occurred at Enfield, in 1891, in the course of an experiment to ascertain the effect of hardening and tempering in diminishing wear and erosion. Barrels in the rifled stage were hardened in oil and reduced to spring temper. They were tested to ascertain what stress they would endure without bursting. The charges, both of lead and powder, were gradually increased to 1,700 grains of lead and 220 grains of powder without effect. A charge consisting of 200 grains of powder, a felt wad, an air space of 1 inch, a plug of clay 1 inch, then 2,700 grains' weight of bullets—the latter occupying about 15 inches of the bore—was fired. The load was forced forward about 6 inches, but still remained in the barrel. In this state two of the barrels were screwed to bodies and fired with service cartridge in the chamber. One only was bulged ; the other burst at the rear of the impediment, but without moving it or affecting the breech-mechanism. The burst was caused by a sudden local increase of pressure when the bullet struck the impediment. In the other instance, on opening the breech, the cartridge-case was blown out by the imprisoned gas. The body and bolt were uninjured. There is no reason to suppose that the pressure exceeded thirty tons to the square inch, except the local pressure in the last trial."

THE RELATIVE STRENGTH OF EXPLOSIVES.

The explosives—other than black gunpowder—used in small guns for the most part consist of granulated gun-cotton. These powders are supposed to approximate black gunpowder in ballistic effect, and chiefly differ from it in producing a smokeless combustion. The strength, or explosive force, as registered by firing in a closed vessel, of gun-cotton and black gunpowder is as 7·5 to 1. If the gun-cotton therefore was not toned down, or by some means caused to burn more slowly, it would be quite useless for employment in small-arms. There is a possibility of these conditions or means not sufficing in some circumstances, and then pressures more nearly approaching the maximum strength of gun-cotton will be produced by the combustion. Unfortunately, all these nitro-compounds are more prone to "detonate" than is black gunpowder; their combustion is accompanied with greater heat, and they are more susceptible to slight changes in the method or intensity of the ignition. Another ingredient now entering generally into the composition of explosives used in small-arms is nitro-glycerine, and the relative strength of nitro-glycerine to black gunpowder is as 10 to 1, and its susceptibility to detonation greater far than that of gun-cotton, though this quality is lessened by its admixture with other explosives, or non-explosive ingredients. The other point of first importance is the quality high explosives possess of generating heat in excess of that desirable for the combustion of the powder with best ballistic effect.

EXCESSIVE PRESSURES WITH NITRO-COMPOUNDS.

When gun-cotton or its chemical equivalent is taken as the basis for an explosive to be used in small arms, it is usually granulated, and coated with some "deterrent" to retard the ignition of contiguous grains ; the grains are usually small because each grain, when it is ignited, decomposes so rapidly that its explosion is practically a detonation. It does not burn from the outside to the centre, as a pellet of gunpowder does ; so to increase the size of each grain would tend to quicken the explosion instead of to retard it. The grains are rounded, instead of being angular, because that shape renders the ignition of each grain more difficult.

In other respects a charge of gun-cotton pellets, or of any similar nitro-compound, resembles in its behaviour a charge of black gunpowder grains. If the load is too heavy, the combustion takes place within the cartridge-chamber, and before the load of shot is started, and excessive pressures result. If too great a charge of the explosive is used, the heat generated is so much in excess of that needed that a part at least of the charge remaining is detonated, and excessive pressures result. In short, the nitro-compounds may be said to give ballistic results similar to those obtained from the very fine-grain black gunpowder, and when used in small arms require to be used with care, discretion, and knowledge.

It is unfortunate that makers of the nitro-compounds, in their attempts to produce explosives suitable for use in fire-arms intended for the ordinary black gunpowder, have not always adhered to the rule of giving approximately the same strength bulk for bulk with black. An explosive which gives greater pressure than

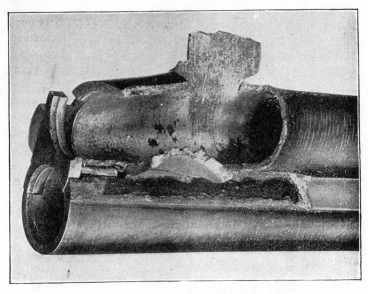

Barrel burst with Quick-burning Nitro.

the same bulk of black is a fertile source of mistake, and the mistakes not unfrequently prove highly dangerous to human life, especially when, as is the case with some explosives made on the Continent, a charge of the same bulk as the ordinary load of black gunpowder produces in the gun such heat or pressure as will "detonate" the nitro-compound. Many accidents are attributable to a commonly made mistake, and one which the makers of the explosive ought to have prevented. The above illustration represents a gun burst with an *ordinary* sporting load of a foreign-made explosive.

The owner of the gun obtained his cartridges directly from the agent of the powder-makers, so that in this case the question of over-loading or of improper loading cannot enter. It must be taken as representing the result of a nitro-compound too quick and violent in its action for use in sporting shot-guns, although, as shown, this one is of ample thickness. The gun was of Belgian manufacture, and of good quality. The burst is instructive as illustrating the sudden nature of the explosion, generating a *local* pressure, the result being that the metal has gone from the breech for the whole length of the chamber, but the barrel forward of the chamber remains uninjured.

Nothing short of legislation will protect the sportsman from this source of danger ; he has the right to expect protection from over-powerful explosives, as at present he is guarded from the issue of weak guns.

The next illustration shows a 16-bore gun of which both barrels were burst

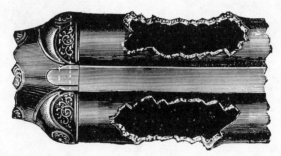

16-bore Gun burst with Regulation Charge of a Foreign Nitro-powder.

through the use of a foreign nitro-compound. The first barrel was burst by the owner when using cartridges loaded with only the regulation 27 grains ; he then returned the gun with some of the same cartridges to the gun-maker, to have them tested. The very first shot fired by the maker burst the second barrel in a similar manner to the first, as will be seen by the illustration. Particular attention is called to the position of these bursts ; two pieces of metal forming nearly half the circle of the barrel have been blown out bodily from the chamber, showing the exceedingly rapid combustion which must have taken place, for forward of the chamber-cone the barrel is intact.

EXCESSIVE CHARGES OF NITRO-EXPLOSIVES.

The effect of an ordinary charge of too strong an explosive being as shown, it is clear that the effect of an overcharge of such an explosive could only differ in degree.

There are other nitro-compounds which burn more slowly and may be considered dangerous only when fired in excessive quantities. The result then is similar to that obtained from a "detonation" of a fine-grain black gunpowder in a rifle.

One characteristic feature resulting from firing an overcharge of a suitable nitro-compound is the excessive pressure generated in the barrel at a distance from the breech. Whether the barrel stands the increased strain, bulges, or bursts, depends

Barrel burst towards the Muzzle by Nitro-powder.

wholly upon the amount of pressure generated. Usually, these bursts are about midway between breech and muzzle, occasionally they are much nearer the muzzle, and occur when there is no possibility of an explanation being traced to an obstruction in the barrel, or any bulge or weakness within it. Nor is such explanation necessary; the nitro-compounds are for the most part soft of grain, and very little pressure is needed to compress them firmly into a practically solid mass. It may be done by excessive ramming; much more probably it is the result of a strong ignition detonating a few of the pellets nearest the flash-hole and the gases so freed jamming the unexploded grains against the base of the projectile, forcing them and the shot into the barrel, where they subsequently explode, and in some instances with such violence as to burst the barrel.

It must not be forgotten that in their endeavours to supply an efficient "deterrent" each grain, flake, or pillule, is rendered non-inflammable save with certain conditions of heat and flame. Time, therefore, is necessary in order to get the ignition of the charge, and for this reason the projectile is made tightly fitting—even the slight delay caused by the extra turning-down of a paper case affords the required moment-ary delay for the combustion of a larger portion of the powder within the chamber; the result, as already stated, is the combustion of the remainder of the charge at a higher temperature. The correct limit may be passed easily, then a burst barrel results; just as easily it may not be attained, and unburnt grains of powder are shot out of the gun or rifle.

Unless the right amount of combustion is got within the cartridge-chamber, good results are not obtained with nitro-compounds. That all of them produce greater heat, and are, to a great extent, burnt in the barrel, is proved by the fact that with most nitro-explosives gun-barrels get hot at the muzzle first; with black gunpowders the barrels first heat at the breech end.

FOULING.

More than one-half of the constituents of black gunpowder are non-gaseous. During the combustion they are in a liquid form, and as finely-divided particles afterwards escape from the barrel in the form of smoke, or as more or less solid residue adhere to the sides of the barrel. In large cannon this solid deposit is not unfrequently three-quarters of an inch thick at the breech end. Fouling possesses the quality of so acting upon the gases of the explosives subsequently burnt in the gun as to diminish the mechanical effect derivable from the explosive; probably by reducing the temperature generated by the combustion, or possibly by some chemical combination of the residue with the gaseous product. If very foul, the resistance to the projectile may be so great that a dangerous local pressure is set up in the barrel, but usually the loss is a loss of velocity only in the projectile.

EROSION.

is the wearing away of the metal of the barrel by the action of the solid particles driven by the gaseous product of the explosion against the surface of the barrel: its effect is the same as that of a sand blast upon steel. The softer the metal and the greater the heat of the explosion, the greater the amount of erosion. In small arms used with black powder its effect is barely appreciable; the ·303 with cordite is particularly subject to the effect of erosion, and it has been found necessary to harden the steel barrels inside, the better to withstand its ravages. An excellent demonstration of the effect of erosion is supplied by the Maxim ·303 machine-gun. Mr. Maxim stated that the life of a barrel was 3,000 rounds, or, when hardened and tempered inside, about 20,000 rounds. After 8,000 rounds from a soft barrel an enlargement of the bore was noticed just in front of the cartridge chamber; after 12,000 rounds had been fired it appeared to be scooped out egg-shaped, and the recoil fell off to such an extent that there was not enough energy remaining to work the gun. The velocity of the bullet diminished proportionally.

THE BURSTING STRAIN OF GUN BARRELS.

In 1858 the late W. Greener stated the strength of a laminated steel barrel, 3-16ths of an inch thick, to be equal to a strain of 6,022 lbs., and that, providing the tube be filled with powder for 1 inch in length, and 1 oz. of shot, the explosive force will be equal to 40,000 lbs., or 1,700 lbs. to the inch; if 1½ oz. of shot, 2,550 lbs.; and if 2 ozs. shot, 3,400 lbs. From the results of later experiments these figures seem to be approximately correct. Experiments made by the late Mr. J. H. Walsh, of the *Field*, and Mr. R. W. S. Griffith, of the Schultze Powder Company, showed that a 12-bore gun, fired with 2½ drams of powder and one ounce of shot, gives 1,640 lbs. pressure *per square inch* at one inch from the breech, 1,448 lbs. at 2¼ inches from the breech, and 916 lbs. at six inches from the breech.

The usual sporting charge of 3 drams and 1⅛ ozs. give 2,090 lbs. at 1 inch, 1,796 at 2¼ inches, and 1,046 at 6 inches from the breech, whilst the not unusually heavy 12-bore charge of 4 drams and 1¼ ozs. gives 3,770 lbs. at 1 inch, 3,210 at 2¾ inches, and 1,321 at 6 inches from the breech—more than 70,000 lbs. pressure on the barrel. Equal measure of " Schultze " gunpowder gives *less* pressure upon the barrel at the first distance; but *more* at the other distances with heavy charges. The charge of 3 drams (42 grains) and 1⅛ ozs. gives 1,850 lbs. at 1 inch, 1,910 at 2¼ inches, and 1,067 at 6 inches. With charges up to and including 3 drams and 1 oz. the Schultze gives less pressure than does black gunpowder, but with heavier charges it gives increased pressure at 2¼ and 6 inches; but with *all* charges gives less pressure at 1 inch from the breech than does the proportionate charge of black.

The illustration shows a section of the breech-end of the barrel of an ordinary double 7-lb. 12-gauge gun, giving exact size and shape of cartridge-chamber, and thickness of metal. The thinnest part is at the commencement of the cone, at the extremity of the cartridge-chamber, and it is here also that the greatest strain of the explosion is exerted, and where all guns first bulge, if a strong explosive or a large charge is used; but to prove that even at this point there is sufficient metal to ensure safety with ordinary heavy charges, a 12-gauge barrel was reduced until it

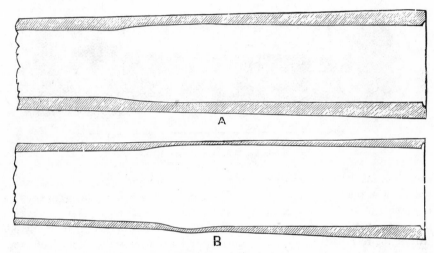

A

B

Section of Breech-end of Gun Barrels.

presented the appearance of B, the metal at the *weakest* point being but ·05 in. thick. It bulged slightly after repeated firing with 3¼ drs. of best Alliance No. 4 powder and 1¼ oz. shot. An exact representation of the bulge is given at B in the illustration.

At 6 in. from the breech the barrel was but 1-48th in. thick, and there was no sign of any bulging.

Another barrel, thicker at the breech, but the same thickness (1-48th in.) 6 in. from the breech-end, was burst with a charge of 42 grs. Schultze powder and 1⅛ oz. shot, the barrel presenting the appearance as shown at C on illustration, page 580. At a distance of 18 or 20 in. from the breech there is relatively little strain. The thickness indicated by the line D is the exact thickness of a 12-bore gun barrel from 17 to 25 in. from the breech, which was not in any way bulged or injured by repeated firing of the usual charge, the barrel remaining intact until ripped up with an ordinary penknife without any trouble. A transverse cut in this portion of the barrel does not appear to dangerously weaken it. A cross-slit was made in a barrel sufficient to pass in a threepenny-bit; the barrel was then fired with the usual charge, without appreciably opening the slit or bulging the barrel.

As before mentioned, the weakest part of a barrel is at the cone of the chamber, caused by the great reduction in the thickness of the metal there. According to

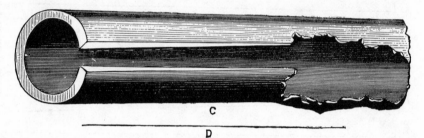

Section of Fore-end of Gun Barrel.

some law, minerals, but especially iron and steel, are more prone to break where a reduction in the thickness occurs. For instance, take a rod of steel gradually taper-ing from 1 in. to $\frac{1}{4}$ in. in thickness, make an incision near the thicker extremity, re-ducing the rod to $\frac{3}{4}$ in. thick, and it will more readily break there than at any other part of the rod; if the incision be but 1-16th deep, but extends completely round the rod, it will still break at the incision, and even much more readily than before. Yet even lately it has been argued by scientific theorists that the cone of the chamber should be made more sudden, or even a square shoulder left, against which the end of the cartridge-case may bed. All who still hold these opinions should remember that shortly after the introduction of breech-loaders the plan was tried and abandoned. The cartridge cases were not, and cannot be, made to such a nicety that they will bear evenly against the bottom of the chamber, so that the very object for which the square shoulder was left was not obtained, and the shape of the chamber weakened the barrel very considerably; and, as it is impossible to remove all residue from a square-shouldered chamber, the acids quickly eat into the metal *there*—at the weakest part—rendering the gun in a short time dangerous.

Behind the cone, the barrels, as now constructed, are sufficiently strong for all purposes. To prove this a longitudinal incision was made in a barrel, extending half the length of the cartridge-chamber, and a transverse slit severing $\frac{1}{8}$ of the circumference, the two incisions forming a **T** on one side of the cartridge-chamber. With ordinary charges these slits were not appreciably opened, but with 50 grs. Schultze and 1⅛ oz. of shot, the longitudinal slit widened ·o8 in., the transverse ·o45 in.

In guns of smaller bore the proportionate pressure per square inch is greater than that upon 12-bores with the same charge of powder. The charge of 2½ drams and ⅞ oz. of black in a 20-bore gave 2,825 lbs. at 1 inch, 2,015 at 2¾ inches, and 1,080 at 6 inches; with like charge of Schultze, 1,772 at 1 inch, 1,890 at 2¾ inches, and 1,046 at 6 inches. Again, with 20-bores, if the charge of Schultze be increased beyond 3 drams and 1 oz. it will give a greater pressure at 6 inches from the breech than will a like charge of black, but a less pressure at 1 inch from the breech.

The following tables give the pressures obtained by Mr. R. W. S. Griffith, of the Schultze Powder Company, and the time required by the shot to traverse various short lengths of the barrel :—

TABLE OF PRESSURES IN A 12-BORE BARREL, IN TONS PER SQUARE INCH, TAKEN BY LEAD CRUSHERS.*

At from the Breech.

	1 in.	2½ in.	6 in.	9 in.	12 in.	18 in.	24 in.
Black No. 2	3·16	2·90	1·42	1·28	1·25	1·25	1·15
,, No. 4	2·60	2·40	1·45	1·28	1·25	1·25	1·20
,, No. 6	2·15	2·04	1·55	1·40	1·28	1·28	1·25
Schultze...	2·55	2·62	1·48	1·30	1·25	1·25	1·20
Nitro in Coned Case	2·10	2·25	1·50	1·25	1·20	1·15	1·05
Ditto in Ordinary Case ...	3·45	2·56	1·50	1·25	1·20	1·15	1·05

TIME TAKEN IN TRAVEL OF SHOT IN A 12-BORE BARREL, TAKEN AT VARIOUS POINTS BY A SMITH CHRONOGRAPH, IN 100,000THS SECOND.†

	Cap to 3″	3″—6″	6″—12″	12″—18″	18″—24″	24″—30″	Total Time in Barrel in Seconds.
Black No. 2	72	45	55	45	35	30	·00282
,, No. 4	138	52	61	50	40	34	·00375
,, No. 6	162	55	65	56	45	37	·00420
Schultze	275	46	57	48	40	34	·00500
Condensed in Coned Case ...	72	44	57	48	42	37	·00300
Ditto in Ordinary Case... ...	100	45	58	49	42	36	·00329

Several things—as variation in the caps used for ignition, the form of the flash-hole and shape of the cartridge cases and wads—will alter the amount of pressure recorded, but the chief cause in producing an increased pressure is the presence of an obstruction in the barrel.

* Comparatively correct, but not necessarily approximately accurate in terms.

† The state of the atmosphere greatly affects ignition, and therefore the reading at 3 inches from the breech, but not the other readings.

The following figures refer to tests made with an ordinary pressure gauge gun. The obstruction consisted of a tight "Field" wad, thick felt and card wad, 1⅛ ozs. of No. 6 Chilled Shot, and card wad over the shot. Measurements taken from the breech to the "Field" wad. Charge used 3 drams, and 1⅛ ozs. of No. 6 shot.

	At 1 inch.	At 2¾ inches.	At 6 inches.
Without any obstruction	... 1,835 ...	... 1,907 ...	... 1,058 lbs. pressure.
Obstruction at 24 in.	... 1,820 ...	... 1,907 ...	... 1,076 ,, ,,
,, 18 in.	... 1,832 ...	... 1,900 ...	... 1,114 ,, ,,
,, 12 in.	... 1,805 ...	... 1,918 ...	... 1,132 ,, ,,
,, 9 in.	... 1,826 ...	... 1,930 ...	... 1,147 ,, ,,
,, 7 in.	... 1,835 ...	... 1,977 ...	... 1,290 ,, ,,
,, 6 in.	... 1,850 ...	... 2,030 ...	... 1,266 ,, ,,

The pressure at the obstruction has not yet been ascertained. Some obstructions will invariably burst some barrels, whilst other obstructions are not such as to produce a bursting pressure. A felt wad ⅜ inch thick, and fitting the barrel tightly, if placed at 6 inches from the breech, will not cause the barrel to burst when the next charge is fired. Neither will such obstruction as shot wads, cobwebs, or leaves, cause a barrel to burst; a barrel, however, plugged at the muzzle with *mud*, will, if fired with the obstruction in, burst at the muzzle, and snow *may* sometimes effect the same result, but the author has never found it to do so.

A charge of shot which shall slip to the muzzle, or be kept between the wads in the barrel at a distance from the charge, *may*, and indeed, probably will, cause the barrel to burst if the charge of powder, also loose, be fired, and it will certainly produce a burst if a charge of shot be fired through the barrel having this obstruction.

Owing to defective cartridges, it sometimes happens that the charge is not blown from the muzzle, but only into it, and sportsmen—not having noticed the very weak discharge—again load and fire.

The looser the shot, *i.e.* the greater the distance between the two wads, the worse the burst.

RECOIL.

Recoil is the movement of the gun in the opposite direction to that of the projectile. The breech and barrel being virtually one mass—a vessel closed by the projectile—the gun would remain stationary until the projectile left the muzzle, were it not for the resistance of the air to the motion of the bullet within the barrel. The internal pressure produced by the combustion of the explosive is merely a rending force, acting equally in all directions, and drives out the bullet because its resistance is soonest overcome. If the gun be placed on a ramrod, and the projecting end of the ramrod supported by a resistance equal to the weight of the gun, the ramrod is not shot out of the gun, but the gun shot off the ramrod. In like manner, but in less degree, the resistance of the air to the bullet tends to drive the gun off the bullet and towards the rear.

The resistance of the air varies with the velocity of the bullet. After the bullet has left the muzzle the air resists the outrushing gases, and these, spreading as they issue from the muzzle, widen the base of resistance, so that the effect upon the gun is the same as though the gases, instead of being driven *from* the gun, were, with equal velocity, rushing in and pressing upon the breech. The extra *kick* of the gun, or increased energy of recoil, due to firing an overcharge of powder, is due to the increased blast of powder gases after the bullet has left the barrel, most of the powder being only in part consumed. The extra kick from a fine-grained or quick-burning powder may be due to the denser nature of the gases which produce an increase of resistance from the atmosphere *after* the projectile has left the muzzle.

Recoil chiefly depends upon the relative weights of the rifle and the projectile and the rate of combustion of the explosive. Other things being equal, the velocity of recoil is inversely proportionate to the weight of the gun; hence additions to the weight of the gun tend to convert the blow of recoil into a push.

The backward momentum of the gun varies with that of the projectile; additions to the weight of the projectile, or an increase of its velocity, add to the velocity of recoil.

In practice the weight of the gun is so much in excess of that of the projectile, and the explosive so suited to the work required of it, that the motion of the recoil scarcely commences until the projectile is at, or has left, the muzzle. With some long-barrelled small arms this is not always the case, but even with them the movement is slight, and always in a line backwards, varied by the position of the greatest resistance—*i.e.* by the position of weight in the weapon itself, or by the relative position of the object against which it is bearing.

Theoretically, the recoil should commence as soon as the projectile is set in motion; but, as it requires more *time* to move a heavy gun from a condition of rest than it takes to overcome the inertia of the light projectile and drive it from the muzzle, the effect of most of the recoil is not observable until the conditions which produce it have ceased.

By photography it has been ascertained that in firing a 25-ton gun the shot was clear of the muzzle before the gun moved. In the case of a 6-inch breech-loading cannon it was ascertained by electricity that the shot was within two inches of the muzzle before the first movement of the gun occurred. Another cannon showed that the recoil of the gun was only 1·1 of an inch whilst the projectile passed down the bore. Other experiments show that the movement of recoil is always *first* in a line with the axis of the bore of the gun.

It would be possible to increase the weight of the weapon until the inertia of its mass overcame the energy of the recoil, when no *movement* would take place in the gun either before or after the projectile left the muzzle.

The weight of the Martini is 9 lbs., and its projectile is 480 grains ; the weapon therefore is 110 times heavier than the projectile. A 7-lb. shot-gun is only 100 times heavier than the 1⅛-oz. of shot usually fired from it, but the ·303 Lee-Metford is 300 times heavier than its bullet.

The larger the bore, the greater the recoil, because the resistance of the air is greater—both to the bullet and to the larger blast of the gases issuing from the gun.

It is this blast that produces what is commonly called the "kick" of a gun. Its power is much greater than is popularly supposed. It has been estimated by Professor Boys that with the service rifle about 2 per cent. of the velocity is due to the force of the blast upon the base of the bullet *after* the projectile has left the barrel. By augmenting the charge or shortening the barrel the force increases ; with short barrels the pressure on the base of the steel-coated bullets has been found so great as to rip off the coating and turn it completely inside out. A too heavy charge in a shot-gun, as all sportsmen know, spoils the closeness of the pattern ; it is because the blast scatters the pellets when they have left the muzzle.

Jump is a motion of recoil, but not in a line with the axis of the barrel. It differs with each rifle, and doubtless is due to the irregular expansion of the metal by the force of the explosion and passage of the bullet. At first the barrel is depressed at the muzzle, then, as the projectile passes along the muzzle, is raised above the right line of alignment, and it varies with any change in the charge. It is almost invariably found that, with black powder charges, a rifle bullet will strike at a point lower than it should do if the actual zero corresponded with the constructive one, but with the Lee-Metford rifle and cordite ammunition the bullet will strike above the constructive zero. The zero point will vary with the way in which the rifle is held, whether as regards the position of the points at which it is supported or the amount of grip or pressure with which it is held.

Flip is a term used to denote the lateral deflection of a rifle barrel due to the same or similar causes as the vertical deflection termed "jump."

A shot-gun lately tried in a rest, by the Editor of *Land and Water*, with only the toe of the stock resting against an immovable block, but with the barrel free to jump, was found to shoot 18 inches higher than when shot from the shoulder. This proves that recoil does affect direction in the fowling-piece.

HOW SHOT EMERGES FROM A SPORTING GUN.

An interesting article on this subject, written by Mr. W. D. Borland, appeared in the *Field* of August 15th, 1908, and the author is indebted to Mr. Borland and the Editor for permission to reproduce the illustrations, taken from actual photographs, and to make the following extracts therefrom :—

"Fig. 1 represents the charge of 1⅛ oz. of shot propelled by 33 grains of E.C. powder from the true cylinder barrel; the coiled wire, by which the discharge at the spark cap is induced at the moment contact is made with the straight wire, is 25 inches from the muzzle of the gun. The front face of the mass of shot is therefore, to all intents and purposes, recorded at 24 inches from the muzzle.

"The mass of shot is quite compact, and its front face shows a distinct outline of some ten pellets. The form is not cylindrical, but more suggestive of a truncated cone, with the card wad pressing into the base of the cone, and being of smaller diameter than the mass of shot; in fact, at this distance from the muzzle, the diameter of the shot charge is about 25 per cent. greater than that of the barrel; but there is no dispersion of individual pellets so far observable. The felt wad follows at a short interval, and this, too, is very nearly in a normal position; finally, the first card wad brings up the rear, and has obviously twisted to an angle of about 45 degrees with the line of fire. It is not unreasonable to conclude, from the examination of this illustration, that the shot emerges from the cylinder barrel in the form of a flat-topped cylinder of the diameter of the barrel, with at least the card wad close up to the base of the cylinder. On the exit of the last card, that is to say, the card over the powder, the powder-gases emerge from the muzzle at a much higher velocity than the shot, and press the wad next to the shot into closer and closer contact. The shot, being no longer confined in the barrel, is free to flow in a lateral direction, and the mass widens first of all at the base, leaving an annular area around the wad unprotected against direct gas-blast. The overshot wad in Fig. 2 (not reproduced), seen in contact with the spiral, has evidently split right open, and scattered many of its particles about the field of view. The particles observable in this illustration proceed partly from the breaking up of the overshot wad and partly from the paper tube of the cartridge case; they may often be observed when firing a gun in bright sunlight, and are not to be confused with solid particles of unburnt or partially burned powder, or mineral residue from explosives of crude composition.

"If the above interpretation is correct, then it follows that any device or procedure which will protect all or any given proportion of the shot from the combined action of wad and powder gases will result in a reduced dispersion,

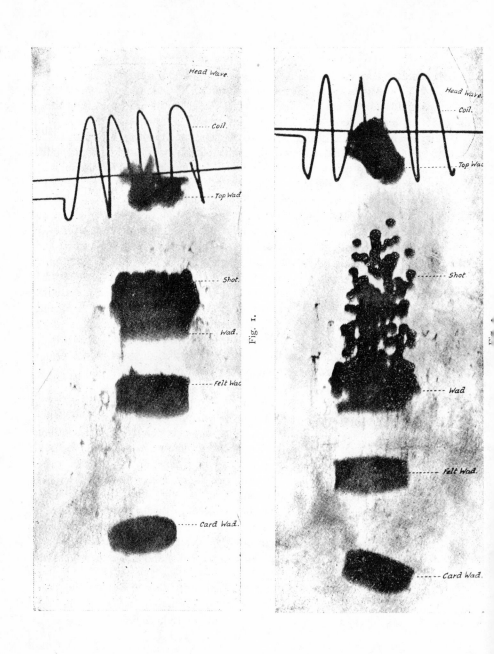

Fig. 1.

and this is what the choke is calculated to effect. The outer layers of shot, on meeting the resistance to their movement offered by the reduction of diameter of the barrel at the choke, may naturally be supposed to be delayed in their passage, permitting the inner layers to pass through and out. When the whole of the shot has run the gauntlet of the choke, the wadding in its turn meets the obstruction, and is delayed thereby for an infinitesimal period, but sufficiently long to delay the issue of the powder gases and to diminish the pressure of the card wad upon the base of the mass of shot. It must be remembered that the shot mass possesses a high momentum and a low co-efficient of friction as compared with the wads, and therefore the delaying action of the choke is more marked in its result upon the wads than on the shot ; this means that the powder gases are also held back for a very small period, and when they do catch up the moving shot they have lost some of their energy by expansion and cooling, and consequently are less able to disturb the formation of the shot charge. In addition to this, by the direct effect of the constricted diameter of the barrel the mass of shot has already been caused to assume a smaller diameter and a greater length than it does when propelled from a cylinder barrel, therefore less of it is exposed to the effect of pressure by the wad or the effect of the gas blast upon the basal portion unguarded by the wad.

"An examination of Fig. 3 supports this view. Here we find, as in Figs. 1 and 2, the overshot wad well ahead of the mass of shot, making the necessary electrical contact at the spiral for the production of the spark. The head wave of air compression is seen on the left close to the spiral. The mass of shot is entirely different in its form from the cylinder projection ; it occupies an actual length of $1\frac{3}{4}$ inches, as compared with $\frac{1}{2}$ inch in the case of the cylinder. On the other hand, its diameter only very slightly exceeds that of the 12-bore wad. The shot pellets are loosely grouped, and the card wad is not bedded against the base of the mass in anything approaching the definiteness observed in Figs. 1 and 2.

"The modelling or shading of the individual pellets is a curious effect due to the fact that the electrical spark is not a geometrical point, but a very short line, and therefore gives rise to penumbra.

"Very noteworthy is the absence of the clearly defined striations in the gases parallel to the line of fire, indicating that from the choke bore the powder gases do not possess the energy in the neighbourhood of the shot mass that they do from the cylinder bore. In a very large number of records this effect is consistently observed, and the differences between cylinder and choke bore shadow-graphs are now regarded by the writer as typical and constant.

"Of course, it is well known that a choke bore can be caused to produce abnormal dispersion by the use of an amount of powder considerably in excess of that for which the gun was standardised, and in the light of the knowledge now gained this simply means that the gas blast from the muzzle possesses sufficient energy to overcome the delaying action of the choke, and causes it to behave more or less like a cylinder.

"A subject of this sort opens up endless avenues of experiment and deduction, and the writer has not sought to do more in the present contribution than indicate broad lines and show typical results."

CHAPTER XXIV.

AMMUNITION AND ACCESSORIES.—CARTRIDGES.

NOTE ON THE HISTORY OF CARTRIDGES.

THE first cartridges were merely charges of powder wrapped up separately to enable the shooter to load more quickly and dispense with the cumbrous powder horn. Capo Bianco, writing in 1597, states that cartridges had long been in use among Neapolitan soldiers. Other authorities state that the troops of Christian I. were the first to use cartridges, and they fix the date as 1586. In the Dresden Museum there are Patronenstocke and other evidence to fix the use of cartridges so early as 1591, and doubtless throughout the seventeenth century their use became general. The first mention of cartridges in the records of the British Patent Office is in 1777, when William Rawle patented several "instruments for carrying soldiers' cartridges," which consisted of cartridge boxes having numerous divisions. The military cartridges were tied round at each end with string, and the end that contained the powder had to be bitten off and the powder poured down the barrel, and the bullet and paper rammed down, the paper thus serving as a wad or patch. In 1827 a patent was obtained for a wire-shot cartridge by Joshua Jenour; the cartridge was made from woven wire, with meshes so wide as to allow the shot to be scattered. In 1828 Edward Orson patented a shot cartridge made in two parts, so that the powder might be easily separated from the shot, cases made to break on issuing

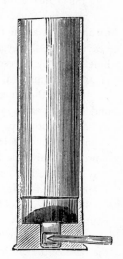

Section of the
Lefaucheux Pin-fire
Cartridge Case.

from the barrel, and so scatter the shots. Augustus Demondion in 1831 patented a breech-loader (page 125) and cartridge for the same. The cartridge had a tube containing detonating powder projecting from its base. It was exploded by a hammer attached to the end of the mainspring, and striking upwards. Another cartridge was patented in the same year by the Marquis of Clanricarde. The cartridge consisted of many sections of a cylinder so united as to form a cylinder. These were intended to be scattered when fired, and the barrel was made bell-mouthed for that purpose. In 1831 a similar cartridge to that used in the Prussian needle-gun was patented in England by Abraham Adolphe Moser; this cartridge had the detonating powder attached to the wad placed between the bullet and in front of the powder. This cartridge was first used in a needle-gun loaded from the muzzle, the breech-loading needle-gun not being invented till 1838. M. Lefaucheux in 1836 produced a breech-loading gun and cartridge. The cartridge as shown is of paper with a metal base; the cap was placed in a chamber with its cup end pointing upwards. A loose brass rod projected from the cup of the cap upwards through the cartridge case, and was struck by the hammer and driven down into the cap, thus causing the discharge. From this cartridge may be dated the success of the modern breech-loader : for, by the expanding at the moment of discharge, escape of gas at the breech is rendered impossible : though, if not well made, or if heavily loaded, they, in common with all pin-fire cartridges, will burst at the pin-hole and allow an escape of gas through it. The cartridge as used by Lefaucheux is still the same as that now commonly supplied for pin-fire guns.

In 1840 the breech-loading needle-gun and cartridge were patented in England ; and in the same year Joshua Shaw invented and patented a novel means of exploding the charge in firearms. A small rod or piston is passed through a cylindrical touch-hole ; upon the end of the rod is a cap, which is struck through the powder-chamber and exploded against the opposite side. The ends of the rod may be made hollow, and contain detonating powder ; the rods may be kept ready prepared with their caps or powder in the gun-stock or elsewhere.

In 1841 a bullet or projectile was patented by Hanson and Golden that contained in a recess in its base a charge of fulminating powder which served to shoot out the projectile. The discharge was effected by a needle striking against the base of the projectile, and was intended for use in a breech-loading arm. In 1847 a similar method was patented by Stephen Taylor, but he used the ordinary powder, and covered the base of the projectile with a cap provided with a touch- or match-hole for igniting the charge by means of gun-cotton or other explosive matter. The projectiles are to be contained in a magazine consisting of a self-acting feeding-tube, which is attached to the barrel of the piece, and as one projectile is discharged, another is to be pulled forward into the breech of the barrel and fired in succession. In 1852 Robert Adams patented improved ball cartridges :—" A metal chamber, by preference made of thin sheet copper, is affixed to a bullet and wad, and contains the charge of powder. The end of the chamber is closed with paper and other suitable material." In 1852 Mr. Needham's gun and cartridge were introduced and patented ; a full description of this cartridge is given, with his gun, on page 143. In 1853 a metal cartridge case was patented, made of tin and coated with flock or fibre. In 1854 William Greener patented a metal cartridge case, made of an alloy which melts at a low temperature, as zinc, lead, and bismuth. In 1855 Prince patented a self-consuming cartridge case, for use in his single rifle. It was made of paper steeped in a mixture of nitre and sulphuric acid. In the same year a soft paper cartridge case was patented by John Norton. The cartridge was loaded first with fulminating powder or gun-cotton, then powder, and afterwards the projectile. The flash from the cap was sufficient to penetrate the cartridge case and fire the fulminate or cotton, thus obviating the tearing of the cartridge cases. In April, 1853, William Terry patented a cartridge for the Terry rifle. The cartridge is made with a conical bullet having a hollow hemispherical base. It may be enclosed in two or three folds of paper, which are readily pierced by the flash of the cap. A disc of paper is attached to the backs of the cartridges, and behind this a wad is placed, which is left in the barrel after the discharge.

In June, 1855, a patent cartridge, chiefly used for revolvers, was patented by Messrs. Samuel Colt and William Eley. The bullet is cast with a rivet and an annular groove at its rear end. The powder-case is formed of sheet foil, and the caps are secured by waterproof cement. The case when charged is attached to the bullet by cement and pressure ; a layer of grease is run round the cartridge at the junction of the powder-case and bullet.

The further history of the cartridge has already been given in the introductory note to the chapter on Modern Breech-loaders.

VARIETIES OF THE CENTRAL-FIRE CARTRIDGE CASE FOR THE SHOT-GUN.

In the modern central-fire cartridge case the base is of metal and the cylinder of coiled paper. The base of the cartridge is filled with hard cardboard, pressed into the case when in a pulpy state. The cap chamber is separate from the base of the case, and is pierced at the point of the dome to allow of the flash reaching the powder. The anvil is shaped like an escutcheon, and is inserted in the cup of the cap, with the point against the detonating powder. Two anvils were once used, as they were supposed to fill up the cap much better and render the ignition more certain· The cap is of copper, and may be made either with enclosed anvils of brass, or the anvils may be separately inserted when re-capping. This case has been improved in the best qualities by inserting in the interior of the cylinder a lining of metal foil, which greatly strengthens the case. The manufacture of this case has been improved since its invention, but the principle and general make of the cartridge are identical with that used by the inventor. A short time after its first introduction a M. Schneider brought out a modification of the Pottet cartridge, which was at the time considered an improvement, but has since proved not so good. Schneider's cartridge was introduced into this country by Mr. G. H. Daw, and shown by him in

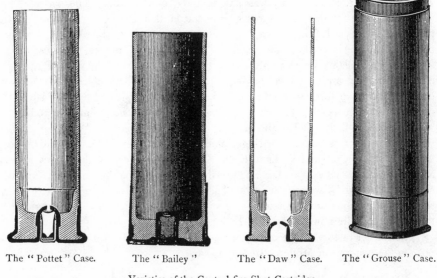

The " Pottet " Case.   The " Bailey "   The " Daw " Case.   The " Grouse " Case.

Varieties of the Central-fire Shot Cartridge.

the Exhibition of 1862. This cartridge differed from the Pottet cartridge in the form of anvil used. In the Schneider case the anvil is made of a short piece of wire, having four fluted grooves running along it. One end of the wire was inserted in the cap, and the other bore against the dome of the cap chamber. Upon being struck, the flash from the cap passed along the fluted grooves in the anvil, and reached the powder through a hole in the dome of the cap chamber. The shell of this cartridge is shown in the accompanying illustration. It will be seen that the cap chamber is not riveted to the base of the cartridge as in the Pottet case, and consequently is not so strong. The "Bailey" case, designed especially to prevent the escape of gas into the lockwork of hammerless guns, had a brass-foil cap completely covering the base of the cartridge ; although thinner metal was used in the percussion cap, miss-fires were frequent, and it has now been abandoned. In later models the capsule, instead of covering the whole of the base of the cartridge, extends only to about one-half the distance ; but this is quite as effectual as a gas-check, and still further lessens the liability the capsule had to sag and thus produce miss-fires. The " Grouse " case more recently introduced has a gun-metal covering extending nearly the whole length of the case to resist damp and facilitate the ejection after firing.

THE MANUFACTURE OF CARTRIDGES.

The manufacture of cartridges is a trade apart from gun-making, and has been carried to a high state of perfection. For metal cases, Birmingham stands pre-eminent in England. At the present time there are several manufactories near Birmingham, of which that of Kynoch, Limited, is the largest. At this manu-factory several hundreds of machines may be seen at work in the one shop, and cartridges, cartridge cases, caps, and ammunition of every description (except powder and shot) made. The metal for the cartridge cases is also mixed and prepared upon the ground. The manufacture of solid-drawn brass cartridge cases is the most interesting branch carried on here, and the various processes may be shortly described. The blanks are first punched from sheet metal. No. 1 (p. 594) represents a full-size blank for a Mauser rifle case. The blank is placed under a drawing machine, and forced by a descending plug through a tapering aperture, from which it is ejected of the shape shown in No. 2 ; the thimble is then annealed, cleaned with sulphuric acid, forced through the drawing machine again, from which it issues of the shape No. 3. The processes of annealing, cleansing, and drawing have to be repeated several more times, until it is of the dimensions and appearance of No. 4. The cap chamber is then formed by a plug in a horizontal punching machine. The neck is afterwards contracted in a press that gives it the bottle-necked appearance as in No. 5, which represents the finished cartridge case. The head and rim of the cartridge case are then formed by quickly forcing it against a die. This is accomplished in a complicated horizontal punching machine having great speed and power. The cartridge case is dropped in the machine and caught upon a steel plug fixed to a heavy piston, which forces the head of the case against the die by a strong elbow-joint motion ; the form is then given to the head or base of the case, as No. 6, and is all accomplished in one blow. The flash holes in the cap chamber are then pierced, which operation is shown completed in No. 6. The case is then cut off to the required length, the rim of the case turned, and it is ready for the cap or primer. In the Mauser cartridge case the anvil is left solid in the cap chamber; but in most sporting cartridge cases the anvil or anvils are separate from the case. The cartridge cases are placed upside down, the caps placed upon

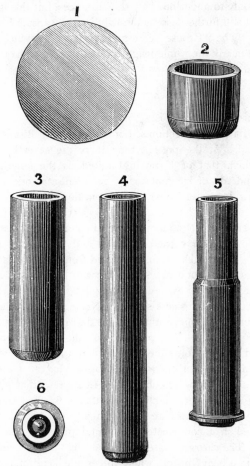

Cartridge Blanks, Cylinder, and Finished Cartridge.

the base and forced into the cap dome by a descending rammer; the cases when primed are ejected from the wheel by an ascending plug, and are ready for loading.

The processes are practically the same for all solid-drawn metal cartridges, whether for pistols, rifles, shot-guns, punt guns, or "quick-firing" ammunition for cannon. They are *fewer* for the small short cartridges, and for the larger sizes— up to 6 inches in diameter—the drawing is accomplished by hydraulic pressure.

The metallic caps or primers are made from copper blanks pierced from rolled sheet metal, and formed into a small cup or thimble. For priming they are placed in an indented plate, and this plate is covered with two other plates having holes drilled through them to coincide with the position of the caps when the three plates are fixed upon the loading frame. The top plate slides horizontally about one-eighth of an inch ; that causes the holes in it to move clear of the holes in the bottom plate, which thus forms a bottom to the holes in the top plate. The detonating mixture, whilst quite damp, is carefully spread over the top plate, and the holes in it are filled when in this position. The surplus powder is brushed off with velvet. The top plate is then moved until the holes correspond with those of the bottom plate and the caps, when the charge of detonating powder falls through into the caps. The caps thus charged are removed to a press, and a tightly-fitting tinfoil disc pressed upon the charge of detonating powder, which, in some cases, is after- wards varnished over with a thick coating of spirit varnish, and thus rendered thoroughly waterproof and capable of being soaked for seven or eight days in water without any deterioration.

Cap-filling is a dangerous process, and is considered so dangerous that by Act of Parliament only one person is allowed in the priming room ; the same rule applies in making up the detonating mixture. Muzzle-loading caps are pierced from sheet copper and swedged into the required cap form at one operation. The machine first cuts the blank either a square, a cross, or star shaped, and forces the blank through a tapered orifice, from which it issues perfectly shaped and ready for priming. Fluted caps are made in the same manner at one operation. Best caps are ground upon the edges after they are formed, and military caps have flanges upon them. By improved machines, military caps are now turned out flanged and shaped at one operation.

Paper cartridge cases, as now commonly used in shot-guns and old-fashioned rifles, have solid brass-drawn bases, which are manufactured from blanks, as already described in the drawing of solid brass rifle cartridge cases. The paper is coiled round a quickly-revolving mandrel whilst damp, and covered with paste ; the tubes of paper are then dried. The paper tube and the metal base have to be joined ; this is done in a press ; the paper tubes are first inserted in the open metal base, and a quantity of cardboard pulp placed in the cartridge. A swedge is then pressed over the outside of the case, and a plug descends with considerable force into the inside and compresses the pulp, and spreads it firmly and evenly over the base. The case is allowed to stand until dry, when the pulp, becoming hard, forms an effectual wedge in the base of the taper case, and prevents the brass base and paper tube from coming apart.

In some cases the cap chamber is separate from the base of the case. It is made of brass, and is of such a shape as to firmly bind the paper and metal cartridge cases together when riveted in its place.

The cartridge cases are glazed by burnishing them, or are varnished. Pegamoid cases which are waterproof are now made by Messrs. Eley. This is paper rendered waterproof with dissolved gun-cotton. Theoretically it looks dangerous; in practice it is not. A new waterproofed case, called "The Bonnaud," has also been introduced by Messrs. Joyce and Co.

MANUFACTURE OF BULLETS.

Bullets when required in quantities are made by machinery, not cast. The lead is carefully prepared and mixed with zinc or tin to harden it. The alloy is then forced out into long round "ropes" of metal, which are coiled and placed upon a rotating vertical spindle of the bullet-making machine. The best machines are self-feeding, cut off the proper length of metal, shape it into a bullet, and eject into a box. The machine cuts off the lead and forces it into a die with a conoidal punch, thus forming the bullet at one blow. When taken from the machine the bullets are "regulated" in a press to ensure a perfect cylindrical form. Each bullet is then placed in a rapidly-revolving lathe and wrapped with the paper patch, which is cut off and twisted whilst revolving. The patches are then waxed on to the bullet, and the whole is ready for use.

Bullets so made are much more uniform in weight and shape than cast bullets, there being no possibility of air-holes or rings occurring in or upon the bullets.

Composite bullets of the type known as the Rubin, and similar to the jacketed bullets used in the ·303 and modern small-bore rifles, have the cases made by processes identical with those followed in the production of metal cartridge cases as already described. The metal used for the jacket is an alloy; a good one is 80 parts of copper, 20 of nickel—containing small quantities of manganese, iron, and silicon: this metal is tough, hard, and allows of a highly-burnished surface being obtained that is not readily tarnished. It has a tensile strength of 27 tons to the square inch. Ordinarily silicon-spiegel is added to nickel and the metal rolled into sheets of ·04 inch thickness; it is then cut out and cupped at one operation and drawn out to the required length. Annealing after each drawing is not necessary, and seven drawings suffice to elongate the blank into the case for the ·303 bullet. The cores are of lead, with 2 per cent. of antimony, and are squirted into rods of the required diameter, cut to length, sized, placed in the jacket by hand, and the bullet is then forced into a die, the jacket thus turned down over the base, and the finishing processes consist of adjusting diameter and ringing.

LOADING RIFLE CARTRIDGES.

When loaded in large quantities, rifle cartridges may be cheaply and accurately done by machinery. The cases are first placed in frames, 100 in each. The frames are then conveyed to the loading room, where one person fills them with powder. The powder is contained in a magazine affixed to the wall on the outside of the loading room. An india-rubber pipe runs from the magazine into the loading room. The cartridges are placed beneath the pipe, and by means of an accurately constructed measuring machine affixed to the end of the pipe the exact charge may be deposited in the cases. The measure is worked with one hand, whilst with the other the loader guides the machine from case to case with such rapidity that 30,000 a day may easily be loaded by one person. The cases when loaded are taken into a separate room, where the wads are introduced and pushed home with hand rammers. When wadded the bullets are placed in the cartridge, pressed home, and the whole cartridge inserted in a swedge, to close in the lip of the case and make it accurately fit, and clip the bullet to prevent it slipping from the cartridge case. Cartridges so made and loaded may be placed under water for a fortnight and will not be injured or rendered useless.

Numerous machines have been produced during the last decade for the automatic loading of rifle and revolver ammunition. Some of these are very accurate and perform the work required of them well and with greater uniformity than is ordinarily obtained by hand labour, whilst the cost is less. Factory loaded rifle ammunition as supplied by the leading manufacturers is much superior to that likely to be produced either by the amateur loader or the jobbing gunsmith.

Special machinery is indispensable for weighing, cutting, and loading the strings of cordite explosive for the ·303 ammunition.

WADDING.

The wadding used in the shot-gun is of three varieties : first, the simple cardboard wad; second, a felt wad; third, a hard felt paper-faced wad, known as the "pink edge" or the "Field" wad. A cardboard or waterproof (pitch-paper) wad must be placed over the powder; this must be followed by a lubricating felt wad, usually 3-8ths of an inch in thickness. The top wad over the shot should be of thin cardboard. Pink-edged, pink-faced, "Field," and thick cardboard wads, cloth wads, and black wads are used for special purposes, as specified in the note on cartridge loading.

The best felt wads are elastic, of a light pink colour, deeper at the greased edge. Cheaper qualities are of a deeper tint, and the commonest are brown in colour and not close in texture. The "Field" wad is black (pitched paper) on one face, pink paper on the other; the edge is greased. Pink-edged wads are greased at the edge, and have paper faces of a light pink tint; they should be of elastic felt.

Felt wadding *must* be used between the powder and shot; a wad $\frac{3}{16}$ inch thick is enough for a 28-bore, and $\frac{3}{4}$ inch would not be too thick for an 8-bore; as there is

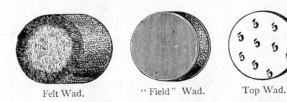

Felt Wad.　　　　　"Field" Wad.　　　　　Top Wad.

not a wad so thick, one or two pink-edged wads must be used as well; $\frac{3}{8}$ or $\frac{7}{16}$ is the correct thickness for a 12-bore wad. A wad slightly larger in diameter than the bore of the gun ($11\frac{3}{4}$ for 12-bores) has been found to give better results with some of the earlier nitro-powders, and especially so with large charges.

Wads need not fit the case tightly. There is little doubt but that the wads are expanded in the cartridge case before the shot is started. The felt wad serves to clean the fouling in the barrel left from the firing of the previous charge.

Numerous wads have been designed with a view to act as concentrators in confining the charge of shot in its flight, but for the most part they act but imperfectly even with cylinder guns, and are quite useless with choke-bores. Wads of hard brittle material, which will crumble to dust when the gun is fired, are sometimes used over shot, though the thin card wad is still employed generally.

Another wad is so constructed that immediately it leaves the muzzle of the gun it falls to dust, and this wad, if fixed over the shot, slightly increases the pattern at short ranges; if over the powder without other wadding, it reduces both pattern and penetration. One firm of English gun-makers use an oily preparation of soft wood sawdust for wadding.

In the United States a metal top wad is sometimes used to *fix* the shot in paper or brass cases.

The Swedish cup wad is made of a pulpy material, with concavities at each end. It is used in place of the ordinary wads between powder and shot, and it tends to make the gun shoot much closer with nitro-powder; it also increases the internal pressure, and with it the penetration. For its performance see "Trap Guns."

For other special wads and the employment of ordinary wadding to modify the shooting of guns by causing the pellets to scatter or concentrate, see the paragraphs on "Cartridge Loading."

METHOD OF CHARGING SHOT CARTRIDGES.

In loading shot cartridges in quantities, most gun-makers make use of the Erskine machine. Another plan is to use the Erskine machine as a tray only to hold the cartridge cases for the insertion of the wads, the methods of measuring both the powder and shot being not sufficiently accurate to obtain the best or uniform results. The powder should be either weighed into the cases, or accurately measured by a machine similar to the one employed in loading military cartridges. The wads are then inserted by using the Erskine machine and rammer. The Erskine machine is simply a block of wood chambered to take a number of cartridge cases—usually 100. These chambers support the cases mouth upwards for loading, and to some extent prevent bulging of the cases whilst the wads are being rammed home in them. Over the block is a sliding tray bored with holes to correspond with the chambers in which the cases are placed; each hole is a measure for the powder charge. The explosive is poured over the tray, and, the holes filled, the surplus is scraped off with a straight-edged rule. A glance at the tray shows whether or not each hole is filled with gunpowder. When all are filled and level with the top of the tray, the part of the tray constituting the powder measures is slid forward, and the measures are brought over holes in the false bottom to the measuring tray and the powder drops through into the cartridge cases. A similar tray with tapered holes in which the wads are placed is then put over the cartridge holding block and the wads rammed home. The shot may be measured in by means similar to that adopted for the powder charges, or the pellets may be counted in by the Greener shot counter hereafter described. The top wads are next placed over the cartridge and pushed home just as was done with the powder wads; the false bottom from below the case block is withdrawn, the machine lifted off and the hundred loaded cartridges are left upon the table ready for being turned over in the usual manner.

The Erskine loader ensures the charging of all the cartridges, providing ordinary care is used. With other machines it is possible to miss a cartridge case occasionally, and the case without its powder charge is subsequently wadded, shotted, and turned over. Such a cartridge may easily escape detection, as the felt wad is prevented from reaching the bottom of the case by the metal lining, and when fired in a gun the force of the cap may drive the shot and wads a few inches only; then, if another cartridge is inserted in the barrel and fired, the barrel will most certainly burst.

Of the many purely mechanical devices designed for loading shot cartridges, not one, so far as the author knows, possesses any means for safe-guarding against the mischance to which allusion has just been made. From most of the steam-driven automatic machines, cartridges without powder but loaded with wads and shot have been taken, and for this reason the author prefers the method of loading he has described. The smaller machines have this fault just as the larger, and most machines feeding by gravitation do not allow of sufficient time for the full charges or loads to be measured in every cartridge, and some, again, provided with automatic cut-offs for measuring the shot are found to cut, mutilate, or otherwise spoil the shape of some of the pellets of the load.

The turning over may be done efficiently with the ordinary hand machine; better, perhaps, by special lathes fitted with automatic devices to ensure uniform pressure being used for all cartridges of the same load and length of case.

With nitro-explosives, as elsewhere stated, the regularity of the shooting is impaired if the wadding be not uniform or too tightly rammed. Still greater will be the irregularity if the crimping or turning down of the cartridge case is unequal. The crusher gauge shows that with a nitro-explosive a slight increase only in the amount of the cartridge case turned down there will be an increase in the pressure exerted in the chamber by the explosion. With one-eighth of an inch extra turn-over the pressures increased equal to an increase of the powder charge by five grains. All nitro-explosives are not to the same extent susceptible, but all with which the author has experimented have shown some variation, according to the amount of turn-over to which the cartridge case was subjected.

RELOADING SHOT CARTRIDGES.

Cartridge cases do not pay to reload; it is false economy in England to reload paper cases or "Perfects"; abroad it may be necessary to do so occasionally, but no case fires so well a second time. Paper and brass cases both quickly lose their elasticity if reloaded and fired time after time, and in reloaded cases there will always be a greater percentage of miss-fires than in new ones. The de-capping must be done as soon after firing as convenient. New anvils will be required to some cases ; and care must be taken that the cap and the anvil are both got well " home " in the cap chamber when re-capping, or miss-fires will certainly ensue.

THE " GREENER " SHOT COUNTER.

This simple contrivance was devised by the author as an instrument accurately loading shot cartridges with a given number of pellets—a matter of great importance when producing cartridges to test a gun's performance. The variation in the size of the pellets of even the most regular shot will cause several pellets' difference in the load by weight ; $1\frac{1}{4}$ ounce of No. 6 of 270 to the ounce should be 338 pellets ; if weighed, it may reach 350 or contain as few as 330, so that to the gun tester the

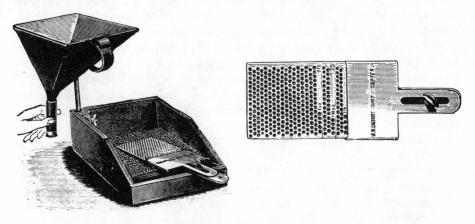

W. W. Greener's Shot-counting Apparatus.

shot-counting machine is an instrument of the first importance. It is easily made and absolutely accurate, and consists, as shown, of a scoop for taking up from a box of shot just the number of pellets required.

By drilling holes of the requisite size and depth in a sheet of hard brass, a species of trowel is formed, in which the pellets of shot will stick when the trowel is forced into a mass of shot and slowly withdrawn. For the use of sportsmen a pattern is now made, with a sliding cover, by which the number of holes exposed in the trowel may be varied according to the charge of shot it is wished to load into the cartridge.

As already stated, the charge of shot is in this manner regulated by *number ;*

270 pellets of No. 6, Greener's Standard, weigh one ounce, and in very good shot, if this number should turn the scale, it will be found that 265 will not; 304 holes for 304 pellets are allowed for the $1\frac{1}{8}$ oz., or standard charge, and beyond this charge the graduation may be varied with the greatest nicety.

In order to obtain exact results it is absolutely necessary that the *same number* of pellets are loaded into the cartridges; if the number varies—although the weight of the charge may not—there will be a variation in the pattern, which will probably prove misleading, and as it is easily avoided by using the counting trowel, the weighing of charges of shot without also counting should be discontinued.

The use of the trowel, with a plentiful supply of shot and the specially-made square—or ribbed—tundish, enables anyone to load cartridges accurately with great speed and ease, and it is a method far in advance of any system of weighing or measuring shot charges. A glance at the trowel as it is withdrawn filled from the shot-box will show whether any undersized or misshapen pellet is on the trowel, any irregularity in size, shape, or number of the pellets being instantly discernible, as each pellet occupies a separate cell and is seen distinctly.

The price, with box, tundish, and stand, is so trifling—viz. 21s. (and the one counter will load three sizes: 5, 6, or 7)—that everyone who loads cartridges should give this method of loading a trial. It will be found satisfactory, and a properly made trowel will load millions of cartridges before the holes become so worn that it has to be discarded.

The author uses this counting trowel in loading all his cartridges, and has done so for many years. Sportsmen who do not load their own cartridges should see that the maker with whom they deal counts the pellets of the charge into the cartridges, or states the number of pellets to the ounce used.

HOW TO LOAD A GUN.

The standard loads of guns for various gauges have already been given in Chapter XV. The sportsman must, however, remember that the closeness of a gun's shooting may generally be improved by the use of Schultze gunpowder, if the gun is full or modified choke. The No. 4 is the black powder that is usually best suited to guns from four to twenty-eight gauge.

As to the size of shot, No. 6 of 270 to the ounce is the standard for 12-bores, in which also every size may be used.

The 28-bore will do relatively better with eight or seven than with six or five, and with a 4-bore gun anything smaller than No. 3 is wasted power.

Modified choke-bores and cylinders give a larger killing circle the smaller the

TABLE SHOWING (APPROXIMATE) NUMBER OF PELLETS IN VARIOUS LOADS, OF ANY SIZE OF NEWCASTLE CHILLED SHOT.

Weight of Load.	NUMBER.																						
	1.	2.	3.	4.	5.	6.	6.*	7.	8.	9.	10.	11.	12.	0.	3A.	2A.	A.	3B.	2B.	B.	SG.	SSG.	SSSG.
¾ ozs.	78	92	105	129	164	203	225	255	338	435	638	780	938	1275	30	36	42	48	57	65	6	8	11
⅞ ,,	91	107	123	151	191	237	262	298	394	508	744	910	1094	1488	35	42	49	56	66	77	7	10	13
1 ,,	104	122	140	172	218	270	300	340	450	580	850	1040	1250	1700	40	48	56	64	76	88	8	11	14
1⅛ ,,	117	137	158	194	245	305	337	383	506	653	956	1170	1406	1913	45	54	63	72	85	99	9	13	16
1¼ ,,	130	152	176	216	272	340	375	426	562	726	1062	1300	1562	2125	50	60	70	80	95	110	10	14	18
1⅜ ,,	143	167	193	237	299	375	401	469	618	799	1168	1430	1718	2338	55	66	77	88	104	121	11	15	19
1½ ,,	156	183	210	258	327	405	450	510	675	870	1275	1560	1875	2550	60	72	84	96	114	132	12	17	21
1⅝ ,,	169	198	228	280	354	439	487	553	731	943	1381	1690	2031	2763	65	78	91	104	123	143	13	18	23
1¾ ,,	182	213	246	302	381	473	525	596	787	1016	1487	1820	2187	2975	70	84	98	112	133	154	14	19	24
1⅞ ,,	195	228	263	323	409	507	562	639	843	1089	1593	1950	2343	3188	75	90	105	120	142	165	15	21	26
2 ,,	208	244	280	344	436	540	600	680	900	1160	1700	2080	2500	3400	80	96	112	128	152	176	16	22	28

* Corresponding to London size No. 6.

NOTE —There is a slight difference in the specific gravity of lead of commercial qualities; the specific gravity of the Newcastle Chilled Shot varies very little, and is usually nearly 11°. The specific gravities of two samples of shot chosen at random were: Chilled, 10·966; Soft, 11·250. Hard shot gives rather higher velocity than soft; soft gives slightly higher pressure.

shot. At the ordinary winged game of Great Britain 20- and 16-bore cylinder barrels may be used with greater success if charged with No. 7 than with 5 or 6. In 12-bore guns No. 6 shot may be used for partridge, and No. 5 for grouse or pheasant shooting; for quail and young partridge shooting No. 7 may be employed to advantage, and for shore shooting even larger size than No. 4. When using large shot, the load may with advantage be slightly increased. But the sportsman must remember that when he uses the large shot he is sacrificing closeness of shooting for the extra benefit he obtains from the increased range and smashing power of the large shot. Cartridges loaded with nitro-compounds must always be well turned down.

Good close shooting in guns of any bore can only be obtained by using cartridges loaded rationally, and to be rationally loaded there must be good wadding between the powder and the shot. The secret of good shooting is in the employment of a first-class felt wad over the powder; and it is imperative that this wad be of good quality. The texture must be close and firm, but the relative hardness or softness of the wad is of less moment. It should be of the same diameter as the internal diameter of the cartridge-case in which it is to be used—$\frac{3}{8}$ or $\frac{7}{16}$ thick for 12-bores, thinner for smaller bores, and thicker for larger bores. To protect the *powder* from the injurious effect which may result from continuous contact with the chemically-prepared felt wad, a thin card wad or a waterproof wad should first be inserted; and it is supposed to be conducive to closer shooting with some nitro-powders if this protective wad, instead of being a simple card wad, be a compound paper and felt wad—technically known as the "pink-edged" or "Field" cloth wad. This "Field" wad should always be used when loading with the older non-waterproof nitro-compounds; with black powders its use is not so imperative. It is customary to place a third wad, of thin card, between the thick felt wad and shot, but it is very doubtful if any benefit will accrue from its use.

The cartridge loaded for close shooting will therefore be charged as in the illustration (page 605).

Loading with two pink-edge wads over the powder, and one pink-edge wad over the shot, as is often done in the United States, causes the charge to scatter, and such loading will lower the pattern from 5 to 10 per cent. in a gun fully choke-bored.

If charged with "Schultze" or "E.C." gunpowder, the wads used will be the pink-edged or "Field," the thick felt and the thin card, or Swedish cup wad, as shown.

For use with concentrated nitros, such as Ballistite, a cartridge case of less capacity is needed, and the conical base case, on the following page, is that used generally. The ordinary case must be packed with wadding, or there is left a too great length of case for turning down. Advantages in recoil and pressure were once claimed for the conical base, but experiments prove that beyond filling up the case there is no appreciable benefit; and it is possible that with concentrated powders this end would be attained more satisfactorily by shortening the cartridge case and chamber and using specially constructed guns.

 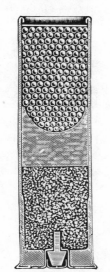 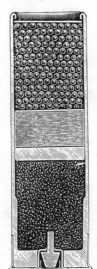 

| For Close Shooting with Black Powder. | Greener's Patent Swedish Cup Wad. | For Close Shooting with Nitro-Gunpowder. | Conical Base, with Ballistite Powder. |

If brass cases are to be loaded for close shooting, put the wads, as illustrated, between the powder and shot, and crimp the case, or use Swedish wad.

The author's experience of the Swedish cup wad, described on page 599, has convinced him that the best results with nitro-powders are to be obtained by its use. The nature of the composition of this wad seems to be adapted for developing the full force of nitro-powders, probably by offering more resistance, and consequently any series of patterns will be more uniform, no one of them containing many more shots than another. This lack of uniformity has always been noticeable when using nitro-powders, although they give higher individual patterns, having always one or two in a long series which are far below the standard of even black powder. This is shown particularly in the record of the Explosive Trial of 1878, and the defect still exists, though in a less degree. Any wadding which will tend to remedy this, therefore, must be a great advantage for pigeon shooting, and the author recommends this wad for this purpose particularly.

To load choke-bore guns so as to scatter the shot at close quarters the rule is to diminish the thickness of the wadding between the powder and the shot. This is usually effective, but to obtain the widest spread by this means the best way is to load as illustrated, separating the load of shot by two thin cardboard wads. This will cause a full-choke-bore gun to make a pattern of 140 at 40 yards instead of

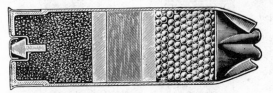

Brass Cartridge Case wadded for Close Shooting.

220. A still smaller pattern may be obtained by using one ounce of shot instead of the ounce and eighth, and still further by substituting No. 5 for No. 6 shot. If it scatters too much, separate the shot by one wad instead of two, or by simply using one pink-edged wad only over the powder, and one over the shot.

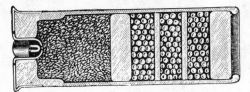

Cartridge loaded to scatter the Shot.

Winans' Shot-spreader.

The scatter-charge has good penetration at 30 or 40 yards, but of course not so much as a cartridge loaded for close shooting.

A still wider spread is obtainable by the use of a special wad—Winans' invention —which divides the shot longitudinally. The wad, as tried by the author, is cruciform, and thus the shot is contained in four separate compartments; with this wad a full-choked 12-bore gun will spread the pellets well over a 30-in. circle at even 15 yards' range. Possibly, by dividing the shot in the same way, but into three instead of four equal compartments, the spread would not be quite so great.

The Shrapnel shell consists of two segments, bolted together by a light wire spindle, its lower end being fixed to ordinary wadding slightly larger in circumference than the shell. The shell is put into the cartridge case instead of loose shot.

This shell differs from ordinary concentrators, and, according to the inventor, the following is the theory of its action :—The opening of the shell is regulated by the length of the spindle, yet for a certain period during its flight the spindle is locked in the shell owing to the temporary distension of the two segments by the contained shot pressing to the circumference of the shell. When the contained pellets acquire a uniform velocity, they settle down, the shell relaxes, and the spindle is snatched away. When the atmosphere begins to withdraw the spindle, it

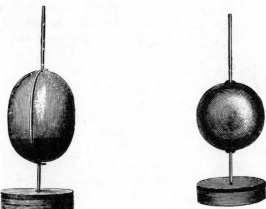

The Shrapnel Spherical and Elongated Shot Shells.

is then that the length of spindle tells, and by the time the spindle is withdrawn from the shell the pellets have all acquired their own path, and cease to jostle each other; at 120 yards a circle four feet in diameter should include the whole of the pattern. Owing to the temporary locking of the spindle, the spherical shell has a minimum range of 90 yards; that is to say, it flies as a bullet for that distance, but it is effective at from 95 to 140 yards.

The Shrapnel shells, wire cartridges, cardboard rings, and other concentrators, if of any use, are only so in guns cylinder-bored.

THE TIME REQUIRED FOR IGNITION.

Different makes of cartridge-cases, being furnished with different caps, are not alike in the method of ignition of the explosive, nor in the time occupied in igniting the powder.

The time actually passed between the pulling of the trigger of a good C. F. 12-bore gun and the exit of the shot from the muzzle of the gun should not exceed ·0075 of a second; with the "Life" cases this is reduced to ·0065 of a second, and if quick powder, as "basket" or No. 3, is used, it is again reduced to ·0060 of a second or less. With smaller bores the time is less. When the time taken is ·03 of a second or more, a "hang fire" is perceptible; when ·06 of a second, a click is heard between the pulling of the trigger and the report.

The difference in the time occupied by the ignition is small; if the time occupied from the instant of pulling the trigger to the pellets of the charge striking the object at 35 yards' distance be ·1237 sec., which is about the average when using the standard charge in a 12-bore gun, the periods may be divided as follows:— Time occupied from pulling of trigger to striker touching the cap, ·0022 sec.; cap to muzzle of gun, ·0055 sec.; and muzzle to object, ·1160 sec., which is a mean velocity for the 35 yards of 905 feet. With the larger cap and Schultze powder the mean velocity will be 910 feet per second, but the total time will be ·1235 secs., as, although the time occupied by the ignition and combustion of the Schultze is ·0004 more than that required by No. 4 black powder, the force generated throws the pellets the 35 yards in ·0006 less time than the black. In Schultze gunpowder the slowness of ignition is compensated for by the greater amount of gas liberated by the combustion; and if the ignition of the powder be quickened by the use of a large cap and more fulminate, the pressure exerted by this larger body of gas is such as to cause the pellets it projects to travel at a greater speed than it is possible to project them with an equal charge of black powder.

The difference in the strength of caps increases or diminishes the time required for the ignition of the gunpowder; but this variation of the cap shows more appreciably in the amount of pressure generated by the explosion.

A clever instrument invented by Mr. Borland, of the "E.C." Powder Company, for registering differences in the strength of caps, and ascertaining to what extent the variation of force they generate is determined by the force of the blow used to explode them, has already been referred to. Unfortunately it is but little used, and irregular action of the cap is even more prevalent than lack of uniformity in the nitro-explosives now commonly used.

The shape of the flash-hole between the cap-chamber and the cartridge considerably affects the ignition. The old-fashioned "Eley" cap was used in connection with a small flash-hole in the centre of the dome, so that the flame from the detonation of the fulminate was slightly delayed before reaching the charge of gunpowder, and the impingement of the flame caused an increase of heat and regulated the ignition of the powder. This cap, after numerous experiments, was found unsuitable for some of the nitro-explosives. Some of the other ammunition makers also use special caps for the nitro-cartridges. The author has for many years used and advocated the " Life " cases as being the best suited to both nitro and black gunpowders. The difference between the two cases, as shown in the illustration, consists chiefly in the form of the anvil and the shape of the flash-hole, but the cap of the " Life " case is also stronger than the ordinary Eley cap. The new concentrated nitro-powders have again necessitated new primers, and Messrs. Eley and others have attempted to meet the necessity.

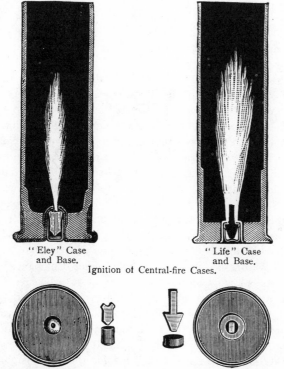

" Eley " Case and Base.   " Life " Case and Base.

Ignition of Central-fire Cases.

View of the Cap chambers and Sections of Caps and Anvils of the " Eley " and " Life " Cases.

It is generally admitted that the stronger the ignition of the explosive the stronger the shooting. Messrs. Eley have, in their ordinary central-fire cap, an article which may be absolutely relied upon for freedom from miss- and hang-fires. That they were loth to depart from their standard pattern is not surprising, but certain of the nitro-compounds now in use requiring such, they produced a cap charged more heavily with detonating material, but otherwise of the same shape and style as their usual primer. The cut shows the exact size of the orifice through which the flash must pass, both in the Eley case 1 and the " Life " case 2 ; it will be seen that there is a wide difference. The cap of the " Life " case 2 is larger, and the anvil of a different shape. The flash with the " Life " cases is very full and fills the case; from the smaller cap, with the cap-chamber pierced with a small round hole only, the flash is much smaller in volume, as well as being of inferior force.

SHOT.

Lead shot is of two kinds : that which is moulded, as large buckshot, and that which is " dropped," as the ordinary small shot, the size of which varies from about 3,000 to 40 pellets in the ounce.

Chilled shot had been used in Germany for some time before its introduction into England by Messrs. Lampen and Roberts, late directors of the Newcastle Chilled Shot Company. It was first manufactured in this country at Wylam by Mr. Lampen, who was considerably handicapped at the outset of the venture by lack of capital. He had no machinery ; the shot was dropped down the shaft of a disused coal-mine, and the sieving was carried on in a most primitive fashion by women, who sorted the shot into their aprons. Still, the results were good, and, by a strange coincidence, the first sample of No. 6 brought to the author's notice counted exactly 270 to the ounce. This shot so well in the author's guns, that its use was continued, and the adoption of this size and count at the *Field* trials led to its wide acceptation as the standard for all tests of a gun's shooting capabilities.

Drop shot should be made of lead without a tin alloy ; it may be hardened by the patented process of the Newcastle Chilled Shot Company. Hard shot is preferable to soft for all purposes, but is usually more expensive. The hardest lead shot will not injure a gun-barrel, even if the barrel be of soft Belgian metal.

To make shot, the lead, when molten, is poured through a sieve which has a tremulous motion conveyed to it by a geared machine; this motion causes the cooling lead to form itself into small globules, and these globules retain their shape as they fall down the shaft into the water placed for them. A large percentage of these globules are not perfectly spherical. From the best quality of shot *all* ill-shapen pellets are removed, and care is taken that the shots of one nominal size are all as nearly as possible the same. The size is controlled, to some extent, by the size of the holes in the sieve through which the molten metal runs, but it requires to be carefully sifted subsequently. In casting, say, No. 6 of 270 to the ounce, a very large proportion of the shot dropped is not of that size at all. Under the best method known, and with the latest appliances, 40 per cent. of the lead cast will be unusable. These unspherical pellets must be re-melted and again cast. Of the remaining 60 per cent., quite 10 per cent. *ought* to be thrown back as unfit for use, and in the best shot this is done; but as they have a certain rotundity, more are sold with the bulk or passed with inferior makes of shot. Of perfect pellets of the exact size required not more than 15 per cent. will be obtained, 40 to 50 per cent. will be such sizes above and below the mean as may be included in No. 6, and the shot will average 270 to the ounce. The majority of the remnant may be used for Nos. 5, 7, and 4. Good shot will have all pellets nearly of one size, a standard obtained by passing through two sieves of mesh almost the same size, and rejecting all that will not pass through the larger mesh, and which do pass through the smaller. This excellence is rarely obtained in any other but the very best make of shot, and that only in No. 6 size, the practice being with other sizes to use meshes of greater difference. The author has tested many makes of shot during the last thirty years, and has found nothing to equal in quality the patent shot originally made by the Newcastle Chilled Shot Company. He has tested other makes, some samples of which were so bad that not a single pellet of even passable sphericity could be found in them.

The nearer to a perfect sphere each pellet of a charge is when the charge leaves the muzzle, the nearer perfect will be the flight of that charge. In passing through the barrel the pellets, by pressing against one another and the barrel, become deformed, unless they are of hardened metal. Chilled shot will improve the shooting of any gun; it does not lead so much as the softer shot, and, if made as it was by the Newcastle Chilled Shot Company, is of the same specific gravity, and freer from poison than soft shot, whilst as a projectile it is superior in every way.

The pellets which fly erratically are usually of irregular shape; hard shot alone leaves the muzzle as nearly spherical as when loaded into the cartridge. The force of the explosion compresses the load of shot in the chamber at starting and forces soft shot much out of shape. It matters not whether the gun be cylindrical or choked, as the damage is effected in the chamber, and the author's experiments have proved that the shot from a choke is not more deformed than that fired from a cylinder with the same conditions. Hard shot is disagreeable to the teeth; but so is soft shot. Hard shot is necessary to good shooting; soft shot is prone to erratic flight, and has, of course, inferior penetration and inferior mean velocity, though possessing equal muzzle velocity.

American and Continental shot is not so regular, either in size or shape, as the English; and there are frequent discrepancies between the printed list of sizes and the actual dimensions of the shot. In America, as in England, there seems to be no association of manufacturers for the purpose of producing shot of standard gauges; and as it is impossible to determine the merit of a gun's performance at the target without knowing the number of pellets contained in the charge, the following tables of sizes of the leading manufacturers may be found useful; but it would be better if, in lieu of arbitrary numbers and letters, the size of shot was designated by the number of pellets to the ounce; for instance, 270 instead of No. 6.

The author seems to be alone in insisting upon having shot exactly to size, but if sportsmen and others would bear the extra expense this incurs, the comparison of the performances of different guns might be made possible. With the present irregularity of shot sizes, no comparisons can be perfectly trustworthy.

The following are the standard sizes of the two leading makers :—

WALKER, PARKER, LIMITED, LONDON AND GATESHEAD.		THE ABBEY IMPROVED CHILLED SHOT CO., NEWCASTLE-ON-TYNE.	
Size.	No. of Pellets to the Ounce.	Size.	No. of Pellets to the Ounce.
A A A A	30	A A A	40
A A A	35 to 40	A A	48
A A	40	A	56
A	45	B B B B	56
B B B	50	B B B	64
B B	58	B B	84
B	75	B	98
1	80	1	104
2	112 to 120	2	122
3	135	3	140
4	175 to 180	4	172
5	218 to 225	5	218
6	278 to 290	5½	240
7	340	†6	270
8	462	6*	300
9	568	7	340
10	985	8	450
Dust.	1672	9	580
* S G	11	10	850
* S S G	15	11	1040
* S S S G	17	12	1250
L G	5½	Large Dust.	1700
M G	9	Small Dust.	2600
—	—	L G	6
—	—	S G	8
—	—	S S G	11
—	—	S S S G	15

* Walker, Parker & Co., London Sizes.

† No. 6 of 270 to the ounce is the standard size.　**No. 6*** is much used both by London loaders and for export, and No. 5½ is sometimes called "medium game" size.

SIZES OF AMERICAN DROP SHOT.

T. N. Sparks, Philadelphia.		Tatham Bros. New York.		N.Y. Lead Co., New York.		Le Roy Co., New York.		St. L. Shot Co. St. Louis, Mo.		Selby Co., San Francisco.	
Size.	Pellets	Size.	Pellets	Size.	Pellets	Size.	Pellets	Size.	Pellets	Size.	Pellets
F	22	FF	24	—	—	TTTT	24	000	29	—	—
TT	36	F	27	—	—	TTT	27	00	32	—	—
T	41	YY	31	TT	32	TT	32	0	40	—	—
BBB	48	T	36	T	38	T	38	BBB	46	—	—
BB	55	BBB	42	BBB	44	BBB	44	BB	53	BBB	46
B	63	BB	50	BB	49	BB	49	B	63	BB	55
1	80	B	59	B	58	B	58	—	—	B	68
2	90	1	71	1	69	1	69	1	79	1	79
3	118	2	86	2	82	2	82	2	98	2	89
4	130	3	106	3	98	3	98	3	116	3	118
5	182	4	132	4	121	4	121	4	163	4	134
6	245	5	168	5	149	5	166	5	181	5	170
7	305	6	218	6	209	6	209	6	252	6	215
8	426	7	291	7	278	7	278	7	306	7	303
9	615	8	399	8	375	8	375	8	426	8	420
10	950	9	568	9	560	9	560	9	584	9	592
11	1660	10	848	10	822	10	822	10	981	10	874
12	3316	11	1346	11	982	11	982	11	1603	11	1404
Dust	5910	12	2326	12	1778	12	1778	12	2305	12	2030
—	—	—	—	—	—	—	—	—	—	—	—.

SIZES OF AMERICAN SHOT. (*Continued.*)

Chicago Co., Chicago, Ill.		Merchant's Co., Baltimore.		Dubuque Co., Dubuque, Iowa.		Montreal Rolling Mill Company.		
Size.	Pellets.	Size.	Pellets.	Size.	Pellets.	Diameter in Inches.	Size.	Pellets.
—	—	TTTT	22	—	—	32-100	SSG	10
000	27	TTT	26	000	27	30-100	SG	11
00	33	TT	30	00	33	28-100	SS	15
0	38	T	34	0	38	23-100	AAAA	24
BBB	46	BBB	39	BBB	46	22-100	AAA	27
BB	53	BB	45	BB	53	21-100	AA	32
B	62	B	52	B	62	20-100	A	38
1	75	1	60	1	75	19-100	BBB	44
2	92	2	77	2	92	18-100	BB	49
3	118	3	94	3	118	17-100	B	58
4	146	4	115	4	146	16-100	1	69
5	172	5	140	5	172	15-100	2	82
6	246	6	180	6	246	14-100	3	98
7	323	7	225	7	323	13-100	4	121
8	434	8	365	8	434	12-100	5	166
9	596	9	610	9	596	11-100	6	209
10	854	10	1130	10	854	10-100	7	278
11	1414	11	2200	11	1414	9-100	8	375
12	2400	12	3200	12	2400	8-100	9	560
—	—	13	12200	—	—	7-100	10	822
—	—	—	—	—	—	6-100	Dust	982

CONTINENTAL SIZES OF SHOT.

| FRENCH. | | | | | | ITALIAN. | | BELGIAN. | | AUSTRIAN. | | PRUSSIAN. | |
| Paris. | | Lyons. | | Marseilles. | | | | | | Ramer & Co. | | Cologne. | |
Size.	Pellets.	Size.	Pellets.	Size.	Pellets.	Size.	Pellets.	Size.	Pellets.	Size.	Pellets.	Size.	Pellets.
00000	28	0000	28	0000000	28	000000	36	000000	40	0000	—	0	2 to 3
0000	40	000	30	000000	33	00000	41	00000	48	000	—	00	3 to 4
000	48	00	33	00000	35	0000	46	0000	56	00	21	000	4 to 5
00	54	0	34	0000	39	000	51	000	66	0	23	0000	5 to 6
0	62	1	37	000	49	00	56	00	84	1	26	AAA	19
1	74	2	43	00	54	0	64	0	98	2	—	AA	26
2	85	3	53	0	62	1	79	1	104	3	35	A	29
3	99	4	81	1	71	2	96	2	122	4	41	BB	38
4	113	5	86	2	75	3	120	3	140	5	—	B	43
5	170	6	178	3	97	4	175	4	172	6	59	1	50
5	221	7	184	4	114	5	220	5	218	7	69	2	64
7	260	8	261	5	144	6	270	6	270	8	82	3	82
8	402	9	443	6	150	7	340	7	340	9	92	4	97
9	686	10	721	7	190	8	450	8	450	10	124	5	123
10	963	11	1254	8	229	9	580	9	580	11	155	6	167
11	1770	12	2218	9	312	10	850	10	850	12	203	7	230
12	3824	—	—	10	485	11	1040	11	1040	13	283	8	336
—	—	—	—	11	920	12	1250	12	1250	14	303	9	442
—	—	—	—	12	1177	13	1480	—	—	15	652	10	696
—	—	—	—	—	—	14	1700	—	—	16	809	11	1223

The pellets are counted to the English ounce, which equals 28 grammes.

GUN CASES AND IMPLEMENTS.

The gun that is worth owning is worth preserving. If kept in a gun-rack—or, better still, a dust-proof gun cupboard—it will last longer, and if put away clean will always be ready for use. To take guns from place to place, a case is necessary; if they are to be sent, a substantial oak case, leather-covered, is the best—such a case, well made, is worth about £5. It affords complete protection to the gun, and will itself withstand the roughest usage.

Sole leather cases—that is to say, cases in which best leather is *sewn* to pine frames—are light and handy, and do well to carry guns in, but they must not be used as packing-cases; and although they will upon occasion stand several trips to the Rocky Mountains, they are not adapted to the rough usage they receive in the goods van, and do not protect the gun as will the oak covered case. A best sole leather case is worth £4. The leg-of-mutton case affected by trap shooters does not give much protection to the gun, but it is very light, and serves well to carry the gun; the cost is £2. A case to carry the gun at full length has been recommended, but its bulk makes it inconvenient in many situations where the shorter case is no incumbrance.

It is preferable to carry cartridges in a separate magazine than in a tray in the gun cases. These magazines are made to carry 50—the neat little case carried by the trap shooter—and 100, 200, 300, 400, or 500, the last a substantial trunk heavily made, and able to withstand luggage-porters' careless handling.

The divisions are preferable, as in the English magazine, for the cartridges then travel better, and are more easily packed into and removed from the magazine.

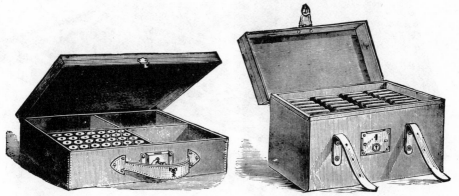

American Cartridge Magazine.   English Cartridge Magazine.

The impedimenta in England may be restricted to a full set of cleaning implements, including pocket cleaner and chamber brushes, action brush, tow, rag, flannel, and oil. A pocket extractor is useful, and a pair of turnscrews may be kept in the cases.

Cartridge loading apparatus will be found useless in England, where ammunition is cheap, and it is not the rule to reload cases.

When travelling abroad, powder and shot measures should be taken; also a rammer, turnover, de- and re-capper, and supply of caps, gunpowder, wadding, and a little shot.

Brass cartridge cases are preferred by travellers and explorers who need to reload the cases.   Thin brass, as being lighter and capable of being reloaded several times, are recommended, a few dozen thick heavy brass being taken for emergencies, and possibly "converters," or brass or steel shells fitted with nipples instead of caps, so that with them the gun may be used as a muzzle-loader.   The thin brass case requires a Greener "crimper" to fix the top wad, which by any other method of turning over is liable to *start*, and so allow the shot to escape

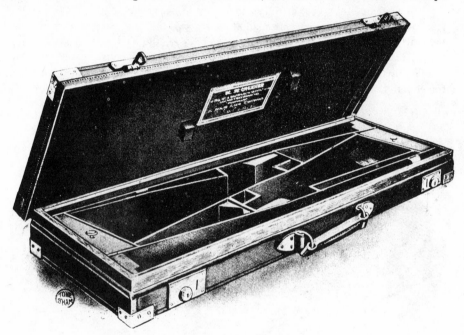

The English Gun-case, to hold a Pair of Guns and Implements.

into the barrel before the cartridge is fired.   The crimper takes up no more room than the ordinary turning-over machine; the loaded cartridge is pressed into it against a die, which corrugates the fore-part of the case, as shown on page 618, or it may also be made to close the case over upon the wad, as shown in the illustration on page 606.

The best chronometer oil should be used for the lock-work; best lubricating oils, Rangoon, refined neats'-foot, or oils of greater body, may be used in the action and parts readily accessible, and these and many other oils and greases are

used as rust preventatives. Two of the latest cleansers and preservatives are
" Greenerene " and " Greener's Gun Grease," the former a perfect fouling remover,
the latter a rust preventative. After using smokeless powders containing nitro-
glycerine a hard deposit
is often left in the barrel ;
various cleansing fluids are
sold to remove it. The mixture used in the Service is
composed of 99 parts of
Russian petroleum oil and
1 part of a saturated solution
of caustic soda or methylated
spirit ; for foreign use it is
thickened with vaseline.

Cartridge belts cannot be
recommended for ordinary
shooting, although there are
times when they are very
useful, if not indispensable.
Cartridge bags are mostly
used by keepers or loaders
to carry their employers'
reserves. Two small bags
feel much lighter than one
large one. The Quellan
patent cartridge carrier is
very handy, but is open to
the same objections as the
bag — viz. the weight always

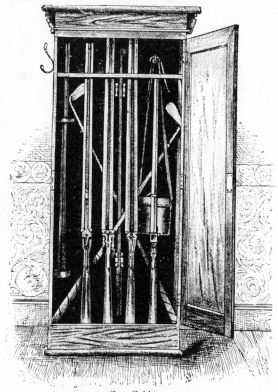

Gun Cabinet.

bearing upon the one shoulder tires more quickly than if the load be distributed in
the pockets of a shooting jacket.

Gun and rifle slings are of various designs ; most of the practical devices allow of
the weapon being carried with a minimum of discomfort and leaving the hands
free for other purposes—as driving. Unfortunately most of these slings require the
weapon to hang from the shoulder in such a position as not to be instantly available
for purposes of sport or defence. The Greener pattern sling is an exception : the butt
of the weapon is attached to the sling by an ordinary swivel hook, and this by a double

swivel link connects to a
ring sliding along the sling.
The strap is passed over the
shoulder and under the right
a r m — bandolier fashion ;
there is a strap from the
sling which forms a loop
for the barrels and *hooks* to
the sling. It is instantly
detachable, and as easily
refastened with one hand
—which may also grip the
barrels. Without freeing the
gun at the butt, it may be
fired from either shoulder

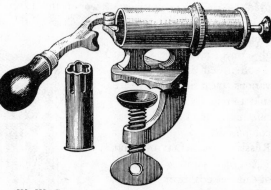

W. W. Greener's Brass Cartridge Case "Crimper" or
Wad Fixer.

or hips, and, in addition to being carried as shown in the illustration, the position
may be altered to under the arm, across
the back, or varied in any way at will, and
as found convenient or least tiring.

HAND GUARD AND SIGHT ALIGNER.

Many patterns of hand guards or protec-
tors have been offered to sportsmen, but none
of them have so rapidly achieved the popularity accorded to the "No-mis-gard" introduced some years ago by the author.   This
guard, in addition to serving the customary
dual purpose of protecting the hand from
the heat of the barrel and the browning from
the rub of the hand, also aids the shooter
rapidly to align his gun, the two ears
serving as a sight between which the
"Game" may be instantly spotted. The
illustration shows clearly the object of
the device, and a trial will quickly convince
the sportsman of its utility.

The Greener Patent "No-mis-gard."

W. W. Greener's Sling.

CHAPTER XXV.

THE HISTORY OF RIFLING AND ITS DEVELOPMENT.

DEFINITION OF RIFLING.

RIFLING consists of the cutting away of the interior of the barrel of a firearm so as to form spiral grooves upon its surface. The object of this spiral grooving is to guide the projectile down the barrel, force it to turn upon its own axis, and impart to it a rotary motion which it shall maintain during its flight, and by this means equalise any irregularities, and so lessen the tendency to depart from a straight line.

The grooving is done by a machine which forces a cutter through the barrel and is so arranged that any angle, pitch, or turn may be given to the groove, and, of course, any shape. The parts of the barrel untouched by the grooves are termed " lands."

THE INVENTION OF RIFLING.

Most writers assign the invention of spiral-grooved musket-barrels to Gaspard Kollner, a gun-maker of Vienna in the fifteenth century ; and other authorities assert that his barrels had straight grooves and attribute the invention to Augustus Kotter, of Nuremberg, fixing the date as 1520. It had long been the practice in Germany to fashion the bolts shot from crossbows so that they rotated during their flight. This was effected by the shape of the bolt-head or by affixing pinions of leather or metal to the shaft. In some crossbows the bolts are shot through a spiral-grooved guiding tube fixed upon the shaft of the bow, thus giving a rotary motion to the bolt ; but whether such bows were produced before or after the first use of spiral grooving in firearms there is no trustworthy evidence to show. Sometimes cannon were made with straight grooves, in order to admit a tight-fitting bullet ; the great fouling with the ungrained powder so quickly reducing the bore that the bullets could be forced home only with great difficulty. The grooves were to accommodate this fouling and so relieve the bullet, and it has been suggested that this grooving was used as rifling when it was found that the bullets took the impression of the grooved bore.

FORMS OF RIFLING.

Straight, parallel, half-round, narrow channels, probably not more than two in number, constituted the rifle in its most primitive form; later, 3, 5, 7, 9, and 12 grooves were more common. When the grooves were made to take a spiral direction the double-grooved barrel was not common. It reappeared in 1725 in Spain, practically in the form introduced in 1835 as the Brunswick rifle.

The amount of turn varies very much in these old rifles; one turn in from 2 to 3 feet is commonly found, but as often there is not more than a half or three-quarter turn in the same length. In some the grooves have a regular spiral; in some they increase as they approach the muzzle, in some they are quicker at the breech, and Mr. Deane states that he has seen an old rifle in which the greatest amount of spiral is midway in the length of the barrel, the turn increasing from the breech to that culminating point, then decreasing at the same speed. So with the depth of grooving which was tried variously; in short, every device appears to have been resorted to in the hope of perfecting the arm. The American "freed bore" and "gaining twist," common at the beginning of the nineteenth century, are said to have been found in very much older weapons of European make.

The form of groove also varied; square, round, triangular, ratchet-shape, and even comma-shaped. This last, known as the *rayures à virgule*, was one of Berner's plans, produced about 1835, and consisted of two, three, or four wide grooves, leaving almost unapparent ridges in the bore but at the muzzle showing the bore to have a comma-like circumference.

With reference to the long-continued use of straight grooving, it seems to have been the common belief that, notwithstanding the spiral grooving, the bullet took a straight path down the barrel, or, as a rifleman would say, "stripped"; and even so late as 1775 a technical journal states, not only that this must be so, but also that the flight of the bullet is in a straight line—that is, not rotating—whatever the arm from which it is fired.

The science of gunnery—mathematical gunnery, or ballistics—received most adequate treatment from Professor Leutmann, of St. Petersburg, about 1730; from Euler the mathematician, Borda, Gussendi; and in this country from Mr. Robins, whose notable treatise was published in 1747.

EARLY USE OF THE RIFLE.

For military purposes rifles were not much used until quite recently—the first rifle generally issued to the English infantry was not produced until 1852—though

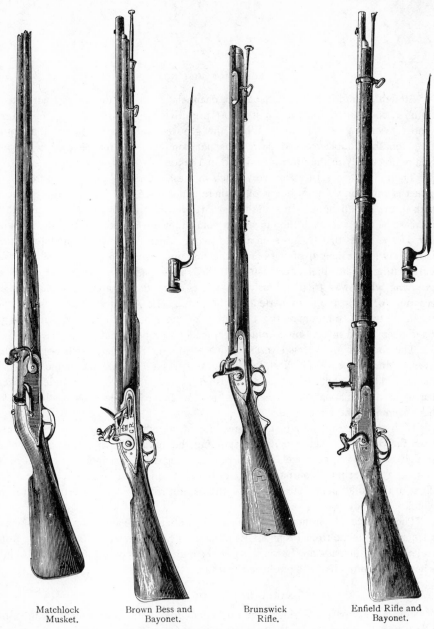

Matchlock
Musket.

Brown Bess and
Bayonet.

Brunswick
Rifle.

Enfield Rifle and
Bayonet.

Early Army Muskets : Regulation Patterns.

there are instances of their occasional employment in the seventeenth and eighteenth centuries. The greater range and accuracy they possessed caused them to be much used for target practice—always a favourite sport of the Teutonic race—and they were also used for hunting.

In 1631 the Landgraf of Hesse had a troop of riflemen, and ten years later Maximilian of Bavaria had several troops armed with rifled arquebuses ; Louis XIII. armed his body-guard with rifles, and later ordered that two men from each of the light cavalry regiments should be similarly equipped. These riflemen were afterwards formed into a regiment of carabineers, but the first regulation carbine was not issued till 1793.

Napoleon withdrew the rifle from the troops, to whom it had been issued during the wars of the Republic, nor did the French make any considerable use of it again until 1830, when the Chasseurs d'Orléans were armed with it for the invasion of Algeria. The French riflemen thought that the Arab guns had greater range than their rifles ; but this is explained by the fact that the Arabs aimed high, whilst the French fired according to the musketry instructions and hit nothing beyond 200 yards. The English learnt their value during the American War of Independence, when the Government subsidised Continental *Jägers* possessed of rifles to oppose the American backwoodsmen, whose rifle-shooting was most deadly.

THE FIREARMS OF THE BRITISH ARMY.

The relative value of modern improvements and inventions will be the more apparent if the results obtainable from them are contrasted with those got from earlier arms ; and as the rifle is altogether a modern weapon from the military point of view, it will not be out of place here to enumerate the chief infantry firearms that preceded it.

The hand cannon, first introduced in 1471, was quickly superseded by the matchlock, which remained in use until the Commonwealth. About 1530 the wheel-lock was first brought to this country, and a few were supplied to English soldiers until the time of Charles II. In the reign of James I. some flint-locks were issued to leading regiments, and in the reign of William III. they came into general use, and from them was developed the renowned " Brown Bess " which, for a century and half, was the regulation musket of the British army. Thus the weapon that won Waterloo was of the same type as our ancestors used at Ramillies and Blenheim.

In the Brown Bess and similar military muskets it was customary to use a bullet two sizes smaller than the bore, wrapped up in a loosely-fitting patch, which formed the cartridge. Thus they were easy to load even when foul; whereas the muzzle-loading rifle employed in connection with a close-fitting ball never was, and could not have been, used by troops generally, the force required to push home the bullet rendering its use as a weapon of war almost impossible.

But with the muskets a very low average of accuracy and range was considered satisfactory. W. Greener, writing in 1841, states that "the immense escape of explosive matter past the ball prevented the possibility of any velocity worthy of the name being given to the ball, and the range is the most contemptible of any kind or description of gun I know : 120 yards is the average distance at which the balls strike the ground when fired horizontally at five feet above the level."

Evidence has already been quoted as to the comparative value of bow and musket (page 12), and it is supposed that, but for being a convenient handle for a bayonet, and so convertible into a pike, its use as the chief offensive weapon would not have been continued.   Though officially effective at 200 yards, it was the rule of the soldier not to fire until he saw the whites of his enemy's eyes; and, if this working rule was adhered to, it is calculated that more often than not the soldier was obliged to fire away his own weight in lead for every man killed ; but how far this was due to bad marksmanship is not known.   The values of musket and rifle fire are contrasted, and some particulars concerning them given, in the paragraphs in the chapter on " Modern Military Rifles."

The table shows clearly how recent are the changes made in the infantry equipment.   Workmen are still living in Birmingham who, as journeymen, made for the British Government the old flint-lock muskets of practically the same pattern as used at the battle of Blenheim and identical with those used at Waterloo.   The conservatism is proved by the fact that the percussion system came into general use for sporting purposes nearly a quarter of a century before being adopted by the Government.   The new method of ignition was fully tested at Woolwich in 1834, and some muskets were converted in 1839, but the system was not really adopted until 1842, and even in that year the Government were still having flint-lock muskets made in Birmingham.

It is sometimes asserted that the Duke of Wellington was to blame, he obstinately refusing to countenance any change in the arms with which he had won Waterloo ; and the fact that the Enfield rifle was issued shortly after his death, at first sight seems to confirm this ; but, on the other hand, the assistance and encouragement given by the Duke to inventors, and the part he took in regard to the Minié system and suppression of the " Brown Bess," shows that he was, at least, ready to admit the superiority of newer weapons.   The reasons why the rifle did not supersede the

THE MUZZLE-LOADING WEAPONS OF THE BRITISH ARMY.

No.	Name and Date	Calibre		Powder	Bullet		Weight of weapon with bayonet	Length of barrel	Rifling		Sights	Range
		Diam.	Bore	Grains	Weight in grs.	Diam.			Grooves	Turn		
1	Matchlock Musket, 17th C.	·729	12	165			20 lbs.	48″	none		plain	
2	Old Army Musket, 1750	·753	11	124	490		11 lbs. 4 oz.	42″	none		corn	200 yds.
3	Brown Bess, 1800	·753	11	70	490		11 lbs. 2 oz.	39″	none		corn	200 yds.
4	Baker's Rifle, 1800	·612	20	70			9 lbs. 8 oz. (no bayonet)	30″	7	1 in 120″		
5	Brunswick Rifle, 1835	·704	13	124	557		11 lbs. 5 oz.	33″	2	1 in 30″	corn	400 yds.
6	Percussion Musket, 1842*	·753	11	70	490	·670	11 lbs. 6 oz.	39″				
7	Jacob Rifle (double)	·526	32	70				24″	4	$\frac{4}{5}$ in 24″	2000	
8	Minié Rifle, 1851	·702	14	70	680	·690	10 lbs. 8¾ oz.	39″	4	1 in 78″	1000	1000 yds.
9	Enfield Rifle, 1853	·577	25	70	530	·568	9 lbs. 3 oz.	39″	3	1 in 78″	1000	1200 yds.
10	Short Enfield Rifle, 1855†	·577	25	70			8 lbs. 7 oz.	33″	5	1 in 54″		
11	Enfield Rifle, 1857‡	·577	25	85	538	·550			5			
12	Whitworth (Military)	·450	52		530	·442		40″	6 (hexagonal)	1 in 20″		

* Afterwards grooved for Minié's bullet of 825 grains, ·731 in diameter, 84 grains powder, then known as "Sea Service Rifles."
† Also made in 1858 with grooves having 1 turn in 48 inches for sea service and rifle brigade.
‡ Bullet lengthened from 1·05 to 1·09 in 1858, and grooves progressing in depth from ·015 at breech to ·005 at muzzle. See parts made interchangeable in 1860.

plain musket for military purposes will be made apparent in the subsequent history of rifling.

The Baker and Brunswick patterns were issued to special regiments only ; of the Minié pattern 28,000 were issued ; a certain proportion to each regiment, and the arm was not a success. Later, special corps—as the sappers—were armed with the Lancaster oval-bore, but practically the muzzle-loading rifle never was, and could not be made, satisfactory as a military weapon, from the standpoint of the expert.

THE HISTORY OF THE BAYONET.

The means of converting a military firearm into a pike, and so enable it to be used as either an offensive or defensive weapon, originated first in France. Some peasants of the Basque provinces, whilst on an expedition against a company of bandits, having used all their ammunition, were driven to the desperate necessity of inserting their long knives in the mouths of their arquebuses, by which means they routed their adversaries. This event became well known, and led to the construction, in 1641, of the *bayonnette* at Bayonne, a village in the south of France, from which place it took its name. In 1649 the pike was replaced by a long narrow blade fixed to a short wooden handle, which was inserted in the muzzle of the musket, but the advantage gained was inconsiderable, owing to the firearm being rendered useless for the time ; the wooden handle also, not giving sufficient solidity to the blade, was shortly afterwards dispensed with, and the iron itself made to screw into the muzzle of the gun.

In the illustration No. 8 is the knife bayonet ; No. 4 is the same type of bayonet furnished with two rings on the shaft, which, slipped over the muzzle of the musket, held it in position, and permitted the gun to be fired with the bayonet so fixed. This, according to Grose, is the origin of the socket bayonet. It is said that during the reign of William III. an English regiment was surprised by a charging troop of French foot-soldiers, who, although they had bayonets fixed, halted during the charge and fired a volley, causing considerable consternation. It would appear, therefore, that the socket bayonet was of French origin. It is known that Vauban, the famous general of Louis XIV., caused all the French foot-soldiers to be supplied with socket bayonets, and the pike became an obsolete weapon in France.

The bayonet-blades were at first flat rods of iron pointed—sometimes with a long, at other times with a short, neck. The Regulation bayonet of the Brown Bess was triangular, with the top side flat, the other two fluted, and it weighed 1 lb. 2 oz. The Enfield bayonet has all three sides fluted. The bayonet-socket has been improved at various times. In the Enfield bayonet the socket was so

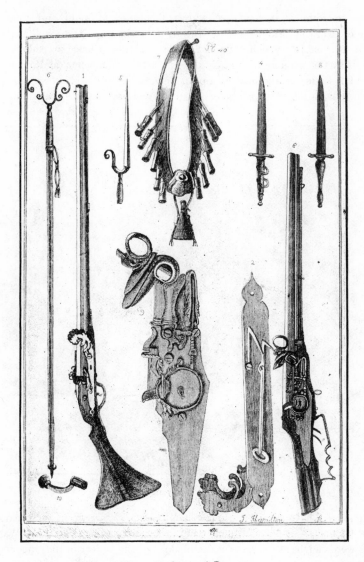

Military Muskets and Bayonets.

shaped as to admit of its being passed over the block foresight, and secured by a half turn of a bayonet-ring. In the Brown Bess bayonet a stop slipped over a spring in the stock, which retained it in position. The sword-bayonet was introduced by the French in 1844 on the rifle of the Chasseurs de Vincennes, and has since been adopted by most European Powers.

Since the introduction of breech-loaders the bayonet has been but seldom

" Crossed Bayonets."

requisitioned. The method of using it hand-to-hand is shown in the illustration of "crossed bayonets"—a term frequently met in accounts of the Peninsular War. The bayonets were caught at the base of the blade, and the object of the opponents was by sheer strength to force the muzzle back until his own bayonet point reached his antagonist.

The weight of the bayonet on the muzzle of the rifle barrel, especially of the sword-bayonet, greatly affected the accuracy of fire, so that from time to time it has been shortened and lightened until at the present time it is little more than a knife. The dimensions of these bayonets are given, with the descriptions of modern military rifles, in a subsequent chapter.

THE DEVELOPMENT OF THE MUZZLE-LOADING RIFLE.

In England the first regiment to be armed with rifles was the 95th, later known as the Rifle Brigade, to which Baker's rifle was issued in 1800.

The Brunswick rifle was next produced; in this there were but two grooves, and a belted bullet was used similar in every respect, it is said, to one produced by a Spanish officer in 1725, and reproduced by Captain Berner, of the Brunswickers, in 1835, which belt enabled the bullet to catch the groove instantly, and, when wrapped in a greased patch, to descend easily without the necessity of hammering.

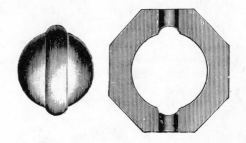

The great objection to the use of the rifle for military purposes was the difficulty experienced in loading. With the Baker, mallets were issued to hammer the bullets into the muzzles ; and, on the other hand, if the diameter of the bullet was so reduced as to admit of its easy insertion, it took but little of the grooving, " stripped," and allowed much of the powder gas to escape as windage. Various endeavours were made to overcome this difficulty : the Brunswick belted bullet was one. M. Delvigne, in 1826, fitted a breech with abrupt shoulders, on which the spherical bullet was rammed down until it expanded and filled the grooves. The objection was that the deformed bullet had an erratic flight. The " tige," or anvil, consisting of a steel stud fixed centrally, was substituted for the shouldered chamber, but with no better success.

The difficulty was not overcome until in 1835 the late W. Greener produced the first perfect expansive bullet. It consisted of an oval ball, a diameter and a half in length, and had a flat end, also a perforation extending nearly through it, a cast metallic taper plug with a head like a round-topped button. The end of the plug being slightly inserted in the perforation, the ball was put into the rifle either end foremost, and upon the explosion taking place the plug was driven home, and the bullet, expanding, filled up the grooves of the rifling and prevented windage.

A trial of the Greener bullet was made in August, 1835, at Tynemouth, by a party of the 60th Rifles, under the command of Major Walcot, R.H.A., and the

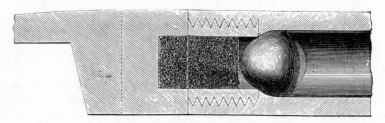

The Delvigne Bullet and Chamber.

success of the trials far surpassed the expectations of the military experts present.   It was proved that the Greener bullet enabled rifles to be loaded as easily as smooth-bore muskets, whilst the range and accuracy of the rifle were retained.   Fifty rounds with Greener bullets were fired into a sandbank, and upon recovery of them the

W. Greener's Expanding Bullet.

marks they bore showed the impress of the grooves exactly, thus proving that the expansion was complete.   The report of the trial, although very favourable to the invention, received scant consideration by the authorities, the invention being rejected on the ground that the bullet was a compound one.

The matter was resuscitated when, in 1852, the Government awarded M. Minié, a Frenchman, £20,000 for a bullet of the same principle adopted into the British service.   Mr. Greener then made several unsuccessful attempts to obtain from the British Government some recognition of his claims to the invention ; but not until Mr. Scholefield, the member for Birmingham, moved in the House of Commons for copies of the correspondence between the Board of Ordnance and Mr. Greener, and the papers connected therewith, was this act of injustice truly exposed. Eventually the Government, after much trouble, admitted Mr. Greener's priority, and awarded him £1,000 in the Army Estimates of 1857, for "the first public suggestion of the principle of expansion, commonly called the Minié principle, in 1836."

Mr. Greener stated in his work, " Gunnery in 1858," " that there is no evidence that either Delvigne or Minié had any profound knowledge of the science of gunnery; and their knowledge of the principles of expansive rifle bullets was so meagre as to justify the assumption that their only connection with its production was that of copying from the *Times*, or from my works, published in 1842 and 1846."

Between the date of the invention of the expansive bullet by Greener and its adoption as the Minié numerous other ways of overcoming the difficulty of loading and windage were attempted.   Some of the most important inventions may be briefly summarised.

It was found that the belted bullet of the Brunswick rifle was unequal to others for accuracy, for the bullet tilted soon after leaving the muzzle.   To reduce this tendency, General Jacobs proposed the four-grooved rifle and cross-belted bullet.

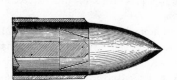

The Jacobs Bullet.

The Minié Bullet.

This was the outcome of extensive and costly experiments, and his rifle certainly possessed greater range and accuracy.   General Jacobs offered this invention to the Indian Government in the year 1846, by whom it was rejected with the plea that " the Brunswick, being considered good enough for the British Army, was good enough for service in the Honourable East India Company."

Notwithstanding this rebuff, the gallant officer continued his experiments, hoping to discover a better bullet than the spherical ball, which last, with no known system of rifling, could be depended upon as accurate beyond 350 yards.

After numerous experiments—many of which were attended with curious results

—a conical ball with a globular spheroidal base, and heavier than the former bullet, was adopted ; this gave excellent shooting at 600 and 800 yards.

Soon after this invention the Minié bullet was introduced ; General Jacobs immediately set himself the task of improving upon it, and succeeded in producing a projectile of the form illustrated. It contained a charge of powder in a copper tube, the front of which was primed with detonating powder and exploded upon impact.

The principal outcome of General Jacobs' elaborate trials and experiments was a double-barrel 32-bore four-grooved rifle, deep grooves $\frac{4}{5}$ turn in 24 inches, which was sighted up to 2,000 yards, with leaf and tangent sight ; also the projectiles before mentioned.

The French artillerists arrived at the same conclusions as General Jacobs with respect to the shape of projectile best fitted for rifles, but by different ways. The battering of the Delvigne bullet in ramming caused Colonel Pontcharra to interpose a *sabot* or cupped wad of wood between the ball and the anvil. His plan answered so well that ammunition of the kind was issued ; next a metallic *sabot* was tried in lieu of the wooden one ; this formed a second projectile and destroyed accuracy. In 1841 a colonel of artillery tried a *sabot* soldered to the base of the ball, and thus an elongated projectile was obtained, but M. Delvigne was the first to announce the fact that elongated bullets, hollowed at the base, were expanded and forced into the grooves of the rifle by the gas evolved in the explosion of the powder, and he patented such a bullet in 1841.

The practical results appear to have advanced little until in 1847 M. Minié suggested an iron cup being placed in the hollow base. One of the early bullets on his principle was a cylindro-ogive in form, with a groove on its cylindrical base intended for a greased patch ; the groove was dispensed with, but the performance was not so good, and experiments showed that alterations in the shape or position of the groove affected the shooting. Efforts were made to construct bullets heavier forward both by flattening the front and by grooving the hollowed base, but the principal rings or cannelures proved the best.

The comparative values of the Minié rifle and improved smooth-bore percussion musket of 1842 pattern were determined by numerous trials. In the following table the results are given of the scores made by twenty men with both the Minié rifle and the plain musket, ten rounds each man, five in file and five in volley, firing at each distance against a target 6 feet high and 20 feet broad. It was remarked that, whereas the shots that missed the target from the musket fell from 15 to 20 feet wide of the target, those from the Minié fell within two or three feet.

RESULTS.

Distances.	Percussion Musket.		Minié Rifle.	
Yards.	No. of Hits.	Per Cent.	No. of Hits.	Per Cent.
100	149	74·5	189	94·5
260	85	42·5	160	80·0
300	32	16·	110	55·
400	9	4·5	105	52·5

THE MINIÉ RIFLE AND PERCUSSION MUSKET.

The great fault of the Minié, in addition to its tendency to foul quickly, was that, owing to irregularities in the bullets, the iron cup used to expand the base, when driven forward, occasionally expanded so much that the bullet was cut in two, the ring base being left in the barrel and pushed down by the next bullet. This was sometimes repeated again and again, the rings remaining in the rifling until the weapon was unloadable. The author has seen as many as sixteen of these rings extracted from the one barrel, which had been returned as " foul."

THE LANCASTER RIFLE.

The difference between the Lancaster oval-bore and the Brunswick rifle consists in the shape of the two grooves. In the first they are very wide and comparatively

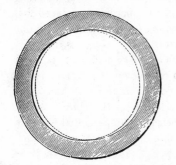

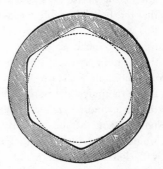

Lancaster Oval-bore Rifling, and Whitworth Rifling and Bullet.

shallow; in the latter, of the ordinary depth and width. The idea of an elliptic bore is an old one—it was used by Captain Berners in a musket in 1835—and its advantage with a muzzle-loading rifle was that the weapon could be more easily loaded ; there was no forcing of the bullet into grooves and less trouble from the fouling, but there was an increase of windage.

THE WHITWORTH RIFLE.

In the year 1852 Viscount Hardinge, then Master-General of Ordnance, experimented with a view to testing the comparative merits of various rifles submitted for the purpose by the Government factories and private gunmakers. He was much discouraged by the discovery that no two of the new rifles could be made to shoot quite alike, and sought the aid of Mr. Whitworth, the first mechanician of the day, in perfecting the machinery for the production of rifles. But Mr. Whitworth thought the fault was to be found in the principle of the rifle rather than in the methods of manufacture, and ultimately he was commissioned to make exhaustive experiments at the cost of the Government, in order to discover the best form of rifling and fittest type of weapon. An enclosed range 500 yards long was erected for the experiments, and fitted with movable targets and every appliance ingenuity could devise ; this range was completed in 1854, and was destroyed by a great storm in the same year, so that it was not until the following spring the tests were commenced. In the meantime, Mr. Whitworth had made some model cannon of polygonal bore, and determined to adapt the same form to musket barrels. Then he experimented with a view to discovering the best form of bullet-projectile.

The advantage of the conical bullet had long been demonstrated, but in attempting to use an elongated ball with the usual spiral he was baffled by finding that the ball invariably " capsized " or " turned over." He became convinced that this was due to the slow spiral, and eventually, after testing every gradation from one turn in 78 inches to one in 5, he found that one turn in every 20 inches increased the rotation sufficiently to impart the required steadiness to the ball, and caused it to maintain a flight parallel to its axis. For the form of grooving he determined to adopt the polygonal bore—which, by-the-bye, he was not the first to use—and found that a cylindro-conoidal bullet expanded sufficiently to fill up the corners of the polygon and at the same time dropped straight down the rifling, so that no time would be lost by the soldier in loading. The experiments showed that with each variation of the bore a different charge of powder was required to give the best results, and that ·450 calibre gave the most satisfactory shooting with the charge and weight of lead to which he was restricted.

Mr. Whitworth patented the hexagonal bore in 1854. By machinery he produced hexagonal bullets corresponding to the bore of the rifle, and these gave the best results; but, as already stated, the long cylindrical bullets "set up" or shortened by the force of the explosion to the degree requisite for filling the angles of the bore. It was questioned whether the greatly increased twist did not retard the bullet, but the velocity was proved by a trial against the Enfield rifle, when the hexagonal bullet passed through fifteen thicknesses of elm to the Enfield's six, under the same conditions and using the same powder charges. Mr. Whitworth even constructed a rifle in which the bullet actually travelled a greater distance round the barrel on its own axis than it did forward—the turn being one turn in one inch. The sum-total of Mr. Whitworth's experiments were—an improved system of rifling, a turn in the spiral four times greater than in the Enfield, a bore in diameter one-fifth less, and an elongated projectile capable of a mechanical fit.

The new rifle was tried at Hythe, 1857, in the presence of the Minister of War and a large company of distinguished officers, and it beat the Enfield of the Government factories by 3 to 1; its mean deviation at 500 yards was $4\frac{1}{2}$, while the recorded best of any rifle previously tried was 27. The annexed table gives the results of both rifles at different ranges; the two diagrams of the shooting at 500 yards are from Sir J. E. Tennant's "Story of the Guns."

Description of Rifle.	Distance : Yards.	Angle of Elevation.	Deviation.	Remarks.
Enfield...............	500	18·32	2·24 feet.	
Whitworth		1·15	·37 ,,	
Enfield	800	2 45	4·20 ,,	
Whitworth		2·22	1·00 ,,	
Enfield...............	1100*	4·12	8·00 ,,	
Whitworth		3·8	2·62 ,,	
Enfield...............	1400*	...	...	{ Shooting so wild no
Whitworth		5·0	4·62 ,,	diagram taken.
Whitworth	1800*	6·40	11·52 ,,	Enfield not fired.

* These trials were made from a fixed rest.

The committee of experts reported that "they acknowledge the relative superiority of his small-bore rifle, even as a military weapon, over all other rifles of similar calibre that have been under trial, and are of opinion that the Whitworth rifle, taking all other points into consideration, is superior to all other arms as yet produced, and that this superiority would be maintained if Mr. Whitworth could ensure all the arms being made with equal mechanical perfection." It was advanced against the rifle that it wore badly, and that there was a difficulty in procuring a sufficient supply of suitable ammunition. The rifle was never adopted into the Government service, but Mr. Whitworth was fortunate in securing an order for the forty rifles with which the Queen's Prize was to be shot for at the 1860 meeting of the National Rifle Association; but at the meeting other chief prizes were taken with rifles of competing makers. Mr. Whitworth, not having the advantage of practical training in the manufacture of guns, was unable to produce

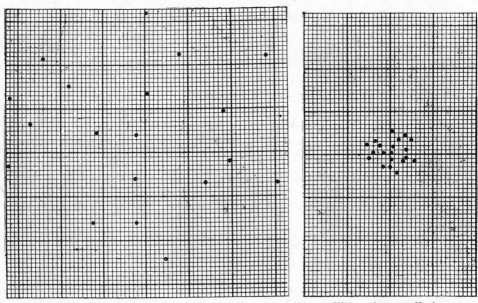

Enfield at 500 Yards. (Target 6 ft. 6 in. square.)   Whitworth at 500 Yards.

weapons as perfect as his competitors. The ignition of the Whitworth was very faulty, and when the barrels did foul the mechanically-fitting bullets jammed in the bore in loading. The gun-makers benefited by his experiments and example, and beat him with rifles of the same calibre and of similar form to that which will always be associated with his name. The Henry rifling, yet to be described, is very like the Whitworth, and muzzle-loaders so made were also used with mechanically-fitting bullets.

The most important points settled by Mr. Whitworth's experiments include the advantages resulting from a sharp twist, and from a small bore and elongated projectile.   The Whitworth principle failed because it possessed the faults common to muzzle-loaders, and presented no conspicuous advantage as a breech-loader—in fact, as a breech-loader, if mechanically-fitting bullets had to be used, it was at a decided disadvantage with those in which a cylindrical bullet could be used any side topmost.

HISTORICAL NOTE ON SPORTING RIFLES.

For most sporting purposes smooth-bore ball guns were generally preferred prior to 1845.   Such rifles as were used by English sportsmen in the East Indies were generally of 16-bore, and fired a charge of $1\frac{1}{2}$ drams of powder with a spherical ball weighing one ounce.   This type of rifle was sighted to 200 yards, and fair accuracy could be obtained at known ranges, but the trajectory was high, the penetration and striking force weak ; and these objections, added to the great difficulty of loading a foul rifle, led sportsmen to prefer the smooth-bore, which, when loaded with a double charge (6 drams) and an ounce spherical hardened ball, gave a lower trajectory, higher velocity, and greater penetration, but beyond fifty yards accuracy was not obtainable.

Polygroove Rifling, as used for Muzzle-loaders.

THE SPHERICAL BALL RIFLE OF LARGE BORE.

To obtain a more efficient weapon for large game shooting, the late Sir Samuel Baker tried rifles of greater calibre.   In 1840 he drew up a plan for an experimental rifle to burn large charges of powder, in order to get a high velocity, low trajectory, and great power.   The plan was successfully carried out by Mr. Gibbs, of Bristol, who produced a rifle weighing 21 lbs., to fire a charge of 16 drams with a 3-ounce spherical or 4-ounce conical bullet.   The barrel was 36 inches long, with rifling exceedingly deep, two broad grooves having one turn in the length of the barrel. Twelve months afterwards his experience with it in Ceylon elephant shooting led him to order a battery of double-barrel 10-bores constructed on the same principle.

According to Captain Forsyth and others, up to 1860 there was no known rifle suitable for sporting purposes in India.

The long-range rifles, such as the Enfield or Jacobs, were not adapted for game-shooting, on account of the high trajectory and lack of striking force, so even at this time smooth-bores were still preferred for large game. The great fault of the rifles made for spherical ball was the rifling; the twist was much too rapid, and caused the bullet to strip when used with heavy charges of powder.

Captain Forsyth concluded that one turn in ten feet was ample for a 12-gauge spherical ball rifle; that the grooving should be shallow and broad; and that the bullet should be of the same diameter as the bore. In this he was correct; the system was perfect, and is the same as used to-day for large-bores using spherical and short conical projectiles. When using a thin patch, the loading was easily effected, the bullet being uninjured by hard ramming; when firing, the patch (instead of the bullet) took the grooving, and imparted a rotary motion to the bullet, which retained its sphericity, and so offered less resistance to the atmosphere. Any charge of powder could be used without the bullet stripping. With the breech-loader the only modification is an increased size bullet, which fills up the grooves entirely, and a reduction in the number of grooves. The characteristics of this rifle are: velocity equal to a smooth-bore of the same calibre, accuracy sufficient for sporting distances, flat trajectory, and great striking energy. It was held in high esteem by Indian sportsmen for some years, but is now superseded by the " Express," which in turn is being to some extent replaced by the more modern " High Velocity Cordite " rifle.

THE ORIGIN OF THE "EXPRESS."

Though this large bore was well adapted for sport in the Indian jungle, where game is shot at comparatively close quarters, a very different rifle is required for South Africa, where wide undulating plains permit of the game being sighted and shot at much longer ranges.

In 1855, before Mr. Whitworth had perfected his system, the late W. Greener was engaged, as were a few other makers, in building a rifle suitable for South African sport. The " Cape Rifle " was of the following specification :—Calibre either 40 or 52 (corresponding to the later ·500 and ·450); rifling, two grooves with one turn in 30 inches; grooves broad and deep, in order to admit the bullet easily; the bullet had wings cast upon it corresponding with the grooves which they fitted when used with a patch. Stripping of the bullet was prevented in spite of what was considered to be the excessively sharp twist and the large charge of powder used. Weight of rifle, 12 lbs. ; sighted up to 2,000 yards.

The extreme range of 2,000 yards was obtained without the bullets key-holing. This rifle proves that the sharp turn, long range, and mechanically fitting bullets were used with success before Mr. Whitworth produced a rifle which is popularly supposed to have been the first to obtain accuracy at long ranges. Mr. Purdey built two similar rifles, one (40 calibre) for the late Lord H. Bentinck, and the other (50 calibre) for the late Sir George Gore, and, as the pattern became popular, Mr. Purdey produced others of this type, to which model he gave the name of "Express Train," and since that date (1856) the word "Express" has come into general use to signify a rifle possessing a long point-blank range and low trajectory.

In America small-bore rifles were used earlier in the century; the celebrated Kentucky rifles were of various sizes; some fired spherical balls of 90 to the pound, others 60 and 40; the small bore being due to the fact that the rifles were used by backwoodsmen who had few opportunities for replenishing their stock of lead and

Cape Rifle Bullet.

Muzzle of "Cape" Rifle.

could carry more light bullets than heavy ones. The usual charge was measured by placing the ball in the palm of the hand and then pouring over it sufficient powder to completely hide the bullet. It is supposed by some that the Express rifle originated either in America or was developed from the Kentucky rifle; for this type of weapon was renowned for its long point-blank range—the special feature of the "Express." At anything under 100 yards the aim was taken point-blank with the same sight; and, consequently, it made no difference whether the squirrel squatting on a branch, or the wild turkey's head, was 20, 50, or 90 yards away; only cover it truly with the bead fine or full, and down it went.

Colonel G. Hanger, writing in 1814, contended that he had such a rifle as the Express; the secret of its production he discovered in America, and that it might not fall into other hands he sawed his rifle barrel in half and threw the pieces into the Thames. The Express principle, still more highly developed than in sporting rifles, has been utilised for modern military weapons, some patterns of which have a longer point-blank range and lower trajectories than even the most heavily-charged Express rifle of usual sporting type.

THE BREECH-LOADING RIFLE.

By loading the rifle at the breech, instead of from the muzzle, it is possible to use a bullet of a size sufficient to fill the grooves ; thus windage is prevented, and, the bullet taking the rifling perfectly, accurate shooting is possible. Instead of deep grooving and a long soft bullet, which were necessary to easy loading and expansion at or near the breech of the barrel with even the best principle of rifling for muzzle-loaders, shallow grooves and hard bullets may be used successfully in breech-loaders, and such bullets have a better trajectory, for they leave the bore more nearly cylindrical than any from the muzzle-loaders.

Unfortunately, this point appears to have been overlooked by the experts who had to decide upon the rifle to be adopted as the service arm, and they declared for the Henry form of rifling, which at the time gave the most satisfactory results with muzzle-loaders ; it remained for the gun-makers and match rifle shots to demonstrate that shallower grooves, quicker twist, and larger bullets produced greater accuracy.

The progress made in the service may be ascertained from the tables. Shortly, the Enfield rifle had three grooves ten-thousandths of an inch deep at the breech and only five-thousandths deep at the muzzle. This same principle of *progressive* grooving was followed in the Martini-Henry, the seven grooves all being nine-thousandths deep at breech and seven at the muzzle, but the twist was increased from one turn in seventy-two inches, or 135 calibres, to a turn in twenty-two inches, or in 48·8 calibres. Similar rifling, but grooves of uniform depth, was generally adopted by the chief Powers for the rifles issued to their armies between 1860 and 1886.

It has been superseded by the principle of rifling used for match rifle-shooting with most success—the principle of shallow grooves and long, hardened bullets.

The rifling with which the name of Mr. Metford is so closely associated consists of wide grooves, narrow lands ; or the lands and grooves of equal width ; the grooves of a uniform depth of four-thousandths of an inch, and the twist an *irregularly increasing* spiral, finishing at one turn in seventeen inches, but making in the whole barrel of thirty-four inches but little more than one complete turn. The projectile, long cylindro-conoidal in shape, and of hardened lead so that it shall grip better in the shallow grooves. This rifling and bullet are shown in the illustration ; the dotted lines indicate the position of the grooves cut in the bullet by the *lands* of the rifling when it left the chamber : as it passed along the barrel, the increasing spiral altered the original shape of these grooves, until, when it left the muzzle, the bullet was grooved as shown in the figure, but the indentations are so shallow that its flight is but slightly impeded by them. Mr. Metford increased the spiral according to formulæ based upon the theory that gunpowder of a given size of grain and density generates its strength irregularly, and that more powder is burnt in one portion of the barrel than in another of equal capacity, and so the spiral must be proportionate to the strength of the powder. In practice, various powders differing considerably in their speed of combustion give equally good results in the Metford rifle.

Apart from the extra trouble to manufacture and to clean, the increasing spiral is unsuitable for use in military arms, and has been discontinued by the Government, the quicker twist adopted by Mr. Metford for the finish being used throughout the length of the barrel, and its speed even exceeded in some instances—a turn in 10 inches, or 33 calibres, being used in England, and a turn in 9·45 inches, or 30 calibres, by France and Russia.

The shallow grooves lessen liability to windage, for the bullets are usually made

The Metford Match-rifling, and Bullet after Firing.

of a diameter equal to the bore of the barrel and the depth of a groove. The liability is still further lessened in the ·303, for the bullet is the calibre of the barrel *plus* the depth of *two* grooves—that is to say, is ·311 inch in diameter. Wads are of little value ; but it is important that the bullet should be of harder and stronger material than lead, in order to withstand the crushing force generated by the high explosives now used. These explosives produce little fouling, and lubrication is effected either by smearing the bullet with wax or grease, or by filling a cannelure with the lubricant. A thin card wad prevents any possibility of fouling reaching the surface of the bore in front of the bullet.

The same principle, suitably modified in detail, is superseding the older methods of rifling for sporting and target weapons ; particulars of the exact forms at present preferred are given in the following chapters, and tabulated in the details of Modern Military Arms.

CHAPTER XXVI.

MODERN SPORTING RIFLES.

CLASSIFICATION OF SPORTING RIFLES.

THE modern sporting rifle may be classed according to its bore and range. The large-bore is the older type, and to this class belong the weapons used for elephant-shooting; the smaller bore is used with proportionately heavier charges and lighter bullets, and to this class belong the various Express rifles and the latest military calibres, which are of the same "Express" type, but have greater range, and may be termed "long-range Express rifles." The third class consists of long-range rifles of various sporting calibres, and the last class consists of miniature loads used for rook- and rabbit-shooting.

All the rifles may be made single- or double-barrelled, though it is unusual for those for rook-shooting to be other than single-barrel, and all the single barrels may have the breech mechanism on the drop-down principle, as usual with shot-guns, or may have one or other of the fixed breech-block or breech-bolt mechanisms more commonly used for military arms.

LARGE-BORE RIFLES.

The use of the large-bore rifle is restricted to the hunting of large and dangerous game, for which purpose many experienced hunters deem them indispensable. The rifle should be double-barrelled; the weight is required to lessen the recoil, and the second barrel is decidedly advantageous. The double 4-bore with barrels 20 inches long will weigh from 14 to 18 lbs., and fire a charge of 12 to 14 drams and a spherical bullet of 1,510 grains. The recoil is undoubtedly heavy, but an Indian hunter of great experience in their use states that it is not noticeable when firing at game, and that on one occasion a rifle with 12 drams and a four-ounce bullet went off both barrels together, but he did not notice the recoil. The great weight of the rifle, as much as its recoil, is against its general use; sportsmen who possess 4-bores of this type usually hold them as weapons in reserve. It is not usual to groove the barrels of the 4-bore ball gun; it is intended for use at short ranges only, and the accuracy of the smooth-bore is serviceable to 60 yards, beyond which distance the 4-bore is

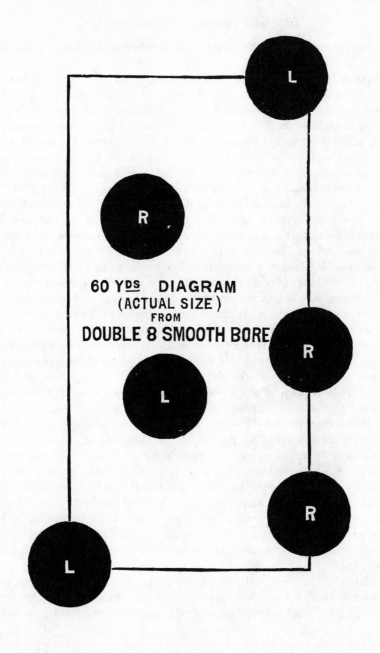

60 YDS DIAGRAM
(ACTUAL SIZE)
FROM
DOUBLE 8 SMOOTH BORE

seldom, if ever, used, whilst the muzzle velocity is greater than from the rifled barrel.

The author, whose experience of manufacturing these large weapons has been great (he having for many years made a study of their construction and powers), is of opinion that the double 8-calibre for brass cases is the better sporting weapon. It is lighter, much more handy, has greater range, and does not recoil excessively. This rifle, unlike the ordinary paper-case 8-bore, which shoots a spherical ball of about 1,092 grains, if specially rifled, will fire a two-ounce ball or a conical bullet weighing three ounces—sufficiently large for the biggest game, and a thoroughly practical weapon. With 20-inch barrels it can be made to weigh as light as $11\frac{1}{2}$ lbs. ; with 24-inch barrels the usual weight is 15 lbs. A charge of 10 or even 12 drams may be used with the spherical ball. The range and velocity of this and other large-bore rifles will be found in the tables, where they may be more readily compared with those obtained with Express and long-range rifles. Possibly the best weapon for large game is this 8-bore with short barrels; but, using the light spherical bullet only, and eight or more drams of powder, the double rifle then need not weigh more than $11\frac{1}{2}$ lbs., as the recoil will be so much less ; and the velocity and penetration at the short ranges at which large game is almost invariably shot will be more than sufficient to penetrate and kill even the largest elephant, whether head or side shot be taken.

The accuracy of the large-bore rifles and ball guns is very good up to 60 yards with the smooth, and 120 with the rifle. The diagrams on page 646 are fairly representative, and should be compared with the shooting obtained with large-bore rifles at the *Field* Rifle Trials of 1883, of which a condensed report is given. The first diagram was obtained with a Greener double 8-bore with spherical ball and 10 drams of powder; distance 50 yards. The eight shots are in a square $2\frac{3}{8}$ by $1\frac{9}{16}$ inches. The next diagram was made by the late Mr. A. Henry, of Saigon, with a Greener double 8-bore rifle weighing only 13 lbs., charge 10 drams, and spherical ball —147 out of 163 shots fired at various times in a 12-inch circle at 110 yards.

Mr. Henry wrote the author that with this rifle he considered he was sure of an elephant at 100 yards ; the author also has in his possession the skull of a large elephant shot by Mr. Carter ("Smooth-bore") of Madras, which shows that the bullet —from a similar 8-calibre rifle of the author's manufacture—passed right through the skull from the right to the left side, the wound increasing in magnitude as the bullet flattened.

Considering the accuracy and power of these weapons, it is possible that sportsmen may prefer them to the ·577 " Express " of about the same weight ; but the 16-, 15-, and 10-calibre rifles on this principle do not seem to present any marked

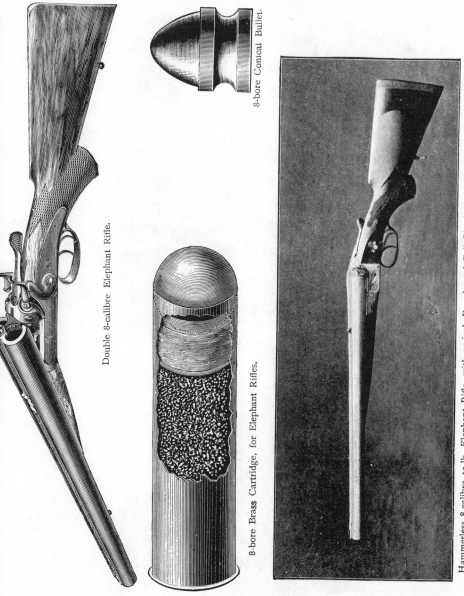

Double 8-calibre Elephant Rifle.

8-bore Conical Bullet.

8-bore Brass Cartridge, for Elephant Rifles.

Hammerless 8-calibre 13-lb. Elephant Rifle, with 22-inch Barrels and Full Pistol Hand and Cheek Piece to Stock.

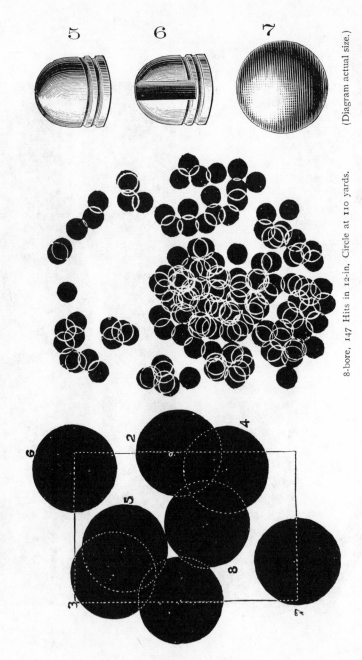

8-bore, 147 Hits in 12-in, Circle at 110 yards. (Diagram actual size.)

Bullets.—No. 5, a short, blunt, conical bullet, sometimes used in spherical ball rifles; it increases the weight of the projectile considerably. No. 6, a hollow shell for the purpose of lightening the bullet; or it may be filled with detonating powder, when it becomes an explosive shell. No. 7 is the exact size of a 4-bore bullet, to fit into a No. 4 brass cartridge-case.

advantage for sporting purposes over the lighter and handier smaller calibre weapons of the " Express " type.

LONG-RANGE SPORTING RIFLES.

The ordinary type of long-range rifle used for sporting and general purposes in South Africa is probably more accurately defined as a modified match-rifle than as either sporting or military. The charge of powder, weight, shape and construction of the bullet are such as conduce to *accurate* shooting at *long* ranges; a high trajectory is not objected to, and most of the cartridges used give no better flight than does the Martini regulation ammunition, but there is less recoil with the lighter charges, better bullets, and improved shapes of cartridge. The powers of these rifles may be gathered from the table of trajectories; the breech-action may be the Martini, the cheapest and most widely understood mechanism, or the Field, or other of the single rifle breech-action systems may be used. A rifle of this type is undoubtedly the best all-round cheap weapon for South Africa; for target-shooting, large game hunting, or as a weapon of offence or defence it is quite trustworthy.

For the ·303 barrel, if the Martini breech-loading mechanism be used, it must be fitted with a breech-block of special construction, or the extra strain caused by using cordite, and similar explosives, will soon so alter the shape of the block that it will not work. To a smaller extent the same thing is noticed in the Lee-Metford rifle itself.

MINIMUM WEIGHTS OF RIFLES SUITABLE FOR BLACK POWDER OR AN EQUI-VALENT CHARGE OF NITRO-POWDER, WITH DIFFERENT LENGTH BARRELS.

Description of Rifle.	Bore.	22	23	24	25	26	27	28	29	30
		Lengths of Barrels in Inches.								
Express (Double Barrel)	·577	...	...	...	...	10½	11	11½	...	...
,, ,,	·500	...	...	...	...	8¼	8½	8¾	...	...
,, ,,	·450	...	...	...	...	8	8¼	8½	...	..
,, ,,	·400	...	...	...	...	7	7¼	7½	...	...
,, ,,	·360	...	...	...	...	6	...	6¾	...	...
Long-range Express	·303	...	...	...	...	8¼	8½	8¾	...	...
Large-bore (Double Barrel)	4	15½	16½	18	..	...	...	...	...	...
,, ,,	8	12½	13¼	14	Special weight of 20-inch is 11 lbs.					
,, ,,	10	...	...	10	10½	11	11½	...	...	..
,, ,,	12	...	...	8	8½	9	9½	...	...	...
,, ,,	16	...	...	7	7¼	7½	...	...	...	...
,, ,,	20	...	...	6	6¼	6½	...	...	...	...
Choke-bore Rifles	8	11	12	12¼	12½	13	...	...	...	...
,,	10	...	...	...	8	8¼	8½	9	...	...
,,	12	...	...	..	...	7	...	7½	...	8½
,,	16	...	...	...	6¼	...	6½	6¾	...	...
,,	20	...	...	...	6	...	6¼	6½	...	...

Weights in lbs.

VARIETIES OF THE SPORTING "EXPRESS" RIFLE.

The signification of the word "Express" as applied to rifles is high velocity; earlier this quality was termed "long point-blank range," an expression which is defined by Captain Forsyth, in "The Sporting Rifle," as "the distance up to which a shot may be taken without considering elevation at all—that is, covering exactly the object intended to be hit."

The flight of a rifle bullet is a curve, but at sporting ranges the deviation from the line of sight may be so slight that for all practical purposes it may be considered as identical.

The high velocity cannot be maintained beyond 150 yards or thereabouts with the ordinary Express type of rifle; with heavier bullets, lower muzzle velocity, and a higher elevation, greater range is attained, but the Express principle is lost, for then the line of flight widely differs from the line of aim.

The nearest approach to a "long-range Express" is attained by the modern small-bore military rifles; they possess qualities long sought in sporting rifles, and although the projectiles used are not altogether suitable for game-shooting, they may be, and are, so modified as to prove useful for the purposes of the sportsman, and with special bullets may be adapted to most requirements of the hunter of large game.

The value of a flat trajectory in a sporting rifle can hardly be over-appraised. This, and this alone, is the reason why the ·303 military rifle and other modern small-bore arms of its type are favoured for sporting purposes. Indeed, the Lee-Metford, by reason of its long point-blank range and exceptionally high velocity, is to be classed as an Express, since the true meaning of Express, as applied to rifles, is a rifle giving a higher initial velocity than 1,600 feet per second, with a trajectory flat enough to admit of one sight for distances up to 200 yards. The ·303-bore has all the qualities of the Express in the highest degree; in fact, it surpasses by far the usual standard of Expresses in point of velocity and trajectory.

To better illustrate the advantage of the flat trajectory: with the ·303 rifle, it is necessary only to use one sight for any distance up to 200 yards, a fine sight being taken for 100 yards and a full sight for 200 yards; this is sufficient allowance to obtain the correct elevation.

The illustrations here given are designed expressly with the object of showing at a glance the advantage of a flat trajectory for rifles intended for sporting purposes. The same system has been repeated in each case for the various bores, in order that comparison may be easy.

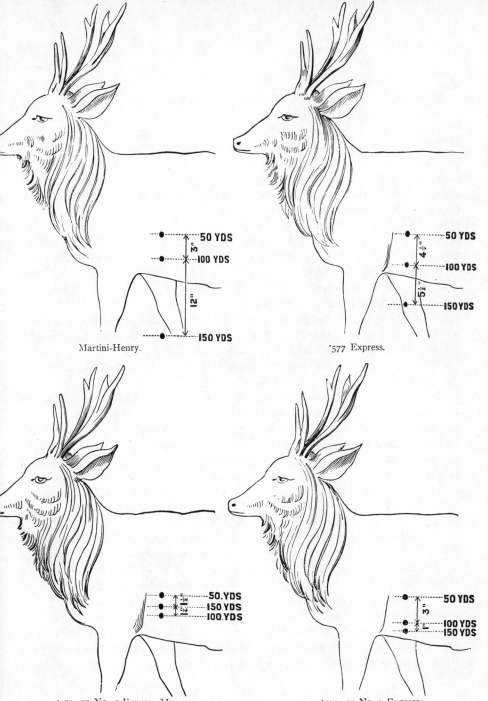

Martini-Henry.

·577 Express.

·450, or No. 1 Express Magnum.

·500, or No. 2 Express.

Diagrams showing Positions of Shots fired from 50, 100, and 150 yards using 50-yard Sight only.

The drop of the bullet is indicated in inches on each woodcut for three distances: 50, 100, and 150 yards.

These diagrams were made at all distances with the 50-yard sight.

With the ·500 and ·450 Expresses the mean drop is so slight at distances between 50 and 150 yards (being only 4½ inches and 3 inches respectively), that it gives command of the vital portions of any ordinary-sized animal's frame from any point within the longer range. With the ·577 Express the average drop is 10 inches; and with the Martini-Henry, 15 inches.

In the ·450 diagram the shot fired from 150 yards is shown higher or nearer the 50-yard shot than is the 100-yard shot; this is in utter disagreement with all laws governing the flight of projectiles, and can only be attributed to the peculiar effect of the "jump" action of the rifle in firing, which gives an increased elevation in addition to the permanent angle of the sight adjustment. In a lesser degree it is also shown in the diagram of the ·500-bore.

With a 12-bore rifle firing a spherical ball with 7 drams of powder a diagram would be obtained very similar to that of the Martini. The mean drop between the 50 and 100 yard ranges is about 2½ inches, and 14 inches in the next 50 yards.

With the ·303 bore the diagram should show less vertical deviation than with the ·450 express.

There is less in so far as deviation is due to difference of mean trajectory, but the shooting with cordite is characterised by some of the shots "dropping," showing variations in velocity. The deviation to right or left is less than might be expected, and in the diagram shown on page 692, each shot, right and left barrel, kept practically to the same vertical line, but both barrels shot high and low of the common centre. But for this variable velocity the diagrams made would often surpass those with Express rifles at short ranges. At long ones they are, of course, much superior.

BLACK POWDER RIFLES SUITABLE FOR AN EQUIVALENT CHARGE OF NITRO-POWDER.

·577 *Express.*—This is the largest Express rifle manufactured suitable for black powder; it possesses great smashing power, and is particularly useful where the boar is allowed to be shot, and among dangerous game. The bullet weighs 520 grains, the powder 160 grains; but it is sometimes, now usually, made for a much heavier bullet (610 grains). Its effective range is a little over 220 yards, point-blank about 120 yards; 11 lbs. is the lightest weight for this bore rifle.

·500 *Express.*—This is of exactly ½-inch bore, and was at one time considered by most Indian sportsmen to be the most effective all-round weapon for that country; it has great smashing power, good penetration, and it is not too cumbrous to cover moving game. The bullet weighs 340 grains, the charge of powder is usually 130 grains, the range is about 300 yards, and the point-blank range 130 yards, but it can also be made for heavier bullets for longer ranges. The minimum weight for the rifle is 8¼ lbs.

·450 *Express.*—This is an excellent all-round weapon ; it is not too large for deer and antelope, whilst it is equally effective among tapirs, seals, and bears, and may be successfully used at leopards, panthers, tigers, and the larger soft-skinned carnivora. The bullet weighs 270 grains, powder 110 grains. The lightest weight for a rifle of this bore is 8¾ lbs. The extreme range is 500 yards with a 360-grain bullet, and point-blank range 150 yards.

Rifles of this bore, when firing bullets of 360 grains, have been successfully used by Mr. Selous and other African sportsmen at lions and, with a still heavier bullet, even at elephants, and its accuracy to 500 yards is trustworthy.

·400 *Express.*—This is a hard-hitting and handy weapon and suitable for deer-stalking generally. The bullet weighs 209 grains, the powder charge is 82 grains, and the rifle, with 26-inch barrels, weighs from 7½ lbs. It has an effective range of 250 yards, and a point-blank range of 160 yards.

·360 *Express.*—This, the smallest calibre sporting Express rifle, is suitable for shooting bustard, gazelle, roe-deer, and the smaller ante. lopes. The bullet weighs 150 grains, the powder charge is 50 grains, the rifle from 6¾ lbs. ; the range is 250 yards, the point-blank range 130 yards. A " magnum " 360 is made for a bullet of 190 grains and a powder charge of 55 grains.

ACTUAL DIAGRAM
10 CONSECUTIVE SHOTS
100 YARDS
FROM A
Double·450
EXPRESS
By·W·W·GREENER

Bullets.—The tendency during the past few years has been to make use of heavier bullets in all the Express rifles, as they give greater accuracy and smashing power. Instead of being hollow, these heavier bullets are solid and generally have cannelures—thus the ·360 has a solid bullet 215 grains, and the ·577 is used with a bullet as heavy as 650 grains.

Light hollow bullets are not suitable for dangerous game ; the 270 grain ˙450 bullet has been known to fly to pieces against the skull of a tiger at close quarters. Solid bullets give the required penetration.

"HIGH VELOCITY" SPORTING RIFLES.

The chief advantages possessed by the Cordite Express rifles over those designed for black powder are smokelessness and greater velocity, and this, not through the greater penetrative power of the bullet, but simply from the lower trajectory. That this is a great advantage no game hunter will deny, and it is all-sufficient to warrant the adoption of the modern weapon in preference to the less powerful, but still sufficiently powerful, older pattern. The necessity for a strictly correct estimate of distance is not so great. More often than not it happens that a shot must be taken so quickly that there is no time for the adjustment of sights to the estimated distance, and the allowance has to be made on the object. In such cases the advantage of a flat trajectory is appreciated, for in 200 yards the difference between the two types of rifle may mean the loss of an animal. In strange surroundings it is not difficult to misjudge to the extent of 50 yards, more or less, over a 150 yards' range. The difference in the trajectory over 200 yards between the ˙450 Cordite and the ˙450 Black Powder Rifle is about 10 inches.

Against this great advantage must be placed several disadvantages, such as extra cost, weight, recoil (in the larger bores), and a shorter "life" than have the Black Powder Rifles firing lead bullets.

Penetration, as apart from velocity, deserves a little consideration from the sportsman ; and he should, and doubtless will, choose his rifles for their suitability to his special requirements. In the Sporting Press several advertisers announce the armour-piercing qualities of certain rifles and bullets. No sportsmen the author has yet met with desire to sink ironclads, or to use their rifles for girder-punching. As a matter of fact, the bullet that is suitable for armour piercing is the most unsuitable for sporting purposes under any circumstances. No bullet which goes through an animal can be of much use, and hence with the nickel-covered bullets some intelligence must be used by the sportsman in the selection of the bullet for the quarry, otherwise nothing but disappointment will result. The object should be for the "bullet to come to rest within the animal," thus ensuring all its energy being used to the best effect. The numerous patterns of bullets now made give plenty of choice. For all general purposes at close ranges the soft-nosed bullet is to be commended most. All big game should be, and generally is, shot at close range—say, within 50 yards—but there are many antelope and deer which cannot readily be approached, and are sometimes shot at from 500 to 600 yards away. Then a hollow-pointed bullet should be used.

It must not be forgotten in this connection that there are many things which tend to reduce the velocity of these Cordite (or other High-velocity) rifles. Should the velocity fall below 1,400 feet per second, none of the nickel-covered bullets can be absolutely relied upon to break up on impact with a soft-skinned animal. Even a solid lead one will not "mushroom" at 1,200 feet per second velocity unless it strikes a bone.

In choosing a rifle the sportsman will be guided by the sport he is likely to get, neither carrying unnecessary weight in rifle or ammunition, nor, on the other hand, under-arming himself for the work to be done. It is better to over- than under-do it in this respect. For jungle work, or for dangerous game, or for those who can only carry one gun, the Choke-bore Rifle is the very best weapon extant. The importation into India of the ·303 and any rifle of ·450 bore is forbidden, as also is their ammunition, and in the South African Colonies south of Rhodesia the ·303 can only be imported by special permission. Further, no rifle can be imported into India which is sighted to more than 300 yards. Sportsmen going to out-of-the-way parts, or on exploring expeditions, should take a good supply of ammunition. Under no circumstances can a sportsman be recommended to load or reload his own cartridges for the High-power Cordite rifles.

The ·450 *Cordite Express* is the largest bore rifle recommended. Anything larger is unnecessary, as the energy developed by this powerful cartridge is so enormous that there is a difficulty in utilising all of it to advantage in the killing of the animal. It is suitable for elephant, rhino, gaur, grizzly bear, &c., with solid bullets, and soft-skinned dangerous game, such as lion, tiger, &c., with hollow-pointed bullets; weight about 11½ lbs. Recoil considerable, but not too severe.

The ·375 *Bore* is probably the most useful of this class. The game animals which it will not kill are few indeed. It is recommended to those who prefer a small bore for all game up to buffalo, rhinoceros, and elephant, and, though not the ideal rifle for these animals, it has sufficient power for any of them when the 320 grain bullet is used. For most of the African antelope or Indian deer this rifle is sufficiently powerful with the solid soft-nosed 270-grain bullet. It is as accurate as any of the high velocity semi-military Express rifles, while neither the weight of the rifle nor the recoil is more than the average man can sustain under the trying circumstances of tropical shooting, and it fires the minimum weight projectile that the author considers should be used for big or dangerous game. Weight of rifle, 8¾ lbs. Recoil very moderate.

The ·303 *Bore*, with suitable bullets, has had considerable success as a "Sporting Rifle," and where there are no restrictions against its importation it should be in the "battery" of every sportsman.   It is not recommended for dangerous game, though it has been successfully employed for everything up to elephants.   Doubtless the fact that the ammunition is generally procurable throughout the Empire (India excepted) is a great consideration.

Double-barrelled built either hammerless or with hammers it must have a very

Muzzle End of ·303.

strong breech-mechanism (preferably with the author's treble-wedge-fast cross-bolt).   The standard charge of black gunpowder is $71\frac{1}{2}$ grains, of cordite 30 grains, of "Rifleite" 38 grains; the muzzle velocity with black is 1,850 feet per second, with cordite 2,000 feet.   The exact size of the bore of the barrel at the muzzle is here shown.

For deer, antelope, chamois, &c., it is an excellent weapon, but owing to the lightness of the bullet it is not a big game rifle.   For small buck in the open, and where shots to 500 yards are the rule, it is at its best.   It is preferable to either the Mannlicher ·256 or the Mauser ·276 bore, although both these rifles, together with other military calibres, are now adapted for sporting purposes and are made as either single- or double-barrelled rifles of the usual types.   The solid military bullet should be rarely, if ever, used ; the hollow-pointed and solid soft-nosed patterns are the bullets mostly to be commended.   Weight of double ·303 bore rifle, $8\frac{1}{4}$ to $8\frac{3}{4}$ according to grade.   Recoil light.

Colonel Patterson, in his interesting book, "The Man Eaters of Tsavo," relates some thrilling adventures amongst lions.   His experience with the ·303 bore rifle proves conclusively the unsuitability of this calibre for use on dangerous game. Describing a most exciting lion hunt, he says : "I accordingly waited until he got quite close—about twenty yards away—and then fired my ·303 at his chest. I heard the bullet strike him, but unfortunately it had no knock-down effect, for, with a fierce growl, he turned and made off.   I managed to have three more shots, and another growl told me the last of these had also taken effect."   The following day he tracked the same animal, and writes : "I at once took careful aim and fired.   Instantly he sprang out and made a most determined charge down on us.   I fired again and knocked him over, but in a second he was up once more and coming for me as fast as he could in his crippled condition.   A third shot had no apparent effect, so I put out my hand for the Martini.   The first shot I fired from this seemed to give him his quietus, but to my surprise he jumped up and attempted another charge ; this time, however, a Martini bullet in the chest, and another in the head, finished him for good and all. On examination, we found no less than six bullet-holes in the body, and embedded only a little way in the flesh of the back was the slug which I had fired into him about ten days previously."

The ·310 Bore rifle and cartridge, designed and introduced originally by the author for cadet use and target practice, met with such unprecedented success and were so often used on game that it was necessary to develop the cartridge for this purpose, and to produce also a rifle in sporting style and finish. The double ·310 bore Miniature Express rifle is eminently suitable for small buck and other animals of not more than 120 lbs. weight, and for distances up to 300 yards.

It has been used most successfully on black buck in India, Duiker and Oribi and the smaller antelope in South Africa, and many flattering testimonials have been received from different countries claiming virtues for it which the designer hesitates to accept.

It will break a stag's neck at 120 yards, but the author does not recommend it for red deer, although the remarkable accuracy of this rifle enables the shooter to rely upon putting his shot exactly where he wishes, providing he is sure of his distance. The rifle will be found so useful that no one who has once used it will be without one. It comes into use when the shot gun is out-ranged, and it is practically noiseless. The solid bullet, 125 grains, is most suitable for target practice, long shots at birds, or when specimens are required for natural-history collections. The hollow-pointed 125-grain bullet is for game animals, and the light 80-grain hollow-pointed bullet for rabbits and vermin. The latter bullet is specially designed to easily break up on impact and for use in restricted areas, and is not very accurate at distances over 70 yards. Weight about 5½ lbs. Recoil imperceptible.

BREECH-MECHANISMS FOR SPORTING RIFLES.

There is only one breech-mechanism for double-barrelled large-bore and Express rifles, whether hammer or hammerless, and that is the author's treble-wedge-fast cross-bolt action, of which full particulars have been given in connection with shot-guns. The double-grip was used for Express and large-bore rifles until the gradually increasing weights of bullets employed and heavier stresses from the introduction of smokeless powders rendered the use of the very strongest breech-mechanism imperative. Of late years the cross-bolt system has been most extensively employed by gun-makers in this country and on the Continent; but even it, unless specially made, is unequal to some of the tremendous strains to which a breech-action is subjected. The ·303 rifles made at Enfield are usually tested to a degree computed equal to a strain of 30 tons to the square inch at the breech, and, as this is much in excess of that usual in shot-guns, the ·303 double Express must be fitted with lumps and bolts of unusual strength and thickness. The face of the breech-action body also must be either of steel case-hardened or be fitted with hardened and tempered steel discs; only the very best material and workmanship will enable the rifle to safely withstand the use to which it is subjected. Steel barrels are preferable to Damascus for rifles, as the metal grooves more evenly, and, the weight of the weapon necessitating a stout barrel, the thickness of the metal ensures the requisite strength and a safe margin, even with the ·303 calibre. The author's "Wrought Steel" barrels are specially adapted for the latter, as they possess a degree of hardness not found in any other make, which enables them to resist the excessive wear to which such rifles are subjected.

UNDER-AND-OVER RIFLES.

It was once thought that the difficulty experienced in making the ordinary double-barrelled rifle shoot both its shots to a centre could be overcome if the

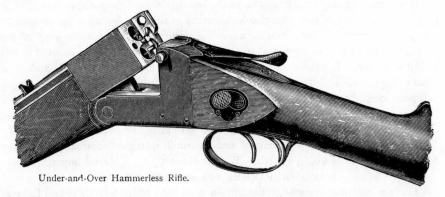

Under-and-Over Hammerless Rifle.

barrels were placed under and over, instead of side by side; for in the ordinary double-barrel rifle the shots are generally thrown outward—the right to the right and the left to the left—and this was put down to the recoil pulling the gun over at the moment of firing. To prove this the author made several under-and-over rifles, but found that the two barrels still shot away from one another, the upper one high and the lower one low, proving clearly that there was some cause other than recoil —probably the unequal expansion of each barrel due to the proximity on one side of the barrel attached to it. With the under-and-over plan, therefore, the same principle of putting the barrels together has to be followed. It is as successful as the side-by-side double-barrel, but slightly more costly to manufacture. The advantages are an easier and better grip of the rifle by the left hand and more ready alignment.

The author has made weapons on this type in several bores; the one illustrated is a double ˙360 hammerless " Express " with holding-down bolts fitted to engage between the barrels instead of upon the under lump. Other successful sizes include a double 12-bore, which was used with great effect at large game in Cochin China by an enthusiastic sportsman whose hands were so small that to grip a double 12 firmly was beyond their span. As a rifle and shot, the plan answers admirably—the sizes best adapted being 16-bore shot-gun barrel with 450 rifle, the rifle-barrel topmost.

THE BEST KIND OF GROOVING FOR SPORTING RIFLES.

With a muzzle-loader the shape and depth of the grooves are of considerable

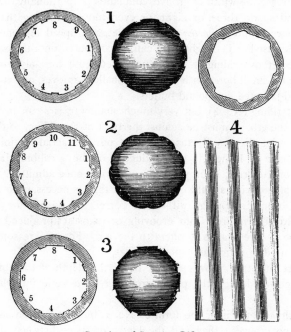

Grooving of Sporting Rifles.

importance; with a breech-loader a bullet *larger* than the bore of the barrel at any point may be fired, and so made to take the rifling whatever shape or depth the grooves may be. Shallow grooves are preferable, as easy to clean, and they alter but slightly the shape of the bullet; with very hard bullets, or those cased with hard metal, shallow grooves are of the first necessity, and the nearer the rifle attains to the smooth-bore the better the results.

The London Rifle Trial of 1883 failed to prove to gun-makers the best kind of rifling adapted for Express or other rifles. The Henry, Lancaster oval-bore, Rigby ratchet, and rounded-grooved riflings were in no one case used.

The Metford, or "increasing spiral," is not better fitted for sporting than for military purposes. A shallow groove, the grooves and bands of equal width, is probably as good as any for all-round purposes with lead or hardened lead bullets. Most gun-makers prefer to have the lands somewhat narrower than the grooves, as shown in No. 1 ; but of late it has been the fashion to decrease the number of the grooves and increase the width of grooves and lands proportionally. Seven grooves answer well, and so do three, or eight, or even more, providing that the *twist* is suited to the *length* and *diameter* of the bullet, and speed of combustion in the charge of powder used. The right twist can be computed on a theoretical basis.

The rounded-groove rifling is now much used, both for poly-grooved rifles of large bore, and for small bores with very wide shallow grooves, and it is as good as any for the hard-jacketed compound bullets.

The ratchet rifling (No. 4), but very much shallower, is again in fashion. The deeper part of the groove must be against the twist of the rifling, so that the bullet, when rotating during flight, will cause the least possible aerial friction. A mistake as to this was made at Enfield in the production of the ·4 calibre Martini, and the radical nature of the error, when pointed out, was at once admitted.

The depth of grooving should not be greater than is necessary to grip the bullet and prevent it from "stripping" within the barrel ; the nearer the bullet is to a perfectly cylindrical form, free from grooving or rugosities produced by the rifling, the less will be the resistance it offers to the air. For this reason the patch is still commonly used in match and sporting rifles.

In a perfect rifle the grooves should be of the depth of the thickness of the patch—·008 inch—and then, the patch dropping off, a perfectly cylindrical bullet should be left.

The grooving adopted is of the form of No. 1, but the fashion now is to have but five or seven grooves ; they and the lands, or space between them, being of equal width. In smaller bores fewer grooves are required, and the lands are wider because of the extreme difficulty of cutting such wide grooves with only very narrow lands to guide the tool.

SIGHTS FOR SPORTING RIFLES.

There are various forms of both back- and fore-sights in general use in sporting rifles. The best of each are illustrated.

No. 1, a bead sight, is a good form for large-bore rifles. Nos. 2 and 4 are suitable for Express or Target rifles. No. 3 is considered the best for fine shooting ; the **V** is broad, and extends the whole width of the leaf, having a platinum line to mark the centre ; sometimes a small slot is preferred, as in No. 4. No. 3 is also adapted for rough work, and is not easily broken. No. 6 is a leaf sight roughed to prevent reflection. The muzzle sights are put in lengthways instead of across the barrel, as formerly, and are frequently inlaid with platinum for jungle shooting.

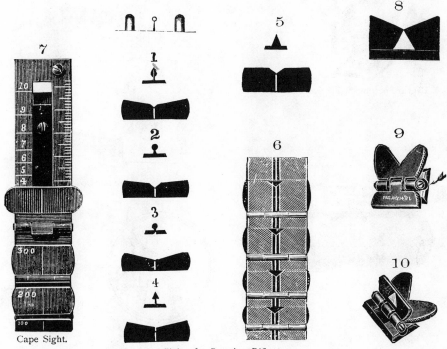

Sights for Sporting Rifles.

A favourite back-sight with South African sportsmen is the combined leaf and tangent sight, shown in No. 7, for it is suitable both for game-shooting and target practice, for which purposes most single rifles sold in South Africa are adapted. It consists of a standard and two leaf sights up to 300 yards, and a slide which can be raised to take sight at any range up to 1,000 yards.

No. 8 shows Greener's "Pyramid" ivory or platinum back-sight, with the open **V**

Beach Peep Sights.

Lyman Sporting Sight.

Seen through Deep **V**.

Seen through Open **V** Sight.

Enamelled Night Sight.

Seen through Lyman's Sight No. 1.

Lyman Combination and Open Fore-sights.

—a most useful sight for all sporting purposes, as it shows up well against all back-grounds, and can be seen in almost any light. It may be used either with the ordinary or in combination with the interchangeable fore-sights.

Nos. 9 and 10 show the Lyman leaf sight; the two leaves are for the same elevation; one has an open **V**, the other is a straight bar with an ivory centre, and, as both leaves fold down flat with the barrel in different directions, the view is not obstructed when using the Lyman or other long-range sights.

For shooting at running shots the American Lyman sight has been much recommended, and it is particularly applicable to single, long-range, Winchester and rook rifles. For double rifles the open patterns, with wide **V**, are preferable. The sight consists of an open globe on a screw stem fixed on the hand of the gun, as an

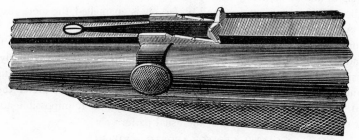

Rigby's Adjustable Sight for Sporting Rifles

orthoptic sight on a match rifle. It is frequently used in conjunction with the Beach combination fore-sight—a globe and pyramid sight pivoted in sight-block, and used either side up; but this is optional. The idea is to obtain a more clear and unobstructed view of the game and its surroundings than is possible with sights placed further from the eye of the shooter.

The two cuts illustrate the difference. The deep **V** of the Winchester—the favourite in America, and excellent for fine shooting at a fixed mark—obstructs almost wholly a view of the deer, except for an instant, whereas with the Lyman the deer is always in full view, and correct aim may be taken without the hesitancy experi-enced when only a part of the mark aimed at is to be seen. Mr. Lincoln Jeffries used one of these sights at the London Rifle Trial of 1883, and spoke highly of it.

To elevate the sight when after game is seldom necessary with an Express rifle, as these guns possess a point-blank range sufficient for any distance that can be judged with any certainty. But with a spherical-ball rifle, or the Winchester and other solid-bullet rifles with high trajectories, sometimes used for sporting purposes, to do so quickly is an advantage. The Winchester sight is a spring raised by a stepped wedge sliding along the centre of the top flat of the barrel. For large-bore rifles the adjustable sight invented by Mr. Rigby is superior. It consists of a steel spring screwed upon the top rib, with one extremity set at right angles to form the **V** sight. A rack travels along each side of the rib, as shown, and is moved by sliding the button on the barrel with the left hand whilst grasping the gun ; by drawing the rack towards the breech the sight is raised. With Express rifles, and all other sporting rifles tending to increased point-blank range, the use of adjustable elevation is less than it formerly was ; with some of the new military rifles also the range from the single standard back-sight is applicable at all distances up to 300 yards.

The night-sight shown consists of a small flap sight fitted in front of the ordinary head fore-sight, and so contrived as to fold flush with the rib when not in use. The disc may be of any convenient size, and preferably is enamelled, the more readily to catch the eye of the shooter in a faint light.

The ordinary back-sight may be dispensed with for night shooting, for the usual standard greatly obstructs the view ; and as the range is necessarily short the front-sight is sufficient alone, the line being taken down the rib, or the rifle simply handled as a gun is when snap-shooting. Some sportsmen prefer the plain rib, just as in a shot-gun, for boar shooting, and many find it impossible to shoot quickly at moving game with sights of the usual pattern.

CARTRIDGES FOR SPORTING RIFLES.

Solid drawn brass cases are now always used for sporting rifle cartridges (except, perhaps, for a few of the larger bores), and their manufacture has already been described on page 594. Their shape may be either a "straight taper" from base to bullet, or "bottle necked" where they clip the bullet in order to hold an increased powder charge, and this latter is the shape of most Express cartridges. When very heavy or "magnum" charges are employed the shape is generally again altered to a straight taper and the case considerably lengthened, as the very deep shoulder might prove dangerous with these extreme charges.

The following tables give the standard loads for rifle cartridges as generally supplied by Messrs. Eley Bros. and Kynoch, Ltd. Cartridges loaded by them with these charges are usually obtainable through all storekeepers and gun dealers and may be relied upon as correct.

The calibres given are those which in the author's opinion have best stood the test of time, or are the most meritorious among the more recently designed cartridges, although it is a matter of personal fancy more than any advantage gained that would lead to the selection of any particular one of the high-power nitro cartridges.

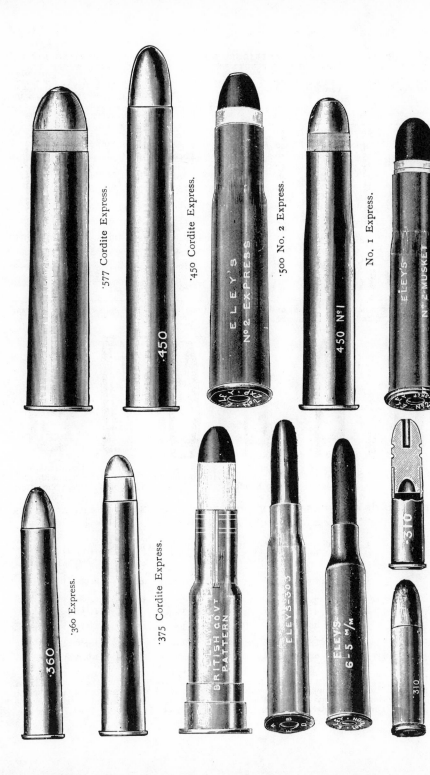

·577 Cordite Express.

·450 Cordite Express.

·500 No. 2 Express.

No. 1 Express.

·360 Express.

·375 Cordite Express.

·310 Hollow Pointed.

·310 Solid.

TABLE OF PARTICULARS OF CARTRIDGES FOR HIGH VELOCITY SPORTING RIFLES.

Bore of Cartridge.	Length of Case.	Weight of Cartridge.	Charge of Cordite.	Weight of Bullet.	Muzzle Velocity.	Trajectory at 100 yards over 200 yards.	Striking Energy at 100 yards.	Approximate Weight for Hammerless Double Rifle.
	inches.	grains.	grains.	grains.	ft. secs.	inches.	ft. lbs.	lbs.
·303	2·2	423	30	215	2,000	5·66	1,343	8¼ to 8¾
·360	2¼	465	30	300	1,650	8·8	1,466	8¼
·375	2½	487	40	270	2,000	6·2	1,870	8¾
·375	2½	547	40	320	1,900	6·5	2,000	8¾
·400/360	2¾	571	40	300	1,900	6·4	2,070	8½
·450/400	3¼	770	60	400	2,150	5·0	3,385	10½
·450	3¼	868	70	480	2,150	5·1	4,024	11½
·450 No. 2	3½	934	80	480	2,175	5·30	4,126	11½
·475	3¼	860	75	480	2,175	4·5	4,030	11¾
·500	3	980	80	570	2,100	5·4	4,532	12½
·577	3	1230	100	750	2,050	5·6	5,680	13½
·600	3	1440	100	900	1,850	7·3	5,337	14
Miniature Express	$1\frac{3}{32}$	195	6½	125 Hollow	1,500	13·0	429	5½
·310	$1\frac{3}{32}$	192½	5½	125 Solid	1,250	17·0	315	5½

The above can be loaded with any of the following pattern bullets, but the author particularly recommends Nos. 1, 2, and 3 for Big Game Shooting.

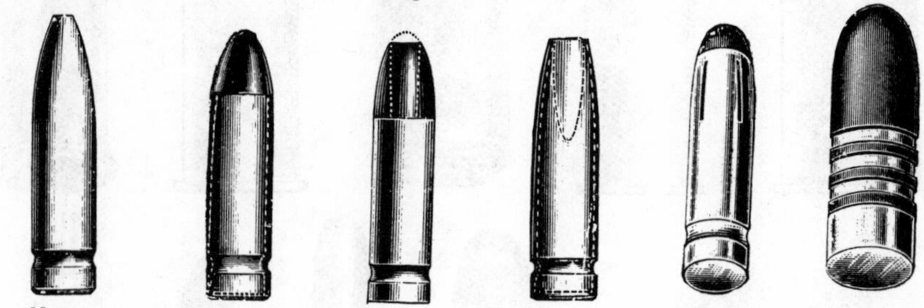

No. 1. Dum Dum. — No. 2. Solid Express. Soft Nosed. — No. 3. Soft Nosed. Hollow Pointed. — No. 4. Hollow Pointed. — No. 5. Solid Soft Nosed Split. — Nickel Base Bullet as used with Equivalent Nitro-Cartridge.

PARTICULARS OF CARTRIDGES FOR EXPRESS RIFLES, DESIGNED FOR BLACK POWDER OR EQUIVALENT NITRO.

Bore of Cartridge.	Length of Case.	Weight of Cartridge.	Charge of Black Powder.	Weight of Bullet.	Muzzle Velocity.	Trajectory at 100 yards over 200 yards.	Striking Energy at 100 yards.	Approximate Weight for Hammerless Double Rifle.
	inches.	grains.	grains.	grains.	ft. secs.	inches.	ft. lbs.	lbs.
·360	2¼	325	50	190	1,525	10·0	700	6¾
·450/400	2⅜	472	80	230	1,850	8·0	1,152	8
·500/450 No. 2 Musket.	$2\frac{5}{16}$	806	76	480	1,300	15·0	1,420	9¼
·450 No. 1	2¾	735	110	270	1,900	8·4	1,386	9½
·577/500 No. 2 Express	$2\frac{13}{16}$	847	130	340	1,850	8·0	1,663	10
·577 Exp.	2¾	960	160	520	1,775	9·56	2,473	11½

These Cartridges can be supplied loaded with a suitable charge of Smokeless Powder (according to weight of bullet) and Nickel Base Bullets. They give a slightly higher pressure and velocity than the Standard Black Powder Cartridges, but are perfectly safe to use in a well-constructed Black Powder rifle.

BULLETS FOR EXPRESS RIFLES.

The peculiar feature of the Express bullet is the hollow point to ensure the expansion of the projectile at impact. This expansion is in part due to the high velocity the bullet possesses at sporting ranges, and its effect is to diminish the

·400   ·360   ·450   ·600   ·500   ·500   ·577

Express Rifle Bullets.

| ·303 Nickel-covered Bullet. Regulation Pattern. | ·303 Soft-nosed Tweedie Bullet after passing through wood 12 in. thick. | ·303 Nickel Bullet after passing through 45 in. of solid wood. | ·577 Bullet of Pure Lead extracted from tiger. |

1	2	2	3	4	6	7
Section showing lead interior. 215 grs.	Express Bullet. 215 grs.	Do. showing lead core and nickel-covered *base*. The Tweedie Patent. 215 grs.	Hollow-pointed. 192 grs.	Hollow-pointed, copper-tubed. 195 grs.	Soft-nosed solid-pointed. 215 grs.	Solid Express, split. 214 grs.

penetrative power, and thus allow of the velocity of the bullet at impact being translated into energy used up, or, as it is usually called in this sense, " shock."

Sir Samuel Baker says :—

" A bullet of pure lead, ·577 bore, with a velocity of 1,650 feet per second, will assume the form of a button mushroom immediately upon impact, and increase in diameter as it meets with resistance upon its course, until when expanded beneath the elastic hide upon the other side, it will have become fully spread, like a mature mushroom. I prefer pure lead for lions, tigers, sambur deer, wapiti, and such large animals, which are not thick-skinned, as the bullet alters its form and nevertheless remains intact ; the striking energy being concentrated within the body."

An expansive bullet may be made of pure lead, but if greater penetration is required it may be hardened, and the expansiveness of both is increased proportionally to the size of hollow in the point. Solid expansion bullets should be of pure lead only. Nickel-coated bullets, except for ·303 and special rifles of that class, need to be used with great caution or the rifle will be injured ; for instance, those made for the Martini cartridge are ·008 of an inch too large for the usual ·450 calibre, and require a specially constructed rifle of ·461 calibre.

The smashing power of the Express, combined with a good deal of the

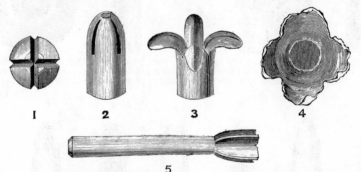

Lord Keanes' Cruciform Expanding Bullet and Core Peg : ·450.

penetration of the solid bullet, is obtained with Lord Keanes' cruciform expanding projectile. A special core-plug is required for casting it, as shown in the illustration, and to be fully effective the bullet should be made of hardened metal.

The bullet is cast with the upper half slit or divided into four equal sections, as in No. 1. It is then placed in a swedge, and the sections brought as close to each other as possible, as shown in No. 2.

The bullet when passing through an animal opens out as in No. 3, and the real appearance of the bullet is shown in No. 4, which represents it after having been fired into a tub of clay. No. 5 is the core-plug required to form the bullet, with slits or transverse cuts. The advantages of this bullet are that it makes a small hole only in passing through the skin, but afterwards flattens out even more effectually than the ordinary Express, whilst it does not flatten *outside* the skin, as is sometimes the case with soft Express bullets, and makes a more deadly wound than the solid Express bullet.

EXPLOSIVE BULLETS.

The best-known of the explosive projectiles is the original Forsyth shell, of which an illustration is here given. The first shells invented contained a small charge of black gunpowder, which was ignited by an ordinary percussion cap placed

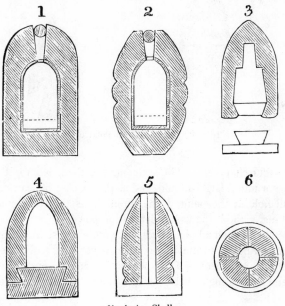

Explosive Shells.

on the point of the bullet and which exploded upon striking. The Jacobs shell is to some extent an improvement, being a copper tube open at one end, containing both detonating and black powder, and a modification of the shell is still used by some Indian sportsmen in small-bore rifles. The Forsyth swedge shell is cast in two segments, the detonating compound is then put in, the base of the bullet is joined to the other part, and passed through a screw swedge, which, if properly made, makes the bullet appear as one piece. These shells are only adapted for large-bore rifles—16-, 12-, or 10-bores. The apparatus for making them is rather bulky and expensive, consisting of two pairs of moulds and a swedging machine.

In the illustration, Nos. 1 and 2 are the copper-bottle, No. 3 is the Forsyth, No. 4 figure represents the Forsyth swedge shell, Nos. 5 and 6 the later segmental shell. No. 5 is cast in a mould by means of a core-peg having four wings, which divides

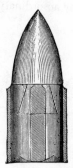

Iron-pointed Bullet, and Point detached.

the mould into four chambers. The segments are then tied together, placed on a thin core-peg, put into a larger mould, and a thin jacket of lead cast round them, leaving a small hole at the point. The intention is that the bullet shall fly into pieces on striking, without the use of detonating powder.

The copper-bottle shell alluded to above is merely cast in a simple mould, first placing the copper-bottle inside, fixing it on a core-peg; this keeps it in a proper position to receive the lead. This peg is withdrawn, and leaves the opening to admit of the detonating powder being put in; the orifice is then closed with wax.

Several attempts have been made from time to time to introduce some projectile that shall be more effective for large game shooting than the ordinary leaden bullet, and for the better penetration of the pachydermata a zinc or iron-pointed bullet has been tried. General Jacobs was the great advocate for its adoption. The illustrations show his bullet with point, and also show the steel point separate. The bullet was made by placing the point at the bottom of the mould, and casting the remainder in the usual way. A great drawback to this bullet was the imperfect junction of the lead and steel, so that when it struck against a tough surface the lead stripped off and the iron point alone penetrated, but this is only when the steel point is too small. It should be of equal size with the bore ; then this difficulty is never experienced, even when firing into hard wood. A much better plan is to make the bullets of type-metal, and this undoubtedly is the best composition of which to make them. Chilled shot makes excellent hardened bullets, but it is too expensive to come into general use. The best way of hardening bullets is to use mercury, 9 parts of lead to 1 part of mercury. Only sufficient metal should be melted to cast 9 bullets, the mercury or quicksilver then added, and the bullets immediately cast, as the mercury volatilises rapidly. Hardened bullets are also made by the admixture of lead and tin. The best proportions are 1 part tin to 9 of lead, 1 part to 12 of lead, or 1 to 15 of lead ; the latter is used for long-range bullets.

EXPERIMENTS WITH EXPLOSIVE SHELLS.

Shells for large-bore rifles, such as the " copper-bottle " and Forsyth swedge shell, have been thoroughly tried on every kind of large game, and their utility in instantly stopping an animal is well known.

The effect of an explosive shell on an animal is much more paralysing than a wound from a solid bullet.

There is an impression among sportsmen that a small quantity of detonating compound, such as is used in the Forsyth shell, would not answer in small-bore shells. The author loaded an ordinary Express bullet by filling up the hollow with the explosive compound and closing the point with wax, firing it with a charge of 3 drams of powder into the head of a bullock. The bullet penetrated the skull and entered the brain, and on examination there appeared merely a small hole in the forehead ; but on opening the head the brain was found to be completely destroyed ; the shell had burst into small pieces, fracturing the bones. A ·450 Express bullet, weighing 300 grains, was next tried in the same manner. The hole in this bullet, being smaller, did not contain so much detonating powder, but the results were about the same, with the exception of the penetration ; this was greater in consequence of the increased charge, which was 4 drams. The shell exploded more at the back of the head, completely shattering it. The rifle was fired at distances of 15 and 40 yards respectively with the same results.

THE EXPLOSIVE COMPOUND FOR SHELLS.

This should be mixed as follows :—Take sulphuret of antimony and chlorate of potash, pounded separately, and mix carefully equal parts by weight with a bone knife, on a plate or other smooth surface.

ROOK AND RABBIT RIFLES.

For rook and rabbit shooting, single breech-loading rifles are generally used. There are at present many sizes in the market, the most popular bores being :—

Bore.	Powder.	Bullet.
·22 Long Rifle	4 grs.	40 grs.
·297/230	3¼ grs.	38 grs.
,, long	5½ grs.	38 grs.
·297/250	6½ grs.	56 grs.
·300	10 grs.	80 grs.
·310	2½ grs. Cordite	80 grs.
·360 No. 5	14 grs.	134 grs. } Same Rifle
·380 long	12 grs.	124 grs. }

The breech-actions applicable to rook rifles are : the Martini, the top-lever, the side-lever, and the hammerless.

The top-lever hammer rook rifle has the ordinary bottom holding-down bolt, half pistol-hand, rebounding lock and octagonal barrel. The extracting is effected

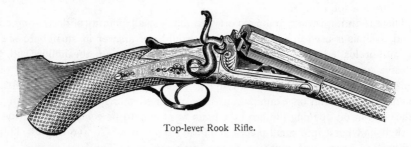

Top-lever Rook Rifle.

by a strong lever on the side of the breech action engaging with the extractor. Such rifles are sold at prices varying from 6 to 10 guineas, according to the quality and style of finish.

The well-known Martini action is most suitable for small rifles when properly made, and for the cheaper qualities is recommended in preference to a cheap and

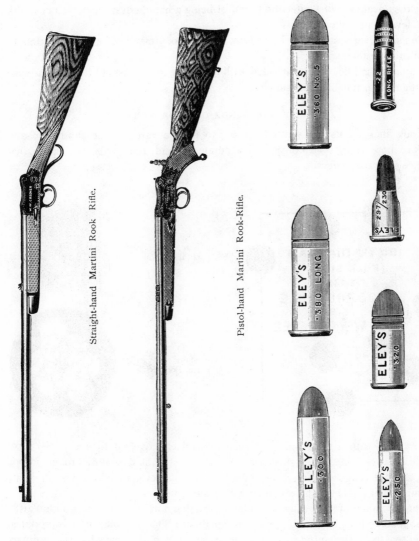

Straight-hand Martini Rook Rifle.

Pistol-hand Martini Rook-Rifle.

Rook and Rabbit Rifle Cartridges (sizes in general use).

generally unreliable hammerless. It is neat in appearance and easy to manipulate. It has the advantage of a safety-bolt, and of being a hammerless ejector, since a jerk of the lever expels the fired case.

The side-lever system may be had by those who prefer a drop-down action to the Martini system.

Hammerless rifles are constructed with a suitable mechanism of the Anson type; they are strong, reliable, and simple.

ACCURACY AND RANGE OF ROOK RIFLES.

Rook rifles are usually sighted up to 150 or 200 yards. The short ·360 and the ·320 bore cannot be considered accurate beyond 100 yards, but up to that distance they are perfect.

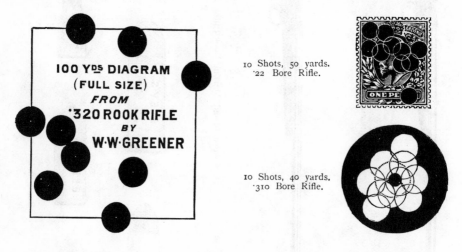

100 YDS DIAGRAM (FULL SIZE) FROM ·320 ROOK RIFLE BY W·W·GREENER

10 Shots, 50 yards. ·22 Bore Rifle.

10 Shots, 40 yards. ·310 Bore Rifle.

The ·380, with a solid bullet, is accurate and effective up to 200 yards. For naturalists these rifles offer special advantages, as the skin is only broken in one place, and the range is greater, thus enabling the collector to add to his bag many specimens that could not be obtained with a shot-gun.

The accuracy of rook rifles is excellent; the diagram made at the London Rifle Trials, good as it is, has frequently been equalled. The facsimiles here reproduced are chosen from the author's file of factory records, and show what the ordinary rook rifle does in the hands of a competent shot; they also prove that the sighting and adjustment of the rifles are as accurately done as for the much more expensive match and Express sporting rifles.

In this country, and in all probability in many others, it is of the first importance that the rook rifle should have but a very limited range. It is often used at a great elevation, shot at angles which would cause a long-range or match rifle to propel its

Mechanism of Holland's Hammerless Rook Rifle.

bullet to the extreme limit of its range—considerably over 1,000 yards. What is required in a rook rifle is great accuracy up to (say) 100 yards, and sufficient striking force to kill the game at that distance, but beyond the bullet to be as harmless as any spent bullet can be. The ·360 with spherical bullet appears to best fulfil this

W. W. Greener's Hammerless Ejector Rook Rifle.

condition. The ·250, with hollow pointed bullets, is the smallest calibre effective at rabbits and small game. The ·220 may be used with the long rim-fire cartridge at rooks ; but, as far as experience proves, it is too small for rabbit-shooting.

A top-lever hammerless rook rifle has been introduced by Messrs. Holland and Holland. The illustration on page 673 shows the mechanism, which is most simple, and the general appearance of the arm is good.

The principle of cocking consists in the compressing of the flat main-spring by pressure on the stud of a slotted cylinder. By turning the top lever to withdraw the holding-down bolts the two planes, one on the lever tumbler the other on the mainspring, are brought into contact, and the mainspring is forced down until the tumbler is caught in full cock by the scear.

An adaptation of the fore-end ejecting mechanism to the "Facile Princeps" hammerless action has now been made by the author, and this probably forms the highest development of the single barrel rook and rabbit rifle.

RIFLED SHOT-GUNS AND CHOKE-BORED RIFLES.

The endeavours of gun-makers towards producing a good all-round weapon have resulted in such inventions as rifled shot-guns and choke-bored rifles, from which both shot and ball cartridges may be indiscriminately fired. The rifled shot-gun (Fosbery's Patent) has the barrel of an ordinary choke-bored shot-gun rifled for the last few inches of its length, a sharp spiral is adopted, and a grooving of sufficient sharpness to turn a conical-cannelured bullet. Such weapons shoot shot moderately well—better than the ordinary cylinder shot-gun, but not so closely as the perfectly choked gun—and conical bullets with accuracy to 100 yards.

The oval-bore rifle, if the spiral be not too sharp, will throw shot closely and well at ordinary ranges, but a still better weapon than either of these is the choke-bore rifle, in which a rifle with modern shallow grooving is choke-bored at the muzzle (Greener's Patent) and has a perfectly smooth surface throughout its entire length.

These weapons are treated by the Government Proof Houses as rifles, and are subjected to special tests with ball. They are usually made of light weight—say, $7\frac{1}{2}$ lbs. 12-bore—and for both bear and boar shooting they offer many advantages, and as a second rifle they fill a need which many a hunter of large game, pioneer and explorer has often felt. Wherever large game is *occasionally* to be met with, they form the best armament of the sportsman.

They shoot spherical bullets with a large charge of powder, and are chosen therefore by many who desire a second weapon for use against buffalo or other thick-skinned animals.

They have the accuracy and force of the heavy rifle combined with the lightness and handiness of the shot-gun. Firing black powder and a conical bullet at 100 yards, diagrams measuring about 4 inches by 3 can be readily obtained. Suitable smokeless cartridges can also be used with satisfactory results. Muzzle velocity of the 12-bore varies from 1,050 to 1,200 ft. secs., with striking energy at 100 yards of 1,722 ft. lbs. to 1,822 ft. lbs., according to load and bullet used.

RIFLE AND SHOT-GUNS.

The combination of a rifle and shot-gun in one double-barrelled weapon is much esteemed by South African sportsmen. The rifle barrel, usually the left, may be rifled on any system. Henry rifling is still most in favour at the Cape, and may be of ·450 or ·500 bore ; the proper proportions of the two being ·450 rifle barrel and 16-bore shot barrel, or ·500 rifle barrel and 12-bore shot barrel. These arms are only useful in countries where the kind of game that may be met with cannot be determined beforehand, and for emigrants who cannot afford more than one gun.

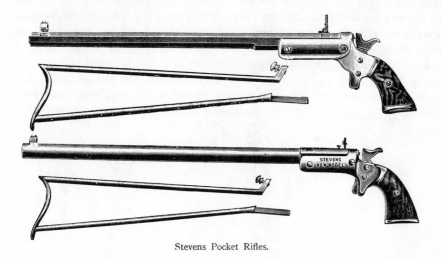

Stevens Pocket Rifles.

They have many drawbacks. The weapon is too heavy as a shot-gun, and makes flying shots almost an impossibility. The balance, of course, is bad. As a rifle the weapon is too light, and the recoil with some of the heavier-loaded cartridges is considerable.

The heavy rifle barrel not giving way in the least causes the shot barrel to become the more easily dented and damaged ; a fall to a rifle and shot-gun generally finishes most disastrously for the shot barrel. The rifle may be chambered for either of the Express cartridges or the long-range No. 2 musket-case; the last-named is most in favour in the South African Colonies. The Government regulation ammunition may also be employed, as in the combination of ·303 and 16-bore.

In all cases where practicable, a single rifle and a double shot-gun are far preferable to the rifle and shot-gun.

AMERICAN POCKET RIFLES.

A product peculiarly American is the pocket rifle, made by the Stevens Arms and Tools Company, which, though seemingly a toy—and it would, no doubt, be called such in this country—has an extraordinary accuracy for its short barrel. As shown in the illustration (page 675), the stock or rest is detachable, so that both parts can readily be placed in the pocket, the length being only 18 or 24 inches for calibre from ·22 to ·44, and the weight from 5 to 5¾ lbs. A still smaller model is made for ·22, ·25, and ·32 calibres, weighing from 2 to 2¾ lbs., the barrel being 10 to 18 inches long. A. C. Gould gives some extraordinary results. With the 22-in. ·250 bore, using regular charge of powder and the 86-grain bullet, ten shots were placed in or on a 7-in. circle at 200 yards; and with the smaller model, 18-in. barrel, ·22 cal., ten consecutive shots were placed in the regulation bull's-eye of 8 inches at 200 yards. These results were, of course, obtained from a rest.

CHAPTER XXVII.

EXTERNAL BALLISTICS.

TRAJECTORIES.

IN the chapter on "Internal Ballistics" it was sought to explain the nature and manner of working of the force which so acted upon the projectile within the gun as to move it from a state of rest and propel it beyond the muzzle; similarly, the following remarks will indicate the nature of the changes which tend to overcome the *energy* of the moving projectile and reduce its motion to a condition of rest, and specify the methods by which the ballistic value of the bullet at any position in its flight may be estimated.

Prior to the seventeenth century it was thought that the path of a bullet was straight for a distance, that it then curved, and later fell perpendicularly. Galileo held that it must describe a parabola, save as diverted by the resistance of the air. It is not the intention of the author to attempt any exposition of the theories of mathematicians, or explain the almost insurmountable difficulties which the problem presents. Full particulars of the formulæ used to calculate velocities and values are given in most gunnery text-books, and with elucidatory comments in the late Mr. Walsh's work, "The Modern Sportsman's Rifle," to which the reader is referred. There are certain elementary truths with which everyone who uses a gun or rifle should be acquainted; one is the object of rifling. It is to prevent a tendency of the bullet to rotate upon its shorter axis—a tendency produced by the air-resistance. Rifling, therefore, is of greater importance when a conical or elongated projectile is used than when the bullet is spherical. It follows that the greater the length of the bullet in proportion to its diameter, the greater the need of rifling, and, other things being equal, the greater must be the speed of rotation. The twist—the rate of which may be correctly calculated, but in practice is usually fixed by actual experiment—is reckoned either in the number of inches or feet in which a complete turn is made, or in calibres; the latter being the more exact, for it is evident that if a 500 calibre and a 300 calibre each have one turn in ten inches the rifling cannot be identical, but if the two rifles made the complete turn in the same number of their calibres the twist of the rifling would be the same.

The resistance of the air varies with differences in the sectional area, shape, and velocity of the projectile and the density of the atmosphere. The sectional area of an elongated projectile is circular, and the resistance increases as the square of the diameter. The increase of resistance to increase of velocity is fairly regular, but no law has been discovered which accurately accounts for its degree of variation. The shape of the head of the bullet causes the resistance to vary; taking the hemispherical head as the unit of value, the ogival head of one diameter offers less resistance, relatively as 0·83 is to 1, the ogival head of 2 diameters less, being as 78 and equal to the hemispheroidal head, whilst the flat or blunt head offers greater resistance, relatively as 1·53 to 1. The variation due to changes in atmospheric density are not inconsiderable in long-range shooting, or at high altitudes, and allowance is made by scientific shots and by practical hunters. When shooting on highlands or mountain peaks, a *fine* sight must be taken, as the rifle shoots high, but ordinarily sportsmen rarely allow for it when game-shooting.

Retardation of the bullet also varies according to the power of the bullet to overcome the resistance by reason of *sectional density*, or the relation existing between the weight of the bullet and the area of its cross section. The value is signified as $\frac{d_2}{w}$; or, conversely, the ranging power of the bullet may be taken; this, being proportional to its weight and inversely to its area, is stated as $\frac{w}{d_2}$, and the sum called the " ballistic coefficient."

The force of gravity is the sole cause of the curved path of the bullet; but the curve is sharpened by the resistance of the air, because, reducing the velocity of the bullet, less travel is made in each successive fraction of time whilst the force of gravitation is acting constantly and without variation. In vacuo the longest range would be obtained by firing at an angle of 45°; owing to the air resistance, the angle must be lessened, and varies with different rifles and ammunition, the maximum range seldom being attained if the angle of elevation much exceeds 35°.

The position of the bullet, relative to its trajectory, is much disputed. Many contend that at some points the nose of the bullet is above, at others below, the line ; others, that at *all* points the axis of the bullet is at a tangent to the trajectory. *Drift* is a deflection of the bullet due to its rotation and the resistance of the air to the peripheral friction, the theory being that the bullet rolls on the air in the direction in which the bullet rotates. Professor Bashforth contends that there is also a *vertical drift*, or deviation, due to difference in density above and below the rotating bullet.

These matters are, however, of small importance in comparison with the value of a flat trajectory. In order to obtain it, the projectile must have a high initial velocity, which ensures flat trajectory at short ranges, and a favourable sectional density to maintain it at long ranges.

The bullet must fall by gravitation, about 16 feet during the first second of its flight, 48 feet during the second, and so on in accordance with the rule of increasing effect of gravity; elevation is given in order to give the bullet time to traverse before drawn to the earth. The advantages of flat trajectory are:—Greater accuracy, the direction of the bullet to the mark being less curved, errors in aiming or in judging distances are of less importance, harder hitting (because the velocity is higher), and greater efficiency in covering the ground—or longer range—because the resistance of the air is overcome at a quicker rate.

The methods by which the trajectory curves are calculated are various, but all require tables of air values to allow of accurate approximations being ascertained; the same tables, with the known values of initial velocity, $\frac{w}{d_2}$, etc., enable the velocity at any range to be calculated, or the stored energy in the bullet to be computed as foot-pounds. Conversely the *time* of flight over a given range may be calculated, and from the work done, the striking force of the bullet and weight of the recoil computed.

Elevation is calculated from the zero, but the zero of each rifle differs slightly, and it is rare that the actual zero is parallel to the axis of the bore. With black powder a rifle bullet will strike lower than it should if the actual zero coincided with the constructive one, that is, with the line of sight; but with the Lee-Metford and cordite the bullet at very short range ($12\frac{1}{2}$ feet) strikes above the constructive zero. The phenomenon is usually attributed to the recoil, the motion of the gun commencing with the motion of the bullet, but not in a line with the axis, because the centre of the gravity of the rifle and the line of resistance to the recoil are below the line of the axis. Or it may be that the expansion of the barrel at the breech, due to the explosion, causes the muzzle to dip, the barrel not being so free to expand underneath, where it is supported, as it is above, where there is no downward pressure. As stated in the chapter on " Internal Ballistics," the motion of recoil is *first* in a line with the axis of the bore, and is not important until the bullet is at or near the muzzle. The action of recoil has never been satisfactorily demonstrated; to the author it seems incredible that very accurate shooting with guns giving great recoil—as with the light double 8-bore already instanced—would be possible, unless upon the hypothesis that the projectile is either at or clear of the muzzle *before* the movement of the recoil commences.

The variations in ballistic value of the different calibres and the charges and loads used in them, as well as of the explosives and projectiles which may be used are far too numerous to specify, but a few particulars are given in connection with descriptions of sporting, military, and target rifles, and at greater length in the following condensed report of the *Field* Rifle Trials and comments thereon.

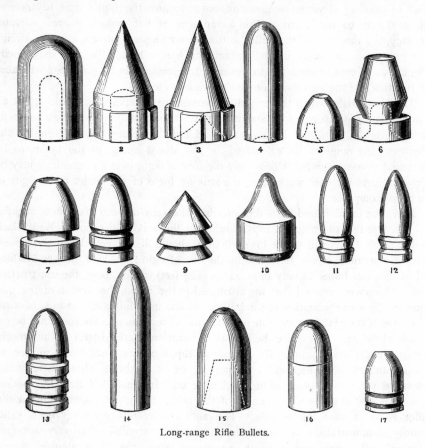

Long-range Rifle Bullets.

BULLETS AND SPECIAL PROJECTILES.

Almost every form of projectile has been experimented with as to its fitness for weapons of ordinary or special type. The round ball is, of course, the earliest and simplest ; the history of the development of the elongated bullet has already been given in the history of rifling. A few of the more generally used, obsolete, and latest modern types will now be described. In the illustration (page 680) No. 1 is one of the earliest forms of the cylindro-conoidal bullet; Nos. 2 and 3 are early French and German mechanically fitting conical bullets, with hollowed, or cupped, bases; No. 4 is the Martini-Henry regulation bullet; Nos. 5, 6, and 7 are bullets used by

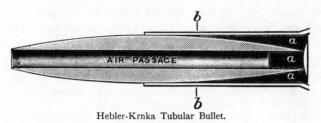

Hebler-Krnka Tubular Bullet.

the French during, and for a short time after, the Crimean War; Nos. 8 and 9 are German bullets, with deep cannelures; No. 10 is a Sardinian bullet; Nos. 11 and 12, Swiss long-range cannelured bullets; No. 13 is a bullet once used in the United States Service, and No. 14, the American Long-Range Rifle "Picket"; No. 15 is the modification of the Minié bullet, adapted for use in the ·577 Sporting Snider Rifle; No. 16 is the ·450 wrapped carbine bullet; and No. 17 the flattened ·44 bullet used in the Winchester Repeating Rifles.

A tubular bullet was proposed by Mr. Krnka some ten years ago; later Professor Hebler, of Zurich, whose work in connection with hard-coated bullets and small-calibre rifles is well known, produced the steel projectile illustrated above.

"The tubular bullet for the 8 m/m and larger calibres may be made of lead or soft metal, with the hard metal jacket common to the Hebler projectiles. For the 5 m/m better results are said to accrue if the projectile is made wholly of steel or of steel furnished with a narrow external band of copper round its greatest circumference. It is held to be of some ballistic advantage, but otherwise of little importance, that the projectile shall be ogival at both ends, also that the tube shall be slightly enlarged at the base and at the muzzle. To give greater stability to the projectile the tube of the jacketed bullet may be lined with a hard metal tube. The bullet is seated in or upon a shoe wad or 'sabot' of paper or other suitable material, and its double purpose is to prevent the loss of gas and oscillation of the projectile during its passage through the barrel. On leaving the muzzle of the rifle, the sabot is immediately separated from the bullet. The theory advanced on behalf of the tubular projectile is that the resistance offered by the air to the bullet is caused by the condensation or compression of air strata immediately in front of the bullet and the formation of a vacuum behind it, both tending to lessen the velocity; the tubular bullet pointed at both ends, and having a passage through it, therefore diminishes the retardation arising from either cause. The air in front passes over the tapered nose and rapidly over the tapered rear, while the central passage is filled by an air current which, issuing at the rear, fills the vacuum caused by the flight of the projectile through the air. The correctness of the theory is supported by the evidence photographs of bullets during flight afford, and is further proved by the results obtained with the tubular bullets in target and velocity experiments."

In the 1888 pattern, 8 m/m rifle, the bullet with hardened jacket weighs 14·5 grammes; the tubular bullet is but 10·8 grammes, a reduction which is equal to ten more rounds to each infantry-man without increasing his burden. The internal pressure is reduced by the bullet from 3,300 to 2,200 atmospheres, and the velocity, commencing at 720 metres per second, is well maintained, being 510 metres a second at 2,000 metres range. In the 5 m/m rifle it is claimed that, with a pressure of 3,100 atmospheres, a muzzle velocity of 4,000 feet per second may be attained.

" With the 8 m/m the maximum effective range is 4,402 metres, duration of flight 9·16 seconds, remaining velocity at this range 337 metres and a penetration of 27·8 centimetres; the extreme calculated range is 8,101 metres (8,850 yards). With the 5 m/m rifle a tubular bullet weighing 3·30 grammes, with a load of 1·64 grammes of Koln-Rottweil smokeless powder, gives a pressure of 2,400 atmospheres, a muzzle velocity of 1,050 metres (3,450 ft.), and the penetration (into soft pine-boards) is 204 c. (7 ft.)."

The author's experiments with this bullet confirm the general verdict that its accuracy is poor, a fact which will militate against its general acceptance in small arms, however useful it may prove for machine-guns.

In addition to lead bullets jacketed with steel, copper, and numerous alloys, tungsten, which is a heavier metal, has been tried as a case, and also, experimentally, as the material for solid bullets.

THE LONDON *FIELD* RIFLE TRIAL.

These trials were held at Putney the first week of October, 1883. The classes were for rook rifles, double ·400, ·450, ·500, and ·577 Express rifles, and for double 12-, 8- and 4-bore rifles. There were but six competitors—Messrs. Adams, Bland, Holland, Jeffreys, Tranter and Watson. The rifles were tried for accuracy at one, two, and the Expresses at three ranges : the recoil, trajectory and velocity of each winning rifle were taken.

The trial resulted in Messrs. Holland being declared winners of every class ; but to the gun trade, and to sportsmen in general, the trial cannot be considered to have been fully satisfactory, nor to have produced the conclusive proofs that were expected.

It is unfortunate that so few makers competed—a fact probably traceable to the short notice given of the contest. There was not sufficient time to make special weapons, or even to determine by experiment which weapons were most likely to show to best advantage in the trial; accuracy, trajectory, and recoil had all to be

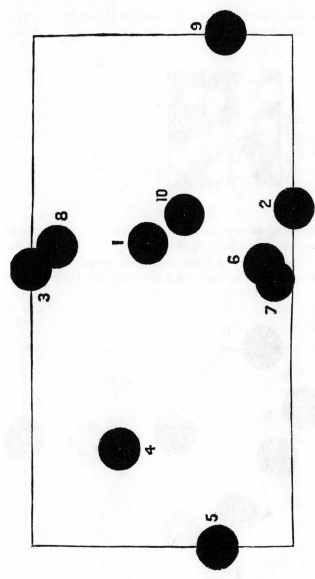

Diagram of Holland's ·450-bore at 100 yards.

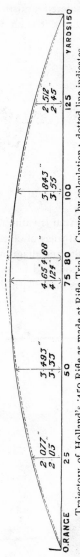

Trajectory of Holland's ·450 Rifle as made at Rifle Trial. Curve by calculation ; dotted line indicates flight as per screens.

considered, and the loads most suitable for the rifles already made might not secure for that rifle such a place in the competition as the weapon from its merits deserved.

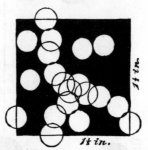

Holland ·295 Diagram, 20 shots at 50 yards.

The trial is valuable because it is the only one of its kind—the only public trial—in which rifles of certain kinds have ever figured ; and it must be remembered that the results and diagrams are authentic beyond dispute and were made in actual competition, and it is therefore unfair to compare them with diagrams selected from a series made with the same rifles and loads.

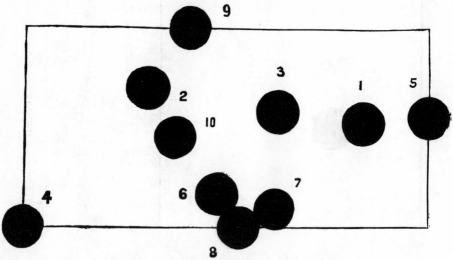

Diagram of ·450-bore at 50 yards. (Actual size.)

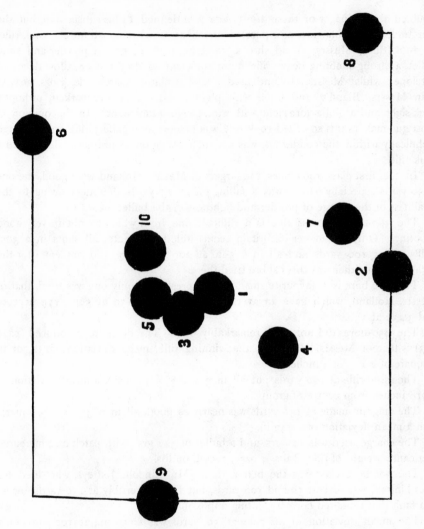

Diagram of ·450-bore Rifle at 150 yards.

The best grooving or system of rifling has not been proved : the merits of rival systems still remain undecided. The terms "Express" and "point-blank," that so troubled the manager of these trials, *have been* defined to his satisfaction, but the gun trade and public are now puzzled afresh as to what constitutes a rook rifle. As rook rifles, Messrs. Bland shot a ·380-bore, with 14 grs. of powder and solid bullet, a strong-shooting heavy rifle quite sufficient to drop roe or fallow deer and antelope ; whilst Messrs. Holland used a ·295 miniature match rifle, 3 ozs. heavier than Messrs. Bland's, and fitted with platinum-edged, Vernier-marked, orthoptic back-sight and a globe fore-sight with wind-gauge attachment. In the opinion of most gun-makers this so-called rook rifle was practically a gallery rifle, and although technically within the conditions, was not such a weapon as ordinarily designated a rook rifle.

In the first-class rook rifles the targets of Messrs. Holland were good, the one at 50 yards especially ; there was a falling off at 75 yards, doubtless owing to the smallness of the charge of powder and lightness of the bullet.

The ·360-bore Express rifle is a difficult one from which to obtain very good shooting. Only one maker in Britain seems able to guarantee all shots in a 3-in. bull's eye at 100 yards and all in a 5-in. at 200 yards ; he did not enter for the Rifle Trials, neither was this calibre tried there.

The ·400-bore is a favourite small-bore Express ; yet only one was tried, that of Messrs. Holland, which gave an average deviation of 1·139 at 50, 2·179 at 100, and 3·232 at 150.

The ·450-bores did not shoot remarkably well. The diagram reproduced (page 683) is that of Messrs. Holland's, the winning rifle, mean deviation 1·132, or in a square of 2·1 × 4·3 inches.

The same rifle at 100 yards put all in a 2·9 × 5·4 square, a mean deviation of 1·318 inches from centre of group.

The diagram made at 150 yards was nearly as good, all in a 3·9 × 4·9 square, with a mean deviation of 1·449 in.

The charge used was 110 grs. and a bullet of 322 grs., with patch and mercurial lubricant ; weight of rifle, 8 lbs. 4 ozs. ; recoil, 96 lbs.

The ·500-bore class was the better tried. Mr. Lincoln Jeffreys, who fired his rifles himself, was first at 50 and 100 yards, but fell off terribly at 150 yards, owing to a fault that rendered correct sighting impossible.

The mean deviation of his rifle at 50 yards was 1·052 in., at 100 yards only 1·004 in., but at 150 yards 4·124 in. At 50 yards all would have been in a square of 1·9 × 3·6, and of 2 × 2·8 at 100.

The best diagram at 150 yards was made by the rifle of Mr. Adams ; mean deviation at 150 yards of 2·400, or the shots in a square 4·7 × 6.

The ·577 class was restricted to rifles under 12 lbs.; the best diagram at 50 yards was made by Mr. Adams, with a 10 lb. 11 oz. rifle, mean deviation 1·056 in., or all in a square of 1·8 × 2·6, this with 164 grs. and bullet 507 grs.

Messrs. Holland, with same charge, but a bullet of 598 grs., had a mean deviation of 1·128 at 50 yards, but of 2·098 at 100, and 2·418 at 150, or in 4·8 × 6·3 and 4·8 × 7·7 respectively, coming out first in the aggregate owing to their better shooting and heavier bullet.

RIFLE TRIALS.

The trials of large-bore rifles were made at Nunhead. The shooting of Messrs. Holland's 13½ lb. 12-bore rifle, which was only fired at 50 yards, as were all other large bores, was, indeed, mediocre. With 7 drs. of powder, the recoil was 141 lbs. and the mean deviation ·993 in., but it surpassed that of its one competitor by several points.

The 10-bore shot weighed but 12 and 12½ lbs. respectively, and with 8 drs. 5 grs.

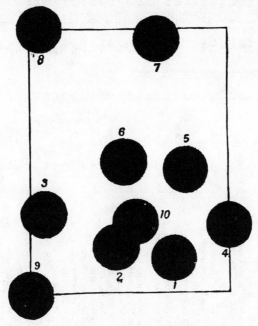

Diagram of Lincoln Jeffreys' ·500 Rifle at 100 yards. (Actual size.)

TABLE SHOWING THE VELOCITY, PENETRATION, AND TRAJECTORY OF AMERICAN AMMUNITION FIRED FROM WINCHESTER RIFLES.

Names of Cartridges.	Length of Barrels. Inches.	Accuracy.	Powder in Grains.	Weights of Bullets. Grains.	Velocities of Bullets per second. Feet.	Penetration of Bullets — Plain Lead. Boards.	Penetration of Bullets — Metal Patched. Boards.	100-Yards Trajectory. Height at 50 Yards. Inches.	200-Yards Trajectory. Height at 100 Yards. Inches.	300-Yards Trajectory. Height at 150 Yards. Inches.
'22 Winchester Rim Fire	24		7	45	1137	4		4·05		
'22 Winchester Centre Fire	26		13	45	1481	5		2·71	12·63	33·67
'236 U.S. Navy	30		36	135	2396		62	1·02	5·96	9·57
'25-20 Winchester Centre Fire	24		17	86	1300	9½		4·30	3·78	34·69
'25-20 W. C. F. Smokeless	24		19	86	1300	9½		4·33	13·01	32·18
'25-20 W. C. F. Smokeless	28		19	86	1304	6¼		3·35	13·61	34·68
'25-35 W. C. F. Smokeless, Metal Patch Soft Point	26		26	117	2000		10	2·4	5·13	13·86
'30 W. C. F. Smokeless	26		30	160	1970		35	2·1	5·22	13·57
'30 U.S. Army	30		40	220	2066		58	1·46	5·10	14·14
'32 Winchester	24	B	20	115	1177			3·46	15·37	37·21
'32-40	30	Ah	40	165	1385	6½	8	2·72	11·32	28·33
'38 Winchester	24		38	180	1268	8½		3·19	14·42	35·68
'38 Winchester Smokeless	24	Ah	38	189	1300	7½		4·13	12·84	34·87
'38-55	30		48	255	1285		14	2·97	12·92	31·98
'38-90 Winchester Express	30		90	217	1546	9½	17	2·16	8·62	22·83
'38-56 Winchester	26		56	255	1359	9	14½	2·82	12·23	30·14
'38-70 Winchester	26	B	68	255	1449	11	19	2·58	10·58	27·17
'40-70 Sharp's Straight	28		45	330	1229	10		3·30	13·40	32·86
'40-60 Marlin	28	B	60	260	1419	11½		2·97	11·81	29·40
'40-60 Winchester	30		62	210	1475	8½		2·61	11·65	30·11
'40-90 Sharp's Straight	26	h	90	370	1357	9½		2·73	10·76	26·85
'40-65 Winchester	26	Bh	65	260	1325	16	14½	2·85	12·00	30·67
'40-70 Winchester	26		70	330	1349	9	19½	2·89	11·79	29·44
'40-82 Winchester	26		82	260	1445	13	17½	2·56	11·92	30·32
'40-110 Winchester Express	30	C	110	260	1555	12½		2·07	8·95	23·63
'44 Winchester	24	B	40	200	1245	9		3·36	15·27	37·39
'44 Winchester Smokeless	24		40	200	1300		10½	4·60	15·92	40·42
'45-75 Winchester	30	B	75	350	1344	14½		3·04	12·41	30·62
'45-60 Winchester	26		62	300	1271	11½		3·16	13·67	33·10
'45-70-500 U.S. Govt.	26		70	500	1179	18		3·66	14·36	34·36
'45-70-405 U.S. Govt.	26		70	405	1271	14		3·29	13·07	32·32
'45-70-405 U.S. Govt., Smokeless	26		70	405	1286		16½	4·12	12·33	29·00
'45-70-350 Winchester	26		70	350	1307	13		2·79	13·13	31·76
'45-70-330 Gould Hollow	26		90	330	1338	10	20	2·82	12·66	32·35
'45-90 Winchester	26		90	300	1480	13		2·44	10·25	31·76
'45-90 Winchester Smokeless	26	Bh	90	300	1479			3·59	11·91	28·79
'45-125 Winchester Express	30	C	125	300	1633	9½		2·19	9·01	25·11
'50-110 Winchester Express	30	D	110	300	1536	11		2·53	11·91	32·52
'50-100-450 Winchester	26		100	450	1383	16		2·85	11·94	30·69
'50-95 Winchester Express	30		95	300	1493	10		2·48	12·57	33·51

NOTE.—Smokeless charge of equal charge nominal. Accuracy, Col. Gould's classification : A, nearly all shots into a 6-inch circle at 200 yards ; B, in an 8-inch circle ; C, into a 12-inch circle ; D, into a 20-inch circle ; h are recommended for game-shooting.

TABLE OF THE TRAJECTORIES OF SPORTING RIFLES.

Rifle.	Bore, Inches.	Powder, Grains.	Bullet, Grains.	$\frac{D^2}{W}$	Weight of Weapon.	Recoil.	Muzzle.	100 Yards.	150 Yards.	200 Yards.	500 Yards.	1,000 Yards.	Extreme Range.	Muzzle.	100 Yards.	150 Yards.	200 Yards.	100 Yards.	150 Yards.	200 Yards.
	CHARGE.				RECOIL.		VELOCITIES in Feet Second.							ENERGIES at Ranges in Foot-Pounds.				TRAJECTORY.		
1. Lee-Speed	·303	70	200	3·213	8	12·0	1850	1619	1507	1404	...	...	2000	1528	1170	1014	880	1·42	3·57	7·55
2. Long-range	·360	40	220	4·124	7	6·8	1350	1142	1063	1010	...	...	1000	895	640	554	501	3·25	7·55	15·09
3. Express	·360	90	250	3·629	7½	19·5	1810	1551	1432	1328	...	...	250	1828	1342	1144	977	1·56	3·89	8·27
4. Long-range	·450	85	480	2·953	9	18·8	1313	1167	1104	1053	864	661	1000	1841	1450	1297	1188	2·74	6·82	14·79
5. Express	·450	130	350	4·05	9½	32·6	1880	1567	1434	1313	911	...	...	2703	1918	1606	1347	1·51	3·76	8·10
6. Express	·450	150	270	5·173	9	31·5	2000	1611	1439	1286	837	...	300	2431	1578	1258	1011	1·33	3·42	7·72
7. Express	·450	150	360	3·15	9½	39·6	1910	1623	1490	1367	930	...	300	2948	2117	1784	1502	1·42	3·50	7·50
8. Express	·450	150	342	5·115	9	31·5	1946	1569	1402	1258	827	...	...	2872	1867	1490	1210	1·43	3·61	8·10
9. Express	·500	138	444	3·94	8¼	28·6	1784	1507	1382	1270	855	...	...	3134	2237	1893	1598	1·62	3·97	8·62
10. Express	·500	138	467	3·47	10	49·9	1800	1534	1413	1302	...	...	...	3364	2437	2067	1756	1·61	3·96	8·58
11. Express	·500	164	505	3·45	10¼	51·2	1738	1498	1388	1288	...	...	...	3390	2518	2163	1862	1·71	4·21	8·90
12. Express	·500	160	480	4·85	10	48·4	1780	1418	1278	1159	830	...	...	3282	2154	1750	1439	1·81	4·60	10·02
13. Express	·577	191	710	3·282	12	78·1	1730	1480	1397	1302	890	...	...	4743	3471	3093	2686	2·16	4·01	8·80
14. Express	·577	191	550	4·237	11¼	59·0	1790	1494	1360	1243	...	...	...	3934	2740	2271	1897	1·65	4·18	9·01
15. Express	·577	191	600	3·884	12	62·3	1760	1480	1367	1259	911	...	...	4149	2973	2503	2123	1·69	4·24	9·01
16. 12-bore	·725	191	599	6·211	13	50·3	1584	1111	968	852	...	...	...	3356	1650	1253	1033	2·55	7·40	15·11
17. 12-bore	·725	110	547	6·801	7¼	42·5	1384	985	865	771	...	...	...	2324	1185	914	726	3·17	8·55	17·88
18. 10-bore	·775	273	670	6·275	11	79·8	1600	1117	970	869	...	...	...	3829	1866	1407	1182	2·50	6·75	12·51
19. 8-bore	·835	10	862	5·662	16	85·0	1654	1193	1038	...	...	...	...	5232	2720	2069	...	2·2	5·9	...
20. 4-bore	1·052	12	1250	6·197	20	102·4	1460	1099	980	...	...	...	...	5912	3351	2869	...	2·7	7·07	...
21. 4-bore	1·052	14	1882	4·116	24	158·4	1450	1217	1124	1050	...	...	...	8832	6222	5307	4632	2·84	7·07	13·50

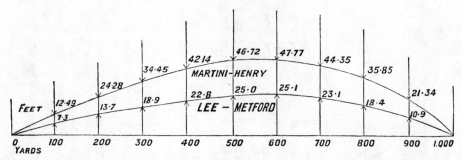

Diagram of Comparative Trajectories of the Martini-Henry and the Lee-Metford.

TRAJECTORY OF LEE-METFORD ·303 WITH CORDITE AMMUNITION.

Range in Yards.	Height of Trajectory in Feet above Line of Sight.												
	100	200	300	400	500	600	700	800	900	1,000	1,100	1,200	1,300
200	0·4												
300	1·0	1·1											
400	1·6	2·3	1·8										
500	2·3	4·7	3·9	2·8									
600	3.1	5·3	6·4	6·0	4·0								
700	4·0	7·1	9·0	9·6	8·5	5·3							
800	5·0	9·1	12·0	13·5	13·4	11·3	7·0						
900	6·1	11·3	15·3	17·9	19·9	17·9	14·6	8·7					
1,000	7·3	13·7	18·9	22·8	25·0	25·1	23·1	18·4	10·9				
1,100	8·6	16·3	22·9	28·0	31·5	33·0	32·3	28·9	22·7	13·1			
1,200	10·0	19·2	27·2	33·8	38·7	41·6	42·3	40·4	35·7	27·5	15·8		
1,300	11·6	22·3	31·8	40·0	46·5	51·0	53·2	52·9	49·6	43·0	32·9	18·6	0

TRAJECTORY OF MARTINI-HENRY ·450.

Range in Yards.	Height of Trajectory in Feet above Line of Sight.									
	450	500	600	700	800	900	1,000	1,100	1,200	1,300
500	3·570	0								
600	11·06	8·492	0							
700	18·85	17·33	11·00	0						
800	27·02	26·59	22·56	13·93	0					
900	35·72	36·43	34·85	28·76	17·48	0				
1,000	44·83	46·77	47·72	44·28	35·80	21·27	0			
1,100	54·44	57·66	61·31	60·64	55·11	43·71	25·71	0		
1,200	64·71	69·26	75·80	78·11	75·71	67·66	53·14	31·11	0	
1,300	75·37	81·39	90·93	96·34	97·21	92·60	81·74	63·52	36·54	0

NOTE.—The height approximating most closely to the " culminating point " of each trajectory is printed in larger type.

and 8 drs. made mean deviations of 1·092 and 1·843 respectively, with a recoil ot 163 lbs.

The 8-bore of Messrs. Holland, weighing 17 lbs. 8 ozs., and fired with 10 drs.— a very light charge for this calibre, some of the more renowned elephant-hunters using as much as 12 and 14 drs. in this bore. The mean deviation was 1·452 at 50 yards, or all in a square of 4·2 × 5·0. The recoil was 185 lbs.

The 4-bore, weighing 23½ lbs., and fired with 12 drs. only (full charge 16 drs.), made a higher recoil than 200 lbs., so could not be registered, and made a better diagram than the 8-bore, the mean deviation being only ·782 in.

A 12-bore smooth-bore ball-gun of Messrs. Holland's was then fired, but the diagram is so outrageously wide that we cannot think of publishing it as a standard. A smooth-bore shot-gun, choked or cylinder, should make a better diagram in good hands.

The following table gives the trajectories and velocities of the better shooting Express rifles :—

Maker.	Bore.	Muzzle Velocity.	Average Trajectory at					
			25 yards.	50 yards.	75 yards.	80 yards.	100 yds.	120 yds.
Holland	·400	1873·6	1·77	3·12	4·35	4·45	3·28	2·28
,, ...	·450	1776·	2·03	3·33	4·65	4·68	3·55	2·45
,, ...	·500	1784·	2·12	3·43	4·72	4·82	3·63	2·47
Jeffreys	·500	1946·	1·79	3·01	3·58	—	3·36	2·23
Holland	·577	1663·4	1·92	3·44	4·84	4·84	3·72	2·68

ACCURACY AND RANGE OF SPORTING RIFLES.

For most sporting purposes, the condition of accuracy is held to be filled if all the shots are grouped within a 6-inch circle at 100 yards, and this degree of accuracy is possible of attainment without sacrificing the velocity of the bullet or discarding the enormous advantage of the second shot obtainable from the double Express.

Selected rifles, under favourable circumstances, are capable of making finer diagrams, but much depends upon the circumstances and the man behind the rifle. The first diagram is an exact reproduction of the shooting made at 100 yards with a W. W. Greener double-barrel No. 1 Express, by the editor of *Sportens* at Helsingfors ; a finer diagram has never been made with a double Express rifle. The next diagram was made with a Greener rifle of ·303 bore ; it is just above a No. 1 Express average. For comparison a diagram with a ·450 Martini-Henry at 100 yards is given. At 200 yards and over the heavier the bullets the better the shooting.

The ·303 has not made any diagram to equal the best on record from rifles having

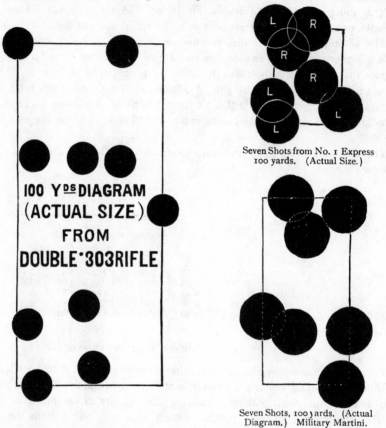

100 YDS DIAGRAM
(ACTUAL SIZE)
FROM
DOUBLE·303 RIFLE

Seven Shots from No. 1 Express
100 yards. (Actual Size.)

Seven Shots, 100 yards. (Actual
Diagram.) Military Martini.

a lower velocity and higher trajectory. Nevertheless it may be taken that the ·303 has sufficient accuracy for all sporting purposes at any range at which it is likely to be used. The deviation is greater in a vertical than a lateral direction, but as the one sight is good for all ranges up to, say, 300 yards, this vertical deviation is of no practical moment. It gives, on the average, better shooting at short—200, 300, 500 yards—ranges than the Martini-Henry, and at longer ranges is immensely its superior. At these longer ranges the ordinary "Express" is of no use whatever. In a word, the shooting of the ·303 is the "best" attainable, but, as elsewhere explained, it needs as much care as a match rifle.

VELOCITY AND PENETRATION.

Just as the shooter has to bear the force of the recoil, plus the weight of the rifle, so the object struck by the bullet has to sustain the force at impact—which is usually expressed as energy, and calculated in foot-pounds. In game shooting this value is not always realised, because a projectile at a high velocity passes through the animal and thus there has to be deducted the energy so lost—which is equal to the weight of the bullet multiplied by the square of the velocity it possessed at the point of separation, but divided by 64 and a fraction, or twice gravity—that is, the speed it had when it left the body of the animal through which it had passed.

The bullet and charge which give the highest percentage of work—whether the work is stated as velocity, striking force or energy, range or penetration—are not necessarily the best for sporting purposes, because the value of the work done is not always fully realised within the animal. In firing at an impenetrable plate the work realised by a soft lead ball will be greater than that of an iron bullet, because the latter will rebound and the energy required to produce that rebound is force lost. In the same manner, if an iron projectile pierces a wooden post and passes on, whilst a lead ball of equal weight and travelling at the same speed remains in the post, the post has to sustain more strain from the blow of the lead bullet than from the iron one.

In estimating the value of penetration, therefore, regard must be paid to only so much as is translatable into force at impact by striking the game. Modern military small arms, with their hard projectiles and high velocity, have too great penetration for ordinary game shooting ; the shock is less than that caused by a larger or heavier projectile at a lower velocity. In order to prevent too great penetration the express bullet is made hollow at the point, so that it expands as it meets resistance on striking, and realises its full value at impact. If the bullet is very soft the expansion is too great and the wound made is only a flesh wound ; if the ·450 or ·500 bullet is hardened by using one part of tin to nine of lead the bullet will mushroom sufficiently to prevent its piercing the animal struck, whilst possessing sufficient penetration to reach the vitals. In like manner, by using a bullet with a smaller hollow, making a heavier projectile and reducing the velocity, greater penetration is obtained. If the bullet is too hard it will break up into fragments if it meets with a solid bone, and the wound will not be sufficient to kill the animal. Methods have been tried to adapt the ·303 bullet to sporting purposes by making it open at the point and by other means elsewhere described.

ON THE CHOICE OF A SPORTING RIFLE.

With most sportsmen the occasions for firing a rifle at large game are comparatively few ; they will consider it false economy to purchase a cheap weapon, especially if such weapon is less efficient and likely to fail them when favourable opportunities for using the rifle occur.

In hunting large and dangerous game, it is better to be able to fire two shots in one second than to have four, or six, or a dozen available at intervals of two or three seconds each ; as a hunting weapon, or sporting weapon, the double rifle is superior to the magazine rifle, no matter on what principle the breech mechanism is constructed. The next point is, not to be underarmed ; that is to say, the weapon must be fully up to the maximum work it will be called upon to do. Either the ·450 or ·500 double Express is probably the best all-round weapon for general Indian shooting, although the importation of the former has for the time being been prohibited by the Indian Government ; if bison is likely to be met frequently the ·577 is preferable ; for, notwithstanding the heavy charge it takes, and the great velocity obtained, it is accurate at even long sporting ranges, as the following letter to the author testifies :—

" As regards the shooting qualities of the guns you made me, they were absolute perfection when I was fit and not shaky from fever. I could do as good shooting with either the ·450 or ·577 as I could with the ·300 or ·360. My best record was 25 buck and a pig, out of 27 shots (·577) ; pig badly wounded, got away ; otherwise I should have bagged 26 head game. My 16 hippopotami out of 17 shots is a matter of history in the Shire Highlands (·577 and hard bullets)."

Count Samuel Teleki says :—

" In my trip in Africa I killed 18 elephants with the ·577, 3 of these animals being killed with a single bullet each, shot in the head, at distances ranging from 90 to 100 yards ; 1 from 250 yards. My experience is that when it is necessary to shoot big game at fairly long range the ·577 is an invaluable weapon, and infinitely more valuable than a Winchester. In all, I killed 82 rhinoceri, 75 of them being bagged with the ·577 at various ranges ; I also bagged 84 buffaloes, some with the ·500, shooting the solid bullet, and nearly all the rest with the ·577 ; on one or two occasions the bullet went quite through the body of the animals. I have always found, in shooting big game, that the shock conveyed by the heavy bullet driven by a fairly large charge of powder is a most desirable feature in a rifle, and absolutely essential when shooting game at anything like close quarters."

Another sportsman writing to the *Field*, says :—

" At the time I was shooting best, in March, being strong and well, I bagged with the ·577 alone (a rifle weighing 10 lbs. 6 ozs.) 25 head of game, comprising buffalo, zebra, wart-hog, bush-pig, hippo, and lion, in 27 consecutive shots."

The 8-bore, owing to its great weight, has been discarded by many sportsmen in favour of the ·577, which is capable of good work, as the following extracts from Sir Samuel Baker's book testify :—

" The ·577 solid bullet of 650 grains and 6 drachms of powder will produce an astonishing effect, and will completely paralyse the attack of any lion or tiger, thus establishing a thorough confidence in the heart of its proprietor.

"A very large tiger may weigh 450 lbs. ; a ·577 bullet of 650 grains, propelled by 6 drachms of powder, has a striking energy of 3,520 foot-pounds. This may be only theoretical measurement, but the approximate superiority of 3,500 lbs. against a tiger's weight (450 lbs.) would be sufficient to ensure the stoppage of a charge or the collapse of the animal in any position, provided that the bullet should be retained within the body, and thus bestow the whole force of the striking energy."

The question of accuracy combined with a high degree of efficiency—that is, striking power and range—is obtainable in the " Express," if properly constructed and the right ammunition is used. It is not often that the "Express" is used at such distances as 300 yards, but that it is available at extreme sporting ranges is proved by the following extract from a letter to the author :—

" I have just made a bag with my ·450 ejector, killing 3 very fine markhor (mountain goats) in three shots at about 300, 250, and 180 yards. I must say it is a lovely rifle, and at sporting ranges, if held straight, never fails."

The following extracts may be accepted as trustworthy testimony of the value of ·303 from the sportsman's point of view :—

" The ·303 rifle I tried, and was very pleased with the result. I had a large shooting party out the day I tried it ; unfortunately, the day was very much against me—blowing ' great guns' as the Cape expression goes—but, notwithstanding, half the bag of the day fell to the ·303 Greener : namely, 23 out of 46 buck."
"GRAAFF REINET, 1893."

" We have received the six ·303 rifles and the cartridges ; they are most satisfactory. I tried mine, and made the largest bag in the shortest time on my record : viz., 11 bucks in an hour.
"J. R."

Extract from the " Kimberley Independent."

" A curious thing connected with the gun is that it has scarcely any recoil and but a slight report. The penetration is very great ; two shots fired at a heavy stinkwood post by Mr. A. J. Wright went right through, and left a hole as clean and unsplintered as if it had been made with a gimlet. At 200 and 300 yards the point-blank shooting was all that could be desired. At 400 yards Mr. Wright made 5 consecutive bulls ; at 500 yards he made 3 bulls and 1 centre ; at 800 yards, 2 centres and 1 bull. Time being short, the remaining trials were made without a marker ; but at 1,000, 1,500, and 1,800 yards Mr. Wright and Mr. Finlason succeeded in hitting the target five times out of six shots. In order to try the extreme ranges, four shots were fired at 2,500 yards, and Mr. Wright missed the target by only a couple of yards ; while Mr. Finlason highly astonished himself by dropping a bullet just over the target on to the mound. Half in jest, the party went back to Mr. Wright's house, and aimed at the Diamond Fields Horse cannon target ; and with the aid of a field-glass the bullets, on two occasions, were distinctly seen to strike over the target.　The distance is about 3,500 yards.　This is an extra-ordinary range for any rifle.　Exactly the same results were obtained from the Martini, which has been adapted to the magazine ·303 rifle cartridge.　The rifles were made by W. W. Greener."

As already stated, much depends upon the loading of the Express.　Mr. F. C. Selous, in his "Travel and Sport in South-East Africa," says that ·450 express bullets lighter than 360 grains should not be used for hartebeest, lions, and other similar game.　And again on the choice of a rifle—

"Should any of my readers acting on my advice determine to buy a ·450 rifle, let them be very careful about the kind of bullet they use.　For large game, long, heavy, solid bullets, and for large antelope and lions, the best kind of bullet is one weighing about 360 grains, with a small hollow point, good thick walls round the hollow part, and a heavy end.　Such a bullet will mushroom on striking an animal, but will also have great penetrating power.

The bore of the rifle will sometimes appear to be of less importance than the weight of the arm.　No one can use a heavy rifle effectively if he has also to carry it long distances ; and in countries where a gun bearer or attendant is not available, the weight of the arm will be of greater importance.　Unnecessary weight has long been a conspicuous cause of complaint against American rifles.

Mr. A. C. Gould writes of the American rifles :—

"There seems no good reason why a ·32 or ·38 calibre rifle, shooting 40 grains of powder, or even less, and a light bullet, should weigh nine or ten pounds, when six or seven is sufficient weight.　This, however, is one of the results of manufacturing rifles in quantity by machinery. A weight calculated to suit a majority of rifle-shooters (and that would probably mean target shooters) has generally been selected by manufacturers, and the rifles on that model would be of standard weight.　As target shooters, as a rule, prefer a heavier rifle than game shooters it has often been found difficult to find rifles light enough to satisfy those who hunt with a rifle. Recently several have been put on the market which are light, but it is a question if they are not as objectionable as the excessively heavy ones ; for, in order to avoid unpleasant recoil, they are charged with pistol cartridges, and the bullets made to fit the barrels so loosely as to almost drop through the barrel.　By use of such ammunition the recoil is reduced, but certain desirable features are sacrificed."

Surely nothing could more eloquently express the dilemma in which the American sportsman is fixed by having to take a hunting rifle which is inadequate, or over-burden himself with a target rifle which is little better.

It has already been stated that none of the American rifles are so powerful as the English ·500 Express, but there are weapons of the same bore, and of those the weights are excessive for double rifles, although the Americans are single, with or without a magazine.　At the Trajectory Trial rifles of the following weights were entered : ·400 calibres —11 lbs. 1 oz., 10 lbs. 3½ ozs., 10 lbs. 6 ozs. ; ·450 calibres— 10 lbs. 8 ozs., 10 lbs. 3 ozs., 9 lbs. 11 ozs. ; ·500 calibres, with the exception of a military musket and one of 8 lbs. 11 ozs., no magazine, all were over 10 lbs.

The trajectories of the American expresses were nearly twice as high as of the English ·450, against which they were tested.

At the *Field* Rifle Trials, London, 1883, as reported, the ·450 bore diagram at 50 yards showed in ten shots, five from each barrel, a mean deviation of 1·032 ; the winning rifle had a mean deviation of 1·132 at this range, 1·318 at 100 yards, 1·449 at 150 yards. A ·500 bore at 100 yards had a mean deviation of 1·004 inch only, yet its muzzle velocity was 1,946 feet, the average trajectory 1·79 at 25 yards, 3·01 at 50, 3·58 at 75, 3·36 at 100, and 2·23 at 120 yards. When a rifle of this power, weighing only 8¼ lbs., is proved capable of giving a force at impact at 100 yards of 1,867 foot-pounds, and with a charge of 138 grains and a bullet of 342 puts five consecutive shots from each barrel within a square 2 × 2·8 inches, it seems unnecessary to seek for a better sporting weapon for the general purposes of large game shooting, for this rifle comes nearer the ideal than any yet proposed or produced.

Compare it, first with the American hunting rifles, taking as the best that proposed by Mr. Gould in "American Rifles," the ·45-·75 Winchester, with a 330 grain bullet. He states that the most satisfactory results were obtained with this charge, but does not give any figures or diagrams ; the same make of rifle was, however, tested at the Forest and Stream Creedmoor Trials in 1885, with a bullet only 20 grains heavier, and the trajectory was—50 yards, 8·592 ; 100 yards, 11·979 ; 150 yards, 9·359. Major Hinman, in Mr. Gould's book, gives the trajectory as 11·4 at 100 yards, which is only fractionally lower ; no velocities are given.

A test of the ·450 calibre Winchester, with a powder charge of 90 grains and a solid bullet of 200 grains, was made at a London shooting-ground in December, 1893 ; the results, as published in the *Field* of December 9th, showed that the muzzle velocity obtained was 1,527 feet, at 200 yards 1,051 feet, energy at muzzle therefore 1,557 foot-pounds, at 200 yards 738 foot-pounds, being thus greatly inferior to the ordinary English Express of ·450 gauge, with 110 grains and 320-grain bullets, which gives 1,776 feet muzzle velocity, 1,218 at 200 yards, energy at muzzle 2,254 foot-pounds, and at 200 yards 1,066 foot-pounds.

It is, of course, possible to secure better results for special work by permitting an excess of one feature and sacrificing others ; and in the American rifle, as a sporting weapon, too much appears to have been sacrificed to accuracy, possibly because, as Mr. Gould states, "I believe fully twenty shots are fired at an inanimate target to one at game."

In order to show that accuracy is not all that the sportsman finds essential in the sporting rifle, the following account, for the truth of which the author can vouch, unmistakably proves :— .

"A short time ago I had an extraordinary experience when shooting fallow-deer from a position up a tree with a ·44 Winchester rifle. I selected an animal for my mark on the outside of a herd some 40 yards away, the only point offered being behind the left ear. My aim was perfectly true, the bullet striking the root of the ear and passing down under the brain cavity and out under the right eye ; this was a good shot, but it failed to bring the doe down. A second shot, taken a short time afterwards, struck behind the right ear, taking exactly the same direction corresponding with the first shot, until it met the course of the first bullet, which it adopted, passing out of the same hole under the right eye. After chasing the herd for an hour and a half, the doe, dropping out, gave an opportunity for another shot, which was taken at the neck, behind the ears ; the bullet passed through the muscles above the spinal column, taking away a piece of the bone. The fourth, a side-shot, struck through the tear hole (an inch below the eyes).

"The fifth hit low in the neck. This at last brought her to the ground, enabling me to get up to her and complete my work with a knife.

"I was afterwards asked why I did not try the shoulder shot. In the first place, behind the ears was the only mark offered ; and, secondly, I had previously taken a shot with the same rifle at a doe, which struck only three inches behind the heart, and it was not until after a two hours' run that this animal was secured."

The skull showing traces of the bullets was, for a time, in the author's keeping. This shooter then discarded the Winchester for an Express ·450. He gives the following respecting its performance :—

"At a doe going away, at a distance of 50 yards, aim was taken between the ears ; the bullet carried away about three or four inches of the top of skull, exposing the brain and killing instantly.

"Another curious shot demonstrates the value of velocity : a deer, in the act of jumping, was struck by a 450 Express bullet just below the knees, which knocked off both legs at the joints, leaving the upper sides of the joints as though severed with a knife."

This correspondent has since had much experience in deer-shooting, and affirms that he never had occasion to fire a second shot at a deer with a ·450 Express. Neither does he remember seeing a deer hit with a ·450 bullet run more than 20 yards before falling.

Mr. Gould thinks that the double Express rifle is not sufficiently accurate for the requirements of the American sportsman. The rifle trials, made more than ten years ago, demonstrated the possibilities of this description of arm ; and it must be remembered that although Mr. Lincoln Jeffreys, with his ·500 bore, giving nearly 2,000 feet velocity, and such wonderful shooting at 100 yards, was unable to get equally satisfactory results at 150, another rifle, giving a velocity of 1,784 feet, got all ten consecutive shots within a square 4·7 × 6 at the longer range.

Long ago it was discovered that a high trajectory was undesirable in hunting rifles, because the shooter is called upon to shoot at once, without having time to arrange sights or calculate fine allowances for wind or elevation ; and the "Express" rifle, with its flat trajectory, having what is commonly termed "a long point-blank range," being therefore *more* accurate at unknown ranges than the slower target or military rifle, and exerting also greater force at impact within sporting ranges than other types of weapon, enjoys the popularity it merits among sportsmen who have had opportunities of testing it thoroughly.

Sportsmen unhesitatingly pronounced in favour of the ·303 with its high velocity, low trajectory, and immense striking force (with soft-nosed bullets) for all large game shooting, but, unfortunately, the weapon is too delicate for every-day work, and has disappointed gunmakers and sportsmen alike. In the first place the strain is so great that no metal will stand repeated firing without giving way. Even in the military weapon it is not unusual for the chambers to enlarge; then the cartridge cases cannot be extracted. Another frequent cause for complaint is that the breech-block is indented. The chamber is then too long, and with successive firing is quickly extended until the breech shoe is injured by the escape of gas, due to the enlargement of the chamber near the extractor. Unless kept absolutely clean, the strain is increased and the barrel will bulge—probably at or near the muzzle—or the breech action will give way; or, still more rarely, the breech action and barrel will give way simultaneously. The ·303 rifle has but a short life; in tropical climates, where possibly the explosive is affected by the heat, it gives way soonest. It is not a matter of faulty design or poor workmanship, but solely that the metal used is inadequate to the immense strains to which it is subjected, and it is most important that the cartridges be only obtained through a gunmaker who is in a position to test them for himself, and who can state that the powder is made to the Government specification, and only gives pressures within the limits laid down for the cordite to be used in Government rifles. The rifles issued from the Government factories, like those made by private firms, are liable to bulge in the barrel at any part of its length, but more particularly, perhaps, near the muzzle. The rifle should be thoroughly cleaned as soon after it has been used as is possible, then cleaned again a few hours after. These two cleanings may not be sufficient; a used rifle should be examined carefully day by day to see that it is without stain, and be kept perfectly clean. If these precautions be taken, and every care used in handling the rifle, the ·303 is quite the best all-round weapon made in England; but as to lasting qualities, it is so far inferior to rifles of ordinary sporting type that two weapons should invariably be taken instead of the one that used to be all-sufficient for the hunter and explorer.

THE SPORTING RANGE FOR GAME SHOOTING.

Most large game is shot at very close quarters, thirty to fifty yards as a rule, sometimes much nearer. Mr. A. Haggard writes of Count Teleki, the noted

African hunter, that his method of shooting was "to induce the animal to charge, to charge in return, step aside on meeting the animal, and fire into the neck at barely a foot distance." This plan has been followed by other African hunters, and all familiar with the books treating of large game hunting in Africa, will remember that the ranges at which most shooting was done were very short. Colonel Sanderson, of the Indian Elephant Keddahs at Decca, in his "Thirteen Years among the Wild Beasts of India," gives evidence of the same practice. Captain Forsyth says of jungle shooting : "One-half at least are shot at under fifty yards, three-fourths under seventy-five yards, and all, without exception, under 100 yards." On the hills a shot at 150 yards may sometimes be made, but the proposition to utilise the extreme long-range ·303 Lee-Speed military rifle for game shooting in India has been strenuously opposed by Anglo-Indian sportsmen, who contend that the additional range is disadvantageous. So in the far East, Annam, Siam, Java, Borneo, Sumatra, the thick jungle does not admit of firing at long ranges, and in the clearings the use of the long-range rifle is likely to prove a source of danger. In Europe bear are often shot at a few feet ; at deer and boar drives on the Continent the range is usually less than fifty yards, and even for deer-stalking in Scotland, a shot at more than 150 or 200 yards was rarely risked before the introduction of the ·303.

In America very little game is shot at even 200 yards. Mr. T. S. Van Dyke, in the "Still Hunter" (page 317), writes :—

"My rule has been to shoot at nothing beyond 150 yards, if there is an even chance of getting closer to it, and not to shoot even that far if there is a fair prospect of shortening the distance. I fully believe I have gotten more deer by it. I certainly know that there have been fewer broken-legged cripples. For deer and antelope on the plains another fifty yards might be added to this distance ; for elk another fifty. Beyond this point you had better make it a rule to get closer."

So Mr. A. C. Gould, in "Modern American Rifles" (page 116) :—

"In many sections most of the game is killed within a range of 100 yards ; but it is also a fact the cariboo, in the barrens of Maine and New Brunswick, are often shot at a distance beyond 250 yards, and antelope on our plains are many times killed from 200 yards upward. I have seen antelope killed with a shot gun, but my experience and the testimony of others lead me to believe that more of these animals are shot at a range of over than under 200 yards. The bighorn and mountain goat are often shot at a long range, but the Virginia deer and moose are chiefly killed within 100 yards."

In South Africa, on the open veldt, the larger antelope are not infrequently shot at a long distance—upwards of 500 yards—but the shooter usually prepares by dismounting, carefully estimating the distance, choosing an appropriate elevation by raising the correct flap sight, and then, if not taking quite as much care and acting as deliberately as if firing at the butts of the local rifle club, the hunter adopts practically the methods of long-range target shooting.

CHAPTER XXVIII.

SINGLE-SHOT MILITARY RIFLES.

HISTORICAL NOTE ON MILITARY BREECH-LOADERS.

THE value of the breech-loading principle, as applied to the infantry rifle, was proved in the Prussian Wars of 1864 and 1866, in the American Civil War, and unmistakably corroborated by the Franco-Prussian War of 1870. European Governments, in their hurry to arm their regiments with breech-loaders, and not wishing to discard as useless the large stocks of muzzle-loading rifles but recently made, determined to convert them. Possibly, therefore, some of the systems thus used and made famous were not the highest development of the breech-loader at that date, but were the best suited to the need of the various Governments at the time. In England it was the Snider system which was employed, and subsequently many thousand new rifles were made on that principle. In France the Tabatière was its equivalent, but this soon gave place to the Chassepot; in Russia a very similar mechanism was used for the same purpose. From the American Civil War until the adoption of the Lebel repeating rifle by France in 1888 the breech-loading systems in use were not modified so much because of the faults or qualities they possessed, but the changes were wrought by improvements in the barrel and ammunition, and, when forced to adopt a smaller bore rifle, the Governments availed themselves of the opportunity to use whichever system of breech-loading offered the greatest advantages; but it is doubtful whether, prior to the Lebel, any change would have been made solely on account of better qualities possessed by any particular breech-loading mechanism.

The lines upon which breech-loading systems applicable to single rifles have developed are so diverse that classification by rule is barely possible, and to enumerate them in chronological order would be confusing. To give an adequate idea of the multiform changes the various mechanisms have undergone is beyond the scope of this work; and the author, to make the most of the space at his disposal, is forced to tabulate much information and pass by many inventions without comment.

Further to economise space the particulars given are often scanty, but by dealing at greater length with at least one type of each group, the author hopes to give a more complete idea of their general characteristics than would be possible by simply cataloguing the arms available for description.

Roughly, the military weapons will be dealt with in the following order :—First, the mechanisms of the simple breech-loading rifles adopted by the British Government; those of some of the foreign armies; and then other mechanisms which have attained some renown; magazine and repeating rifles in their historical order; and lastly automatic firearms.

THE SNIDER MECHANISM.

The success of the Prussian "needle-gun" in the 1864 Danish War led to the appointment of a special Committee to decide upon the best means for arming the British infantry with a breech-loader, and to avoid delay it was determined to convert the Enfield muskets. Of the fifty different mechanisms submitted for trial the Snider was deemed the best suited for the purpose, and in 1867 it was adopted with a metallic central-fire cartridge-case adapted by Colonel Boxer, of Woolwich.

The Snider Cavalry Carbine.

About two inches of the upper part of the breech-end of the Enfield barrel is cut away at the top, for the admission of the cartridge and bullet, which are pushed forward by the thumb into a taper chamber, formed by slightly enlarging the barrel at the breech. The space behind the cartridge is closed by a solid iron breech-block, hinged upon the right side of the barrel, and is opened by lifting sideways by the thumb of the right hand. The block forms a false breech and receives the recoil from the base of the cartridge. A piston or striker passes through this breech-block, the point being flush with the face of the breech and immediately opposite the cap of the cartridge, and a blow from the hammer upon its other end —which projects above the breech and is kept in position by a sloping nipple— drives it forward and strikes the cap with sufficient force to explode the cartridge.

The empty cartridge-case is withdrawn by a claw extractor attached to the breech-block, which, when open, is drawn back with it about half an inch. The cartridge-case is brought entirely out of the barrel, and by turning the rifle sideways the empty case falls to the ground. A spiral spring fitted upon the hinge-rod takes the block and the extractor back into position.

This principle of breech-loading cannot claim any particular originality; many specimens, similar in construction, may be seen in museums of ancient arms. The success of this mechanism was due to the adoption of the metallic form of cartridge; for only a perfectly gas-tight cartridge would answer. The first Snider rifles submitted took a pasteboard cartridge with a metallic base on the central-fire

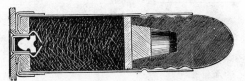

Boxer Cartridge, used in the Snider Rifle.

or " Pottet " principle, similar to those now used in sporting breech-loaders. This cartridge was not exactly suited to this particular weapon, but it proved to the Committee that a cartridge containing its own ignition, and being at the same time thoroughly gas-tight, was preferable to all others. Having decided to adopt the Snider, the experts turned their attention to the cartridge, and referred the matter to Colonel Boxer, of the Royal Laboratory, who, after many experiments, succeeded in producing a cartridge so well adapted for this rifle that it made it a decided success. No greater proof of the advantage of the breech-loading principle could be adduced. Using practically the same charge of powder and the same ball, it converted a weapon, notorious for its ill shooting, into one that at the shorter ranges can hardly be beaten for accuracy by even the most modern rifle.

THE MARTINI-HENRY RIFLE.

The British army being temporarily provided for by the conversion of the Enfield to Sniders, the Committee in 1867 were free to decide upon the merits of rival systems submitted as suitable for the new arm. Previous competitive trials showed that in the manufacture of arms of this class less attention had been given to the accuracy of shooting than to the mechanism for closing the breech. The rifles which shot best were of ·577, ·500, and ·451 calibres ; but, as these did not attain to that standard of accuracy demanded, the work was divided. The barrel was considered apart from the breech mechanism, and *vice versâ ;* the former confined to the barrels which had performed best in preliminary trials, the latter open to world-wide competition.

In 1869 the Committee reported, recommending a combination of the block breech-mechanism submitted by Mr. Martini, and as modified at the Enfield factory, and the ·450 barrel of Mr. Henry, to be used with Boxer cartridge cases and a

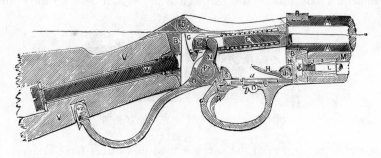

The Martini-Henry Breech-loader and its Parts.

AA Barrel.	J Rod and fore-end holder.	R Trigger.
BB Body.	K Rod and fore-end holder	S Tumbler-rest.
CC Block.	screw.	T Trigger and rest axis-pin.
D Block axis-pin.	L Ramrod.	U Trigger and rest-spring.
E Striker.	M Stock, fore-end.	V Stock-butt.
F Main-spring.	N Tumbler.	W Stock-bolt washer.
G Stop-nut.	O Lever.	Z Lever catch-bolt spring and
H Extractor.	P Lever and tumbler axis-pin.	a Locking-bolt. [pin.
I Extractor axis-pin.	Q Trigger-plate and guard.	b Thumb-piece.

bullet of 480 grains. The arm was definitely adopted in April, 1871, the twenty-two pattern rifles issued in October, 1870, having proved satisfactory.

Since this arm was adopted by the English Government as the national arm it has been much improved, and is now an efficient weapon—one of the best non-repeating mechanisms.

It is actuated by depressing the lever O with the thumb ; this opens the breech by lowering the hinged breech block, the fired case being automatically ejected as soon as the breech block falls upon the arm H of the extractor. At the same time the rifle is cocked, and, a fresh cartridge being inserted and the lever returned to its place, the rifle is ready for firing.

The barrel is 33 inches long, rifled upon Henry's principle, consisting of seven grooves, ·03 inch of the original bore being left between each groove as lands, and, as shown in the figure, the lands and the *centres* of the grooves are contained in the same circle. The twist is right-handed, uniform, one turn in 22 inches, the grooves ·009 deep at breech, ·007 at muzzle; weight of rifle, 8 lbs. 10 ozs.

The bottle-necked cartridge was a later development by the ordnance factories, the long taper case used in the first 200 trial weapons not being wholly satisfactory. The charge is 85 grains, the bullet 480 grains, ·450 inch in diameter, 1·27 inch in

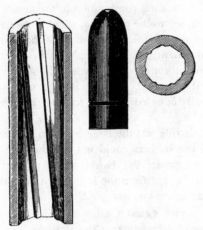

The Henry Rifling and Bullet.

length, and the cartridge over all 3·15 inches in length, and a bundle of ten weighs 1 lb. 2 ozs. if of coiled brass, 2¼ ozs. heavier if solid.

The Martini-Henry carbine has a 22-inch barrel, and the charge used with it is 70 grains in the coiled case, 65 grains in the solid case, the bullet weighing 410 grains and being 1·115 inch in length, the cartridge 2·98 over all. In a later pattern the bore was reduced to ·400 bore, and some thousands of rifles were so made. It was given up shortly after, on account of the decision to adopt a magazine arm, when a still smaller bore was also considered necessary.

THE PRUSSIAN NEEDLE-GUN.

This gun, which did such wonderful service in the wars of 1866 and 1870, was invented by Herr Dreyse, of Sommerda, in 1838, and adopted by the Prussian Army in 1842. The mechanism is of the "door-bolt" principle ; but in the earliest guns the first movement was to withdraw the needle and cock the gun by pulling out the striker by the stud at the breech extremity of the bolt, an action performed automatically in later patterns. The knob or lever-handle of the bolt is then grasped, lifted over to the left, and drawn backwards, so as to leave a sufficient opening to receive the cartridge ; by reversing this motion the cartridge is pushed forward, and the rifle is then ready for firing. The bolt is hollow ; it contains the spiral spring and needle from which the gun derives its name, and by which the explosion of the charge is effected. By pulling the trigger this needle is released and shoots forward into a patch of detonating composition in the centre of the cartridge. The bullet is enclosed in a papier-mâché envelope, which answers the purpose of a wad, being about a quarter of an inch thick at the base of the bullet. The bore is 16 or ·660. The patch of detonating powder is placed in the rear of the wad. The needle, therefore, passed through the powder charge within, and became not only rapidly fouled and corroded, but not infrequently was broken. The solid cartridge was subsequently adopted and the form of breech-mechanism developed into that of the Mauser.

The worst fault of this rifle was the large escape of gas at the breech, which was so great that it is said the soldiers could not fire the rifle from the shoulder after the first few shots ; for when the barrel was foul and the strain increased the men were obliged to fire it from the hip. Its range was about 400 yards, but even at 200 yards the accuracy was not good.

THE FRENCH CHASSEPOT RIFLE.

This arm is in principle the same as the Prussian needle-gun, but is certainly an improvement both in the action and barrel. The piece is cocked by the thumb as is the needle-gun ; and the bolt then turned one-quarter of a circle to the left, and drawn back ; the cartridge is put in and pushed home by the bolt, whose face is furnished with an indiarubber washer to prevent the escape of gas. This bolt is turned one-quarter of a circle to the right, and the piece is then ready for firing. The cartridge is ignited by a cap at the base ; the needle enters the cap, which is so placed that the opening is towards the breech ; thus the needle strikes the inside of the cap instead of the outside. The Chassepot barrel is ·434 calibre, made of steel, and takes a charge of 85 grains, and a solid conical bullet of 380 grains. The bullet for the Chassepot is larger than the bore of the barrel, is driven through it, and thus fills up the grooves, preventing windage. This causes great friction, and the barrel also leads very quickly; the bullet leaves the barrel nearly square, which is a bad form for any projectile, although it was

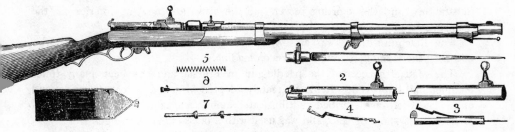

The Prussian Needle-gun.

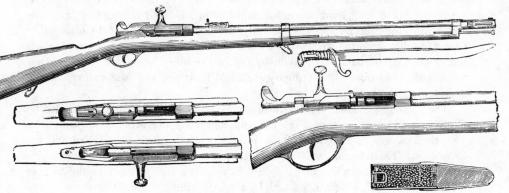

The French Chassepot.

claimed that the rifle had an extreme range of 1,800 yards. The rifling is four deep grooves, with one turn to the left in each $21\frac{3}{4}$ inches. The cartridge was self-consuming and the breech-action fouled quickly; there was found to be much difficulty in loading in consequence, and not a few accidents resulted. Subsequently the rifle was converted to take a metallic gas-tight cartridge-case.

MISCELLANEOUS SYSTEMS FOR RIFLES.

Little interest attaches to most of the mechanisms of military rifles which have fallen into desuetude, and no useful purpose would be served by here describing them in detail. Only a few need any explanation other than is conveyed in the illustrations, and the sporting powers of the arms are now as inferior as the mechanisms, and therefore call for no particular mention.

The Braendlin-Albini was an English mechanism used by the Belgians, who also used the Comblain system of breech-loading.

The Mauser succeeded the needle-gun in Prussia, and has been many times modified and improved. It was ultimately adopted for use as a repeating rifle, and in this latest form is described and illustrated among magazine rifles. The original Mauser was 60-bore or ·420, and was used with a brass-drawn cartridge.

The Roberts system of breech-loading was adopted by the United States Government for converting the Springfield muzzle-loading rifle. The mechanism consists of an iron frame or shoe screwed on to the barrel. The breech-block is placed in this shoe, and works upon an elbow-joint. The block is extended backwards, forming a lever lying along the grip of the gun. By raising this lever, the front part of the breech-block is sufficiently depressed as to admit of the insertion of a short cartridge into the barrel. The extractor is a curved lever fixed on the left side of the chamber and acted upon by the breech-block when it descends below the cartridge chamber. An ordinary lock and firing-pin are used to explode the cartridge.

The Russian Berdan is of American origin ; it was subsequently superseded by the Krnka, and that, in turn, has been supplanted by the Monzai magazine rifle. The Berdan is a combination of the principles of the Braendlin-Albini and the Chassepot. There is a hinged block which turns over the barrel and extracts the cartridge-case. It is locked in position for firing by a bolt resembling the cock of the Chassepot. The lock is worked by a spiral spring. The blow given by the locking-bolt is communicated to a striker working in the breech-block.

The Werndl rifle, so long used in Austria, is on the block system ; the breech-block being hinged below the bore of the barrel ; by turning the breech-block to the left with the thumb it opens to allow of the cartridge being inserted, as shown in the illustration (page 710). The bore originally was 13·9 mm., reduced to 10·7 or ·420 in 1867, and used with a solid brass-drawn cartridge. It has been supplanted by the Mannlicher repeater in the Austro-Hungarian army.

The Peabody, an American invention, was one of the first with a drop-block

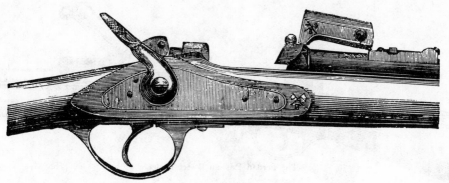

The Braendlin-Albini.

The Mauser Rifle.

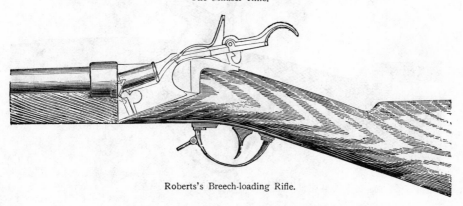

Roberts's Breech-loading Rifle.

The Berdan Russian Breech-loader.

The Austrian Werndl Breech-loader.

The Werndl Cartridge.

The Peabody Breech-loading Rifle.

hinged at the rear. The mechanism was fully tested by the Ordnance Board of the United States, and the rifle was subsequently adopted for use in the Turkish army and the forces of some of the South-Eastern principalities. It is still used in Europe side by side with the ordinary English Martini, the Remington, and other systems.

SOME EARLY AMERICAN SYSTEMS.

The first rifle manufactured by the American Government at Harper's Ferry, where the first arms made upon the interchangeable principle were produced, is of sufficient interest to warrant its illustration. It is a muzzle-loading, flint-lock rifle, and is contemporary with the English " Brown Bess " musket.

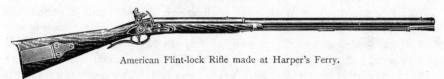

American Flint-lock Rifle made at Harper's Ferry.

The Sharp carbine was one of the earliest and best known of the American breech-loaders; it was used with success by the United States army in Mexico, and also during the Civil War. This breech-loader was at first used with a made-up linen cartridge, ignited by a percussion cap, and afterwards by an improved magazine primer, called " Maynard's." This was placed in front of the cock, and worked by the hammer in the act of cocking. This increased the rapidity of the arm: it could be fired ten times per minute. The breech-action is a dropping-block; by pressing downwards the trigger-guard, which is fitted with a hinge-joint,

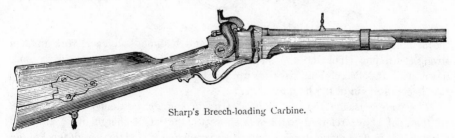

Sharp's Breech-loading Carbine.

the breech-block is depressed, and allows the cartridge to be inserted in the chamber, the top edge of which is sharpened, so as to cut off the end of the cartridge, and expose the powder to the igniting flash which passes through the block. This breech-loader was submitted to the American Board of Ordnance at Washington, in November, 1850, who declared it to be superior to any other arm loading at the breech that had up to that date been submitted to them.

Some of the English cavalry were also supplied with Sharp's carbine in 1857, but it was found objectionable on account of the escape of gas at the breech. To such an extent did it escape that it would burn through a handkerchief if tied round the breech-joint. There is no arrangement to prevent this escape, which, if not dangerous, is most inconvenient, the liability to clogging making it difficult to load after a number of shots have been fired. The Sharp's Company afterwards improved this arm by making it take a metallic central-fire cartridge.

THE REMINGTON RIFLE.

This rifle was tried at Wimbledon as long ago as 1866, and attracted considerable attention at that time, in consequence of the extraordinary rapidity with which it was loaded and fired : as many as fifty-one shots were discharged within three minutes. Many patterns of this rifle exist; the original has been much modified, but its characteristics have never been lost. The mechanism consists essentially of two pieces, one being the breech-piece and extractor, and the other

Mechanism of the Remington Rifle.

the hammer breech-bolt. This breech-piece and hammer-bolt each work upon a strong centre-pin. The letter A shows the breech-piece, closed; B C, the hammer down, with the breech-bolt backing up the breech-piece; D, the spring, holding the breech-piece until the hammer falls.

The bore is usually 500, but it is also made 450 for bottle-necked cartridges. At the trial above referred to, it was shot with the small charge of $1\frac{1}{2}$ dram of powder. It is now made to take a much larger charge (85 grains) and the Berdan cartridge. The breech arrangement is simple, but lacks solidity. The method of holding the breech-block up to the barrel is quite original, but it can scarcely be considered truly scientific, as the breech-piece should receive its support from immediately behind the cartridge.

Other mechanisms which attained considerable popularity in the United States, as the Maynard, Ballard, and Whitney, did not receive sufficient support from military experts to lead to their adoption as service weapons, and their use as breech-mechanisms for sporting rifles is not likely to continue now that the bolt and automatic repeating arms are rapidly growing in favour.

SOME ENGLISH MECHANISMS.

The adoption of the Martini principle by the British Government undoubtedly tempted the inventive genius of the English gunmakers to follow generally the principle of the service arm in designing new mechanisms. The Swinburn, for instance, is almost identical with the Martini, the chief difference being the use of the ordinary **V** mainspring for the spiral spring of the Martini. Where the mechanisms departed radically from the Martini type was in the substitution of a sliding for a hinged block; some gunmakers, as Westley-Richards and Field, had rifles of each type, and the Birmingham and London gun-makers usually chose whichever breech mechanism they deemed best adapted to the purpose they had in view when choosing an action for a sporting weapon. None of the mechanisms were to any extent used for military purposes.

THE HENRY BREECH-LOADING RIFLE.

This rifle resembles the Sharp carbine, already described and illustrated; the breech is closed by a sliding vertical block, which, for the admission of the cartridge, is depressed by a lever underneath the trigger-guard. The only difference between the two principles is, the former has the lever and trigger-guard in one piece, and the latter has a separate lever fitting over the trigger-guard.

Mr. Henry improved this breech-loader by making it hammerless, and fitting an extractor similar to the Martini, retaining the same breech-block, but dispensing with the side-lock. This reduced the movements to the same number as the Martini. The barrel of this rifle can be cleaned from the breech-end, which is a great advantage, and it can be made any bore.

THE FIELD MECHANISM.

This breech-loading mechanism is made on two distinct plans: in one the breech-block slides downward, as in the Sharp and Henry; in the other it is hinged, as in the Martini, but is actuated by a side lever, as shown.

The chief point in which the mechanism differs from other single breech-actions is that the lever, which is upon the right-hand side, is pushed forward to depress the breech-block and raise the hammer. From the illustration of the section of the mechanism it will be seen that the centre of the hammer-pivot is immediately behind that of the action-lever pivot, so that the projecting breast of the hammer may rest upon a toe or small cam projecting from the action-lever pivot. The block is depressed by a two-armed cam placed upon the action-lever pivot. A stud upon the extremity of each of the arms of the cam engages with a

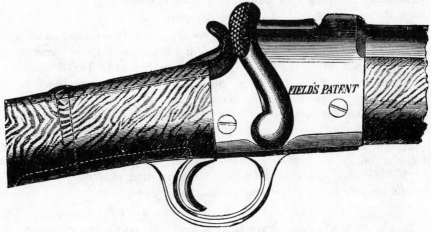

The Field Rifle.

diagonal slot on each side of the breech-block. Upon the action-lever being pushed forward, the arms of the cam also move forward, and the studs, running up

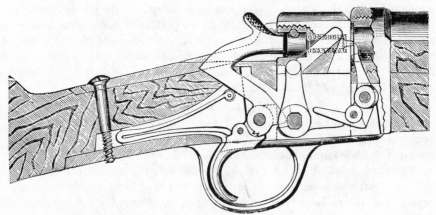

Section of the Field Rifle.—Sliding-block Pattern.

the diagonal slots, depress the breech-block. The hammer is raised at the same time by the toe on the action-lever raising the breast of the cock until the scear slips into full-cock. When closed, the breech-block is propped up by the armed cam. The sliding block possesses the great advantage of ready access to the barrel for inspection or cleaning; the action-lever, too, is easily manipulated, and the mechanism has proved efficient in arms of all sizes from ·320 to ·577 Express.

THE WESTLEY-RICHARDS SLIDING-BLOCK RIFLE.

This breech-action, the joint production of Messrs. Deeley and Edge, has been, and is, extensively used in match rifles, for which type of arm it is well suited, although originally intended for a military weapon.

The Westley-Richards Sliding-block Rifle.

The mechanism consists of a vertically-sliding breech-block, which contains the tumbler, main-spring, and other lock work. The guard and lever are in one, and are pivoted to the body of the action, beneath the barrel. By depressing the guard the breech-block descends, as in the Henry carbine, the hammer—or rather tumbler—cocked, and the cartridge extracted.

It possesses a signal advantage over the Martini and Swinburn by allowing the barrel to be cleaned from the breech—certainly always a convenience, and a desideratum in match rifles.

CHAPTER XXIX.

EARLY REPEATING RIFLE MECHANISMS.

NOTE ON MAGAZINE ARMS.

No part of the mechanism of any arm is more distinctly modern than the magazine and feeding mechanism of the latest repeating arms. To fire shot after shot from the one barrel, commencing with that nearest the muzzle, is, as has been shown, an idea almost as old as the hand-gun ; but in the modern repeating breech-loader the ammunition is taken from a magazine which may be replenished by one movement, and in some of the latest arms the mechanism is worked automatically by utilising the force of the recoil, or other similar means.

In describing these weapons the following arrangement is followed :—The early breech-loading arms are placed first in their chronological order; the varieties of the Winchester target and sporting weapons are also included. Next are described and illustrated the newest repeating rifles of the leading Governments, and the repeating arm when considered as a military weapon. This section is followed by descriptions of one or two specimens of modern repeating mechanisms, which, by reason of their simplicity or other qualities, merit attention, although they have not been definitely adopted as the mechanism for any service weapon. The section concludes with some illustrations of the automatic repeating mechanisms—a system of breech-loading which will probably be employed in the future.

REPEATING OR MAGAZINE RIFLES.

The Spencer appears to have been the first successful breech-loading magazine rifle ; it was patented in the United States in 1860. The illustration represents the original model, with the magazine in the butt. To load, the muzzle is pointed downwards, the magazine lock is turned to the right, the inner magazine tube is withdrawn, the cartridges are dropped into the outer magazine, ball foremost, then the tube is inserted and locked. There is a spiral spring fitted in the magazine, which forces the cartridges up to the breech-chamber. The first cartridge is forced forward into the chamber of the barrel by moving the guard-lever downwards, as shown by the engraving, and immediately drawing it back. It can be loaded with the hammer down, but should be kept at half-cock while the cartridge remains in the chamber. To fire, bring the hammer to full-cock, and, by pulling the trigger, it strikes the percussion slide, forcing it against the rim of the cartridge, and exploding it. The discharged shell is withdrawn by the opening motion; there is a carrier-block that moves the shell-drawer over the cartridge guide, which is then depressed by a spring. This same guide aids in conducting the new cartridge to the chamber. It can be fired seven times in ten seconds, but only fifteen times in one minute; it

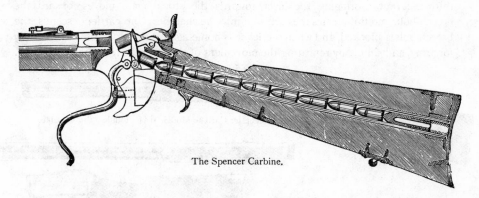

The Spencer Carbine.

can also be used as an ordinary breech-loader. Subsequently the rifle was modified to use a central-fire case and to cock automatically. In the Civil War it was used with success, one man so armed being considered equal to seven using muzzle-loaders. It was liable to explode in the magazine, and was superseded by the Winchester.

THE HENRY REPEATING RIFLE.

This arm chiefly differed from the Spencer in having the cartridge magazine under the barrel; it was the precursor of the better-known "Winchester," and was used in the American Civil War by the Federals with considerable success. Its speed is said to have been thirty shots a minute, and it was the earliest rifle in which the simple motion of the lever extracted the fired case, cocked the lock, reloaded the gun, and closed the breech.

THE "WINCHESTER" RIFLES.

The original Winchester closely resembled the Henry; the form of the cartridge extractor and the working of the magazine were the most noticeable differences.

In the earlier patterns the magazine tube is under the barrel, the cartridges are put in from the breech, point first, and a coiled spring in the tube forces them back towards the breech, and so into position in the "carrier." The action of depressing the lever unlocks, then withdraws, the breech-bolt, causing it to slide back in a direct line with the barrel; its rear extremity engages with the hammer and forces that into full-cock, and its fore extremity has an extractor by which the fired case is gripped and so withdrawn. Further travel of the action lever raises the carrier until it is in line with the barrel and its top sides have raised the empty case and thrown it out. Bringing the lever towards the stock again moves forward the breech-bolt, and this pushes the cartridge into the chamber; the carrier descends, the breech-bolt is blocked, and when the lever is home against the stock the rifle is ready for firing, and simply by repeating the movement of the lever the reloading is effected.

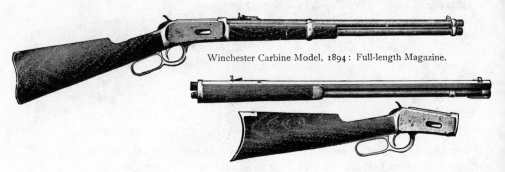

Winchester Carbine Model, 1894 : Full-length Magazine.

In the hands of an expert the Winchester is very quick, and, as some of the long magazines contain as many as twenty shots, the advantages the arm possesses over all single-loaders are considerable.

The disadvantages are—with rim-fire ammunition, the possibility of accidental discharge in the magazine; with central-fire cartridges, the feebleness of the powder-charge and shot load, and the slight leverage available to extract a bad cartridge.

In the 1894 model the breech-bolt is not only stronger, and so better fitted to withstand the strain of heavier charges, but it is locked by a bolt sliding up and down in the action frame, and having a firm bedding both on sides and at the rear. Greater leverage is obtained for extracting, the carrier is of an improved type, and the weapon is in every way more efficient. The improvements of details are numerous, covered by many patents, and, although outwardly the type is little changed, the principle upon which the various parts of the mechanism are worked is quite different from that employed in the early patterns.

The Winchester is also made as a "take-down" rifle; that is, the barrel and

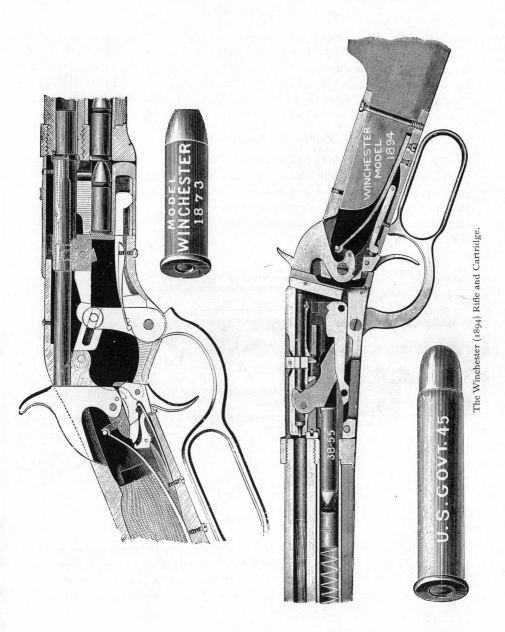

The Winchester (1894) Rifle and Cartridge.

magazine tube are detachable from the stock and breech-action, and are locked in place by a simple device. The various models of the "Winchester" rifle, and particulars of the ammunition which may be used with them, are enumerated in the table given on page 688. Two of the best-known patterns are illustrated, and the cartridges shown are of the exact size, and will give some idea of the magazine capacity requisite for several shots.

THE COLT "LIGHTNING" RIFLE.

The Colt rifle differs from the Winchester chiefly in the substitution of a straight pull slide for the hinged action-lever. Instead of depressing and raising the lever the left hand, gripping the fore-end, is brought towards the breech, to open and cock the gun, and is pushed out towards the muzzle to close the mechanism. Other parts of lock, and carrier work also, widely differ from the Winchester, as shown in the illustration.

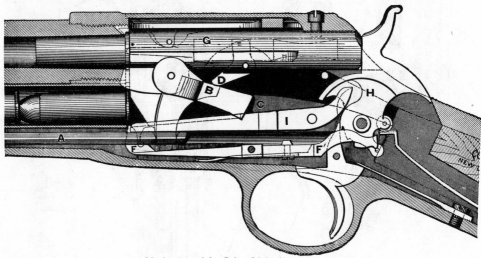

Mechanism of the Colt "Lightning" Rifle.

When the hammer is at full- or half-cock, the action is released by lowering the hammer. To load and fire, grasp the handle or slide A with the left hand, and draw it to the rear. The first part of this rear movement raises the locking-brace B from the abutment C, acts upon the firing-pin lever D, withdraws the firing-pin, and releases the magazine gate F, causing it to hold back the cartridge in the magazine, and, as the bolt G moves to the rear, ejects the cartridge shell, cocks the hammer H, and raises the carrier I, so that when the movement is finished the cartridge is in proper position to enter the chamber.

Then push the slide A forward. This movement carries the bolt G forward, drives the cartridge into the chamber, throws down the carrier I into position to receive, and withdraws the magazine gate F to release another cartridge, throws the brace B against the abutment C, and the rifle is then ready for firing.

After the piece has been fired, or when the breech is closed, the handle and slide may be locked by half-cocking the hammer. This action causes a projection on the magazine gate lever (shown just behind the letter F in the cut), to engage a corresponding recess in the under side of the slide, thus locking it, and preventing it and the breech-bolt from moving. As may be seen from the drawing, the handle and slide can only be released by bringing the hammer to the down position. In the other positions of the hammer—viz. full- and half-cock—the slide, handle, and breech-bolt are positively locked. A feature peculiar to this rifle is, the breech-bolt is brought clear forward, and the extractor is hooked over the cartridge in the barrel *before* the magazine gate will allow another cartridge to be fed to the carrier, and the magazine gate is positively locked, only allowing one cartridge at a time to pass from the magazine, thus preventing blocking of the breech action, and the escape of cartridges under the carrier. The firing-pin is held back positively until the cartridge has entered the chamber, when the bolt is locked so that premature explosion is impossible. The hammer is automatically locked and unlocked by the hook near the end of the magazine lever F′. By this arrangement the rifle may be loaded and discharged by the reciprocating motion of the slide, keeping the trigger constantly pressed back during the motion by the trigger finger. The magazine can be charged only when the slide is drawn to the rear.

The Colt rifles are made in various sizes for different cartridges, as enumerated in the table of " American Rifles."

THE MARLIN SYSTEM.

The mechanism of the Marlin rifle differs from that of the Winchester chiefly in the form of the cartridge carrier, which is pivoted, instead of sliding perpendicularly. The extracting mechanism is stronger under the later models, which have been considerably simplified and improved; there is a bolting block, E, to secure the breech-block I in position during discharge.

Both the Marlin and the Winchester are made to take down—that is to say, the barrel and tubular magazine may be detached from the stock for convenience in carriage.   In the Winchester an interrupted screw is used to attach the barrel to the action-frame; to dismount the rifle it is necessary only to partly withdraw the magazine tube, release the catch, and give the barrel a quarter turn.   In the Marlin

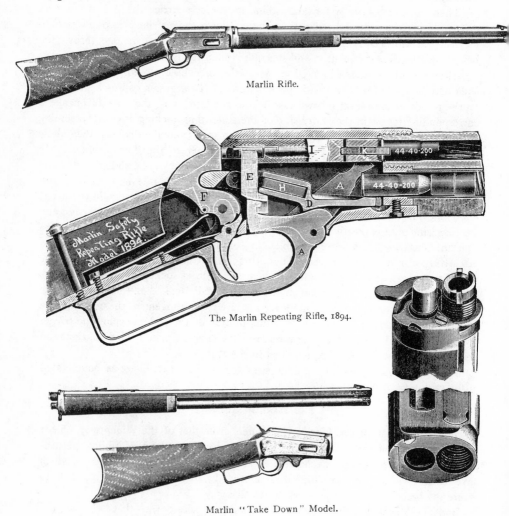

Marlin Rifle.

The Marlin Repeating Rifle, 1894.

Marlin "Take Down" Model.

the screw is not interrupted, but turns easily, and by an ingenious wedge-lever the joint is tightened and barrels and action made rigid. This wedge also acts as a compensator for any loss by wear in screwing and unscrewing the barrel.

AMERICAN BOLT-ACTION REPEATING MECHANISMS.

The Lee, which has been adopted by Great Britain, appears to be the only bolt-action American repeating-rifle which has received particular favour. The United States (*vide* pages 736, 737) are armed with rifles of European design, but the Hotchkiss repeater was reported upon favourably by the Ordnance Committee at the conclusion of the earlier stages of the tests. This magazine is on the butt, and contains six ·450-bore cartridges; they pass through a hollow trigger, and are forced to a position in front of the breech-bolt by a spiral spring.

The magazine may be cut off by a stop placed on the side of the arm; and by a modification, suggested by Lieutenant Russell, of the United States Army, a detachable magazine containing four cartridges may be placed in the stock. There is a spiral mainspring and needle plunger. The extractor is affixed to the breech-bolt, as in the Winchester.

The author, in earlier editions of this book, criticised this mechanism adversely, and the opinion he formed appears to have been fully justified by the subsequent career of the rifle. The Lee is illustrated and described in the succeeding chapter.

THE SCHULHOF REPEATER.

This principle, the invention of Mr. J. Schulhof, of Vienna, possesses several novel points, the chief of which are a commodious and handy magazine, a powerful and effective cartridge-carrier, and a unique trigger.

As will be seen from the illustration, the breech-action is of the common bolt form. The trigger is a raised catch on the top of the grip of the stock. The cartridges—any number up to twenty-eight—are carried in the stock, which has a large lid on the one side; a circular tube or cartridge way leads from the magazine to the lifter immediately under the breech-bolt. In this tube works a transport rail extending the length of the tube, and linked to the breech-bolt. The action of the parts is as follows :—The magazine being filled, the breech-bolt is turned half over and withdrawn; this cocks the gun and pushes the transport rail to its furthest extent towards the heel of the stock; the cartridges—three or four, depending on the number of compartments in the magazine—fall into the way, and spring teeth on the transport rail engage on the base of the cartridge-rims; on the breech-bolt being returned home, the rail with its load advances the length of the cartridge springs; stops projecting in the cartridge-way prevent any retrograde movement on the part of the cartridge; so that upon the block being again opened the spring teeth of the transport rail glide over the cartridges towards their base, and each time engage and hitch up fresh cartridges; thus, at every movement each cartridge in the "way" is carried one step nearer the barrel chamber. When underneath the breech-block, the arm being open, a spring under the lifter raises it, and the cartridge is brought into a line with the barrel, to be pushed home by the lever.

Gear is added to disconnect magazine, to bolt the trigger, and to cover up breech-action. The salient points of this truly novel arm are the arrangement of the cartridges in the magazine, and the strong carrier—both so arranged that the cartridges cannot possibly come into contact with each other—a simple lifter (automatic in action), a strong extractor, and an easy pull-off. The mechanism is all too complex to commend itself to military experts, and since its production numerous mechanisms much more simple and equally efficient have been made public.

THE NEEDHAM MAGAZINE RIFLE.

This mechanism is of English invention. Like the Schulhof, it is not of a type likely to commend itself to either military experts or sportsmen, but it possesses several points which are decidedly novel; for it combines the principles of the ejecting hammerless gun and the ordinary revolver with a tubular magazine gun.

The cartridges, which are of special design, are forced by a spiral spring, base first, into the chamber; to actuate the gun an under-lever is depressed and raised; linked to this lever are lifters engaging with a ratchet-wheel upon a centre spindle to which the chamber is keyed. The lowering of the lever carries the revolving chamber the fourth of a circle, partly raises the hammer by another ratchet, and allows it to fall, an arm from it striking the base of the fired case and thus ejecting it from the chamber *forwards*. On bringing the lever back to the stock, the revolving chamber is carried round another fourth of the circle, bringing the loaded chamber in a line with the barrel, the empty chamber in a line with the tubular magazine, and cocking the arm.

The cartridge, shown separately, consists of two pieces, the base having no rim, and the sides tapering toward the base instead of from it; at the mouth a collared cap fits tightly the exterior of the case, and projects some way into the interior of the case. The internal diameter of this collared cap is that of the bore of the rifle, and into this collar the bullet is fitted. The percussion cap—ordinary

The Schulhof Magazine Gun.

The Needham Magazine Gun and Cartridge.

pattern—is in the base of the cartridge. When fired, the collar is driven forward, and, expanding, prevents any escape of gas at the joint of the barrels and chamber, and, being taper and short, the cartridge never fails to be ejected. The powder in the cartridge case lies all around the bullet, as well as at the base; in fact, the bullet is embedded in the charge of powder. Experiments fail to detect any injury to the bullet or shooting by this arrangement; all the powder is apparently burnt, and its full energy obtained.

CHAPTER XXX.

MODERN MILITARY MAGAZINE RIFLES.

HISTORICAL NOTE ON THE SMALL BORE.

PRIOR to 1850 it was generally held by military experts that the bore of the infantry musket must be large and the projectile heavy in order to stop a cavalry charge; bullets, even if driven at greater velocity, thus giving equal striking force, would not, it was contended, have the same effect, as they would pierce and wound, but not smash and instantly disable the advancing foe. Since 1850 the *rifle* has been generally adopted, and the tendency has been always to reduce the bore, when changing the type of infantry weapons, in every army. It has been found, by experiment, that the increased velocity of the bullet makes good what it loses in weight, whilst the efficiency of the weapon is increased by its greater range and the larger quantity of ammunition the soldier can carry. The costly experiments of Sir Joseph Whitworth proved that the half-inch bore gave the best ballistic results; this was owing to the explosive used. With the adoption of nitro-compounds, it was found advantageous to still further decrease the calibre and the weight of the ammunition. At present preference is given to rifles from ·256 to ·315 inch in diameter, and most of the Continental infantry are now supplied with weapons of this size—*i.e.* 6·5 to 8 millimetres. It is believed by experts that the calibre will shortly be still further reduced, the 5 mm. rifles having developed remarkable qualities. The history of the development of calibre is shown by the annexed table :—

TABLE SHOWING DIMINUTION IN CALIBRE OF MILITARY RIFLES.

Year.						
1850.	England used the	... ...	11-bore "Brown Bess"	of ·750 inch or	19·2	mm.
1850.	England made 20,000 ...	...	14-bore "Brown Bess"	of ·693 ,,	,, 17·85	,,
1852.	England adopted the ...	...	25-bore "Enfield" ...	of ·577 ,,	,, 14·8	,,
1854.	Austria adopted the ...	...	28-bore rifle	of ·550 ,,	,, 13·8	,,
1860.	Sweden adopted the ...	...	40-bore rifle ...	of ·488 ,,	,, 12·6	,,
1866.	France adopted the ...	...	59-bore rifle	of ·433 ,,	,, 11·0	,,
1867.	Austria adopted the ...	...	62-bore rifle	of ·420 ,,	,, 10·7	,,
1869.	Switzerland adopted the	...	75-bore rifle	of ·400 ,,	,, 10·4	,,

TABLE SHOWING DIMINUTION IN CALIBRE OF MILITARY RIFLES (*continued*).

Year.				
1871.	Germany adopted the ...	58-bore rifle ...	... of ·433 inch or 11·0 mm.
1871.	England adopted the ...	51-bore rifle ...	... of ·450 ,, ,, 11·43 ,,
1871.	Spain and Holland adopted the	58-bore rifle ...	... of ·433 ,, ,, 11·0 ,,
1874.	France adopted the ...	58-bore rifle ...	... of ·433 ,, ,, 11·0 ,,
1878.	Sweden adopted the ...	76-bore rifle ...	... of ·396 ,, ,, 10·15 ,,
1880.	Servia adopted the ...	76-bore rifle ...	... of ·396 ,, ,, 10·15 ,,
1886.	France and Portugal adopted the	145-bore rifle ...	... of ·315 ,, ,, 8·0 ,,
1887.	Turkey adopted the ...	150-bore rifle ...	... of ·350 ,, ,, 9·5 ,,
1887.	England made the " Enfield " Martini	... of ·400 ,, ,, 10·25 ,,
1888.	Germany adopted the ...	156-bore rifle ...	... of ·311 ,, ·,, 7·9 ,,
1888.	Austria adopted the ...	150-bore rifle ...	... of ·315 ,, ,, 8·0 ,,
1889.	England adopted the ...	173-bore rifle ...	... of ·303 ,, ,, 7·7 ,,
1889.	Belgium adopted the ...	172-bore rifle ...	... of ·301 ,, ,, 7·65 ,,
1889.	Denmark adopted the ...	150-bore rifle ...	... of ·315 ,, ,, 8·0 ,,
1889.	Switzerland adopted the	·295 ,, ,, 7·5 ,,
1891.	Italy adopted the	·256 ,, ,, 6·5 ,,
1891.	Russia adopted the	·300 ,, ,, 7·62 ,,
1892.	Spain adopted the	·276 ,, ,, 7·0 ,,
1892.	Holland and Roumania adopted the	·256 ,, ,, 6·5 ,,
1893.	The United States of America adopted the	·300 ,, ,, 7·62 ,,
1895.	The United States of America (Navy) adopted the ...	·236 ,, ,, 5·87 ,,

BOLT-ACTION SYSTEMS.

The breech mechanisms of modern breech-loading military rifles are one and all modifications of the door-bolt principle, the oldest known system of breech-loading. Until the unmistakable advantages of the magazine or repeating rifle were appreciated by military experts, it appeared possible that some other form of breech-action might supersede the hinged and falling block rifles in use ; but now that the magazine arm is imperative the mechanism which best lends itself to the exigencies of a magazine feed is that of the bolt-gun. The French Chassepot and the Prussian needle-gun, therefore, are the prototypes of the modern rifle action, not any of the arms which have been described in the account of the weapons of the British Army. The numerous mechanisms upon other principles no longer demand special notice, but the reader curious to know details of their construction may consult the author's earlier books, where many are described and illustrated.

The breech-bolt mechanisms may be arranged in two broad divisions : first, those in which the motion of the bolt is a straight to-and-fro movement in a line with the barrels, and, second, those in which the bolt, in addition to this movement, turns or is turned upon its own axis.

The second division is the more general ; the simplest form is that of the needle-gun already described (page 707), but sometimes the handle or lever which is grasped does not turn with the bolt, but is attached by a sleeve, or other means, in which the breech-bolt itself is turned by suitable grooves in the shoe of the breech-action body engaging studs on the bolt, or *vice versâ*. A few typical mechanisms, although now somewhat out of date, may be described, in order that the more recent models may be better understood.

THE VETTERLI REPEATING RIFLE.

The Vetterli repeating arm is named after its inventor, a Swiss, who has made three separate models, the earliest in 1869, the second in 1871, and in 1874 the one now illustrated. It will be seen that the gun is loaded by raising the locking lever and then drawing backward the sliding breech-block; a stud upon the bolt presses

The Vetterli Magazine Gun.

against one arm of a bell crank lever when the bolt is drawn backward; the other arm of the lever raises the cage containing the cartridge on a level with the chamber in the barrel; then the breech-block, returned to its place, forces the cartridge into the chamber, and the cage falls to a level with the magazine under the barrel, and receives another cartridge. The cartridges are inserted at the side of the arm, and the magazine cage and extractor are similar to that employed in the Winchester rifle

The Lebel Rifle.

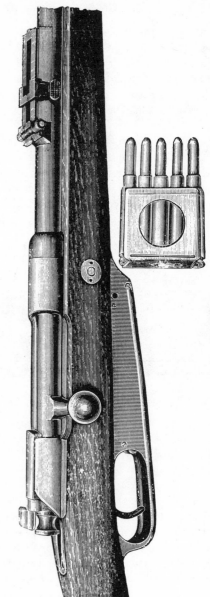

The Mauser Magazine Rifle (Model '88).

THE LEBEL RIFLE.

This is the breech mechanism approved by the French Commission of Artillery Experts in 1886, and consists of a slight modification of the Gras-Kropatschek action previously in use by some of the French regiments. In the original model a tubular magazine is used, but this is to be discontinued and a detachable magazine provided. In the Lebel breech mechanism the peculiar feature is a double tenon in the fore-part of the breech-bolt, which securely holds the bolt close up to the cartridge base, and it is further supported by the handle having a bearing upon the breech, as in the Lee-Speed, the Prussian needle-gun, and other weapons of the breech-bolt type. The cartridges are fed into the barrel from the top right-hand side when the gun is used as a single loader.

THE MAUSER MAGAZINE RIFLE.

The Mauser has been many times and in many ways improved; a modification of its mechanism is still employed as the breech-action of the magazine rifle of the German Army. The bolt-head is interlocking, as in the Lebel, and the lock, firing, and magazine mechanisms have been reduced to the fewest possible parts. The bolt is raised and withdrawn to load, and the opening in the top right-hand side of the breech-action shoe is the position found most suitable for the quick insertion of cartridges when the rifle is used as a single loader. The magazine is fed by the insertion at once of a clip containing five cartridges, arranged as shown in the illustration.

THE MANNLICHER SYSTEMS.

The development of the Mannlicher breech mechanism is of itself an instructive study in the history of modern rifle-making. The arm illustrated in the first figure— a type of gun which was tentatively introduced about fifteen years ago—shows how very different was the original design from that model of the same inventor which has now been generally approved by the leading military authorities in Europe. The next gun is decidedly superior as a weapon; the position of the magazine is objectionable, but the enormous advance made towards simplifying the various parts of the breech mechanism is at once noticed. The improved Mannlicher (Austrian model, 1888), has a straight pull-and-push bolt, the breech-bolt being secured in position during firing by a self-acting drop-catch slipping down between the bolt and the shoe of the breech-action. Another modification of the same gun, made by Mr. Krnka, has a loose bolt-head somewhat similar to that of the Lebel,

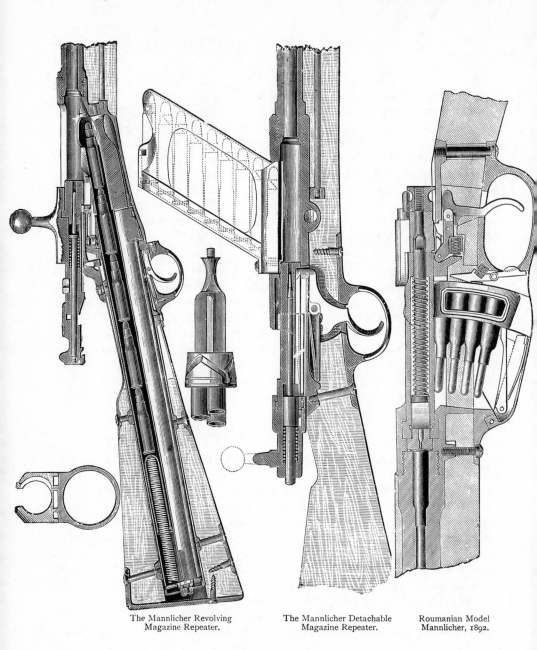

The Mannlicher Revolving
Magazine Repeater.

The Mannlicher Detachable
Magazine Repeater.

Roumanian Model
Mannlicher, 1892.

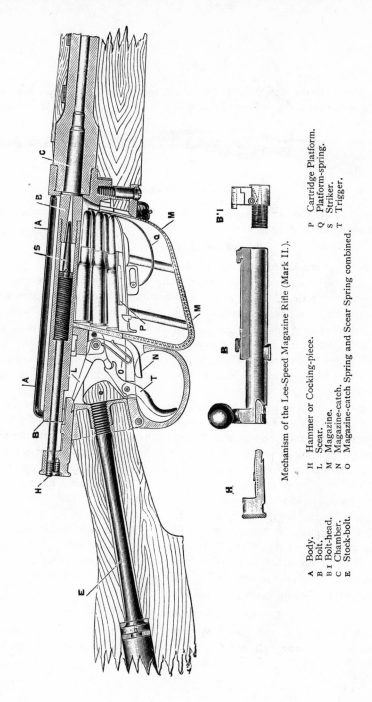

Mechanism of the Lee-Speed Magazine Rifle (Mark II.).

A Body.
B Bolt.
B 1 Bolt-head.
C Chamber.
E Stock-bolt.

H Hammer or Cocking-piece.
L Scear.
M Magazine.
N Magazine-catch.
O Magazine-catch Spring and Scear Spring combined.

P Cartridge Platform.
Q Platform-spring.
S Striker.
T Trigger.

which, with only the straight push forward of the bolt, is turned by a helical groove and locks automatically. There is another and later invention of Mr. Mannlicher's

The Mannlicher Rifle.

illustrated in the chapter on automatic arms. The last one to be noticed here is the Roumanian model of 1892.

THE LEE-SPEED MAGAZINE RIFLE.

This rifle was adopted upon the recommendation of a Committee appointed to test the repeating arms which had been offered to the British Government. The invention is American, with certain modifications made at the instance of the Committee and Mr. Speed of Enfield. The infantry arm, " Mark I.," weighs 9 lbs. 8 ozs. unloaded—$10\frac{1}{2}$ lbs. fully loaded. It has a length over all of 50 inches, and is fitted with a knife straight bayonet only 12 inches long in the blade and $16\frac{3}{4}$ inch over all. The " Mark II." has been improved in several details, the weight reduced 4 ozs., rifling changed, and sighted to 2,800 yards ; other particulars are given in the table.

The chief parts of the breech mechanism are enumerated, and the illustration will make clear the action of the various parts. The bolt is actuated by lifting and pulling the knob, and, the spring in the magazine having forced another cartridge into place, the bolt is pushed forwards, and then the knob turned down. This turning motion has been adopted in preference to the straight pull-and-push, because it brings other muscles into play, and is found to be less fatiguing than the simple pull-and-push action of the Mannlicher and similar rifles.

The magazine is $3\frac{1}{4}$ by 2, and holds eight cartridges ; a " cut-off" of the simplest description, in the shoe of the rifle, blocks the exit of the magazine, and converts the weapon into a single-shot arm. A wooden shield or hand-guard is fixed round the breech of the barrel, so that the rifle may be fired when the barrel is too hot to hold with the naked hand. There is no ramrod or cleaning stick, but a " pull-through " and oil bottle are carried in the butt.

MINOR DETAILS OF CONSTRUCTION.

With reference to the breech-bolt, the Mannlicher of the Roumanian 1892 pattern has a rotating bolt with a straight-push. In the other arms both handle and bolt turn, or the movement is straight pull-and-push, as in the Austrian Mannlicher.

The barrels are for the most part shorter than 30 inches; the longest is the Portuguese, 32·30 inches; the shortest, the Turkish, 28·40 inches. The rifling differs but slightly; it is in every case four-grooved, except in the Lee-Metford, which has seven, the Danish Krag-Jorgensen six, the Lee-Enfield five, and the Swiss Schmidt-Rubin, which has but three. There is about an equal division of opinion as to the worth of the "cut-off" to the repeating mechanism. The English Lee-Metford and Lee-Enfield, Danish, French, Norwegian, Portuguese, and American rifles have a "cut-off"; the other rifles are not furnished with any mechanism of the kind.

With reference to bayonets, Russia is the only country using the old stabbing bayonet; theirs is now quadrangular, and 16·88 inches long. Sword-bayonets about 20 inches in length are still used by the French, Portuguese, and Turks; the short knife-bayonet—sometimes 12 inches long, but usually an inch shorter—has been adopted by the other Powers. All the knife-bayonets weigh less than one pound.

BALLISTICS OF MILITARY RIFLES.

The range, pressure, and velocity may be ascertained from the table; with reference to the recoil, it is usually less than 8 ft.-lbs., but in the new United States rifle is 11, in the Roumanian only 5. Penetration depends not only on velocity but also on the form and constitution of the composite bullet. The French rifle will penetrate at 165 feet 1·18 inch of masonry, or ·31 inch of steel; at 6,560 feet 1·18 inch of oak. The Norwegian rifle penetrates $35\frac{1}{2}$ inches of pine wood at 328 feet. A writer in the *United Service Magazine* says that at this distance it pierced 11 inches of light sand, but at 1,640 feet the penetration was 17 inches; a paradox ascribed to the great deforming action of sand upon a bullet travelling at a great velocity. The new 1893 Mauser is said to penetrate 55 inches of pine wood at 39 feet; the German rifle penetrates 31·5 inches at 327 feet; the Roumanian Mannlicher penetrates 49 inches of joined pine planks at 130 feet; and the ·303 has penetrated 30 inches of oak at 20 feet. In fact, of all modern rifles the penetration may be regarded as more than sufficient for every purpose to which they are likely to be applied.

MODERN MILITARY RIFLES COMPARED.

The more important differences between the magazine rifles which have been adopted by the leading military Powers are shown by the annexed table, and have

Calibre.		Rifle.		Barrel.					Name of System.	Country.	
					Grooving.			Sighted			
In.	Mm.	Length. ft. ins.	Weight. lb. ozs.	Length.	Depth.	Twist. 1 turn in inches.	to yards.			
·315	8·0	4 2	8 5½	30·12	·008	9·842 (r)	2,132	Mannlicher, 1895 ... {	Austria, Bulgaria, and Greece }	a
·301	7·65	4 2·25	8 0½	30·67	·0065	9·842 (r)	2,187	Mauser, '89 ...	Belgium ...	b
·315	8·0	4 4·4	9 6	33·00	·0055	11·80	2,078	Krag-Jorgensen, 1889	Denmark ...	c
·315	8·0	4 3·12	9 3½	31·50	·0059	9·45 (l)	2,187	Lebel, 1886 to 1893	France ...	d
·311	7·9	4 1·4	9 0	29·05	·0065	9·39 (r)	2,187	Mauser, 1898 ...	Germany ...	e
·303	7·0	4 1·5	9 4	30·19	·0065	10·00 (l)	2,800	Lee-Enfield, MK. I*	Great Britain...	f
·303	7·7	3 8·5	8 2½	25·20	·0050	10·00 (l)	2,800	Short Lee-Enfield, 1903	Great Britain...	g
·256	6·5	4 2·7	9 8	31·10	·0059	7·874 (r)	2,187	Mannlicher, 1895 ...	Holland ...	h
·256	6·5	4 2·75	8 6½	30·70	·0051	7·87	2,187	Paravicini-Carcano	Italy	i
·256	6·5	4 1·2	8 4	29·10	·0049	7·87 (r)	2,187	Mauser	Japan... ...	1
·256	6·5	4 1·50	8 13	30·00	·0059	7·87	2,406	Krag-Jorgensen ...	Norway ...	k
·315	8·0	4 4	10 3	31·633	·0075	11·00 (r)	2,406	Kropatschek, '86 ...	Portugal ...	l
·256	6·5	4 0·5	8 12¾	28·60	·0059	7·874 (r)	2,187	Mannlicher, 1893 ...	Roumania ...	m
·3	7·62	4 3·875	8 15¼	32·25	·007	9·5 (r)	2,096	"3-line" Nagant, 1894	Russia ...	n
·276	7·0	4 0·625	9 6¾	29·031	·055	8·68 (r)	2,187	Mauser, 1896 ...	Spain	o
·295	7·5	3 7·12	8 8	23·33	·0039	10·63 (r)	1,312	Schmidt-Rubin Short Rifle, 1900 ...	Switzerland ...	p
·301	7·65	4 0·6	9 1	29·134	·0055	10·00 (r)	2,187	Mauser, 1893 ...	Turkey ...	q
·300	7·62	3 7·2	8 11	24·00	·0040	10·00	2,000	New Springfield ...	United States	r
A		B	C	D	E	F	G	H	I	

NOTES.

B. The lengths are without bayonets. There is a difference of 14¼ inches between the longest and shortest rifle when bayonets are fixed.

C. This column is weight of rifle with magazine empty. The difference in weight with magazine filled is more marked.

E—F. All rifles have four grooves, except the Swiss, which has three, the Danish and Japanese, six, and the English, which has five.

G. The dividing of the sight varies from 200 yards in the English, the finest, to 547 yards in the Portuguese and Turkish. There is also a long-range sight for two miles in the Austrian, and for 2½ miles in the German. The extreme range is not indicated by the sighting. The German rifle has an extreme range of 4,350 yards, and the trajectory at 2,400 yards, the highest point, is 1,640 feet; the elevation required is 32 degrees. The new naval rifle of the United States will give a point-blank range of 725 yards.

| | | Cartridge. | | | | | Explosive. | | Ballistics. | | | Magazine and No. of Shots. | *Danger Zone. |
| | | Complete Ctge. | | Bullet. | | | | | | | | | |
	Rim or Rimless.	Total weight in grs.	Total length in inches.	Material of Envelope.	Length in inches.	Weight in grains.	Kind.	Charge in grs.	Muzzle Velocity f. s.	W/d²	Chamber Pressure in tons of sq. in.		Yards.
a	Rim	455	3·0	Steel.	1·24	244	M., 1892	42·44	2,034	·334	19·7	F.B.C. 5	579
b	Rimless	441	3·055	C.-N.	1·205	219	Wettern	37	2,034	·333	19·7	D.B.S. 5	577
c	Rim	460	3·0	C.-N.	1·187	237	S. flake	33·95	1,968	·325	15·1	F.B.S. 5	558
d	Rim	447	2·952	Solid Copper Alloy.	1·221	231	Vielle B.F.	42·43	2,073	·320	17·75	T.U.B. 8	587
e	Rimless	431	3·22	S. C. N.	1·235	227	S. flake	40·75	2,093	·322	21	F.B.S. 5	754
f	Rim	415	3·05	C.-N.	1·25	215	Cordite	31·5	2,060	·3205	15·25	D.B. 10	579
g	Rim	415	3·05	C.-N.	1·25	215	Cordite	31·5	2,060	·3205	15·75	D.B.S. 10	562
h	Rim	338	3·05	S. C. N.	1·23	162	{ Nitro-cellulose }	36·26	2,433	·334	--	F.B.C. 5	612
i	Rimless	331·8	3·00	Cupro-N.	1·182	163	Ballistite	30·09	2,295	·337	17·1	F.B.C. 5	610
j	Semi-rimless	348·5	2·98	Copper.	1·28	140	{ Nitro-cellulose }	32	2,950	·337	—	F.B.S. 5	873
k	—	326·7	3·125	Nickel-Steel	1·250	156	Ballistite	—	2,396	—	—	U.L. 5	657
l	Rim	546	3·189	Steel.	1·279	248	Black	70	1,750	·34	15·75	T.U.B. 9	—
m	Rim	350	3·05	Cupro-N.	1·244	162	Troisdorf	36	2,400	·334	—	F.B.C. 5	62
n	Rim	363	3·025	Cupro-N.	1·194	214	Pyroxiline	33	1,985	·324	17·47	F.B.S. 5	568
o	Rimless	373·5	3·08	Cupro-N.	1·21	172·8	{ Nitro-cellulose }	38·35	2,296	·313	22·3	F.B.S. 5	626
p	Rimless	424	3·043	Nickel plated Steel envelope over point.	1·18	212·5	S. flake	30·7	1,920	·337	17·1	D.B.S. 6	567
q	Rimless	416	3·07	S. C.-N.	1·212	211·3	Rothweil	40·2	2,066	·325	19·7	D B.S. 5	577
r	Rim	444·5	3·08	C.-N.	1·26	150	{ Peyton-Dupont }	38·56	2,700	·337	—	F.B.S. 5	723
	J	K	L	M	N	O	P	Q	R	S	T	U	V

NOTES—(Continued).

M. The bullets are mostly composite. Steel on lead, nickelled-copper on lead, nickelled-steel on lead, nickel on lead, cupro-nickel, nickel-steel, or cupro-nickel-steel. The density of the bullets varies from ·330—·340; the heaviest is the Austrian Steel Lubricated, 244 grs.; the lightest, the C.N., 150 grs., U.S.A. New Springfield.

P. All the powders are more or less smokeless.

U. The magazines are subject to alteration; the clip, or charger system of feeding the cartridges into the frame of the rifle appears to be growing in favour with experts. The author was the first to suggest this method. U.L. is under breech-lock; U.B. under barrel; F. fixed; D. detachable; C. clip; S. strip charger; B. the box magazine of the English rifle; T. Tube.

* *i.e.* Range at which summit of trajectory is exactly the average height of a man = 66·9 inches, above the line of sight. The author is indebted to Mr. Angier's table, printed in Mr. Blanch's book, "A Century of Guns," for this information.

been referred to in the preceding notes. It may be of interest to state how far the armament with the new type of weapon has gone, and what results have been already obtained.

The Austrian Mannlicher has taken the place of the Werndl with the regular troops of the kingdom of Austria and Hungary; and its ballistic properties, elsewhere referred to, are probably better known than those of any modern rifle. In France the Lebel, having supplanted the ·433-calibre rifles of 1874, 1878, and 1884-85 patterns, has given place to a ·315-bore Lebel with a tube magazine holding eight cartridges.

The new pattern German Mauser, 1898 model, is supplanting the earlier models issued, and is declared by leading technical journals to be the best repeating rifle produced. Its calibre is ·311 inch.

The Regular forces of the British Army are now armed with the Short Lee-Enfield; this is of the clip loader type, five cartridges being pushed into the magazine from a clip at one operation. The back-sight is a complete departure from previous English models, and is furnished with screw lateral adjustment as well as a Vernier scale elevation; a U instead of the customary V opening is provided, and the protected fore-sight is a knife-edge instead of the ordinary barleycorn. The barrel is completely covered with wood, and weight of rifle and length of barrel have both been reduced.

The Territorials are armed with a compromise between the earlier Lee-Enfield and the latest Short Lee-Enfield rifle. The "Territorial" model is fitted with a wind-gauge back-sight and protected fore-sight; it is a clip loader, the magazine carrying 10 cartridges; in other respects it is the same as the Mark I. Lee-Enfield rifle.

In Holland the Mannlicher of ·256 bore, and a very good model of this favourite weapon, is gradually supplanting the Beaumont-Vitali, ·433 calibre, which was adopted in 1878.

Italy has issued a ·256-calibre rifle in place of the ·408-calibre Vetterli-Vitali of 1887 pattern.

The Japanese "Year '30th" pattern rifle did satisfactory service in the Russo-Japanese War, but the troops are now being armed with the ·256-calibre Mauser of the 1906 model.

Norway has still the Jarmann of ·396 calibre in use, but has recently adopted the Krag-Jorgensen of ·256 calibre

Mark III. Short Rifle.

for the cavalry, artillery and engineers, in addition to which some of the "line" Regiments are armed with the Remington carbine of 1890 model and 8 mm. calibre.

Sweden, still armed with Remingtons, is converting them into ·315 calibre rifles.

Portugal has discarded the ·530 Snider of 1872 pattern for the ·315 calibre Kropatschek.

Roumania leads the way in choosing small-calibre rifles, and the present ·256-calibre Mannlicher is an excellent weapon, possessing a remarkably low trajectory, great accuracy, and good penetration.

Russia has issued large numbers of the "3 line." This rifle follows the 1891 and 1894 models of the same type, known by the designations 3-line Nagant and Mossin.

The new infantry rifle of the United States, the ·3-bore New Springfield, is undoubtedly an efficient weapon.

Between the others there is probably little to choose, for the new Mauser closely approximates the Roumanian Mannlicher; the English, French, and German infantry rifles show no marked superiority over each other, and, in placing them in order of merit, they would change places according to the opinion of the expert as to which of several points were most advantageous in a rifle. The English Lee-Enfield rifle is the heaviest, yet fires proportionally the lightest bullet; its ballistic qualities are good, but with other explosives than cordite they may be improved, and, in addition to its great cost of production, the rifle is severely criticised as a military weapon on account of the hybrid magazine attached to it.

In comparing the qualities of the various weapons, it must be remembered that quick firing is a great advantage, and is enhanced if the ammunition used whilst available at a long range is so light that many rounds may be carried. The enormous consumption of ammunition with even a comparatively slow-firing arm, as the Lee-Speed-Metford, may be appreciated from the following fact. In the Mopla rising in Malabar, in 1894, fewer than thirty fanatics charged a force of fifty men of the Dorset regiment, armed with the Lee-Metford magazine rifle, and about a hundred native police with Sniders. They had less than fifty yards to run, yet a few of them actually reached the line and fell upon the bayonets, although there were fired at them over seven hundred shots from the Metford rifles and three hundred from the Sniders. This indicates that the stopping power of the small-calibre rifle is not so great as believed : an indication confirmed by some incidents of the Chino-Japanese War and the Anglo-Boer War.

It may serve to cite for comparison some figures as to the number of shots fired in earlier wars.

At the battle of Salamanca only 8,000 men were put *hors de combat*, although 3,500,000 cartridges were fired, not including the 6,000 cannon balls (besides which there were cavalry charges and hand-to-hand engagements), so that it is estimated that only one musket-ball in 437 took effect. In the *Spectator* of March 19th, 1859, is the following :—" An officer engaged at Waterloo says that he could not see more than three or four saddles emptied by the fire of one side of a square of British infantry upon a body of French cavalry close to them." It is evident therefore that the marksmanship of the soldiers was as bad as the musket itself. In 1859 Colonel Wilford stated in a lecture at the United Service Institution that during a single engagement in the Caffre War 80,000 cartridges were fired and only 25 of the enemy fell! In the Crimean War the French fired away 25,000,000 cartridges, and certainly did not hit 25,000 men, and the *Times*, about the same period says, " We believe the calculation used to be one bullet in 250 carried death ; and that estimate is probably not far from the truth." In 1838 a series of experiments were undertaken by the officers of the Royal Engineers to ascertain the real properties of the Service musket, with the result that they instructed the soldier to aim 130 feet above a man at 600 yards if they wished to hit him !

OTHER MILITARY MAGAZINE RIFLES.

There are many more systems of breech-loading applied to repeating rifles than have been, or are ever likely to be, adopted as service weapons. In order to show how simple may be the mechanism of a repeating rifle on the bolt principle, two specimens are illustrated.

THE BERTHIER RIFLE.

The breech-loading mechanism consists of the breech-bolt A, with locking projections at its fore-extremity, being in this particular similar to the Lebel ; the lock and firing mechanisms are of the ordinary simple construction. The stock and fore-part are in one piece, and, instead of a detachable magazine, the cartridges, fixed to a strip or held in a clip, are inserted by uncovering the carrier below the breech-block. The trigger action, and the lifting mechanism, by which the cartridges are fed to the level of the barrel, are both of unusually simple design ; and it is claimed that the rifle is one of the cheapest patterns to manu_ facture.

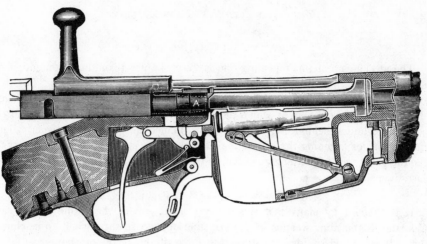

The Berthier Rifle.

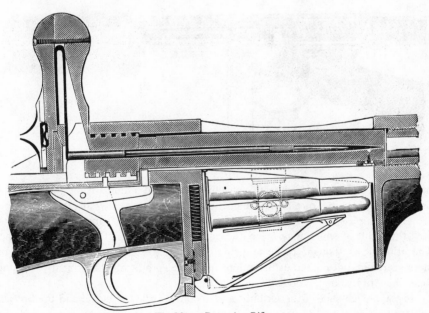

The Marga Repeating Rifle.

THE MARGA REPEATING RIFLE.

The mechanism of this repeating-rifle is even simpler than the last-mentioned, and special pains have been taken to make it as compact as possible. For this reason the magazine is made continuous with the breech-action (the cartridges being introduced from above), which then forms the bearing for the bolt in a closed socket or cylinder behind the magazine, and immediately over the trigger. The arrangement for fastening the breech to the stock is very strong, and makes it easy to take the gun apart. The magazine, too, is especially strong and serviceable, as the illustration shows.

AUTOMATIC REPEATING RIFLES.

It is thought by many that the military small arm of the future will be an automatically repeating weapon of the principle applied so successfully to machine-guns. It is a modern idea to utilise the force of the recoil or the power of a portion of the gases generated in the chamber for the purpose of actuating the

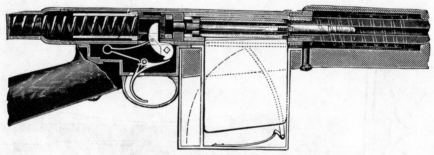

The Griffiths and Woodgate Automatic Rifle.

breech and lock mechanisms, and effecting the feed automatically; and at the present moment the question is being considered by nearly all the European Powers. The British Government has invited inventors to submit their ideas for trial, the result of which may mean the entire re-arming of the armies of Europe. The principle is thought to be fully protected by a French patent now fifteen or more years old, but numerous inventions have been protected subsequently; among them the Griffiths and Woodgate and the Srogen.

In the breech-shoe of the Griffiths and Woodgate rifle the barrel and the breech-bolt are both free to slide, the shoe being stopped at the rear by a cap, and the forward movement of the barrel is regulated by a locking nut. In the breech-piece

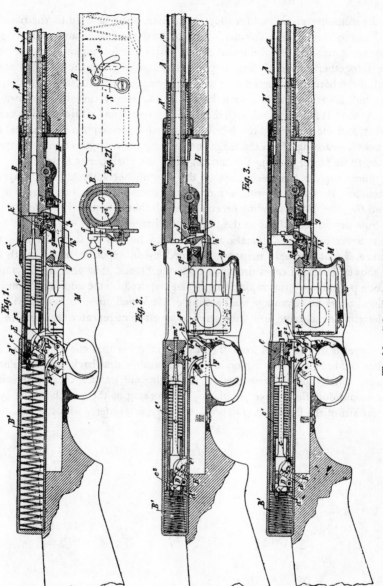

Fig.1.

Fig.2.

Fig.3.

Fig.21.

The Mannlicher Automatic Rifle.

there is the usual breech-bolt with extractor, the bolt being held up to the barrel by the spiral spring at its base. The motion for opening the breech and extracting the cartridge-case is imparted by the recoil of the barrel, the locking-nut holding barrel and breech together sufficiently long to prevent escape of gas at the breech, but with the travel of the barrel it is turned by a cam on it engaging with a stop in a slot, and then, the bolt being free, it is driven back, and the empty case is withdrawn and ejected. As soon as the bolt is released the barrel is stopped and returned to its position by a spring, and the recoiling breech-bolt has actuated mechanism of the usual type to feed another cartridge from the magazine, and, by the strength of the rear spring, is returned to its place, pushing the cartridge into the chamber as it travels.

Still more simple is the mechanism of the Mannlicher automatic gun, in which the breech-bolt is dispensed with, a momentary contact of the breech-end of the barrel and the face of the standing breech being all that is required to safeguard the shooter from any escape of gas at the time of discharge.

The speed in firing the automatic rifle is said to be very great. With one rifle, for instance, a photographic negative, obtained by an exposure of one-tenth of a second, showed five fired cases dropping from the breech, thus making the rate of firing 3,000 per minute; but rapid firing, when acquired by the addition of intricate mechanism, offers no advantage, and a simple rifle which, upon occasion, will gear with a detachable magazine, and thus serve as an efficient repeater, is the arm now sought.

The removal of the finger from the trigger, in order that the right hand may manipulate the breech-bolt or action-lever, is certainly a drawback, and an efficient mechanism which could be worked by a single pull on the trigger, as with a revolver. would doubtless prove popular. The working of the breech-action by the sliding forward of the left hand is deprecated, since it interferes with the aim.

CHAPTER XXXI.

TARGET RIFLES.

CLASSIFICATION OF TARGET RIFLES.

As already stated, rifles were first produced for the purpose of shooting at targets; their adoption for military and sporting uses came much later. The sport of shooting at the target has many times changed its character, for the range and accuracy of weapons has been the theme of endless discussions; and to this day no one knows exactly what it is possible to do with a rifle. This uncertainty adds to the interest of the sport, and, as rifles have again and again been improved so as to shoot at different distances with greater accuracy, marksmen have striven to excel, and with fresh zest attempted and achieved feats thought to be impossible.

The conditions of the sport have changed, are ever changing, and to define them is almost impossible. The ruling condition—that which divides rifle-shooting into distinct varieties—appears to be the range or distances at which the trials are made. The shorter the range, the less deviation must there be from absolute accuracy; the longer the range, the greater the latitude allowed to overcome the difficulties presented. The rifle which will shoot with least deviation at, say, 200 yards, is not the best type of arm for use at 1,000 yards, or even 500, but the long-range rifle will be beaten hollow by it at the shorter range. This is due to the fact that the velocity requisite to overcome the resistance of the air at the long ranges can be obtained only by more work in the rifle; thus the strain on the shooter is proportionately heavier.

Range, therefore, governs the construction of the target rifle. Other limitations —as of the powder charge to be used, weight of the bullet and rifle—are arbitrarily imposed in order to encourage marksmen in the acquisition of a difficult art by starting competitors from a common base line.

Long-range rifle-shooting is the most difficult, requiring finer training, wide-knowledge, steadier nerve, and better physique than is demanded of the follower of any other sport. The long-range match rifle is not the superior of the military rifle as a *weapon*, but as a shooting instrument is considerably ahead of any arm produced.

The ordinary target rifle is a hybrid arm—a combination of the points found in long-range match, modern military, and the best sporting rifles.

The miniature match rifle, as now made, is a weapon of marvellous accuracy at short ranges, and is the practice weapon of the rifleman.

There is still another class of target rifle—a sort of scientific toy with which the rifleman attempts absolute accuracy, and allows himself every artificial aid his ingenuity suggests. It is doubtful whether this instrument of precision should not be regarded rather as a miniature cannon than a rifled small arm; but to the gun-maker and scientist it is as interesting as any of the other models which conform more nearly to the accepted standard.

HISTORICAL NOTE ON TARGET SHOOTING.

There was a rifle club established in Geneva early in the seventeenth century, but as to the feats of its members and of generations of marksmen who succeeded them it is idle to write. Has not the rifle always played an important part in stories of war, in legends of the chase, and in romance? Was not the weathercock at Nuremberg decorated ages ago with the nine shot-holes figuratively arranged by the cleverest marksman of the time? In the nineteenth century, did not a member of the Rifle Brigade fire from the Bull Ring, in Birmingham, and pierce the weather-vane on St. Martin's spire? How these feats were accomplished is not known. "Skill," says the hero-worshipper. "Fluke," says the cynic. "Never were done," says the incredulous one.

Although some sportsmen and soldiers became skilled shots, the bulk of the people knew little or nothing of marksmanship with the rifle or musket; hence, perhaps, the surprise and admiration fine shooting excited. Until the Crimean War directed attention to the best means of defence in the event of a foreign invasion, target shooting as a sport or a business was rarely practised in this country. Then Volunteer Rifle Brigades were established, and ranges obtained for shooting practice. The faults of the weapons became apparent to the general public, and the inadequacy of the weapons to the work expected of them led to much money and thought being expended in efforts to improve the accuracy and range of the rifle. It must not be forgotten that the interest taken in rifles and marksmanship, if not wholly due to the National Rifle Association, has at least been fostered by that society to a very large extent, and the movement has been practically kept alive by its meetings and by the clubs associated with it.

From the beginning of the century up to 1844 the rifle in general use had a poly-grooved barrel ·630 inch in diameter, with spherical ball, and the arm weighed from

11 to 15 lbs. It was not fired in the military fashion. There was fixed upon it a handle extending downwards immediately in front of the trigger-guard, and this, when grasped by the left hand, permitted of the left arm being steadied against the body in a manner that is impossible if the rifle is held by the barrel in the modern way.

The body-rest position is shown in the illustration of the British rifleman; the modern position was not assumed until the establishment of rifle corps, half a century later.

British Rifleman about 1800.

The same method of shooting is still followed by the Swiss riflemen, and is customary at the German shooting clubs, both on the Continent and in the United States. The Swiss and the Americans were accredited the finest rifle shots in the world, and doubtless they remain first when the firing is at medium ranges and the

conditions to which they are habituated are allowed; but at long ranges, notwithstanding the excellent results the American shots achieved twenty to twenty-five years
ago, they are far behind the standard of shooting ruling in this country and the

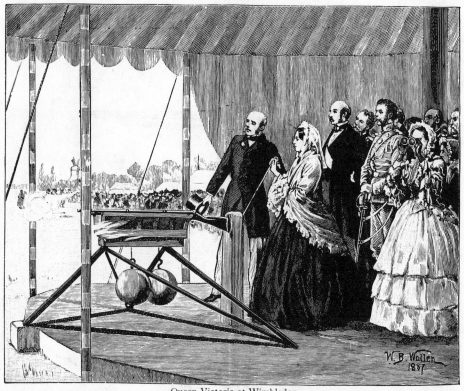

Queen Victoria at Wimbledon.

(Her Majesty opened the first meeting of the National Rifle Association on Wimbledon Common on July 1st, 1860.)

British Colonies. As a sport, long-range rifle-shooting is dead in America; the
medium range is that now practised. Recent triangular competitions at short ranges
with ·22-calibre rifles, between representatives of Great Britain, Australia, and the
United States of America, have resulted in decisive victories for the British teams,
which would point either to their greater skill with the "low power" rifles, or to the
superior accuracy of the British-made rifles.

The first meeting of the British National Rifle Association was held at Wimbledon in 1860. The first shot was fired by Queen Victoria, from a Whitworth rifle on a machine rest, at 400 yards, and struck the bull's-eye at $1\frac{1}{4}$ inches from its centre. The Whitworth muzzle-loading rifle won most of the important prizes at it, and at subsequent meetings until 1871—for its use was compulsory in the Queen's Prize, except in the years 1865–66–67. Most of the Swiss riflemen who attended the meeting had their weapons taken from them in France, and were forced to use others; nine took the Whitworth, but they used it with such success as to unmistakably demonstrate their superior skill, one making the top score of nine hits at 500 yards, one seven, and several six; the Swiss took the Duke of Cambridge's Prize for shooting at 800 and 1,000 yards; and three out of five of the prizes offered by the N.R.A., with scores of 11 (the top score of 12 was made by an Englishman). The Swiss also took three out of five prizes contested at 300 yards, two Lancaster rifles, Duke of Wellington's second prize, Lord Vernon's Prize, Mr. Coutts' prize at 1,000 yards; in fact, the cream of the shooting was theirs.

In the Wellington competition, a Swiss, with his own rifle and hair trigger, made, at 400 yards, on a target six by three, 3 bulls, 2 inners, 1 outer, out of ten shots.

The Swiss managed the Whitworth rifle best. The Swiss who won the Coutts Prize had a Whitworth; his compatriots and competitors used Enfields; and in the official account published of the visit, on their return to Geneva, it is stated that the shooters were at a great loss, owing to firing with a style of rifle to which they were not accustomed, at ranges—1,000 yards—of which they had absolutely no experience, and also because there was no signalling from the target to advise them of *how* they were shooting.

In Switzerland the sport of rifle-shooting at fixed marks has been practised continuously from mediæval times; a rifle club held meetings in Geneva in the seventeenth century; and at medium ranges, and from a rest, excellent shooting is recorded to have been made early in the nineteenth century. It was reported in the *Field* that at the Tir Cantonal, held at Zurich in August, 1860, a rifleman succeeded in making 153 bull's-eyes in one day, the range being about 200 yards, and the bull's-eye only $2\frac{1}{2}$ inches in diameter. This score was phenomenal, and at the time considered to be unparalleled, either in Switzerland or any other country.

Dr. Scoffern says :—

"As regards the Swiss system of loading and firing, both are peculiar. The Switzer unslings a powder-flask of large dimensions and turns in a charge of about $2\frac{1}{2}$ drams of powder. From a side pocket he next extracts a linen patch, and, putting it into his mouth, turns it round and round, very much as Jack turns his quid. The Switzer's object is to saturate his patch with saliva. This is his way of solving the lubrication difficulty, and, mind me, it is not a bad one. His next move is to lay the patch upon the bore, and the picket upon that ; which being done, he takes the ramrod in both hands and drives the picket home with one thrust. To be assured that it is home the Switzer jerks the ramrod down upon it with a ringing thwack. ' Bad practice,' you say ; ' he meals the powder.' Not a bit of it ! At the end of the ramrod there is a flat iron boss, which only permits it to fall down to a fixed and unvarying extent. Well, the anxious moments of firing are now come round. See how the Switzer employs them. He begins by planting his legs wide apart—left leg foremost. He tries the ground under him for a moment or so, to find whether it be soft, and if he can wriggle out two little graves, one for each foot, the better. Should you have turned away your eye for a moment, and then direct your glance at the Switzer again, you will have found him half as big again as he was when you last saw him. He has puffed himself out with a deep breathing, like the frog who aspired to become a bull. By this deep inspiration the Switzer has stiffened himself, just after the way one takes the limpness out of a macintosh cushion—by filling it full of wind. The Switzer is firm planted and rigid now—he could no more bend from side to side than can a hard-rammed sausage. If he were obliged to hold his wind as long as we take to tell our tale, it would be bad for him—he would burst outright, like an overcharged rifle. Well, with legs apart (like a little Rhodian Colossus) and bated breath, the Switzer shoulders his piece. At the end of the stock is a boss, which he tucks between his right arm and right ribs. Gathering his two hands close together, he rests his rifle on his left hand, placed close in front of the trigger guard ; pressing his left elbow, not on the left knee, indeed, but upon the left hip. Lot's wife could hardly be more rigid. Limited power of motion, nevertheless, the Switzer has. Heavenward you see his rifle pointing, and if you observe the Switzer's nose (that organ given only for ornament, as some affirm), it is turned to a purpose of utility. The Switzer is steadying the butt-end of his rifle against it ; his nose is a lateral rest. By this time that nose is red on the tip, the face turgid, the eyes projecting. The Switzer's whole position is decidedly not graceful—one very suggestive of extrusion. Heavenward you see it pointing. Gradually down and down it drops. The blank is seen, the trigger pressed. Rifle crack and Switzer's grunt follow on the heels of each other. He could not hold his breath for ever. Picket and unpreserved breath fly together. Behold him now, panting and puffing like a Cingalese pearl-diver fresh from the worrying of a ground shark. Decidedly, our style of rifle-firing is more graceful and more quick."

The progress of rifle-shooting in Britain may be studied in the reports of the National Rifle Association's annual meetings. Here space allows only of such items as bear directly upon changes in the weapons used. In 1861 the Henry grooving, a modification of the Whitworth, made its first appearance and was professedly produced in order to allow of a cylindrical bullet being used instead of a mechanically-fitting one ; but with the Henry mechanically-fitting bullets were used, as they gave better results. The Enfield was brought out with grooves of diminishing depth. In 1863 five competitors tried to oust Whitworth from his position as purveyor of the most accurate rifles—that is, those with which the Queen's competitions were shot. The Whitworth again proved its superiority, and the next year maintained its position. In 1864 Mr. Rigby tied with Whitworth upon the figure of merit obtained by the shooting of six rifles from the machine rest at 1,000 yards. It was hinted that the use of the rest permitted a particular aim to be favoured, or the reverse, for as the rifle became foul, and the bullets in consequence dropped, by increasing the pressure on the butt the elevation was slightly raised to counteract the tendency At a subsequent trial, Mr. Rigby obtained first place and supplied the rifles for the next year's meeting.

In 1865 Mr. Rigby's rifles were tried at Enfield, and gave a group of 20 shots at 1,000 yards with a mean deviation of 1·11 feet only—a figure of merit never before

Method of holding Rifle and Position of Swiss Rifle Shot.

reached in a public trial; and in the Queen's competition the shooting was better than that of previous years. Mr. Metford's grooving first appeared at this meeting, being used by Sir H. Halford in the Elcho Shield competition. Shallow grooving, an increasing spiral, and a long cylindrical bullet of hardened lead were the features of the Metford, and some wonderful results were obtained, although these, in part, are supposed to be due to the much better quality of the powder used. At the next meeting (1866) there was a noticeable trend against the mechanically-fitting bullet. In 1867 Mr. Rigby produced his new model long-range rifle, on the lines followed by Mr. Metford ; and the breech-loading rifle, using metallic ammunition, appeared in the field. The Westley-Richards capping breech-loader with soft cartridges had often distinguished itself at Wimbledon, but the Henry breech-loader this year came conspicuously to the front. The next year no distinct advance was made by the breech-loader, but in 1869 the work of the Government Committee caused a great impulse to be given to experimental rifle manufacture, and the " Henry " barrel came well to the front when used as a breech-loader.

In 1870 the Martini-Henry, the new arm of the service, won the Duke of Cambridge's prize, the extreme range in this competition being 800 yards. In 1871 the Enfield-Snider breech-loader replaced the Enfield muzzle-loader, and the Martini-Henry replaced the Whitworth in the second stages—800, 900, and 1,000 yards ranges—of the Queen's. The Metford barrel also was used in breech-loaders, and the Duke of Cambridge's prize—for the first time fired at 1,000 yards—fell to it.

In 1872 the muzzle-loader lost ground and the military breech-loader advanced. A team shoot between five a side, breech-loader and muzzle-loader respectively, 30 shots per man at 1,000 yards, somewhat equalised matters, the muzzle-loader team winning with an average of 15 points per man. Metford and Henry barrels tied for top score in the Queen's ; and with a muzzle-loader Mr. Ross won the Wimbledon cup with a highest possible score at both 600 and 1,000 yards. In 1873 the military breech-loader at least held its own, but the year following it made a decided advance ; for very fine shooting the muzzle-loader seemed hard to equal, and this year the Irish team, armed with Rigby muzzle-loader rifles, visited Creedmoor, U.S.A., and were defeated by three points only by an American team armed with the breech-loader rifles. The story of this visit is told in a volume of 216 pages published by Stanford, London, in 1875.

In 1875, American riflemen made their first visit to Wimbledon armed with " army pattern " breech-loading rifles, and practised the swabbing out of the barrel after every shot. They had defeated the Irish team at Dublin and showed the superiority of the breech-lóader cleaned out after each shot over the muzzle-loader not cleaned out. The hints given by the Americans led to some noteworthy changes later. A feature of their shooting was the " back position," regarded as a novelty, although a few English rifle-shots had long practised it. The best score was in the Elcho Shield competition—2 magpies, then 13 bull's-eyes : eleven of the latter in succession. In 1876 the Duke of Cambridge's prize was won very easily with a Metford breech-loader, and the same type of rifle did well in other long-range competitions. The great contest at Creedmoor took place this year, Ireland, Scotland, Australia, and Canada sending teams, the conditions being those of the

Elcho Shield competition. A United States team secured first place ; the Irish team were a close second. Mr. J. K. Milner, of the Irish team, made a highest possible : fifteen consecutive bull's-eyes at 1,000 yards : for long the record score.

Some of the finest shooting ever recorded was made in 1877 both in this country and in the United States. The American teams defeated those of the United Kingdom, and the superiority of the American system of rifle-shooting, the superiority of the cleansable and cleansed breech-loader over the increasing fouling and foulness of the muzzle-loader, was demonstrated beyond question. In England, too, the breech-loader deprived the muzzle-loader of first place ; but the muzzle-loader did not at once disappear. In 1878 the highest scores ever made with the muzzle-loader in this country were recorded, greater care being taken to clean the rifles after every shot. In 1879—the year of the " Marking Scandal "—the American rifle carried away notable long-range prizes, and in 1880 the English breech-loader in the hands of the Irish team made wonderful scores, being 28 points ahead of the highest record, in 1878, for the same competition. The military breech-loader Martini-Henry had been quite ousted from pride of place in long-distance competitions, and more and more its use became confined to the competitions from which " any " rifles were barred. In 1881 the muzzle-loader was deprived of the " Duke's " prize, the last it had held successively since 1873. In 1882 the American rifle went back somewhat ; no American came to Wimbledon, but a match took place at Creedmoor between a team of British Volunteers and one chosen from the U.S.A. National Guard, and was won by the British with low scores ; 99 out of a possible 105 was the best score at long range.

In 1883 the National Rifle Association Council altered the conditions, believing that the American system was not worthy of encouragement from the military and gunmakers' points of view. Wiping out after each shot was forbidden, but muzzle-loaders were not disqualified ; the result was that the American type of rifle has disappeared. The poor shooting of the Martini at 1,000 yards induced the Council to reduce the range for the Queen's competition, the maximum distance being 900 yards—a retrograde step hardly complimentary to the military authorities, though undoubtedly justified by the inferior shooting of the Martini at that distance.

In 1885 the shooting was of the usual description ; the Martini-Enfield ·4-calibre was proposed as the new regulation rifle, but was not tried at the meeting, and the following year saw no marked improvement in the shooting of either match or military rifles. In 1887 Mr. Winans with a Purdey rifle beat Earl Grey's record score of 24 in the Hillhouse or moving target (running deer) competition. Mr. Winans made the record score of 25.

In 1890 the National Rifle Association first met at the new ranges at Bisley ; the meeting was opened by the Princess of Wales firing a rifle aligned by Sir Henry Halford, and this scored a central bull's-eye.　In the competitions Major Thorburn made the highest possible at 1,000 yards with a Gibbs' rifle, and other highest possible scores were made at long ranges, although the wind allowance necessary was more than twelve feet.　This year was noticeable for the excellent shooting made in the any rifle competitions by the Gibbs' match rifle.　The accepted type was ·461 calibre, 7 grooves, ·0045 inch in depth, 80 grains of special black gun-powder, and a bullet of 570 grains.

At the 1892 meeting the only highest possible score at 1,000 yards was made by Captain Davidson in the " Tyro" competition, 10 shots at 1,000 yards.　Many of the " Regulars " used the Lee-Metford with cordite, and the Queen's Prize was won with a very low score compared to the average shooting made with match rifles— the difference between the accuracy of the military and match rifles being very marked at this meeting.

In 1893 there was seen to be a steady improvement in the shooting of the public school teams, due to the issue of the Martini in 1885, since which date the perform-ances improved year by year.　This year the Metford was used by the Army team with cordite ammunition, and this led to the withdrawal of the Volunteer team from the contest for the United Service Challenge Cup, a trophy they had won and held successively from 1880 to 1891.　The superior shooting made by the ·303 in this proved that the Volunteer team was justified in refusing to compete.

In 1894 the match rifle-shooting of Captain Gibbs was remarkable ; he used copper-coated bullets, and made top scores in most competitions in variable and boisterous weather, and although no highest possible scores were made at 1,000 yards, he in one competition made nine successive bull's-eyes at that range, and in the Wimbledon Cup (shot for at 1,100 yards, 15 shots) scored 71 out of the possible 75 points.

In 1895 many of the match rifle-shots used copper-coated bullets, following the lead of Captain Gibbs.　The nitro-powder competitions proved that at every range the scoring was not likely to surpass that achieved with black gunpowder ; at long ranges the scores were generally lower than the average of recent years, and the ·303 was equalled, and in some instances beaten, by the smaller calibre Mannlicher rifle, which, owing to its lighter bullet, ought to have been at a disadvantage.　The cordite cartridges were not satisfactory, not ten per cent. of the competitors using them being able to fire ten shots at 800 or 900 yards without making a miss, and the ricochets showed that there was considerable variation in the velocity.　Much of the erratic shooting was attributed to the fact that the bullets stripped or "ringed" in the barrel. Sir E. Loder had two hits scored to him from one shot ; one due to the lead core and the other to the nickel jacket. A service rifle was burst with a nitro-compound, but it was shown that this was not wholly, if at all, the fault of the explosive.

No remarkable shooting was made with the match rifle at the 1896 meeting, but the ·256 Mannlicher proved itself not only a capital target weapon, but a handy rifle for sporting purposes, excellent shooting at the moving targets being made with it by Mr. Littledale, Mr. Ranken, and others, and it defeated the ·303 in the contest for the Duke of Cambridge's Cup. The ·303 proved its superiority over the ·450 Martini, the team of regulars defeating the volunteers by 33 points. The chief advantage was shown at the longest range, although at 200 yards, when shooting off-hand, the lighter recoil of the smaller bore told slightly in its favour. Numerous complaints were made as to the quality of the Martini ammunition supplied by the Government ; and this, of course, made the older pattern weapon appear to be even worse than it was, and, as the shooting in the Queen's proved— the lowest winning score but one on record taking the gold medal—the best the rifle is capable of achieving was not shown. This meeting practically closed the series of contests with both the Martini and the Military Match rifles. The Territorials are now armed with the ·303, and both the King's and St. George's Competitions are competed for with that bore.

RECORD SCORES.

The best score ever placed on record is probably that made by Mr. Gibbs on the private range at Wistow and authenticated by Sir Henry Halford.

This proves that the match rifle is capable of registering the highest possible score in any competition ; if the conditions are favourable and the marksman capable, a full score may again and again be recorded without any further improvement in rifles.

A score that held the record for fifteen years was made at Dollymount, Ireland, in 1880, on the occasion of the American team's visit, when Dr. S. J. Scott made 74 out of a possible 75. Appended is a facsimile of the diagram. During the same match highest possible scores were made at 900 yards by both Col. Clark and Mr. Rathbone, all three scores being for the American team. The top score of the Irish team was 72 at 1,000 yards and two highest possible at 800 yards.

A very good score was made at Hounslow in 1879 by Major S. S. Young with a Farquharson-Metford breech-loading match rifle, 10 lbs. weight, 73 out of 75 at

Fifty Consecutive Shots; distance, 1,000 yards ; from a ·461-bore Metford rifle, by Gibbs, of Bristol, and a ringing bull's-eye. Shot by Mr. G. C. Gibbs at ordinary first-class targets, with 3-feet bull's-eye, and without cleaning bore, on October 11th, 1886, at Wistow.

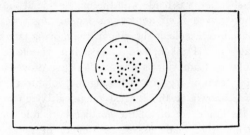

5 5 5 5 5 4 5 5 5 5 5 5 4 5 5 5 5 5 5 5 5 5 5 5 5 5 5 5 5 5 5 5 5 5 5 5 5 5 5 5 5 5 5 5 5 5 5 5 5 5—total, 248.

1,000 yards.   All these scores were made with orthoptic sights and cleaning rifle *ad libitum.*

In 1891 Mr. Whitehead made 71—75 at 1,000 yards in the Wimbledon Cup

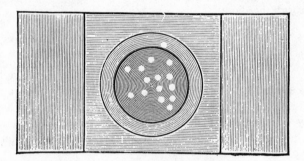

Diagram of Dr. Scott's Target at 1,000 yards.

competition, and in the same competition in 1894 Captain Gibbs scored 71 at 1,100 yards, in both cases with the Metford rifle.   In 1892 both Captain Gorvan and Private Boyd scored 74 out of 75 at 1,000 yards in the Elcho Shield competition with the same make of rifle.

Among the best long-range scores on record with military rifles and ammunition, plain sights, and no wiping out of the barrel, mention must first be made of that credited to Major S. S. Young at Hounslow on November 4th, 1879, with a Field-

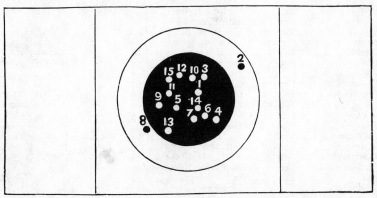

Diagram of Target made with a Farquharson-Metford Match Rifle.

Turner rifle, 9 lbs. weight. The appended diagram shows that the value of the score is 68 out of a possible 75.

It is very difficult to judge the relative value of the scores made in the Queen's

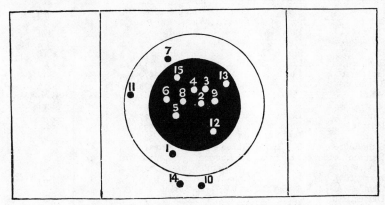

Diagram of Target at 1,000 yards, with Military Rifle.

and similar competitions, as the conditions have so many times been altered. The winning scores in the final stage are given in the following table :—

WINNERS OF THE QUEEN'S PRIZE, 1860-1900, AND THE KING'S PRIZE, 1901-1909.

Year.	Name and Rank of Winner.			Scores made.	Highest possible scores.	Rifle used.
*1860	Ross ...	... Pte.	... 7th North York ...	24 points	60	Whitworth M.L
*1861	Jopling ...	... Pte.	... South Middlesex ...	18 ,,	42	,, ,,
1862	Pixley ...	... Sgt.	... Victoria Rifles ..	44 marks	84	,, ,,
1863	Roberts ...	... Sgt.	... 12th Shropshire ...	65 ,,	,,	,, ,,
1864	Wyatt ...	... Pte.	... London R.B. ...	60 ,,	,,	,, ,,
1865	Sharman ...	... Pte.	... 4th West York ...	64 ,,	,,	Rigby. [Co. M.L.
1866	Cameron, A.	... Pte.	... 6th Inverness ...	69 ,,	,,	Birmingham S. A.
1867	Lane ...	... Sgt.	... Bristol Rifles ...	57 ,,	,,	Gov. Whitwth M.L.
1868	Carslake	... Lt.	... 5th Somerset ...	65 ,,	,,	,, ,,
1869	Cameron, A.	... Crp.	... 6th Inverness ...	71 ,,	,,	,, ,,
1870	Humphries	... Pte.	... 6th Surrey ...	66 ,,	,,	,, ,, [B L.
1871	Humphry	... Ens.	... Cambridge Univ. ...	68 ,,	,,	Gov. Martini-Henry
1872	Michie ...	... C.Sgt.	... London Scottish ...	65 ,,	,,	,, ,,
1873	Menzies...	... Sgt.	... Queen's Edinburgh	60 ,,	,,	,, ,,
1874	Atkinson	... Pte.	... 1st Durham ...	64 ,,	105	,, ,,
1875	Pearse ...	... Cpt.	... 18th Devon... ...	73 ,,	,,	,, ,,
1876	Pullman	... Sgt.	... South Middlesex ...	74 ,,	,,	,, ,,
1877	Jamieson	... Pte.	... 15th Lancashire ...	70 ,,	,,	,, ,,
1878	Rae ...	... Pte	... 11th Stirling ...	78 ,,	,,	,, ,,
1879	Taylor ...	... Crp.	... 47th Lancashire ...	83 ,,	,,	,, ,,
1880	Ferguson	... Pte.	... 1st Argyle ...	74 ,,	,,	,, ,,
1881	Beck ...	... Pte.	... 3rd Devon ...	86 ,,	,,	,, ,,
1882	Lawrance	... Sgt.	... 1st Dumbarton ...	65 ,,	,,	,, ,,
1883	Mackay ..	... Sgt.	... 1st Sutherland ...	79 ,,	100	,, ,,
1884	Gallant ...	... Pte.	... 8th Middlesex ...	110 ,,	150	,, ,,
1885	Bulmer ...	... Sgt.	... 2nd V.B. Lincoln ...	307 ,,	380	,, ,,
1886	Jackson ...	... Pte.	... 1st V.B. Lincoln ...	265 ,,	330	,, ,,
1887	Warren ...	... Lt.	... 1st Middlesex ...	274 ,,	,,	,, ,,
1888	Fulton ...	... Pte.	... 13th Middlesex ...	280 ,,	,,	,, ,,
1889	Reid ...	... Sgt.	... 1st Lanark Engrs. ...	281 ,,	,,	,, ,,
1890	Bates ...	... Sgt.	... 1st V.B. Warwick...	278 ,,	,,	,, ,,
1891	Dear ...	... Pte.	... Queen's Edinburgh	269 ,,	,,	,, ,,
1892	Pollock ...	... Maj.	... 3rd V.B. A. & S. H.	277 ,,	,,	,, ,,
1893	Davies ...	... Sgt.	... 1st V.B. Welsh Rgt.	274 ,,	,,	,, ,,
1894	Rennie ...	... Pte.	... 3rd Lanark ..	283 ,,	,,	,, ,,
1895	Hayhurst	... Pte.	... Canada ...	279 ,,	,,	,, ,,
1896	Thomson	... Lt.	... Queen's Edinburgh	273 ,,	,,	,, ,,
1897	Ward	... Pte.	... 1st V.B. Devon ...	304 ,,	,,	Gov. Magazine Rifle, ·303 bore.
1898	Yates	... Lt.	... 3rd Lanark... ...	327 ,,	380	,, ,,
1899	Priaulx ...	... Pte.	... Guernsey	336 ,,	,,	,, ,,
1900	Ward ...	... Pte.	... 1st V.B. Devon ...	341 ,,	,,	,, ,,
1901	Ommundsen	... L. Crp.	... Queen's Edinburgh	310 ,,	355	,, ,,
1902	Johnson...	... Lt.	... 1st London ...	307 ,,	,,	,, ,,
1903	Davies ...	... C. Sgt.	... 3rd Glamorgan ...	311 ,,	,,	,, ,,
1904	Perry, S. J.	... Pte.	... Canada ...	321 ,,	,,	,, ,,
1905	Comber, A. J.	... A. Sgt.	... 2nd V.B. E. Surrey	315 ,,	,,	,, ,,
1906	Davies, R. ff.	... Capt.	... 1st Mx. V. R. C. ...	324 ,,	,,	,, ,,
1907	Addison, W. C.	... Lt.	... Australia	318 ,,	,,	,, ,,
1908	Gray, G.	... Pte.	... 5th Scottish Rifles	325 ,,	,,	,, ,,
1909	Burr, H. G.	... Cpl.	... London R. B. ...	324 ,,	,,	,, ,,

* No bull's-eye at long ranges. To 1881 inclusive was shot at 800, 900, and 1,000 yards; from 1882 not beyond 900 yards ; and of late years has been shot for in three stages at 200, 500, 600 ; 500, 600, 800, 900, and 1,000 yards.

The Lee-Metford.—The ·303 was used with singular success as a match rifle by Sir H. Halford at the Bisley meeting, 1894. In the Doyle competition he made the highest possible score at 900 yards, 7 consecutive bull's-eyes, the only full scores registered at the distance with the ·303 rifle during the meeting. Miss Leale in the Ladies' any rifle made the next best score, 34 out of 35, with the same rifle.

MODERN AMERICAN TARGET RIFLES.

In America there are three recognised departments of target shooting—the off-hand shooting, shooting from a simple rest to lean the barrel on, and shooting from a fixed machine rest, with telescopic or any other sight. For the first two classes the bores of the rifles are smaller than used in this country, ·380 being the most in favour, though still smaller calibres are becoming popular, but nothing larger than ·38 is now used. The usual weight is from 8 to 10 lbs.; the length of barrel either 28 or 30 inches. It is said that the reduction to these small bores resulted in great improvement in American target practice, on account of the lessening of the recoil, few men being able to continue shooting with the heavily-charged larger bores, on account of the strain of the recoil on the nerves resulting in flinching at the moment of firing; whilst with the smaller bores double the shots or more can be easily fired, and the increased practice thus secured the improved accuracy. As this target shooting is followed entirely for itself the larger charges necessary for a sporting or military rifle are sacrificed to accuracy at comparatively short ranges. In the ·38 bore only 55 grs. of powder are employed with a 330 grain bullet, as this charge is found to give the best results at 200 yards. The Americans have found out that the very small bores are not trustworthy in all weathers, as in that admirable work "Modern American Rifles," Mr. A. C. Gould writes:—"It is a mistaken idea that a ·25 calibre with 20 grains and an 86 grain bullet shoots more accurately than a ·32 calibre with 35 or 40 grains of powder and the usual target bullets; or that the ·32 calibre will do finer and more reliable work than the ·38 calibre. The work and target of the ·25 or ·32 calibre are often wonderful, but they are selected and made under favourable conditions, and I have never yet seen regular and continuous work in all kinds of weather with the 25 and 32 which would compare favourably with the work of the larger bores."

In the second class—that of rest shooting—the barrel is longer and the weight increased to just under 12 lbs. A long, heavy barrel is the correct pattern, as with it the recoil is less and a better sight is obtained. The bore is generally ·38. When the rest shooting was first introduced, it was thought the old pattern long-range match rifles of ·450 calibre (nominal) might be utilised, but it was found that they were not so accurate at the shorter distances. The range is 200 yards, at the American standard ringed-bull target.

Most of the American rifles have a much hollowed-out butt-plate, which they call the Swiss Plate. Mr. A. C. Gould condemns it in his book, already mentioned, thinking that it tends to make the rifleman shoot from the arm, instead of from the muscles of the shoulder, which he considers is the natural place to put a gun against; and that one can better stand the recoil when shooting from there, as well as escaping the shock to the nerves to some extent.

The third class of target shooting is not much practised. A machine rest is used, and generally telescopic sights. Every kind of rifle is employed; therefore, usually they are large bore, and weigh anything from 20 to 60 lbs. The shooter is provided with flags at varying distances from the target, and watches for a lull in the wind before touching off his hair trigger.

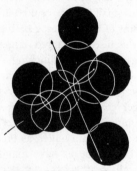

Diagram of Mr. Gove's Target.

The annexed diagram was made by C. Gove, of Denver, with one of these rifles, at 100 yards; a muzzle-loader, 500 bore, weighing 45 lbs. Telescopic sights and conical bullets were used. The average deviation of the ten shots is ·4 of an inch.

The long-range breech-loading match rifle, with which so much fine shooting was done when wiping out after each shot was allowed, was a heavy weapon; the breech mechanism any falling block, as the Sharp's, Farquharson, Deeley and Edge, or Wiley, that would admit of the insertion of the cleaning-rod at the breech. The barrel weighed within an ounce or two of 6 lbs. in a 10 lb. rifle; length, 32 to 34 inches; seven or more grooves, about ·003 to ·005 in depth, and having a complete turn in 20 inches. A sharp continual spiral and very shallow grooves constituted the feature of the American plan.

Mr. Rigby's plan was similar, but one turn in 18 inches and eight grooves, the lands being about half the width of the grooves. In the Wiley the grooves were fewer and wider. The Metford is an increasing twist, starting at the pitch of one turn in sixty and finishing at a turn of one in twenty, or sharper.

The usual bore, ·458 for one cartridge, ·461 for another; powder, 76 grains of No. 6 or of special "fouling" rifle powder; the bullet a long picket, ·450 in diameter naked, ·458 with paper patch, and weight 540 grains. Later rifles were made for 90 grains, 95 grains, and, if the fouling powder was used, as much as

105 grains. The patch dropped from the bullet immediately it left the barrel. The expansion of the bullet was less than $\frac{1}{5000}$ths of an inch.

The pull-off was lighter than 3 lbs.; the butt of shot-gun shape; often with pistol hand, and the sights allowed of elaborate pattern.

CONTINENTAL MATCH RIFLES.

The target rifle with which such accurate shooting at medium ranges is made by the Continental marksmen is a modification of the old pattern Swiss rifle, to which reference has already been made in connection with the reports of the early meetings of the National Rifle Association.

In the newer type the main features are retained : the scroll-guard, hollowed butt-plate, and hair trigger. This last, a valuable adjunct to accurate shooting, but dis-

The Old Pattern Swiss Target Rifle : 1840-45.

allowed in military arms, is a development of the old "tricker-lock" which was used in seventeenth-century wheel-locks. Its object is to free the tumbler from the scear without any pull on the trigger sufficient to influence the aim. It is accomplished by converting the leverage of the trigger into a *blow* upon the scear-tail. A suitable spring and catch are provided to act upon the trigger, which is "set" after the gun is cocked, and when it is ready for firing, and retained by a small hair trigger. The lightest pressure upon this trigger releases the larger trigger, which is forced by the spring against the scear, and the blow given drives it from bent and the tumbler falls. To prevent the scear catching in half-bent—as it would do, there being no continuous pull upon the trigger, as is the case when it is pressed by the finger— an oscillating tongue, called a detant, is pivoted on the tumbler, and its office is to guide the scear nose past the notch in the tumbler as the hammer falls. When the hammer is raised it is pushed backward by the scear and then discloses the half-bent notch, and allows the scear to engage with it.

The detant was formerly much used in both muzzle-loading and breech-loading rifles; it disappeared with the introduction of the rebounding lock from all sporting weapons, and, having been discountenanced by the military authorities, its use is now almost entirely confined to target rifles fitted with hair triggers.

MILITARY MATCH RIFLES.

The military match rifle is not a rifle of any regulation infantry pattern, but such a modification of some military rifle as will, when modified, conform with the rules of the National Rifle Association and permit of its use in the M.B.L. competitions at the Bisley meeting. Up till 1894 the M.B.L. rifle was usually ·440 bore. On the adoption of the ·303 Lee-Speed by the Government, the Council of the Association altered the rules, so that the calibre of rifles of this class must not exceed ·315 inch, thus admitting not only the English rifle, but Continental patterns of modern type. This was done with a view to Continental arms being used in competition, and thus possibly demonstrating the capabilities of these arms and their ammunition at long ranges in comparison with the shooting obtained with the regulation British rifle.

By the present rule, the M.B.L. must not exceed $8\frac{3}{4}$ lbs. in weight; calibre, ·315 or less; pull-off, not less than 4 lbs.; sights may be of any description except telescopic or magnifying, but must be affixed to barrel—spirit levels are allowed. All sights must be strong enough for military purposes and capable of use from prone position. The stock must be strong and fitted with swivel for sling; no pad or shoe for heel of the butt is allowed.

The use of aperture sights of various forms is now permitted for military rifles; the simplest is the windgauge bar sliding on the military tangent, but the aperture in this is too far from the shooter's eye to be of much value. The latest and most popular form is illustrated on page 763; this is affixed to the sight spindle of the present auxiliary backsight on the side of the Lee-Enfield rifle; it allows of rapid as well as minute adjustments, and when not in use lies snugly out of the way on the side of the stock.

The results of the 1895 year's meeting proved that rifles of the ·303 class, and the ·303 British rifle particularly, are not so good viewed from the point of the match rifle shooter. The light bullets are more subject to deflection by the wind at long ranges than the heavier, speed-retaining bullets of the larger bores; in strong,

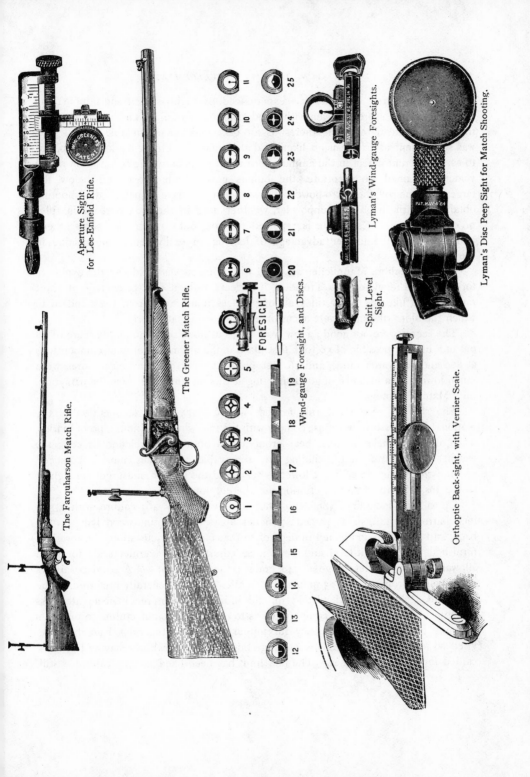

Aperture Sight
for Lee-Enfield Rifle.

The Greener Match Rifle.

The Farquharson Match Rifle.

FORESIGHT

Wind-gauge Foresight, and Discs.

Lyman's Wind-gauge Foresights.

Spirit Level
Sight.

Lyman's Disc Peep Sight for Match Shooting.

Orthoptic Back-sight, with Vernier Scale.

variable winds great difficulty was experienced by highly-skilled shots in making even fairly high scores. Even with good conditions of light and wind, which to the rifleman mean so much, there was an occasional unaccountable miss. This was so frequent as to be in no likelihood attributable to erratic marksmanship, but to some inherent defect in the ammunition; in all probability due to variation in the velocity obtained from cordite, the bullets going both above and below the target. None of the nitro-powders used seem to have equalled the shooting obtainable with the black gunpowder, whether used in the ·303 bore or in rifles of other calibres. Cannonite is reported to have done better than some others, and to possess the further advantage of leaving an easily removable residue in the barrel.

The ·256 calibre Mannlicher was used with some success, and with the explosive for which it is regulated, viz. Troisdorf, it appears to be above the average at short ranges ; but, like the other rifles, at long ranges it fell away from the standard to which the older rifle-shots were accustomed when using ·461 bores.

The scores were not good ; a few were fair, but none really good. A score of 48 out of a highest possible of 50 took first place in the unlimited series of competitions at 800 and 900 yards' range, and 46 first place at 1,000 ; the average scores were much lower. An instance of good shooting at this meeting is given in the paragraph on " Match Shooting."

The "M.R." or match rifle for use in the "any" rifle competition of the National Rifle Association must comply with the following conditions : proof marks ; when of British make, it must bear proof marks both on barrel and breech ; the weight of the barrel, not including any removable appliances, must not exceed 3¼ lbs. ; the maximum calibre allowed is ·325, and the pull off must not be lighter than 4 lbs. Sights of any description may be employed.

Up to (and including) 1896, the rifles usually were of ·461 calibre, with a 34-inch barrel, aperture sights placed 47 inches apart for shooting when lying on the back, and the sight graduated in degrees to that radius for elevation, the foresight furnished with a spirit-level and screw-rack adjustment by vernier scale for wind allowance. The bullet weighed 540 grains ; the charge of *black* powder—always used—varied from 70 to 105 grains, the smaller charges generally preferred. The stock had a short fore-end, pistol-grip, and indiarubber anti-recoil heel-plate. As the object of the "any" rifle competitions is to encourage manufacturers to produce weapons of the highest efficiency for military purposes, the rules have been revised so as to exclude rifles of such large bores, the old calibres having been discarded for military purposes. The new limit has been fixed at ·325 calibre. Still,

"Off-hand" Position.

if experts are to be encouraged to perfect the rifle, some latitude of calibre and ammunition must be allowed them—a fact the Council of the National Rifle Association are not likely to overlook, and the match rifle of the future, like the military weapon of the present, may be of still smaller calibre—probably under rather than over ·300 of an inch in diameter.

POSITIONS FOR RIFLE-SHOOTING.

Of positions in rifle-shooting, Mr. A. C. Gould, in " Modern American Rifles," writes :—" A rifleman is generally able to shoot well in almost any position, if the object shot at be large, and at short ranges ; but when he aims at the 8-inch bull's-eye at a distance of 200 yards, or one proportionately reduced at a shorter distance, it is found that it is impossible to hold the rifle perfectly still, and the attempt is made to find a position in which one can hold the rifle best. Undoubtedly, the physique of a person has its influence on the choice of positions, for nearly every rifleman sooner or later decides on some position which suits him best, and takes it when shooting.

" Young riflemen very naturally study the position of experts, but, as they find fine shots shooting in various attitudes, it generally follows that they try the different positions until they find a preferred one."

The best positions are known as : off-hand, kneeling, sitting, prone, and back positions. The beginner should practise rifle-shooting in the prone and kneeling positions ; then, when to some extent master of the rifle, and able to aim with confidence and fire steadily, the off-hand position may be tried with advantage, but the shooting, of course, will not be as accurate as in the steadier and easier positions, which should always be assumed for shooting at long ranges and when time allows.

The correct off-hand military position is shown in the illustrations. Steadiness is essential, and this is acquired only by practice. It is assumed by taking a half-turn to the right ; the right foot is placed away from the left, and almost at right angles to the target, but the legs not wider spread than necessary to give a firm stand ; in short, to shoot well the position must be a comfortable one.

The position then is such that, at the " present," the rifle is well across the chest, and the left-hand, therefore, can the more easily grip the rifle well forward without the elbow joint being straightened much.

The kneeling position is, like the standing position, useful both for sporting and target purposes, and is the best position for firing heavy elephant rifles. It is steadier and easier than the standing position, and easily assumed on almost any

"Off-hand" Position for Short Range.

kind of ground. For target shooting and when practising the position, the rifleman should be careful to sit well down on the right heel and lean forward sufficiently to get the left elbow-joint just over the left knee, the elbow not resting on the thigh, but as shown in the illustration. The left fore-arm may be almost upright. The left foot should point to the right front ; kneeling on the right knee with the right foot well behind the left, the lower part of the leg will then be at right angles to the rifle. In this, as in the standing position, care must be taken to have the rifle

Kneeling Position

across the chest ; it is easier and allows a steadier aim, but in both positions, especially in windy weather, target shooting is considered uncertain work by even the best shots, and snap-shots must be taken with such conditions. Some men find advantage in swaying the rifle slowly across the target and pressing the trigger as the fore-sight nears the edge of the bull's-eye, but this plan is not recommended to beginners.

The sitting position is very little used by military experts, but it is a very good position, especially when shooting on a steep slope, when it is uncomfortable either to lie "prone" or even to kneel. Sit with the face half-right from the target, rest an elbow on each knee, and then a very steady shot is possible at either a stationary or moving object.

The prone position is the best position for beginners, the easiest, and the steadiest, unless the ground slopes steeply down to the front, or an extreme elevation is required in the rifle; in such circumstances the back position is

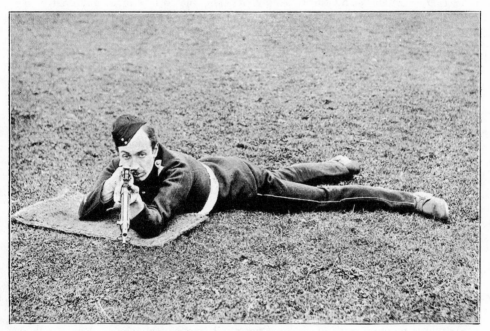

"Prone" Position.

preferable. The essential feature of a good prone position is having the legs disposed well to the left; they may be crossed or extended at choice, well apart for steadiest shooting. The left arm must be brought well under the rifle, and the fore-arm as nearly perpendicular as the elevation of the rifle allows. If the body is at the right angle to the mark, the rifle will come well across the chest. The fore-end and barrel should be firmly grasped with the left hand, but there must be no straining of the muscles or a tremulous motion will be set up which is fatal to good shooting;

in fact, one of the most important factors in obtaining steadiness in any position is to feel perfectly easy in the position adopted ; this is soon gained by practice.   The right hand should grip the small of the stock firmly, and the forefinger be placed so far round the trigger as to press it with the second joint ; the pressing must not be sudden, but a very gradual increase of pressure until the scear is released.   After a little practice, one knows exactly what amount of pressure is required ; but it is a point upon which the beginner should be most careful.   It should be practised in every position many times, simply snapping the lock without any charge in the barrel ; the eye should be kept on the sights steadily, and any movement of the sights from the correct aim when pressing the trigger should be noticed, and the practice continued until the trigger can be pulled without any movement of the rifle.   This is of more importance to the beginner than it at first appears, for if he commences to shoot without this position and aiming practice, the recoil and smoke will prevent him observing possible errors of aim due to the pull upon the trigger.

Large-bore rifles, or any which give great recoil, must not be fired from the prone position.   A well-known professional shot, having to shoot an elephant rifle, foolishly adopted the prone position, the better to command the rifle ; but the great recoil, as he should have known, would be doubly severe when the body was so disposed that it would not yield to the pressure.   His collar-bone was badly fractured, for the butt of the rifle is supported higher on the shoulder in this position than is the case when the shooter is more or less in an upright attitude.

The back position is variously assumed ; the illustration shows that permitted by the National Rifle Association's rules for military competitions, and it is as good for all practical purposes as any of the different fancy positions tried by shooters of long-range match rifles.   It is not likely to be of much use to the sportsman except in very open country.   It is the best for very long ranges, where a high elevation of the rifle is required, and for shooting down hill from a steep slope.   To take this position readily and correctly, sit on the ground facing the target, holding the rifle across the body ; lie on the back, then turn sufficiently on to the right side to allow of the right thigh being almost squarely on the ground ; the legs should then be drawn up placing the left foot on the ground, toe pointing to the right front, with the knee almost upright, but inclining slightly to the left.   The right knee should be bent round the left foot so that the outer side, or that next to the ground, rests on the left instep.

The barrel of the rifle should be laid on the right knee ; the left hand, grasping the top of the stock close in front of the heel-plate, pulls it into the hollow of the shoulder more between the body and arm than in the other positions; raise the head and take a small portion of the left coat-sleeve at the wrist between the teeth to steady the head.

The right elbow rests on the ground, and the right hand, gripping the stock lightly, has little to do but press the trigger as usual.

Back Position, as allowed by the National Rifle Association in Military Competitions.

From this position aim can be taken comfortably and accurately, especially at long ranges, with the aid of orthoptic and spirit-level sights.

The position, although possessing the advantage of steadiness and better vision for long ranges, requires more practice.

AIM.

The beginner should first make himself acquainted with the rifle he is about to use; that is to say, he should understand something of the trajectory and the elevations required for the distances he is likely to shoot at. This and the mechanism of the lock should be his first study. Then comes the correct method of aiming.

Aim is dependent upon the quality of eyesight, the care with which it is applied, and the steadiness of hand.

The system of aiming adopted by almost every good shot, and undoubtedly the best method, is to align the rifle beneath the centre of the bull's-eye and gradually raise it until the tip of the foresight appears to almost touch the bottom edge, care being taken to keep the rifle perfectly upright. A small space should always intervene—the amount should be just as little as the eye can recognise without any strain, as shown in the illustration. To aim at an object, it must be seen; if the object and the foresight be of one colour, no definite spot can be chosen by placing one over the other, as both will appear to merge into one.

As the Bull's-eye should appear above the Sight.

To aim correctly, take more or less of the foresight over the true centre of the backsight; but never more at one time than another. It is best to take a full sight, that is, the whole of the bead of a sporting foresight, or with a military rifle a half-sight—the half of the barleycorn.

It has been found in practice that a rifleman shoots higher when he fires from the prone, or from the kneeling position, than when shooting from a standing position; further, that if the target be brightly illuminated it tends to high aim, while a dull target may lead one to aim low.

THE PRINCIPAL POINTS TO OBSERVE ARE:

(1) Backsight to be kept perpendicular, *i.e.* not leaning either to right or left.

(2) Aim to be taken with foresight in centre of backsight, and the eye to be focussed upon the object aimed at.

(3) The same amount of foresight to be seen through backsight notch for each shot.

(4) The trigger to be gently "squeezed off," not jerked.

THE "RIFLE CLUB" MOVEMENT.

It is generally admitted that the Americans were the first to recognise the necessity for and advantages of a rifle firing a bullet of smaller bore than that in general vogue for target practice and small game shooting, and even in the muzzle-loading days of the eighteenth century their rifles were acknowledged to be unrivalled for accuracy at short ranges.

The invention of the metal cartridge in 1853 marked a distinct advance in the manufacture of rifles. The American manufacturers quickly grasped this improvement, and by the introduction of the ·220 bore rim fire cartridge opened up a new field to the rifle shot. This cartridge, which was, and is still, made in various lengths, is the smallest reliable cartridge made, and for many years it—together with the American rifle—held sway throughout the world for short range shooting.

Later the ·250 bore cartridge was introduced, and like the ·220 bore, it quickly attained a popularity which it has held until the present day. Unlike America, England had for many years treated the miniature rifle question with complete indifference, and prior to the year 1900 the English rifle manufacturer may be said to have entirely ignored this branch of the "trade," beyond the construction of a few highly-priced rifles for rook and rabbit shooting, but few single-barrelled rifles were made in this country, the cheaper American and Belgian rifles commanding the greater portion of our home trade, and entirely dominating our foreign markets.

For many years rifle clubs had been looked upon by both Americans and Swiss as a means of providing a healthy recreation for the people, and at the same time of training a reserve force of men capable of taking up arms at short notice, should the necessity arise, in defence of their Fatherland. The British Government, resting upon laurels won, and lulled to sleep by years of peace, failed to realise that in the preparedness of her people lay the country's strength, and the terrible tragedies of the Anglo-Boer War drew the attention of the whole world to the necessity for accurate marksmanship with the rifle, as opposed to "pipe-clay drill," which had for so long been looked upon as the chief essential to the efficiency of the British Army. The woeful ignorance of many of our hastily gathered levies of even the rudiments of rifle shooting, and consequent failure in the field, quickly brought home to the public mind the absolute need for some preliminary training in this "art."

Unfortunately but little was done by the authorities to foster the rifle club movement ; in fact, many obstacles were placed in the way of those clubs who were so fortunate as to secure sufficient space for open-air ranges, the stringent and ofttimes ridiculous regulations imposed upon them by the War Office rendering the construction of the range in such a way as to meet with the approval of the officials an extremely difficult and expensive undertaking—so much so that but few clubs were able to avail themselves of this class of shooting.

Lord Salisbury's memorable statement that he would like to see a rifle in every cottage in the land, acted like a torch upon the then inflammable minds of the people, and in spite of all obstacles rifle clubs were formed in all parts of the country, and the movement forged slowly but surely ahead. At this period a leader arose in the person of Lord Roberts, who by letter and speech sought to impress upon the Government and the people the lessons he had learned in the Boer War, and it will be readily admitted by all that the energy and enthusiasm with which he has taken up the cause have done much to establish the rifle-club movement upon a firm basis. With the rapid increase in the number of clubs it became evident that outdoor ranges for all were an impossibility, and very soon indoor ranges were established in every important town and in hundreds of villages throughout the kingdom, while the ·220 bore rifle, of which the author's " Miniature Club" and " Martini Service" models are the most generally used, was quickly acknowledged to be the most suitable calibre for indoor shooting.

Continual pressure eventually convinced the Government that the " clubs" had

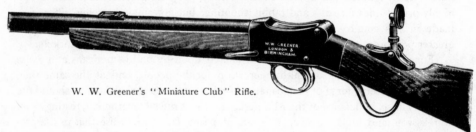

W. W. Greener's "Miniature Club" Rifle.

come to stay, and in conjunction with the National Rifle Association it was decided that members of all clubs affiliated to that Association might claim exemption from the Excise tax in respect of the rifles used at their clubs. Later the Society of Miniature Rifle Clubs was officially recognised, and its members were granted the same privileges as those of the N.R.A.

This *résumé* of the movement would be incomplete without reference to the part taken therein by the working men of Birmingham. Unable to obtain long ranges, they quickly demonstrated their adaptability to the circumstances, and by utilising the air gun were enabled to obtain much excellent practice in an ordinary room. A league was formed, and this later became a national organisation, which also received, through the N.R.A., Government recognition. The first English-made air guns and rifles were manufactured by the author, and were so distinctly in advance of the foreign-made weapons previously available, that they speedily became very popular, and at the present time two other English manufacturers are turning out air guns and rifles in large numbers, both for the home and export trade.

THE MORRIS TUBE AND "ADAPTORS."

The difficulty of obtaining open-air ranges in close proximity to densely populated towns had many years previously shown the necessity for providing some form of rifle practice at short ranges, and the invention of the Morris tube solved the problem for a time, so far as the Army and Volunteers were concerned. This tube consists of a small rifled barrel which exteriorly is less than the bore of the weapon into which it is fitted. A self-centering adjustment at the muzzle enables it to be fixed with little trouble; then, with the ordinary sights firing and extracting mechanism, the tube is usable as a miniature rifle — for instance, the ·450 or ·303 bore rifle may, with this tube, which is usually chambered for the 297/230 bore cartridge, be made available for short range practice, and fairly accurate results will be obtained within the range of the cartridge.

The targets employed with this tube were originally drawn to a special scale, so that when firing at 10 yards the target, according to its size, would present the same appearance to the shooter as the regulation target at 200, 500, or 600 yards· The Morris tube was adopted by the War Office, and there can be but little doubt that it afforded an excellent means of training, enabling the recruit to learn quickly and cheaply how to hold the rifle, align the sights, and pull off correctly.

A more recent invention, adapting the ·303 rifle for practice at short ranges, consists of a dummy cartridge case into which a short cartridge, having a bullet of the same calibre as the bore of the barrel, is fixed. Many ingenious methods have been devised to secure the practice cartridge in the dummy case, and allow of its extraction after firing, but they are too numerous to describe here.

It is a well-known fact that no tube or "adaptor" used from a heavy rifle can be so satisfactory as a rifle specially constructed for use at short ranges, and complete in itself. The chief objection to the former combination is that owing to the weight of the bullet being so much out of proportion to the weight of the rifle, and consequent lack of recoil, one fails to obtain a true knowledge of the weapon's behaviour at the moment of firing.

THE FIRST ENGLISH MINIATURE TARGET RIFLE.

The author may justly claim to have had a considerable share in the initial success of the Rifle Club movement. He had long recognised the fact that a well-made English rifle of absolute accuracy, and produced at a low price, would command a ready sale, and he was the first English maker prepared to meet the demand that rapidly arose for such a weapon.

The first rifle introduced by him was upon the Martini principle, which is still undoubtedly, for its purpose, the best extant, being exceedingly strong, simple in construction, and consequently less liable to get out of order than other more complicated mechanisms. It was of ·310 calibre, the cartridge also being specially designed by him, and suitable for all ranges from 50 yards to 300 yards.

THE "SHARPSHOOTER'S CLUB" RIFLE.

This weapon was quickly adopted by all the leading clubs having outdoor ranges and its name, "The Sharpshooter's Club" rifle, became a household word amongst riflemen, synonymous with "absolute accuracy."

In the year 1901 the author commenced what is now the most popular of the many miniature rifle competitions at Bisley, under the title of "The Greener," and at the first meeting a record was established with the Greener ·310 bore rifle at 100 yards, which record has never yet been beaten by any other rifle in a public competition.

In the same year a long series of public trials were arranged by the proprietors of the *Navy and Army Illustrated*, in order to determine the best rifle for club purposes. Here, also, Greener rifles were easily first both with the ·310 and ·220

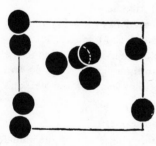

10 Shots at 100 yards with Greener ·310-bore Rifle, Bisley.

calibre. The diagram made with the latter rifle at 50 yards was of such excellence that it not only beat those of all other competitors—English and foreign—but has only since been beaten by users of Greener rifles, and that owing to the vastly superior ammunition now in use.

In 1905 the War Office invited several manufacturers—the author being amongst the number—to submit samples of rifles suitable for the use of cadet corps and miniature rifle clubs. Several models were sent in for inspection, none of which were accepted in their entirety, but eventually a model was evolved, presumably from the designs submitted, which accorded with the ideals of the Army Council, and which is officially described as the War Office miniature rifle, ·22 bore. The chief points of the rifle are the bolt action and the wind-gauge backsight, both of which are intended to accustom the user to the manipulation of the Service rifle.

The Cadet movement is showing signs of revival in England, but greater encouragement will be required from the authorities before it acquires such popularity as it now has in the Colonies. The Commonwealth of Australia have set an excellent example, and have made provision for the training of upwards of 150,000 cadets, the type of arm adopted being the Greener Sharpshooter's Cadet rifle, of ·310 bore for the elder boys, and the miniature pattern of 297/230 bore for the juniors.

10 Shots, 50 yards,
22 bore Rifle.

In the early days of the movement there were not wanting detractors who argued that nothing but practice with the Service rifle could be of any practical value in the field.

The author has always contended that the primary principles of rifle shooting

The W. O. Miniature Rifle.

could be learned as easily with the miniature rifle at a short range as with a heavier rifle at a greater distance.

The advent of the air gun afforded an excellent opportunity of testing this theory, and in 1905 a match was arranged by Mr. Lincoln Jeffries and Mr. Hirst between two teams of seven men aside. The team captained by Mr. Jeffries was composed of ex-soldiers or Volunteers who had served their country in the South African War, and who presumably had a sound knowledge of rifle shooting. That under Mr. Hirst's leadership consisted of "air gunners," not one of whom had previously fired a military rifle, and whose sole training ground had been at the most a seven yards' range.

Both teams used the Service rifle and ammunition, and each man fired five shots at 100 yards; yet in spite of the fact that some of the air gunners did not even know how to load the rifles, they succeeded in beating Mr. Jeffries' team by thirteen points, proving conclusively that the absolute essentials to success in rifle shooting are not necessarily long range shooting, and an accurate knowledge of wind and light variation, but continuity of practice, whether it be at ten yards or 100 yards.

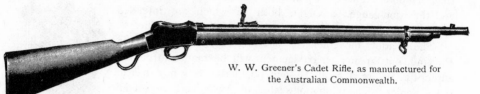

W. W. Greener's Cadet Rifle, as manufactured for
the Australian Commonwealth.

The diagrams shown are actual size, and serve to illustrate not only the remarkable skill of the marksmen, but also the extraordinary degree of perfection

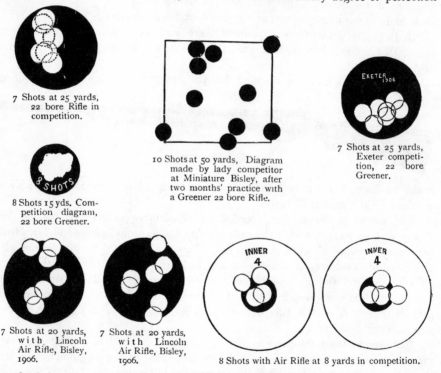

7 Shots at 25 yards, 22 bore Rifle in competition.

8 Shots 15 yds. Competition diagram, 22 bore Greener.

10 Shots at 50 yards, Diagram made by lady competitor at Miniature Bisley, after two months' practice with a Greener 22 bore Rifle.

7 Shots at 25 yards, Exeter competition, 22 bore Greener.

7 Shots at 20 yards, with Lincoln Air Rifle, Bisley, 1906.

7 Shots at 20 yards, with Lincoln Air Rifle, Bisley, 1906.

8 Shots with Air Rifle at 8 yards in competition.

attained by the manufacturer in the rifling and sighting of the weapon; moreover, they may be accepted as showing the line of demarcation between the air rifle and the ·22 bore rifle, there being but little to choose between the two weapons in point of accuracy at from eight to ten yards. Beyond these ranges, however, the ·22 calibre rifle is undoubtedly the superior.

A few details of the principal rifles used by miniature rifle clubs, of which some 2,500 are now affiliated to the various societies in Great Britain, are given as likely to be of interest to the reader. Fuller information on miniature rifle shooting may be obtained from the author's books, " Sharpshooting for Sport and War " and " The British Miniature Rifle."

PARTICULARS OF MINIATURE TARGET RIFLES AND CARTRIDGES.

RIFLES.   AMMUNITION.

Maker.	Name of Rifle.	Calibre.	Type of Action.	Length of Barrel.	Weight.		Calibre.	Weight of Powder	Weight of Bullet.	Muzzle Velocity.	Trajectory at ½-range.
				inches.	lb.	ozs.		grs.		f.s.	50 yds. inches.
Cogswell & Harrison	Certus	22	Bolt	22	4	6	22 Short Smokeless.	—	30	850	1.3
W. W. Greener	Miniature Club Sh'psh'ters	*22	Martini detachable	26	6	8	22 Short Black.	3	30	1,000	0.8 100 yds.
,,	Club	310	,,	26	6	8	22 Long Rifle	5	40	1,100	4.1
Westley Richards	Sherwood	300	,,	—	6	8	297/230 Short	3	37	800	
Savage Arms Co.	Target	22	Bolt	22	4	12	297/230 Long	5	37	1,220	
Stevens	Ideal	*22	{ Falling { block	—	5	12	250	7 Cordite.	56	1,100	100 yds. inches.
,,	Repeater	22	{ Bolt { repeater	—	5	4	300	7	140	1,450	2.44
,,	Favorite	22	{ Falling { block	—	4	8	310	5½	120	1,320	3.25 200 yds.
Winchester	Single Shot	22	Bolt	21	4	4	310	6½ h.p.	125	1,500	13.0
	W. O. Miniature	*22	,,	24	5	4					
W. W. Greener	Service Martini	*22	Martini	30	8	8					
,,	Service Magazine	*22	Lee Speed bolt	30	8	8					

* The majority of these rifles are chambered for the ·22 short, long, and long rifle cartridges, and can also be supplied chambered and bored for 297/230, ·250, ·300, and other calibres.

SIGHTS.

The increasing use of the miniature rifle has led to a corresponding increase in the variety of sights for target shooting. Many have no actual utility, and novelty is their only excuse for existence.

Foremost, and justly so, among the sights in use is the " Orthoptic " or " Peep " backsight. When first patented by Lyman, this sight was the subject of much

FORESIGHTS.

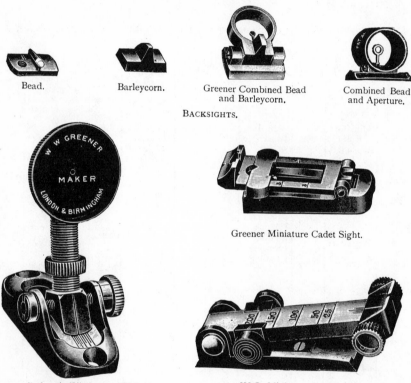

Bead.   Barleycorn.   Greener Combined Bead   Combined Bead
                                          and Barleycorn.   and Aperture.

BACKSIGHTS.

Greener Miniature Cadet Sight.

Greener Orthoptic Wind-gauge Sight.   W.O. Miniature Backsight.

adverse criticism, but experience has proved that by its aid the beginner can learn to shoot more quickly, and the expert can shoot still better.

The Wind-gauge Orthoptic sight illustrated is one introduced by the author some years ago, and its principal advantages are extreme rigidity, rapid and easy elevation, and lateral adjustment, allowing of a fine degree of accuracy. The backsight in general use is of a military pattern, but of reduced size. The foresights are too numerous to describe in detail. A few will be found illustrated on pages 660 and 763, and further illustrations are appended. In conjunction with the Military pattern backsight, a barleycorn, or fine bead sight, is generally used, while for rifles fitted with the Orthoptic the combined bead and barleycorn foresight is an extremely popular and useful combination.

RIFLE SHOOTING AS A SPORT.

To the casual observer the sporting element in rifle shooting seems to be reduced to the veriest minimum. He may, perhaps, on some occasion have witnessed a match between two well-known teams of marksmen; and if entirely ignorant of the sport, the continual ping of the bullets, and monotonous raising and lowering of the signalling discs, occasionally broken by the bugle call, " cease fire," would merely convince him that rifle shooting was but dull sport, and he would in all probability leave the range utterly disgusted with the whole business.

To thoroughly appreciate this pastime one must be an actual performer, and a right understanding of even the rudiments of rifle shooting quickly changes the opinions of the one-time casual observer.

Every shot becomes of interest, whether his own or a fellow rifleman's, and he anxiously awaits the appearance of the marker's disc. Success but breeds the desire for greater success, and whether Territorial or Clubsman he becomes anxious to represent his corps or club in some public competition. The same spirit is evident, whether it be a match fired with one's next-door neighbour in the back garden, or between two of England's crack shots in the final of the " King's." There is always that necessary element of chance which raises rifle shooting from the realms of mere skill and science into true sport.

Rifle shooting in every form of competition calls for the exercise of all the qualities that most ennoble a man—determination, self-possession, faith, self-confidence, admiration for the achievements of others. It is suitable for the elderly, since it makes but a small demand upon the muscle. It is the best schooling for the young, as it requires nerve. It interests all, since it allows—nay commands—the exercise of intelligence. There is no pastime the equal of rifle shooting. Rifle shooting, pure and simple, will satisfy without the adjuncts of applauding crowds, "pots" won or honours received, for the use of the rifle is in itself a sport unsurpassed.

ENGLISH AND METRIC WEIGHTS AND MEASURES.

MEASURES OF LENGTH.

Millimetres.				Inches.
1	...	...	= ...	1-25th
2	...	...	= ...	5-64ths
5	...	...	= ...	13-64ths
10 (1 centimetre)		= ...		13-32nds
20 (2 ,,)		= ...		25-32nds
50·	...	...	= ...	1 31-32nds
50·8	...	...	= ...	2
53	...	...	= ...	2 1-8th
56·4	...	...	= ...	2 1-4th
63	...	...	= ...	2½
68	...	...	= ...	2 3-4ths
70	...	...	= ...	2 25-32nds
75	...	...	= ...	3
87	...	...	= ...	3½
100	...	...	= ...	3 15-16ths
150	...	...	= ...	5 29-32nds
200	...	...	= ...	7 7-8ths
250	...	...	= ...	9 27-32nds
300	...	...	= ...	11 13-16ths
350	...	...	= ...	13 25-32nds
355	...	...	= ...	14
360	...	...	= ...	14 1-4th
365	...	...	= ...	14½
500	...	...	= ...	19 43-64ths
609·6	...	...	= ...	2 feet
762	...	...	= ...	2 feet 6 inches
914·4	...	...	= ...	3 feet

FRACTIONS OF THE INCH.

Inches.		Millimetres.
1/16	=	1·58
1/8	=	3·17
1/4	=	6·35
3/8	=	9·52
1/2	=	12·7
3/4	=	19·05
13/16	=	20·63
7/8	=	22·22
15/16	=	23·81
1	=	25·4
12	=	304·8·0
36	=	914·3·0
39·37	=	1,000 or one metre.

NOTE.—(1) To convert feet into metres, the rule is to multiply the number of feet by 61 and divide by 200.

(2) To find the number of feet in a given number of metres, multiply by 200 and divide by 61.

GRAINS AND GRAMMES.

Grains.					Grammes.
1	...	...	...	...	0·064799
2	..	...	...	...	0·129
3	...	...	...	...	0·194
5	...	...	...	...	0·323
10	...	...	...	...	0·646
20	...	...	..	...	1·392
30	...	...	...	...	2·038
35	...	...	...	...	2·261
36	...	...	...	...	2·328
37	...	...	...	...	2·397
38	...	...	...	...	2·462
40	...	...	...	...	2·591
42	...	...	...	...	2·722
45	...	...	...	...	2·914
46	...	...	...	...	2·980
47	...	...	...	...	3·045
49	...	...	...	...	3·175
50	...	...	...	...	3·240
54	...	...	...	...	3·499
56	...	...	...	...	3·708
60	...	...	...	...	3·887
62	...	...	...	...	3·967
66	...	...	...	...	4·226

POWDER CHARGES.

Drams.		Grains.		Grammes.
1	...	27½	...	1·772
2	...	55	...	3·544
2½	...	69	...	4·428
2¾	...	75¼	...	4·872
3	...	82	...	5·315
3¼	...	89	...	5·758
3½	...	95⅜	...	6·201
3¾	...	102	...	6·645
4	...	109	...	7·088
4¼	...	116	...	7·521
4½	...	123	...	7·964
5	...	137	...	8·52

NOTE.—In cartridge loading the avoirdupois weight is used. One pound contains 16 ounces, or 256 drams, or 7,000 grains, and is equal to the metric weight of 453·592 grammes. The dram is therefore equal to 27½ grains, or to 1·9772. One grain equals 0·064799 grammes, and is usually calculated as 0·065 g.

INDEX.

A.

PRINTED BY CASSELL & COMPANY, LIMITED, LA BELLE SAUVAGE, LONDON. E.C.

ii

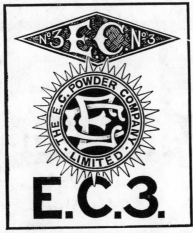

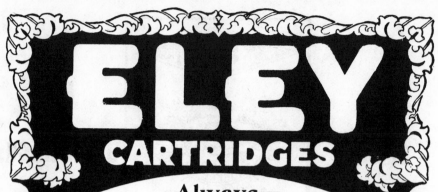

ELEY
CARTRIDGES

Always
Reliable

Shooting accuracy starts with your cartridge! The name 'Eley' on a cartridge is an unfailing guarantee of accuracy and of uniform excellence.

A few 'Eley' Specialities are here illustrated:

'450 Revolver (Target Bullet)

'22 Long Rifle

'455 Revolver (Target Bullet)

'22 Rim

'ELEY' CARTRIDGES have won the highest encomium from some of the most critical sportsmen in the world.

Obtainable from all gunmakers and dealers throughout the world.

ELEY BROS., LTD., LONDON
Birmingham, Glasgow, and
Liége (Belgium)

'303 Marksman

'280 Ross-Eley

7m/m Mauser

Books published by Horace Cox

CARTRIDGES for SHOT GUNS.

W. W. GREENER's Cartridges are loaded by hand, the pellets of the charge being counted into each case, and no variation is possible, 304 pellets always going to the charge of $1\frac{1}{8}$ ounce of No. 6 of 270 to the ounce.   The shot is made specially for Mr. Greener, and the powder is the best procurable at any given time.   Every batch of powder received is personally tested by the chronograph and crusher gun, as well as for pattern and recoil, before being issued.

PRICES FOR 12 BORES.

	Cash.		Booked.	
	s.	d.	s.	d.
Best Selected Powder, in the famous "Sporting Life" case, standard load, and $1\frac{1}{8}$ ounce shot, per 100	10	6	11	6
The "Dead Shot" Nitro (selected) Cartridge, second quality case and Patent shot... ... ...per 100	8	9	9	9
The "Paragon" Cartridge, Nitro Powder, and full load ... per 100	7	6	not booked	

These Prices do not include either Carriage or Packing, which are charged extra, but Carriage will be paid in England on lots of 1,000 and upwards. Cash Prices mean Cash accompanying the Order.

Write for detailed List of Cartridges, free by post.

Prices of W. W. GREENER'S GUNS
HAMMERLESS EJECTOR,
WITH ALL LATEST IMPROVEMENTS.

Grade G. 70.

Grade Presentation.   Under this grade W. W. Greener supplies guns elaborately decorated with gold in relief, and will send prices and photographs on application.

Grade G. 70. "Imperial" quality. The highest development of the modern shot-gun ...	£73	10 0
Grade G. 60. "Royal." Very best material, artistically engraved and finished	63	0 0
Grade F. H. 45. Fore-end Ejector, nicely engraved	47	5 0
Grade F. H. 35. Ditto ditto ... ... ∴.	36	15 0
Grade F. H. 25. Ditto soundly finished and reliable...	26	5 0

GREENER'S HAMMERLESS GUNS.

The "Facile Princeps" Lock Mechanism, the celebrated Treble-wedgefast Breech Fastening, and Patent Side Safety Bolt, with which these guns are fitted, have given satisfaction in all parts of the world.

Grade F. 70. "Imperial." Highest quality Gun	£73	10 0
Grade F. 60. "Royal." Best quality Gun	63	0 0
Grade F. 40. Artistically engraved and finished	42	0 0
Grade F. 30. A thoroughly well-made Gun, nicely engraved	31	10 0
Grade F. 20. "The International" Pigeon Gun	21	0 0
Grade F. 16. Well made and finished, little engraving	16	16 0
Grade D. 13. Improved A and D action, plainly finished	13	13 0

GUN CASES ARE NOT INCLUDED IN THESE PRICES.

W. W. GREENER'S GUNS.

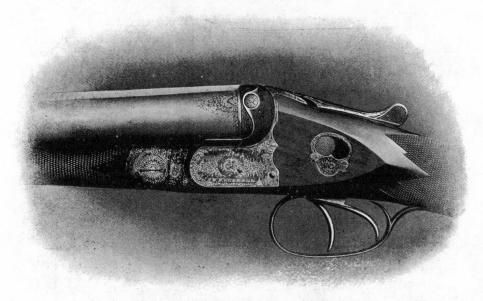

Grade F. 40. Hammerless Gun.

HAMMER GUNS.

Grade A. 60.	Very best quality	£63 0 0
Grade A. 40.	Principally made as a Pigeon Gun, best quality...	42 0 0
Grade A. 25.	Specially recommended for hard work	26 5 0
Grade A. 16.	"The Far-killing Duck" Gun, originally designed for Duck shooting ...	16 16 0
Grade A. 13.	Treble-wedge-fast action, neatly finished	13 13 0
Grade A. 9.	"The Dominion Gun," plainly finished, but thoroughly reliable	9 9 0

SINGLE BARRELLED GUNS.

20, 16, and 12 bores ... ... from 5 to 10 guineas.

DUCK GUNS.

HAMMER.				HAMMERLESS.		
Single 8-bore Duck Guns	...	...	from 16 guineas.	8-bores	...	from 25 guineas.
,, 4-bore ,, ,,	...	...	,, 25 ,,	4-bores	...	,, 35 ,,
Double 8-bore ,, ,,	...	...	,, 20 ,,	8-bores	...	,, 30 ,,
,, 4-bore ,, ,,	...	...	,, 30 ,,	4-bores	...	,, 45 ,,

REVOLVERS.

Greener's Bull-Dog Revolver, ·320, ·380, or ·450 bores...	...	...	...	...	£2 2 0
Greener's self-extracting Revolver, N.P., ·320 or ·310 bores	...	...	...	...	3 0 0
Target Pistols, firing ·22, ·297/·230, or ·310 cartridges ...	...	...	...	from	1 10 0

Air Canes from 55s. ; Air Guns from 21s.
Walking Stick Guns, C.F. ·410 bore, with detachable butt and safety bolt, 50s.

Combined Rifle and Shot-Guns.

The combination of a rifle and shot-gun in one double-barrelled weapon is extremely popular in South Africa. The right barrel is usually full choke 12 bore, and the left rifled, and bored to shoot the No. 2 musket cartridge, 76 grains powder, and 480 grains solid bullet, sighting from 100 to 700 yards with seven leaf flush sight. (Weight 9 to $9\frac{1}{2}$ lb.)

Always made on Greener's treble-wedge-fast principle, as no other system of breech action is adapted so well to withstand the enormous strain produced by the heavy bullet.

A combination ·450 bore rifle and 16 bore shot barrels with 30 in. barrels can be made as light as 8 lbs.

A special combination of a Hammerless ·303 and 16 bore, weighing but $8\frac{1}{2}$ lb., can be made to order. Other combinations to special order.

PRICES.

Hammer Rifle and Shot-Gun combined ... £26 5 0 and upwards.
Hammerless ditto, from   ...   . £31 10 0   ,,

BALL AND SHOT-GUNS.

Specially bored for shooting with either ball, buck shot, or small shot.

The gun is similar in appearance to a shot-gun, but can be fitted with a backsight, and weighs a little heavier. It is not, however, so heavy as a rifle, but quite as accurate within its range, which is from 40 to 50 yards, the larger bores carrying the farther.

The barrels can be bored either choke or cylinder ; but in case one barrel is choke and the other cylinder, care must be taken to see that the bullets are moulded for the *smaller* (i.e. choked barrel).

PRICES (*including Bullet Mould*).

Hammer Guns, from   ...   . 20 guineas.
Hammerless   ,, ... 30   ,,

Send for Special Rifle List, giving particulars.

THE CHOKE-BORE RIFLE.

Hollow Bullet, Copper
Tubed, Weight 710 Grains.

Weight of Bullet,
568 Grains.

Steel-Pointed Bullet.

A PERFECT SHOT-GUN AND A PERFECT RIFLE IN ONE.

It performs equally well with conical and spherical ball, solid and hollow bullets, light and heavy charges of powder, and shoots shot of any size making regular patterns, either cylinder or choke, as ordered.

The grooving is invisible, cannot foul, and is as easily kept bright and clean—*throughout its whole length*—as is the barrel of a shot-gun.

It has the accuracy and force of the heavy rifle combined with the lightness and handiness of the shot-gun, and is, without a doubt, the best weapon for snap-shots at large game. If used as a shot-gun when loaded with expansive conical bullets, it is the best weapon for deer-drives, boar-drives, also bear and elk shooting, or whenever advantage has to be taken of a snap-shot at driven or moving large game.

W. W. Greener's "Wrought Steel," which rifles perfectly, and is stronger than Damascus, is used for all barrels of the Choke-Bored Rifles.

PRICES (for any Bores from 28 to 10 Calibre).

Hammer Gun, Treble-Wedge-Fast, Breech Action ...	**£26 5 0**	and upwards.
Hammerless	**31 10 0**	,,
Self-acting Ejector	**36 15 0**	,,

With a gun on this system, weighing 7 lb., *good diagrams* can be made up to 100 yards, with charges of powder up to 3¾ drams and a spherical ball *without excessive recoil;* 12 bore 28-in. barrels can be made as light as 7 lb.

The "stopping" power of the Spherical Ball is well known to all hunters of large game. The short Conical Bullet, with steel core and point (as illustrated above), has great striking force and penetration. These bullets augment the price of the cartridges 11s. to 15s. per 100.

W. W. GREENER, BIRMINGHAM.

W. W. Greener's BIG GAME RIFLES.

HIGH VELOCITY AND BLACK POWDER EXPRESS.

THE construction of W. W. Greener's rifles is under the direct supervision of members of the firm, who are not only excellent rifle shots, and have attended the meetings of the National Rifle Association for many years, but who have had practical experience in game shooting in all parts of the world. Besides the shooting range at the factory, W. W. Greener has a private range where all long range rifles are shot.

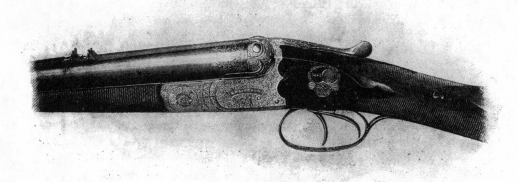

Grade R. F. T. 60.

Prices of Double Barrelled High Velocity Rifles.

Grade R. G. T. 80.	Greener	Unique Ejector Mechanism ...	...	price £84	0 0
,, R. F. H. T. 60.	,,	Fore-end Ejector Mechanism	...	,, 63	0 0
,, R. F. T. 40.	,,	Facile Princeps, Hammerless	...	,, 42	0 0
,, R. D. T. 30.	,,	Improved A. and D., Hammerless	...	,, 31	10 0

Supplied in ·303, ·375, ·450, ·500 *and other calibres.*

Black Powder or Equivalent Nitro Express Rifles.

Grade R. F. T. 30.	Greener	Facile Princeps, Hammerless	...	price £31	10 0
,, R. T. A. 25.	,,	Treble Wedge-Fast Hammer	...	,, 26	5 0
,, R. C. Y. T. 20.	,,	Under Lever Double Grip ,,	...	,, 21	0 0
,, R. D. B. T. 15.	,,	·310 Miniature Cordite	..	,, 15	15 0

W. W. GREENER'S
SINGLE HIGH VELOCITY RIFLES.

These Rifles are made in various bores—·303, ·360, ·375, ·450, &c. The falling block action of the Farqu=harson or Webley type is recommended for the larger calibres.

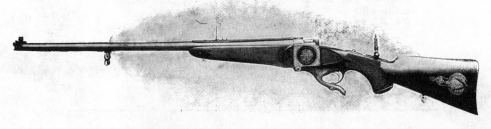

Grade U. 25 . . £26 5 0.

Grade U. 25.	Falling Block Action, Hammerless, Ejector, strengthening pieces on grip (Orthoptic Sights, 21s. extra)	£26	5	0
„ U. 15.	Ditto, plainer finish without strengthening pieces .	15	15	0
„ M. V. 10.	Martini Action, sporting finish	8	8	0

Grade Z. 15.	·303 or ·375 Magazine Action Rifle, sporting finish, and well engraved	£15	15	0
„ Z. 10.	Ditto, plainer finish	10	10	0
„ Z. 8.	Ditto, 21″ barrel (·303 only)	8	8	0

W. W. GREENER,
Rifle Manufacturer,
CONTRACTOR TO THE BRITISH AND FOREIGN GOVERNMENTS,
LONDON, BIRMINGHAM, MONTREAL and NEW YORK.

xv

W. W. GREENER'S
MILITARY RIFLES.
ACCURATE AND RELIABLE.

The Lee-Enfield Service Rifle, ·303 bore, "King's Prize" quality . £8 8 0
The Lee-Enfield Service Rifle, specially sighted and tested for
    Match shooting 10 10 0
The Lee-Enfield Carbine, 21″ barrel 7 7 0

THE NEW SERVICE RIFLE.

The New Short Lee-Enfield Mark I. Rifle, price £8 8 0
    Ditto, specially selected . . . 10 10 0
The Territorial Model 7 7 0

ROOK RIFLES.

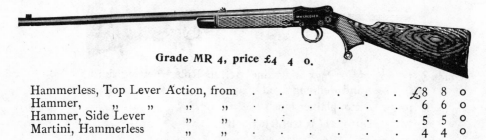

Grade MR 4, price £4 4 0.

Hammerless, Top Lever Action, from £8 8 0
Hammer,   „   „   „ „ 6 6 0
Hammer, Side Lever   „ „ 5 5 0
Martini, Hammerless   „ „ 4 4 0

W. W. GREENER, Rifle Manufacturer,
CONTRACTOR TO THE BRITISH
AND FOREIGN GOVERNMENTS. .
LONDON and BIRMINGHAM.

W. W. GREENER'S
"MINIATURE CLUB" RIFLE.

·22 R.F. ·297/·230 and ·297/·250 Bore.

(ACCURACY GUARANTEED.)

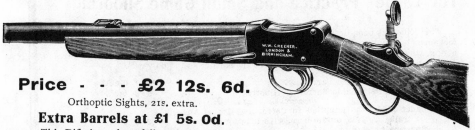

Price - - - £2 12s. 6d.

Orthoptic Sights, 21s. extra.

Extra Barrels at £1 5s. 0d.

This Rifle is made to follow the description of the " Sharpshooters' Club " Rifle, and is specially suited for indoor ranges, and distances up to 100 yards.

MORE RELIABLE THAN ANY FOREIGN MADE RIFLE OF THE CLASS.

A larger number of Prizes have been won with these Rifles than all other makes combined.

The Sights usually supplied on these Rifles are Greener's Special Standard Back Sight and a Bead Foresight, or Military Cadet Back Sight and Barleycorn Foresight.

MATCH AND SPORTING SIGHTS CAN BE FITTED TO ORDER AT FOLLOWING PRICES :—

Greener's Orthoptic Wind Gauge Peep Sight	£0 16 0
Bead or Globe Foresight for same	0 5 6
Fixed Windgauge Foresight with Screw Adjustment	0 16 0
Greener's British-made Orthoptic and Detachable Spirit-level and Windgauge Foresight	3 3 0

(Made with Vernier scale screw adjustment, and to fit over ordinary sporting sight when required. It can be detached instantly when open sights are desired.)

ACCESSORIES.

Small Canvas Case, complete with Cleaning Rod, Oil, etc., suitable for the above Rifles	£0 15 0 each,
Canvas Cover, with Straps for carrying Rifle by hand	0 7 6 each.
" Greenerene," a Special Nitro Cleaning Oil, anti-corrosive	0 1 0 per tin.
Greener's Gun Grease, a perfect preservative	0 0 6 ,, tube.
Cleaning Apparatus for " Club " Rifles	0 2 6 ,, set.

Resizing and Reloading Tools complete for ·310 Cartridge, 25s.
Paper and Card Targets with different sized Bull's-Eye for various distances.

Special Miniature Rifle Catalogue sent Post Free to any Address.

W. W. GREENER, GUN AND RIFLE MAKER,

68, Haymarket, London; St. Mary's Square, Birmingham; and 19, Paragon Street, Hull.

xvii

GUN CASES.

The best are of oak, leather covered, but these are heavy. Solid leather cases, well stiffened and with strong, well-made frames, afford equally good protection, and being much lighter are generally preferred.

The pattern to be recommended is one in which the barrels and the stock lie on the same level; in any case in which barrels are over the stock, injury may occur to the gun in transit. All gun cases are made of the finest selected leather and well-seasoned wood.

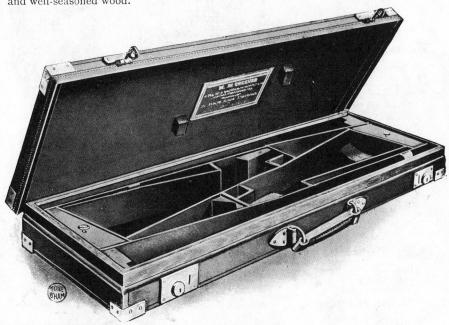

Best Case for Pair of Guns, with Spaces for Cleaning and Loading Implements.

	Gun Case only.				Gun Case only.		
No. 1—Best oak case, covered with dark leather, lined green velvet, and fitted with two spring locks..	**£5**	**5**	**0**	No. 6A—The "Sportsmanteau," to hold gun, stiff limp cover, etc., price, including cover .. **£4 4 0** and	**£5**	**5**	**0**
„ 2—Best leather case, lined green velvet, and fitted with two spring locks ..	**4**	**4**	**0**	„ 7—Best leg-of mutton case, all leather, to take gun only, barrels over stock	**3**	**3**	**0**
„ 3—Second quality leather case, lined red cloth, one slide lock and straps	**3**	**3**	**0**	„ 8—Second quality ditto	**2**	**2**	**0**
„ 4—Plain leather case, lined red cloth, spring lock and straps	**2**	**12**	**6**	„ 9—Special case, for three guns, best quality leather, with brass corners and centre plate, and lined with best cloth. The three pairs of barrels fitted in a polished oak tray, and the stocks on edge in the bottom of the case. All fittings in bottom ..	**10**	**10**	**0**
„ 5—Willesden canvas case, lined red cloth, spring lock and straps ..	**2**	**2**	**0**				
„ 6—Tan canvas waterproof case, lined red cloth, spring lock and straps ..	**1**	**11**	**6**	„ 10—Ditto, extra stout, brass squares fitted in frame for strength ..	**12**	**12**	**0**

Cleaning Implements, suitable for above Cases, 21s. and 42s. per set extra.
Tanned Waterproof Leather-bound Case Covers, to protect Gun Cases, £1 11s. 6d.
Cases for pairs of guns cost double the above prices. Nos. 1 to 6 are adapted for pairs.

HONOURS WON WITH THE GREENER GUN

ENGLISH AND COLONIAL HONOURS.

Purdey Cup. Choke-Bores *v.* Cylinders, 1877.

Championship, Live Birds, Canada, 1910.

Championship Live Birds, New Zealand, 1910.

RECORDS.

The "Sportsman" Championship or the World Challenge Cup.

Record score at Pigeons 199-200, Elliott, 1894.

GUN TRIALS.

The Great London Field Gun-Trial Cup, 1875, beating 68 guns by all best English gunmakers.

CONTINENTAL HONOURS.

Grand Prix du Casino, 1891.

MONTE CARLO.

Grand Prix du Casino, 1878.

AMERICAN HONOURS.

The "American Field" Champion Wing Shot Cup, won 10 times in succession by Mr. Elliott.

Since 1878, more than 120 prizes, worth over £10,000, have been won at Monte Carlo with Greener Guns.

xx

"The Breechloader and How to Use It."

NINTH EDITION—REVISED.

282 pp.
Half Cloth Paper Boards, 2s. 6d.

133 Illustrations.
Cloth, 3s. 6d.

This book is written for those Sportsmen who wish to know whatever is of real use to them about guns and ammunition, and who, while delighting in a day's shooting, have neither the time nor the means to make the sport a life's study.

Published at a popular price, it will, it is hoped, reach many who have hitherto been deterred from shooting, believing it to be an expensive recreation, the author's aim being to induce all who can to participate in a manly Sport, and to advance the interests of those who look to the gun for pleasure, health, or occupation.

SUMMARY OF CONTENTS.

Press Opinions.

" By its aid the young sportsman may not only avoid being swindled in the choice of his gun, but may also gain much valuable information as to its use."—*Liverpool Post.*

"Speaking candidly, we think no sportsman should be without this capital volume."—*Shooting Times.*

"It is wonderful to notice how much valuable information is contained within its covers."—*The Stock-keeper.*

VIEWS OF W. W. GREENER'S FACTORY

THE LARGEST AND MOST COMPLETE

SPORTING GUN FACTORY IN THE WORLD.

BARREL BORING SHOP

A MACHINE SHOP

OFFICE

VIEW OF WORKS FACING BATH ST AND LOVEDAY ST.

WOOD WORKING MACHINE SHOP

PRESS & TOOL SHOP

THE HOME OF THE GUN TRADE.
ST. MARY'S SQUARE, BIRMINGHAM.

INTERIOR VIEWS OF THE FACTORY.

CARTRIDGE-LOADING

VIEWING & FITTING ROOM.

TESTING ROOM.

ACTION FILING SHOP.

SCENES IN THE MAKING & TESTING OF SHOT GUNS

A BARREL FILING SHOP.

ST. MARY'S SQUARE, BIRMINGHAM.

THE abridged Catalogue of W. W. Greener's manufactures is intended primarily for Sportsmen abroad, to whom the delay entailed in writing for a price list is at all times irksome, but W. W. Greener will be pleased to send the following Catalogues, post free, to any address, and to reply fully to any questions relating to guns or shooting.

Price List of Shot-Guns and Accessories.
  „   „   **Single and Double High Velocity Rifles.**
  „   „   **Short and Long Range Target Rifles and Accessories.**
  „   „   **Rook Rifles.**
  „   „   **Shot-Gun Ammunition.**

The following Booklets are also of interest to sportsmen, and will be forwarded on request :—

"The World's Views on Greener Guns."
"Does your Gun Stock fit you?"

With Greener's registered Self-Measurement Form.

Note.—All genuine W. W. Greener Guns are Stamped with the Registered Trade Mark, an Elephant. There are numerous imitations, of which Sportsmen should beware.

TRADE MARK.

FULL DESCRIPTIVE LISTS ON APPLICATION.

W. W. GREENER,
Contractor to British and Foreign Governments,
GUN AND RIFLE MAKER,

St. Mary's Square, Birmingham, England ;
68, Haymarket, London, England ;
19, Paragon Street, Hull, England ;
63 & 65, Beaver Hall Hill, Montreal, Canada ;
44, Cortlandt Street, New York, U.S.A.